Admiralty Record

Volume 1

PUBLISHED ADMIRALTY OPINIONS OF
THE SUPREME COURT OF THE UNITED STATES AND
THE UNITED STATES COURTS OF APPEALS ISSUED DURING
THE CALENDAR YEAR

2013

Cite as: 1 Adm. R. _____

REPORTED BY KIRK N. AURANDT, ESQ.
MEMBER OF THE BAR IN LOUISIANA AND PENNSYLVANIA

ADMIRALTY RECORD PUBLISHING COMPANY, L.L.C.
MANDEVILLE, LOUISIANA, U.S.A.

ISSN 2334-5411
ISBN 978-0-9983853-1-0

Admiralty record : published
admiralty opinions of the Supreme
Court of the United States and the
United States Courts of Appeals
issued during the calendar year ...
Mandeville, Louisiana, U.S.A. :
Admiralty Record Publishing
Company, LLC, 2014-

    KF1104 .A75
    ISSN: 2334-5411

https://lccn.loc.gov/2014200303

PREFACE

Volume 1—the inaugural annual edition of the Admiralty Record—reports published admiralty opinions of the Supreme Court of the United States and the United States Courts of Appeals that were issued during the calendar year 2013. The opinions reported are the original majority, concurring, and dissenting opinions of the Court, with only minor changes in formatting to better suit a dual-column presentation. The pagination found in the original opinion is indicated by the number contained inside of black brackets.

The decision to select an opinion to appear in Volume 1 of the Admiralty Record was made solely by me following an examination of those opinions that each of the above-named courts designated for publication in 2013. Every effort has been made to ensure inclusion of all 2013 federal appellate court admiralty opinions that were designated for publication; however, to the extent that a relevant admiralty opinion has been inadvertently overlooked or otherwise mistakenly omitted, the error is regretted and is solely my own. A few opinions from appeals in civil cases that technically may not have fallen under a federal district court's admiralty or maritime jurisdiction have been reported if they touched upon admiralty matters, or were otherwise deemed to be of potential interest to the admiralty practitioner. Additionally, several opinions from criminal cases involving maritime crimes have been included.

To assist the reader in locating those opinions from 2013 involving subject matters of interest, I have prepared an Index to the opinions. I have also prepared Tables of Authority, which supply page references to the cases, statutes, and rules cited in each opinion. Prior to relying upon any of the opinions reported herein, the reader is reminded to verify the current status of any particular case as valid precedent by checking the case with a reliable citator.

Additional copies of Volume 1, covering 2013, and succeeding-year volumes may be ordered at www.admiraltyrecord.com. I hope that the Admiralty Record will become a valuable and ready reference source for not only the admiralty practitioner, but for anyone who is interested in reading the published admiralty opinions of the federal appellate courts.

KIRK N. AURANDT, ESQ.

This page intentionally left blank

TABLE OF CONTENTS
(Cases arranged chronologically by Court)

PAGE

This page intentionally left blank

Supreme Court of the United States

Supreme Court of the United States

No. 11-626

LOZMAN

vs.

CITY OF RIVIERA BEACH, FLA.

On Writ of Certiorari to the United States Court of Appeals for the Eleventh Circuit

Decided: January 15, 2013

Citation: 568 U.S. ___, 133 S.Ct. 735, 1 Adm. R. 2 (2013).

BREYER, J., delivered the opinion of the Court, in which ROBERTS, C.J., and SCALIA, THOMAS, GINSBURG, ALITO, and KAGAN, J.J., joined. SOTOMAYOR, J., filed a dissenting opinion, in which KENNEDY, J., joined.

[—1—] BREYER, J.:

The Rules of Construction Act defines a "vessel" as including "every description of watercraft or other artificial contrivance used, or capable of being used, as a means of transportation on water." 1 U.S.C. §3. The question before us is whether petitioner's floating home (which is not self-propelled) falls within the terms of that definition.

In answering that question we focus primarily upon the phrase "capable of being used." This term encompasses "practical" possibilities, not " merely ... theoretical" ones. *Stewart* v. *Dutra Const. Co.,* 543 U.S. 481, 496 (2005). We believe that a reasonable observer, looking to the home's physical characteristics and activities, would not consider it to be designed to any practical degree for carrying people or things on water. And we consequently conclude that the floating home is not a "vessel."

I

In 2002 Fane Lozman, petitioner, bought a 60-foot by 12-foot floating home. App. 37, 71. The home consisted of a house-like plywood structure with French doors on three sides. *Id.,* at 38, 44. It contained a sitting room, bedroom, [—2—] closet, bathroom, and kitchen, along with a stairway leading to a second level with office space. *Id.,* at 45-66.

An empty bilge space underneath the main floor kept it afloat. *Id.,* at 38. (See Appendix, *infra,* for a photograph.) After buying the floating home, Lozman had it towed about 200 miles to North Bay Village, Florida, where he moored it and then twice more had it towed between nearby marinas. In 2006 Lozman had the home towed a further 70 miles to a marina owned by the city of Riviera Beach (City), respondent, where he kept it docked. Brief for Respondent 5.

After various disputes with Lozman and unsuccessful efforts to evict him from the marina, the City brought this federal admiralty lawsuit *in rem* against the floating home. It sought a maritime lien for dockage fees and damages for trespass. See Federal Maritime Lien Act, 46 U.S.C. §31342 (authorizing federal maritime lien against vessel to collect debts owed for the provision of "necessaries to a vessel"); 28 U.S.C. §1333(1) (civil admiralty jurisdiction). See also *Leon* v. *Galceron,* 11 Wall. 185 (1871); *The Rock Island Bridge,* 6 Wall. 213, 215 (1867).

Lozman, acting *pro se,* asked the District Court to dismiss the suit on the ground that the court lacked admiralty jurisdiction. See 2 Record, Doc. 64. After summary judgment proceedings, the court found that the floating home was a "vessel" and concluded that admiralty jurisdiction was consequently proper. Pet. for Cert. 42a. The judge then conducted a bench trial on the merits and awarded the City $3,039.88 for dockage along with $1 in nominal damages for trespass. *Id.,* at 49a.

On appeal the Eleventh Circuit affirmed. *Riviera Beach* v. *That Certain Unnamed Gray, Two-Story Vessel Approximately Fifty-Seven Feet in Length,* 649 F.3d 1259 (2011). It agreed with the District Court that the home was a "vessel." In its view, the home was "capable" of movement over water and the owner's subjective intent to remain [—3—] moored "indefinitely" at a dock could not show the contrary. *Id.,* at 1267-1269.

Lozman sought certiorari. In light of uncertainty among the Circuits about application of the term "capable" we granted his petition. Compare *De La Rosa* v. *St. Charles Gaming Co.,* 474 F.3d 185, 187 (CA5 2006)(structure is not a "vessel" where "physically," but only "theoretical[ly]," "capable of sailing," and owner intends to moor it indefinitely as floating casino), with *Board of Comm'rs of Orleans Levee Dist.* v. *M/V Belle of Orleans,* 535 F.3d 1299, 1311-1312 (CA11 2008) (structure is a "vessel" where capable of moving over water under tow, "albeit to her detriment," despite intent to moor indefinitely). See also 649 F.3d at 1267 (rejecting views of Circuits that "'focus on the intent of the shipowner'").

II

At the outset we consider one threshold matter. The District Court ordered the floating home sold to satisfy the City's judgment. The City bought the home at public auction and subsequently had it destroyed. And, after the parties filed their merits briefs, we ordered further briefing on the question of mootness in light of the home's destruction. 567 U.S. ___ (2012). The parties now have pointed out that, prior to the home's sale, the District Court ordered the City to post a $25,000 bond "to secure Mr. Lozman's value in the vessel." 1 Record, Doc. 20, p. 2. The bond ensures that Lozman can obtain monetary relief if he ultimately prevails. We consequently agree with the parties that the case is not moot.

III

A

We focus primarily upon the statutory phrase "capable of being used ... as a means of transportation on water." 1 U.S.C. §3. The Court of Appeals found that the home [—4—] was "capable" of transportation because it could float, it could proceed under tow, and its shore connections (power cable, water hose, rope lines) did not "'rende[r]'" it "'practically incaple of transportation or movement.'" 649 F.3d at 1266 (quoting *Belle of Orleans, supra,* at 1312, in turn quoting *Stewart,* 543 U.S., at 494). At least for argument's sake we agree with the Court of Appeals about the last-mentioned point, namely that Lozman's shore connections did not "'render'" the home "'practically incapable of transportation.'" But unlike the Eleventh Circuit, we do not find these considerations (even when combined with the home's other characteristics) sufficient to show that Lozman's home was a "vessel."

The Court of Appeals recognized that it had applied the term "capable" broadly. 649 F.3d at 1266. Indeed, it pointed with approval to language in an earlier case, *Burks* v. *American River Transp. Co.,* 679 F.2d 69 (1982), in which the Fifth Circuit said:

> "'No doubt the three men in a tub would also fit within our definition, and one probably could make a convincing case for Jonah inside the whale.'" 649 F.3d, at 1269 (brackets omitted) (quoting *Burks, supra,* at 75).

But the Eleventh Circuit's interpretation is too broad. Not *every* floating structure is a "vessel." To state the obvious, a wooden washtub, a plastic dishpan, a swimming platform on pontoons, a large fishing net, a door taken off its hinges, or Pinocchio (when inside the whale) are not "vessels," even if they are "artificial contrivance[s]" capable of floating, moving under tow, and incidentally carrying even a fair-sized item or two when they do so. Rather, the statute applies to an "artificial contrivance ... capable of being used ... *as a means of transportation on water.*" 1 U.S.C. §3 (emphasis added). "[T]ransportation" involves the "conveyance (of things or persons) from one place to [—5—] another." 18 Oxford English Dictionary 424 (2d ed. 1989)(OED). Accord, N. Webster, An American Dictionary of the English Language 1406 (C. Goodrich & N. Porter eds. 1873) ("[t]he act of transporting, carrying, or conveying from one place to another"). And we must apply this definition in a "practical," not a "theoretical," way. *Stewart, supra,* at 496. Consequently, in our view a structure does not fall within the scope of this statutory phrase unless a reasonable observer, looking to the home's physical characteristics and activities, would consider it designed to a practical degree for carrying people or things over water.

B

Though our criterion is general, the facts of this case illustrate more specifically what we have in mind. But for the fact that it floats, nothing about Lozman's home suggests that it was designed to any practical degree to transport persons or things over water. It had no rudder or other steering mechanism. 649 F.3d at 1269. Its hull was unraked, *ibid.*, and it had a rectangular bottom 10 inches below the water. Brief for Petitioner 27; App. 37. It had no special capacity to generate or store electricity but could obtain that utility only through ongoing connections with the land. *Id.,* at 40. Its small rooms looked like ordinary nonmaritime living quarters. And those inside those rooms looked out upon the world, not through watertight portholes, but through French doors or ordinary windows. *Id.,* at 44-66.

Although lack of self-propulsion is not dispositive, *e.g., The Robert W. Parsons,* 191 U.S. 17, 31 (1903), it may be a relevant physical characteristic. And Lozman's home differs significantly from an ordinary houseboat in that it has no ability to propel itself. Cf. 33 CFR §173.3 (2012) ("Houseboat means a *motorized* vessel ... designed primarily for multi-purpose accommodation spaces with low [—6—] freeboard and little or no foredeck or cockpit" (emphasis added)). Lozman's home was able to travel over water only by being towed. Prior to its arrest, that home's travel by tow over water took place on only four occasions over a period of seven years. *Supra,* at 2. And when the home was towed a significant distance in 2006, the towing company had a second boat follow behind to prevent the home from swinging dangerously from side to side. App. 104.

The home has no other feature that might suggest a design to transport over water anything other than its own furnishings and related personal effects. In a word, we can find nothing about the home that could lead a reasonable observer to consider it designed to a practical degree for "transportation on water."

C

Our view of the statute is consistent with its text, precedent, and relevant purposes. For one thing, the statute's language, read naturally, lends itself to that interpretation. We concede that the statute uses the word "every," referring to "*every* description of watercraft or other artificial contrivance." 1 U.S.C. §3 (emphasis added). But the term "contrivance" refers to "something contrived for, or employed in contriving to effect a purpose." 3 OED 850 (def. 7). The term "craft" explains that purpose as "water carriage and transport." *Id.,* at 1104 (def. V(9)(b))(defining "craft" as a "vesse[l] ... for" that purpose). The addition of the word "water" to "craft," yielding the term "watercraft," emphasizes the point. And the next few words, "used, or capable of being used, as a means of transportation on water," drive the point home.

For another thing, the bulk of precedent supports our conclusion. In *Evansville & Bowling Green Packet Co.* v. *Chero Cola Bottling Co.,* 271 U.S. 19 (1926), the Court held that a wharfboat was *not* a "vessel." The wharfboat floated next to a dock; it was used to transfer cargo from [—7—] ship to dock and ship to ship; and it was connected to the dock with cables, utility lines, and a ramp. *Id.,* at 21. At the same time, it was capable of being towed. And it was towed each winter to a harbor to avoid river ice. *Id.,* at 20-21. The Court reasoned that, despite the annual movement under tow, the wharfboat "was not used to carry freight from one place to another," nor did it "encounter perils of navigation to which craft used for transportation are exposed." *Id.,* at 22 (See Appendix, *infra,* for photograph of a period wharfboat).

The Court's reasoning in *Stewart* also supports our conclusion. We there considered the application of the statutory definition to a dredge. 543 U.S., at 494. The dredge was "a massive floating platform" from which a suspended clamshell bucket would "remov[e] silt from the ocean floor," depositing it "onto one of two scows" floating alongside the dredge. *Id.,* at 484. Like more traditional "seagoing vessels," the dredge had, *e.g.,* "a captain and crew, navigational lights, ballast tanks, and a crew dining area." *Ibid.* Unlike more ordinary vessels, it could navigate only by "manipulating its anchors and cables" or by being towed. *Ibid.* Nonetheless it did move. In fact it moved over water "every couple of hours." *Id.,* at 485.

We held that the dredge was a "vessel." We wrote that §3's definition "merely codified the meaning that the term 'vessel' had acquired in general maritime law." *Id.,* at 490. We added that the question of the "watercraft's use 'as a means of transportation on water' is ... practical," and not "merely ... theoretical." *Id.,* at 496. And we pointed to cases holding that dredges ordinarily "served a waterborne transportation function," namely that "in performing their work they carried machinery, equipment, and crew over water." *Id.,* at 491-492 (citing, *e.g., Butler* v. *Ellis,* 45 F.2d 951, 955 (CA4 1930)).

As the Court of Appeals pointed out, in *Stewart* we also wrote that §3 "does not require that a watercraft be used [—8—] *primarily* for that [transportation] purpose," 543 U.S., at 495; that a "watercraft need not be in motion to qualify as a vessel," *ibid.*; and that a structure may qualify as a vessel even if attached—but not "permanently" attached—to the land or ocean floor. *Id.,* at 493-494. We did not take these statements, however, as implying a universal set of sufficient conditions for application of the definition. Rather, they say, and they mean, that the statutory definition *may* (or may not) apply— not that it *automatically must* apply—where a structure has some other *primary* purpose, where it is stationary at relevant times, and where it is attached—but not permanently attached—to land.

After all, a washtub is normally not a "vessel" though it does not have water transportation as its primary purpose, it may be stationary much of the time, and it might be attached—but not permanently attached— to land. More to the point, water transportation was not the *primary purpose* of either *Stewart's* dredge or *Evansville's* wharfboat; neither structure was "in motion"

at relevant times; and both were sometimes attached (though not permanently attached) to the ocean bottom or to land. Nonetheless *Stewart's* dredge fell within the statute's definition while *Evansville's* wharfboat did not.

The basic difference, we believe, is that the dredge was regularly, but not primarily, used (and designed in part to be used) to transport workers and equipment over water while the wharfboat was not designed (to any practical degree) to serve a transportation function and did not do so. Compare *Cope* v. *Vallette Dry Dock Co.,* 119 U.S. 625 (1887) (floating drydock not a "vessel" because permanently fixed to wharf), with *Jerome B. Grubart, Inc.* v. *Great Lakes Dredge & Dock Co.,* 513 U.S. 527, 535 (1995) (barge sometimes attached to river bottom to use as a work platform remains a "vessel" when "at other times it was used for transportation"). See also *ibid.* (citing *Great Lakes* [—9—] *Dredge & Dock Co.* v. *Chicago,* 3 F.3d 225, 229 (CA7 1993) ("[A] craft is a 'vessel' if its purpose is to some reasonable degree 'the transportation of passengers, cargo, or equipment from place to place across navigable waters'")); *Cope, supra,* at 630 (describing "hopper-barge," as potentially a "vessel" because it is a "navigable structure[,] used for the purpose of transportation"); cf. 1 Benedict on Admiralty §164, p. 10-6 (7th rev. ed. 2012) (maritime jurisdiction proper if "the craft is a navigable structure intended for maritime transportation").

Lower court cases also tend, on balance, to support our conclusion. See, *e.g., Bernard* v. *Binnings Constr. Co.,* 741 F.2d 824, 828, n. 13, 832, n. 25 (CA5 1984) (work punt lacking features objectively indicating a transportation function not a "vessel," for "our decisions make clear that the mere capacity to float or move across navigable waters does not necessarily make a structure a vessel"); *Ruddiman* v. *A Scow Platform,* 38 F. 158 (SDNY 1889) (scow, though "capable of being towed ... though not without some difficulty, from its clumsy structure" just a floating box, not a "vessel," because "it was not designed or used for the purpose of navigation," not engaged "in the transportation of persons or cargo," and had "no motive power, no rudder, no sails"). See also 1 T. Schoenbaum, Admiralty and Maritime Law §3—6, p. 155 (5th ed. 2011) (courts have found that "floating dry-dock[s]," "floating platforms, barges, or rafts used for construction or repair of piers, docks, bridges, pipelines and other" similar facilities are not "vessels"); E. Benedict, American Admiralty §215, p. 116 (3d rev. ed. 1898) (defining "vessel" as a "'machine adapted to transportation over rivers, seas, and oceans'").

We recognize that some lower court opinions can be read as endorsing the "anything that floats" approach. See *Miami River Boat Yard, Inc.* v. *60' Houseboat*, 390 F.2d 596, 597 (CA5 1968) (so-called "houseboat" lacking self-propulsion); *Sea Village Marine, LLC* v. *A 1980 Carlcraft* [—10—] *Houseboat*, No. 09—3292, 2009 WL 3379923, *5—*6 (D NJ, Oct. 19, 2009) (following *Miami River Boat Yard*); *Hudson Harbor 79th Street Boat Basin, Inc.* v. *Sea Casa*, 469 F. Supp. 987, 989 (SDNY 1979) (same). Cf. *Holmes* v. *Atlantic Sounding Co.*, 437 F.3d 441 (CA5 2006) (floating dormitory); *Summerlin* v. *Massman Constr. Co.*, 199 F.2d 715 (CA4 1952) (derrick anchored in the river engaged in building a bridge is a vessel). For the reasons we have stated, we find such an approach inappropriate and inconsistent with our precedents.

Further, our examination of the purposes of major federal maritime statutes reveals little reason to classify floating homes as "vessels." Admiralty law, for example, provides special attachment procedures lest a vessel avoid liability by sailing away. 46 U.S.C. §§31341-31343 (2006 ed. and Supp. IV). Liability statutes such as the Jones Act recognize that sailors face the special "'perils of the sea.'" *Chandris, Inc.* v. *Latsis*, 515 U.S. 347, 354, 373 (1995) (referring to "'vessel[s]' in navigation'"). Certain admiralty tort doctrines can encourage shipowners to engage in port-related commerce. *E.g.*, 46 U.S.C. §30505; *Executive Jet Aviation, Inc.* v. *Cleveland*, 409 U.S. 249, 269-270 (1972). And maritime safety statutes subject vessels to U.S. Coast Guard inspections. *E.g.*, 46 U.S.C. §3301.

Lozman, however, cannot easily escape liability by sailing away in his home. He faces no special sea dangers. He does not significantly engage in port-related commerce. And the Solicitor General tells us that to adopt a version of the "anything that floats" test would place unnecessary and undesirable inspection burdens upon the Coast Guard. Brief for United States as *Amicus Curiae* 29 n. 11.

Finally, our conclusion is consistent with state laws in States where floating home owners have congregated in communities. See Brief for Seattle Floating Homes Association et al. as *Amici Curiae* 1. A Washington State [—11—] environmental statute, for example, defines a floating home (for regulatory purposes) as "a single-family dwelling unit constructed on a float, that is moored, anchored, or otherwise secured in waters, and is not a vessel, even though it may be capable of being towed." Wash. Rev. Code Ann. §90.58.270(5)(b)(ii) (Supp. 2012). A California statute defines a floating home (for tax purposes) as "a floating structure" that is "designed and built to be used, or is modified to be used, as a stationary waterborne residential dwelling," and which (unlike a typical houseboat), has no independent power generation, and is dependent on shore utilities. Cal. Health & Safety Code Ann. §18075.55(d) (West 2006). These States, we are told, treat structures that meet their "floating home" definitions like ordinary land-based homes rather than like vessels. Brief for Seattle Floating Homes Association 2. Consistency of interpretation of related state and federal laws is a virtue in that it helps to create simplicity making the law easier to understand and to follow for lawyers and for nonlawyers alike. And that consideration here supports our conclusion.

D

The City and supporting *amici* make several important arguments that warrant our response. First, they argue against use of any purpose-based test lest we introduce into "vessel" determinations a subjective element— namely, the owner's intent. That element, they say, is often "unverifiable" and too easily manipulated. Its introduction would "foment unpredictability and invite gamesmanship." Brief for Respondent 33.

We agree with the City about the need to eliminate the consideration of evidence of subjective intent. But we cannot agree that the need requires abandonment of all criteria based on "purpose." Cf. *Stewart*, 543 U.S., at 495 (discussing transportation purpose). Indeed, it is difficult, **[—12—]** if not impossible, to determine the use of a human "contrivance" without some consideration of human purposes. At the same time, we have sought to avoid subjective elements, such as owner's intent, by permitting consideration only of objective evidence of a waterborne transportation purpose. That is why we have referred to the views of a reasonable observer. *Supra*, at 1. And it is why we have looked to the physical attributes and behavior of the structure, as objective manifestations of any relevant purpose, and not to the subjective intent of the owner. *Supra,* at 5-6. We note that various admiralty treatises refer to the use of purpose-based tests without any suggestion that administration of those tests has introduced too much subjectivity into the vessel-determination process. 1 Benedict on Admiralty §164; 1 Admiralty and Maritime Law §3—6.

Second, the City, with support of *amici*, argues against the use of criteria that are too abstract, complex, or open-ended. Brief for Respondent 28-29. A court's jurisdiction, *e.g.*, admiralty jurisdiction, may turn on application of the term "vessel." And jurisdictional tests, often applied at the outset of a case, should be "as simple as possible." *Hertz Corp.* v. *Friend*, 559 U.S. ___, ___ (2010)(slip op., at 1).

We agree with the last-mentioned sentiment. And we also understand that our approach is neither perfectly precise nor always determinative. Satisfaction of a design-based or purpose-related criterion, for example, is not always sufficient for application of the statutory word "vessel." A craft whose physical characteristics and activities objectively evidence a waterborne transportation purpose or function may still be rendered a nonvessel by later physical alterations. For example, an owner might take a structure that is otherwise a vessel (even the *Queen Mary*) and connect it permanently to the land for use, say, as a hotel. See *Stewart, supra,* at 493-494. Further, **[—13—]** changes over time may produce a new form, *i.e.*, a newly designed structure—in which case it may be the new design that is relevant. See *Kathriner* v. *Unisea, Inc.*, 975 F.2d 657, 660 (CA9 1992) (floating processing plant was no longer a vessel where a "large opening [had been] cut into her hull").

Nor is satisfaction of the criterion always a necessary condition, see Part IV, *infra*. It is conceivable that an owner might *actually use* a floating structure not designed to any practical degree for transportation as, say, a ferry boat, regularly transporting goods and persons over water.

Nonetheless, we believe the criterion we have used, taken together with our example of its application here, should offer guidance in a significant number of borderline cases where "capacity" to transport over water is in doubt. Moreover, borderline cases will always exist; they require a method for resolution; we believe the method we have used is workable; and, unlike, say, an "anything that floats" test, it is consistent with statutory text, purpose, and precedent. Nor do we believe that the dissent's approach would prove any more workable. For example, the dissent suggests a relevant distinction between an owner's "clothes and personal effects" and "large appliances (like an oven or a refrigerator)." *Post*, at 8 (opinion of SOTOMAYOR, J.). But a transportation function need not turn on the size of the items in question, and we believe the line between items being transported from place to place (*e.g.*, cargo) and items that are mere appurtenances is the one more likely to be relevant. Cf. Benedict, American Admiralty §222, at 121 ("A ship is usually described as consisting of the ship, her tackle, apparel, and furniture ...").

Finally, the dissent and the Solicitor General (as *amicus* for Lozman) argue that a remand is warranted for further factfinding. See *post*, at 10-12; Brief for United States as *Amicus Curiae* 29-31. But neither the City nor Lozman [—14—] makes such a request. Brief for Respondent 18, 49, 52. And the only potentially relevant factual dispute the dissent points to is that the home suffered serious damage during a tow. *Post*, at 10-11. But this would add support to our ultimate conclusion that this floating home was not a vessel. We consequently see nothing to be gained by a remand.

IV

Although we have focused on the phrase *"capable* of being used" for transportation over water, the statute also includes as a "vessel" a structure that is *actually* "used" for that transportation. 1 U.S.C. §3 (emphasis added). And the City argues that, irrespective of its design, Lozman's floating home was *actually* so used. Brief for Respondent 32. We are not persuaded by its argument.

We are willing to assume for argument's sake that sometimes it is possible actually to use for water transportation a structure that is in no practical way designed for that purpose. See *supra*, at 12-13. But even so, the City cannot show the actual use for which it argues. Lozman's floating home moved only under tow. Before its arrest, it moved significant distances only twice in seven years. And when it moved, it carried, not passengers or cargo, but at the very most (giving the benefit of any factual ambiguity to the City) only its own furnishings, its owner's personal effects, and personnel present to assure the home's safety. 649 F.3d, at 1268; Brief for Respondent 32; Tr. Of Oral Arg. 37-38. This is far too little *actual* "use" to bring the floating home within the terms of the statute. See *Evansville*, 271 U.S., at 20-21 (wharfboat not a "vessel" even though "[e]ach winter" it "was towed to [a] harbor to protect it from ice"); see also *Roper* v. *United States*, 368 U.S. 20, 23 (1961) ("Unlike a barge, the S.S. *Harry Lane* was not moved in order to transport commodities from one location to another"). See also *supra*, at 6-11. [—15—]

V

For these reasons, the judgment of the Court of Appeals is reversed.

It is so ordered.

(Reporter's Note: Dissenting opinion on p. 10).

[—16—] Appendix to opinion of the Court

APPENDIX

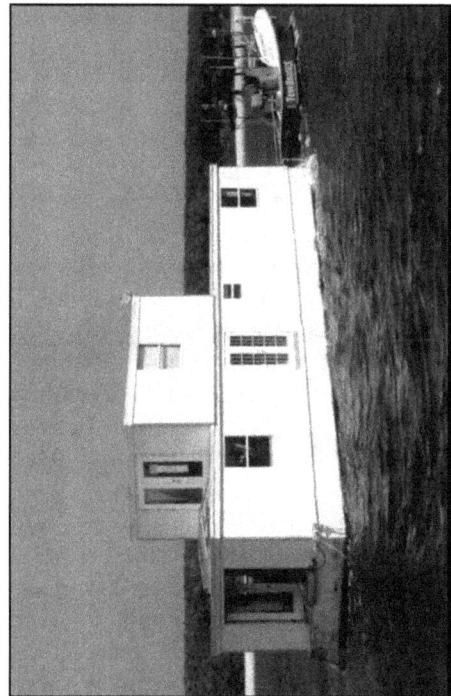

Petitioner's floating home. App. 69.

[—17—] Appendix to opinion of the Court

50- by 200-foot wharf boat in Evansville, Indiana, on Nov. 13, 1918. H. R. Doc. No. 1521, 65th Cong., 3d Sess., Illustration No. 13 (1918).

[—1—] **SOTOMAYOR, J.**, with whom **KENNEDY, J.** joins, dissenting:

I agree with much of the Court's reasoning. Our precedents fully support the Court's reasoning that the Eleventh Circuit's test is overinclusive; that the subjective intentions of a watercraft's owner or designer play no role in the vessel analysis of 1 U.S.C. §3; and that an objective assessment of a watercraft's purpose or function governs whether that structure is a vessel. The Court, however, creates a novel and unnecessary "reasonable observer" reformulation of these principles and errs in its determination, under this new standard, that the craft before us is not a vessel. Given the underdeveloped record below, we should remand. Therefore, I respectfully dissent.

I

The relevant statute, 1 U. S. C. §3, "sweeps broadly." *Stewart* v. *Dutra Constr. Co.*, 543 U.S. 481, 494 (2005). It provides that "[t]he word 'vessel' includes every description of watercraft or other artificial contrivance used, or capable of being used, as a means of transportation on water." This broad phrasing flows from admiralty law's long recognition that vessels come in many shapes and sizes. See E. Benedict, American Admiralty §218, p. 121 [—2—] (1870 ed.) ("[V]essel, is a general word, many times used for any kind of navigation"); M. Cohen, Admiralty Jurisdiction, Law, and Practice 232 (1883) ("[T]he term 'vessel' shall be understood to comprehend every description of vessel navigating on any sea or channel, lake or river . . . ").

Our test for vessel status has remained the same for decades: "Under §3, a 'vessel' is any watercraft practically capable of maritime transportation . . . ." *Stewart*, 543 U. S., at 497; see also *Evansville & Bowling Green Packet Co.* v. *Chero Cola Bottling Co.*, 271 U.S. 19, 22 (1926); *Cope* v. *Vallette Dry Dock Co.*, 119 U. S. 625, 627 (1887). At its core,

vessel status has always rested upon the objective physical characteristics of a vessel (such as its structure, shape, and materials of construction), as well as its usage history. But over time, several important principles have guided both this Court and the lower courts in determining what kinds of watercraft fall properly within the scope of admiralty jurisdiction.

Consider the most basic of requirements. For a watercraft to be "practically capable" of maritime transportation, it must first be "capable" of such transportation. Only those structures that can simultaneously float and carry people or things over water are even presumptively within §3's reach. Stopping here, as the Eleventh Circuit essentially did, results in an overinclusive test. Section 3, after all, does not drag every bit of floating and towable flotsam and jetsam into admiralty jurisdiction. Rather, the terms "capable of being used" and "practical" have real significance in our maritime jurisprudence.

"[A] water craft is not 'capable of being used' for maritime transport in any meaningful sense if it has been permanently moored." *Stewart*, 543 U. S., at 494. So, to take an obvious example, a floating bridge over water does not constitute a vessel; such mooring is clearly permanent. Cf. *The Rock Island Bridge*, 6 Wall. 213, 216 (1867). Less [—3—] dramatically, a watercraft whose objective physical connections to land "evidence a permanent location" does not fall within §3's ambit. See, *e.g.*, *Evansville*, 271 U.S., at 22 ("[The wharfboat] served at Evansville as an office, warehouse and wharf, and was not taken from place to place. The connections with the water, electric light and telephone systems of the city evidence a permanent location"); *Dunklin* v. *Louisiana Riverboat Gaming Partnership*, No. 00–31455, 2001 WL 650209, *1, n. 1 (CA5, May 22, 2001) (*per curiam*) (describing a fully functional casino boat placed "in an enclosed pond in a cofferdam"). Put plainly, structures "permanently affixed to shore or resting on the ocean floor," *Stewart*, 543 U. S., at 493–494, have never been treated as vessels for the purposes of §3.

Our precedents have also excluded from vessel status those watercraft "rendered practically incapable of transportation or movement." *Id.*, at 494. Take the easiest case, a vessel whose physical characteristics have been so altered as to make waterborne transportation a practical impossibility. *Ibid.* (explaining that a "floating processing plant was no longer a vessel where a 'large opening [had been] cut into her hull,' rendering her incapable of moving over the water" (quoting *Kathriner* v. *UNISEA, Inc.*, 975 F. 2d 657, 660 (CA9 1992)). The longstanding admiralty exception for "dead ships," those watercraft that "require a major overhaul" for their "reactivation," also falls into this category. See *Roper* v. *United States*, 368 U. S. 20, 21 (1961) (finding that a liberty ship "deactivated from service and 'mothballed'" is not a "vessel in navigation"); see generally Rutherglen, Dead Ships, 30 J. Maritime L. & Comm. 677 (1999).[1] Likewise, ships that "have been [—4—] withdrawn from the water for extended periods of time" in order to facilitate repairs and reconstruction may lose their status as vessels until they are rendered capable of maritime transport. *Stewart*, 543 U.S., at 496. Cf. *West* v. *United States*, 361 U.S. 118, 120, 122 (1959) (noting that "the *Mary Austin* was withdrawn from any operation whatever while in storage with the 'moth-ball fleet'" and that "[t]he *Mary Austin*, as anyone could see, was not in maritime service. She was undergoing major repairs and complete renovation . . .").

Finally, our maritime jurisprudence excludes from vessel status those floating structures that, based on their physical characteristics, do not "transport people, freight, or cargo from place to place" as one of their purposes. *Stewart*, 543 U. S., at 493. "Purpose," in this context, is determined solely by an objective inquiry into a craft's function. "[N]either size, form, equipment nor means of propulsion are determinative factors upon the question of [vessel status]," though all may be considered. *The Robert W. Parsons*, 191 U. S. 17, 30 (1903). Moreover, in assessing a particular structure's function, we have consistently examined its past and present activities. *Stewart*, 543 U. S., at 495; *Cope*, 119 U. S., at 627. Of course, a seaborne craft is not excluded from vessel status simply because its "primary purpose" is not maritime transport. *Stewart*, 543 U. S., at 497. We held as much in *Stewart* when we concluded that a dredge was a vessel notwithstanding that its "primary purpose" was "dredging rather than transportation." *Id.*, at 486, 495. So long as one purpose of a craft is transportation, whether of cargo or people or both, §3's practical capability requirement is satisfied.

Certainly, difficult and marginal cases will arise. For- [—5—] tunately, courts do not consider each floating structure anew. So, for example, when we were confronted in *Stewart* with the question whether a dredge is a §3 vessel, we did not commence with a clean slate; we instead sought guidance from previous cases that had confronted similar structures. See *id.*, at 490, and n. 5; see also *Norton* v. *Warner Co.*, 321 U. S. 565, 571–572 (1944) (likewise surveying earlier cases).

In sum, our precedents offer substantial guidance for how objectively to determine whether a watercraft is practically capable of maritime transport and thus qualifies as a §3 vessel. First, the capacity to float and carry things or people is an obvious prerequisite to vessel status. Second, structures or ships that are permanently moored or fixed in place are not §3 vessels. Likewise, structures that are practically incapable of maritime transport are not vessels, whether they are ships that have been altered so that they may no longer be put to sea, dead ships, or ships removed

---

[1] The converse category of ships "not yet born" is another historical exclusion from vessel status. See *Tucker* v. *Alexandroff*, 183 U. S. 424, 438 (1902) ("A ship is born when she is launched, and lives so long as her identity is preserved. Prior to her launching she is a mere congeries of wood and iron—an ordinary piece of personal property—as [—4—] distinctly a land structure as a house, and subject only to mechanics' liens created by state law and enforceable in the state courts").

from navigation for extended periods of time. Third, those watercraft whose physical characteristics and usage history reveal no maritime transport purpose or use are not §3 vessels.

II

The majority does not appear to disavow the legal principles described above. The majority apparently accepts that permanent mooring suffices to take a ship out of vessel status, *ante,* at 8, 12,[2] and that "[a] craft whose [—6—] physical characteristics and activities objectively evidence a waterborne transportation purpose or function may still be rendered a nonvessel by later physical alterations," *ante,* at 12–13.[3] No one argues that Lozman's craft was permanently moored, see App. 32 (describing the "deteriorated" ropes holding the craft in place), or that it had undergone physical alterations sufficient to take it out of vessel status, see Tr. of Oral Arg. 13 (Lozman's counsel arguing that the craft was never a vessel in the first place). Our precedents make clear that the Eleventh Circuit's "anything that floats" test is overinclusive and ignores that purpose is a crucial factor in determining whether a particular craft is or is not a vessel. Accordingly, the majority is correct that determining whether Lozman's craft is a vessel hinges on whether that craft had any maritime transportation purpose or function.

---

[2] In discussing permanent mooring, as well as *Stewart*'s rejection of primary-purpose and state-of-transit tests for vessel status, *Stewart* v. *Dutra Constr. Co.,* 543 U. S. 481, 495 (2005), the majority states that our holdings "say, and they mean, that the statutory definition [given by §3] *may* (or may not) apply—not that it *automatically must* apply—where a structure has some other *primary* purpose, where it is stationary at relevant times, and where it is attached—but not permanently attached—to land." *Ante,* at 8. This must mean, by negative implication, that a permanently moored structure never falls within §3's [—6—] definition.

[3] Presumably, this encompasses those kinds of ships "otherwise rendered practically incapable of transportation or movement." *Stewart,* 543 U. S., at 494. That is, ships which have been altered so they cannot travel the seas, dead ships, and ships removed from the water for an extended period of time. *Supra,* at 3–4.

The majority errs, though, in concluding that the purpose component of the §3 test is whether "a reasonable observer, looking to the [craft]'s physical characteristics and activities, would not consider it to be designed to any practical degree for carrying people or things on water." *Ante,* at 1. This phrasing has never appeared in any of our cases and the majority's use of it, despite its seemingly objective gloss, effectively (and erroneously) introduces a subjective component into the vessel-status inquiry.

For one thing, in applying this test the majority points to some characteristics of Lozman's craft that have no relationship to maritime transport, such as the style of the craft's rooms or that "those inside those rooms looked out upon the world, not through water-tight portholes, but [—7—] through French doors or ordinary windows." *Ante,* at 5. The majority never explains why it believes these particular esthetic elements are important for determining vessel status. In fact, they are not. Section 3 is focused on whether a structure is "used, or capable of being used, as a means of transportation on water." By importing windows, doors, room style, and other esthetic criteria into the §3 analysis, the majority gives our vessel test an "I know it when I see it" flavor. *Jacobellis* v. *Ohio,* 378 U.S. 184, 197 (1964) (Stewart, J., concurring). But that has never been nor should it be the test: A badly designed and unattractive vessel is different from a structure that lacks any "practical capacity" for maritime transport. In the majority's eyes, the two appear to be one and the same.

The majority's treatment of the craft's past voyages is also strange. The majority notes that Lozman's craft could be and was, in fact, towed over long distances, including over 200 miles at one point. *Ante,* at 2–6. But the majority determines that, given the design of Lozman's craft, this is "far too little *actual* 'use' to bring the floating home within the terms of the statute." *Ante,* at 14. This is because "when it moved, it carried, not passengers or cargo, but at the very most (giving the benefit of any factual ambiguity to the City) only its own furnishings, its owner's personal effects, and personnel present to assure the home's safety." *Ante,* at 13–14.

I find this analysis confusing. The majority accepts that the record indicates that Lozman's craft traveled hundreds of miles while "carrying people or things." *Ante,* at 1. But then, in the same breath, the majority concludes that a "reasonable observer" would nonetheless conclude that the craft was not "designed to any practical degree for carrying people or things on water." *Ibid.* The majority fails to explain how a craft that apparently did carry people and things over water for long distances was not "practically capable" of maritime transport. [—8—]

This is not to say that a structure capable of such feats is necessarily a vessel. A craft like Lozman's might not be a vessel, for example, if it could only carry its owner's clothes and personal effects, or if it is only capable of transporting itself and its appurtenances. *Jerome B. Grubart, Inc.* v. *Great Lakes Dredge & Dock Co.,* 513 U. S. 527, 535 (1995) ("[M]aritime law . . . ordinarily treats an 'appurtenance' attached to a vessel in navigable waters as part of the vessel itself"). But if such a craft can carry large appliances (like an oven or a refrigerator) and all of the other things we might find in a normal home in addition to the occupants of that home, as the existing record suggests Lozman's craft may have done, then it would seem to be much more like a mobile home (and therefore a vessel) than a firmly rooted residence. The simple truth is that we know very little about the craft's capabilities and what did or did not happen on its various trips. By focusing on the little we do know for certain about this craft (*i.e.,* its windows, doors, and the style of its rooms) in determining whether it is a vessel, the majority renders the §3 inquiry opaque and unpredictable.

Indeed, the little we do know about Lozman's craft suggests only that it was an unusual structure. A surveyor was unable to find any comparable craft for sale in the State of Florida. App. 43. Lozman's home was neither obviously a houseboat, as the majority describes such ships, *ante,* at 5–6, nor clearly a floating home, *ante,* at 10–11. See App. 13, 31, 79 (sale, lease, and surveying documents describing Lozman's craft as a "houseboat"). The only clear difference that the majority identifies between these two kinds of structures is that the former are self-propelled, while the latter are not. *Ante,* at 5–6. But even the majority recognizes that self-propulsion has never been a prerequisite for vessel status. *Ante,* at 5 (citing *The Robert W. Parsons,* 191 U. S., at 31); see *Norton,* 321 U.S., at 571. Consequently, it is unclear why [—9—] Lozman's craft is a floating home, why all floating homes are not vessels,[4] or why Lozman's craft is not a vessel. If windows, doors, and other esthetic attributes are what take Lozman's craft out of vessel status, then the majority's test is completely malleable. If it is the craft's lack of self-propulsion, then the majority's test is unfaithful to our longstanding precedents. See *The Robert W. Parsons,* 191 U. S., at 30–31. If it is something else, then that something is not apparent from the majority's opinion.

Worse still, in straining to find that Lozman's craft was a floating home and therefore not a vessel, the majority calls into question the conclusions of numerous lower

---

[4] To be clear, some floating homes are obviously not vessels. For example, some floating homes are structures built upon a large inverted pyramid of logs. Brief for Seattle Floating Homes Assn. et al. as *Amici Curiae* 14. Cf. App. 38 (Lozman's craft was buoyed by an empty bilge space). These kinds of floating homes can measure 4,000 or 5,000 square feet, see Brief for Seattle Floating Homes Assn. et al. as *Amici Curiae* 4, and may have connections to land that require the aid of divers and electricians to remove, *ibid.* These large, immobile structures are not vessels and have physical attributes directly connected to their lack of navigational abilities that suggest as much. But these structures are not before us; Lozman's craft is.

courts that have found houseboats that lacked self-propulsion to be §3 vessels. See *ante,* at 9–10 (citing *Miami River Boat Yard, Inc.* v. *60' Houseboat,* 390 F. 2d 596, 597 (CA5 1968); *Sea Village Marina, LLC* v. *A 1980 Carlcraft Houseboat,* No. 09–3292, 2009 WL 3379923, *5–*6 (D NJ, Oct. 19, 2009); *Hudson Harbor 79th Street Boat Basin, Inc.* v. *Sea Casa,* 469 F. Supp. 987, 989 (SDNY 1979)). The majority incorrectly suggests that these cases applied an " 'anything that floats' " test. *Ante,* at 9. These cases suggest something different. Many of these decisions in assessing the crafts before them looked carefully at these crafts' structure and function, and determined that these ships had capabilities similar to other long-established vessels, suggesting a significant maritime [—10—] transportation function. See *Miami River Boat Yard,* 390 F. 2d, at 597 (likening houseboat at issue to a "barg[e]"); *Sea Village Marina,* 2009 WL 3379923, *7 ("According to the available evidence, [the houseboats in question] float and can be towed to a new marina without substantial effort . . . "); *Hudson Harbor,* 469 F. Supp., at 989 (houseboat "was capable of being used at least to the extent that a 'dumb barge' is capable of being used" and comparable to a "yach[t]"). Their holdings are consistent with older cases, see, *e.g., The Ark,* 17 F. 2d 446, 447 (SD Fla. 1926), and the crafts at issue in these cases have been widely accepted as vessels by most treatises in this area, see 1 S.Friedell, Benedict on Admiralty §164, p. 10–6, n. 2 (7th ed. rev. 2012); 1 T. Schoenbaum, Admiralty & Maritime Law §3–6, p. 153, n. 10 (5th ed. 2011); 1 R. Force & M. Norris, The Law of Seamen §2:12, p. 2–82 (5th ed. 2003). The majority's suggestion that rejecting the Eleventh Circuit's test necessitates jettisoning these other precedents is simply wrong. And, in its rejection, the majority works real damage to what has long been a settled area of maritime law.[5]

---

[5] The majority's invocation of two state environmental and tax statutes as a reason to reject this well-established lower court precedent is particularly misguided. See *ante,* at 10–11. We

III

With a more developed record, Lozman's craft might be distinguished from the houseboats in those lower court [—11—] cases just discussed. For example, if Lozman's craft's previous voyages caused it serious damage, then that would strongly suggest that it lacked a maritime transportation purpose or function. There is no harm in remanding the case for further factfinding along the lines described above, cautioning the lower courts to be aware that features of Lozman's "incomparable" craft, see App. 43, may distinguish it from previous precedents. At most, such a remand would introduce a relatively short delay before finally ending the years-long battle between Lozman and the city of Riviera Beach.

On the other hand, there is great harm in stretching the facts below and overriding settled and likely correct lower court precedents to reach the unnecessary conclusion that Lozman's craft was not a vessel. Without an objective application of the §3 standard, one that relies in a predictable fashion only on those physical characteristics of a craft that are related to maritime transport and use, parties will have no *ex ante* notion whether a particular ship is a vessel. As a wide range of *amici* have cautioned us, numerous maritime industries rely heavily on clear and predictable legal rules for determining which ships are vessels.[6] The

---

have repeatedly emphasized that the "regulation of maritime vessels" is a "uniquely *federal* are[a] of regulation." *Chamber of Commerce of United States of America* v. *Whiting,* 563 U. S. __, __ (2011) (plurality opinion) (slip op.,at 19) (emphasis added); see also *United States* v. *Locke,* 529 U. S. 89, 99 (2000) (explaining that "the federal interest [in regulating interstate navigation] has been manifest since the beginning of our Republic and is now well established"). Our previous cases did not turn to state law in determining whether a given craft is a vessel. There are no good reasons to do so now.

[6] For example, without knowing whether a particular ship is a §3 vessel, it is impossible for lenders to know how properly to characterize it as collateral for a financing agreement because they do not know what remedies they will have recourse

majority's distorted application of our [—12—] settled law to the facts of this case frustrates these ends. Moreover, the majority's decision reaches well beyond relatively insignificant boats like Lozman's craft, *id.,* at 79 (listing purchase price of Lozman's craft as $17,000), because it specifically disapproves of lower court decisions dealing with much larger ships, see *ante,* at 10 (questioning *Holmes* v. *Atlantic Sounding Co.,* 437 F. 3d 441 (CA5 2006) (finding a 140-foot-long and 40-foot-wide dormitory barge with 50 beds to be a §3 vessel)).

IV

It is not clear that Lozman's craft is a §3 vessel. It is clear, however, that we are not in a good position to make such a determination based on the limited record we possess. The appropriate response is to remand the case for

---

to in the event of a default. Brief for National Marine Bankers Assn. as *Amicus Curiae* 14–15. Similarly, cities like Riviera Beach provide docking for crafts like Lozman's on the assumption that such crafts actually are "vessels," App. 13–21 (Riviera Beach's wet-slip agreement referring to Lozman's craft as a "vessel," "boat," or "houseboat"), that can be "remove[d]" upon short notice, *id.,* at 17 (requiring removal of the craft on three days' notice). The majority makes it impossible for these marinas to know whether the "houseboats" that fill their slips are actually vessels and what remedies they can exercise in the event of a dispute. See *id.,* at 15 ("In addition to any other remedies provided for in this Agreement, [—12—] the Marina, as a provider of necessities to this *vessel*, has a maritime lien on the *vessel* and may bring a civil action *in rem* under 46 United States Code 31342 in Federal Court, to arrest the *vessel* and enforce the lien . . . " (emphasis added)). Lozman's behavior over the years is emblematic of this problem. For example, in 2003, prior to his move to Riviera Beach, Lozman had his craft towed from one marina to another after a dispute arose with the first marina and he was threatened with eviction. App. 76–78. The possibility that a shipowner like Lozman can depart so easily over water and go beyond the reach of a provider of necessaries like the marina in response to a legal dispute is exactly the kind of problem that the Federal Maritime Lien Act, 46 U.S.C. §31342, was intended to address. See *Dampskibsselskabet Dannebrog* v. *Signal Oil & Gas Co. of Cal.,* 310 U. S. 268, 272–273 (1940).

---

further proceedings in light of the proper legal standard. See Brief for United States as *Amicus Curiae* 29–31. The Court resists this move and in its haste to christen Lozman's craft a nonvessel delivers an analysis that will confuse the lower courts and upset our longstanding admiralty precedent. I respectfully dissent.

This page intentionally left blank

United States Court of Appeals for the First Circuit

United States Court of Appeals
for the First Circuit

No. 11-1611

UNITED STATES
VS.
$8,440,190.00 IN U.S. CURRENCY

Appeal from the United States District Court for the
District of Puerto Rico

Decided: June 17, 2013

Citation: 719 F.3d 49, 1 Adm. R. 18 (1st Cir. 2013).

Before **HOWARD, LIPEZ,** and **THOMPSON,** Circuit
Judges.

[—2—] **THOMPSON,** Circuit Judge:

While fleeing from the Coast Guard aboard a go-fast vessel, the claimant Robert Hovito Van Bommel Duyzing ("Van Bommel") and his crew tossed approximately $8 million into the Caribbean Sea. The money was recovered by the Coast Guard and the government filed this action seeking to have the currency, along with some additional money found on the crew members' persons, forfeited to the United States. Van Bommel tried to put a stop to this, claiming that the money was his. The district court dismissed his claim on summary judgment and Van Bommel now appeals. After careful review, we affirm in part and reverse in part.

BACKGROUND

A. The Interdiction

In the late evening hours of June 20, 2009, the United States Coast Guard cutter Harriet Lane was conducting a routine patrol in the waters off of Panama when the crew began tracking a nearby small, fast-moving vessel. A helicopter was launched from the Harriet Lane to initiate visual and radar contact. It was determined that the boat was a go-fast vessel of approximately forty feet in length that had four persons on board, four engines, and no masthead, stern light or sidelights visible as required by maritime regulations. The Coast Guard crew's suspicions were aroused and so the helicopter approached the vessel, which was located in international waters, and fired three warning shots as [—3—] an order to stop. The vessel did not heed the warning and it took a round of disabling fire from the helicopter to bring the vessel to a halt. The helicopter crew witnessed the individuals aboard the go-fast vessel throwing numerous bales overboard.

An inflatable boat was launched from the Harriet Lane and Coast Guard crew members headed to the disabled boat. They boarded to find four men, one of whom is the claimant in this case, Van Bommel.[1] The boat, which contained none of the tell-tale indicators of a vessel's nationality, was determined to be stateless after contact was made with Panamanian authorities.[2] Surface samples were taken from the boat, revealing that certain areas had been in recent contact with cocaine.

The jettisoned bales, which had been marked by the helicopter's crew with strobe lights and a data marking buoy, were found floating in the sea (six bales were never found; it seems they may have sunk or drifted away). The Coast Guard scooped them up. There were approximately twenty-one bales total, all of similar shape and size, as well as a plastic package containing a loaded semi-automatic handgun and ammunition. Aboard the Harriet Lane, thirteen of the bales were opened. Each contained roughly [—4—] $400,000 putting the preliminary estimate of recovered currency at $8.4 million.

Van Bommel and his three companions, who had also been transferred to the Harriet Lane, were advised of their rights and interviewed. Van Bommel stated that he was offered $40,000 to transport the bales of money and was paid $10,000 of it up front. Consistent with his story, Van Bommel had $10,000 cash on his person as did each of his

---

[1] The other crew members were Arnaldo Henao-Serna, Manuel Carrascal-Reales, and Abraham Carrascal-Carrascal. All, including Van Bommel, were from Colombia.

[2] It is unclear whether the Panamanian authorities were contacted simply because the boat was found near the Panama coast or because the crew reported it as being Panamanian.

associates. Van Bommel also told Coast Guard officers that he and his crew had tossed the bales overboard when they saw the helicopter.[3]

B. Van Bommel Talks with Law Enforcement

About a week later, on June 29, Van Bommel was again interviewed by law enforcement officials and he continued talking. Van Bommel said that while drinking at a bar on San Andres Island, he and his three crew members met a man named Tomas (last name unknown). After the group hung out a few times, Tomas cut to the chase. He wanted the four men to participate in a smuggling venture that would involve them moving bales of money from one area of Panama to another. Van Bommel said Tomas then made arrangements [—5—] for all four men to be transported from San Andres Island to Boca de Toro, Panama to board the go-fast vessel.

Also on the day of his interview, June 29, Van Bommel signed U.S. Immigration and Customs Enforcement ("ICE") forms titled "Notice of Abandonment of All Rights and Interest in Property" (the "notices of abandonment"). One form pertained to the twenty-one bales and the other to $10,000 in currency (indubitably the $10,000 found on Van Bommel's person).[4] The forms contained an "Acknowledgment and Abandonment of Claim" that stated:

I understand that I have a right to assert a claim in the seized property

---

[3] The government claims that Van Bommel indicated that he threw the bales overboard to sink them; Van Bommel says he made no such admission. Another point of disagreement: the government alleges that Van Bommel made other incriminating statements, tying himself and the others to illegal endeavors such as drug and weapons trafficking. Van Bommel denies this. This dispute is not material for our purposes.

[4] The form we have pertaining to the twenty-one bales is in English and the form pertaining to the $10,000 is in Spanish. The forms, apart from being in different languages, look identical and appear to provide for the same thing. No party claims otherwise. We therefore treat both forms as containing the same terms.

described above and to seek return of the property. With full knowledge of those rights, I hereby abandon any and all claims I may have to that property. I waive my right to receive notice of future administrative or judicial proceedings involving the property. I also waive any further right to contest the administrative or judicial forfeiture of the property described above.

Van Bommel signed the notices of abandonment, both for the twenty-one bales and the $10,000, and an ICE agent and Drug Enforcement Administration ("DEA") agent signed as witnesses.

C. Criminal Charges

The same day he met with law enforcement, a criminal complaint was filed against Van Bommel (and his three cohorts). It alleged that Van Bommel, by failing to stop his boat when ordered [—6—] to do so by the Coast Guard, had violated 18 U.S.C. § 2237, which makes it unlawful for an operator of "a vessel subject to the jurisdiction of the United States, to knowingly fail to obey" a federal law enforcement officer's order "to heave to that vessel" (in layman's terms, failing to slow down or stop). *See* 18 U.S.C. § 2237(a)(1), (e)(2). Van Bommel was ultimately indicted and pled guilty on December 22, 2009. Van Bommel was sentenced on February 4, 2010 to time already served and a three year term of supervised release was imposed.

D. The Forfeiture Action

We backtrack a little. A few months earlier, on November 25, 2009, the United States filed this action, a verified complaint for forfeiture in rem as to $8,440,190. Relying on an affidavit completed by ICE agent Antonio Rivera, who participated in the investigation of Van Bommel, the government alleged that the $8,440,190 in currency was seized from Van Bommel and his accomplices, and the go-fast vessel that they were traveling on. The complaint indicated that the currency, which represented the $8,400,190 found in the bales and the $10,000 found on each crew member's person, was currently in the custody of the

DEA, ICE, Department of Homeland Security ("DHS"), U.S. Customs and Border Protection ("CBP"), and the Federal Bureau of Investigation ("FBI"). The complaint asserted that the currency should be forfeited to the United States, *see* 46 U.S.C. § 70507, because it [—7—] was involved in a violation of the law, specifically the manufacture, distribution, or possession of a controlled substance on a vessel, *see id.* § 70503. On December 1, the district court ordered that a warrant of arrest in rem be issued for the seized currency. On that same day, the court granted the government's motion to seal the case.

Once Van Bommel and the others' criminal convictions were all wrapped up, the court ordered the forfeiture case unsealed. A week or so later, on March 19, 2010, Van Bommel filed a verified claim of ownership with the district court for $8,410,190 of the currency—representing all the money in the bales plus the $10,000 found on Van Bommel's person. The claim, after detailing the amount of money and where it was presently being held,[5] simply indicated that Van Bommel was the owner of the currency. He signed the document under the pain of perjury. That same day, Van Bommel filed a motion to dismiss the complaint. In essence, Van Bommel argued that the government had not established that he was involved in a drug smuggling venture and he also took issue with the timing of the complaint and the fact that it was sealed. Attached to the motion to dismiss were three more verified claims of ownership (one each pertaining to the $10,000, $4,200,000, and $4,200,190) that again simply averred that Van Bommel was the owner. [—8—]

The government then filed an amended complaint, which Van Bommel moved to dismiss. He also filed an answer. Motion practice continued with the government moving for summary judgment. It argued that Van Bommel did not have Article III standing under the United States Constitution to challenge the forfeiture because he had no colorable interest in the seized currency. The government said Van Bommel's claim for the money should be stricken. Van Bommel objected, arguing among other things that he did have standing and that the district court lacked jurisdiction over the in rem action. Van Bommel reiterated his lack of jurisdiction argument in a motion to quash the arrest warrant in rem.

Given the various filings going back and forth, the district court decided that an evidentiary hearing was needed to flesh out the standing issue. The hearing took place on August 19, 2010. Though billed as an evidentiary hearing, neither side ended up offering factual evidence or testimony. Van Bommel, for his part, had by then been deported to Colombia.[6] The government had two agents at the ready to testify—the ones who interviewed Van Bommel and witnessed his signing the notices of abandonment—however they were never ultimately called. The attorneys did make [—9—] their pitches though. Van Bommel's argued that his client never intended to abandon the property—supposedly he planned to retrieve it from the sea later—and that Van Bommel's sworn claims of ownership were sufficient to establish standing. The government persisted that Van Bommel abandoned the property, pointing not only to the fact that he tossed it into the sea but also that he signed notices of abandonment. Van Bommel's attorney countered: he intended to go back for the bales and he only signed because he was not fully advised of his rights and was threatened with prosecution for drug smuggling. After a little more back and forth, the hearing came to a close.

---

[5] It indicated that $10,000 was being held by the FBI, $4,200,000 by the DEA, and $4,200,190 by the CBP.

[6] Van Bommel's attorney, who also participated in Van Bommel's deportation proceeding, never filed a motion with the court or approached the prosecutor seeking to keep his client in the country for this evidentiary hearing. In fact, when the government sought to stay the deportation so that Van Bommel could be deposed, Van Bommel's counsel opposed it.

A few months later,[7] on March 15, 2011, the district court issued its decision. It found that the claims of ownership filed by Van Bommel, which were unsupported by any evidence other than his affidavit, were inadequate. Van Bommel, it held, had also given up any right he might have had to the loot by signing the notices of abandonment. Because Van Bommel had not shown a colorable interest in the seized currency, the court concluded that he had failed to establish Article III standing to challenge the forfeiture. The government's motion for summary judgment was granted, and Van Bommel's claim of ownership and pleadings were [—10—] dismissed with prejudice.[8] The court also dismissed Van Bommel's various motions to dismiss and motion to quash as moot.

E. This Appeal

Van Bommel now appeals the district court's grant of summary judgment. He advances two grounds: the district court did not have jurisdiction over a portion of the defendant currency, and the court erred in finding that he has no standing.

ANALYSIS

A. Jurisdiction

Van Bommel, though he never argued this below, contends that the warrant for arrest in rem pertaining to just the $4,200,190 in the custody of CBP was never executed.[9] To

---

[7] Van Bommel, in between the hearing taking place and the decision issuing, filed yet another motion to dismiss.

[8] To be clear, this was a grant of partial judgment. Full judgment in favor of the government on its forfeiture complaint was not granted at this time. One of the other members of Van Bommel's crew, Henao-Serna, also had a claim pending that had to be sorted out. When Henao-Serna ultimately failed to prosecute this claim, the court dismissed it. With no claims left pending, the court (over a year after partial judgment was entered against Van Bommel) entered final judgment in favor of the United States and closed the case.

[9] Van Bommel raised a somewhat related argument below in his motion to quash, which the district court twice denied (once without

support [—11—] this theory he claims that no return of service was filed for that portion of the money. According to Van Bommel, the failure of the government to execute a warrant for that part of the defendant currency results in the district court having no in rem jurisdiction over it. The government offers no response to this argument because it was not addressed by the district court. The government suggests that if we find standing we should remand to the district court to address this issue. We will not take the government's proffered approach. Van Bommel challenges the district court's jurisdiction and this court has an obligation to satisfy itself that the court had jurisdiction. *See Steel Co. v. Citizens for a Better Env't*, 523 U.S. 83, 95 (1998); *Sindicato Puertorriqueño de Trabajadores v. Fortuño*, 699 F.3d 1, 8 (1st Cir. 2012). And so we take up Van Bommel's argument, although it does not get him far.

Though Van Bommel says that the warrant was never executed for the $4,200,190 held by the CBP, we do not see any record support for this contention. While Van Bommel is not specific about what portion of the record he is relying on (in his [—12—] brief he simply says

---

explanation, and then again as moot based on its award of summary judgment to the government). Van Bommel argued that the warrant of arrest in rem for the entire defendant currency, which was issued on December 1, 2009, was not timely executed because, according to the process receipt and return, it was executed on May 10, 2010, one-hundred and sixty-one days later. Van Bommel averred that the one-hundred plus days did not satisfy the requirement of Rule G of the Supplemental Rules for Admiralty or Maritime Claims and Asset Forfeiture Actions, which requires that warrants in forfeiture in rem actions must be executed "as soon as practicable." Rule G(3)(c)(ii). However, as the government [—11—] correctly noted in its opposition, this argument is without merit because Rule G specifically provides that the "as soon as practicable" requirement does not apply when "the property is in the government's possession, custody, or control" which the defendant currency was here. Rule G(3)(c)(ii)(A). When Van Bommel made this argument below he made no mention of his current assertion that the warrant was never executed as to the $4,200,190.

the "docket sheet" reveals that the warrant was never executed), we think it safe to assume that he is focusing on the Process Receipt and Return (the "process receipt") and so we take a close look at that. The process receipt, which is the same document that Van Bommel relied on to say that the warrant was not executed in a timely manner, indicates that the warrant of arrest in rem was served on the United States Marshals on May 10, 2010. We assume that Van Bommel is honing in on a section of the process receipt called "Special Instructions or Other Information That Will Assist in Executing Service." This section contains the following language: "Ten Thousand Dollars ($10,000.00) in U.S. Currency-09-FBI-004982" and "Four Million Two Hundred Thousand Dollars and Zero Cents ($4,200,000.00) in U.S. Currency 09-DEA-520362." There is no reference to the $4,200,190 held by the CBP. This omission, however, is not sufficient to establish that the warrant was never executed on the $4,200,190.

The defendant listed at the top of the process receipt is "$8,440,190.00 in U.S. Currency," in other words, the entire amount of the defendant currency. There is nothing to indicate that the special instructions section alters or in any way limits this amount. The type of process to be served is listed as the complaint, amended complaint, the warrant of arrest in rem, and an unspecified order (the most likely candidate being the court order granting the government's motion to issue the warrant). All of [—13—] these documents speak in terms of the entire $8,440,190. None of them excludes the $4,200,190. Indeed none of the documents even distinguish between, or parse out, the different amounts being held by the different government agencies, other than to say that the defendant currency is being held by various agencies.

The warrant of arrest in rem, in particular, provides that "a complaint has been filed in this Court praying for the forfeiture of the above captioned defendant property" and that "we do hereby command that you seize said defendant property, which is described in the caption of the complaint, and to detain the same in your custody until further order of the Court." The caption on the warrant, and on the complaint, reads "$8,440,190.00 in U.S. Currency, Defendant." The warrant of arrest in rem clearly calls for the arrest of the entire property. And there is nothing on the face of the process receipt to indicate that the warrant was not executed for all of the money. The fact that the special instructions, which are simply meant to assist in expediting service, do not reference the $4,200,190 held by the CBP does not clearly indicate that the warrant for that portion of the money was never executed.

That is all we need to say on this point. Because the record does not support the underlying premise that the warrant for arrest in rem for the $4,200,190 was never executed, we need not [—14—] get into the merits of Van Bommel's claim that the alleged failure to execute the warrant divests the district court of jurisdiction.[10]

B. Standing

We move on to the main question on appeal: whether Van Bommel has constitutional standing under Article III to challenge the forfeiture.[11] Van Bommel thinks the answer is yes, alleging that his verified claims of ownership are sufficient to give him standing to contest the entire $8,410,190 and that it is a disputed issue of fact whether he voluntarily abandoned the money or waived his right to it. The government continues to contend that Van Bommel has not shown any

[10] Van Bommel had a follow-up argument too. He contended that if the government were to now attempt to fix its alleged failure to execute the warrant, it would be too late because the suit would be untimely. Since we find no merit in his claim that the warrant was not executed, we do not need to get into this claim.

[11] Standing in forfeiture actions "has both constitutional and statutory aspects." *United States v. One-Sixth Share of James J. Bulger in All Present & Future Proceeds of Mass Millions Lottery Ticket No. M246233*, 326 F.3d 36, 40 (1st Cir. 2003). The government only challenged Article III standing before the district court and the court deemed it uncontested that Van Bommel had statutory standing. The government does not challenge that finding on appeal. Therefore only Article III standing is at issue here.

possessory or ownership interest in any of the confiscated money.

Our review, since this case comes to us on a grant of summary judgment, is de novo. *Kenney v. Floyd*, 700 F.3d 604, 608 (1st Cir. 2012). Facts are viewed in a light most favorable to Van Bommel, the non-movant; all reasonable inferences are also drawn in [—15—] his favor. *Rared Manchester NH, LLC v. Rite Aid of N.H., Inc.*, 693 F.3d 48, 52 (1st Cir. 2012). Ultimately, summary judgment is called for when the movant, here the government, demonstrates that "there is no genuine dispute as to any material fact" and that it "is entitled to judgment as a matter of law." Fed. R. Civ. P. 56(a). Genuine issues are those capable of being resolved in favor of either party and material facts have the potential to impact the case's outcome. *Vera v. McHugh*, 622 F.3d 17, 26 (1st Cir. 2010).

After careful review, we conclude that the answer to the standing question is different depending on which amount of money one is talking about— the approximately $8 million in the bales versus the $10,000 on Van Bommel's person. We take the two groups of currency separately.

i. The $8 Million in the Bales

In general, there are three components that must be satisfied for Article III standing: a concrete and particularized injury, a causal connection between that injury and the wrongdoer's conduct, and the likelihood that prevailing in the action will rectify the injury in some way. *Antilles Cement Corp. v. Fortuño*, 670 F.3d 310, 317 (1st Cir. 2012); *United States v. U.S. Currency, $81,000*, 189 F.3d 28, 34 (1st Cir. 1999). "Standing is a threshold consideration in all cases, including civil forfeiture cases." *United States v. One-Sixth Share of James J. Bulger in All Present* [—16—] *& Future Proceeds of Mass Millions Lottery Ticket No. M246233*, 326 F.3d 36, 40 (1st Cir. 2003).

In forfeiture cases, the property is the defendant and therefore defenses against forfeiture can only be brought by a third-party intervenor, here Van Bommel, who generally must have independent standing. *See id.* When faced with a motion seeking to strike a claim, as Van Bommel is here, the burden is on the party contesting the forfeiture (the claimant) to establish standing by a preponderance of the evidence. Supplemental Rule for Admiralty or Maritime Claims and Asset Forfeiture Actions G(8)(c)(ii)(B). To have such standing, the claimant must start by demonstrating an ownership or possessory interest in the seized property. *One-Sixth Share*, 326 F.3d at 41. At the initial stages of intervention, the requirements are not arduous and typically "any colorable claim on the defendant property suffices." *Id.* (addressing the claimants' standing at the motion to intervene/motion to set aside a judgement phase); *see also U.S. Currency, $81,000*, 189 F.3d at 35 (considering standing at the motion to dismiss stage); *United States v. One Parcel of Real Prop. with Bldgs., Appurtenances & Improvements Known as 116 Emerson St.*, 942 F.2d 74, 78-79 (1st Cir. 1991) (deciding the claimant's standing at the motion to intervene stage). An allegation of ownership, coupled with some evidence of ownership, is sufficient to establish constitutional standing to contest a forfeiture. *U.S. Currency, $81,000*, 189 F.3d at 35. [—17—]

This case comes to us not at the early stages of intervention but following a hearing that the district court ordered specifically to address the issue of standing.[12] This was a hearing that the court had every right to order as the burden is on the claimant to prove

---

[12] We do not go so far as to say that a distinct test should be applied to civil forfeiture actions at the summary judgment phase. In fact, in *United States v. Union Bank for Sav. & Inv. (Jordan)*, 487 F.3d 8, 22 (1st Cir. 2007), this court, in deciding whether summary judgment was properly granted, decided that a claimant had standing using the forgiving "colorable claim" requirement that is typically applied at the early stages of intervention. However, that case was very different from this one in that the court did not need to delve into the factual underpinnings of the claimant's ownership because it was undisputed that the money the government was seeking forfeiture of was seized from the claimant's bank account. *See id.* As we said, the court here actually ordered an evidentiary hearing to flesh out the standing considerations.

standing, *see One-Sixth Share*, 326 F.3d at 41 (explaining that the onus is on the party seeking to challenge the forfeiture to demonstrate the necessary ownership or possessory interest to establish standing), and the court was entitled to flesh out what evidence Van Bommel had, *see, e.g., United States v. Union Bank for Sav. & Inv. (Jordan)*, 487 F.3d 8, 13 (1st Cir. 2007) (the district court held an extended summary judgment hearing to consider whether the claimant bank was the owner of the seized currency for standing purposes); *U.S. Currency, $81,000*, 189 F.3d at 37 (the district court sifted through evidence, including grand jury testimony of the claimant, to address whether he had an [—18—] ownership interest for standing purposes). In short, Van Bommel's evidence was minimal.

In fact, the only evidence Van Bommel offered, in support of his verified claim for the money, was his own affidavit (proffered in connection with his summary judgment opposition) in which he referred to the bales as "my bales" and indicated that he concealed "my ownership of the defendant currency." This evidence of ownership, minimal in its own right, was contradicted by the other evidence on the record. Namely, the uncontradicted evidence, which came in the form of the affidavit from the ICE agent, that Van Bommel tossed the bales into the sea and told law enforcement that he was paid to move the bales for someone else as part of a smuggling venture. Van Bommel does not disagree that he did these things.

To be more specific, it is undisputed that Van Bommel twice affirmatively indicated to law enforcement that he was simply a paid courier, transporting someone else's money for them. Van Bommel went so far as to give specifics about how he came to transport this money (recall his story about Tomas and the bar on San Andres island). The $10,000 found on Van Bommel's person, along with the $10,000 each of his cohorts had, fit into the story he gave law enforcement. In fact, not one thing in the record suggests that the $8 million was really Van Bommel's except his own after-the-fact affidavit in which he made vague references to [—19—] owning the bale

money. Even crediting the conclusory, self-serving statements made in the affidavit, *see SMS Sys. Maint. Servs., Inc. v. Digital Equip. Corp.*, 188 F.3d 11, 20 (1st Cir. 1999) (noting that conclusory, self-serving testimony need not be credited on summary judgment), the "'mere existence of a scintilla of evidence' in favor of the nonmoving party is insufficient to defeat summary judgment," *Barreto-Rosa v. Varona-Mendez*, 470 F.3d 42, 45 (1st Cir. 2006) (quoting *Anderson v. Liberty Lobby, Inc.*, 477 U.S. 242, 252 (1986)). We do not have any more than that here.

Furthermore, Van Bommel abandoned the property by tossing it into the middle of open ocean. His affidavit claim that he intended to go back and retrieve the bales defies common sense. Not only did Van Bommel toss the bales out in plain sight of a Coast Guard helicopter, but there is no indication in the record that the bales had any built-in feature that would keep them floating in place as opposed to sinking or drifting away. In fact, six of the bales disappeared, presumably sinking or floating away themselves. Again, more than a scintilla of evidence is called for here. *See Barreto-Rosa*, 470 F.3d at 45. And though Van Bommel persists that there is a factual dispute about whether he intended to abandon the money to the sea, this dispute is of his own making based solely on an after-the-fact affidavit that is uncorroborated by any evidence and, like we said, contradicted by common sense. Even viewing the facts in a light most favorable to Van Bommel, we [—20—] do not see a genuine dispute of material fact. *See Webb v. Lawrence Cnty.*, 144 F.3d 1131, 1135 (8th Cir. 1998) (holding that a "non-movant cannot simply create a factual dispute; rather, there must be a genuine dispute over those facts that could actually affect the outcome of the lawsuit").

The common theme here is that not until after the forfeiture action was filed did Van Bommel try to reverse course. He alleged through verified claims and his affidavit that the money was really his all along and that he did not mean to give up his right to it. But when the district court ordered an evidentiary hearing specifically for the purpose of evaluating Van Bommel's standing and clearing up any factual discrepancies, Van Bommel offered no evidence. Not only did he not submit to a deposition beforehand but at the hearing, Van Bommel did not testify[13] and did not offer an additional affidavit to firm up his claim of ownership. For instance, it strikes us that evidence about how he came to own the $8 million and why he was racing across the sea with it in the dark of night would have helped buttress his claim. There was none of this.

For the reasons detailed above, Van Bommel did not have the requisite ownership interest in the $8 million needed to [—21—] establish standing in a forfeiture action. As we said, standing requires an injury that is caused by the wrongdoer and likely to be redressed by the relief sought. *See Antilles Cement Corp.*, 670 F.3d at 317; *U.S. Currency, $81,000*, 189 F.3d at 34. With no ownership interest in the $8,400,190, there is no possible way that Van Bommel can be injured by the forfeiture of the money. Dismissal of Van Bommel's claim as to the approximately $8 million contained in the bales was appropriate.

ii. The $10,000 Van Bommel Was Carrying

The $10,000 Van Bommel was carrying is a different story. Not only did Van Bommel assert in his verified claims and affidavit that he was the owner, but other evidence corroborated this. Specifically, Van Bommel was found with the $10,000 on his person (he did not toss this into the ocean) and, at the time of his capture, he told law enforcement that he was paid $10,000 as the first part of a $40,000 payment to transport the bales. Consistent with his story, all three of his crew members were found with $10,000 on their persons. The tale continued to jibe when Van Bommel later told law enforcement that he and his crew were hired by Tomas for a smuggling venture. Given all of this evidence, we find that Van Bommel demonstrated the requisite ownership interest in the $10,000 to

---

[13] As we said earlier, Van Bommel was deported before the hearing but the record indicates that his counsel did not seek any relief from the district court to stay the deportation and even opposed the government's efforts to keep Van Bommel here.

have standing to contest its forfeiture. *See One-Sixth Share*, 326 F.3d at 41. At this stage in the proceedings, Van Bommel need not prove the full merits of his claim, just that [—22—] he has a colorable interest in the proceedings such that he satisfies prudential standing requirements. *See U.S. Currency, $81,000*, 189 F.3d at 35. He has done that.

The fact that Van Bommel signed a notice of abandonment—this is the fact that the district court harped on with respect to the $10,000—does not change things. In his affidavit, Van Bommel indicated that he "involuntarily and unintelligently" signed the notice after he was "threatened to be prosecuted for drug smuggling if [he] did not abandon the currency." He added that law enforcement did not advise him of his due process rights and that the notice of abandonment did not advise him "of the full panoply of rights counsel later explained to me," such as the right to present evidence and to have a jury determine whether forfeiture was warranted.

The dissent would have us disregard this affidavit on the grounds that it is hearsay. We are not convinced such an approach makes sense. First, the government did not raise any hearsay objection to the affidavit, nor is it making such an argument on appeal. Indeed it would be surprising if it was since the government, in support of its motion for summary judgment, relied heavily on its own affidavit—the affidavit completed by ICE agent Antonio Rivera, which detailed what happened the night the money was seized and Van Bommel's conversations with law enforcement. The district court also raised no hearsay concerns. [—23—]

Second, in analysis section B, i of this decision, which the dissent agrees with and has signed on to, we utilize not only Van Bommel's affidavit to explain why he has not proffered enough evidence to establish standing to contest forfeiture of the bale money, but we also rely on the government's affidavit. Given our reliance on these affidavits to decide Van Bommel's standing to contest the forfeiture of the bale money—again, the dissent does not disagree with that analysis—it seems inconsistent to now say that Van Bommel's affidavit should not be considered on the issue of whether he waived his right to contest the $10,000 because it is hearsay.

Finally, and perhaps more fundamentally, we disagree that Van Bommel's affidavit should be treated as inadmissable hearsay. While the district court called the parties in for an evidentiary hearing, no evidence was in fact taken at the hearing. The judge stated: "Well, I think that takes care of what we intended today, which was basically I wanted to receive additional information on certain issues, more so concerning the issue of standing. But as it stands today it will have to be a determination made on the record." Van Bommel's affidavit was never offered into evidence; its admissibility was not at issue. Affidavits are of course typically relied on to support or defend against motions for summary judgment. *See* Fed. R. Civ. P. 56(c)(1)(A). While it is true that such affidavits "must be made on personal knowledge" and [—24—] "set out facts that would be admissible in evidence," Fed. R. Civ. P. 56(c)(4), and it "is black-letter law that hearsay evidence cannot be considered on summary judgment for the truth of the matter asserted," *Kenney*, 700 F.3d at 609 (internal quotation marks omitted), such hearsay concerns are not present here.

Furthermore, the case that the dissent cites for the proposition that claimants cannot establish Article III standing through hearsay, *United States v. All Funds in the Account of Prop. Futures, Inc.*, 820 F. Supp. 2d 1305 (S.D. Fla. 2011), is not on all fours with this case. The affiant in that case, who was the attorney for the claimant company, attested to a company vote taking place even though he was not present at it. *Id.* at 1331-32. The court disregarded the evidence as inadmissable hearsay because the facts attested to by the affiant were not within his personal knowledge; instead the facts were only known to him because the claimants told him about them. *Id.* at 1332. This is not the situation here. Everything in Van Bommel's affidavit, including the facts relating to his signing the notices of abandonment, were

within his personal knowledge. We see no reason why we should not consider Van Bommel's affidavit.

Thus, on the issue of Van Bommel's knowing and voluntary waiver of his interest in the $10,000 we are left with his affidavit; an affidavit, which despite the dissent's characterization, is not conclusory or cursory. Rather, Van Bommel [—25—] clearly explained the threats that the law enforcement agents allegedly made and what rights he was not advised of. And no evidence on record contradicts his claims. The notice of abandonment, signed and dated by Van Bommel and witnessed by two government agents, indicated that Van Bommel understood his "right to assert a claim in the seized property" and to seek its return and that with "full knowledge of those rights," he was giving them up. Indeed the notice of abandonment does not go into detail (though we are not saying it necessarily had to) about Van Bommel's specific rights. And, more importantly, there is nothing in the record to contradict Van Bommel's claim that law enforcement did not advise him of certain rights and bullied him into signing the notice by dangling the threat of drug smuggling prosecution over his head. The government offered no affidavit evidence on this point, and the law enforcement officers ready to testify at the evidentiary hearing never testified. Furthermore, though the burden is on Van Bommel to convince us of his standing, it is important to remember that this case comes to us on the government's motion for summary judgment. Thus, facts are viewed in a light most favorable to Van Bommel and all reasonable inferences go in his favor. *See Rared Manchester NH, LLC*, 693 F.3d at 52.

The dissent's focus, on what it perceives as Van Bommel's gamesmanship in avoiding having his deposition taken and not [—26—] appearing at the hearing, is misplaced. We are reviewing the district court's grant of summary judgment, of course making our review de novo. *See Kenney*, 700 F.3d at 608. This review centers on the record evidence, not the parties' tactics or course of conduct. The attention the dissent devotes to the latter two things strikes us as a tack more appropriately taken when we are operating under an abuse of discretion standard and giving the district court a wide berth to make discretionary calls about the parties' demeanor and behavior. But that is not the state of affairs here.

Given all this, we conclude that Van Bommel presented enough evidence to demonstrate constitutional standing to contest the forfeiture of the $10,000 found on his person. While the dissent disagrees with us on this point, we think the dissent's approach gets close to collapsing the issue of Van Bommel's standing with the merits of his forfeiture claim, something courts should not do. *See One-Sixth Share*, 326 F.3d at 41 ("Courts should not, however, conflate the constitutional standing inquiry with the merits determination that comes later.") On this narrow issue of standing, we find that Van Bommel established the necessary ownership interest and has alleged an injury at the hands of the government that can be remedied by forfeiture of the $10,000 not going forward. *See U.S. Currency, $81,000*, 189 F.3d at 34-35. To be clear, we are saying nothing more than Van Bommel has the right [—27—] to contest the forfeiture. Whether he will ultimately prevail on his assertion that the property should not be forfeited is up to the district court to decide.

CONCLUSION

To sum things up, there is no merit to Van Bommel's contention that the district court lacked jurisdiction over a portion of the defendant currency. As for Van Bommel's standing, he does not have constitutional standing to contest the forfeiture of the $8,400,190 found in the bales. He does, however, have standing to contest the forfeiture of the $10,000 found on his person. The district court's grant of summary judgment resulting in the dismissal of Van Bommel's claim for the $8,400,190 is affirmed. The court's grant of summary judgment as to the $10,000 is reversed and Van Bommel's claim for the $10,000 is reinstated.[14] Each side shall bear its own costs.

-Concurring and Dissenting Opinion Follows-

(Reporter's Note: Concurring and dissenting opinion on p. 28).

---

[14] The dissent suggests that, even assuming the district court erred, reversal with reinstatement is not the proper disposition. Rather it would have us vacate the grant of summary judgment and give the parties a chance to have a full evidentiary hearing. We disagree. We are asked to decide this appeal on the record at hand. Here the court scheduled an evidentiary hearing but ended up deciding the government's motion for summary judgment on the record. The question we are faced with is whether, based on the evidence that was considered by the court, this grant of summary judgment was erroneous. As we explained above, we think it was as to the $10,000. Reversal is proper.

[—28—] HOWARD, Circuit Judge, concurring in part and dissenting in part:

I concur in the majority's opinion, except for its conclusion that Van Bommel demonstrated constitutional standing to contest the forfeiture of the $10,000 found on his person. Van Bommel did not prove by a preponderance of the evidence that he had a colorable interest in that money; he therefore lacks standing to contest its forfeiture.

As the majority explains, there is every reason to believe that Van Bommel was paid $10,000 to transport the bales of currency that he later threw into the sea. Thus, at one point Van Bommel had a colorable claim of ownership of that $10,000. But he signed a waiver that stated, in Spanish,

> I understand that I have a right to assert a claim in the seized property described above [i.e., the $10,000] and to seek return of the property. With full knowledge of those rights, I hereby abandon any and all claims I may have to that property. I waive my right to receive notice of future administrative or judicial proceedings involving the property. I also waive any further right to contest the administrative or judicial forfeiture of the property described above.

I think the majority would agree that if this waiver is valid, Van Bommel has no claim to the $10,000 and no standing to participate in this action. Van Bommel argues, however, that his waiver is void because it was involuntary and unintelligent. The majority believes that Van Bommel has produced sufficient evidence in support of this argument. For the reasons below, I disagree. [—29—]

I. Background

Throughout this case, Van Bommel has worked tirelessly to prevent discovery of facts relating to his standing. I recount the relevant procedural history.

The government began this action by filing a complaint for forfeiture in rem on November 25, 2009. On December 22, 2009, Van Bommel pleaded guilty to conspiring to fail to heave to a helicopter, and on February 4, 2010, he was sentenced to time served. On February 26, 2010, Van Bommel's counsel advised the government that Van Bommel was scheduled for a final removal hearing before an Immigration Judge just four days later, on March 2. Van Bommel's counsel stated that the Immigration Judge had previously rejected a request for Van Bommel to remain in the United States pending the outcome of the forfeiture proceedings, so he "encourage[d] [the government] to complete any matters pertaining to any intended discovery, that would require Mr. Van Bommel's presence in this district, before he is removed from the United States." It appears that at the hearing, the Immigration Judge ordered that Van Bommel be removed on March 26. On March 4, the government responded to Van Bommel's counsel that it was trying to stay Van Bommel's removal so that he could be deposed, and it asked for dates on which Van Bommel's counsel would be available for the deposition. Van Bommel's counsel did not respond, and the government contacted him again on March 18 to arrange a deposition [—30—] on March 24. Van Bommel's counsel told the government that he would check his schedule to confirm the date. Instead of doing so, the next day he filed a claim in the forfeiture action for the seized bales of currency and the $10,000 found on his person. On the same day, he also filed a motion to dismiss the government's complaint and unilaterally canceled the deposition, considering it "unnecesary [sic] based on the arguments raised in our motion." The motion to dismiss featured Van Bommel's bare, unexplained claims of ownership of the $10,000 and the bales of currency, but it nowhere mentioned that Van Bommel's waiver of ownership was involuntary or unintelligent. When the government informed Van Bommel's counsel that it intended to conduct the deposition with or without Van Bommel, he filed an emergency motion for a protective order staying the deposition, which the court granted without a response from the government.

For reasons that are not clear from the record, Van Bommel's removal was postponed. He was still in the United States on April 13, when the government moved for summary judgment, asking the court to strike Van Bommel's claim for lack of standing. The government argued that Van Bommel had waived his ownership of the seized currency, and it attached to its motion Van Bommel's signed waivers of ownership of the bales of currency and the $10,000. As the government pointed out, a motion to strike a claim "must be decided before any motion by the claimant to dismiss the action." **[—31—]** Rule G(8)(c)(ii)(A), Supplemental Rules for Admiralty or Maritime Claims and Asset Forfeiture Actions ("Supplemental Rules").

Van Bommel was removed from the United States a week later, on April 20.[1] On May 3, he filed an opposition to the government's motion for summary judgment. Attached to that motion was a declaration, dated April 29, which stated that his waiver of ownership was involuntary and unintelligent:

> During law enforcement interviews I involuntary [sic] and unintelligently signed a Notice of Abandonment of All Rights and Interest in Property. I signed the papers after I was threatened to be prosecuted for drug smuggling if I did not abandon the currency. The law enforcement agents never advised me of any of my Fifth Amendment rights and I was completely unfamiliar with U.S. law. The Notice of Abandonment did not advise me of the full panoply of rights counsel later explained to me, i.e., the standards of proof under [the Civil Asset Forfeiture Reform Act of 2000], right to cross-examine witnesses, present evidence, right to be assisted by Counsel, and the right to have a jury determine the forfeitability of the defendant currency, so as to establish that I made a knowing and intelligent

waiver of these rights and my Due Process right to contest the forfeiture of the defendant currency. Once advised by Counsel of these rights, I asserted my ownership interest in the currency and categorically pursued my right to contest the forfeiture of my currency. **[—32—]**

On July 28, the district court entered an order scheduling an evidentiary hearing "to evaluate disputed issues of fact regarding claimant's standing." Van Bommel's counsel did not notify the court that Van Bommel had left the United States and would be unavailable to testify, nor did he seek assistance from the court or the government with Van Bommel's application to enter the United States on parole for the purpose of testifying. *See* 8 C.F.R. § 212.5(b)(4) (describing authority to parole "[a]liens who will be witnesses in proceedings . . . conducted by judicial, administrative, or legislative bodies in the United States"). Instead, he sprang this information on the court at the evidentiary hearing, which took place on August 19.

At the hearing, the government was prepared to refute Van Bommel's declaration by calling two agents who had secured Van Bommel's signature on the waiver, but the court informed the government that they need not testify.[2] On March 15, 2011, the **[—33—]** court entered an order stating,

---

[1] The government later told the district court that it had requested a stay of deportation to depose Van Bommel, but the motion was denied because of Van Bommel's counsel's opposition. Van Bommel's counsel did not object to this characterization of the facts.

---

[2] The court stated, "Here I take it that the burden remains on the plaintiff to prove that he has the standing. And even assuming that he has it, if there is a waiver that basically supports the relinquishment allegation that the government is presenting or the fact that the property was abandoned. Assuming in the best scenario for the claimant here that he is questioning that, or he has come forward with sufficient evidence to raise doubts as to the voluntariness, I think as far as can I go is to kind of even tip the scale further for no justified reason on the record, and listen to the testimony of the agent as to how this waiver was procured and what were the circumstances under which it was offered just like in a suppression hearing. But still recognizing that if the government puts the witness on the stand it will be at the Court[']s request not because it has the burden of doing so, in order to prove standing or in

Claimant provides no specific facts or details of the alleged coercion in his opposition to the motion for summary judgment, in claimant's opposing statement of uncontested fact[s], or in his verified declaration under penalty of perjury. In fact, aside from a single paragraph of allegations in his own sworn statement, claimant provides no evidence of law enforcement's coercion in obtaining his waiver of rights and signature on the Notice. Nor was claimant able to testify to provide further details in support of his claim. Thus, claimant has failed to establish that his signature on the Notice was both unintelligent and involuntary.

(citations omitted). Therefore, the court held that Van Bommel "has failed to establish standing or raise a material issue of fact as to his Article III standing" and dismissed his claims.

II. Analysis

In a forfeiture proceeding, a claimant's burden to establish standing depends on the stage of the litigation. At the pleading stage, standing is not difficult to establish. *See United States v. $133,420.00 in U.S. Currency*, 672 F.3d 629, 638 (9th Cir. 2012); *United States v. One-Sixth Share of James J. Bulger in All Present and Future Proceeds of Mass Millions Lottery Ticket No. M246233*, 326 F.3d 36, 41 (1st Cir. 2003) ("At the initial stage of intervention, the requirements for a claimant to demonstrate constitutional standing are very forgiving. In general, any colorable claim on the defendant property suffices."). But when the [—34—] court holds an evidentiary hearing, as the district court did here, the burden of proof rises: a claimant "carr[ies] the burden of establishing standing by a preponderance of the evidence." Supplemental Rule G(8)(c)(ii)(B); Supplemental Rule G(8)(c)(ii) advisory committee's note. Thus, Van Bommel "must prove by a preponderance of the evidence that he has a facially colorable

order to prove the [—33—] validity of the document they have in their possession right now."

interest in the res." *United States v. $148,840.00 in U.S. Currency*, 521 F.3d 1268, 1273 (10th Cir. 2008).

To establish standing at an evidentiary hearing, a party must present admissible evidence supporting its claims. *United States v. $543,190.00 in U.S. Currency*, 535 F. Supp. 2d 1238, 1247 (M.D. Ala. 2008); Stefan D. Cassella, *Asset Forfeiture Law in the United States* 381 (2d ed. 2013); *see also Lujan v. Defenders of Wildlife*, 504 U.S. 555, 561 (1992) (holding that "each element [of standing] must be supported in the same way as any other matter on which the plaintiff bears the burden of proof, *i.e.*, with the manner and degree of evidence required at the successive stages of the litigation"). The Federal Rules of Evidence determine whether evidence is admissible in a civil forfeiture action. *See* Fed. R. Evid. 101(a), 1101; *United States v. $92,203.00 in U.S. Currency*, 537 F.3d 504, 509-10 (5th Cir. 2008). Therefore, Van Bommel had the burden to produce admissible evidence that his waiver was unintelligent or involuntary.

Van Bommel's declaration—the linchpin of his claim to [—35—] standing—is inadmissible hearsay, not admissible evidence. Hearsay, of course, is a statement made outside of a trial or hearing, which a party offers in evidence to prove the truth of the matter asserted in the statement. Fed. R. Evid. 801. Van Bommel's declaration is textbook hearsay: it was not made at a trial or hearing, and it was offered to prove that Van Bommel was coerced into signing the waiver. Generally, hearsay is inadmissible.[3] *Id.* 802.

---

[3] We have held that a court may receive hearsay at an evidentiary hearing on a motion for a preliminary injunction. *Asseo v. Pan Am. Grain Co.*, 805 F.2d 23, 25-26 (1st Cir. 1986). In that case, however, we stressed "the need for expedition" that characterizes an injunctive proceeding, and that the hearsay at issue previously had been subject to cross-examination. *Id.* at 26. Neither circumstance exists here. Even if it were appropriate both to extend *Asseo* to an evidentiary hearing regarding standing in a forfeiture action, and to take the further step of *requiring* the affidavit's admission, Van Bommel's declaration would be entitled to little or no weight, given its lack of factual detail and Van Bommel's efforts to prevent cross-examination. *Cf. Mullins v. City of New York*, 626

While there are several exceptions to the rule against hearsay, *see generally id.* 803, 804, 807, none applies here. As a result, Van Bommel produced no admissible evidence whatsoever that his waiver was unintelligent or involuntary.[4] *See United States v. All Funds in the Account of Prop. Futures, Inc.*, 820 F. Supp. 2d 1305, 1331-32 (S.D. Fla. 2011) (holding that claimants could not [—36—] establish Article III standing through hearsay). This alone requires us to affirm the district court's decision.[5]

F.3d 47, 52 (2d Cir. 2010) ("The admissibility of hearsay under the Federal Rules of Evidence goes to weight, not preclusion, at the preliminary injunction stage.").

[4] Van Bommel could have avoided this result by attending his deposition. If he was unable to return to the United States for the evidentiary hearing, he then could have offered his deposition testimony into evidence under Federal Rule of Evidence 804(b)(1).

[5] The district court had no need to address the admissibility of the declaration, since Van Bommel's counsel never tried to move it into evidence. In any event, the transcript of the evidentiary hearing suggests that the court did not consider the declaration to be competent evidence: "The question would be, what is the evidence that you have of the threats? What is the evidence that you have that the waiver was not voluntarily signed?" Even if this was not the basis of the court's decision, we may affirm on any ground supported by the record. *In re Miles*, 436 F.3d 291, 293-94 (1st Cir. 2006).

The majority views it as inconsistent to set aside Van Bommel's declaration when deciding his standing to claim the $10,000, while relying on the government's affidavit when deciding his standing to claim the bales of currency. There is no inconsistency. As to the bales of currency, Van Bommel either failed to counter the government's allegations, or disputed them with allegations that were too vague or incredible to create a genuine dispute of material fact. Therefore, summary judgment was appropriate, without any need for more evidence. As to the $10,000, there was a genuine dispute about the circumstances of Van Bommel's waiver. To prove his standing by a preponderance of the evidence, Van Bommel was obligated to produce something more than his bare-bones declaration.

Even assuming that Van Bommel's declaration could have been considered at the evidentiary hearing, it was not enough to prove, by a preponderance of the evidence, that he had a colorable interest in the $10,000. "[J]udges simply cannot decide whether a witness is telling the truth on the basis of a paper record and must observe the witnesses' demeanor to best ascertain their veracity— or lack thereof." *United States v. 1998 BMW "I" Convertible*, 235 F.3d 397, 400 (8th Cir. 2000) (citing *Goldberg v. Kelly*, 397 U.S. 254, 269 (1970)). As the district court noted, Van [—37—] Bommel offered a single paragraph with "no specific facts or details of the alleged coercion." In determining whether Van Bommel had established his standing by a preponderance of the evidence, the court gave this lone paragraph the short shrift it deserved. *See $133,420.00 in U.S. Currency*, 672 F.3d at 638 ("As we have explained, a conclusory, self-serving affidavit, lacking detailed facts and any supporting evidence, is insufficient to create a genuine issue of material fact." (internal quotation marks omitted)). Courts routinely demand more facts and evidence from claimants than Van Bommel was willing to provide. *See* Stefan D. Cassella, *Asset Forfeiture Law in the United States* 381-82 (2d ed. 2013) (collecting cases). Van Bommel's declaration falls far short of proving his standing by a preponderance of the evidence.

Finally, even if the district court had erred (which it did not), I believe that the majority has chosen the wrong disposition by reversing the grant of summary judgment, rather than vacating it. The government came to the evidentiary hearing with two witnesses prepared to testify about the circumstances under which Van Bommel signed his waiver. Given Van Bommel's failure to offer any evidence at the hearing, the court told the government that the witnesses' testimony would be unnecessary. By reversing the grant of summary judgment and reinstating Van Bommel's claim, the majority punishes the government for complying with the district court's guidance. The more prudent course would be to [—38—] vacate the grant of summary judgment and give the parties another opportunity to present their evidence on standing.

III. Conclusion

By letting this case proceed to the merits, the majority rewards Van Bommel's gamesmanship.[6] Van Bommel's counsel unilaterally canceled Van Bommel's deposition, fought to have him removed from the United States, failed to make a serious effort to secure his attendance at the evidentiary hearing, and kept from the court that he had been removed months before that hearing. It is difficult to imagine a party trying harder *not* to meet its burden of proof. Nevertheless, the district court must now expend judicial resources on an abandoned claim to $10,000. On this point, I respectfully dissent.

---

[6] The majority states that I have focused too much on Van Bommel's conduct and not enough on the record before the district court. This is a false distinction: Van Bommel's efforts at avoiding the development of evidence were well documented in the record. In any event, I focus on this conduct not because I believe that Van Bommel should be punished for it, but because it demonstrates that Van Bommel failed to develop any evidence, despite his burden to prove his standing by a preponderance of the evidence.

United States Court of Appeals for the Second Circuit

United States Court of Appeals
for the Second Circuit

No. 12-834

PADILLA
vs.
MAERSK LINE, LTD.

Appeal from the United States District Court for the
Southern District of New York

Decided: June 25, 2013

Citation: 721 F.3d 77, 1 Adm. R. 34 (2d Cir. 2013).

Before **B.D. PARKER, LOHIER,** and **CARNEY,** Circuit
Judges.

[—2—] PARKER, Circuit Judge:

Defendant-Appellant Maersk Line, Limited ("Maersk") appeals from a judgment of the United States District Court for the Southern District of New York (Leisure, J.) granting summary judgment in favor of a class of seafarers, discharged from service on Maersk ships due to illness or injury. These seafarers sought, and the district court granted, as part of unearned wages, overtime pay that they would have earned from the time of their discharge until the end of their respective voyages. It is not disputed that seafarers on Maersk voyages regularly received substantial overtime payments. Indeed, by Maersk's own calculations, overtime payments regularly exceeded each class member's base wages. The principal issue on this appeal is whether unearned wages recoverable by ill or disabled seafarers under general maritime law include overtime pay that they would have earned had they completed their voyages.

On October 30, 2006, John Padilla began his contract as Chief Cook aboard a Maersk vessel, the MAERSK ARKANSAS. His voyage was scheduled to end on February 26, 2007. However, on Nov. 6, 2006, Padilla sustained an abdominal injury, was relieved of service at the Port of Salalah in Oman and discharged as unfit for duty. The Particulars of Engagement and Discharge indicated that, at the time of his discharge, Padilla was entitled to the balance of his earned wages, which included six days of regular pay plus thirty-four hours of overtime pay.

Maersk voluntarily paid Padilla unearned wages at his base pay rate, along with "maintenance and cure,"[1] for the duration of his contract, but declined to pay him overtime wages. In May 2007, Padilla sued on behalf of himself and a proposed class of similarly situated seafarers **[—3—]** seeking the overtime pay he would have earned on his voyage had he not been injured. As noted above, it is uncontested that prior to his injury, Padilla, like other class members, routinely earned substantial overtime in excess of 100% of base income.

The district court addressed the merits of Padilla's individual claim prior to considering class certification. Padilla moved for summary judgment, which the court granted in March 2009. Padilla contended that his entitlement to unearned wages was governed by general maritime law. Maersk did not seriously contest this proposition but argued that the collective bargaining agreement between Padilla's union and Maersk limited his recovery to unearned wages excluding overtime. The district court correctly concluded that the application of general maritime law could be limited, but not abrogated, in collective bargaining agreements. Turning to the Standard Freightship Agreement ("CBA"), the collective bargaining agreement between Padilla's union, Seafarers International Union, and Maersk, the district court concluded that the CBA did not address the inclusion of overtime pay in the calculation of Padilla's unearned wages. The court then held that unearned wages include overtime pay where the seafarer reasonably expected to earn overtime pay on a regular basis throughout his service in an amount that was not speculative and would have earned it "but for" an illness or injury. The district court found that Padilla satisfied this test and awarded him $13,478.40 in overtime pay.

---

[1] "Maintenance" is the cost of lodging and food and "cure" is medical treatment.

The case was reassigned to Hon. Richard M. Berman, who, in October 2010, certified a class of seamen who suffered illness or injury while in service aboard Maersk ships and who, after discharge, were paid unearned wages, maintenance and cure until the end of their voyage, but were not paid overtime wages as part of unearned wages. After further proceedings, in January 2012, the court awarded damages to the class in the amount of $836,819.40. Following this award and after [—4—] Maersk filed an appeal in this court, Maersk sought to amend the judgment on two separate occasions. In July 2012, the court granted Maersk's first motion to amend to remove from the class two seamen who had filed separate suits. Shortly thereafter, but well after the end of the period allowed for filing a motion under Fed. R. Civ. P. 59(e), Maersk moved to amend the judgment again, this time to remove fifteen officers from the class. Maersk argued that the employment benefits of these officers were governed by a separate collective bargaining agreement, the American Maritime Officers Union Collective Bargaining Agreement ("AMOU CBA"), which expressly limited unearned pay to "benefits/wages only." The district court denied the motion finding that it was untimely, concerned with "wholly independent grounds" from those that led to the amended judgment and that Maersk failed to show "excusable neglect" for its delay in seeking the additional amendment.

On appeal, Maersk argues principally that the class is not entitled to overtime pay because overtime is not encompassed within the definition of "unearned wages" under general maritime law. Padilla argues that, given that overtime was a substantial and routine component of the seafarers' compensation, they were entitled to overtime payments because, under general maritime law, they must be placed in the same position they would have been in had they not been injured or disabled. We agree with Padilla.

We review *de novo* a district court's grant of summary judgment, construing the evidence in the light most favorable to the non-movant, asking whether there is a genuine dispute as to any material fact and whether the movant is entitled to judgment as a matter of law. Fed. R. Civ. P. 56(a); *Miller v. Wolpoff & Abramson, LLP*, 321 F.3d 292, 300 (2d Cir. 2003). [—5—]

DISCUSSION

Under general maritime law, seamen who have become ill or injured while in a ship's service have the right to receive maintenance and cure from the owner of the vessel. *Ammar v. United States*, 342 F.3d 133, 142 (2d Cir. 2003). In addition, a seaman is entitled to recover unearned wages, the wages he would have earned if not for the injury or illness. *Rodriguez Alvarez v. Bahama Cruise Line, Inc.*, 898 F.2d 312, 315 (2d Cir. 1990) ("When a seaman is injured during his employment on a ship, the ship operator is liable not only for the seaman's maintenance and cure, but also for lost wages.") (citing *The Osceola*, 189 U.S. 158, 175 (1903)); *see also Griffin v. Oceanic Contractors, Inc.*, 664 F.2d 36, 39 (5th Cir. 1981) ("The right of an injured seaman to recover unearned maintenance-wages-cure (M-W-C) under the general maritime law of the United States until either (1) the end of the voyage or (2) the end of the contractual period of employment is well established.") (citing *The Osceola*, 189 U.S. at 175), *rev'd on other grounds,* 458 U.S. 564, 73 L. Ed. 2d 973, 102 S. Ct. 3245 (1982). While Padilla bears the burden of proving his right to maintenance and cure, claims for these are construed expansively and doubts regarding a shipowner's liability for maintenance and cure should be resolved in favor of the seamen. *Vaughan v. Atkinson*, 369 U.S. 527, 532 (1962); *Breese v. AWI, Inc.*, 823 F.2d 100, 104 (5th Cir. 1987).

As the district court correctly recognized, while the entitlement to unearned wages arises under general maritime law, rates for unearned wages may be defined and modified in collective bargaining agreements, *see Ammar*, 342 F.3d at 146-47, and Maersk contends that the CBA should control our interpretation of the unearned wages issue. The CBA at issue here was between large parties well-equipped to represent and protect their respective interests. Under these circumstances, the appropriate accommodation between federal maritime law and federal common law for the [—6—] enforcement of collective bargaining agreements is to allow unionized seamen to bargain for the rights and privileges they prefer in exchange for limitations on various components of compensation so long as the negotiations are legitimate and the seamen's interests are adequately protected. *Id.* In light of these considerations, our responsibility is to determine the actual terms agreed to by the parties to the CBA and not to impose a limitation where none was intended or agreed to. *Marcic v. Reinauer Transp. Cos.*, 397 F.3d 120, 131 (2d Cir. 2005). Consequently, as the Ninth Circuit held in *Lipscomb v. Foss Mar. Co.*, 83 F.3d 1106, 1109 (9th Cir. 1996), only if the CBA expressly provides for a different computation of the seafarers' remedies does it modify the general maritime law. Here, however, the CBA does not limit the availability of unearned wages and so we must apply general maritime law.

Because much of Padilla's income was derived from overtime compensation, the district court awarded him overtime pay as part of his unearned wages, reasoning that Padilla was entitled to recover in full the compensation that he would have earned "but for" his injury. We agree with this approach. The record reflects that it was the custom and practice for seafarers working for Maersk to derive substantial income from overtime compensation and that, consequently, such compensation was a common expectation of both the seamen and of Maersk. As noted, Padilla and other Maersk seafarers regularly earned 100% or more of their base pay in overtime wages. Significantly, the district court concluded that the calculation of the overtime Padilla would have worked was not speculative. *Cf. Griffin*, 664 F.2d at 40 (upholding the district court's decision to deny overtime because "[t]he actual amount of overtime was uncertain, and hence any inclusion of such would have been purely speculative"). In fact, the calculations of the overtime pay due to the class were essentially undisputed: a Maersk manager easily calculated each seaman's expectation of [—7—] his overtime from records of past work

for Maersk. Thus we agree that the district court correctly applied the "but for" test.[2]

In reaching this conclusion, we align ourselves with the other circuits who apply the same test. *See Flores v. Carnival Cruise Lines*, 47 F.3d 1120, 1122-24 (11th Cir. 1995) (holding that tips should be included in the measure of unearned wages because a seaman would have earned them but for his injury); *Lipscomb*, 83 F.3d at 1109 (concluding that accumulated time off is part of seaman's unearned wages under general maritime law); *Aksoy v. Apollo Ship Chandlers, Inc.*, 137 F.3d 1304, 1306 (11th Cir. 1998) (calculating unearned wages as average tip income plus guaranteed minimum wage); *Morel v. Sabine Towing & Transp. Co.*, 669 F.2d 345, 346 (5th Cir. 1982) (holding that accumulated leave time is part of total wages and payable in addition to maintenance); *Shaw v. Ohio River Co.*, 526 F.2d 193, 199 (3d Cir. 1975) (same).

II.

Maersk also appeals the district court's decision denying its motion to amend the amended judgment under Rule 59(e) by removing the fifteen officers whose employment was governed by the AMOU CBA. The district court denied the motion because it was six months late, because it concerned "wholly independent grounds" from those that gave rise to a previously amended judgment and because Maersk's explanation that it "overlooked" the AMOU CBA did not

---

[2] Maersk also argues that by including overtime pay in "unearned wages" the district court expanded maritime remedies beyond those in the Jones Act, 46 U.S.C. § 30104, which permits the recovery of overtime only upon proof of negligence and a causal connection between the negligence and unseaworthiness and injury. According to Maersk, "a cause of action that existed before the Jones Act (unearned wages) survived the Jones Act, but damages permitted by the Jones Act (overtime wages) must be limited by the conditions in the Act." Appellant's Brief at 29. These arguments were not raised before the district court, and we decline to consider them here. *Greene v. United States*, 13 F.3d 577, 586 (2d Cir. 1994) ("Entertaining issues raised for the first time on appeal is discretionary with the panel hearing the appeal.").

constitute excusable neglect. On appeal, Maersk argues that the decision to amend the judgment on [—8—] this substantive issue could have been made conveniently and without waste of judicial resources. Maersk also argues that "class actions by their nature should be treated differently under Rule 59 ... [because] subclasses may emerge unexpectedly" and "may have to be decertified in light of the proceedings." Appellant's Brief at 38.

Maersk's arguments are unavailing. We review the denial of a motion to amend the judgment under Rule 59(e) for abuse of discretion. *See Schwartz v. Liberty Mut. Ins. Co.*, 539 F.3d 135, 150 (2d Cir. 2008). "A court abuses its discretion when (1) its decision rests on an error of law or a clearly erroneous factual finding; or (2) cannot be found within a range of permissible decisions." *Johnson ex rel. United States v. Univ. of Rochester Med. Ctr.*, 642 F.3d 121, 125 (2d Cir. 2011). A motion to alter or amend a judgment under this rule must be filed no later than 28 days after the entry of judgment. Fed. R. Civ. P. 59(e). Because Maersk did not meet this time limitation, its motion is considered under Rule 60(b) and Maersk must demonstrate "excusable neglect." *See Stevens v. Miller*, 676 F.3d 62, 67-68 (2d Cir. 2012); *Lora v. O'Heaney*, 602 F.3d 106, 111 (2d Cir. 2010). When assessing claims of "excusable neglect" we look to the following so-called *Pioneer* factors: "(1) the danger of prejudice to the [non-movant], (2) the length of the delay and its potential impact on judicial proceedings, (3) the reason for the delay, including whether it was within the reasonable control of the movant, and (4) whether the movant acted in good faith." *Silivanch v. Celebrity Cruises, Inc.*, 333 F.3d 355, 366 (2d Cir. 2003) (quoting *Pioneer Inv. Servs. Co. v. Brunswick Assocs. Ltd. P'ship*, 507 U.S. 380, 395 (1993)) (quotation marks and brackets in original omitted).

Our Circuit focuses closely on the third *Pioneer* factor: the reason for the delay, including whether it was within the reasonable control of the movant. *Id.* The district court concluded that [—9—] Maersk did not offer a valid reason for its delay since

Maersk stated only that its argument pertaining to the officers had been "overlooked" during the two-year period following class certification. Maersk offered no explanation as to why it did not raise the point that the officers were not entitled to overtime two months earlier when it made its first motion to amend the judgment to remove other plaintiffs. Because a delay attributable solely to a defendant's failure to act with diligence cannot "be characterized as 'excusable neglect'," we see no abuse of discretion by the district court in denying the motion. *Dominguez v. United States*, 583 F.2d 615, 617 (2d Cir. 1978).

CONCLUSION

For the foregoing reasons, we **affirm** the judgment of the district court.

United States Court of Appeals
for the Second Circuit

No. 13-0192

BLUE WHALE CORP.
vs.
GRAND CHINA SHIPPING DEV. CO.

Appeal from the United States District Court for the
Southern District of New York

Decided: July 16, 2013

Citation: 722 F.3d 488, 1 Adm. R. 38 (2d Cir. 2013).

Before **POOLER**, **WESLEY**, and **DRONEY**, Circuit
Judges.

[—3—] **WESLEY**, Circuit Judge:

This admiralty law dispute arises from a distinctly international transaction: a Chinese company contracted to transport goods from Brazil to China aboard a Liberian vessel. The existence of so many foreign interests yields an inherently federal choice-of-law question— one we resolve via application of maritime conflicts-of-law principles.

Background

Plaintiff-Appellant Blue Whale Corporation ("Blue Whale"), a foreign company,[1] entered into a charter party (a maritime contract) with Defendant-Appellee Grand China Shipping Development Company, Ltd. ("Development"), a Chinese company, on May 25, 2011. The charter party provided for transport of 250,000 metric tons of iron ore from Brazil to China aboard a Blue Whale vessel registered in the republic of Liberia. The contract purportedly required Development to pay 98% of the total freight costs [—4—] to Blue Whale within seven days of loading the iron ore; allegedly, Development failed to make this

---

[1] Throughout this litigation, Blue Whale is identified only as a "foreign corporation." We note that Blue Whale lists a business address in Monrovia, Liberia, on a freight invoice issued to Defendant-Appellee Grand China Shipping Development Company, Ltd., and that at least one of Blue Whale's vessels is registered in Liberia.

payment. Blue Whale therefore held the vessel and its contents until Development satisfied the claimed debt, resulting in more than $1 million in damages borne by Blue Whale. Blue Whale commenced arbitration against Development in London pursuant to the charter party's clause specifying that "[a]ny disputes arising under the Contract," if not settled amicably, "shall be referred to arbitration in London [with] British law to apply." The arbitration is ongoing.

On March 26, 2012, Blue Whale filed a complaint in the United States District Court for the Southern District of New York seeking to attach property belonging to Development's alleged alter ego, Defendant-Appellee HNA Group Company, Ltd. ("HNA"), also a Chinese company, in anticipation of a future arbitration award against Development. Rule B of the Supplemental Rules for Certain Admiralty and Maritime Claims ("Rule B") allows plaintiffs to seek an attachment of "defendant's tangible or intangible personal property— up to the amount sued for— in the hands of garnishees named in the process," "[i]f a defendant is not found within the district" at the time the complaint is [—5—] filed. FED. R. CIV. P. SUPP. R. B(1)(a). Blue Whale alleged that Development and HNA "are in fact a single business enterprise" and that the district court should allow Blue Whale to pierce the corporate veil to reach in-district HNA assets of approximately $1.3 million.

On May 17, 2012, the district court (Nathan, J.) issued an order authorizing attachment of HNA's holdings in third party Pacific American Corporation—a privately-held direct subsidiary of HNA based in New York—in an amount up to approximately $1.3 million. HNA subsequently moved to vacate the district court's maritime attachment order under Rule E(4)(f), which provides that a person claiming interest in attached property "shall be entitled to a prompt hearing at which the plaintiff shall be required to show why the arrest or attachment should not be vacated." FED. R. CIV. P. SUPP. R. E(4)(f).

Under Rule B, attachment is only appropriate if, *inter alia*, the plaintiff has a valid prima facie admiralty claim against the defendant. Neither party disputed that Blue Whale had alleged a claim sounding in admiralty and that the court had maritime jurisdiction. However, the parties disagreed over what substantive body of law controlled [—6—] whether Blue Whale had alleged a valid prima facie claim to pierce the corporate veil. HNA argued that English law governed pursuant to the charter party's choice-of-law provision and that Blue Whale had failed to allege sufficient facts to support a prima facie alter-ego claim. In response, Blue Whale argued that federal common law controlled the inquiry because Rule B is procedural in nature and, in addition, because "it is well-settled that 'federal courts sitting in admiralty must apply federal common law when examining corporate identity.'"[2] Memorandum of Law in Opposition to Motion to Vacate Maritime Rule B Attachment, at 8-9, *Blue Whale Corp. v. Grand China Shipping Dev. Co., Ltd., et al.*, No. 12 Civ. 02213 (AJN) (S.D.N.Y. 2012).

The district court separately analyzed the two elements required for Blue Whale's claim: (1) whether the claim sounded in admiralty; and (2) whether the claim was prima facie valid. First, the court held that whether Blue Whale [—7—] adequately pled an admiralty claim was a procedural question governed by federal maritime law because it related to the court's subject matter jurisdiction (a point not disputed by the parties). The court therefore exercised maritime jurisdiction over the claim. Second, the district court held that the substantive question of whether Blue Whale had pled a valid prima facie alter-ego claim was controlled by English law pursuant to the contractual choice-of-law provision. Under English law, the court concluded that Blue Whale had not alleged an adequate prima

facie claim to pierce the corporate veil, and therefore vacated the attachment.[3] [—8—]

Supported by Amicus Curiae White Rosebay Shipping S.A. ("White Rosebay"),[4] Blue Whale appeals from the district court's January 11, 2013 order vacating the prior Rule B maritime attachment order against HNA.

---

[2] Apparently, neither party raised the issue of whether HNA (a non-signatory to the charter party between Blue Whale and Development) could be bound by the English choice-of-law clause. As the district court noted, there are cases that speak to this issue and find that courts may force non-signatories to adhere to choice-of-law clauses. *See, e.g., FR 8 Singapore Pte. Ltd. v. Albacore Maritime Inc.*, 754 F. Supp. 2d 628, 636 (S.D.N.Y. 2010).

[3] The district court also made an alternative ruling supporting vacatur. Under Rule B, attachment is impermissible if a defendant can be "found" within the district. FED. R. CIV. P. SUPP. R. B(1)(a); *see also Aqua Stoli Shipping Ltd. v. Gardner Smith Pty Ltd.*, 460 F.3d 434, 445 (2d Cir. 2006), *overruled on other grounds by Shipping Corp. of India Ltd. v. Jaldhi Overseas Pte Ltd.*, 585 F.3d 58 (2d Cir. 2009). Because HNA had registered to do business in New York State after the district court issued the Rule B attachment order, the district court reasoned that HNA could now be "found" in the district and that vacatur was appropriate under Rule E. On this basis, the court also denied Blue Whale's request to stay its decision and grant Blue Whale an opportunity to obtain limited discovery and to amend its complaint.

Both Blue Whale and HNA recognize that the district court erred by finding that HNA's post-attachment registration to do business in New York State undermined Blue Whale's basis for a Rule B attachment order. *See ProShipLine, Inc. v. Aspen Infrastructures, Ltd.*, 585 F.3d 105, 112 n.4 (2d Cir. 2009) ("The time for determining whether a defendant is 'found' in the district is set at the time of the filing of the verified [—8—] complaint that prays for attachment and the affidavit required by Rule B(1)(b)."); *see also Marimed Shipping Inc. v. Persian Gulf Shipping Co. Inc.*, 567 F. Supp. 2d 524, 527 (S.D.N.Y. 2008). HNA could not be "found" within the district for purposes of Rule B attachment because the text of the rule itself establishes that a defendant is "found within the district when a verified complaint . . . [is] *filed*." FED. R. CIV. P. SUPP. R. B(1)(a) (emphasis added). Thus, the district court's alternative basis for vacating the attachment order fails as a matter of law.

[4] White Rosebay's interest in this appeal stems from its separate commencement of two admiralty veil-piercing actions against HNA (and other parties).

Discussion

"We review a district court's decision to vacate a maritime attachment for abuse of discretion; however, we review de novo any legal determinations on which this discretion rests." *Williamson v. Recovery Ltd. P'ship*, 542 F.3d 43, 48 (2d Cir. 2008). This Court has interpreted Rule B to permit a plaintiff to obtain an order of attachment if it can show that

> 1) it has a valid prima facie admiralty claim against the defendant; 2) the defendant cannot be found within the district; 3) the defendant's property may [—9—] be found within the district; and 4) there is no statutory or maritime law bar to the attachment.

Aqua Stoli Shipping Ltd. v. Gardner Smith Pty Ltd., 460 F.3d 434, 445 (2d Cir. 2006), *overruled on other grounds by Shipping Corp. of India Ltd. v. Jaldhi Overseas Pte Ltd.*, 585 F.3d 58 (2d Cir. 2009). If a plaintiff fails to make this showing when challenged under Rule E, a district court must vacate the prior order of attachment. *Id.*

The principal issue on appeal is whether Blue Whale satisfied its burden of pleading a valid prima facie admiralty claim against HNA in satisfaction of the first prong of *Aqua Stoli*. As the district court recognized, this evaluation requires us to answer two questions: (1) whether Blue Whale's claim against HNA sounds in admiralty; and (2) whether the claim is prima facie valid. Each of these questions, in turn, necessitates determining the governing body of law. For the reasons explained below, we conclude that the district court properly applied federal maritime law to the procedural question of whether Blue Whale's claim sounds in admiralty, and we agree that the claim does sound in admiralty because it arose out of a maritime contract. [—10—]

We also agree with the district court that the issue of the claim's prima facie validity is a substantive inquiry. We conclude, however, that the district court's application of English law to this question was improper because the charter party's choice-of-law provision does not govern Blue Whale's collateral alter-ego claim against HNA. Instead, we draw on maritime choice-of-law principles to hold that although federal common law does not govern every claim of this nature, federal common law does apply here, primarily because of the collateral claim's close ties to the United States. We remand for reconsideration by the district court of the prima facie validity of Blue Whale's alter-ego claim under federal common law.

I. The Rule B Inquiry Is Procedural in Part and Substantive in Part

"There is a split of authority" in the Southern District of New York on the issue of what law governs "whether [a] plaintiff has pled a facially valid admiralty claim . . . and the Second Circuit has not ruled on it." *Al Fatah Int'l Nav. Co. Ltd. v. Shivsu Canadian Clear Waters Tech. (P) Ltd.*, 649 F. Supp. 2d 295, 299 (S.D.N.Y. 2009). Some district courts within this Circuit presume that [—11—] "federal law governs all questions concerning the validity of a Rule B attachment." *Harley Mullion & Co. Ltd. v. Caverton Marine Ltd.*, No. 08-cv-5435 (BSJ), 2008 WL 4905460, at *2 (S.D.N.Y. Aug. 7, 2008) (assessing whether plaintiffs pled a valid maritime claim).[5] Other district courts reason that despite Rule B's "undoubted[ ]" status as a procedural rule, "Rule B itself does not provide the basis for determining the existence of a valid prima facie admiralty claim," and instead, "the

---

[5] *See also Emeraldian Ltd. P'ship v. Wellmix Shipping Ltd.*, No. 08 Civ. 2991 (RJH), 2009 WL 3076094, at *2-3 (S.D.N.Y. Sep. 28, 2009) (applying federal common law without discussion of English choice-of-law clause in charter party); *Euro Trust Trading S.A. v. Allgrains U.K. Co.*, No. 09 Civ. 4483 (GEL), 2009 WL 2223581, at *2-3 (S.D.N.Y. July 27, 2009) (agreeing that "the better view is that federal law governs all questions concerning the validity of a Rule B attachment," but specifically deciding that federal law governs whether plaintiff alleged a valid maritime claim (internal quotation marks omitted)); *Budisukma Permai SDN BHD v. N.M.K. Prods. & Agencies Lanka (Private) Ltd.*, 606 F. Supp. 2d 391, 395-96 (S.D.N.Y. 2009) (discussing choice of law in the context of deciding whether plaintiff had a valid maritime claim).

existence of a valid prima facie claim turns on substantive law." *Al Fatah*, 649 F. Supp. 2d at 300.[6] **[—12—]**

A. Whether a Claim Sounds in Admiralty Is a Procedural Question Governed by Federal Maritime Law

Despite the divide, what is clear is that federal law controls the procedural inquiry, namely, whether a plaintiff's claim sounds in admiralty. *See id.* at 299 n.4; *Euro Trust Trading S.A. v. Allgrains U.K. Co.*, No. 09 Civ. 4483 (GEL), 2009 WL 2223581, at *3 (S.D.N.Y. July 27, 2009). This question is inherently procedural by virtue of its relationship to the courts' subject matter jurisdiction and, thus, is controlled by federal maritime law. Here, the parties do not dispute that Blue Whale's claim sounds in admiralty because it arises out of a maritime contract. The more difficult question is whether federal law also controls a court's assessment of the validity of a plaintiff's prima facie claim.

B. Whether a Claim Is Prima Facie Valid Is a Substantive Question Governed by the Relevant Substantive Law

If the prima facie validity component of the inquiry is **[—13—]** procedural in nature, federal law will control; if it is substantive, the relevant substantive body of law will control. The district courts in the Southern District of New York have laid out the competing arguments for us. In *Harley Mullion & Co. Ltd. v. Caverton Marine Ltd.*, the court explained its reasoning for finding that "the better view is that federal law governs all questions concerning the validity of a Rule B attachment" as follows:

> If, in order to comply with the requirements set forth in *Aqua Stoli*, a claim must be valid under the substantive law that will govern the underlying action, parties initiating or responding to a Rule 4(E) [sic] challenge would be routinely required to litigate issues of foreign law and courts would have to probe into the merits of the underlying claim. This sort of detailed examination is inappropriate at a Rule 4(E) [sic] hearing as it would undermine the prima facie standard and is at odds with the limited inquiry contemplated by *Aqua Stoli*.

No. 08-cv-5435 (BSJ), 2008 WL 4905460, at *2 (S.D.N.Y. Aug. 7, 2008) (internal quotation marks omitted). By contrast, in *Al Fatah*, the district court rejected this position because

> Rule B itself does not provide the basis for determining the existence of a valid prima facie admiralty claim. . . . [T]he existence of a valid prima facie claim turns on substantive law. Where the **[—14—]** substantive law underlying the claim is foreign, it would make no sense to determine the claim's prima facie validity under U.S. law.

649 F. Supp. 2d at 300. Then-District Judge Chin further explained that his "conclusion [was] not inconsistent with *Aqua Stoli*[ ]" because even if an inquiry conducted under foreign law might be "more difficult" than the same assessment under United States law, "it need not necessarily be any more rigorous." *Id.*

We agree with Judge Chin's reasoning. Admiralty law provides the remedy;

---

[6] *See also Indagro S.A. v. Bauche S.A.*, 652 F. Supp. 2d 482, 489-90 & 490 n.9 (S.D.N.Y. 2009) (outlining the dispute and finding that law of the contract governs whether plaintiff pled a valid prima facie claim and federal law governs whether that claim sounds in admiralty); *Kulberg Fins. Inc. v. Spark Trading D.M.C.C.*, 628 F. Supp. 2d 510, 515, 518-19 (S.D.N.Y. 2009) (endorsing "numerous courts['[]" view that "existence of a valid prima facie admiralty claim turns on the . . . law of the contract"); *Precious Pearls, Ltd. v. Tiger Int'l Line Pte Ltd.*, **[—12—]** No. 07 Civ. 8325 (JGK), 2008 WL 3172998, at *2 (S.D.N.Y. July 31, 2008) (without discussion, applying English law pursuant to contract clause to assess whether contingent indemnity claim was ripe); *Sonito Shipping Co., Ltd. v. Sun United Maritime Ltd.*, 478 F. Supp. 2d 532, 536 (S.D.N.Y. 2007) ("The existence *vel non* of a valid maritime claim for purposes of a Rule B writ of attachment turns upon the applicable substantive law, in this case the law of contract.").

substantive law defines the right to the remedy. Assessing the prima facie validity of a claim is a substantive inquiry that should be governed by the relevant substantive law. By contrast, whether a claim sounds in admiralty is a procedural question, the answer to which supplies the source of a court's subject matter jurisdiction.

As the district court here recognized, the decisions incorporating the reasoning in *Harley Mullion* typically do so in the context of resolving a dispute over whether a plaintiff has sufficiently alleged an *admiralty* claim— not whether a plaintiff has pled a *valid prima facie claim*. See *Indagro S.A. v. Bauche S.A.*, 652 F. Supp. 2d 482, 490 [—15—] (S.D.N.Y. 2009) ("Where the question is not whether the claim is maritime in nature, but rather whether the plaintiff has pled a 'valid' claim at all, courts in this District have considered whether the plaintiff alleged a prima facie claim under the substantive law governing the parties' dispute."). As a result, in these cases, statements to the effect that all Rule B queries are procedural in nature and are governed by federal law effectively constitute dicta—no one disagrees that federal law controls the determination of whether a claim sounds in admiralty.

We hold that federal maritime law governs whether a claim sounds in admiralty and that the relevant substantive law governs whether a plaintiff has alleged a valid prima facie claim. We use substantive law to assess the prima facie validity of a plaintiff's claim because substantive law supplies the relevant measure for deciding whether or not the claim is legally sufficient. Of course, this means that courts must apply the correct substantive law—i.e., the law which defines the rights and responsibilities of the parties to the dispute. This introduces the more difficult question in this case: what substantive law controls the validity of Blue Whale's alter-ego claim? [—16—]

II. Federal Maritime Choice-of-Law Analysis Determines the Relevant Substantive Law

There are three approaches for evaluating what law governs Blue Whale's alter-ego claim in this case: invoking the charter party's choice-of-law provision, which specifies English law; automatically applying federal common law because the court is "examining corporate identity"; or engaging in a federal maritime choice-of-law analysis. Because we find that the charter party's choice-of-law clause does not govern this collateral alter-ego claim, we hold that federal maritime choice-of-law principles dictate the proper controlling substantive law. In this case, a maritime choice-of-law analysis yields federal common law as the relevant governing law by virtue of the claim's connection to the United States.

A. The Contractual Choice-of-Law Clause Does Not Control Because the Alter-Ego Claim Is Collateral

First, we reject HNA's contention, and the district court's conclusion, that the charter party's choice-of-law clause requires applying English substantive law to govern this dispute. *Kalb, Voorhis & Co. v. American Financial Corp.*, 8 F.3d 130, 132 (2d Cir. 1993), teaches us that choice-of-law clauses in underlying contracts are [—17—] "irrelevant" to assessing alter-ego claims. In that case, Kalb, the plaintiff, held debentures (collateral-free debts or notes) issued by third-party corporation Circle K. *Id.* at 131. After Circle K filed for bankruptcy under Chapter 11, Kalb sued as a creditor of Circle K to pierce the corporate veil and impose liability for the debentures on the defendant, a former controlling stockholder of Circle K. *Id.* Shortly thereafter, Circle K asserted its own rights to pierce the veil against the defendant; the question in the case was "whether a claim alleging that the debtor or bankrupt is the alter ego of its controlling stockholder" belonged to Circle K or Kalb. *Id.* at 132.

In considering the choice of law in this diversity case, we determined that it was appropriate to apply the choice-of-law principles of the forum state (New York) rather than relying on the choice-of-law clause in the debentures. *Id.* We noted that "[t]he choice of law provisions in the debentures [were] irrelevant [because t]he issue is the limited liability of shareholders of a corporation—not Circle K's obligations under the debentures." *Id.*

Similarly, here the issue is HNA's legal status as an alter ego of Development, not the obligations under or **[—18—]** subsequent alleged violations of the charter party between Development and Blue Whale. Blue Whale's claim against HNA sounds in admiralty because it arose from this maritime contract—however, the substance of the attachment claim concerns whether HNA is an alter ego of Development. This corporate identity inquiry is indeed distant from the dispute over the charter party's provisions regarding the transport of iron ore. For this reason, we find that "the issue of piercing the corporate veil is collateral to the contract, and thus this Court is not bound by the choice of law provision." *United Trade Assocs. Ltd. v. Dickens & Matson (USA) Ltd., Inc.*, 848 F. Supp. 751, 759 (E.D. Mich. 1994); *see also Wehlage v. EmpRes Healthcare Inc.*, 821 F. Supp. 2d 1122, 1127-28 (N.D. Cal. 2011); *JSC Foreign Economic Ass'n Technostroyexport v. Int'l Dev. and Trade Servs., Inc.*, 295 F. Supp. 2d 366, 385-86 (S.D.N.Y. 2003) (determining that action to enforce judgment was "in no way connected to or related to the performance of the shipment contracts" and that arbitration clause did not govern).[7] **[—19—]**

B. Federal Common Law Does Not Apply Automatically for "Examining Corporate Identity"

Second, we reject the proposition advanced by Blue Whale and White Rosebay that federal common law *automatically* governs the alter-ego claim. Blue Whale and Amicus Curiae White Rosebay cite numerous cases for the proposition that

> courts in this Circuit have consistently held . . . [that] '[f]ederal courts sitting in admiralty must apply federal common law when examining corporate identity.'

Clipper Wonsild Tankers Holding A/S v. Biodiesel Ventures, LLC, 851 F. Supp. 2d 504, 507-08 (S.D.N.Y. 2012) (quoting *In re Holborn Oil Trading Ltd.*, 774 F. Supp. 840, 844 (S.D.N.Y. 1991)).[8] However, many of these cases, as well as matters **[—20—]** cited more broadly in support,[9] are focused principally on the scope of courts' admiralty jurisdiction, rather than on the source of substantive law. Admiralty jurisdiction and federal maritime law need not go hand–in–hand, *see, e.g.,*

---

[7] There are a number of cases that indicate that had Blue Whale prevailed at the London arbitration proceeding in advance of bringing an action for attachment or enforcement in the United States, federal common law and not English law would govern the court's evaluation of HNA's alleged alter-ego status. *See, e.g., Bridas S.A.P.I.C. v. Gov. of Turkmenistan*, 345 F.3d 347, 353, **[—19—]** 358-60 (5th Cir. 2003) (remanding after applying federal common law instead of contractually-specified English law to determine whether Government of Turkmenistan was subject to arbitration, and thus liable for arbitration award, as alleged alter ego of contracting party) (*cited favorably in Compagnie Noga D'Importation et D'Exportation, S.A. v. Russian Federation*, 361 F.3d 676, 686 (2d Cir. 2004)).

[8] *See also Constellation Energy Commodities Grp. Inc. v. Transfield ER Cape Ltd.*, 801 F. Supp. 2d 211, 223 (S.D.N.Y. 2011) (applying federal common law to evaluate plaintiff's claim to enforce arbitration award against alleged alter-ego defendants); *Emeraldian*, 2009 WL 3076094, at *2-3 (applying federal common law to assess validity of plaintiff's prima facie alter-ego maritime claim without discussing applicability of English choice-of-law provision); *Arctic Ocean Int'l Ltd. v. High Seas Shipping Ltd.*, 622 F. Supp. 2d 46, 53 (S.D.N.Y. 2009) (same).

[9] *See Swift & Co. Packers v. Compania Colombiana Del Caribe, S.A.*, 339 U.S. 684 (1950); *Williamson*, 542 F.3d at 49-50; *see also Williamson v. Recovery Ltd. P'ship*, No. 06 Civ. 5724 (LTS)(FM), 2007 WL 102089, at *2 (S.D.N.Y. Jan. 16, 2007) ("The choice of law clauses, whatever their significance in the ultimate determination of the merits of the dispute, do not divest the federal court of subject matter jurisdiction."); *see also Budisukma*, 606 F. Supp. 2d 391 (adopting *Harley Mullion* analysis to decide primary issue of whether plaintiff's claim was maritime in nature and not specifying whether reasoning for applying federal common law, instead of English law, to assess validity of alter-ego claims was on a similar basis).

Lauritzen v. Larsen, 345 U.S. 571 (1953), even in the context of examining corporate identity.

It appears that this Court's decision in *Kirno Hill Corp. v. Holt*, 618 F.2d 982 (2d Cir. 1980) (per curiam), is at the root of the principle that federal common law governs the analysis of corporate identity. *Kirno Hill* did not involve Rule B, a contract specifying choice of law, international parties or contracts, or, in fact, any quarrel over choice of law. Instead, the case centered around a dispute over personal liability for obligations under a charter party. *Id.* at 984. We applied federal maritime law, "which is the law we apply in an admiralty case," to [—21—] determine whether an undisclosed principal was bound by contracts made by an agent acting within his authority. *Id.* at 985.

Subsequent cases citing *Kirno Hill* for the proposition that federal common law dictates whether or not a maritime plaintiff has sufficiently pled a claim to pierce the corporate veil tend to proceed along one of two lines. First, there are cases like *Clipper Wonsild Tankers Holding A/S v. Biodiesel Ventures, LLC*, 851 F. Supp. 2d 504 (S.D.N.Y. 2012), opining that courts must choose between state law and federal common law. In *Clipper*, alleged alter-ego defendants argued that plaintiffs' Rule B claims should be governed by Texas law because of the parties' diversity and defendants' status as Texas corporations. *Id.* at 506-07. The district court disagreed because plaintiffs had expressly (and properly) invoked the court's admiralty jurisdiction since a charter party lay at the center of the dispute. *Id.* at 507-08. This result strikes us as correct. When the choice is between state law and federal common law, the federal interest in maintaining uniformity in the quintessentially federal realm of admiralty supersedes any competing interest in applying state law. *See generally Am. Dredging Co. v. Miller*, 510 U.S. 443 (1994). [—22—]

Second, there are Rule B attachment cases in which district courts must grapple with foreign parties' disputes that arose (or sometimes sank) in foreign waters. In *Arctic Ocean International, Ltd. v. High Seas Shipping Ltd.*, 622 F. Supp. 2d 46 (S.D.N.Y. 2009), for example, a Russian plaintiff-company secured a Rule B attachment order in the Southern District of New York against a Marshall Islands defendant-company and an alleged alter-ego Canadian defendant-company. *Id.* at 47-48. In evaluating the alleged alter ego's attack on the attachment order,[10] the district court assessed the prima facie validity of plaintiff's alter-ego claim under federal common law. *Id.* at 53-56. The district court applied federal common law instead of Russian law, Marshall Islands law, Canadian law or English law (which was specified by the charter party's arbitration choice-of-law provision, *id.* at 48) because "federal courts sitting in admiralty have tended to apply federal maritime common law," *id.* at 53 (citing *In re Holborn*, 774 F. Supp. at 844). [—23—]

Although the district court may well have reached the correct result in *Arctic Ocean*, we do not believe that *Kirno Hill* (or its progeny) compels courts "examining corporate identity" to apply federal common law. That said, we recognize that district courts frequently have found value in using federal common law to evaluate the validity of collateral claims in Rule B attachment proceedings. Our aim today is to clarify that the decision of which body of law to apply should be the product of a maritime choice-of-law analysis.

C. Maritime Choice-of-Law Analysis Shows that Federal Common Law Controls Because United States Law Has the Strongest Connection to the Relevant Transaction

The Supreme Court first announced the maritime conflicts-of-law test in *Lauritzen v. Larsen*, 345 U.S. 571 (1953). "The rule of

---

[10] The alleged alter-ego defendant moved to dismiss the complaint under Rules 12(b)(2) and 12(b)(6) rather than challenging the attachment under Rule E(4)(f) because no property had actually been attached in the approximately eleven months that the Rule B order had been in force. *Arctic Ocean*, 622 F. Supp. 2d at 50. However, as the district court recognized, defendant's arguments "would have similar force at a Rule E(4)(f) hearing." *Id.*

Klaxon Co. v. Stentor Electric Mfg. Co.[ ], under which a federal court exercising its diversity jurisdiction looks to the choice-of-law doctrine of the forum state, does not govern suits invoking the court's admiralty jurisdiction." *Itel Containers Int'l Corp. v. Atlanttrafik Exp. Serv. Ltd.*, No. 86 Civ. 1313 (RLC), 1988 WL 75262, at *2 (S.D.N.Y. July 13, 1988). Thus, when parties properly invoke admiralty jurisdiction, courts apply federal maritime choice-of-law rules. *Id.* [—24—]

In *Lauritzen*, a Danish seaman brought suit in the Southern District of New York under the Jones Act, 46 U.S.C. § 688, alleging that he was negligently injured aboard a ship of Danish flag and registry while in Havana harbor. 345 U.S. at 573. The ship was owned by a Danish citizen, and the injured seaman had signed the ship's articles providing that disputes would be governed by Danish law. *Id.* Nevertheless, he sought to invoke United States law. *Id.*

Recognizing that "[m]aritime law . . . has attempted to avoid or resolve conflicts between competing laws by ascertaining and valuing points of contact between the transaction and the states or governments whose competing laws are involved," *id.* at 582, the Supreme Court laid out a multi-factor choice-of-law test,[11] "[t]he purpose of [which] [—25—] is to assure that a case will be treated n [sic] the same way under the appropriate law regardless of the fortuitous circumstances which often determine the forum," *id.* at 591.

---

[11] Supplemented by subsequent case law, the non-exhaustive list of factors includes: "(1) the place of the wrongful act; (2) the law of the ship's flag; (3) the domicile of the injured party; (4) the domicile of the shipowner; (5) the place of the contract; (6) the inaccessibility of the foreign forum; (7) the law of the forum; and (8) the shipowner's base of operations." *Carbotrade S.p.A. v. Bureau Veritas*, 99 F.3d 86, 90 (2d Cir. 1996) (citing *Hellenic Lines Ltd. v. Rhoditis*, 398 U.S. 306, 309 (1970); *Romero v. Int'l Terminal Operating Co.*, 358 U.S. 354, 382 (1959); *Lauritzen*, 345 U.S. at 583-92). Though the *Lauritzen* factors speak more directly to tort claims, a modified framework may be invoked in contract actions. *See Rainbow Line, Inc. v. M/V Tequila*, 480 F.2d 1024, 1026-27 (2d Cir. 1973); *see also Itel Containers*, 1988 WL 75262, at *2.

In *Lauritzen*, the balance of factors clearly pointed to application of Danish law: the injured seaman had minimal contacts with the United States beyond the intangible—his desire to invoke this nation's more favorable maritime tort law. *Id.* at 592.

Here, by contrast, Blue Whale initiated this proceeding in the United States, and specifically in the Southern District of New York, because that is where HNA owns property. Blue Whale did not invoke the Southern District of New York's admiralty jurisdiction by serendipity—the presence of HNA's property enabled this action and, along with it, the application of federal maritime law. Furthermore, the basic tenet upon which *Lauritzen* is premised will be satisfied here by using federal common law because its application reflects an implicit "resol[ution of] conflicts between competing laws by ascertaining and valuing points of contact between the transaction and the states or governments whose competing laws are involved." *Id.* at 582. [—26—]

As is often the case in admiralty, we deal here with multi-national foreign parties locked in dispute as the result of an alleged breach of an international shipping contract. Indeed, part of the reason we authorize maritime attachment is the "peripatetic" nature of maritime parties, the "transitory" status of their assets, *Aqua Stoli*, 460 F.3d at 443, and the need for parties to obtain security "[i]n a world of shifting assets, numerous thinly-capitalized subsidiaries, flags of convenience and flows of currencies," *Navalmar (U.K.) Ltd. v. Welspun Gujarat Stahl Rohren, Ltd.*, 485 F. Supp. 2d 399, 404 (S.D.N.Y. 2007) (citing *Aurora Maritime v. Abdullah Mohamed Fahem & Co.*, 84 F.3d 44 (2d Cir. 1996)).

This particular case arose from a charter party between a Chinese company, Development, and another foreign company, Blue Whale, to ship iron ore from Brazil to China on a Liberian vessel. This narrative yields several potential sources of law; none have a particularly strong connection to the transaction. The facts here contrast strongly with the facts in *Lauritzen*, where all parties, the ship, and the contract itself exhibited strong ties to Denmark. 345 U.S. at 573. [—27—]

Importantly, however, the relevant "transaction" in this case is *not* Development's alleged failure to comply with the charter party—it is Blue Whale's claim to pierce the corporate veil. The district court in this Rule B action is charged only with determining whether Blue Whale stated a prima facie valid alter-ego claim against HNA in furtherance of its motion to attach HNA's property in New York. Accordingly, United States law has the strongest "points of contact" with this claim by virtue of the location of HNA's property, Blue Whale's corresponding choice of forum and the unavailability of an alternative forum, and the absence of a dominant foreign choice of law.

On a final note, we recognize the value of simplifying the judicial process required for Rule B attachments and Rule E motions to vacate when feasible. *See generally Aqua Stoli*, 460 F.3d at 443-44. As we have articulated, this does not excise the judicial obligation to apply the governing substantive law to assess the prima facie validity of a Rule B admiralty claim when challenged in a Rule E proceeding. But here, for the reasons discussed, we identify federal common law as the proper substantive body of law to govern Blue Whale's alter-ego claim against HNA. This follows from the ideas underpinning the *Lauritzen* [—28—] choice-of-law analysis and from our aim of ensuring uniformity in admiralty law whenever possible. Accordingly, we vacate the district court's order and remand for reconsideration of the prima facie validity of Blue Whale's Rule B alter-ego claim under federal common law. *See Williamson*, 542 F.3d at 53; *Clipper*, 851 F. Supp. 2d at 509-10.

Conclusion

For the foregoing reasons, the order of the district court is hereby VACATED and REMANDED.

United States Court of Appeals
for the Second Circuit

No. 11-1644

NORTHEAST RESEARCH, LLC
vs.
ONE SHIPWRECKED VESSEL

Appeal from the United States District Court for the Western District of New York

Decided: September 5, 2013

Citation: 729 F.3d 197, 1 Adm. R. 47 (2d Cir. 2013).

Before **POOLER**, **HALL**, and **LIVINGSTON**, Circuit Judges.

[—2—] **LIVINGSTON**, Circuit Judge:

This action arises from the chill depths of Lake Erie, where lies the intact shipwreck of an early nineteenth century wooden schooner. In 2004, Plaintiff-Appellant Northeast Research, LLC ("Northeast") filed an *in rem* action in federal court laying claim to the shipwreck under admiralty law as the finder and salvor of the sunken vessel. Claimant-Appellee the State of New York ("New York") intervened, asserting title to the wreck under state law and the Abandoned Shipwreck Act ("ASA," or the "Act"), 43 U.S.C. § 2101 *et seq.*, which vests title to certain abandoned shipwrecks in the state on whose land they rest. [—3—]

On summary judgment, the parties disputed whether, as Northeast proposed, the shipwreck was actually the *General Wayne*, which participated in the Battle of Lake Erie during the War of 1812, or, as New York argued, an abandoned and "nameless 1830s schooner that sank carrying grain." The district court found that the wreck is abandoned, that no material issue has been raised to the contrary, that New York accordingly proved its claim under the ASA, and that Northeast is not entitled to a salvage award. *See Northeast Research, LLC v. One Shipwrecked Vessel*, 790 F. Supp. 2d 56, 64-66 (W.D.N.Y. 2011). On appeal, Northeast seeks review of the district court's holding that New York has title to the wreck pursuant to the ASA, an inquiry that requires this Court to articulate the standard of proof for abandonment under the ASA and whether abandonment of a shipwreck must be express, or may be inferred circumstantially. For the reasons stated below, we conclude that abandonment may be inferred from circumstantial evidence, and we affirm the judgment of the district court on the basis: (1) that the record demonstrates by clear and convincing evidence that the shipwreck is abandoned within the meaning of the ASA; and (2) that Northeast has failed to raise a material dispute of fact on this issue. [—4—]

BACKGROUND

I. Facts

In review of the district court's grant of summary judgment to New York, we view the facts in the light most favorable to Northeast. *Anemone v. Metro. Transp. Auth.*, 629 F.3d 97, 113 (2d Cir. 2011). Accordingly, the following facts, unless otherwise noted, are undisputed or construed in Northeast's favor.

A. Discovery and Arrest of the Shipwreck

Richard Kullberg formed Northeast in 2004 for the purpose of searching the bottom of Lake Erie for old shipwrecks. Kullberg, who had purchased a set of GPS coordinates indicating the potential location of Lake Erie wrecks, discovered the Defendant-Res in 2003 while searching for another shipwreck by means of a remote-operated vehicle.[1] Known as the "Dunkirk Schooner" for the nearby port of Dunkirk, New York, the wreck lies at an approximate depth of 170 feet on submerged New York land in the eastern basin of Lake Erie, where the water temperature remains around 37 degrees Fahrenheit. The depth of the freshwater covering the wreck and the cool temperature have combined to preserve the wooden vessel in relatively pristine condition. Northeast avers that its "ultimate goal" is to raise the Dunkirk Schooner and

---

[1] Northeast's statement of undisputed facts asserts that Northeast first dived the wreck in the early 1990s, but that assertion is not supported in the record.

place it on permanent display in a museum on the Buffalo, New York waterfront. [—5—]

On August 6, 2004, Northeast filed the instant *in rem* admiralty action in the Western District of New York, seeking title to the Dunkirk Schooner under the maritime[2] law of finds, or, in the alternative, a salvage award, and requesting a preliminary injunction prohibiting any rival salvors from diving or conducting salvage operations within two nautical miles of the wreck site. Northeast also moved for issuance of a Warrant of Arrest[3] of the shipwreck and to be appointed her Substitute Custodian in place of the U.S. Marshals. The district court granted both motions, directing Northeast to provide public notice of the action and arrest of the shipwreck, and for any person claiming an interest in the Dunkirk Schooner to make an application to the court. In September 2004, New York responded to that call by filing an answer to the complaint asserting that the Dunkirk Schooner is the sole and exclusive property of the State pursuant to the ASA, the Submerged Lands Act, 43 U.S.C. § 1301 *et seq.*, and New York Education Law § 233. [—6—]

B. Excavation of the Dunkirk Schooner

In 2004, following its appointment as custodian of the Dunkirk Schooner, Northeast engaged Kenneth Vrana and Robert Reedy of the Center for Maritime & Underwater Research Management ("CMURM") as the "archaeological team" that would lead the investigation of the Dunkirk Schooner. Vrana, the president of CMURM, is an underwater archaeologist who specializes in the survey and assessment of historic shipwrecks; Reedy is also an underwater archaeologist and experienced diver. Kullberg, Vrana, and Reedy hoped to partner with New York in order to establish the identity of the wreck and avoid an extended legal battle.[4] To that end, Vrana and Reedy prepared a "research design" to guide further archaeological and historical research of the Dunkirk Schooner, a process that included documentation and survey of the site without intrusive testing or excavation. Northeast, through its archaeological team, arranged to store any recovered artifacts at Mercyhurst College in Erie, Pennsylvania. On May 16, 2008, CMURM applied to the New York State Museum, a division of the New York State Education Department, for a permit to collect and excavate archaeological materials at the wreck site. On June 4, 2008, pursuant to New [—7—] York Education Law § 233,[5] the State granted a permit allowing excavation of the Dunkirk Schooner through August 30, 2008. Eventually, the State extended the permit through September 30, 2008. The permit contained a number of conditions, including that "[i]n the event that human remains are recovered from the shipwreck, the State Museum must be contacted in decision-

---

[2] Admirality and maritime "are used synonymously today" and we do not depart from this usage. Thomas J. Schoenbaum, 1 *Admiralty and Maritime Law* § 1-1 (5th ed. 2011). Traditionally, however, they are distinct terms. "[M]aritime law . . . refer[s] to the entire body of laws, rules, legal concepts and processes that relate to the use of marine resources, ocean commerce, and navigation. Admiralty law . . . is narrower in the sense that it refers only to the private law of navigation and shipping; it is broader in that it covers inland as well as marine waters." *Id.* (emphases omitted and internal footnote).

[3] "In an *in rem* admiralty action, the arrest of a shipwreck is the procedure by which a salvor establishes jurisdiction in federal court." *Great Lakes Exploration Grp., LLC v. Unidentified Wrecked & (for Salvage-Right Purposes), Abandoned Sailing Vessel,* 522 F.3d 682, 686 (6th Cir. 2008).

[4] In his deposition, Kullberg explained, "I filed for a museum permit, a [New York Education Law §] 233 permit, so we could work together, so the State of New York would know what I was doing and we could work together, you know, step-by-step, to find out the great history on the shipwreck."

[5] New York Education Law § 233 provides in relevant part that "no person shall investigate, excavate, remove, injure, appropriate or destroy any object of archaeological, historical, cultural, social, scientific or paleontological interest situated on, in or under lands owned by the state of New York, without the written permission of the commissioner of education." N.Y. Educ. Law § 233(4).

making related to the removal and/or analysis of these remains."[6]

The primary objective of Northeast's physical investigation of the Dunkirk Schooner was to determine the identity of the ship, which remained a mystery, by taking measurements, excavating its cargo, and collecting artifacts. The [—8—] process included "desilting" parts of the wreck, obtaining core samples of the forward hold, and a limited inspection of the after hold. Due to the depth of the wreck, excavating and documenting the Dunkirk Schooner required "technical" diving, "a form of self-contained diving using various mixed gases and requiring special training and experience."

Although Northeast's efforts, including the work of Vrana and Reedy, discovered no identifying marks on the vessel, they did unearth a trove of clues. Core samples from the forward hold yielded a mixture of wheat and barley. The after hold, although not fully excavated, contained hickory nuts. Divers recovered a range of artifacts indicative of daily life aboard a sailing vessel, including ceramic wares, watches, two compasses, lamps, crockery, period furniture, jewelry, book bindings, brass buttons, and coins with

---

[6] The permit also required that Northeast prepare and submit a report on the project to the State Museum by November 30, 2008, and that, "[i]f the shipwreck site is ultimately determined by the court to be under the jurisdiction of the State of New York," Northeast enter into a curation agreement with the State Museum for any artifacts recovered. A letter from the New York State Museum approving the permit and detailing conditions included the following disclaimer:

The approval by the parties to this agreement and any determination by the State with respect to this application shall not prejudice any claim or defense of either party in this litigation but rather is being done as a gesture of good faith within the context of the instant underlying admiralty litigation. Further, any granting of a permit by the State pursuant to this application shall not prejudice or commit either party with respect to the need for, or the denial of, any subsequent applications by Northeast, or with respect to any position of the State with respect to enforcement of its laws.

dates from 1797 to 1834. Divers working for Northeast—apparently without the knowledge of Vrana and Reedy—also found human bones. Northeast submitted some of these bones to a lab for DNA analysis, which revealed that they mostly likely came from an individual of Caucasian origin.

Toward the end of the summer of 2008, the relationship between Northeast and CMURM hit rough waters, in part as a result of the discovery of the human remains, and Vrana and Reedy took no part in field investigations after August 15, 2008. On October 21, 2008, the State Museum notified Vrana [—9—] of alleged violations of the excavation permit, including the recovery of human remains without notification to the State, continued diving by Northeast after the expiration of the permit on September 30, 2008, and the removal of planks from the roof of the Dunkirk Schooner's cabin.[7] Vrana and Reedy eventually submitted a Report of Investigations on the Dunkirk Schooner (the "CMURM Report") to the State, detailing their excavation work through August 30, 2008.

On March 4, 2009, based on an application by the New York State Office of Parks, Recreation and Historic Preservation, the National Park Service deemed the Dunkirk Schooner Site eligible for placement on the National Register of Historic Places.

II. Procedural History

A. *The Dispute Over the Identity of the Dunkirk Schooner*

On July 31, 2009, New York moved for summary judgment on the ground, *inter alia*,

---

[7] Northeast maintains that other unauthorized divers damaged the shipwreck, and that it took every effort to protect the Dunkirk Schooner from further destruction, including requesting an injunction from the district court (which was denied) and installing mooring blocks so that vessels could tie up without damaging the wreck. Northeast also maintains that it never removed the human bones from the wreck site, but placed them in a "bone bag" on the shipwreck; however, it is undisputed that Northeast sent certain bone fragments to a lab for DNA analysis.

that the Dunkirk Schooner is abandoned within the meaning of the ASA such that title automatically vests with the State.[8] Northeast filed a cross- [—10—] motion for partial summary judgment on August 4, 2009, disputing New York's claim to title and, in the alternative, requesting a salvage award. The parties' summary judgment arguments and materials in the record, including the CMURM Report and other analyses, focused largely on the issue of abandonment, specifically, whether the Dunkirk Schooner could be positively identified as the *General Wayne*, which Northeast asserted was not abandoned.

Kullberg proposed the *General Wayne*, originally christened the *Caledonia*, as a possible candidate for the identity of the Dunkirk Schooner after he and Northeast's videographer discovered a line drawing of the *Caledonia* in the Erie Maritime Museum. Vrana and Reedy's archival research into the *Caledonia*, as detailed in the CMURM Report, laid bare the following history: Built in 1799 in present-day Windsor, Canada, the *Caledonia* was a merchant vessel for the North West Company and was employed in the fur trade on Lake Erie. When the War of 1812 transformed Lake Erie into a battle front-line, the British armed the *Caledonia* with cannons and deployed her in the attack on Fort Michilimackinac in 1812. She was later captured on the Niagara River and converted into an American warship, and in that guise the *Caledonia* played a role in Commodore Perry's key victory in the Battle of Lake Erie in 1813. By [—11—] 1814, an American captain reported that "[t]he *Caledonia* is unseaworthy, from natural decay," and recommended her for sale. Newspaper accounts and a bill of sale show that in 1815, John Dickson and Rufus S. Reid of Erie, Pennsylvania bought the *Caledonia* and retrofitted or rebuilt her, renaming her

the *General Wayne*. The last reported mention of the *General Wayne* was in the year 1818. No reliable reports of her sinking or other disposition have surfaced.

In the CMURM Report, Vrana and Reedy discussed four possible historic ships, including the *General Wayne*, that could be the Dunkirk Schooner, but refrained from offering a definite conclusion regarding the identity of the wreck and recommended that further historical and archival research is necessary to positively identify the shipwreck. The CMURM Report does conclude that the Dunkirk Schooner's probable career dated from the 1820s to the 1840s, and that her cargo of hickory nuts and mixed grains was typical of ingredients used in the production of whiskey in distilleries around the Great Lakes in the nineteenth century. During his deposition, Vrana reiterated that he had no opinion "either which way" regarding whether the Dunkirk Schooner is the *General Wayne*.

In support of its motion for summary judgment, New York offered the expert report of Arthur B. Cohn, executive director of the Lake Champlain Maritime Museum. Cohn concluded "with a high degree of confidence" that the Dunkirk Schooner is not the *General Wayne*, but an unidentified merchant [—12—] vessel built shortly before 1829 and which sank sometime between 1834 and 1844. He reached this conclusion based in part on the architecture and measurements of the Dunkirk Schooner, which he found were consistent with ships built to traverse the Welland Canal, completed in 1829,[9] and inconsistent with the drawing of the

---

[8] Additionally, New York asserted title to the Dunkirk Schooner under the federal Submerged Lands Act and New York law, and argued that the Eleventh [—10—] Amendment divested the district court of admiralty jurisdiction over the action, that equity mandated that Northeast's claims should fail as a matter of law, and that sovereign immunity barred Northeast's salvage claim.

[9] As the CMURM Report explains,

Maritime commerce between Lake Erie and Lake Ontario during this time period was greatly enhanced by the completion of the Welland Canal in 1829. However, the dimensions of the Welland Canal also affected the design of vessels by shipwrights in order to take advantage of commercial opportunities between the upper and lower lakes. . . . The dimensions of the Dunkirk Schooner are less than the dimensions of the [Welland Canal], and therefore, indicate that this vessel could have participated in the Lake Ontario trade after 1829.

Caledonia in the Erie Maritime Museum.[10] The *General Wayne*, Cohn noted, had a reported length of 56 feet, which is nearly 20 feet shorter than the length of the shipwreck. [—13—]

Cohn also offered testimony to support New York's contention that the Dunkirk Schooner was abandoned long ago. Cohn opined that the technology to locate and recover the vessel existed at or about the time of its sinking. He alluded, specifically, to the salvage of the Steamboat *Atlantic*, which sank in about 160 feet of water in Lake Erie in 1852, and was salvaged by hardhat divers working in 1852 and 1855 and descending to 139 feet and 155 feet, respectively. Cohn noted that the Dunkirk Schooner's masts rise to about 100 feet from the surface, making it at least a potential candidate for salvage, and yet there is no evidence that any salvage effort was ever made. Cohn opined, finally, that the schooner's "mixed cargo of grain and hickory nuts would not have provided the economic incentive to drag the lake and attempt to recover the cargo, despite the technological feasibility of that type of effort at the time."

In support of Northeast's assertion that it had found the wreck of the *General Wayne*, Northeast submitted an archaeological site assessment by James Sinclair (the "Sinclair Report").[11] The Sinclair Report concluded that the cumulative physical evidence, including the Dunkirk Schooner's distinctive "fiddlehead" bow, the notched rudder, measurements taken by divers, and other architectural features, "substantiates the fact that the Dunkirk Schooner is none [—14—] other than the storied former warship and Underground Railroad freedom boat, the *CALEDONIA/GENERAL WAYNE*." According to Sinclair, all other theories for the identity of the shipwreck could be scuttled based on inconsistencies with the Dunkirk Schooner. Sinclair also noted that the Dunkirk Schooner's lack of identifying markings would be consistent with the purported use of the *General Wayne* in the smuggling of slaves to freedom. Sinclair reported that the *General Wayne*'s owners, Reid and Dickson, were active in the abolitionist movement and their houses in Erie, Pennsylvania, "feature extensive labyrinths of underground passageways reputedly used to hide fugitive slaves prior to their final journey to freedom in Canada." He speculated that the ship may have been carrying fugitive slaves at the time it sunk.

Northeast also commissioned an opinion paper from Rindlisbacher, the marine artist who specializes in Great Lake vessels, regarding the "likelihood that the Dunkirk wreck is actually the CALEDONIA" based on the shipwreck's "design features, deck fittings and present conditions." Rindlisbacher compared the Dunkirk Schooner with known examples of the design features of ships contemporary to the *Caledonia*, concluding that the shipwreck's "design features, deck fittings and other characteristics . . . are consistent with the supposed appearance of the CALEDONIA to a significant extent," and that nothing had "convincingly exclude[d]" the *Caledonia* as a possible candidate. Rindlisbacher [—15—] recognized, however, that "[v]ery little" is known about the physical aspects of the historic *Caledonia*, a circumstance which "adds increased difficulty

---

[10] Cohn's expert report and the CMURM Report both note that the line drawing of the *Caledonia* in the Erie Maritime Museum is a modern-day rendering by maritime artist Kenneth Atkins in 1997, and was based on secondary sources, identified as the "tonnage reports, Bell draught, [and] proportions of *General Hunter*[, another ship], and pictures." As Cohn explained, "The rendering is drawn from images of boats contemporary with *Caledonia* to create a reasonable estimation of what a boat of that time period and with those dimensions might have looked like." Northeast, in order to bolster the reliability of the Atkins drawing as proof of the *Caledonia*'s physical appearance, submitted an affidavit by Peter J. Rindlisbacher, a marine artist specializing in vessels of the Great Lakes, attesting that Atkins usually sought primary sources as the basis for his drawings and that "Mr. Atkins' renderings . . . of the *CALEDONIA* can be relied upon as highly accurate depictions of the historic vessel."

[11] Sinclair holds an M.A. in Historic Maritime Archaeology and is the vice president of a firm specializing in the "private-public management of shipwreck resources."

51

to evaluating whether the present wreck is actually the original CALEDONIA." Rindlisbacher also acknowledged that the "most difficult fact" weighing against identifying the shipwreck as the *General Wayne/Caledonia* is that, assuming that she sank sometime after 1834 (the date of the newest coin on the wreck), she would have been at least 35 years old at her sinking (based on a 1799 launch date), and "[t]he general wisdom is that these early schooners seldom had that long a lifespan." Nevertheless, "if we allow that CALEDONIA was repaired or refurbished at least once and perhaps additionally through her career, and finally foundered in an end-stage barge condition," Rindlisbacher offered, "it is conceivable that she might have been afloat for all those 35 or more years before her loss."

Finally, Northeast located Hannah Reed Mays, one of the descendants of Rufus S. Reid, the *General Wayne*'s co-owner. Northeast obtained from her an assignment to Northeast of her ownership interest in the *General Wayne* (the "Mays Assignment"), which it proffered as additional evidence in support of its claim that the Dunkirk Schooner is not abandoned.[12] [—16—]

B. The District Court's Decision

In a Report and Recommendation dated May 27, 2010, the magistrate judge (Leslie G. Foschio, *Magistrate Judge*) to whom the case was referred recommended granting New York's motion for summary judgment and denying Northeast's request for a salvage award. *See Northeast Research,* 790 F. Supp. 2d at 66-89 (appending Report and Recommendation). With regard to New York's claim under the ASA, Magistrate Judge Foschio found that "even if the . . . [v]essel is, as [Northeast] urges, the *Caledonia/General Wayne,*" *id.* at 81, "clear and convincing evidence in the record establishes an inference

of abandonment," *id.* at 80, and thus the State has title to the Dunkirk Schooner.[13]

Northeast filed objections to the Report and Recommendation, and the district court held oral argument on September 9, 2010. *Id.* at 61. On March 25, 2011, the district court issued a Decision and Order finding that New York had established its claim that the Dunkirk Schooner is abandoned and that Northeast had failed to raise a material issue to the contrary, entitling the State to title pursuant to the ASA. The court adopted the Report and Recommendation "to the extent set forth herein," granted the State's motion for summary judgment, and denied Northeast's salvage award request. *Id.* at 66. [—17—] In reaching these conclusions, the district court identified a purported split among circuit courts regarding whether abandonment under the ASA must be proved by express relinquishment of title or may be inferred from surrounding circumstances, and decided to adopt an inferential standard for proving abandonment. *Id.* at 63-64. The court also agreed with the magistrate judge that abandonment must be shown by clear and convincing evidence, rather than a preponderance of the evidence. *Id.* at 64. The district court referenced Cohn's opinion that the technology to salvage the vessel has existed since 1850 and noted that Northeast had "provided no evidence to support" its assertion that the Dunkirk Schooner could not have been discovered, much less salvaged, without the advent of modern technology. *Id.* at 65. "Moreover," the district court continued, "even if a salvage operation would have been unsuccessful, as plaintiff contends, there is no evidence that any salvage effort was attempted." *Id.* The court determined that the Mays Assignment was insufficient to create a material dispute on the issue of abandonment, particularly as no evidence demonstrated any effort by descendants "to locate the vessel in the 150 years since its sinking." *Id.* at 66. "In sum," the district court held,

---

[12] The record also contains the affidavit of Nancy Potter, a descendant of John Dickson, affirming that Northeast contacted her and requested that she assign her ownership interest in the *General Wayne* to Northeast, but that she refused to do so.

---

[13] Magistrate Judge Foschio first determined that the Eleventh Amendment did not divest the court of jurisdiction over the suit, even though New York had a "colorable" claim to the shipwreck. 790 F. Supp. 2d at 74-76.

the passage of over 150 years since the sinking of the vessel along with the absence of any effort to locate or salvage the vessel by the owners or their de[scendants] despite the existence of technology to do so demonstrates an intent to abandon by clear and convincing evidence.

Id.

This appeal followed. [—18—]

DISCUSSION

On appeal, Northeast argues that the district court erred in granting New York's motion for summary judgment. Northeast principally asserts that, in finding that the Dunkirk Schooner is abandoned, the district court failed to apply the proper burden of proof, made impermissible factual findings, and failed to draw reasonable inferences in favor of Northeast.[14] We address each of these arguments in turn.

---

[14] Northeast spends a considerable portion of its brief arguing that, under *California v. Deep Sea Research, Inc.*, 523 U.S. 491 (1998), because New York does not have actual possession of the Dunkirk Schooner, the state cannot have its ownership claim adjudicated until Northeast completes its salvage operations. This argument holds no water. *Deep Sea Research* held only that the Eleventh Amendment does not bar federal jurisdiction over an *in rem* admiralty action so long as the state does not have actual possession (as opposed to constructive possession) of the *res* to which it claims ownership. *Id.* at 507-08; *see also Fairport Int'l Exploration, Inc. v. Shipwrecked Vessel (Fairport III)*, 177 F.3d 491, 497 (6th Cir. 1999) (*Deep Sea Research* "definitively instructs us that, if a State does not possess a shipwreck, the Eleventh Amendment does not prevent a federal court from entertaining claims under the ASA to the shipwreck."). We agree with the district court that the Eleventh Amendment does not bar the exercise of jurisdiction here—an argument that New York has, in any event, abandoned on appeal. We also conclude, however, that Northeast's reliance on *Deep Sea Research* is misplaced, as *Deep Sea Research* did not discuss and does not clarify a salvor's rights, if any, in the absence of a state's actual possession of the wreck.

A. Standard of Review

We review *de novo* a district court's grant of summary judgment, "construing the evidence in the light most favorable to the non-moving party and drawing all reasonable inferences in its favor." *Fincher v. Depository Trust & Clearing Corp.*, 604 F.3d 712, 720 (2d Cir. 2010) (internal quotation marks [—19—] omitted). "[W]e affirm only where we are able to conclude . . . that 'there is no genuine issue of dispute as to any material fact and the movant is entitled to judgment as a matter of law.'" *Costello v. City of Burlington*, 632 F.3d 41, 45 (2d Cir. 2011) (quoting Fed. R. Civ. P. 56(a)).

B. The Abandoned Shipwreck Act

The ASA provides in relevant part that the United States asserts title to any abandoned shipwreck that is:

(1) embedded in submerged lands of a State;

(2) embedded in coralline formations protected by a State on submerged lands of a State; or

(3) on submerged lands of a State and is included in or determined eligible for inclusion in the National Register [of Historic Places].

43 U.S.C. § 2105(a). If a shipwreck qualifies as property of the United States under § 2105(a), the ASA automatically transfers title to the state "in or on whose submerged lands the shipwreck is located." *Id.* § 2105(c). Thus, "[f]or a state to acquire title to a shipwreck [under the ASA] it must be (1) abandoned and (2) on or embedded in the submerged lands of a state." *Sea Hunt, Inc. v. Unidentified Shipwrecked Vessel or Vessels*, 221 F.3d 634, 640 (4th Cir. 2000). As it is undisputed that the Dunkirk Schooner is a wreck embedded in the submerged lands of New York, this case turns on whether a material issue of fact exists as to its abandonment. [—20—]

The ASA displaces the maritime law of salvage and the law of finds that otherwise govern shipwrecks not falling within the Act's terms. *See* 43 U.S.C. § 2106(a) ("The law of salvage and the law of finds shall not apply to abandoned shipwrecks to which section 2105 of this title applies."); *Great Lakes Exploration Grp., LLC v. Unidentified Wrecked & (For Salvage-Right Purposes), Abandoned Sailing Vessel*, 522 F.3d 682, 688 (6th Cir. 2008). Although "there appears to be no clear line of demarcation between property that is 'salvaged' and 'finds,'" *Adams v. Unione Mediterranea Di Sicurta*, 220 F.3d 659, 670 (5th Cir. 2000) (internal quotation marks and alterations omitted), traditionally, courts have applied the law of salvage when the original owner of a ship or cargo lost at sea retains an ownership interest in the property— albeit also granting a "very liberal" award to the salvor for its recovery of the *res*.[15] *Columbus-Am. Discovery Grp. v. Atl. Mut. Ins. Co.*, 974 F.2d 450, 459 (4th Cir. 1992); Thomas J. Schoenbaum, 2 *Admiralty and Maritime Law* § 16.7 (5th ed. 2011); *cf. Int'l Aircraft Recovery, L.L.C. v. Unidentified, Wrecked & Abandoned Aircraft*, 218 F.3d 1255, 1258 (11th Cir. 2000) ("The law of salvage generally governs efforts to save vessels in distress. Under the law of salvage, rescuers take possession of, but not title to, the distressed vessel and its contents."). Conversely, the law [—21—] of finds vests title to property that is abandoned, or which has never been owned, in the finder. *See Martha's Vineyard Scuba Headquarters, Inc. v. Unidentified, Wrecked & Abandoned Steam Vessel*, 833 F.2d 1059, 1065 (1st Cir. 1987) (applying "the ancient and honorable principle of 'finders, keepers,'" to steam vessel the *Republic*, "given the passage of so many decades" since its sinking); *cf. Columbus-Am. Discovery Grp.*, 974 F.2d at 460 (noting that "[a] relatively recent trend in the law . . . has seen the law of finds applied to long lost and abandoned shipwrecks"). But since the ASA, where applicable, precludes application of both the law of salvage and finds, "[i]f a diver now discovers a long-lost ship embedded in the submerged lands of a State, a finding of abandonment leaves the diver with neither title nor a salvage award." *Fairport Int'l Exploration, Inc. v. Shipwrecked*

Vessel (*Fairport III*), 177 F.3d 491, 498 (6th Cir. 1999).

In enacting the ASA, Congress sought to preserve and protect abandoned, embedded and historic shipwrecks by entrusting states with their management and encouraging states to develop sound policies for: (1) the protection of natural resources and habitat associated with such wrecks; (2) the guarantee of recreational exploration of shipwreck sites; and (3) the appropriate recovery of wrecks so as to protect historical values and the integrity of the shipwrecks and [—22—] their sites. *See* 43 U.S.C. §§ 2101, 2103.[16] The ASA does not prohibit the activities of commercial salvors but rather encourages states to regulate "private sector recovery of shipwrecks consistent with the protection of historical values and environmental integrity

---

[15] Technically, "[b]y performing a voluntary and successful [salvage] act, the salvor obtains a maritime lien on the salved property, which he can enforce in rem in an admiralty court." *Adams*, 220 F.3d at 670 (internal quotation marks omitted).

---

[16] The ASA's "Congressional statement of findings" provides:

(a) States have the responsibility for management of a broad range of living and nonliving resources in State waters and submerged lands; and
(b) included in the range of resources are certain abandoned shipwrecks, which have been deserted and to which the owner has relinquished ownership rights with no retention.

43 U.S.C. § 2101. Moreover, the ASA states that

[I]t is the declared policy of the Congress that States carry out their responsibilities under this chapter to develop appropriate and consistent policies so as to—

(A) protect natural resources and habitat areas;
(B) guarantee recreational exploration of shipwreck sites; and
(C) allow for appropriate public and private sector recovery of shipwrecks consistent with the protection of historical values and environmental integrity of the shipwrecks and the sites.

Id. § 2103(a) ("Access rights"). In that vein, "States are encouraged to create underwater parks or areas to provide additional protection for such resources." *Id.* §2103(b) ("Parks and protected areas").

of the shipwrecks." 43 U.S.C. § 2103(a). The Act reflects Congress's judgment, however, that states are the best guardians of abandoned wrecks of historical significance found in their waters (and of other abandoned shipwrecks embedded in state lands), and that a policy of settling ownership of such shipwrecks with states promotes the best interests of the public. *See Zych v. Unidentified, Wrecked & Abandoned Vessel, Believed to Be* **[—23—]** *the "Seabird,"* 19 F.3d 1136, 1140 (7th Cir. 1994) ("Congress passed the ASA to clear up any confusion over who owns certain abandoned shipwrecks.").

1. Abandonment under the ASA

Northeast concedes that the Dunkirk Schooner is a historically significant shipwreck embedded in the submerged lands of New York, but disputes that it is "abandoned" within the meaning of the Act. As Magistrate Judge Foschio succinctly explained, "[i]f . . . the Dunkirk Schooner is not abandoned, then neither the ASA nor the maritime law of finds applies, and although title would vest in neither North[e]ast nor New York, [Northeast] could be granted a salvage award." *Northeast Research*, 790 F. Supp. 2d at 78. If the wreck is abandoned, then it belongs to New York pursuant to the ASA.

The ASA does not define the term "abandoned." However, the Supreme Court has stated that "the meaning of 'abandoned' under the ASA conforms with its meaning under admiralty law." *California v. Deep Sea Research, Inc.*, 523 U.S. 491, 508 (1998). In admiralty cases, courts do not assume that ship owners have abandoned their vessels simply because the vessels have wrecked. *See Dluhos v. Floating & Abandoned Vessel, Known as "New York,"* 162 F.3d 63, 74 (2d Cir. 1998). Rather, courts employ an "assumption of nonabandonment," anchored on the "realistic premise that property previously owned but lost at sea has been taken involuntarily out of the owner's possession and control by the **[—24—]** forces of nature at work in oceans and waterways." *Columbus-Am. Discovery Grp.*, 974 F.2d at 460-61 (quoting *Hener v. United States*, 525 F. Supp.

350, 356- 57 (S.D.N.Y. 1981)); *see Fairport III*, 177 F.3d at 498 ("Intent on protecting the property rights of owners, admiralty courts recognize a presumption against finding abandonment."). Thus, abandonment under admiralty law "means much more than merely leaving the property, for it has long been the law that when articles are lost at sea the title of the owner in them remains." *Columbus-Am. Discovery Grp.*, 974 F.2d at 461 (internal quotation marks and alteration omitted).

As a consequence of the presumption against abandonment, courts in this Circuit and elsewhere have traditionally imposed a stringent burden of proof of abandonment in the admiralty context. *See, e.g., The C.P. Minch*, 73 F. 859, 865 (2d Cir. 1896) (holding that circumstances must show abandonment of a vessel was "absolute, without hope or expectation of recovery"); *Adams*, 220 F.3d at 671; *Trueman v. Historic Steamtug New York*, 120 F. Supp. 2d 228, 233 (N.D.N.Y. 2000); Schoenbaum, 2 *Admiralty and Maritime Law* § 16-7 (stating that application of law of finds "requires strong proof" that the property was lost). Those circuits that have decided the issue, moreover, have adopted a heightened "clear and convincing evidence" standard for states attempting to prove abandonment under the ASA. *See Fairport III*, 177 F.3d at 500-01 **[—25—]** (holding that state must prove abandonment by clear and convincing evidence); *Sea Hunt*, 221 F.3d at 644 (same). We agree that the clear and convincing "burden of proof accords with maritime law and with the protection of private property rights against appropriation by the state," *Fairport III*, 177 F.3d at 501, and therefore hold that abandonment for ASA purposes must be shown by clear and convincing evidence by the party arguing for abandonment—the state.

We also agree with the district court that abandonment pursuant to the ASA need not be proved by express or explicit statements of intent to abandon, but rather may be inferred from circumstantial evidence (provided such evidence is sufficiently strong as to satisfy the clear and convincing burden). Although the district court identified a circuit split regarding inferential abandonment under the

ASA, those Circuits that have broached the subject in fact agree on the following: that for ships last owned by a private party, abandonment may be inferred from circumstantial evidence in appropriate cases, at least when there is no owner presently claiming an interest in the vessel.[17] *Compare Fairport III*, [—26—] 177 F.3d at 500 (holding that "a State may prove by inference that a shipwreck last owned by a private party is 'abandoned'"), *and Deep Sea Research, Inc. v. Brother Jonathan*, 89 F.3d 680, 688 (9th Cir. 1996), *vacated on other grounds by California v. Deep Sea Research*, 523 U.S. 496 (1998) (applying "traditional approach" to abandonment that "allows abandonment to be inferred on the basis of circumstantial evidence"), *with Sea Hunt*, 221 F.3d at 641 (noting that "[a]n inference of abandonment is permitted, but only when no owner appears").

This approach comports with the treatment of abandonment in admiralty cases. Indeed, even before enactment of the ASA, courts applying traditional admiralty principles had begun to reject the notion that "[d]isposition of a wrecked vessel whose very location has been lost for centuries" must proceed "as though its owner were still in existence." *Treasure Salvors, Inc. v. Unidentified Wrecked & Abandoned Sailing Vessel*, 569 F.2d 330, 337 (5th Cir. 1978). *See Martha's Vineyard Scuba Headquarters*, 833 F.2d at 1065 (applying law of finds to long-lost ship without requiring express abandonment); *Dluhos*, 162 F.3d at 74 (recognizing trend away from legal fiction "under which an owner . . . retains title" to a ship that has "rested for centuries under fathoms of open ocean"). As the Ninth Circuit has observed:

> Traditionally, maritime law has found abandonment when title to a vessel has been affirmatively renounced, or when

circumstances give rise to an inference that the vessel has been abandoned; courts [—27—] have found abandonment, for instance, when a vessel is "so long lost that time can be presumed to have eroded any realistic claim of original title."

Deep Sea Research, 89 F.3d at 688 (quoting *Martha's Vineyard Scuba Headquarters*, 833 F.2d at 1065). Requiring express abandonment in all ASA cases would be inconsistent with these admiralty cases and, as the Sixth Circuit has observed, would "render the ASA a virtual nullity," since "such explicit action is obviously rare indeed," *Fairport Int'l Exploration, Inc. v. Shipwrecked Vessel Known as the Captain Lawrence (Fairport II)*, 105 F.3d 1078, 1085 (6th Cir. 1997), *vacated on other grounds by* 523 U.S. 1091 (1998).

In determining whether clear and convincing circumstantial evidence supports inferring abandonment, courts consider a variety of factors, including lapse of time, the location and circumstances of the wreck, whether parties presently claim ownership, whether such parties have attempted to locate or salvage the vessel, and the availability of technology to do so. While mere nonuse and lapse of time alone may not be enough to establish abandonment, "a combination of several facts, proved clearly and convincingly, . . . may support a finding than an owner has abandoned a shipwreck." *Fairport III*, 177 F.3d at 500; *see also Trueman*, 120 F. Supp. 2d at 234; *Moyer v. Wrecked & Abandoned Vessel, Known as The Andrea Doria*, 836 F. Supp. 1099, 1105 (D.N.J. 1993) ("Factors such as lapse of time and nonuse by the owner may give rise to an [—28—] inference of intent to abandon. Other factors include the place of the shipwreck as well as the actions and conduct of the parties having ownership rights in the vessel." (citations omitted)). For example, an owner's failure to salvage a vessel despite the availability of technology to do so may support an inference that the owner has abandoned his property, while the technical infeasibility of salvage may deprive the owner's inaction of evidentiary significance. *Compare Zych v. Unidentified, Wrecked &*

---

[17] The Sixth Circuit limited its holding in *Fairport III* to shipwrecks last owned by a private party and "express[ed] no view" as to whether express abandonment is required as to "vessels initially owned by the United States." *Fairport III*, 177 F.3d at 500. *See also Sea Hunt*, 221 F.3d at 643 (applying express abandonment test in context of *in rem* action against two Spanish ships claimed by Spain). We similarly limit our holding and analysis.

Abandoned Vessel Believed to be the "SB Lady Elgin", 755 F. Supp. 213, 216 (N.D. Ill. 1991) (finding that insurance company "was not required to engage in efforts to recover the wreck in order to avoid abandoning its interest when such efforts would have minimal chances for success" due to lack of enabling technology) *with Fairport Int'l Exploration, Inc. v. Shipwrecked Vessel (Fairport IV)*, 72 F. Supp. 2d 795, 798-801 (W.D. Mich. 1999) (inferring abandonment based in part on evidence of failure to attempt salvage despite technological feasibility), *and Moyer*, 836 F. Supp. at 1105 (insurer's "failure to engage in salvage efforts" not excused where technology to salvage the wreck was available shortly after its sinking).

For obvious reasons, discovering the identity of a vessel, if ascertainable, is helpful in determining whether it is abandoned. *See Fathom Exploration L.L.C. v. Unidentified Shipwrecked Vessel or Vessels*, 857 F. Supp. 2d 1269, 1272-73 n.4 (S.D. Ala. 2012) (in suit involving claims under the ASA, noting that "the [—29—] identity of Shipwreck #1 is of vital importance to the parties' underlying claims and rights in this matter"). But it does not follow that a shipwreck *must* be positively identified in order to adjudicate a state's claim to title under the ASA. *See id.* at 1279 (provisionally identifying shipwreck as British barque the *Amstel* for purposes of determining whether it was abandoned pursuant to the ASA even absent any "hard evidence" to support that theory as the "definitive truth"); *cf. Klein v. Unidentified Wrecked & Abandoned Sailing Vessel*, 758 F.2d 1511, 1514 (11th Cir. 1985) (in pre-ASA case, applying law of finds to determine ownership of unidentified shipwreck); *Smith v. Abandoned Vessel*, 610 F. Supp. 2d 739, 754 (S.D. Tex. 2009) (inferring that unidentified and potentially nonexistent vessel was abandoned). Common sense suggests that in some circumstances, especially in the case of old and ancient wrecks, "100% certainty as to the vessel's identity is not possible," even after "untold hours of laborious research[.]" *Fathom Exploration*, 857 F. Supp. 2d at 1272 n.4. Imposing such a requirement (which, at any rate, is not to be found in the text of the ASA) would thus undermine the statute by condemning some wrecks and the artifacts associated with them to a watery limbo, vulnerable to further deterioration and destruction. Thus, although ascertaining the identity of a vessel is certainly helpful in making the determination whether the vessel has been abandoned, this is not a precondition for determining abandonment under the ASA. [—30—]

C. The Dunkirk Schooner is Abandoned under the ASA

The question before this Court is whether the district court erred in determining that New York established its case by clear and convincing evidence, and that Northeast failed to raise a material issue of fact as to whether the Dunkirk Schooner is abandoned. We conclude that the district court did not err in granting summary judgment to New York. There are admittedly questions of fact regarding the identity of the Dunkirk Schooner— questions that Lake Erie has perhaps permanently obscured. But in this case, the district court properly determined that this mystery need not impede adjudication of title to the shipwreck.

In reviewing the grant of summary judgment to New York, we view the evidence in the light most favorable to Northeast and assume that the Dunkirk Schooner is the War of 1812 battleship the *General Wayne,* née *Caledonia.* Even so, New York has demonstrated abandonment by clear and convincing evidence: there were no efforts to locate the wreck for over 150 years; *General Wayne*'s poor working condition and spoilable contents strongly call into question the economic worth of the vessel and the then-owners' continued interest in recovery; and the alleged owners' descendants have no proof of their ownership of the vessel, further suggesting abandonment by the original owners. We [—31—] therefore uphold the district court's conclusion that the Dunkirk Schooner was abandoned.

Proceeding on the assumption that Northeast discovered the wreck of the *General Wayne,* the following undisputed facts emerge: Originally built in 1799, the *Caledonia,* a wooden schooner, sank sometime after 1833 with some unfortunate souls on board. This means that she was at least 34 years old when she sank and, as Northeast's own evidence suggests, nearing the end of her expected lifespan even if she was retrofitted in 1815, after her purchase by Dickson and Reid.[18] At the time of her disaster, the hold of the *Caledonia*, renamed the *General Wayne*, contained grain and hickory nuts, which were undoubtedly ruined by the water and rendered valueless. After 1818, moreover, the *General Wayne* disappears from the history books, and there is no record of her sinking. Assuming, then, that the Dunkirk Schooner is the *General Wayne*, she has rested at the bottom of Lake Erie for at least 150 years. And there is no evidence—none—that her former owners Reid and Dickson (or anyone else connected to the ship) ever tried to locate her or took any actions indicative of a continued interest prior to her discovery by Northeast in 2003. [—32—]

Pointing to the abolitionist ties of Reid and Dickson and the lack of identifying markings on the Dunkirk Schooner, Northeast speculates that the *General Wayne* was used to ferry fugitive slaves to Canada as part of the Underground Railroad—so that Reid and Dickson had an incentive *not* to attempt to find the vessel containing proof of their illegal activities immediately after it sunk. However, even if we assume that the *General Wayne* was carrying escaped slaves when it wrecked—an inference supported only by Sinclair's bald speculation—that fact still does not support a finding of non-abandonment. While in some circumstances, "lack of overt efforts to claim the ship may comport as much with a concern for secreting [treasure] as with an intent to abandon the ship," such is not the case here. *Fairport III*, 177 F.3d at 501 n.4 (discussing possible intent of ship's owner to

return to gold that might lie with the ship). Whereas the "secreting" of treasure is presumably done with the intent to return to the booty and retain a claim to it, a decision to leave the evidence of an illegal act carries no such implication—especially where the evidence, as here, was an old ship and a ruined cargo.

The parties disagree about whether the technology existed to salvage the *General Wayne* after it sank, and whether the Mays Assignment is a legitimate claim of ownership that creates a genuine issue of material fact regarding abandonment. On the issue of technology, we agree with Northeast that the [—33—] district court erred in concluding that no issue of fact exists as to whether hardhat divers could have recovered the Dunkirk Schooner beginning in 1852. New York's expert, Cohn, noting that the Dunkirk Schooner's masts rise to about 100 feet from the surface of Lake Erie, based his conclusion that hardhat divers could have salvaged the Dunkirk Schooner near the time of its wreck on his observation that "[o]n Lake Erie the Steamboat *Atlantic* which sank in 160 feet of water in 1852 was salvaged by hardhat divers descending to 139 and 155 feet in 1852 and 1855." However, the record also contains evidence that "technical diving," which relies on modern technology, is required today to reach the wreck. Moreover, the ability of hardhat divers to reach the top of the *General Wayne*'s mast (the ship itself lies at 170 feet) hardly demonstrates the technological feasibility of recovery, let alone a likelihood of successful salvage. *See Zych*, 755 F. Supp. at 216. Based on our review of the record, we therefore conclude that the technological possibility of salvage in the mid-1850s remains a disputed issue.

Nevertheless, even assuming that technological infeasibility barred recovery in the 1850s, the Dunkirk Schooner remained undisturbed for 150 years thereafter, despite advances in deep-water salvage in the intervening years. *See Columbus-Am. Discovery Grp.*, 974 F.2d at 467 (mentioning "drastic advances in deep water salvage" by the late 1970s). Long past fear of repercussion for [—34—] illegally helping fugitive slaves,

---

[18] Rindlisbacher, Northeast's expert witness, opined that the Dunkirk Schooner was not in a "normal working state" when she sank, since "[h]er stand rigging had been removed, along with essential spars, which do not indicate that she was sailing very effectively prior to her sinking. This is consistent with a ship which, being at the end of her working life, was unable to tolerate the working loads of being under sail."

and long past any time in which deep-water salvage was out of the question, no owner of the *General Wayne*, or any successor in interest, made efforts to locate or recover the wreck. To the extent Northeast relies on the Mays Assignment as a demonstration of continued owner interest, moreover, this applies to Mays as well.

Regarding the Mays Assignment, we conclude, contrary to Northeast's claim, that it creates no genuine issue of material fact necessitating trial on the issue of abandonment. The validity of Mays's ownership claim, and thus of the assignment to Northeast, depends on several significant assumptions: first, that Mays's great-great-great grandfather Rufus Reid did not abandon the *General Wayne* during his lifetime; second, that Reid bequeathed the *General Wayne* to his children (or that title otherwise passed to them) rather than to someone else; third, that title to the *General Wayne* thereafter passed to Reid's descendants; and fourth, that those descendants did not abandon the *General Wayne*. Although Mays's declaration attests to her family lineage and the fact that her ancestor Reid purchased a half-ownership in the *General Wayne* in 1816, it offers no documentary or other proof, *or even personal belief*, that the *General Wayne* remained in the family or that Mays inherited an ownership interest in the ship. Thus, while the assumption that the Dunkirk Schooner is the *General Wayne* has some (albeit limited) support in the record, there is no evidence supporting [—35—] any of the assumptions necessary to transform the Mays Assignment into legitimate proof of ownership when faced with 150 years of non-interest. In these circumstances, no reasonable inference against abandonment may be drawn from the Mays Assignment. *See Scotto v. Almenas*, 143 F.3d 105, 114 (2d Cir. 1998) (stating that "[t]he non-moving party may not rely on conclusory allegations or unsubstantiated speculation[ ]" to defeat a motion for summary judgment).

Considering all of the known factors, the clear and convincing evidence proves that even assuming the Dunkirk Schooner is the *General Wayne*, this ship has rested at the bottom of Lake Erie, utterly forgotten and undisturbed, for at least 150 years. As further circumstantial evidence of abandonment, the *General Wayne*'s hold was filled with spoilable goods and she was nearing the end of her working days. While the lack of technology available to salvage a shipwreck at the time of its disaster might in some cases excuse inaction, that factor does not suffice to create a material dispute of fact necessitating trial here, where the ship has gone undisturbed for such a lengthy period during which no recovery effort was ever made. *See Anderson v. Liberty Lobby, Inc.*, 477 U.S. 242, 247-48 (1986) ("[T]he mere existence of *some* alleged factual dispute between the parties will not defeat an otherwise properly supported motion for summary judgment; the requirement is that there be no *genuine* issue of [—36—] *material* fact."); *cf. Fairport Int'l Exploration, Inc. v. The Captain Lawrence (Fairport V)*, 245 F.3d 857, 863-64 (6th Cir. 2001) (affirming district court's conclusion that state proved abandonment despite evidence of owner's financial inability to return to shipwreck). The "lapse of time, alone, does not necessarily establish abandonment, and an owner's failure to return to a shipwreck site does not necessarily prove abandonment." *Fairport III*, 177 F.3d at 499 (citation omitted). But here, given the surrounding circumstances, the Dunkirk Schooner is a vessel "so long lost that time can be presumed to have eroded away any realistic claim of original title," *Martha's Vineyard Scuba Headquarters*, 833 F.2d at 1065. Northeast has failed to point to any fact in the record sufficient to create a genuine issue of material fact to the contrary. *See Scotto*, 143 F.3d at 114 ("[T]he non-movant [opposing a motion for summary judgment] must produce specific facts indicating that a genuine factual issue exists." (internal quotation marks omitted)). Accordingly, summary judgment was properly granted to New York. [—37—]

CONCLUSION

We have considered Northeast's remaining arguments and find them to be without merit. We conclude that dismissing the case on summary judgment was proper because the

Dunkirk Schooner is abandoned and title vests in New York pursuant to the ASA. For the foregoing reasons, we AFFIRM the judgment of the district court.

United States Court of Appeals
for the Second Circuit

No. 12-4505

AMERICAN PETROLEUM AND TRANSP., INC.
vs.
CITY OF NEW YORK

Appeal from the United States District Court for the Southern District of New York

Decided: December 6, 2013

Citation: 737 F.3d 185, 1 Adm. R. 61 (2d Cir. 2013).

Before **NEWMAN**, **RAGGI**, and **LYNCH**, Circuit Judges.

[—2—] **NEWMAN**, Circuit Judge:

The issue on this appeal is whether, under maritime law, an owner of a vessel may be awarded damages for economic loss due to negligence in the absence of physical damage to its property. For many years a number of courts have derived from the Supreme Court's opinion in *Robins Dry Dock & Repair Co. v. Flint*, 275 U.S. 303 (1927), a "rule" prohibiting such damages. Plaintiff-Appellant American Petroleum and Transport, Inc. ("American") appeals from the October 11, 2012, judgment of the United States District Court for the Southern District of New York (Paul A. Engelmayer, District Judge), granting a motion to dismiss by Defendants-Appellees City of New York and the New York Department of Transportation ("City"). *See American Petroleum and Transport, Inc. v. City of New York*, 902 F. Supp. 2d 466 (S.D.N.Y. 2012).

Although we conclude that *Robins Dry Dock* has been overread to establish a rule barring damages for economic loss in the absence of an owner's property damage, we believe the rule has been so consistently applied in admiralty that it should continue to be applied unless and until altered by Congress or the Supreme Court.

Background

American is a corporation in the business of transporting petroleum products by water. At all relevant times, American was the registered owner of a barge, the *John Blanche*, [—3—] and the demise charterer[1] of a tug, the *Caspian Sea*. The City operates a drawbridge, the Pelham Parkway Bridge, over the Hutchinson River. In March 2011, the tug and the barge, after passing upstream on the Hutchinson River under the opened bridge, requested the City to open the bridge for the downstream voyage. Due to a mechanical malfunction, which American alleges was the result of negligence, the City did not open the bridge, delaying the tug and the barge for approximately two and one-half days.

As a consequence of the delay, American alleges that it suffered $28,828 in economic losses. American acknowledges that it did not suffer any property damage.

In May 2012, American brought claims against the City for common law negligence and for violation of 33 U.S.C. § 494, which requires that a drawbridge over navigable water "be opened promptly by the persons owning or operating such bridge upon reasonable signal for the passage of boats and other water craft."[2] In October 2012, the District Court, relying on *Robins* [—4—] *Dry Dock v. Flint*, 275 U.S. 303 (1927), granted the City's motion to dismiss under Fed. R. Civ. P. 12(b)(6). *See American Petroleum*, 902 F. Supp. 2d at 468-71. The Court stated:

The issue presented by the City's motion to dismiss is whether the "*Robins Dry Dock* rule," as the case law has come to refer to it, precludes American from recovery here. American is quite correct that, on its facts, *Robins Dry Dock* itself does not address the situation here: a claim for economic

---

[1] In a demise or bareboat charter, the charterer is owner *pro hac vice* of the vessel, and the charterer is treated as the owner of the vessel with a sufficient property interest to recover lost profits. The demise charter is "tantamount to, though just short of, an outright transfer of ownership." *Guzman v. Pichirilo*, 369 U.S. 698, 700 (1962).

[2] The District Court ruled that the City's Department of Transportation was an improper defendant, and American does not challenge that ruling on appeal. *See American Petroleum*, 902 F. Supp. 2d at 467 n.1.

damages by a vessel's owner (as opposed to a time charterer). However, since that decision, the courts in this Circuit have extracted from it a broader prohibition with respect to maritime tort suits that is fatal to American's negligence claim here.

Specifically, as the Second Circuit has stated, the *Robins Dry Dock* rule "effectively bars recovery for economic losses caused by an unintentional maritime tort absent physical damage to property in which the victim has a proprietary interest."

902 F. Supp. 2d at 468-69 (quoting *G & G Steel, Inc. v. Sea Wolf Marine Transportation, LLC*, 380 Fed. Appx. 103, 104 (2d Cir. 2010) (summary order), and citing *Gas Natural SDG S.A. v. United States*, No. 07-2129-CV, 2008 WL 4643944, at *1 (2d Cir. Oct. 21, 2008) (summary order)). Although both *G & G Steel* and *Gas Natural* were non-precedential summary orders, *see* 2d R. 32.1.1(a), we had unequivocally stated in the latter decision, "[T]here exists a bright line rule barring recovery for *economic losses* caused by an unintentional maritime tort absent physical damage to property in which the victim has a *proprietary* [—5—] *interest*." *Gas Natural*, 2008 WL 4643944, at *1 (internal quotation marks and citations omitted) (emphases in original).

The District Court also concluded that most Circuits have held that 33 U.S.C. § 494 does not give rise to an implied private right of action. *American Petroleum*, 902 F. Supp. 2d at 470.

Discussion

In *Robins Dry Dock*, a dry docking company damaged a propeller on a steamship, rendering the vessel unusable for two weeks. The steamship's time charterer sued the dry dock company to recover its lost profits resulting from the delay. The Supreme Court denied recovery. *See Robins Dry Dock*, 275 U.S. at 308-10. The Court first ruled that the time charterer could not prevail as a third-party beneficiary of the contract between the

vessel owner and the dry docking company. *See id.* at 307-08. Turning to the time charterer's tort claim, the Court first stated generally that whether the dry dock company repaired the owner's vessel "promptly or with negligent delay was the business of the owners and of nobody else," and more specifically that "[t]he injury to the propeller was no wrong to the [time charterer] but only to those to whom it belonged." *Id.* at 308. The Court next considered what effect, if any, the charterparty had on the time charterer's claim: "But as there was a tortious damage to a chattel [the propeller of the owner's vessel] it is [—6—] sought to connect the claim of the [time charterer] with that in some way." *Id.* The Court observed that the time charterer's loss "arose only through their contract with the owners," *id.*, and then rejected the time charterer's claim in the passage most often quoted from *Robins Dry Dock*:

> [A]s a general rule, at least, a tort to the person or property of one man does not make the tort-feasor liable to another merely because the injured person was under a contract with that other unknown to the doer of the wrong. The law does not spread its protection so far.

Id. at 309 (internal citation omitted).[3]

Robins Dry Dock made two explicit rulings. The first ruling—that the time charterer was not the third-party beneficiary of the contract between the vessel owner and the drydocker— has no relevance to the pending case. The drawbridge operator has no contract with anyone. The second ruling was that the fact that the time charterer had a contract with the vessel owner whose property had been damaged by an unintentional tort gave the time charterer no right to recovery of its economic losses. This ruling, which we will

---

[3] The Court also rejected the theory, which our Court had used to uphold the time charterer's claim, *see Flint v. Robins Dry Dock & Repair Co.*, 13 F.2d 3, 6 (2d Cir. 1926), that the time charterer should receive an appropriate portion of the damages that the drydocker paid to the owner for loss of use because the owner could have sued on the time charterer's behalf. *See Robins Dry Dock*, 275 U.S. at 309-10.

call the "narrow ruling" of [—7—] *Robins Dry Dock*, also seems to have no relevance to the pending case: American Petroleum is not grounding its claim for economic losses on a contract between the negligent operator of the drawbridge and some other party whose property was damaged. Therefore, if American Petroleum's claim is barred, as the District Court held, by a *Robins Dry Dock* "rule" that economic losses cannot be recovered for an unintentional maritime tort in the absence of physical damage to the claimant's property, it must be because either there is some additional broader ruling implicit in that decision, or the narrow ruling has been extended, whether justifiably or not, into a broader ruling.[4]

Justice Holmes's text, however, gives no hint of either an implicit broader ruling or a basis for an extended broader ruling. He stated the *Robins Dry Dock* rule in narrow terms, explicitly declining to permit recovery just because the claimant has a contract with a party damaged by the tort. "[A]s a general rule, at least, a tort to the person or property of one man does not make the tort-feasor liable to another merely because the injured person was under a contract with that other unknown to [—8—] the doer of the wrong." *Robins Dry Dock*, 275 U.S. at 309. Moreover, the three cases Justice Holmes cited as a "good statement," *id.*, of the "general rule" all involved a claimant seeking recovery because of its contract with the tort victim. *See The Federal No. 2*, 21 F.2d 313 (2d Cir. 1927)[5]; *Elliott Steam Tug Co. v. Shipping Controller*, 1 K.B. 127 (1921); *Byrd v. English*, 117 Ga. 191, 43 S.E. 419 (1903).[6] Nowhere in the text

[—9—] of *Robins Dry Dock* is there a broad statement that economic losses for an unintentional maritime tort are not recoverable in the absence of physical damage to the claimant's property.

A leading treatise on maritime law has candidly acknowledged that the broad rule is not to be found in *Robins Dry Dock*. Referring to the broad rule, Professor Schoenbaum states, "This is the interpretation *accorded to* the case of *Robins Dry Dock and Repair Co. v. Flint*, 275 U.S. 303 (1927)." 1 Thomas J. Schoenbaum, *Admiralty and Maritime Law* §5-16, at 317 n.3 (5th ed. 2011) (emphasis added), and also acknowledges that the "*Robins Dry Dock* holding was later *transformed* into a bright-line rule against liability for pure economic loss that has been consistently applied in admiralty in a wide

---

working. The seaman could have sued for negligence but did not. The owner of the barge was required by its contract with the seaman to provide maintenance and cure, and did so. The barge owner then made a claim against the tug to recover the cost of providing maintenance and cure, *i.e.*, the hospital expenses. We ruled against recovery. After pointing out the barge owner had no right of subrogation, we said that "damage suffered by one whose interest in the party or thing is contractual is too remote for recovery, unless the wrong is done with intent to affect the contractual relations." 21 F.2d at 314. Interestingly, we cited our decision in *Robins Dry Dock v. Flint*, 13 F.2d 3 (2d Cir. 1926), before it was reversed by the Supreme Court.

In *Elliott Steam Tug*, a time charterer sued the agency that had requisitioned the vessel, seeking lost profits. In dictum, before the Court upheld a statutory indemnity claim, the Court said that the plaintiff had no claim at common law for injury to its contractual rights. *See* 1 K.B. at 140.

In *Byrd*, a printing company lost power for several hours during which it lost profits it could have earned. The loss of power resulted from the excavation of a nearby site, which [—9—] caused a quantity of earth to fall on underground conduits through which an electric company's power lines ran. The plaintiff sued the company doing the excavating, relying on the plaintiff's contract with the company that supplied electric power. The Court rejected the claim, ruling that the wrong was done to the power company, and that the plaintiff had only a claim against the power company, not the excavating company. *See* 43 S.E. at 420-21.

---

[4] Dissenting in *State of Louisiana ex rel. Guste v. M/V TESTBANK*, 752 F.2d 1019 (5th Cir. 1985), Judge Wisdom contended that the narrow rule of *Robins Dry Dock* "has been expanded now to bar recovery by plaintiffs who would be allowed to recover if judged under conventional principles of foreseeability and proximate cause." *Id.* at 1039 (Wisdom, J., with whom Rubin, Politz, Tate, and Johnson, JJ, join, dissenting) (footnote omitted).

[5] *The Federal No. 2* was "abandoned" by our Circuit in *Black v. Red Star Towing & Transportation Co.*, 860 F.2d 30, 34 (2d Cir. 1988).

[6] In *The Federal No. 2*, a seaman was injured due to the negligence of a tug whose towing hawser swept the deck of the barge on which he was

variety of contexts . . . ." 2 Schoenbaum, *supra* § 18-4, at 319 (emphasis added).

Since *Robins Dry Dock*, the Supreme Court has cited it three times, all without illuminating its meaning. In *Aktieselskabet Cuzco v. The Sucarseco*, 294 U.S. 394, 404 (1935), the Court only distinguished the narrow contract rule of *Robins Dry Dock*. In *Caldarola v. Eckert*, 332 U.S. 155, 158 (1947), it [—10—] simply noted that no claim was made under the narrow contract rule of *Robins Dry Dock*. The third case, *East River Steamship Corp. v. Transamerica Delaval, Inc.*, 476 U.S. 858 (1986), was a products liability ruling, made under maritime law. The Court's narrow holding was that "a manufacturer in a commercial relationship has no duty under either a negligence or strict products-liability theory to prevent a product from injuring itself." *Id.* at 871. Notably, the Court explicitly left open the question whether a broad rule is to be derived from *Robins Dry Dock*:

> We do not reach the issue whether a tort cause of action can ever be stated in admiralty when the only damages sought are economic. *Cf. Ultramares Corp. v. Touche*, 255 N.Y. 170, 174 N.E. 441 (1931). *But see Robins Dry Dock & Repair Co. v. Flint*, 275 U.S. 303 (1927).

East River, 476 U.S. at 871 n.6.

Two opinions of Courts of Appeals have thoughtfully endeavored to explain why the broad rule attributed to *Robins Dry Dock* exists: *State of Louisiana ex rel. Guste v. M/V TESTBANK*, 752 F.2d 1019, 1022 (5th Cir. 1985) (*in banc*), and *Barber Lines A/S v. M/V Donau Maru*, 764 F.2d 50 (1st Cir. 1985).

The argument that such a broad rule is implicit in the narrow rule that Justice Holmes stated was expressed by Judge Higginbotham for the 10-5 majority of the in banc court in *Guste*. *Guste* involved numerous claims for economic losses suffered as [—11—] a result of the temporary closing of the Mississippi River Gulf outlet because of chemicals that had spilled into the outlet after a collision of two vessels. None of the plaintiffs claimed to have had a contract with either of the vessels involved in the collision.[7] After noting the plaintiffs' attempt to limit *Robins Dry Dock* to claimants relying on a contract with the victim of a maritime tort, Judge Higginbotham seemed to find the broader rule implicit in what he terms Justice Holmes's "delphic" opinion. *Guste*, 752 F.2d at 1022. Judge Higginbotham stated:

> If a time charterer's relationship to its negligently injured vessel is too remote, other claimants without even the connection of a contract are even more remote.

752 F.2d at 1023.

For Judge Higginbotham, the rationale animating the narrow rule of *Robins Dry Dock* was the avoidance of recovery for losses thought to be too remote from a defendant's negligence, from which he reasoned that claimants without a contract to a party suffering a tort are more remote than claimants with a contract. Although we agree that remoteness of losses is always relevant to tort recoveries, a concept usually expressed in terms of the extent of the tortfeasor's duty, *see Palsgraf v. Long Island R.R.*, 248 N.Y. 339, 162 N.E. 99 (1928), or foreseeability [—12—] or proximate cause, *see In re Kinsman Transit Co.* ("*Kinsman II*"), 388 F.2d 821, 823 (2d Cir. 1968),[8] we are not as sure as Judge Higginbotham that the losses of a claimant without a contract with a tort victim are inevitably more remote from the tort than the losses of those with such a contract.[9] Even if

---

[7] The opinion does not indicate which vessel was considered the maritime tort victim, perhaps because negligence was apportioned between the two colliding vessels.

[8] "In the final analysis, the circumlocution whether posed in terms of 'foreseeability,' 'duty,' 'proximate cause,' 'remoteness,' etc. seems unavoidable." *Kinsman II*, 388 F.2d at 825.

[9] In dissent, Judge Wisdom has endeavored to refute Judge Higginbotham's argument that a claim for economic losses in the absence of a contract with the tort victim is inevitably less meritorious than a claim invoking such a contract:

> This argument would be sound in instances where the plaintiff suffered no loss

the drydocker [—13—] in *Robins Dry Dock* could not reasonably foresee that the vessel owner would charter his vessel, which strikes us as an unlikely supposition, the drawbridge operator in the pending case could surely have expected that its negligent delay in opening the bridge for a vessel not chartered would likely cause economic losses.

Judge Higginbotham also explained *Robins Dry Dock* as based on "a principle . . . which refused recovery for negligent interference with 'contractual rights,'" *Guste*, 752 F.2d at 1022, and on what he called the "well established" principle "that there could be no recovery for economic loss absent physical injury to a proprietary interest," *id*. at 1023. Although this principle has been articulated by distinguished torts commentators, *see, e.g.*, 4 Fowler V. Harper, Fleming James, Jr., Oscar S. Gray, *The Law of Torts* § 25.18A, at 619 (2d ed. 1986), these same commentators have noted that "[c]ourts are, however, beginning to disclaim the existence of any such 'absolute rule,' and to refer instead to the applicability of pragmatic considerations," *id*. at 619-20 n.1, and have more recently observed that the "rule" is permeated with numerous exceptions, *see id*. at 326 n. 9a (cumulative supp. 2005). Several of these

---

but for a contract with the injured party. We would measure a plaintiff's connection to the tortfeasor by the only line connecting them, the contract, and disallow the claim under *Robins [Dry Dock]*. In the instant case [involving an economic loss resulting from a collision of two ships producing an oil spell that blocked a Mississippi outlet to all shipping], however, some of the plaintiffs suffered damages whether or not they had a contractual connection with a party physically injured by the tortfeasor. These plaintiffs do not need to rely on a contract to link them to the tort: The collision proximately caused their losses, and those losses were foreseeable. These plaintiffs are therefore freed from the *Robins [Dry Dock]* rule concerning the recovery of those who suffer economic loss because of an injury to a party with whom they have contracted.

Guste, 752 F.2d at 1040 (Wisdom, J., with whom Rubin, Politz, Tate, and Johnson, JJ, join, dissenting).

exceptions are catalogued in *Union Oil Co. v. Oppen*, 501 F.2d 558, 565-68 & n.9 (9th Cir. 1974). [—14—]

Barber Lines, like *Guste*, also involved an oil spill caused by a ship's negligence, this one causing economic losses to a vessel delayed from docking at its assigned berth. Unlike Judge Higginbotham, however, then-Judge Breyer did not contend that the rationale of *Robins Dry Dock*, which he called "[t]he leading 'pure financial injury' case," 764 F.2d at 51, was the remoteness of the claimed economic losses. On the contrary, he "assume[d] that the [financial] injury was foreseeable." *Id*. Nor did he express the view that the absence of a contract between the claimant and a tort victim made the claim more remote than that of a claimant with a contract. Indeed, he stated that "[t]he authority that Justice Holmes says contains a 'good statement' of the legal principle does not, however, turn so much on the existence of a formal contract as on the existence of limitations upon tort recovery for financial injury." *Id*. (citing *Elliott Steam* and *Byrd*).[10] [—15—]

Instead of relying on remoteness, he simply embraced what he understood to be the holdings of post-*Robins Dry Dock* cases, which, he stated, "refuse to hold a defendant liable for negligently caused financial harm

---

[10] In a somewhat perplexing attempt to show that the circumstances of the claim in *Barber Lines* were not significantly different than those of the claim in *Robins Dry Dock*, then-Judge Breyer explicitly rejected a distinction based on the time charterer's contract. He stated that "the present appellants must have had a 'right' to use the dock," that "interference with that 'right' caused the loss," and that "[i]t is difficult in this instance to see why the technical legal label applied to that right should make a legal difference." 764 F.2d at 51. We can accept that the claimant in *Barber Lines* likely had a right to use the dock, which is arguably similar in law to the time charterer's contract with the vessel owner in *Robins Dry Dock*, but this [—15—] comparison overlooks the very point Justice Holmes was making: the time charterer was trying to benefit from a contract it had with the victim of a tort; the dock in *Barber Lines* suffered no tort injury, and the claimant was not trying to use its right (or contract) to dock to support its claim.

without accompanying physical injury or other special circumstances." *Id.* at 53. And he candidly acknowledged that he favored the broad rule claimed to be derived from *Robins Dry Dock* because of "pragmatic or practical administrative considerations which, *when taken together*, offer support for" the broad rule. *Id.* at 54 (emphasis in original). Among these, he noted, were that "[t]he number of persons suffering foreseeable financial harm in a typical accident is likely to be far greater than those who suffer traditional (recoverable) physical harm," *id.*; the share of amounts paid by tort suit defendants to victims is less than the share of premium dollars earned by insurance companies that is paid out to victims who insure themselves; and the typical victim of financial losses is a business firm that is able to purchase first-party insurance, *see id.* at 54-56. Judge Higginbotham also invoked these considerations. *See Guste*, 752 F.2d at 1029. [—16—]

Other circuits have also found in *Robins Dry Dock* a broad rule barring economic losses for unintentional maritime torts in the absence of physical injury. *See Channel Star Excursions, Inc. v. Southern Pacific Transportation Co.*, 77 F.3d 1135, 1137-38 (9th Cir. 1996); *Getty Refining & Marketing Co. v. MT FADI B*, 766 F.2d 829, 831-33 (3d Cir. 1985); *Kingston Shipping Co. v. Roberts*, 667 F.2d 34, 35 (11th Cir. 1982); *see generally* Trey D. Tankersley, *The Robins Dry Dock Rule: The Tar Baby of Maritime Tort Law*, 25 Tul. Mar. L. J. 371 (2000) (The "Tar Baby" allusion is borrowed from Judge Wisdom's dissent in *Guste*, 752 F.2d at 1035.). In the Fourth Circuit, *Robins Dry Dock* was followed to disallow a time charterer's claim for lost profits, but its claim for the amount it paid the owner for the period the vessel was out of service was allowed. *See Venore Transportation Co. v. M/V Struma*, 583 F.2d 708, 710-11 (4th Cir. 1978). The Ninth Circuit has made exceptions to a broad *Robins Dry Dock* rule for seamen's lost wages, *see Carbone v. Ursich*, 209 F.2d 178, 181-82 (9th Cir. 1954), and commercial fishermen's lost profits resulting from an oil spill, *see Union Oil*, 501 F.2d at 565-71.

Our Circuit's view of the broad rule attributed to *Robins Dry Dock* has followed a somewhat uneven course. Prior to the Supreme Court's decision, our Court had allowed the time charterer's claim for economic losses when the case was here, *see Flint v. Robins Dry Dock & Repair Co.*, 13 F.2d 3, 5-6 (2d Cir. [—17—] 1926), *rev'd*, 275 U.S. 303 (1927), deeming the economic losses to have been the "proximate results" of the tortfeasor's negligence, *id.* at 6.

Our first direct reckoning with the Supreme Court's decision in *Robins Dry Dock* occurred in *Agwilines, Inc. v. Eagle Oil & Shipping Co.*, 153 F.2d 869 (2d Cir. 1946).[11] *Agwilines* is a slightly more complicated version of *Robins Dry Dock*. The owner of a time chartered ship, the *Agwidale*, sued the owner of the *San Veronica*, with which it had collided. Pursuant to the charterparty, the time charterer paid the *Agwidale's* owner for an interval when the *Agwidale* was out of service. The *Agwidale's* owner then sued the *San Veronico's* owner for what was alleged to be the time charterer's loss. Judge Learned Hand's opinion for a divided panel[12] rejected the claim stating: [—18—]

[The Supreme Court] thought that the only basis for charging the drydocker with liability was because he had prevented the performance of the charterparty by the promisor—the

---

[11] Two prior decisions had cited *Robins Dry Dock* for the accepted proposition that liability would exist for an intentional interference with contractual relations. *See New York Trust Co. v. Island Oil & Transport Corp.*, 34 F.2d 649, 652 (2d Cir. 1929); *Sidney Blumenthal & Co. v. United States*, 30 F.2d 247, 249 (2d Cir. 1929). A third prior decision, *The Toluma*, 72 F.2d 690, 693 (2d Cir. 1934), *aff'd sub nom. Artieselskabet Cuzco v. The Sucarseco*, 294 U.S. 394 (1935), had cited *Robins Dry Dock* for what we have called the "narrow rule," but found the rule inapplicable because of the special circumstances that the claim was for return of a cargo owner's contribution in general average, which had been made pursuant to a so-called "Jason clause," (named for *The Jason*, 225 U.S. 32 (1912)). *See The Toluma*, 72 F.2d at 693-94.

[12] Judge Clark dissented. *Agwilines*, 153 F.2d at 872.

owner—and that interference by a third person with the performance of a contract was an actionable wrong only if it was intentional. The Court thought it irrelevant that this resulted in exonerating the drydocker from nearly all liability through the fortuity that the profitable use of the ship had been divided between the owner and the charterer: The difficulty went deeper; the drydocker had committed no legal wrong against the charterer a[t] all, though he had caused it serious damage.

Id. at 871. Thus, *Agwilines* appears to have recognized both a narrow *Robins Dry Dock* rule—the contract with the owner does not help the time charterer—and a broad rule—a negligent tortfeasor has no legal liability for economic losses in the absence of physical damage.

Our next significant consideration of *Robins Dry Dock* occurred in *Kinsman II*, 388 F.2d 821 (2d Cir. 1968), so named because it was preceded by *In re Kinsman Transit Co.* ("*Kinsman I*"), 338 F.2d 708 (2d Cir. 1964).[13] The *Kinsman* litigation [—19—] concerned an extraordinary series of calamities of the sort more likely found in a law school torts exam than occurring in the real world. In brief, a vessel, inadequately moored, drifted down the Buffalo River, and collided with another vessel; both vessels drifted farther down the river and collided with a third vessel; a lift bridge farther downstream was not raised

despite a warning; the second vessel crashed into the bridge causing a tower to fall into the river; the obstruction formed by the first two vessels and ice caused water to overflow the river banks; the overflowing water damaged a grain elevator located three miles upstream. The facts are more fully elaborated in *Kinsman I*, 338 F.2d at 711-713, 714-16.

Judge Friendly upheld the various claims for physical injuries to property, deeming them foreseeable under traditional tort principles. He acknowledged, however, that "[s]omewhere a point will be reached when courts will agree that the link [between negligent conduct and injury] has become too tenuous—that what is claimed to be consequence is only fortuity." *Id.* at 725. In the absence of a claim for economic losses, he had no occasion to consider *Robins Dry Dock*. [—20—]

Claims for economic losses were before us, however, when the same litigation returned four years later in *Kinsman II*. Cargill, Inc., sought to recover the expenses of its extra transportation and storage costs incurred because the river flooding prevented it from unloading wheat on a vessel in the Buffalo harbor, and it was obliged to obtain replacement wheat to fulfill its contracts. *See Kinsman II*, 388 F.2d at 823. Cargo Carriers, Inc., sought to recover the extra expenses of unloading its cargo of corn from yet another vessel that had been struck by the original two colliding vessels, the damage to this vessel necessitating special equipment for unloading cargo. *See id.*

Judge Kaufman began his consideration of these claims by noting that the District Court, in the absence of proof of intentional interference with contracts, had rejected what the Court deemed interference-with-contract claims on the authority of *Robins Dry Dock*. *See id.* He then stated, "We too deny recovery to the claimants, but on other grounds." *Id.* Leaving what he termed "the rock-strewn path of 'negligent interference with contract,'" he grounded decision on "more familiar tort terrain." *Id.* at 824. Judge Kaufman rejected the claims as simply "too 'remote' or 'indirect' a consequence of defendants' negligence." *Id.*

---

[13] Decisions of our Court citing *Robins Dry Dock* after *Agwilines* and before *Kinsman I* and *II* shed no new light on its proper interpretation. *See Paragon Oil Co. v. Republic Tankers, S.A.*, 310 F.2d 169, 175 (2d Cir. 1962) (bailee entitled to value of damaged goods); *Hanlon v. Waterman Steamship Corp.*, 265 F.2d 206, 207 (2d Cir. 1959) (claimant not third-party beneficiary of contract); *International Brotherhood of Electrical Workers v. NLRB*, 181 F.2d 34, 38 & [—19—] n.11 (2d Cir. 1950) (referring generally to tort of interference with contractual obligation); *Conmar Products Corp. v. Universal Slide Fastener Co.*, 172 F.2d 150, 155 & n.2 (2d Cir. 1949) (same); *Ozanic v. United States*, 165 F.2d 738, 743 (2d Cir. 1948) (vessel owner's contract to pay part of economic losses of crew members could not create liability for second vessel with which first vessel collided).

Rather than invoking the narrow rule of *Robins Dry Dock*, [—21—] rejecting a claim for economic losses sought to be based on the victim's contractual relation to an injured vessel, or the broad rule identified in *Agwilines*, rejecting all claims for economic losses in the absence of physical injury, Judge Kaufman used the traditional tort concept of foreseeability and rejected the claims as too remote. *Id.* at 825. All that he drew from *Robins Dry Dock* was Justice Holmes's statement, appended to his rejection of a contract-related claim, that "[t]he law does not spread its protection so far." *Id.* (quoting *Robins Dry Dock*, 275 U.S. at 309).[14]

Seven years later, however, a panel with two members from the *Kinsman II* panel (Judges Kaufman and Feinberg) explicitly applied *Robins Dry Dock* to reject a time charterer's claim for economic losses. *See Federal Commerce & Navigation Co.* [—22—] *v. M/V Marathonian*, 528 F.2d 907, 908 (2d Cir. 1975). The per curiam opinion noted an effort "to justify the [narrow] rule [of *Robins Dry Dock*] on the basis of remoteness of injury," and added, perhaps nostalgically, "If free to do so, we might question whether at least the damage to the principal time charterer is not so reasonably to be expected as to justify recovery." *Id.* (citing *Kinsman II*). The retreat from *Kinsman II* is brought into sharp focus by the District Court's opinion, which our Court labeled "considered and thorough," *id.* at 907, in which Judge Canella had written:

---

[14] In *Guste*, Judge Higginbotham endeavored to enlist *Kinsman II* in support of his categorical rejection of economic losses in the absence of physical injury by claiming that Judge Kaufman had recognized "the need for the imposition of limitations on recovery for the *foreseeable* consequences of an act of negligence," an analysis he deemed "compatible with our own." *Guste*, 752 F.2d at 1026 (emphasis added) (footnote omitted). In fact, Judge Kaufman had rejected liability because he thought the claimed losses were not foreseeable. *Kinsman II*, 388 F.2d at 824-25. As Judge Wisdom noted in *Guste*, *Kinsman II* "rejected the requirement of physical damages without even bothering to distinguish *Robins*, and instead relied on customary negligence principles." *Guste*, 752 F.2d at 1042 (Wisdom, J., with whom Rubin, Politz, Tate, and Johnson, JJ, join, dissenting).

[W]ere this Court . . . not constrained by the weight of precedent, we would reject the negligent interference with contract doctrine in favor of a negligence-causation-foreseeability analysis, such as that adopted by Chief Judge Kaufman in *Petition of Kinsman Transit Co.* [*Kinsman II*].

Federal Commerce & Navigation Co. v. M/V Marathonian, 392 F. Supp. 908, 913 (S.D.N.Y. 1975).

Our Court's next three encounters with *Robins Dry Dock* before today were all non-precedential summary orders, each of which, without elaboration, approved or announced what has become the broad rule that economic losses for an unintentional maritime tort are not recoverable in the absence of physical injury. In *Allders International (Ships) Ltd. v. United States*, 100 F.3d 942 (2d Cir. 1996) (summary order), we rejected a claim by a [—23—] concessionaire that lost revenue when a cruise ship canceled voyages because of a grounding accident. We affirmed "for substantially the same reasons set forth" in the District Court's opinion, *id.* at 942, in which Judge Martin had dismissed as dicta the tort-based approach of *Kinsman II* in favor of a "bright line approach." *Allders International (Ships) Ltd. v. United States*, No. 94 CIV. 5689, 1995 WL 251571, at *1-2 (S.D.N.Y. Apr. 28, 1995). Next came the two summary orders on which Judge Engelmayer relied in the pending case, *Gas Natural*, 2008 WL 4643944, at *1 (stating "a bright line rule barring recovery for economic losses caused by an unintentional maritime tort absent physical damage to property in which the victim has a proprietary interest") (emphases and internal quotation marks omitted), and *G & G Steel*, 380 Fed. App'x at 104 (same).

Although, since *Marathonian*, we have not considered *Robins Dry Dock* in a published opinion, the district court decisions in our Circuit, in addition to Judge Engelmayer's decision in the pending case, have regularly invoked the "bright line rule" barring economic losses in the absence of physical damage. *See G & G Steel, Inc. v. Sea Wolf Marine Transportation, LLC*, No. 06 Civ.

1840, 2008 WL 192049, at *3 (S.D.N.Y Jan. 23, 2008); *Gas Natural SDG S.A. v. United States*, No. 04 CIV. 8370, 2007 WL 959259, at *6 & n.5 (S.D.N.Y. Mar. 22, 2007); *Conti Corso* [—24—] *Schiffahrts-GMBH & Co. KG NR. 2 v. M/V "Pinar Kaptanoglu"*, 414 F. Supp. 2d 443, 446-47 (S.D.N.Y. 2006); *Brown v. Royal Caribbean Cruises, Ltd.*, No. 99 Civ. 11774, 2000 WL 34449703, at *5 (S.D.N.Y. Aug. 24, 2000); *American Dredging v. Plaza Petroleum Inc.*, 845 F. Supp. 91, 93 (E.D.N.Y. 1993); *Plaza Marine, Inc. v. Exxon Corp.*, No. 92 Civ. 1189, 1992 WL 197398, at *1 (S.D.N.Y. Aug. 5, 1992).

Having surveyed the field and our own slightly wavering contribution to it, we now explicitly accept the broad rule attributed to *Robins Dry Dock* that economic losses are not recoverable for an unintentional maritime tort in the absence of physical injury, mindful that for some categories of claims, exceptions may well be appropriate. We see little point in endeavoring to determine whether the broad rule that has been attributed to *Robins Dry Dock* was implicit in that decision or has resulted from an unstated extension of the narrow rule there announced. Instead, as then-Judge Breyer did in *Barber Lines*, we simply accept the broad rule, and do so for four main reasons. First, the rule has been accepted by a clear consensus of courts throughout the country, including many district courts within our Circuit. Second, Congress, possessing full authority to legislate on maritime matters, *see Panama Railroad Co. v. Johnson*, 264 U.S. 375, 386 (1924), has neither altered the broad [—25—] rule nor made any serious attempts to do so.[15] Third,

the rule has the virtue of certainty.[16] Fourth, the context in which the broad rule primarily applies—financial losses incurred in the course of commercial shipping—is marked by the well recognized availability of first-party insurance to cover such losses and the frequent purchase of such insurance.[17] [—26—]

We are not unsympathetic to the Appellant's earnest plea that, even if a broad *Robins Dry Dock* rule exists, recovery could be allowed in this case without countenancing an unbounded exposure of maritime tortfeasors to a vast number of economic loss claims that would stretch the concept of foreseeability up to and often beyond any discernible limit. It was surely foreseeable that an operator who had opened a drawbridge to let vessels move upriver and negligently failed to open the bridge when the vessels returned will cause economic losses to at least some of the vessels expecting to pass under the bridge. And when that operator is a governmental entity, the burden of such foreseeable losses can be spread narrowly through user fees or broadly

---

[15] Judge Rubin, in dissent in *Guste*, has replied to this point:

> The constitutional grant of jurisdiction to federal courts over cases and controversies not only empowers but requires us . . . to decide . . . cases within our jurisdiction whether or not Congress has provided a rule of decision and even when we think Congress should have acted and has not done so.

Guste, 752 F.2d at 1053 (Rubin, J., with whom Wisdom, Politz, and Tate, JJ, join, dissenting).

---

[16] Even in dissent, Judge Wisdom acknowledged this virtue:

> There is only one justification for the requirement of physical injury: If *Robins* [*Dry Dock*] establishes a policy of restricting the type of plaintiff who can recover for a defendant's negligence, physical property damage furnishes an easily discernible boundary between recovery and nonrecovery.

Guste, 752 F.2d at 1045 (Wisdom, J., with whom Rubin, Politz, Tate, and Johnson, JJ, join, dissenting).

[17] In dissent in *Guste*, Judge Wisdom disputed the validity of this factor:

> The *Robins* [*Dry Dock*] approach restricts liability more severely than the policies behind limitations on liability [—26—] require and imposes the cost of the accident on the victim, who is usually not in a superior position to obtain insurance to cover this loss.

752 F.2d at 1052 (Wisdom, J., with whom Rubin, Politz, Tate, and Johnson, JJ, join, dissenting).

through taxation.[18] Although the argument for a fact- [—27—] specific exception to *Robins Dry Dock* gives us pause, we ultimately conclude that the case for such an exception on the particular facts here is outweighed by the benefits of adhering to the general rule that denies recovery for economic losses from unintentional maritime torts in the absence of physical damage. In weighing the case for exceptions to the general rule, the benefits of its certainty, the customary use of first-party insurance to mitigate or eliminate its effects, and its long recognized establishment within maritime jurisprudence weigh heavily.[19]

Conclusion

The judgment of the District Court is affirmed.

---

[18] Discussing the liability of the municipal operators of a drawbridge, the negligently delayed opening of which contributed to a variety of claims for physical damage, Judge Friendly wrote:

> Here it is surely more equitable that the losses from the operators' negligent failure to raise the Michigan Avenue Bridge should be ratably borne by Buffalo's taxpayers than left with the innocent victims of the flooding.

Kinsman I, 338 F.2d at 726.

[19] American seeks to draw support for its position from 33 U.S.C. § 494, which imposes duties upon bridge owners and operators. Recognizing that the statute does not create an implied private right of action, American nonetheless contends that it states a federal policy that we should enlist to narrow the broad rule of *Robins Dry Dock*. We are not persuaded. Accepting American's suggestion would effectively adopt a statutory private right of action in the guise of a tort rule.

United States Court of Appeals for the Third Circuit

United States Court of Appeals
For the Third Circuit

No. 10-4710

MALA
VS.
CROWN BAY MARINA, INC.

Appeal from the District Court of the Virgin Islands

Decided: January 7, 2013

Citation: 704 F.3d 239, 1 Adm. R. 72 (3d Cir. 2013).

Before **SMITH**, **HARDIMAN**, and **ROTH**, Circuit Judges.

[—2—] **SMITH**, Circuit Judge:

K elley Mala sued Crown Bay Marina after his boat exploded. The District Court conducted a bench trial during which Mala represented himself and after which the court rejected his negligence claims. Mala now contends that the court should have provided him with additional assistance because of his status as a pro se litigant. He also contends that the court wrongfully denied his request for a jury trial and improperly ruled on [—3—] a variety of post-trial motions. We reject these contentions and we will affirm.

I

Mala is a citizen of the United States Virgin Islands. On January 6, 2005, he went for a cruise in his powerboat near St. Thomas, Virgin Islands. When his boat ran low on gas, he entered Crown Bay Marina to refuel. Mala tied the boat to one of Crown Bay's eight fueling stations and began filling his tank with an automatic gas pump. Before walking to the cash register to buy oil, Mala asked a Crown Bay attendant to watch his boat.

By the time Mala returned, the boat's tank was overflowing and fuel was spilling into the boat and into the water. The attendant manually shut off the pump and acknowledged that the pump had been malfunctioning in recent days. Mala began cleaning up the fuel, and at some point, the attendant provided soap and water. Mala

eventually departed the marina, but as he did so, the engine caught fire and exploded. Mala was thrown into the water and was severely burned. His boat was unsalvageable.

More than a year later, Mala sued Crown Bay in [—4—] the District Court of the Virgin Islands.[1] Mala's pro se complaint asserted two claims: first, that Crown Bay negligently trained and supervised its attendant, and second, that Crown Bay negligently maintained its gas pump. The complaint also alleged that the District Court had admiralty and diversity jurisdiction over the case, and it requested a jury trial. At the time Mala filed the complaint, he was imprisoned in Puerto Rico. Although the record is silent on the reason for his imprisonment, it is fair to say that he is a seasoned litigant—in fact, he has filed at least twenty other pro se lawsuits.[2] See Appellee's Br. at 21-22.

Mala's original complaint named "Crown Bay Marina Inc." as the sole defendant. But Mala soon amended his complaint by adding other defendants—including Crown Bay's dock attendant, Chubb Group Insurance Company, Crown Bay's attorney and "Marine Management Services Inc., [a] registered corporation entity duly licensed to conduct business in the State of Florida ..., d/b/a Crown Bay Marina Inc., [ ] a corporate [—5—] entity duly licensed to conduct business in St. Thomas Virgin Islands of the United States." JA 55. The District Court allowed Mala to amend his complaint a second time by adding his wife as a plaintiff—though the court dismissed her loss-of-consortium claim shortly thereafter. Mala later attempted to amend his complaint a third time by adding Texaco as a defendant. The District Court rejected this attempt for failing to comply with Federal

---

[1] Chief Judge Curtis Gomez was initially assigned the case, but Judge Juan Sanchez took over in the middle of 2010 and presided over the trial.

[2] Mala requested a court-appointed attorney in this case, but the District Court denied the request because his history of filing frivolous lawsuits prevented him from securing in forma pauperis status. See 28 U.S.C. §1915.

Rule of Civil Procedure 15 (a)(2) (requiring the other side's consent or the court's leave).[3]

As the trial approached, two significant incidents took place. First, the District Court decided on its own to identify the parties to the case. It concluded that the only parties were Mala and "Marine Services Management d/b/a Crown Bay Marina, Inc." JA 132. It thereby dismissed all other defendants that Mala had named in his various pleadings.

Next, Crown Bay filed a motion to strike Mala's jury demand. Crown Bay argued that plaintiffs generally do not have a jury-trial right in admiralty cases—only when the court also has diversity jurisdiction. And Crown Bay asserted that the parties were not diverse in this case, which the court itself had acknowledged in a previous [—6—] order. In response to this motion, the District Court ruled that both Mala and Crown Bay were citizens of the Virgin Islands. The court therefore struck Mala's jury demand, but nevertheless opted to empanel an advisory jury.

The trial began at the end of 2010— nearly four and a half years after Mala filed his complaint. The delay is partly attributable to the District Court's decision to postpone the trial until after Mala's release from prison. At the close of Mala's case-in-chief, Crown Bay renewed a previous motion for summary judgment. The court granted the motion on the negligent-supervision claim but allowed the negligent-maintenance claim to go forward. At the end of the trial, the advisory jury returned a verdict of $460,000 for Mala— $400,000 for pain and suffering and $60,000 in compensatory damages. It concluded that Mala was 25 percent at fault and that Crown Bay was 75 percent at fault. The District Court ultimately rejected the verdict and entered judgment for Crown Bay on both claims.

After his loss at trial, Mala filed a flurry of motions, asking the court to vacate its judgment and hold a new trial. These motions contained numerous overlapping objections. A magistrate judge prepared three Reports and Recommendations that summarized Mala's claims and urged the District Court to reject all of them. Judge Sanchez adopted these recommendations [—7—] and explained his reasoning in an eight-page opinion.

This appeal followed. Mala argues that the District Court made three reversible errors. First, the court failed to accommodate Mala as a pro se litigant. Second, it improperly denied his request for a jury trial. Third, it erroneously adopted the magistrate's recommendations. We consider and reject these arguments in turn.[4]

II

Mala first argues that the District Court did not give appropriate consideration to his status as a pro se litigant. Specifically, he claims that the District Court should have provided him with a pro se manual—a manual that is available to pro se litigants in other districts in the Third Circuit and throughout the country. We conclude that pro se litigants do not have a right to general legal advice from judges, so the District Court did not abuse its discretion by failing to provide a manual. [—8—]

According to Mala, "[t]here is comparatively little case law regarding the responsibility of courts to provide information and assistance to the *pro se* party." Appellant's Br. at 7. A more accurate statement is that there is *no* case law requiring courts to provide general legal advice to pro se parties. In a long line of cases, the Supreme Court has repeatedly concluded that courts are under no such obligation. *See, e.g.*, *McKaskle v. Wiggins*, 465 U.S. 168, 183-184 (1984) ("A defendant does not have a constitutional right to receive

---

[3] Because the District Court refused to add Texaco as a defendant, *see* JA 94 n. 2, we have omitted "Texaco Puerto Rico" from the case caption.

[4] The District Court had admiralty jurisdiction under 28 U.S.C. § 1333(1). Mala argues that the court also had diversity jurisdiction under 28 U.S.C. § 1332. This argument determines the outcome of Mala's jury claim, so we will discuss it in Part III. At all events, we have jurisdiction under 28 U.S.C. § 1291.

personal instruction from the trial judge on courtroom procedure. Nor does the Constitution require judges to take over chores for a *pro se* defendant that would normally be attended to by trained counsel as a matter of course."); *McNeil v. United States*, 508 U.S. 106, 113 (1993); *Faretta v. California*, 422 U.S. 806, 834 n. 46 (1975).

The Supreme Court revisited this line of cases nearly a decade ago. In *Pliler v. Ford*, 542 U.S. 225 (2004), the Court rejected the idea that district courts must provide a specific warning to pro se litigants in certain habeas cases. It concluded that "[d]istrict judges have no obligation to act as counsel or paralegal to *pro se* litigants." *Id.* at 231. After all, a "trial judge is under no duty to provide personal instruction on courtroom procedure or to perform any legal 'chores' for the defendant that counsel would normally carry out." *Id.* (quoting *Martinez v. Court of Appeal of Cal., Fourth Appellate Dist.*, 528 U.S. 152, 162 (2000)) (quotation [—9—] marks omitted). Because of this general rule, courts need not, for example, inform pro se litigants of an impending statute of limitation. *See Outler v. United States*, 485 F.3d 1273, 1282 n. 4 (11th Cir. 2007) ("[N]o case has ever held that a *pro se* litigant should be given actual notice of a statute of limitations.").

The general rule, then, is that courts need not provide substantive legal advice to pro se litigants. Aside from the two exceptions discussed below, federal courts treat pro se litigants the same as any other litigant. This rule makes sense. Judges must be impartial, and they put their impartiality at risk—or at least might *appear* to become partial to one side—when they provide trial assistance to a party. *See Pliler*, 542 U.S. at 231 ("Requiring district courts to advise a *pro se* litigant … would undermine district judges' role as impartial decisionmakers."); *Jacobsen v. Filler*, 790 F.2d 1362, 1364 (9th Cir. 1986); *see also* Julie M. Bradlow, Comment, *Procedural Due Process Rights of Pro Se Civil Litigants*, 55 U. Chi. L. Rev. 659, 671 (1988) ("[E]xtending too much procedural leniency to a pro se litigant risks undermining the impartial role of the judge in the adversary system."). Moreover, this rule eliminates the

risk that judges will provide bad advice. *See Pliler*, 542 U.S. at 231-32 (noting that warnings and other legal advice "run the risk of being misleading themselves"); *see also* Robert Bacharach & Lyn Entzeroth, *Judicial Advocacy in Pro Se Litigation: A Return to Neutrality*, 42 [—10—] Ind. L. Rev. 19, 42 (2009) ("[G]iving legal advice is prohibited by multiple canons of judicial conduct.").

To be sure, some cases have given greater leeway to pro se litigants. These cases fit into two narrow exceptions. First, we tend to be flexible when applying procedural rules to pro se litigants, especially when interpreting their pleadings. *See, e.g., Higgs v. Att'y Gen.*, 655 F.3d 333, 339 (3d Cir. 2011) ("The obligation to liberally construe a *pro se* litigant's pleadings is well-established."). This means that we are willing to apply the relevant legal principle even when the complaint has failed to name it. *Dluhos v. Strasberg*, 321 F.3d 365, 369 (3d Cir. 2003). And at least on one occasion, we have refused to apply the doctrine of appellate waiver when dealing with a pro se litigant. *Tabron v Grace*, 6 F.3d 147, 153 n. 2 (3d Cir. 1993). This tradition of leniency descends from the Supreme Court's decades-old decision in *Haines v. Kerner*, 404 U.S. 519 (1972). In *Haines*, the Court instructed judges to hold pro se complaints "to less stringent standards than formal pleadings drafted by lawyers." *Id.* at 520; *see Erickson v. Pardus*, 551 U.S. 89, 94 (2007).

We are especially likely to be flexible when dealing with imprisoned pro se litigants. Such litigants often lack the resources and freedom necessary to comply with the technical rules of modern litigation. *See Moore v. Florida*, 703 F.2d 516, 520 (11th Cir. 1983) [—11—] ("Pro se prison inmates, with limited access to legal materials, occupy a position significantly different from that occupied by litigants represented by counsel"). The Supreme Court has "insisted that the pleadings prepared by prisoners who do not have access to counsel be liberally construed and [has] held that some procedural rules must give way because of the unique circumstance of incarceration." *McNeil v. United States*, 508 U.S. 106, 113 (1993) (citations omitted). Accordingly, the Supreme Court has concluded that pro se prisoners successfully file a notice of appeal in habeas cases when they deliver the filings to prison authorities—not when the court receives the filings, as is generally true. *Houston v. Lack*, 487 U.S. 266, 270-71 (1988) ("Such prisoners cannot take the steps other litigants can take to monitor the processing of their notices of appeal and to ensure that the court clerk receives and stamps their notices of appeal before the 30-day deadline.").

Yet there are limits to our procedural flexibility. For example, pro se litigants still must allege sufficient facts in their complaints to support a claim. *See Riddle v. Mondragon*, 83 F.3d 1197, 1202 (10th Cir. 1996). And they still must serve process on the correct defendants. *See Franklin v. Murphy*, 745 F.2d 1221, 1234-35 (9th Cir. 1984). At the end of the day, they cannot flout procedural rules— they must abide by the same rules that apply to all other litigants. *See McNeil*, 508 U.S. at 113 ("[W]e have never suggested that procedural rules in [—12—] ordinary civil litigation should be interpreted so as to excuse mistakes by those who proceed without counsel."); *Kay v. Bemis*, 500 F.3d 1214, 1218 (10th Cir. 2007).

The second exception to our general rule of evenhandedness is likewise narrow. We have held that district courts must provide notice to pro se prisoners when converting a motion to dismiss into a motion for summary judgment. *See Renchenski v. Williams*, 622 F.3d 315, 340 (3d Cir. 2010). In particular, courts must tell pro se prisoners about the effects of not filing any opposing affidavits. *Id.*; *see also Somerville v. Hall*, 2 F.3d 1563, 1564 (11th Cir. 1993); *Neal v. Kelly*, 963 F.2d 453, 457 (D.C. Cir. 1992); *Klingele v. Eikenberry*, 849 F.2d 409, 411 (9th Cir. 1988) (concluding that the rule applies only to pro se prisoners). *But see Williams v. Browman*, 981 F.2d 901, 903-04 (6th Cir. 1992) (holding that such notice is unnecessary); *Martin v. Harrison City Jail*, 975 F.2d 192, 193 (5th Cir. 1992)(same).

Similarly, the Supreme Court has required district courts to provide notice to pro se litigants in habeas cases before converting any motion into a motion to vacate under 28 U.S.C. § 2255. *See Castro v. United States*, 540 U.S. 375, 383 (2003). The underlying principle is simple: when a court acts on its own in a way that significantly alters a pro se litigant's rights—for example, by converting one type of motion into a different type of [—13—] motion— the court should inform the pro se party of the legal consequences. But as the Supreme Court made clear only a few months after *Castro*, notice is the exception. Nonassistance is the rule. *See Pliler*, 542 U.S. at 231, 233-34.

That brings us back to Mala's claim. Mala argues that the District Court should have provided him with a pro se manual. Various district courts have created manuals to help pro se litigants navigate the currents of modern litigation. *See, e.g.*, U.S. District Court for the Eastern District of Pennsylvania, *Clerk's Office Procedural Handbook* (2012), http://www.paed.uscourts.gov/documents/hand book/handbook.pdf; U.S. District Court for the Western District of Pennsylvania, *Pro Se Package: A Simple Guide to Filing a Civil Action* (2009), http://www.pawd.uscourts.gov/Documents/For ms/PROSE_manual_2009.pdf; U.S. District Court for the District of New Jersey, *Procedural Guide for Pro Se Litigants* (2006), http://www.njd.uscourts.gov/rules/proselitguid e.pdf. These manuals are generally available online and in the clerk's office. They explain how to file a complaint, serve process, conduct discovery, and so forth. In addition, public-interest organizations have supplemented these manuals by publishing their own guides for pro se litigants. *See, e.g.*, Columbia Human Rights Law Review, *A Jailhouse Lawyer's Manual* (9th ed. 2011), http://www3.law.columbia.edu/hrlr/jlm/toc/. [—14—]

These manuals can be a valuable resource for pro se litigants. They may help litigants assert and defend their rights when no lawyer is available. And they can reduce the administrative burden on court officials who must grapple with inscrutable pro se filings. Because these manuals do not provide case-specific advice and because they are available to all litigants—not just to pro se litigants— they do not impair judicial impartiality. *See* Nina I. Van Wormer, Note, *Help at Your*

Fingertips: A Twenty-First Century Response to the Pro Se Phenomenon, 60 Vand. L. Rev. 983, 1018 (2007) ("By providing pro se litigants with easy, understandable, and reliable access to both procedural and substantive law, court systems can uphold their mandate their impartially administer justice to all, while at the same time increasing the efficiency with which they can manage their dockets."). Without a doubt, these manuals are informative, and inexperienced litigants would do well to seek them out.

That said, nothing requires district courts to provide such manuals to pro se litigants. *See Pliler*, 542 U.S. at 231 ("District judges have no obligation to act as counsel or paralegal to *pro se* litigants."). To put it another way, pro se litigants do not have a right—constitutional, statutory, or otherwise—to receive how-to legal manuals from judges. *See McKaskle*, 465 U.S. at 183-184 ("[T]he Constitution [does not] require judges to take over chores for a *pro se* defendant that would [—15—] normally be attended to by trained counsel as a matter of course."). And Mala has less reason to complain than the neophyte pro se litigant, having filed more than twenty suits in the past. *See* Appellee's Br. at 21-23. His experiences have made him well acquainted with the courts. *See Davidson v. Flynn*, 32 F.3d 27, 31 (2d Cir. 1994) (refusing to be flexible when interpreting a complaint because the plaintiff was "an extremely litigious inmate who [was] quite familiar with the legal system and with pleading requirements"); *Cusamano v. Sobek*, 604 F.Supp.2d 416, 445-46 (N.D.N.Y. 2009). The District Court's failure to provide Mala with a pro se litigation manual was not an abuse of discretion.[5]

---

[5] We would reject Mala's claim even if the District Court had an obligation to provide a pro se manual. For one thing, Mala never identified anything that he would have done differently if he had access to such a manual. Moreover, it is unclear why he needed a pro se manual from the District Court of the Virgin Islands. He could have received a manual from other district courts or from public-interest organizations. These manuals are easy to access through an internet search,

Mala also suggests that the District Court abused its discretion by not considering his status as a prisoner during the early stages of litigation. His problem, [—16—] however, is that he has not identified anything in particular that the court should have done differently. In fact, the court was solicitous of Mala's needs as an incarcerated litigant—delaying the trial until his release from prison and allowing him to amend the complaint at least once despite his noncompliance with Rule 15(a). Contrary to Mala's suggestion, the court accommodated his status as a prisoner.

III

Mala next argues that the District Court improperly refused to conduct a jury trial. This claim ultimately depends on whether the District Court had diversity jurisdiction. The court concluded that it had only admiralty jurisdiction, and Mala urges us to conclude otherwise. We generally exercise plenary review over jurisdictional questions, but factual findings that "undermine a court's determination of diversity jurisdiction ... are subject to the clearly erroneous rule." *Frett-Smith v. Vanterpool*, 511 F.3d 396, 399 (3d Cir. 2008) (citation and quotation marks omitted). Here, the District Court found that both Mala and Crown Bay were citizens of the Virgin Islands. These findings were not clearly erroneous, and so we conclude that Mala did not have a jury-trial right.

The Seventh Amendment creates a right to civil jury trials in federal court: "In Suits at common law ... the right of trial by jury shall be preserved." U.S. Const. [—17—] amend. VII. Admiralty suits are not "Suits at common law," which means that when a district court has only admiralty jurisdiction under 28 U.S.C. § 1331(1) [sic], the plaintiff does not have a jury-trial right. *Complaint of Consolidation Coal Co.*, 123 F.3d 126, 132 (3d Cir. 1997) (citing *Waring v. Clarke*, 46 U.S. (5 How.) 441, 458-60 (1847)). But the saving-to-suitors clause in § 1333(1) preserves state common-law remedies. *U.S. Express Lines Ltd v. Higgins*, 281 F.3d 383, 390 (3d Cir.

---

which Mala could have performed while doing his legal research at the local library. Any error therefore would be harmless.

2002). This clause allows plaintiffs to pursue state claims in admiralty cases as long as the district court also has diversity jurisdiction. *Id.* In such cases, § 1333(1) preserves whatever jury-trial right exists with respect to the underlying state claims. *Gorman v. Cerasia*, 2 F.3d 519, 526 (3d Cir. 1993) (noting that the saving-to-suitors clause saves "common law remedies, including the right to a jury trial"); *see also Ross v. Bernhard*, 396 U.S. 531, 537-38 (1970).

Mala argues that the District Court had both admiralty and diversity jurisdiction. As a preliminary matter, the court certainly had admiralty jurisdiction. The alleged tort occurred on navigable water and bore a substantial connection to maritime activity. *See Jerome B. Grubart, Inc. v. Great Lakes Dredge & Dock Co.*, 513 U.S. 527, 534 (1995) (explaining the two-part test for admiralty jurisdiction under § 1333(1)).

The grounds for diversity jurisdiction are less [—18—] certain. District courts have jurisdiction under 28 U.S.C. § 1332 only if the parties are completely diverse. *Barefoot Architect, Inc. v. Bunge*, 632 F.3d 822, 836 (3d Cir. 2011). This means that no plaintiff may have the same state or territorial citizenship as any defendant. *Id.* The parties agree that Mala was a citizen of the Virgin Islands. He was imprisoned in Puerto Rico when he filed the suit, but his imprisonment is of no moment. Prisoners presumptively retain their prior citizenship when the gates close behind them. *See Hall v. Curran*, 599 F.3d 70, 72 (1st Cir. 2010); *Smith v. Cummings*, 445 F.3d 1254, 1260 (10th Cir. 2006); *Sullivan v. Freeman*, 944 F.2d 334, 337 (7th Cir. 1991). No one challenges that presumption here.

Unfortunately, for Mala, the District Court concluded that Crown Bay also was a citizen of the Virgin Islands. Mala rejects this conclusion, stating that the sole defendant was Marina Management Services—a Florida corporation that operated Crown Bay Marina as one of its divisions. For its part, Crown Bay acknowledges that Marina Management Services managed the day-to-day operations at Crown Bay Marina, but Crown Bay argues that the two were separate legal entities. We

recognize that the District Court could have done more to clarify the relationship between these [—19—] two entities.[6] Even so, Mala's claim must fail.

Mala bears the burden of proving that the District Court had diversity jurisdiction. *McCann v. Newman Irrevocable Trust*, 458 F.3d 281, 286 (3d Cir. 2006) [—20—] ("The party asserting diversity jurisdiction bears the burden of ... proving diversity of citizenship by a preponderance of the evidence."). Mala failed to meet that burden because he did not offer evidence that Crown Bay was anything other than a citizen of the Virgin Islands. Mala contends that Crown Bay admitted to being a citizen of Florida, but Crown Bay actually denied Mala's allegation that Crown Bay Marina was a division of "Marine Management Services." *Compare* JA 55 ¶ 9 (alleging that Crown Bay Marina was a "corporate entity" under "Marine Management Services"), *with* JA 61 ¶ 9 (admitting that "Marine Management Services" is a Florida corporation but denying everything else).[7]

---

[6] A few months before trial, the District Court decided to "clarify the pre-trial status of [the] case." JA 131. Because no one else had been served, the court dismissed all defendants other than "Marine Services Management d/b/a Crown Bay Marina, Inc." JA 132. The acronym "d/b/a" stands for "doing business as" and typically indicates that the second name (here, "Crown Bay Marina, Inc.") is the party's trade name, whereas the first name (here, "Marine Services Management," which seems to be a reference to Marina Management Services) is the party's legal name. *See, e.g., Tai-Si Kim v. Kearney*, 838 F.Supp. 2d 1077, 1090 (D. Nev. 2012). This suggests that a Florida corporation was the sole defendant.

On the other hand, during the pre-trial proceedings, Crown Bay claimed to be a Virgin Islands entity, separate from Marina Management Services, *see* JA 122, and later provided testimony to support that claim, *see* Trial 12/6 at 75-76. Also, the District Court concluded that it lacked diversity jurisdiction. *See* JA 96, n. 3. This suggests that the sole defendant was a Virgin Islands business and that Marina Management Services was a separate entity.

[7] Mala also points out that during a pretrial hearing, Crown Bay's attorney introduced himself as "Mark Wilczynski on behalf of Marina Management Services, Inc." JA 144. But this statement does not appear to be an admission that

Absent evidence that the parties were diverse, we are left with Mala's allegations. Allegations are insufficient at trial. *McCann*, 458 F.3d at 286 (requiring a showing of diversity by a preponderance of the [—21—] evidence). And they are especially insufficient on appeal, where we review the District Court's underlying factual findings for clear error. *Smith*, 511 F.3d at 399. Under this standard, we will not reverse unless "we are left with the definite and firm conviction" that Crown Bay was in fact a citizen of Florida. *Id.* (quotation mark omitted). Mala has not presented any credible evidence that Crown Bay was a citizen of Florida—much less evidence that would leave us with the requisite "firm conviction."

Mala tries to cover up this evidentiary weakness by again pointing to his pro se status. He argues that we should construe his complaint liberally to find diversity. But Mala's problem is not a pleading problem. It is an evidentiary problem. Our traditional flexibility toward pro se pleadings does not require us to indulge evidentiary dificiencies. *See Brooks v. Kyler*, 204 F.3d 102, 108 n. 7 (3d Cir. 2000) (indicating that pro se litigants still must present at least affidavits to avoid summary judgment). Accordingly, the parties were not diverse and Mala does not have a jury-trial right.[8] [—22—]

Crown Bay was the same entity as Marina Management Services. Indeed, Crown Bay's attorney might have introduced himself this way simply because the District Court had previously identified the defendant as "Marine Services Management d/b/a Crown Bay Marina, Inc."

[8]At various times, Mala suggested that the District Court also had supplemental jurisdiction. It is unclear whether he was referring to supplemental jurisdiction under 28 U.S.C. § 1367, or whether he was calling diversity jurisdiction by the wrong name. Either way, the argument fails. As noted above, the parties were not [—22—] diverse. And even if he was referring to supplemental jurisdiction under § 1367, such jurisdiction exists only when there is no independent basis for federal jurisdiction. *See* 28 U.S.C. § 1367(a) (stating that supplemental jurisdiction is limited to "other claims" over which district courts do not have "original jurisdiction"). Here, the District Court had admiralty jurisdiction over all parts of Mala's claim, as both parties

Mala also claims that the District Court erred by rejecting the advisory jury's verdict. Federal Rule of Civil Procedure 39(c) states that "[i]n an action not triable of right by a jury, the court, on motion or on its own … may try any issue with an advisory jury." District courts are free to use advisory juries, even absent the parties' consent. *Compare* Fed. R. Civ. P. 39(c)(2) (requiring consent for a nonadvisory jury when the party does not have a jury-trial right), *with id.* 39(c)(1) (not requiring consent for an advisory jury); *see also Broadnax v. City of New Haven*, 415 F.3d 265, 271 n. 2 (2d Cir. 2005). District courts are also free to reject their verdicts, as long as doing so is not independently erroneous. *Wilson v. Prasse*, 463 F.2d 109, 116 (3d Cir. 1972) ("[F]indings by an advisory jury are not binding."). As a result, the District Court did not err in this case by empanelling an advisory jury or by rejecting its verdict. [—23—]

IV

Mala's final claim is that the District Court erroneously ruled on a handful of post-trial motions. After losing at trial, Mala asked the court to vacate the judgment under Federal Rule of Civil Procedure 60 (b) and to grant a new trial under Rules 50(b) and 59. These motions contained several overlapping arguments.[9] A magistrate judge recommended that the District Court reject these motions, and the court adopted the magistrate's recommendations. We conclude that the court did not make a mistake in doing so.

In reviewing a district court's decision to adopt a magistrate's recommendations, "[w]e exercise plenary review over the District Court's legal conclusions and apply a clearly erroneous standard to its findings of fact." *O'Donald v. Johns*, 402 F.3d 172, 173 n. 1 (3d

---

acknowledge. The court did not need supplemental jurisdiction.

[9] Among other things, Mala claimed that he should have a received a jury trial, that the District Court improperly ignored evidence, that the court did not have jurisdiction once Mala had filed a recusal motion, and that Crown Bay had committed fraud on the court.

Cir. 2005) (per curiam). Mala claims that "the Court stubbornly maintained that its rulings were correct and proper; no real review took place of the facts of the case, especially on the issue of jurisdiction allowing the Plaintiff a jury trial, nor acknowledging that the Court's decision to [—24—] empanel an advisory jury during the pretrial conference was unclear and confusing to the Plaintiff at best." Appellant's Br. at 23.

Mala's claim has little substance. The magistrate prepared three Reports and Recommendations that discussed Mala's arguments and urged the District Court to deny his motions. Judge Sanchez explained his reasons for doing so in an eight-page opinion. Both judges were meticulous and thorough. Mala has given us no reason to accept his general argument that "no real review took place."

Beyond this general argument, Mala alleges two specific shortcomings. First, he bemoans the District Court's refusal to conduct a jury trial. As noted above, this was not an error. Although the court could have been clearer about Crown Bay's citizenship, Mala nevertheless failed to meet his burden of proving diversity. Second, Mala asserts that he failed to understand that the jury's findings would be nonbinding. This was not the District Court's fault. The court plainly stated that the jury would be advisory. *See* JA 147 ("[CROWN BAY'S ATTORNEY]: And is that in fact the Court's position that there will be an advisory jury? THE COURT: Yes."). We therefore reject Mala's final claim.

* * *

Mala is a serial pro se litigant. In this case, he [—25—] convinced a jury of his peers to award him over $400,000 in damages. Unfortunately for Mala, the jury was advisory, and the District Court rejected the verdict. We conclude that the court did not err by using an advisory jury or by rejecting its verdict. Nor did the court err by adopting the magistrate's recommendations or by failing to provide a pro se manual. For these reasons we will affirm the District Court's judgment.

United States Court of Appeals
for the Third Circuit

No. 11-2576

IN RE FRESCATI SHIPPING CO.

Appeals from the United States District Court for the
Eastern District of Pennsylvania

Decided: May 16, 2013

Citation: 718 F.3d 184, 1 Adm. R. 80 (3d Cir. 2013).

Before **AMBRO, GREENAWAY, JR.,** and **O'MALLEY,***
Circuit Judges.
*Hon. Kathleen M. O'Malley, United States Court of
Appeals for the Federal Circuit, sitting by designation.
[—6—] AMBRO, Circuit Judge:

Table of Contents

A s the oil tanker *M/T Athos I* neared
Paulsboro, New Jersey, after a journey
from Venezuela, an abandoned ship
anchor lay hidden on the bottom of the
Delaware River squarely within the *Athos I*'s
path and only 900 feet away from its berth.
Although dozens of ships had docked since the
anchor was deposited in the River, none had
reported encountering it. The *Athos I* struck
the anchor, which punctured the ship's hull
and caused approximately 263,000 gallons of
crude oil to spill into the River. The cleanup
following the casualty was successful, but
expensive.

This appeal is the result of three interested
parties attempting to apportion the monetary
liability. The first party (actually two entities
consolidated as one for our purposes) includes
the *Athos I*'s owner, Frescati Shipping
Company, Ltd., and its manager, Tsakos
Shipping & Trading, S.A. (jointly and
severally, "Frescati"). Although Frescati states
that the spill caused it to pay out $180 million
in cleanup costs and ship damages, it was
reimbursed for nearly $88 million of that
amount by the United States (the
"Government")—the second interested party—
pursuant to the Oil Pollution Act of 1990, 33
U.S.C. § 2701 *et seq.* In order to recoup the
unreimbursed losses, Frescati made claims in
contract and tort against the third interested
party—a set of affiliates known as CITGO
Asphalt Refining Company, CITGO Petroleum
Corporation, and CITGO East Coast Oil
Corporation (jointly and severally,
"CARCO")—which requested the oil shipped
on the *Athos I* and owned the marine terminal
where it was to dock to unload its oil.
Specifically, Frescati brought a contract claim
for CARCO's alleged breach of the safe
port/safe berth warranty (jointly and
severally, "safe berth warranty") it made to an
intermediary—Star Tankers, Inc.—
responsible for chartering the *Athos I* to
CARCO's port, and alleged negligence and
negligent [—8—] misrepresentation against
CARCO as the owner of the wharf the *Athos I*
was nearing when it was holed. The
Government, as a statutory subrogee that
stepped into Frescati's position for the $88
million it reimbursed to Frescati under the Oil
Pollution Act, has limited its claim for
reimbursement from CARCO to Frescati's
contractual claim pursuant to a limited
settlement agreement.

Following a 41-day bench trial, the District
Court for the Eastern District of Pennsylvania
held that CARCO was not liable for the
accident under any of these theories. The
Court, however, made no separate findings of

fact and conclusions of law as required by Federal Rule of Civil Procedure 52(a)(1). That calls for a remand to set out these mandated matters. However, for the sake of efficiency, we discuss—and, to the extent necessary, make holdings on—the legal issues appealed.

In regard to the contractual safe berth warranty, the Court determined that Frescati (and the Government as a subrogee) could not recover on their contractual claims. First, Frescati was not a party to the agreement that contained the warranty between CARCO and Star Tankers, and was not an intended beneficiary of that agreement. Furthermore, even if Frescati could claim the protection of the warranty, it was only a promise by CARCO to exercise due diligence and not an unconditional guarantee; moreover, sufficient diligence existed here. In any event, the warranty was excused because CARCO specified the port ahead of the *Athos I*'s arrival, placing the burden on the *Athos I*'s captain to accept it as safe or reject it under what is called the "named port exception."

For reasons elaborated below, we disagree with all three of these rulings. Instead, we hold that the *Athos I*—and by extension, its owner, Frescati—was an implied beneficiary of CARCO's safe berth warranty. We conclude as well that the safe berth warranty is an express assurance of safety, and that the named port exception to that warranty does not apply to hazards that are unknown to the [—9—] parties and not reasonably foreseeable. We cannot be sure, however, that this warranty was actually breached, as the District Court made no finding as to the *Athos I*'s actual draft nor the amount of clearance actually provided.

If on remand the District Court rules in favor of Frescati on its contractual warranty claim, its negligence claim becomes unnecessary. If this issue is reached, we do not agree with the District Court's conclusion that CARCO cannot be liable in negligence because the anchor lay outside the approach to CARCO's terminal—the area in which CARCO had a duty to exercise reasonable care in proving a safe approach. As such, the District Court would need to resolve the

appropriate standard of care required, whether CARCO breached that standard, and if so, whether any such breach caused the accident. Conversely, we find no error with the Court's holding that CARCO's alleged misrepresentation as to the depth of its berth was geographically (and hence factually) irrelevant to the ultimate accident. In addition, we conclude that the Government has waived reliance on a partial settlement agreement with CARCO that, the Government contends, precludes CARCO from making certain equitable defenses to the Government's subrogation claims. In this context, we affirm in part, and vacate and remand in part for additional factfinding on the contractual (and possibly negligence) claims.

I. Factual and Procedural Background

A. The Tanker and Its Charters

At the heart of this dispute is the *Athos I*, a single-hulled oil tanker measuring 748 feet long and more than 105 feet wide. It was owned by Frescati at all relevant times. At the time of the accident, however, the *Athos I* had been chartered into a tanker pool assembled by Star Tankers, who is not a party to this consolidated action. In order to transport a load of heavy crude oil [—10—] from Venezuela to its asphalt refinery in Paulsboro, New Jersey, CARCO sub-chartered the *Athos I* from the Star Tankers pool.

In admiralty, these contracts for service are known as "charter parties."[1] In specific regard to Star Tankers, the *Athos I* was enlisted into the tanker pool in October of 2001 pursuant to a *time* charter party." "Under a time charter, the owner [Frescati] remains responsible for the navigation and operation of the vessel and

---

[1] The term "charter party" may be confusing in that it does not refer to an entity, but a document. This is due to its historical genesis, deriving from the phrase "*charta partita, i.e.,* a deed of writing divided." *Black's Law Dictionary* 268 (9th ed. 2009) (quoting Frank L. Maraist, *Admiralty in a Nutshell* 44-45 (3d ed. 1996)). The *charta partita* was literally a divided document, the owner and the charterer each retaining one half of the agreement. *Id.*

the charterer [Star Tankers] assumes responsibility for arranging for the employment of the vessel, providing fuel and paying for certain cargo-related expenses." Terence Coghlin *et al.*, *Time Charters* ¶ 1.59 (6th ed. 2008). The time charter party gave Star Tankers, an intermediary or "middleman," the right to sub-charter the *Athos I* although Frescati remained responsible for keeping the vessel staffed and serviceable.

In contrast, CARCO's employment of the *Athos I* for the specific voyage was pursuant to a "*voyage* charter party" with Star Tankers. Unlike a time charter party in which a "vessel's employment is put under the orders of . . . charterers" for a period of time, under a voyage charter party the ship is hired "to perform one or more designated voyages in return for the payment of freight."[2] Julian Cooke *et al.*, *Voyage Charters* ¶ 1.1 (3d ed. 2007). [—11—] CARCO's particular voyage charter party, based on a standard industry ASBATANKVOY form, contained what are customarily known as "safe port" and "safe berth" warranties (already defined, for convenience, as a "safe berth warranty"). It provided that

> [t]he vessel . . . shall, with all convenient dispatch, proceed as ordered to Loading Port(s) named . . . , or so near thereunto as she may safely get (always afloat), . . . and being so loaded shall forthwith proceed, as ordered on signing Bills of Lading, direct to the Discharging Port(s), or so near thereunto as she may

---

[2] It has been observed that

> [t]he fundamental difference between voyage and time charters is how the freight or "charter hire" is [—11—] calculated. A voyage charterparty specifies the amount due for carrying a specified cargo on a specified voyage (or series of voyages), regardless of how long a particular voyage takes. A time charterparty specifies the amount due for each day that the vessel is "on hire," regardless of how many voyages are completed.

David W. Robertson *et al.*, *Admiralty and Maritime Law in the United States* 335 (2d ed. 2008).

safely get (always afloat), and deliver said cargo.

J.A. at 1222 (Tanker Voyage Charter Party, Part II, ¶ 1). It further directed that "[t]he vessel shall load and discharge at any safe place or wharf, . . . which shall be designated and procured by the Charterer [CARCO], provided the Vessel can proceed thereto, lie at, and depart therefrom always safely afloat . . . ." *Id.* at 1222 (Tanker Voyage Charter Party, Part II, ¶ 9). We note that, in the time charter party between Frescati and Star Tankers, the latter contracted to provide a similar safe berth warranty, but this warranty was qualified whereby Star Tankers obligated itself to exercise "due diligence to ensure that the vessel is only employed between and at safe places . . . ." *Id.* at 1157 (Time Charter Party [—12—] ¶ 4). Following the accident, Frescati began arbitration with Star Tankers regarding its claims for damage of the *Athos I*, but that proceeding has been stayed pending the outcome of this case. Oral Arg. Tr. 4:8–15, Sept. 20, 2012.

In preparation for the arrival in Paulsboro of the *Athos I*, its master[3] was provided with a copy of CARCO's Port Manual. This Manual indicated that the allowable maximum draft at the Paulsboro facility was 38 feet, but that this "may change from time to time and should be verified prior to the vessel's arrival." J.A. at 1095 (CITGO Terminal Regulations for Vessels ¶ 2). On November 22, 2004, four days before the *Athos I* arrived, CARCO reduced this maximum draft to 36 feet. The *Athos I* was not informed of this modification.

B. The Accident

On November 26, 2004, the *Athos I* was nearing its ultimate destination, CARCO's asphalt refinery in Paulsboro, New Jersey. When the *Athos I* reached the mouth of the Delaware River, only 80 miles remained of its 1,900-mile journey. Although Captain Iosif Markoutsis was the ship's master, the seven-hour upriver transit was aided by Delaware River Pilot Captain Howard Teal. At

---

[3] A ship's master is its commander and captain. *Black's Law Dictionary*, *supra*, at 1065.

approximately 8:30 p.m., while the *Athos I* was still navigating up the River channel, Docking Pilot Captain Joseph Bethel boarded the vessel (Captain Bethel was employed by non-party Moran Towing of Pennsylvania). The Docking Pilot relieved the River Pilot at about 8:40 p.m.

CARCO's Paulsboro facility sits on a jetty on the New Jersey side of the Delaware River. Federal Anchorage Number Nine ("the Anchorage" or "Anchorage Number Nine") separates the River channel from CARCO's port waters. As pictured in [—13—] Appendix A to this opinion, the Anchorage's border runs diagonally to CARCO's waterfront, ranging between 130 and 670 feet from the face of its ship dock. Across the Anchorage, the River Channel begins less than 2,000 feet from CARCO's berth, a little more than two-and-a-half lengths of the *Athos I*. Customarily, a tanker of the *Athos I*'s size would come up the River, make a starboard (right) 180° turn into the Anchorage, and would then be pushed sideways by tugs (*i.e.*, parallel parked) into CARCO's pier. The *Athos I* was following this procedure when, at 9:02 p.m., it suddenly listed to the port (left) side, and oil became visible in the water. It was later determined that an abandoned anchor had punched two holes in the *Athos I*'s hull, causing (as already noted) roughly 263,000 gallons of crude oil to spill into the River. At the time of the allision,[4] the *Athos I* was only 900 feet from CARCO's berth, approximately halfway through the Anchorage. The tide was relatively low at the time of the accident after having reached its lowest point only 50 minutes prior. J.A. at 2102.

The anchor was eventually exhumed. Inspection revealed that it weighed roughly nine tons and measured 6′8″ long, 7′3″ wide, and 4′6″ high. J.A. at 2192 (United States Coast Guard Marine Casualty Investigation Report). The Coast Guard further reported that the anchor was ultimately found lying prone with its blade reaching 54 inches above the floor of the River. *Id.* at 2196. Although

the District Court made no finding of fact as to the exact position of the anchor at the time of the allision, it found persuasive the testimony of oceanographer and ocean engineer Dr. Peter Traykovski, who opined that the anchor was lying horizontal at the time of the accident with a height of only 41 inches above the bottom of the River. Traykovski Test., 24:25–25:13, Nov. 4, 2010. The Court also did not make any finding as to the depth of the [—14—] Anchorage where the anchor lay, though the record before us seems to indicate that the depth was between 40.3 and 41.45 feet deep at low tide. *Id.* at 49:12–25; J.A. at 2196.

The District Court also did not make any finding as to the draft of the *Athos I*—that is, the distance between the lowest point of the ship and the waterline—but assumed, for purposes of analysis, that it was drawing 36′7″ as represented by Frescati at the time of the accident. The Court also failed to resolve the anchor's depth or position, although it noted that there was "persuasive evidence" that the anchor was lying down at the time of the accident. *In re Frescati Shipping Co., Ltd.*, Nos. 05-CV-00305-JF, 08-cv-02898-JF, 2011 WL 1436878, at *7 (E.D. Pa. Apr. 12, 2011). The parties, however, stipulated that the anchor had been in the same approximate location for at least three years because it was detectable from a sonar scan performed by the University of Delaware in 2001 as part of an independent geophysical study.[5] The owner of the anchor has never been determined, but the Court speculated that the anchor likely was used for dredging operations at the time it was lost.

C.   The Cost of the Accident

Frescati claims that the accident cost it, as the "responsible party" under the Oil Pollution Act, approximately $180 million in clean-up costs and damages to the ship. (The Act was

---

[4] An allision is "[t]he contact of a vessel with a stationary object such as an anchored vessel or a pier." *Black's Law Dictionary, supra,* at 88.

[5] The stipulation suggests that the anchor was not mentioned in the report ultimately issued by the University of Delaware professors. *See* J.A. at 1310–12. Instead, it seems that it was not until after this litigation began that the parties obtained the 2001 side scan sonar data and agreed that it revealed the anchor's presence.

passed in the wake of the Exxon Valdez accident in 1989, and was designed to facilitate oil spill cleanups by requiring "responsible parties" to pay initially for removal costs and damages. *See* 33 U.S.C. §2702(a).) Because the Act sets liability limits for cooperative responsible [—15—] parties, *see id.* at § 2704(a), an incentive exists for responsible parties to respond quickly and competently in order to limit the extent of their financial exposure. *See Unocal Corp. v. United States*, 222 F.3d 528, 535 (9th Cir. 2000) ("'The purpose of [the Oil Pollution Act] . . . was to encourage rapid private party responses.'" (quoting *In re Metlife Capital Corp.*, 132 F.3d 818, 822 (1st Cir. 1997))). Responsible parties in compliance with the Act may file a claim with the Oil Spill Liability Trust Fund, controlled by the United States Government, for reimbursement of costs beyond the liability limit. 33 U.S.C. §2708(a)(2). Specifically, Frescati was able to limit its liability for cleanup to $45,474,000, thus allowing it to recover cleanup costs exceeding that amount from the Fund.[6] It was ultimately reimbursed for approximately $88,000,000 of its cleanup costs, and the Fund became subrogated as to that amount under 33 U.S.C. §§ 2712(f) and 2715(a).

D. Control of the Waters

The casualty here occurred squarely within Anchorage Number Nine. As the term implies, an anchorage ground is "a place where vessels anchor or a place suitable for anchoring." *Webster's Third New Int'l Dictionary* 79 (1971). Section 7 of the Rivers and Harbors Act of 1915 authorizes the establishment of "anchorage grounds for vessels in all harbors, rivers, bays, and other navigable waters of the United States whenever it is manifest . . . that the maritime or commercial interests of the United States require such anchorage grounds for safe [—16—] navigation . . . ." 33 U.S.C.

§ 471. By 1930, a "lack of adequate anchorage room" was creating a hazard on the Delaware River between navigating vessels and those "awaiting accommodation at the wharves, or awaiting cargo or orders." H. Doc. No. 71-304, 24 (1930). Anchorage Number Nine, also known as the Mantua Creek Anchorage, was established in 1930. Pub. L. No. 71-520, 46 Stat. 918, 921 (1930). Today it runs for approximately 2.2 miles along the Delaware River channel (*see* Appendix A) and provides a place for ships to anchor so long as they do not "interfere unreasonably with the passage of other vessels to and from Mantua Creek." 33 C.F.R. § 110.157(a)(10).

Anchorage Number Nine, though only a few hundred feet from CARCO's pier, is neither controlled nor maintained by CARCO. Instead, the federal Government's Army Corps of Engineers (the "Corps") conducts hydrographic surveys and dredges as necessary in an attempt to maintain the Anchorage's depth at 40 feet. The Corps also regulates any construction or excavation within the navigable waters, including the issuance of dredging permits, 33 U.S.C. § 403, and its regulatory jurisdiction "extend[s] laterally to the entire water surface and bed of a navigable waterbody, which includes all the land and waters below the ordinary high water mark," 33 C.F.R. § 329.11. The National Oceanic and Atmospheric Administration conducts surveys on occasion for various federal projects. No Government entity, however, is responsible for preemptively searching all federal waters for obstructions, and the District Court found that the Government does not actually survey the Anchorage for hazards. If, however, the Government is alerted to the presence of a threat, the Corps will remove the obstruction if it is a hazard to navigation and, if not removable, the Coast Guard will chart it. Ultimately, the "[p]rimary responsibility for removal of wrecks or other obstructions lies with the [obstruction's] owner, lessee, or operator." 33 C.F.R. § 245.10(b). [—17—]

CARCO maintains a self-described "area of responsibility" directly abutting its Paulsboro terminal, "a roughly triangular-shaped area ... comprising the waters of the berth footprint

---

[6] In February 2007, Frescati applied to have its liability exonerated pursuant to 33 U.S.C. §2703(a)(3). That subsection directs that a responsible party is not liable for the acts or omissions of a third party. In this case, that third party would have been the unknown anchor-dropper. It is unclear why Frescati withdrew this claim in 2008.

and the immediate access area next to it where vessels enter and exit the footprint." CARCO's Br. at 19. This area, also set out in Appendix A to this opinion, runs essentially the length of CARCO's facility and extends offshore to the border of the Anchorage. It is based on a permit to dredge for maintenance purposes that was issued by the Corps to CARCO's predecessor in 1991. The scope of such a permit is derived from the initial request; put another way, it is self-defined subject to approval by the Corps. This area of responsibility is not large enough to rotate the 748 foot-long *Athos I*.

In maintaining its area of responsibility, CARCO retained a consulting engineering firm, S.T. Hudson Engineers, Inc., to perform hydrographic surveys. While CARCO had inspected that area for depth, it never specifically searched for debris or other hazards. Hudson interpolated the area's depth from a grid of pinpointed, single-beam sonar depth soundings at 50-foot intervals. This particular procedure is poor at detecting sunken objects because it is unlikely that any given hazard would fall within the exact spot measured, and if it did, it would not necessarily indicate that there was an object but only the depth of that object as indistinguishable from the bottom of the waterway. Long Test., 78:8–79:5, Nov. 17, 2010; Fish Test., 59:11–18, Sept. 29, 2010.

CARCO's Port Captain William Rankine estimated that approximately 250 ships with a draft of 36′6″ or greater either entered or departed CARCO's port between 1997 and 2005. Rankine Test., 22:25–23:15, Nov. 22, 2010. In specific regard to arriving vessels, from the time the anchor was spotted by the University of Delaware in August 2001 until the *Athos I* casualty, the record reflects that 61 ships with a draft of 36′6″ or greater arrived at CARCO's facility. J.A. at 1788–94. The record does not reflect at what time these ships docked, and high tide adds [—18—] approximately six feet of depth to the River. Moreover, Frescati points out that— unlike the *Athos I*— 21 of these ships would have been required to dock within three hours prior

to high-water due to their excessive drafts.[7] *Id.* at 1622–24.

E. The District Court Proceedings

In January 2005, Frescati filed in the District Court a Complaint for Exoneration From or Limitation of Liability pursuant to the Shipowner's Limitation of Liability Act, 46 U.S.C. § 30501 *et seq.* (formerly 46 App. U.S.C. § 181 *et seq.*). In that Complaint, Frescati sought a declaration that it was not liable for any losses stemming from the accident or, in the alternative, a limitation of liability to the value of the *Athos I* and its pending freight. CARCO was among the parties who asserted claims in that action, seeking recovery against Frescati for its lost oil in an amount in excess of $259,217. Frescati then filed a counterclaim against CARCO for all costs incurred beyond those reimbursed by the Fund.

In June 2008, the Government filed a separate suit against CARCO seeking compensation on its subrogated right, pursuant to 33 U.S.C. §§ 2712(f) and 2715(a), to the approximately $88 million disbursed by the Fund. In a pretrial settlement agreement, the Government waived its negligence claims against CARCO in return for the latter's agreement not to pursue negligence claims against the United States. The Government, believing that CARCO [—19—] was advancing against it negligence theories in violation of the settlement agreement, moved for partial summary judgment against CARCO's counterclaim for equitable recoupment. That motion was denied.

As noted, these two actions were consolidated, and they were tried over 41 days before Judge Fullam. After trial, the Court issued an 18-page opinion holding that CARCO could not be held responsible under contract or tort for any of the losses stemming

---

[7] The Docking Pilot Association ("DPA") Guidelines provide directives for the appropriate docking times for vessels of different sizes. The DPA Guidelines were developed after discussion with CARCO's previous Port Captain and were based in part on CARCO's desire to maximize the number of vessels that could dock at its berth. J.A. at 1104; Quillen Dep. 11:12–20, Sept. 2, 2010.

from the accident. *See In re Frescati,* 2011 WL 1436878.

On the contractual safe berth warranty, the Court determined that Frescati had no standing for relief, as it was not a third-party beneficiary to the voyage charter party between CARCO and Star Tankers, and that, in any event, CARCO did not breach those warranties because they are not unconditional guarantees but instead "'impose[ ] upon the charterer a duty of due diligence to select a safe berth,'" a duty satisfied here. *Id.* at *6 (quoting *Orduna S.A. v. Zen-Noh Grain Corp.,* 913 F.2d 1149, 1157 (5th Cir. 1990)). The Court further ruled that, even if a stricter warranty applied, the naming of the port in advance precluded recovery under the named port exception, which, as a general matter, protects a charterer when the port is named ahead of arrival and the master proceeds there without protest.

The Court also held that CARCO was not negligent in failing to search for or detect the abandoned anchor that lay within the Anchorage. As the Court deemed it outside the approach to CARCO's berth, detection and notification to others of its presence thus fell beyond CARCO's obligation to provide a safe entry to that berth. The Court also held that there was no negligent misrepresentation in CARCO's failure to alert the *Athos I* that— only four days prior to its arrival—the allowable maximum draft at CARCO's facility had been reduced from 38 feet to 36 feet. It reasoned that this was an internal determination pertaining to the [—20—] area at the berth and outside the Anchorage, and therefore was "factually irrelevant to the casualty." *Id.* at *5.

In sum, the District Court concluded that the anchor-dropper rather than any of the named parties was at fault, and rejected all of Frescati's and the Government's arguments as to CARCO's liability.

II. Jurisdiction and Standard of Review

The District Court had admiralty jurisdiction pursuant to 28 U.S.C. § 1333(1).

We have jurisdiction over this appeal under 28 U.S.C. § 1291.

Findings of fact made during a bench trial are reviewed for clear error, and will stand unless "'completely devoid of minimum evidentiary support displaying some hue of credibility, or . . . bear no rational relationship to the supportive evidentiary data.'" *In re Nautilus Motor Tanker Co.,* 85 F.3d 105, 115 (3d Cir. 1996) (alteration in original) (quoting *Haines v. Liggett Grp. Inc.,* 975 F.2d 81, 92 (3d Cir. 1992)). Following a bench trial, we review *de novo* a district court's conclusions of law. *McCutcheon v. Am.'s Servicing Co.,* 560 F.3d 143, 147 (3d Cir. 2009) (citation omitted). "[C]onstruction of an unambiguous contract is a matter of law and subject to plenary review." *Colliers Lanard & Axilbund v. Lloyds of London,* 458 F.3d 231, 236 (3d Cir. 2006) (citing *U & W Indus. Supply, Inc. v. Martin Marietta Alumina, Inc.,* 34 F.3d 180, 185 (3d Cir. 1994)). Similarly, we exercise "plenary review over the legal question of 'the nature and extent of the duty of due care . . . .'" *Andrews v. United States,* 801 F.2d 644, 646 (3d Cir. 1986) (quoting *Redhead v. United States,* 686 F.2d 178, 182 (3d Cir. 1982)). [—21—]

III. Rule 52

Federal Rule of Civil Procedure 52(a)(1) provides that "[i]n an action tried on the facts without a jury or with an advisory jury, the court must find the facts specially and state its conclusions of law separately." Fed. R. Civ. P. 52(a)(1). This is a mandatory requirement. *H. Prang Trucking Co., Inc. v. Local Union No. 469,* 613 F.2d 1235, 1238 (3d Cir. 1980) (citing 9 Charles Alan Wright & Arthur R. Miller, *Federal Practice and Procedure* § 2574, at 690 (1st ed. 1971)); *Scalea v. Scalea's Airport Serv., Inc.,* 833 F.2d 500, 502 (3d Cir. 1987) (*per curiam*). Typically, a Rule 52 violation occurs when a district court's inadequate findings render impossible "'a clear understanding of the basis of the decision,'" *H. Prang Trucking,* 613 F.2d at 1238 (quoting Wright & Miller, *supra,* § 2577, at 697), and those "'findings are obviously necessary to the intelligent and orderly presentation and proper disposition of an appeal,'" *Bradley v. Pittsburgh Bd. of Educ.*, 910 F.2d 1172, 1178 (3d Cir. 1990) (quoting *Mayo v. Lakeland Highlands Canning Co.*, 309 U.S. 310, 317 (1940)). *See also Berguido v. E. Air Lines, Inc.*, 369 F.2d 874, 877 (3d Cir. 1966) ("If a full understanding of the factual issues cannot be gleaned from the District Court's opinion, we would be obliged to remand for compliance with Rule 52(a)."). Although Rule 52 does not require hyper-literal adherence, *see Hazeltine Corp. v. Gen. Motors Corp.*, 131 F.2d 34, 37 (3d Cir. 1942), "an appellate court may vacate the judgment and remand the case for findings if the trial court has failed to make findings when they are required," *Giles v. Kearney*, 571 F.3d 318, 328 (3d Cir. 2009) (citing *H. Prang Trucking*, 613 F.2d at 1238–39).

Instead of presenting his findings in accord with Rule 52, the trial judge here elected to "set forth in narrative fashion [his] findings of fact . . . and conclusions of law." *In re Frescati*, 2011 WL 1436878, at *1. Unfortunately, what followed leaves us unable to discern what were his intended factual findings. Moreover, in arriving at his particular legal conclusions, the trial [—22—] judge held back making many of the factual findings that would support those conclusions, in effect going from first base to third across the pitcher's mound. While we do not endorse or require a panoply of extraneous factual findings, the overall dearth of clear factual findings, much less those pertaining to the heart of this matter— such as the draft of the *Athos I*—falls below what is required by Rule 52.

Because we cannot derive a full understanding of the core facts from the District Court's opinion, this was a violation of Rule 52 and itself a basis for remand. *Giles*, 571 F.3d at 328. In light of the legal determinations set out below, factual clarification is required in any event.

IV. The Contractual Safe Berth Warranty

CARCO's promise to Star Tankers that the *Athos I* would be directed to a location that "she may safely get (always afloat)" is a provision known in context as either a safe port or safe berth warranty (to repeat again, we use for shorthand "safe berth warranty"). *See* Cooke *et al.*, *supra*, ¶ 5.121 (citation omitted). This language triggers two separate protections: a contractual excuse for a master who elects not to venture into an unsafe port, and protection against damages to a ship incurred in an unsafe port to which the warranty applies. *See* 2 Thomas J. Schoenbaum, *Admiralty and Maritime Law* §11-10, at 32–33 (5th ed. 2011). In this case, only the second benefit of the safe berth warranty is at issue, as the *Athos I* was damaged in an allegedly unsafe port. Specifically at issue are the scope and applicability of this warranty, topics we explore below. [—23—]

A. Was Frescati a Third-Party Beneficiary of the Safe Berth Warranty?

"'Before a stranger can avail himself of the exceptional privilege of suing for a breach of an agreement, to which he is not a party, he must at least show that it was intended for his direct benefit.'" *Robins Dry Dock & Repair Co. v. Flint*, 275 U.S. 303, 307 (1927) (quoting *German Alliance Ins. Co. v. Home Water Supply Co.*, 226 U.S. 220, 230 (1912)). As Frescati is not a party to CARCO's promise to Star Tankers to provide a safe berth, there must be a compelling showing that it was nonetheless an intended beneficiary. The District Court held that this was not the case because the testimony at trial failed to reveal any intent by CARCO to benefit Frescati. The Court, however, failed to inquire whether the contract itself established a third-party beneficiary relationship, a question of law. *See Pierce Assocs. v. Nemours Found.*, 865 F.2d 530, 535 (3d Cir. 1988). We conclude that, although Frescati is not a named beneficiary to the safe berth warranty within the charter party between Star Tankers and CARCO, the *Athos I* benefits from this warranty, and Frescati, as the vessel's owner, is thus a third-party beneficiary.

Maritime contracts "must be construed like any other contracts: by their terms and consistent with the intent of the parties." *Norfolk S. Ry. Co. v. Kirby*, 543 U.S. 14, 31

(2004). "When a contract is a maritime one, and the dispute is not inherently local, federal law controls the contract interpretation." *Id.* at 22–23 (citing *Kossick v. United Fruit Co.*, 365 U.S. 731, 735 (1961)). We typically look to the Restatement of Contracts for the federal law on third-party beneficiaries. *Doe v. Pennsylvania Bd. of Prob. & Parole*, 513 F.3d 95, 106 (3d Cir. 2008); *see* Restatement (Second) of Contracts § 302 (1981). A third-party may be a beneficiary to a contract of others where it is "appropriate to effect[ ] the intention of the parties," and "the circumstances indicate that the promisee intends to give the beneficiary the benefit of the promised performance." Restatement, *supra*, § [—24—] 302(1)(b); *see also Cargill Int'l S.A. v. M/T Pavel Dybenko*, 991 F.2d 1012, 1019 (2d Cir. 1993) (holding that a third-party beneficiary to a charter party "must show that 'the parties to that contract intended to confer a benefit on [it] when contracting; it is not enough that some benefit incidental to the performance of the contract may accrue to [it]'" (alterations in original) (quoting *McPheeters v. McGinn, Smith & Co.*, 953 F.2d 771, 773 (2d Cir. 1992))).

In 1959, the Supreme Court held that vessels are automatic third-party beneficiaries of warranties of workmanlike service made to their charterers by stevedores who unload vessels at docks. *Crumady v. The Joachim Hendrik Fisser*, 358 U.S. 423, 428 (1959). This is because "[t]he warranty which a stevedore owes when he goes aboard a vessel to perform services is plainly for the benefit of the vessel whether the vessel's owners are parties to the contract or not." *Id.* This natural relationship between the entities was "enough to bring the vessel into the zone of modern law that recognizes rights in third-party beneficiaries." *Id.* (citation omitted). A year later, the Supreme Court extended this rule a logical step further in holding that "[t]he owner, no less than the ship, is the beneficiary of the stevedore's warranty of workmanlike service." *Waterman S. S. Corp. v. Dugan & McNamara, Inc.*, 364 U.S. 421, 425 (1960).

Although these two Supreme Court cases aid Frescati's position, they do so only by analogy. As CARCO points out, the matter before us does not involve an implied warranty for workmanlike service, but an explicit assurance of safety in a document to which Frescati is not a party. The Court of Appeals for the Second Circuit, however, has applied *Crumady* and *Waterman* to a set of facts similar to the one before us. In *Paragon Oil Co. v. Republic Tankers, S.A.*, 310 F.2d 169, 171 (2d Cir. 1962) (Friendly, J.), a vessel owner (Paragon Oil Co., Inc.) and voyage charterer (Republic Tankers, S.A.) entered into a voyage charter with a safe berth warranty. Republic had executed a contract of [—25—] affreightment (essentially a sub-voyage charter) with a third-party that contained a safe berth warranty identical to the one it promised in the voyage charter. *Id.* From this, the Second Circuit concluded that Paragon (the owner) was "the true party in interest" to the safe berth assurance in the contract of affreightment even though it was not explicitly named in the contract between Republic (the voyage charterer) and the third-party. *Id.* at 175.

We agree with the Second Circuit's reasoning that *Crumady* and *Waterman* counsel in favor of Frescati's third-party beneficiary status.[8] Specifically, we are convinced that a safe berth warranty necessarily benefits the vessel, and thus benefits its owner as a corollary beneficiary.[9]

---

[8] CARCO makes a belated argument that *Crumady* and *Waterman* are of dubious precedential value in light of the 1972 amendments to the Longshore and Harbor Workers' Compensation Act. These amendments required negligence (as opposed to an unsafe condition) for a longshoreman to recover against a ship owner, and abolished the ship owner's right of indemnity against the stevedore. *See* 33 U.S.C. § 905 (b); *Scindia Steam Nav. Co., Ltd. v. De Los Santos*, 451 U.S. 156, 164-65 (1981). This legislative exclusion, however, does not undermine the fundamental premise that a ship owner may benefit from an arrangement between third parties. As such, Judge Posner has noted that, following this amendment, "indemnity has continued to be sought in cases not involving longshoremen and hence not within the scope of the Longshore[ ] and Harbor Workers' Compensation Act." *Hillier v. S. Towing Co.*, 714 F.2d 714, 718-19 (7th Cir. 1983) (Posner, J.).

[9] Insofar as CARCO cites to *Bunge Corp. v. MV Furness Bridge*, 390 F. Supp. 603, 604 (E.D. La.

"[T]he circumstances indicate" that the warranty is intended to endow the vessel with "the benefit of the promised performance." Restatement, *supra*, § 302(1)(b). Because the warranty explicitly covers the safety of the vessel, it would be nonsensical to deprive the vessel's owner the benefits of this [—26—] promise, as the owner is ultimately the one most interested in the vessel's status and is obligated to maintain its condition.[10]

Moreover, it would work an odd windfall if Star Tankers were allowed to collect on CARCO's safe berth warranty but not be required to pass on those remedial dollars to the ship's ultimate owner. That illogical result could occur where the owner (Frescati) received no safe berth warranty from the time charterer (Star Tankers), or where—as in the case before us—Frescati received a less comprehensive warranty from Star Tankers than Star Tankers received from the voyage charterer (CARCO).[11] This would theoretically allow Star Tankers to collect for damages to the ship that were actually paid by Frescati. While we are mindful of the parties' ability to contract differently, there is no indication that Star Tankers bargained for the potential of

---

1974), it is unpersuasive, as its conclusion that the owner was not a third-party beneficiary of the sub-charterer's safe berth warranty is unsupported by any reasoning. Further, this issue was abandoned when the Court later resolved the merits of the claim and held that the sub-charterer had "violated a legal duty [in tort] whether or not it also had a contractual one." *Bunge Corp. v. MV Furness Bridge*, 396 F. Supp. 852, 858 (E.D. La. 1975), *rev'd*, 558 F.2d 790 (5th Cir. 1977). On appeal, the Court of Appeals for the Fifth Circuit agreed that the issue of contractual liability was "irrelevant" because none of the parties could have intended to warrant complete safety of an inadequately small wharf. 558 F.2d at 801–02.

[10] Under the time charter, Frescati remained responsible for insuring, maintaining, and restoring the *Athos I* throughout the term of the charter. J.A. at 1447–48 (Time Charter Party ¶¶ 3, 6).

[11] Although we ultimately conclude that the full safe berth warranty from CARCO to Star Tankers is an express assurance made without regard to the amount of diligence taken by the charterer, *see infra* Part IV.B, Star Tankers only promised due diligence to Frescati, J.A. at 1448 (Time Charter Party ¶ 4).

---

such an unearned windfall—profiting from the mishaps of the vessels within its tanker pool when it did not pay for the repair of those mishaps. Instead, requiring warranties from voyage charterers like CARCO is a way to insure against claims asserted by vessel owners. Per this path, the promise made to protect a vessel flows through the intermediary party(ies) to the ultimate party who bore the pain of an unsafe port, here the vessel's owner.

We discount CARCO's suggestion that it was unaware of Frescati's status as the true owner of the *Athos I*. CARCO had [—27—] completed an internal vetting of the *Athos I* in October of 2004 that identified Frescati as its owner. J.A. at 1318 (Citgo Vetting Report). Regardless, even if the ultimate owner had been undisclosed, CARCO expressly warranted to provide a safe berth, which is a promise made "plainly for the benefit of the vessel." *Crumady*, 358 U.S. at 428. Thus we see no reason why the *Athos I*'s owner would be any less entitled to rely on this warranty, whether it was identified or not. Frescati, as the owner of the *Athos I*, may therefore rely on CARCO's safe berth warranty as a third-party beneficiary.

B. The Scope of the Safe Berth Warranty

That Frescati may benefit from CARCO's safe port/safe berth warranty requires that we delineate its comprehensiveness, a question of first impression in our Circuit. Though the District Court did not need to reach this legal issue after determining that Frescati was not a third-party beneficiary, it nonetheless concluded—as an alternate holding—that the safe berth warranty was not breached because "CARCO fulfilled its duty of due diligence . . . ." *In re Frescati*, 2011 WL 1436878, at *6. We part from this holding, as we believe the Court incorrectly relied on *Orduna S.A. v. Zen-Noh Grain Corp.*, 913 F.2d 1149, 1157 (5th Cir. 1990), which held that the safe berth provision was not a full warranty but required only due diligence.

A port is deemed safe where "the particular chartered vessel can proceed to it, use it, and depart from it without, in the absence of abnormal weather or other occurrences, being exposed to dangers which cannot be avoided by good navigation and seamanship." Cooke *et al., supra*, ¶ 5.137; *Leeds Shipping v. Societe Francaise Bunge (The Eastern City)*, [1958] 2 Lloyd's Rep. 127, 131 (same). Whether a port is safe refers to the particular ship at issue, Cooke *et al., supra*, ¶ 5.68, and goes beyond "the immediate area of the port itself" to the "adjacent areas the vessel must traverse to either enter or leave," Coghlin *et al., supra*, [—28—] ¶10.124. In other words, a port is unsafe—and in violation of the safe berth warranty—where the named ship cannot reach it without harm (absent abnormal conditions or those not avoidable by adequate navigation and seamanship).[12]

This formulation is deeply rooted. In 1888, the Supreme Court held charterers liable for breach of a safe berth warranty in insisting that a ship sail to Aalborg, Denmark, a port that was impossible for the particular ship to reach due to a sand bar and the absence of any reasonably safe place to anchor or discharge. *The Gazelle*, 128 U.S. 474, 485–86 (1888). In a similar fashion, the Supreme Court held in 1902 that charterers failed to provide a safe dock where the ship in question could not reach it without damage. *Mencke v. Cargo of Java Sugar*, 187 U.S. 248, 253 (1902). Specifically, the charterers were aware that the ship's mast was too tall to clear the Brooklyn Bridge when they designated a discharge dock upriver from the Bridge. *Id.* at 250. The Court concluded that this was a warranty violation by analogizing the overhead obstacle to a submerged one: "A ship could not be said to be afloat, whether the obstacle encountered was a shoal or bar in the port over which she could not proceed, or a bridge under or through which she could not pass, nor could she be said to have safely reached a dock if required to mutilate her hull or her permanent masts." *Id.* at 253; *see also*

---

[12] On the facts before us, we need not define the outer geographical bounds of the safe berth/safe port warranty. At oral argument CARCO conceded that the warranty—if applicable—"would include the area in and around Paulsboro," including the Anchorage. Oral Arg. Tr. 62:18–64:3, Sept. 20, 2012.

Carbon Slate Co. v. Ennis, 114 F. 260, 261 (3d Cir. 1902) (concluding that safe berth warranty was violated where the ship "was directed to load at a berth where a full cargo, if taken aboard, would have made it impossible for her, at any stage of water or at any time, to pass out over the harbor bar").
[—29—]

The Court of Appeals for the Second Circuit has long held that promising a safe berth effects an "express assurance" that the berth will be as represented. *Cities Serv. Transp. Co. v. Gulf Ref. Co.*, 79 F.2d 521, 521 (2d Cir. 1935) (*per curiam*), recognized this principle in holding that a master was not liable for damages incurred in reliance on a charter party's safe berth warranty at a particular dock. In *Park S.S. Co. v. Cities Serv. Oil Co.*, 188 F.2d 804, 806 (2d Cir. 1951) (Swan, J.), the same Court elaborated that the purpose of the warranty was to memorialize the relationship between the contracting entities: "the charterer bargains for the privilege of selecting the precise place for discharge and the ship surrenders that privilege in return for the charterer's acceptance of the risk of its choice." *Paragon* continued this tradition in contrasting the duty of a wharfinger (an admiralty term for an "owner or occupier of a wharf," *Black's Law Dictionary* 1733 (9th ed. 2009))—to exercise reasonable diligence in keeping its berth safe for incoming vessels—with that of a charterer who is contractually bound to provide "not only a place which he believes to be safe, but a place where the chartered vessel can discharge 'always afloat.'" 310 F.2d at 173 (citation and internal quotation marks omitted). *See also Venore Transp. Co. v. Oswego Shipping Corp.* 498 F.2d 469, 472 (2d Cir. 1974) (citing *Park S.S. Co.*, 188 F.2d at 804) (sub-charterer had a non-delegable "obligation to provide a completely safe berth," which was breached when it permitted the ship to dock at a berth that it knew was unsafe).

Thus, prior to the Fifth Circuit's decision in *Orduna*, "the law concerning safe ports had a rather secure berth in maritime law and it was well settled that a safe port clause in a charter constituted a warranty given by a charterer to an owner." Cooke *et al., supra*,

¶ 5.124. *Orduna* created quite a splash in veering from the view that a charterer warrants a ship's safety, and established instead for the Fifth Circuit that a safe berth warranty merely "imposes upon the charterer a duty of due diligence to select a safe berth." 913 F.2d at 1157. While *Orduna* acknowledged the Second Circuit's contrary perspective, it dismissed that [—30—] interpretation in deference to critical commentators, namely Professors Grant Gilmore and Charles L. Black. *Id.* at 1156 (citing Grant Gilmore & Charles L. Black, *The Law of Admiralty* § 4-4, at 204–06 (2d ed. 1975)). We do not find their criticism so compelling.[13]

Orduna concluded that "no legitimate legal or social policy is furthered by making the charterer warrant the safety of the berth it selects." *Id.* at 1157. Primarily, the Court reasoned that it is more sensible to impose fault on the "master on the scene" rather than a far away merchant charterer.[14] *Id.* at 1156

---

[13] Gilmore's book has been described as being

more adapted for the teacher than for the active lawyer or judge. As teachers, the authors are interested in controversy. Wherever they can find it, in the long past or in the nearer present, they stir it up, and frequently label it 'confusion.' … It is all very interesting; but in the various admiralty fields—except personal injury and death—most of the old controversies have long been settled. Therefore, our authors tend to give a picture which does not resemble the daily grist of today. Sometimes indeed, straining to keep old battle-fires ablaze, they sprinkle harsh words on the judges who settled the old disputes…. On the whole, this is a teaching book rather than an office and courtroom work of reference; and it must be read as such.

Arnold W. Knauth, Book Review, 58 Colum. L. Rev. 425, 426–28 (1958) (reviewing Grant Gilmore & Charles L. Black, Jr., *The Law of Admiralty* (1957)).

[14] *Orduna* also noted that a due diligence standard would not upset a master's ability to rely on a safe berth warranty in rejecting an [—31—] unsafe port. 913 F.3d at 1156. This goes only so far, as it addresses but half of the safe berth warranty's protection, which is both to provide a master with a

(citing Gilmore & [—31—] Black, *supra*, § 4-4, at 204–06). The appeal of this construction here is illusory. While an owner is liable for its master's superseding negligence, *see* Cooke *et al.*, *supra*, ¶ 5.151, we see no policy reason why a master on board a ship would normally be in any better position to appraise a port's more subtle dangers than the party who actually selected that port. The "commercial reality [is] that it is the charterer rather than the owner who is selecting the port or berth," *id.* ¶ 5.126, and the charterer is more likely to have at least some familiarity with the port it selected. After all, charterers do not select ports without good reason (and, in the case before us, CARCO was directly on the scene, *as it had selected its own berth*). Messrs. Gilmore and Black (famous in other areas of law—Gilmore on commercial law, including secured transactions, and Black on constitutional law) acknowledged that their rationale is undermined in those instances where a charterer has more knowledge of a danger than the master (although they explain that these situations could be remedied through tort liability[15]). We [—32—] disagree. To any extent a charterer, however distant, bargains to send a ship to a particular port and warrants that it shall be safe there, we see no basis to upset this contractual arrangement.

---

contractual excuse for avoiding an unsafe port and to protect for damages actually sustained in unsafe ports. Additionally, to the extent *Orduna* relied on *Atkins v. Fibre Disintegrating Co.*, 2 F. Cas. 78 (E.D.N.Y. 1868), *aff'd sub nom. Atkins v. The Disintegrating Co.*, 85 U.S. 272, 299 (1873), we are similarly unpersuaded. While *Atkins* featured a safe berth warranty, *id.* at 79, it was essentially an application of the named port exception. *See infra* Part IV.D. As the ship's master made outside inquiries and was fully aware of the port's dangers and yet did not object, he waived his right to complain later for damage. *Id.* at 79–80.

[15] Specifically, Gilmore & Black would find an actionable wrong for charterers directing ships to ports with known dangers, and [—32—] suggest that a charterer may sometimes be "so situated as reasonably to be charged with a duty of inquiry, particularly as to berth." Gilmore & Black, *supra*, §4-4, at 205.

We are persuaded that the Second Circuit's longstanding formulation of the safe berth clause is the one we should follow.[16] *See* 2 Schoenbaum, *supra*, § 11-10, at 32–33 (citing *The Gazelle*, 128 U.S. 474 (1888)) ("[I]f the ship reasonably complies with the order and proceeds to port, the charterer is liable for any damage sustained."); Stewart C. Boyd *et al.*, *Scrutton on Charter Parties and Bills of Lading,* Section IX, art. 69, at 127 (20th ed. 1996) (same); 2A Michael F. Sturley, *Benedict on Admiralty* § 175, at 17–25 (7th ed. 2012) (same); Coghlin *et al.*, *supra*, ¶ 10.110 (same). *But see* Gilmore & Black, *supra*, § 4-4, at 204–06.

Beyond the near consensus of these authorities, we are also convinced that an "express assurance" warranty is most consistent with industry custom. *See Park S.S.*, 188 F.2d at 806; *Cities Serv.*, 79 F.2d at 521. Vessel charters are formalized via "highly standardized forms," 2 Schoenbaum, *supra*, §11-1, at 4–5 (citation omitted). That some forms explicitly adopt a due diligence [—33—] standard[17] suggests that the understood default is to impose liability on the charterer without regard to the care taken. *See* Coghlin *et al.*, *supra*, ¶¶ 10.52, 10.54. Reading these warranties as dappled with due diligence would make contractual language explicitly adopting a due diligence metric pointless, and we disfavor contract interpretation "that 'render[s] at least one clause superfluous or meaningless.'" *Sloan & Co. v. Liberty Mut. Ins. Co.*, 653 F.3d 175, 181 (3d Cir. 2011) (alteration in original) (quoting *Garza v. Marine Transp. Lines, Inc.*, 861 F.2d 23, 27

(2d Cir. 1988)). Moreover, the "always afloat" language plainly suggests an express assurance. To the extent the Fifth Circuit in *Orduna* deviated from this well-established standard, we are not persuaded by its reasoning and decline to follow the course it charted.[18] Hence we conclude that the safe berth warranty is an express assurance made without regard to the amount of diligence taken by the charterer.

C. Was the Safe Berth Warranty Breached?

As explained, a berth is deemed safe when a ship may "proceed to it, use it, and depart from it without . . . being exposed to dangers." Coghlin *et al.*, *supra*, ¶ 10.123. As noted above, *see supra* note 11, CARCO conceded at oral argument that the safe berth warranty—if applicable—"would include the area in and around Paulsboro," including the Anchorage, and we therefore need not delineate the geographic sweep of this warranty. Thus having determined that Frescati was a beneficiary of CARCO's [—34—] safe berth warranty and that this warranty applies irrespective of a charterer's diligence, we proceed to whether the warranty was actually breached by the anchor's presence. Specifically, we need to determine whether the anchor rendered CARCO's port unsafe for a ship of the *Athos I*'s agreed-upon dimensions and draft.

That the *Athos I* was injured by the anchor does not automatically indicate that the warranty was breached. CARCO's safe berth warranty was not a blank check; it did not warrant that any ship would be safe at its port, but instead assured that the port would be safe for the *Athos I*. Boyd *et al.*, *supra*, Section IX, art. 69, at 129–30 (citations omitted) ("Whether a port is a 'safe port' is in each case a question of fact and degree and must be determined with reference to the particular ship concerned . . . ."); *In re Lloyd's*

---

[16] Though not dispositive, we also note that adhering to the Second Circuit's view on this issue promotes uniformity of maritime law along the mid-Atlantic seaboard. *See Sea-Land Serv., Inc. v. Dir., Office of Workers' Comp. Programs*, 552 F.2d 985, 995–96 n.18a (3d Cir. 1977) (noting deference pursuant to federal comity and uniformity in maritime law to the Second Circuit, "since [the Third Circuit] shares appellate review with the Second Circuit over the geographical area comprising one of the country's major east coast harbor complexes").

[17] As already mentioned, the time charter party between Star Tankers and Frescati contains such a standard, as it is predicated on a Shelltime 4 form. *See* Coghlin *et al.*, *supra*, ¶ 10.54.

---

[18] We are also unpersuaded that this warranty applies only to known hazards. This would effectively undermine the more strict nature of the warranty by requiring some level of due diligence, which, for the reasons above, we do not believe is the case.

Leasing Ltd., 764 F. Supp. 1114, 1135 (S.D. Tex. 1990) ("The safety of a port is to be determined with reference to the vessel and the circumstances surrounding that vessel's use of the port."). In this regard, the District Court correctly framed the ultimate issue as whether it was possible for a ship of the *Athos I*'s purported dimensions to reach CARCO's berth safely. *In re Frescati*, 2011 WL 1436878, at *6.

The Court, however, neglected to make the necessary factual findings to resolve whether the warranty was actually breached. Instead, it concluded "that the port and berth were generally safe" due to "the volume of commercial traffic that passed without incident," notwithstanding that it was impossible to know how many of those ships had actually passed over the anchor. *Id.* That similar ships had successfully berthed at the port is irrelevant to whether the warranty was actually breached in this case, as "[a] dangerous place may often be stopped at or passed over in safety." *The Gazelle*, 128 U.S. at 485. Instead, the Court should have evaluated whether the port was safe based on the facts particular to the *Athos I* and its arrival. [—35—]

From what we can glean from the record, it appears that CARCO warranted a safe berth with the understanding that the *Athos I* would be drawing as much as 37 feet of water upon its arrival. The Voyage Instructions indicate that the vessel would be filled with a quantity of crude oil "always . . . consistent with a 37 [foot] or less [fresh water] sailing draft at loadport," J.A. at 1242, and Captain Markoutsis confirmed this directive, Markoutsis Test. 199:5–9, Oct. 13, 2010. He testified, moreover, that he was "afraid of that draft," and opted to load the ship to only 36'6".[19] *Id.* at 200:7–25. This latter figure was confirmed by CARCO Port Captain William Rankine, who testified that the *Athos I* reported that it was drawing 36'6", Rankine

---

[19] We note there is minor disagreement as to this particular figure. While the record suggests that the *Athos I* was represented as drawing 36'6", Frescati explains that it was actually 36'7". This one-inch difference is on its face irrelevant to our analysis, as both drafts are less than 37 feet.

Test. 41:5–12, Nov. 22, 2010, and also by Steamship Agent Stephen Carroll, Carroll Test. 63:2–4, Oct. 7, 2010. In any event, the warranty made by CARCO appears to have covered the *Athos I* up to a draft of 37 feet.[20] Yet, as noted throughout this opinion, the District Court made no finding on the [—36—] vessel's actual draft at the time of the accident. This needs to be corrected on remand.[21]

If it is found that the *Athos I* was drawing 37 feet or less and absent a determination of bad navigation or seamanship,[22] that finding

---

[20] Of course, this is ultimately a factual matter for remand. As such, we also note that the Voyage Charter between CARCO and Star Tankers indicates that the "[l]oaded draft of Vessel on assigned summer freeboard [is] 12.423 meters [40.76 feet] . . . in salt water." J.A. at 1220 (Tanker Voyage Charter Party, Part I.A). While we understand this to mean that the *Athos I* could draw over 40 feet in salt water if filled to its summer capacity, the facts before us appear to indicate that it was directed to arrive at CARCO's port drawing 37 feet or less, and that this was the understood basis for the safe berth warranty.

[21] We note that there is record evidence suggesting that the promised 37 feet of clearance was indeed afforded, namely that Dr. Traykovski opined that there was—in his most conservative estimate—between 37.2 and 37.8 feet of water not only above the riverbed but the anchor itself (presumably at low tide). Traykovski Test. 49:12–50:24, Nov. 4, 2010.

[22] Although the warranty exception for abnormal weather conditions is not at issue here, CARCO argues that the exceptions for bad navigation and seamanship apply. CARCO's Br. at 77, 80; *see also* Coghlin *et al.*, *supra*, ¶¶ 10.148, 10.166 (citations omitted); Cooke *et al.*, *supra*, ¶5.151 (citation omitted); *Paragon*, 310 F.2d at 173–74 (quoting *Constantine & Pickering S.S. Co. v. W. India S.S. Co.*, 199 F. 964, 967–68 (S.D.N.Y. 1912)) ("It is true that one liable for violating a safe berth clause 'may lessen the amount of damages for which he is responsible by showing negligence, or even lack of diligence, on the part of the person wronged, in failing to take steps to lessen certain or even probable damages.'").
CARCO argues that the vessel's master and the navigation officer believed they were docking at high tide, and in fact were not (as the tide at the time of the accident was rising but an hour removed from low tide). However, we find no

would indicate that the warranty had been breached because the ship sustained damage. What, if anything, under the water may have caused that margin to be diminished is therefore [—37—] immaterial. It could have been the remnants of a shipwreck, a range of rocks, a jutting reef, or a shoal. In this case, it happened to be an abandoned anchor that protruded into the *Athos I*'s hull. And by its safe berth warranty, CARCO assumes liability for that damage.

If the draft at the time of the accident cannot be determined, or if the *Athos I* is found to have been drawing more than 37 feet, it will be necessary to ascertain the amount of clearance that existed above the anchor to conclude whether the promised 37 feet of water depth was actually provided.[23] Because it appears that CARCO assured a safe berth for a ship drawing 37 feet or less, our concern is whether 37 feet of clearance existed at the time of the accident.

D. The Named Port Exception

CARCO exposes one additional limitation to the broad protection generally afforded by the safe berth warranty—the named port exception. In essence, "[w]hen a charter names a port [—38—] and the master proceeds there without protest, the owner accepts the port as a safe port, and is bound to the conditions that exist there." *Bunge Corp.*

---

indication in the record that the *Athos I* was attempting to dock at an inappropriate time.

[23] If the vessel is found to have been drawing more than 37 feet, this could potentially reduce CARCO's liability even if it were determined that a safe berth was not provided. In this circumstance, the commentators note a trend in which damages resulting from both a breach of a safe berth warranty and the master's negligence may appropriately be split between the parties. Cooke *et al.*, *supra*, ¶ 5.152; 2A Sturley, *supra*, § 175, at 17-26; *see also Ore Carriers of Liber., Inc. v. Navigen Co.*, 435 F.2d 549, 550–51 (2d Cir. 1970) (affirming an order dividing a ship's damages between the owner and charterer where the charterer had warranted a safe port, but the owner nonetheless proceeded "with full knowledge of the probable unavailability of tug assistance," which was hazardous). In any event, these issues can also be resolved on remand.

v. M/V Furness Bridge, 558 F.2d 790, 802 (5th Cir. 1977) (internal quotation marks omitted) (quoting *Pan Cargo Shipping Corp. v. United States*, 234 F. Supp. 623, 638 (S.D.N.Y. 1964), *aff'd*, 373 F.2d 525 (2d Cir. 1967)). The purpose of the exception is to shift liability to the owner once a ship's master has had ample opportunity to discover a port's hazards.[24] As such, the exception may apply in instances in which a master—without lodging any objection—is charged "with full knowledge of local conditions which make it unsafe for that particular voyage." Coghlin *et al.*, *supra*, ¶10.158; *see also* Cooke *et al.*, *supra*, ¶ 5.130 ("[T]he master's conduct in entering a port he considers unsafe without raising a protest may result in a waiver of the safe port warranty.").

This formulation is essentially an application of the above-mentioned rule that negligent seamanship will nullify the safe port warranty: once a particular risk becomes known, it is then the master's responsibility to avoid it through competent seamanship [—39—] or to declare the port unsafe. This application of the exception does not apply to the case before us, however, as there is no suggestion that anyone—much less the master of the *Athos I*—had any inkling as to the anchor's existence in the River.

Instead, and more pertinent to the *Athos I*, the exception is also triggered when a particular port is named in the charter party. *See* Cooke *et al.*, *supra*, ¶ 5.130 ("If the charter names the ports or berths the vessel will call

---

[24] Although it never uses the term "named port exception," *Atkins v. Fibre Disintegrating Co.*, 2 F. Cas. 78 (E.D.N.Y. 1868), *aff'd sub nom. Atkins v. The Disintegrating Co.*, 85 U.S. 272, 299 (1873), is a paradigm for the exception. There, "the peril of the port was such that no vessel of [the ship's] size could get out without making her safety from the reefs dependent entirely upon the continuance of the breeze." *Id.* at 79. Predictably, the breeze failed, and the ship was damaged on the reef. *Id.* at 78. The trial court concluded, however, that the master could not rely on the agent's representation that the port was safe because he failed to object to the port after having "made inquiries . . . as to the character of the port, which was, moreover, fully described in the Coast Pilot [the official publication describing the coast]." *Id.* at 79–80.

at, the general rule is that the ports or berths will have been accepted by the owner as safe, such that the safe port/safe berth warranty is deemed to have been waived."); Coghlin *et al.*, *supra*, ¶ 10.164 (same) (citations omitted). This particular application of the exception is very broad and would seem poised to swallow the rule, but frequently the voyage charter will specify a range of ports, and thus the "safe [berth] warranty continues to play a role in voyage charters." Cooke *et al.*, *supra*, ¶5.123. In fact, this is such a case; the voyage charterer (CARCO) did not specifically name the discharge port in the voyage charter party, but instead directed that the *Athos I* would transit to one or two safe ports located somewhere on the United States Atlantic Coast, Gulf Coast, or the Caribbean Sea. J.A. at 1225 (Tanker Voyage Charter Party, Special Provision 2). CARCO nonetheless maintains that this exception applies even where the port location is not specifically named in the charter so long as some advance notice of the designated port is given. It is unclear how much notice would be required under CARCO's theory of the exception, although CARCO argues that it applies here because there is evidence that the master knew approximately two weeks before the accident that the *Athos I* would be headed to Paulsboro, New Jersey.

We need not address this issue of advance notice because we conclude that the hazard of the submerged anchor was not the sort contemplated by the exception. As explained above, the purpose of the named port exception is to "relieve[ ] the charterer of liability for damage arising from conditions at that port so long as [—40—] those conditions were *reasonably foreseeable*." *Duferco Int'l Steel Trading v. T. Klaveness Shipping A/S*, 333 F.3d 383, 387 (2d Cir. 2003) (emphasis added) (citations omitted). Without at least an opportunity to discover a particular port's specific pitfalls, the identity of the port would be irrelevant. This would defeat the purpose of naming the port, which is to excuse charterers for the results of hazardous conditions known to the master, not to exonerate them completely from all resulting liability.

In sum, here the particular hazard—the submerged anchor—was unknown to the parties. As the naming of CARCO's port ahead of time did not provide the *Athos I* with an opportunity to accept this unknown hazard, the exception does not come into play.[25]

V. The Tort Claims

Should its claim regarding CARCO's contractual liability not succeed, Frescati argues in the alternative that CARCO is liable as the owner of the terminal receiving the *Athos I* under two tort theories: negligence and negligent misrepresentation. The District Court held both theories inapplicable. Although we agree that the negligent misrepresentation claim fails on these facts, we disagree [—41—] with the Court's conclusion that Frescati's negligence claim is necessarily precluded.

A. Negligence

Negligence in admiralty law is essentially coextensive with its common law counterpart, requiring: (1) "[t]he existence of a duty required by law which obliges the person to conform to a certain standard of conduct"; (2) "[a] breach of that duty by engaging in conduct that falls below the applicable standard or norm"; (3) a resulting loss or injury to the plaintiff; and (4) "[a] reasonably close causal connection between the offending conduct and the resulting injury." 1 Schoenbaum, *supra*, §§ 5-2, at 252; *Pearce v. United States*, 261 F.3d 643, 647 (6th Cir. 2001) (citation omitted) (same).

---

[25] The District Court determined that although underwater hazards are a well-known threat, none of the parties had any reason to believe that Anchorage Number Nine was likely to conceal such a menace. *In re Frescati*, 2011 WL 1436878, at *2. To the extent the Court later determined that knowledge "in general of lost or abandoned objects in the river" was sufficient to trigger this exception, *id.* at *7, that amounted to an error of law. This sort of general knowledge cannot be used to impute knowledge of a specific condition, and we see no evidence that the Delaware River was known to be particularly treacherous in this regard.

Because this accident resulted in a clear loss, we address the existence of a duty, the potential breach of that duty, and causation. As discussed above, the wharfinger in this case—CARCO—contracted to provide the *Athos I* a safe berth. In the tort context, however, a wharfinger is not a guarantor of a visiting ship's safety, but is "'bound to use reasonable diligence in ascertaining whether the berths themselves and the approaches to them are in an ordinary condition of safety for vessels coming to and lying at the wharf.'" *Smith v. Burnett*, 173 U.S. 430, 436 (1899) (quoting, with approval, *The Calliope*, [1891] A.C. 11 (H.L.) 23 (appeal taken from Eng.)). This is not an unconstrained mandate to "ensure safe surroundings or warn of hazards merely in the vicinity." *In re Nautilus*, 85 F.3d at 116 (citing *Trade Banner Line, Inc. v. Caribbean S.S. Co., S.A.*, 521 F.2d 229, 230 (5th Cir. 1975)). Instead, a visiting ship may only expect that the owner of a wharf has afforded it a safe approach. *Id.* (citations omitted). In being invited to dock at a particular port, "a vessel should be able to enter, use and exit a wharfinger's dock facilities without being exposed to dangers that cannot be avoided by reasonably prudent navigation and seamanship." *Id.* [—42—]

While CARCO has a duty to maintain a safe approach to its terminal, we must determine the geographic scope of that duty.

i. The Scope of the Approach

The geographic scope of a safe approach has been largely unaddressed by the courts. Frescati argues that the scope should be inferred as a matter of custom and practice, and CARCO counters that the approach should be a function of the wharfinger's exertion of control. The District Court, in attempting to adopt a workable method of analysis, was chiefly concerned about CARCO's lack of control in the Anchorage and the absence of a limiting principle if it were to define the approach as the waters that a ship "naturally would traverse." *In re Frescati*, 2011 WL 1436878, at *4. Accordingly, it opted to limit the approach to "the area 'immediately adjacent' to the berth or within 'immediate access' to the berth." *Id.* (quoting

Western Bulk Carriers v. United States, No. S-97-2423, 1999 U.S. Dist. LEXIS 22371, at *20–21 (E.D. Cal. Sept. 14, 1999)). Such immediacy, we believe, sets too constricted a path to the berth. Instead, we hold that an approach should be understood by its ordinary terms, and that its scope is derived from custom and practice at the particular port in question.

Bouchard Transportation Co. v. Tug Gillen Brothers, 389 F. Supp. 77 (S.D.N.Y. 1975), is helpful in defining the geographic scope of an approach. It partially concerned a claim by a barge owner against the terminal owner for negligence in failing to maintain a safe approach and to warn of an unsafe condition. *Id.* at 79. The District Court there found that the approach began when the barge—traveling mid-channel up the Hudson River—altered its heading such that it was on a straight course to the terminal, which was the normal practice for ships docking there. *Id.* at 80. While executing this procedure, the barge grounded, its hull was [—43—] punctured, and oil was lost.[26] *Id.* at 80–81. *Bouchard* concluded that the terminal owner "was negligent in failing to maintain the approach to its terminal, in particular that area outside the river channel and within its dominion and control, normally utilized as the southerly approach to its ship dock, free of obstruction and safe for vessels approaching said terminal."[27] *Id.* at 81.

---

[26] The grounding in *Bouchard* occurred "immediately adjacent to the ballast dock," approximately 50 feet away. 389 F. Supp. at 81. This "immediately adjacent" language, however, does not refer to the beginning of the approach, but the location of the hazard within the approach. The District Court in our case adopted this language—citing *Western Bulk Carriers*, 1999 U.S. Dist. LEXIS 22371, at *20—as a "reasonable definition of 'approach.'" *In re Frescati*, 2011 WL 1436878, at *4. We believe this interpreted *Bouchard* incorrectly.

[27] CARCO argues that this reference to "dominion and control" is a prerequisite to *Bouchard*'s holding. We do not view control as a requirement, but as a fact of that case where the port was also deemed negligent for failing to warn of shallow waters in an area directly off its dock where it had previously dredged. 389 F. Supp. at 80, 83. Instead, in relying primarily on *Smith v. Burnett*, *Bouchard* held that the terminal owner

Less instructive, but still worth exploring, is *P. Dougherty Co. v. Bader Coal Co.*, 244 F. 267 (D. Mass. 1917). There, an invitation to use a particular dock in a charter party was construed to "extend[ ] to the approaches to the dock, and to the water which would naturally be traversed or used by a vessel discharging there." *Id.* at 270 (citing *Hartford & N.Y. Transp. Co. v. Hughes*, 125 F. [—44—] 981 (S.D.N.Y. 1903)). Although *P. Dougherty* is of limited usefulness on its facts (the Court was interpreting the parties' express agreement to use the dock), its conclusion that the wharfinger's obligation covered "individual approaches," distinguished from "the common channel," is nonetheless helpful. *Id.* More recently, *MS Tabea Schiffahrtsgesellschaft mbH & Co. KG v. Bd. of Com'rs of the Port of New Orleans*, No. 08-3909, 2010 WL 3923168, at *2 (E.D. La. Sept. 29, 2010), *aff'd*, 434 F. App'x 337 (5th Cir. 2011), similarly defined the approach as "the area through which vessels travel in order to move from the main channel of the river to the berth." *See also McCaldin v. Parke*, 37 N.E. 622, 624 (N.Y. 1894) (determining that a cluster of rocks "not in any channel which had to be used to approach the wharf," but potentially "in that part of the river used for general navigation," was not within the approach).

In light of these cases, we are persuaded by the suggestion in the maritime industry associations' *amici* brief that an approach should be afforded its plain meaning. *See* Mar. Indus. Ass'ns *Amici* Br. at 20. As a noun, "approach" is defined as "a drawing near in space or time," and "a way, passage, or avenue by which a place or a building can be approached." *Webster's Third New Int'l Dictionary* 106 (1971). This suggestion is persuasively illustrated by *amici's* reference to an airplane on final approach or a golf ball approaching the green. Both examples capture the intuitive meaning of the term as the beginning of a final, linear path to a fixed point. In fact, *Webster's* specifically

incorporates those examples into its definition, listing "a golfing stroke from the fairway for the green," "the steps and motion of a bowler before he delivers the ball," and the "descent of an airplane toward a landing strip." *Id.*

What is an approach should be given its same plain meaning in the maritime context; when a ship transitions from its general voyage to a final, direct path to its destination, it is on an approach. This is the most logical construction, and it comports with those [—45—] cases suggesting that an approach should be gleaned from actual practice. *See, e.g., Bouchard*, 389 F. Supp. at 80–81 (concluding that the approach began where vessels departed the channel on a direct course to the receiving dock and defined it pursuant to the area "normally utilized"). It also reflects the definition used in the maritime industry. For example, *The Mariner's Handbook* defines "approaches" as "[t]he waterways that give access or passage to harbours, channels, and similar areas." J.A. Petty, *The Mariner's Handbook* 226 (8th ed. 2004). Further, in most cases it will not result in a line-drawing problem, a concern raised by CARCO and shared by the District Court. Entire rivers, bays, and oceans will not be transformed into approaches. Instead, in most instances the approach will begin where the ship makes its last significant turn from the channel toward its appointed destination following the usual path of ships docking at that terminal. This analysis will necessarily vary on the characteristics of a particular port, and there will be close and difficult cases. Accordingly, we believe it may be useful to analogize the final approach of a vessel to a port to that of a driveway leading to a home from the public road.[28] It is the last [—46—]

---

simply "had a duty to ascertain any imminent dangers to [the ship] as it approached." *Id.* at 83. Further, to any extent *Bouchard* does suggest that control is required, we disagree for the reasons explained below.

[28] In *Smith v. Burnett*, the United States Supreme Court quoted a Massachusetts Supreme Court case making a similar comparison where a defendant failed to warn a schooner of a rock it knew of adjacent to its wharf.

This case cannot be distinguished in principle from that of the owner of land adjoining a highway, who, knowing that there was a large rock or a deep pit between the traveled part of the highway and his own

segment of the voyage leading directly to the host's door. Marine navigation is further complicated in that ships sometimes have the luxury of approaching through a variety of different courses across open water. Yet, so long as a ship is not approaching in an illogical, unreasonable, or disallowed manner, it will be deemed within its approach when it is within this final phase of its journey.

ii. Was the *Athos I* Within the Approach to CARCO's Terminal When the Accident Occurred?

Fortunately, the case before us is not one of the difficult ones, for the facts indicate that the *Athos I* was within the approach when it struck the anchor. First, the vessel was following the usual path for ships of its size docking at CARCO's terminal, having turned away from the channel at the usual point and was being pushed by two tugboats in a straight path toward CARCO's pier. Moreover, there were other indicators that the *Athos I* had ceased navigating generally and was within the final phase of its travel, namely that it was rotated sideways and, as noted, assisted by tugs. While not dispositive factors, these trappings indicate that the *Athos I* was no longer voyaging, but was configured solely for docking.

To the extent CARCO argues that the sphere of control exercised by it should be used to limit the scope of its duty,[29] we

___

gate, should tell a carrier, bringing goods to his house at night, to drive in, without warning him of the defect, and who would be equally liable for an injury sustained in acting upon his invitation, whether he did or did not own the soil under the highway. [—46—]

173 U.S. at 434 (quoting *Carleton v. Franconia Iron & Steel Co.*, 99 Mass. 216, 219 (1868) (internal quotation marks omitted)).

[29] In further support of this position, CARCO cites to *Sonat Marine Inc. v. Belcher Oil Co.*, 629 F. Supp. 1319 (D.N.J. 1985), aff'd, 787 F.2d 583 (3d Cir. 1986) (table). That case, however, does not apply on its facts, and uses a wharfinger's assumption of control to *expand*, rather than *limit*, the scope of its liability. Specifically, that wharfinger took the initiative secretly to widen its

[—47—] hold that a failure to exercise control over an area is not conclusive in this analysis. The appeal of *The Moorcock* long-ago dispatched this argument.[30] [1889] 14 P.D. 64 (Eng.). The steamship *Moorcock* was invited to be discharged and loaded at a particular wharf where it would be moored alongside the wharfingers' jetty. *Id.* at 64. Although the ship was expected to rest on the bottom of the River Thames at low tide, the particular section of riverbed was not actually under the wharfingers' control. *Id.* at 69. Even so, the Court explained that it "d[id] not follow that [the wharfingers] · are relieved from all responsibility. They are on the spot." *Id.* at 70. It continued:

> No one can tell whether reasonable safety has been secured except themselves, and I think if they let out their jetty for use they at all events imply that they have taken reasonable care to see whether the berth, which is the essential part of the use of the jetty, is safe, and if it is not safe, and if they have not taken such reasonable care, it is their duty to warn persons [—48—] with whom they have dealings that they have not done so.

Id.; *see also The Cornell No. 20*, 8 F. Supp. 431, 433 (S.D.N.Y. 1934) ("However, it is clear that the obligation of the wharfinger is not limited to the area of the land under water actually owned by it. . . . It impliededly [sic] represents to the master of a vessel who is

___

approach [—47—] because "it recognized that larger vessels had problems entering the barge berth and required a greater margin of safety." *Id.* at 1322. Insofar as the terminal operator had "assumed sufficient control over that area to attempt to ensure a proper approach to the ship and barge terminal," *id.* at 1327, it was deemed negligent for "fail[ing] to use means adequate[, such as side scans or wire drags,] to ensure that the new area where it thought larger barges could safely go was free of obstructions," *id.* at 1325. Control aside, the District of New Jersey Court also noted that a "safe approach to the berth had to include the additional . . . area." *Id.* at 1326.

[30] That the appeal of *The Moorcock* was operating under a theory of an implied contractual warranty does not reduce its import for purposes of this analysis. [1889] 14 P.D. 64 at 68 (Eng.).

induced to bring his vessel to its wharf that the berth and immediate access to it are reasonably safe for the vessel.").

In addition, insofar as the sphere of responsibility exercised by CARCO is a voluntary assumption of duty, it cannot be relied on to restrict the scope of a port owner's duty as a matter of law. Limiting a wharfinger's responsibility to areas in which it has affirmatively assumed responsibility would allow it to define the scope of its own liability regardless of the port's actual approach. Such a construction plays poorly against a policy that places logic and common sense over self-serving limitations of liability in the tort context. Moreover, we are not convinced that CARCO was actually precluded from extending its area of responsibility into the Anchorage. The record reflects that permission to it was not required for sonar scans, for example, and the record lacks an indication that CARCO could not have obtained a dredging permit for the Anchorage if it desired to do so.

We conclude that the *Athos I* was well within the approach to CARCO's terminal when the casualty occurred, and that it therefore had a duty to exercise reasonable diligence in providing the *Athos I* with a safe approach.

iii. Potential Breach of Duty to Maintain a Safe Approach

Having determined that the *Athos I* was within its approach when it was damaged and that CARCO therefore owed it a safe approach, did CARCO satisfy that duty by exercising the standard [—49—] of care required of a reasonable wharfinger under the circumstances? Although the "the nature and extent of the duty of due care is a question of law," factual issues predominate here as they do in most negligence litigation. *Redhead v. United States*, 686 F.2d 178, 182 (3d Cir. 1982). Thus, we review findings of negligence as factual findings for clear error. *See In re Moran Towing Corp.*, 497 F.3d 375, 377–78 (3d Cir. 2007); *Andrews v. United States*, 801 F.2d 644, 646 (3d Cir. 1986). As noted, there were no findings.

Negligence exists where there was a "fail[ure] to exercise that caution and diligence which the circumstances demanded, and which prudent men ordinarily exercise." *Grand Trunk R.R. v. Richardson*, 91 U.S. 454, 469 (1875). The admiralty context is no different, requiring "reasonable care under the particular circumstances." 1 Schoenbaum, *supra*, § 5-2, at 253 (citation omitted); *see also Smith*, 173 U.S. at 436 (remarking that wharfingers are "bound to use reasonable diligence" (citation and quotation marks omitted)). In admiralty, the particular duty required under any given circumstance can be gleaned from statute, custom, or "the demands of reasonableness and prudence." 1 Schoenbaum, *supra*, § 5-2, at 253 (citing *Pennsylvania R.R. v. S.S. Marie Leonhardt*, 202 F. Supp. 368, 375 (E.D. Pa. 1962), *aff'd*, 320 F.2d 262 (3d Cir. 1963)). Of course, "the degree of care which the law requires in order to guard against injury to others varies greatly according to the circumstances of the case." *Richardson*, 91 U.S. at 469–70.

On the facts before us, we are insufficiently informed to delineate the exact standard of care required by CARCO,[31] let [—50—] alone

---

[31] In evaluating the specific nature of this duty, the parties point to no statute on point and our research reveals none. As to custom, it "is only evidence of a standard of care[,] and violation of custom or adherence to it does not necessarily constitute negligence or lack of [—50—] negligence." *In re J.E. Brenneman Co.*, 322 F.2d 846, 855 (3d Cir. 1963) (citations omitted); *Norton v. Ry. Express Agency, Inc.*, 412 F.2d 112, 114 (3d Cir. 1969) ("Although not controlling, custom and practice may be shown to establish the standard of care to which the party charged with the wrongful act may be required to conform.").

The District Court also determined that no industry custom would have "put CARCO on notice that it should scan into the Anchorage." *In re Frescati*, 2011 WL 1436878, at *4. It is unclear if this apparent factual finding refers to other River terminals not searching their full approaches, federal waters generally, or Anchorage Number Nine specifically. Unfortunately, a review of the record leaves us similarly adrift. While several trial witnesses testified that they did not know of any Delaware River terminal taking precautionary action within federal waters, the Chief of Operations Division for the U.S. Army Corps of Engineers suggested that at least one terminal had

whether there was a breach of that standard (a.k.a. duty). That task rests with the District Court on remand should it need to reach the negligence claim.

iv. Causation

On remand, the District Court will also need to determine whether the failure, if any, to meet the standard of care proximately caused the accident. "Questions of causation in admiralty are [—51—] questions of fact." *Stolt Achievement, Ltd. v. Dredge B.E. LINDHOLM*, 447 F.3d 360, 367 (5th Cir. 2006); *see also In re Nautilus*, 85 F.3d at 116 (reviewing, in admiralty, a district court's determination as to causation for clear error).

The purpose of requiring proximate cause is "to limit the defendant's liability to the kinds of harms he risked by his negligent conduct." 1 Dan B. Dobbs *et al.*, *The Law of Torts* § 198, at 681 (2d ed. 2011) (citations omitted). Proximate cause is something of a misnomer in that it "is not about causation at all but about the appropriate scope of legal responsibility." *Id.* at 682. Instead, "proximate cause holds that a negligent defendant is liable for all the general kinds of harms he foreseeably risked by his negligent conduct and to the class of persons he put at risk by that conduct." *Id.* at 682–83; 1 Schoenbaum, *supra*, § 5-3, at 260–61 ("[T]he injury or damage must be a reasonably probable consequence of the defendant's act or omission.").

CARCO argues that proximate cause is lacking on these facts because the presence of an anchor in the anchorage was not foreseeable, especially by virtue of other ships arriving unharmed in the past. Once again, we decline to resolve this issue on the record

before us. CARCO further argues that proximate cause is lacking on the basis that the anchor-dropper was the actual cause of the accident. It is clear, however, "'that there may be more than one proximate cause of an injury.'" *Serbin v. Bora Corp.*, 96 F.3d 66, 75 (3d Cir. 1996) (quoting *Davis v. Portline Transportes Mar. Internacional*, 16 F.3d 532, 544 (3d Cir. 1994)).

More crucially, the issue is whether the accident would have been prevented had CARCO exercised its duty to act as a prudent wharfinger within the approach. At a minimum, this requires "that the injury would not have occurred without the defendant's negligent act." 1 Schoenbaum, *supra*, § 5-3, at 259. Here, the causation inquiry turns on whether prudent behavior—had it been exercised, a factual inquiry—would have prevented the injury. *See* [—52—] Dobbs *et al.*, *supra*, § 184, at 620. In light of CARCO's invitation that the *Athos I* arrive drawing 37 feet or less, *see supra* Part IV.C, it may be that the anchor lay sufficiently deep such that it would not have been detected even if CARCO had acted as a prudent wharfinger. Conversely, it could be the case that—even if the 37 feet of contractual clearance were provided—CARCO's duty as a wharfinger required something more. Should this be put in issue, further inquiry must occur as to what diligence was required of a prudent wharfinger, and only then can the District Court determine whether a failure to implement those procedures proximately caused the accident.[32]

Therefore, because factual issues remain to be resolved if Frescati's negligence claim becomes relevant, we also remand for further proceedings, as necessary, on this claim.

---

surveyed the federal waters preceding its berth. *See* DePasquale Test. 104:20–105:13, Oct. 6, 2010. Ultimately, the record is unhelpful on this point because we do not know if any of the terminals on the River had an approach that also traversed federal waters like CARCO's did. Of course, the only relevant consideration for custom would be similarly situated terminals, and we are unable to make any meaningful assessment of industry custom on these facts.

---

[32] We note that the District Court was "not convinced that had the area been scanned the anchor would perforce have been detected . . . ." *In re Frescati*, 2011 WL 1436878, at *4. We interpret the Court's remark as contemplating the effort required to detect the anchor absent an incident, as the anchor was in fact discovered with the use of side-scan technology.

B. Negligent Misrepresentation

Frescati argues that CARCO's failure to inform the *Athos I* of the reduction in maximum draft at its facility's ship dock prior to the vessel's arrival was a negligent misrepresentation. The District Court held otherwise, reasoning that "the area of concern was not the area where the casualty occurred and the draft at the berth was factually irrelevant to the casualty." *In re Frescati*, 2011 WL 1436878, at *5. We reach essentially the same result.

Negligent misrepresentation stems from a failure to exercise reasonable care in supplying incorrect information during the course of a business transaction. *Coastal (Berm.) Ltd. v. E.W.* [—53—] *Saybolt & Co., Inc.*, 826 F.2d 424, 428 (5th Cir. 1987) (citing *Grass v. Credito Mexicano, S.A.*, 797 F.2d 220, 223 (5th Cir. 1986)). The receiving party must rely on that false information and thereby suffer injury. *Id.* at 428–29 (citing same). This formulation, set out by § 552 of the Restatement (Second) of Torts, implicitly incorporates the standard elements of negligence: duty of care, a breach of that duty, injury, and causation. *See J.E. Mamiye & Sons, Inc. v. Fid. Bank*, 813 F.2d 610, 615 (3d Cir. 1987); 1 Schoenbaum, *supra*, § 5-2, at 252.

CARCO initially explained in its Port Manual that the allowable maximum draft at its Paulsboro facility was 38 feet, but this "may change from time to time and should be verified prior to the vessel's arrival." J.A. at 1095 (CITGO Terminal Regulations for Vessels ¶ 2). On November 22, 2004, four days before the *Athos I* arrived, CARCO's Port Captain Rankine announced internally that "the maximum draft at Paulsboro berth #1 (ship dock) has been reduced to 36-00 feet." J.A. at 1702. No one informed the *Athos I* of the change (and apparently its personnel did not inquire). This meant that the *Athos I* would have to enter CARCO's port under an exception to the maximum draft, and in any event Port Captain Rankine was comfortable with this because the *Athos I* would not be lying in the shallower area next to its dock

that motivated the draft reduction.[33] Rankine Test. 41:22–42:3, Nov. 22, 2010. [—54—]

On its terms, the reduction was limited to CARCO's ship dock. Although Frescati argues that the *Athos I* would not have berthed at CARCO's facility (its actual ship dock, but not the approach to it through the Anchorage) so early in the rising tide if its crew had known of the reduction in maximum allowable draft, this is irrelevant to its decision to enter Anchorage Number Nine—the site of the submerged anchor.

In this context, any misrepresentation about the ship dock is factually irrelevant to the accident because it did not occur at the dock, but rather 900 feet out in the Anchorage. There was no injury sustained that resulted from the failure to note the draft reduction at or immediately adjacent to CARCO's dock. Frescati's negligent misrepresentation claim thus fails on its merits as a matter of law.

VI. Effect of the Government's Settlement With CARCO

In its limited settlement agreement with the Government, CARCO promised not to

demand that the court reduce or offset the damages awarded to the United States against [CARCO] in the Lawsuit based on evidence that the negligence or fault of the United States in failing to detect, mark and/or remove underwater obstructions to navigation in the navigable waters of the Delaware River caused or contributed to the ATHOS I Incident.

---

[33] Rankine testified that such exceptions are common in the industry, and that he was not concerned for the *Athos I* because a ship drawing 37'3" had sat through low water just ten days before without harm. Rankine Test. 38:22-23, 41:22–42:9, Nov. 22, 2010. When the trial judge inquired about the rationale for making regular exceptions, Rankine replied that he was required by the guidelines to make the reduction, but that he did not "have any [—54—] worries about the depth of water in the area where the ship was going to sit." *Id.* at 45:18-25.

J.A. at 95 (Release ¶ 3.1(b)). It thus asks us to preclude CARCO on remand from raising any equitable defense premised on the Government's regulation of the Anchorage. CARCO responds that it retained unspecified equitable defenses relevant to defending [—55—] against, *inter alia*, the contractual claims, and that the Government conflates defenses to these claims with violations of CARCO's promise to forbear making claims against the Government sounding in tort to reduce or offset damages awarded to it.[34]

The Government also argues that the District Court mistakenly denied its earlier motion for summary judgment on CARCO's defense of equitable recoupment,[35] as that defense was really just a disguised attempt for indemnity or contribution payments. After hearing oral argument, the District Court denied the Government's pretrial motion on the ground "that the question of subrogation defenses [by CARCO] is better resolved with the benefit of a full trial record." J.A. at 101. CARCO claims that the Government failed to follow up at trial, and thus waived the issue. We agree, as we see no indication that the Government renewed its [—56—] argument at trial (or argued before us how the issue has not been waived). Thus, we decline to preclude CARCO from revisiting any previously raised

equitable defense to the Government's subrogation claims.

VII. Conclusion

Although remand is appropriate because the District Court failed to set out separate findings of fact and conclusions of law as required by Federal Rule of Civil Procedure 52(a)(1), our legal conclusions also make it necessary to remand for factual findings.

We conclude that the *Athos I*, and Frescati as its owner, are beneficiaries of CARCO's contractual safe berth warranty. This was an express assurance that CARCO's port would be safe for the *Athos I* within the scope of its invitation—that is, drawing 37 feet or less. Therefore, on remand it will need to be determined whether this amount of clearance was actually provided. This analysis may require inquiries into the arriving draft of the *Athos I* and, if the vessel was drawing more than the agreed-upon depth of 37 feet, the depth and positioning of the anchor.

CARCO's assertion of the named port exception is unavailing. Even if it were eligible on the type of notice given to the *Athos I*, its crew did not have an opportunity to accept a hazard (the anchor) that was unknown to the parties prior to the accident, and the exception is inapplicable.

We further conclude that, as this case is primarily a contractual one, analysis of Frescati's negligence claim is required only if the contractual safe berth warranty of CARCO is deemed satisfied. In that event, because we conclude that the accident occurred within the approach to CARCO's terminal, the District Court would need to determine the appropriate standard of care, whether it was breached, and, if so, was that breach a cause of the spill. The negligent misrepresentation claim, however, fails for [—57—] lack of factual causation because the alleged misrepresentation applied to an area unrelated to the accident.

Finally, we conclude that the Government has waived its reliance on its partial

---

[34] The Government argues that CARCO has attempted to circumvent this partial settlement agreement by presenting against it negligence claims couched as equitable defenses. CARCO explicitly retained "the right to raise affirmative defenses under any theory or doctrine of law or equity, the right to assert setoff or recoupment and the right to assert compulsory or non-compulsory counterclaims other than a Claim for Contribution or Indemnity . . . ." J.A. at 97 (Release ¶ 4.2). It was further agreed that the partial settlement would have no force as to CARCO's suit with Frescati. *Id.* at 97–98 (Release ¶ 4.3).

[35] Equitable recoupment is "[a] principle that diminishes a party's right to recover a debt to the extent that the party holds money or property of the debtor to which the party has no right." *Black's Law Dictionary, supra,* at 618. The competing claims must arise from the "same transaction." *Phila. & Reading Corp. v. United States,* 944 F.2d 1063, 1075 (3d Cir. 1991) (quoting *United States v. Dalm,* 494 U.S. 596, 608 (1990)).

settlement agreement in challenging CARCO's defenses to liability.

We thus affirm in part, vacate in part the District Court's judgment orders of April 12, 2011 against Frescati and the Government, and remand for further proceedings consistent with this opinion. Further appeals relating to this case will be referred to the current panel.

[—58—] Appendix A

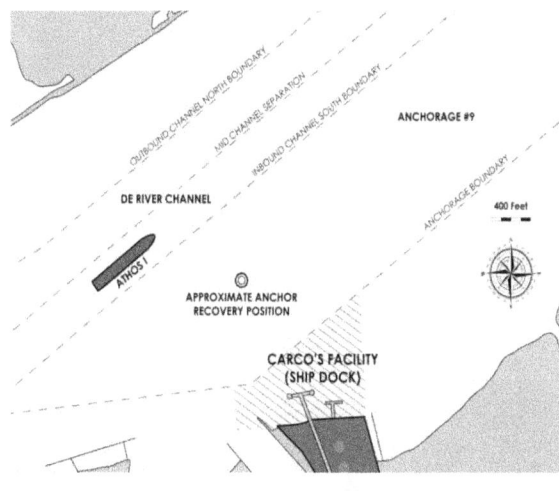

DE RIVER CHANNEL

OUTBOUND CHANNEL NORTH BOUNDARY

MID CHANNEL SEPARATION

INBOUND CHANNEL SOUTH BOUNDARY

ANCHORAGE #9

ANCHORAGE BOUNDARY

400 Feet

ATHOS I

APPROXIMATE ANCHOR RECOVERY POSITION

CARCO'S FACILITY (SHIP DOCK)

This page intentionally left blank

United States Court of Appeals for the Fourth Circuit

United States Court of Appeals
for the Fourth Circuit

No. 11-1900

VITOL, S.A.
vs.
PRIMEROSE SHIPPING CO.

Appeal from the United States District Court for the
District of Maryland

Decided: February 8, 2013

Citation: 708 F.3d 527, 1 Adm. R. 106 (4th Cir. 2013).

Before **MOTZ, AGEE,** and **THACKER**, Circuit Judges.

[—3—] **AGEE,** Circuit Judge:

Vitol, S.A. ("Vitol") brought the underlying action in the district court against Spartacus Navigation Corp. ("Spartacus") and Primerose Shipping Company ("Primerose") (collectively "S&P") seeking to "pierce the corporate veil" and enforce a judgment against S&P it had previously obtained against Capri Marine, Ltd. ("Capri Marine"). After determining that its exercise of admiralty jurisdiction was proper, the district court granted motions to dismiss and to vacate attachment filed by S&P. For the reasons stated below, we affirm the judgment of the district court.

I.

Background and Proceedings Below

In September 2000, the vessel ALAMBRA was involved in a marine pollution incident ("the Oil Spill") while in port in the country of Estonia. The ALAMBRA was owned by Capri Marine and chartered by Vitol at the time of the Oil Spill. Vitol brought suit against Capri Marine in the English High Court of Justice, Queen's Bench Division, Commercial Court, alleging that Capri Marine breached certain warranties of seaworthiness resulting in the Oil Spill and resulting damages. Vitol prevailed in the English court, and obtained a judgment in 2005 against Capri Marine in the amount of $6.1 million plus costs and interest ("the English Judgment"). The English Judgment remains unpaid and now totals over $9 million with accrued interest. During the English litigation, the ALAMBRA was sold for scrap by Capri Marine to Aurora Maritime ("Aurora") for approximately $2 million.

In 2009, Vitol filed a verified complaint (the "Verified Complaint") against S&P in United States District Court for the District of Maryland alleging that S&P (as well as other [—4—] named but not joined defendants)[1] were alter egos of Capri Marine, thereby seeking to enforce the English Judgment against S&P. In conjunction with its Verified Complaint, Vitol filed a motion, pursuant to Rule B(1)(a) of the Supplemental Rules for Admiralty or Maritime Claims and Asset Forfeiture Actions of the Federal Rules of Civil Procedure (the "Supplemental Rules"), requesting an *ex parte* order for issuance of process of maritime attachment, and prayed that the district court attach the vessel M/V THOR (then docked at Baltimore, Maryland), owned by Spartacus.[2]

The district court granted the motion and issued an *ex parte* order attaching the THOR. Shortly thereafter S&P entered a restricted appearance in the district court, posted a security bond, and reached a stipulation for the THOR's release by paying approximately $9 million into the district court as substitute collateral for the THOR (the "THOR Substitute Collateral").[3] Subsequently, S&P moved to vacate the attachment, pursuant to Supplemental Rule E, and to dismiss the Verified Complaint pursuant to Rule 12(b)(6) of the Federal Rules of Civil Procedure.

By order entered February 23, 2010, the district court granted the motions to vacate

---

[1] Capri Marine, Gerassimos Kaligaratos, and other related entities were named as defendants in Vitol's alter ego suit against S&P. These defendants, however, have not been served, were not parties to the district court proceedings, and are not parties to this appeal.

[2] Vitol sought Supplemental Rule B attachment of the THOR to initiate the underlying *quasi in rem* action against the defendants, S&P, who could not be found in the District of Maryland. *See* Fed. R. Civ. P. Adm. Supp. R. B(1)(a).

[3] Although the THOR is owned by Spartacus, it is managed by Primerose as a part of the Primerose fleet.

the attachment and dismiss the Verified Complaint (the "2010 Order"). In the 2010 Order, the district court addressed its jurisdiction over the action, as S&P contended that Vitol failed to state an admiralty claim and [—5—] therefore the district court lacked jurisdiction over the proceedings.

The district court determined that the action filed by Vitol sounded in admiralty even though the English Judgment was issued by the Commercial Court of the English High Court of Justice, not the English Admiralty court. The district court based its ruling on expert witness declarations stating that the underlying English action (relating to the Oil Spill) sounded in admiralty under English law, and could have been brought either in the Commercial or Admiralty court in England. On that basis, the court concluded Vitol's choice of forum in England was not dispositive for purposes of admiralty-based jurisdiction.

Having concluded it possessed competent jurisdiction in admiralty over the proceeding, the district court then held that Vitol had failed to state a claim upon which relief may be granted, and dismissed the Verified Complaint pursuant to Rule 12(b)(6). In early 2011, however, the district court granted Vitol leave to amend and Vitol filed an amended verified complaint (the "Amended Verified Complaint"), and stayed release of the THOR's Substitute Collateral. The Amended Verified Complaint contains the allegations relevant to this appeal.

Although the Amended Verified Complaint contains some thirty pages of detailed allegations related to Vitol's alter ego claim against S&P, the gravamen of that claim can be distilled into a short summary: Capri Marine is owned by Starlady Marine Ltd. ("Starlady"), an entity that is in turn controlled by Gerassimos and Ionnas Kalogiratos. Aurora, the company to which the ALAMBRA was sold for scrap, is actually a dummy corporation owned and operated as part of the Kalogiratos Group— a group of related shipping entities under the control of the Kalogiratos family. After the ALAMBRA was sold to Aurora, Aurora sold the ALAMBRA to a third party (for approximately

$3 million), and the proceeds from [—6—] the sale were used to pay down one of Capri Marine's loans, but not paid towards the Oil Spill damages. Primerose, which is owned by Nicholas Velliades (a non-party), was allegedly established with the remaining proceeds of the ALAMBRA sale. Velliades, the nominal principle of the Primerose fleet, is alleged to be a mere puppet of Gerassimos Kalogiratos ("Gerassimos"). Primerose uses the office facilities of Starlady without charge, engages in extensive comingling of funds and makes undocumented, uncollateralized, and unrepaid loans to Starlady or members of the Starlady fleet. In addition, Spartacus, which is also nominally controlled by Velliades, also shares office facilities with Primerose and Starlady, and put up no funds to secure the release of the THOR from attachment. Rather, the THOR Substitute Collateral was provided by Primerose.

S&P again moved to vacate the attachment and dismiss the Amended Verified Complaint. In an August 22, 2011 order (the "2011 Order"), the district court granted both motions, although it did conclude that Vitol had alleged sufficient facts to support a reasonable belief that Capri Marine is an alter ego of Gerassimos. The court pointed to allegations that Capri Marine was substantially undercapitalized at the time of the Oil Spill, that Capri Marine did not hold business meetings or keep corporate minutes, and that Gerassimos orchestrated the sale of the ALAMBRA to Aurora "for less than fair market value with the intent to defraud Capri [Marine]'s creditors, including [Vitol]." (J.A. 1563).

The court went on to conclude, however, that Vitol had failed to allege with sufficient particularity in the Amended Verified Complaint that S&P were alter egos of either Gerassimos or Capri Marine. The court discussed allegations made by Vitol that Gerassimos, not Velliades, was the "real" owner of Primerose (and related entities) and concluded that the allegations demonstrated only that Velliades' companies have a close relationship with Gerassimos' companies, but a close relationship is not sufficient as a matter of law to prove alter [—7—] ego status.

Further, the court found that dividends paid to the Kalogiratos family from their interest in Deep Blue Maritime S.A. ("Deep Blue") (another company principally owned by Velliades) did not "directly relate to Primerose or Spartacus and [ ] therefore [are] not probative as to whether Primerose or Spartacus are alter egos of Gerassimos." (J.A. 1569).

Because the Amended Verified Complaint failed to make a plausible allegation with sufficiently particularized facts (in accordance with Supplemental Rules B and E) that S&P are alter egos of Capri Marine, the district court found no basis for the further attachment of the THOR's Substitute Collateral and vacated the attachment. The court also found that the allegations were insufficient to show a plausible basis for relief pursuant to Rules 8 and 12, and granted the motion to dismiss the Amended Verified Complaint.

Vitol noted a timely appeal, posted a supersedeas bond, and the district court has stayed the order vacating the attachment of the THOR's Substitute Collateral pending appeal. We have jurisdiction pursuant to 28 U.S.C. § 1291.

On appeal, Vitol claims that the district court erred in vacating the attachment of the THOR and dismissing Vitol's Amended Verified Complaint for failure to state a claim. S&P respond that the district court was without jurisdiction to entertain the complaint in the first instance, and we should affirm the judgment in their favor on that ground. Alternatively, S&P argue that should the jurisdictional ruling be affirmed, the district court correctly held that Vitol's pleadings fail to state a claim upon which relief can be granted. We address the jurisdictional matter first, as we must verify jurisdiction in order to proceed. *See Sucampo Pharms., Inc. v. Astellas Pharma, Inc.*, 471 F.3d 544, 548 (jurisdiction is a "threshold" issue that must be resolved prior to resolving "an issue relating to the merits of the dispute, such as failure to state a claim"). [—8—]

II. Jurisdiction

An issue of the district court's subject matter jurisdiction is a question of law that the Court reviews *de novo*. *See North Carolina ex rel. Cooper v. Tenn. Valley Auth.*, 515 F.3d 344, 347 n. 1 (4th Cir. 2008).

S&P assert the district court's exercise of jurisdiction over this case was improper for two reasons. First, S&P contend the English Judgment is not an admiralty decree, and thus the district court here, sitting only in admiralty, lacked subject matter jurisdiction. Second, even if the district court had admiralty jurisdiction, S&P argue that Supplemental Rule B is a "pre-judgment" remedy only and could not be used to secure the appearance of a party once the English Judgment had been entered. We disagree with S&P's contentions and hold the district court did not err in its determination of jurisdiction.

A. Admiralty Jurisdiction

Congress has vested the district courts with, *inter alia*, original jurisdiction over "[a]ny civil case of admiralty or maritime jurisdiction." 28 U.S.C. § 1333. Central to this appeal, then, is the question of whether Vitol's Amended Verified Complaint sounds in admiralty so as to invoke the district court's admiralty jurisdiction under § 1333.

It is well recognized that federal courts in the United States possess jurisdiction in admiralty over claims to enforce a foreign admiralty judgment. *See, e.g.*, 1 Benedict on Admiralty § 106 ("[A]dmiralty jurisdiction in the United States may be broadly stated as extending to ... any claim to enforce a judgment of a foreign admiralty court."). Even in the earliest days of the Republic, the Supreme Court confirmed that the courts of the United States possess jurisdiction to recognize the admiralty decrees of foreign admiralty courts. *See Penhallow v. Doane's Adm'rs*, 3 U.S. (3 Dall.) 53, 97 (1795) (Iredell, J.) [—9—] ("It was clearly shown at the bar, that a Court of Admiralty, in one nation, can carry into effect the determination of the [C]ourt of Admiralty of another.").

American courts have long and consistently held that admiralty jurisdiction was well-founded to enforce the judgments of foreign admiralty courts. *See, e.g., Otis v. The Rio Grande*, 18 F. Cas. 902, 903 (C.C.D. La. 1872) (No. 10,613), *aff'd* 90 U.S. 458 (1874) ("This court is in duty bound to carry into effect the sentences and decrees, not only of other federal courts, but even of the admiralty courts of foreign countries...."); *The Jerusalem*, 13 F. Cas. 559, 563 (C.C.D. Ma. 1814) (No. 7,293) (admiralty court "will enforce a foreign maritime judgment between foreigners, where either the property or the person is within its jurisdiction"); *Int'l Sea Food Ltd. v. M/V Campeche*, 566 F.2d 482, 485 (5th Cir. 1978) (citing *The Centurion*, 5 F. Cas. 369, 370 (No. 2,554) (D. Me. 1839)) ("[A]n admiralty court has jurisdiction to enforce any judgment of another admiralty court....").

While acknowledging this established precedent, S&P assert that it is inapplicable here because the English Judgment is not an "admiralty judgment" so as to be entitled to recognition by the admiralty courts of the United States. This is so, S&P argue, for two reasons. First, the Commercial Court (rather than the Admiralty Court) of the English High Court of Justice, Queen's Bench Division, issued the English Judgment. Second, in any event, the English Judgment, having been reduced to a judgment debt, is now merely a monetary award that itself lacks any maritime character.

B. Choice of English Forum

The thrust of S&P's first argument is that because Vitol elected to pursue legal action against Capri Marine in the Commercial Court of the English High Court of Justice, rather than the Admiralty Court, the English Judgment was not an [—10—] admiralty judgment and therefore no admiralty jurisdiction can exist in the case at bar. We do not agree.

Vitol and S&P proffered declarations to the district court from their respective experts on English law. Those experts agreed that the type of maritime claim brought by Vitol against Capri Marine could have been brought in *either* the Commercial Court or the Admiralty Court. Julia Dias, *Spartacus'* own expert, averred that there is a "considerable overlap between admiralty claims falling within the Admiralty jurisdiction of the High Court ... on the one hand, and commercial claims on the other." (J.A. 136-37). Dias went on to state that "[Vitol] properly and legitimately elected to commence proceedings and pursue its claim in the Commercial Court rather than the Admiralty Court as it was entitled to do[,]" and noted that "it is entirely commonplace in my experience for claims such as Vitol's which involve issues of unseaworthiness to be brought in and heard by the Commercial Court." (J.A. 138). Finally, Dias stated that "[h]ad Vitol elected to bring the claim in the Admiralty Court, it would almost certainly have proceeded and been handled in much the same way as it actually was." (*Id.*).

Vitol's expert on English law, Luke Parsons, offered a substantially similar declaration with respect to the structure of the English Admiralty and Commercial Courts. Parsons agreed with Dias' assessment that Vitol's claim against Capri Marine could have been brought in either court, and similarly described the jurisdictional overlap between the two. Parsons concluded "the claim made by Vitol in this case, is an 'admiralty claim' within the meaning of [English Law] and are claims which the Admiralty Court and Commercial Court both have the jurisdiction and expertise to hear." (J.A. 360).

The expert declarations are illuminating, particularly to the degree the experts of the adverse parties are in agreement concerning the application of English law. These expert declarations, considered together, plainly demonstrate that Vitol's [—11—] action against Capri Marine could have been brought in the English Admiralty Court, i.e., that it was an admiralty claim as that term is understood by the courts of England. S&P, however, ask this Court to hold that the choice of forum in England, not the subject matter of the underlying claim, is dispositive of whether jurisdiction lies with the district court pursuant to 28 U.S.C. § 1333. In other words, S&P contend that Vitol's choice of forum in the English Commercial Court for an otherwise valid admiralty claim there divests any resulting judgment of its admiralty character in this country so it can no longer be considered as an admiralty matter. We find this argument unpersuasive and unsupported.

The approach advocated by S&P, which looks purely to form at the expense of substance, is unsupported by citation to any case as authority for its position. Indeed, the dispositive question is not whether the English Judgment issued from an "admiralty court," but rather, whether the claim itself is maritime in nature. *See Victrix S.S. Co., S.A. v. Salen Dry Cargo A.B.*, 825 F.2d 709, 713 (2d Cir. 1987) ("[A]n admiralty court has jurisdiction of a claim to enforce a foreign judgment *that is itself based on a maritime claim.*") (emphasis added). Inasmuch as the English Commercial Court exercised jurisdiction over a maritime claim, we agree with the district court's conclusion that "the Commercial Court was an admiralty court with respect to the English Judgment." (J.A. 991-92).

C. Reduction to Monetary Award

We also reject S&P's separate contention on appeal that because the English Judgment has been reduced to a monetary award it now lacks the maritime character necessary to being considered an admiralty judgment which would deprive the district court of jurisdiction in this proceeding. The Fifth Circuit's decision in *Int'l Sea Food Ltd. v. M/V Campeche*, 566 F.2d 482 (5th Cir. 1978) is instructive on this issue.

In *Campeche*, the sole issue before the court was "whether a United States district court has subject matter jurisdiction in [—12—] admiralty to enforce a foreign maritime decree which awarded monetary damages to the plaintiff on a claim for collision." 566 F.2d at 483. In finding the district court possessed jurisdiction, the Fifth Circuit looked to *The Centurion*, 5 F. Cas. 369 (D. Me. 1839) (No. 2,554), which addressed the jurisdiction of an admiralty court to enforce a monetary award made in an arbitration

arising out of a salvage dispute. The *Centurion* court reasoned that

> [a]lthough the admiralty has a general jurisdiction over maritime contracts and quasi contracts, and things done on the sea, it does not follow that the payment of a debt in every form which it may assume can be enforced in the admiralty, simply because it originated in a contract ... which was within the jurisdiction of the court[,]

5 F. Cas. at 370, and concluded that admiralty jurisdiction did not lie to enforce the arbitration agreement award. The *Centurion* court noted, however, that if the underlying matter "had been decided by a regular decree of a court of admiralty by which a specific sum were awarded to the libellant, this court could have taken cognizance of the case, because a court of admiralty has jurisdiction to carry into execution the decree of another court of admiralty." *Id*. Thus, the fact that the debt at issue in *The Centurion* arose from an arbitration award was dispositive. Had the debt been established by way of an admiralty court judgment, then admiralty jurisdiction would be present in a subsequent proceeding to enforce that judgment.

The *Campeche* court thus read the language of *The Centurion* to "suggest[ ] that an admiralty court has jurisdiction to enforce any judgment of another admiralty court *regardless of its lack of maritime flavor.*" 566 F.2d at 485 (emphasis added). The Fifth Circuit accordingly held that the district [—13—] court possessed jurisdiction over the money-judgment enforcement action in that case.[4]

---

[4] S&P urge us to distinguish *Campeche* on the grounds that the underlying dispute revolved around the interpretation of a maritime insurance contract. Thus, the subsequent trial in that case would involve issues of a maritime flavor.

While S&P correctly recite an additional rationale for the *Campeche* court's decision, they are incorrect to suggest that the presence of a second justification somehow undermines the primary basis of jurisdiction: that the money judgment was the decree of an admiralty court. Indeed, the *Campeche* court squarely addressed the

In light of *Campeche*, we are persuaded that the fact that the judgment Vitol ultimately seeks to recognize is now a monetary award does not defeat the district court's admiralty jurisdiction because that prior judgment was rendered by a competent court sitting in admiralty. Consistent, therefore, with a long line of cases confirming American admiralty jurisdiction over actions to enforce foreign admiralty judgments, we reject S&P's argument that the district court lacked admiralty jurisdiction over Vitol's action.

D. Supplemental Rule B

S&P's next contention is that Supplemental Rule B could not be used to attach the THOR. In S&P's view, since they were not parties to the English Proceeding resulting in the English Judgment, the current action is only a post-judgment enforcement action against them and not a maritime claim subject to Supplemental Rule B. In support of their argument, S&P recite language from the Second Circuit's decision in *Williamson v. Recovery Ltd. Partnership*, 542 F.3d 43, 48 (2d Cir. 2008), which states, *inter alia*, that attachment pursuant to Supplemental Rule B is recognized as a "pre-judgment mechanism used by parties in admiralty cases to secure jurisdiction over an absent party and to obtain security for potential judgment where the absent party's assets are transitory." **[—14—]** We find S&P's reading a strained construction and contrary to a long line of precedent in admiralty cases.

Supplemental Rule B provides in pertinent part:

> If a defendant is not found within the district when a verified complaint praying for attachment and the affidavit required by Rule B(1)(b) are filed, a verified complaint may contain a prayer for process to attach the defendant's tangible or intangible personal property—up to the amount sued for—

in the hands of garnishees named in the process.

Fed. R. Civ. P. Adm. Supp. R. B(1)(a).[5]

Initially, we note that the limitation suggested by S&P, i.e., that Supplemental Rule B must be strictly construed as a prejudgment remedy, does not appear in the text of the rule. **[—15—]** Rather, the plain wording of the rule itself requires only that the defendants not be present in the district wherein the Rule B prayer is filed, and that the plaintiff file an affidavit in accordance with Supplemental Rule B(1)(B) that the prospective defendant's property is present in the district. In this case, Vitol has unquestionably complied with both requirements. Indeed, in *Aqua Stoli Shipping Ltd. v. Gardner Smith Pty Ltd.*, the Second Circuit opined that where a plaintiff has satisfied the two-part Supplemental Rule B(1)(B) test, a district court should only vacate attachment in "limited" circumstances: "that

---

[5] The Second Circuit has provided a useful history of the maritime attachment process that aids in our analysis of S&P's argument.

Maritime attachment is a feature of admiralty jurisprudence that antedates both the congressional grant of admiralty jurisdiction to the federal district courts and the promulgation of the first Supreme Court Admiralty Rules in 1844. *Aurora Mar. Co. v. Abdullah Mohamed Fahem & Co.*, 85 F.3d 44, 47 (2d Cir. 1996). In fact, "[t]he use of the process of attachment in civil causes of maritime jurisdiction by courts of admiralty … has prevailed during a period extending as far back as the authentic history of those tribunals can be traced." *Atkins v. The Disintegrating Co.*, 85 U.S. (18 Wall.) 272, 303, (1874). The power to grant attachments in admiralty is an inherent component of the admiralty jurisdiction given to the federal courts under Article III of the Constitution. U.S. Const. art. III, §2. The power's historical purpose has been two-fold: first, to gain jurisdiction over an absent defendant; and second, to assure satisfaction of a judgment. *Swift & Co. Packers v. Compania Colombiana Del Caribe, S.A.*, 339 U.S. 684, 693 (1950).

Aqua Stoli Shipping Ltd. v. Gardner Smith Pty Ltd., 460 F.3d 434, 437-38 (2d Cir. 2006).

---

identical issue before this Court in the case at bar and we find its rationale persuasive.

[the defendant] would be subject to *in personam* jurisdiction in an adjacent district, that [the defendant] was located and subject to personal jurisdiction in the same district as [the plaintiff], or that [the plaintiff] had already obtained sufficient security." 460 F.3d 434, 447 (2d Cir. 2006). S&P do not assert that any of those limited circumstances are present here. Therefore, we conclude the language of Supplemental Rule B did not on its face bar the THOR's attachment.

As the district court recognized, ample precedent reflects that Supplemental Rule B has been used to attach admiralty defendants' property in actions to enforce a foreign admiralty judgment. *See, e.g., Campeche,* 566 F.2d at 483 (finding admiralty jurisdiction where Supplemental Rule B used to garnish judgment debtor's proceeds in district); *Good Challenger Navagante S.A. v. Metalexportimport S.A.,* No. 06-cv-1847 (KMK), 2006 U.S. Dist. LEXIS 97920 at *1 (S.D.N.Y. July 24, 2006) (upholding Supplemental Rule B attachment in action to enforce the judgment of English Commercial Court); *Pink Goose (Cayman) Ltd. v. Sunway Traders LLC,* No. 08-cv-2351 (HB), 2008 WL 4619880, at *1 (S.D.N.Y. Oct. 17, 2008) (upholding Supplemental Rule B attachment in action to enforce foreign arbitration award).

S&P, however, emphasize that courts have described Supplemental Rule B as a "pre-judgment" remedy, *e.g., Williamson,* 542 F.3d at 48, and argue that it should not be used in a case such as this, where a judgment has already issued from [—16—] a foreign admiralty court, and Vitol's claim is one to collect on that judgment. We believe, however, that "pre-judgment," as it is used in the Supplemental Rule B context, must be understood to mean prior to the judgment in the particular case where a plaintiff seeks to use Supplemental Rule B. It makes little, if any, sense to construe Supplemental Rule B otherwise when centuries of settled hornbook admiralty law establish that "admiralty jurisdiction in the United States may be broadly stated as extending to ... any claim to enforce a judgment of a foreign admiralty court." Benedict, *supra,* § 106; *see also Penhallow,* 3 U.S. at 97 (Iredell, J.) ("It was

clearly shown at the bar, that a Court of Admiralty, in one nation, can carry into effect the determination of the [C]ourt of Admiralty of another.").

Vitol seeks, as an absolutely necessary condition precedent to an action to enforce the English Judgment, a prior separate and independent judgment against S&P that those entities are the alter ego of Capri Marine and/or the Kalogiratos group. "It is well established that an admiralty court can review questions of ... alter ego." *Ost-West-Handel Bruno Bischoff GMBH v. Project Asia Line, Inc.,* 160 F.3d 170, 174 (4ᵗʰ Cir. 1998) (citing *Swift & Co. Packers v. Compania Colombiana Del Caribe,* 339 U.S. 684, 689 n. 4 (1950)). Attachment of the THOR under Supplemental Rule B is thus cleary a pre-judgment mechanism in the sense which establishes jurisdiction over S&P for adjudication of the alter ego dispute. This seems the logical conclusion here as Vitol's prayer in the Amended Verified Complaint is for judgment against S&P as the alter ego of Capri Marine. Only armed with that initial judgment can Vitol proceed to enforce the English Judgment.

Moreover, it would be difficult to understand the long line of cases, discussed *supra* at 8-9, extending the admiralty jurisdiction of the United States district courts to actions to enforce the decrees of foreign admiralty courts, if the limitation suggested by S&P was correct. We simply do not believe, based on the text of Supplemental Rule B and the long line [—17—] of admiralty precedent, that a plaintiff seeking to enforce a foreign admiralty judgment could avail itself of the courts of admiralty in the United States, yet be deprived of the use of the district court's power to attach assets: an "inherent component of the admiralty jurisdiction given to the federal courts." *Aqua Stoli,* 460 F.3d at 437.[6]

---

[6] Had Vitol already obtained a judgment in the district court against S&P and a later time then sought to attach their assets to satisfy a previously docketed judgment, in that circumstance, Vitol's attempt to use Supplemental Rule B might be seen as a prohibited post-judgment action. In that limited circumstance, Vitol might be required to

In re Stolt-Nielsen Transp. Grp. B.V., No. 06 Civ. 703 (NRB), 2008 WL 650391 (S.D.N.Y. Mar. 7, 2008), *aff'd sub nom. Stolt-Nielsen Transp. Grp. v. Lio Yag Sanayi Ve Ticaret A.S.*, 330 F. App'x 207 (2d Cir. 2009) (unpublished), cited by S&P in support of their construction of Supplemental Rule B, actually lends support to the construction that we adopt. In that case, the plaintiff initially brought the complaint against the defendant without Supplemental Rule B attachment, apparently because the defendant was located within the district. The defendant left the district and a default judgment was ultimately entered in favor of the plaintiff. Thereafter, the plaintiff attempted to use Supplemental Rule B to attach the defendant's property. The court rejected the plaintiff's attempts, finding that because a default judgment had already been entered by the court, "[plaintiff's] motion is essentially a plea for us to allow it to use [Supplemental] Rule B as [a] judgment collection device." *Id.* 2008 WL 650391, at *2.

By contrast, the district court in the case at bar had not entered any judgment against S&P at the time the *ex parte* motion for Supplemental Rule B attachment was filed by Vitol. What Vitol sought was to establish jurisdiction through Supplemental Rule B in the District of Maryland so its under- [—18—] lying alter ego complaint could be adjudicated; not to enforce the English Judgment in the first instance, although we are not at all certain that usage is barred by the Rule. In any event, Vitol's use of Supplemental Rule B was entirely consistent with the rule's purpose: "to permit the attachments of assets wherever they can be found and not to require the plaintiff to scour the globe to find a proper forum for suit or property of the defendant sufficient to satisfy a judgment." *Transportes Navieros y Terrestres S.A. de C.V. v. Fairmount Heavy Transp. N.V.*, 572 F.3d 96, 103 (2d Cir. 2009).

Accordingly, we reject S&P's arguments either that the district court lacked admiralty

---

use other attachment or judgment enforcement procedures in lieu of Supplemental Rule B. However, that situation is not present in this case and we need not speculate here on what decision would be required should those events occur.

jurisdiction or that the attachment of the THOR was a misuse of Supplemental Rule B.

III. The Merits

Turning to the merits of this appeal, Vitol argues that the district court erred in concluding that the Amended Verified Complaint failed to adequately plead a claim under Rule 8 of the Federal Rules of Civil Procedure or Supplemental Rule E(2)(a). Under Rule 8(a), a pleading must contain "a short and plain statement of the claim showing that the pleader is entitled to relief, in order to give the defendant fair notice of what the claim is and the grounds upon which it rests." *Bell Atl. Corp. v. Twombly*, 550 U.S. 544, 555 (2007) (internal citations, quotation marks, and alterations omitted). A district court should dismiss a complaint pursuant to Rule 12(B)(6) if, accepting all well-pleaded allegations in the complaint as true and drawing all reasonable factual inferences in the plaintiff's favor, the complaint does not allege "enough facts to state a claim to relief that is plausible on its face." *Id.* at 570. Under Rule 12(e), a "party may move for a more definite statement of a pleading to which a responsive pleading is allowed but which is so vague or ambiguous that the party cannot reasonably prepare a response."

By contrast, Supplemental Rule E(2)(a), the governing pleading standard for Supplemental Rule B proceedings, [—19—] states that "the complaint shall state the circumstances from which the claim arises *with such particularity that the defendant or claimant will be able, without moving for a more definite statement, to commence an investigation of the facts and to frame a responsive pleading.*" (emphasis added).

The remedy for failure to comply with the pleading standards of Supplemental Rule E(2)(a) is set forth in Supplemental Rule E(4)(f), which provides that "[w]henever property is arrested or attached, any person claiming an interest in it shall be entitled to a prompt hearing at which the plaintiff shall be required to show why the arrest or *attachment should not be vacated* or other relief granted consistent with these rules." Fed. R. Civ. P.

Adm. Supp. R. E(4)(f) (emphasis added). Thus, the primary remedy afforded for failure to comply with Rule E(2)(a) is vacatur of the attachment. Dismissal of the complaint is not a Rule E remedy. *See Chiquita Int'l Ltd. v. MV BOSSE*, 518 F.Supp. 2d 589, 596 (S.D.N.Y. 2007) ("Rule E(4)(f) allows a motion for vacatur of attachment, but does not provide for dismissal.").

Counsel for S&P, however, suggested at oral argument that dismissal of the complaint automatically flows from vacatur of the Supplemental Rule B attachment because, absent Supplemental Rule B attachment, the courts lacks jurisdiction over S&P. Oral Argument Audio Recording at 33:30.[7] This argument fails as a matter of law.

In *Republic National Bank of Miami v. United States*, 506 U.S. 80 (1992), the Supreme Court rejected the notion that, in an *in rem* civil forfeiture action, the district court's continued [—20—] control of the *res* is necessary for the court to retain jurisdiction over the forfeiture proceedings. *See id.* at 84. In that case, following a civil forfeiture proceeding in which the Government prevailed, the United States Marshal transferred the *res* (the proceeds of a sale of certain assets) from his control to the United States Treasury. *Id.* at 83. Although the claimant timely appealed from the judgment against it, the claimant did not move to stay execution of the judgment or post a supersedeas bond. Once the assets were removed from the court's control, the Government sought to dismiss the claimant's appeal for lack of jurisdiction. The court of appeals granted the motion to dismiss the appeal, but the Supreme Court reversed.

After a lengthy discussion of both maritime and forfeiture cases, the Supreme Court held that "[s]tasis is not a general prerequisite to

the maintenance of jurisdiction. Jurisdiction over the person survives a change in circumstances." *Id.* at 88. The seizure of the *res*, the Court concluded, "and the publication of the monition or invitation to appear, is regarded as equivalent to the particular service of process in the courts of law and equity." *Id.* at 85. In sum, while control over the *res* is a prerequisite to initiation of the *in rem* action, the court does not need to continuously possess the *res* to maintain jurisdiction once established.[8]

The *in rem* principle articulated in *Republic National Bank* has been extended to *quasi in rem* proceedings, including those arising under Supplemental Rule B. *See Stevedoring* [—21—] *Servs. of Am. v. Ancora Transp., N.V.*, 59 F.3d 879, 882 (9th Cir. 1995) ("[The *Republic National Bank* rationale] applies with equal persuasiveness to *quasi in rem* proceedings instituted under [Supplemental] Rule B."). We find the logic of *Republic National Bank* applicable in the case at bar.[9] *See Woodlands Ltd. v. Nationsbank N.A.*, 164 F.3d 628 (table), No. 97-1813, 1998 WL 682156 (4th Cir. Sept. 23, 1998) (applying *Republic National Bank* in a Supplemental Rule B maritime attachment case). Thus, even if the attachment of the THOR was vacated under Supplemental Rule E, that event would not, in and of itself, act to terminate the jurisdiction of the district court as to the Amended Verified Complaint.

---

[7] Although it appears that S&P did not previously advance the argument that dismissal of the complaint flows automatically from vacatur of the attachment, we address the argument because it implicates the subject matter jurisdiction of the district court and "[s]ubject matter jurisdiction cannot be forfeited or waived." *See In re Kirkland*, 600 F.3d 310, 314 (4th Cir. 2010).

[8] The Court acknowledged that "if a defendant ship stealthily absconds from port and leaves the plaintiff with no *res* from which to collect, a court might determine that a judgment would be useless." *Republic Nat'l Bank*, 506 U.S. at 87 (internal quotation marks and citations omitted). Nevertheless, the Court reasoned that "the fictions of *in rem* forfeiture were developed primarily to expand the reach of the courts and to furnish remedies for aggrieved parties, not to provide a prevailing party with a means of defeating its adversary's claim for redress." *Id.* (internal citations omitted).

[9] Moreover, if we were to conclude that dismissal of the complaint automatically flowed from the grant of a motion to vacate the attachment, Supplemental Rule E would effectively subsume Rules 8 and 12 in the context of admiralty and forfeiture cases. No court has extended the supplemental rules in that way and neither do we.

As dismissal of the complaint is not a proper remedy under Supplemental Rule E, and because dismissal does not automatically flow from vacatur of Supplemental Rule B attachment, we must, as the district court endeavored to do, analyze Vitol's claims through the lens of both Supplemental Rule E and Rules 8 and 12. As the district court observed, "it is at least theoretically possible that a Complaint adequate to withstand a Rule 12(b)(6) motion may, nevertheless, not be adequate to avoid the vacatur of an attachment." (J.A. 1551). We now describe the standards under the two sets of rules and then apply those standards to the merits of Vitol's Amended Verified Complaint.

A. Supplemental Rule E Standard

We review the district court's order vacating the attachment of the THOR's Substitute Collateral for abuse of discretion, with legal conclusions underlying the order reviewed *de novo*. *See ProShipLine Inc. v. Aspen Infrastructures Ltd.*, 609 F.3d [—22—] 960, 966 (9th Cir. 2010); *Shipping Corp. of India Ltd. v. Jaldhi Overseas Pte Ltd.*, 585 F.3d 58, 66 (2d Cir. 2009).

After receiving notice of Supplemental Rule B attachment, the defendant is entitled to contest the attachment at a prompt hearing pursuant to Rule E(4)(f). To avoid vacatur of attachment, it is the plaintiff's burden to show that "1) it has a valid prima facie admiralty claim against the defendant; 2) the defendant cannot be found within the district; 3) the defendant's property may be found within the district; and 4) there is no statutory or maritime law bar to the attachment." *Aqua Stoli*, 460 F.3d at 445. "[T]he sole basis for extending this claim to [S&P] is the allegation that [S&P are] ... alter ego[s] of [Capri Marine]. Thus, to survive this motion [to vacate], the Complaint must allege particular facts supporting [Vitol's] alter ego theory of liability to satisfy Rule E(2)(a)'s heightened pleading standard." *Arctic Ocean Int'l Ltd. v.*

High Seas Shipping Ltd., 622 F.Supp. 2d 46, 53 (S.D.N.Y. 2009).[10]

To restate a basic premise, to plead a prima facie admiralty case pursuant to Supplemental Rule E, "the complaint shall state the circumstances from which the claim arises with such particularity that the defendant or claimant will be able, without moving for a more definite statement, to commence an investigation of the facts and to frame a responsive pleading." Fed. R. Civ. P. Adm. Supp. R. E(2)(a). The burden to show why continued attachment is proper is the plaintiff's to bear. *See Equatorial Marine Fuel Mgmt. Servs. Pte. Ltd. v. MISC Berhad*, 591 F.3d 1208, 1210 (9th Cir. 2010).

As we have previously explained, [—23—]

Rule E(2)(a)'s requirement for pleading specific circumstances is one part of the process which guards against the improper use of admiralty seizure proceedings. Thus, the rule's heightened particularity in pleading requirement is always subject to the general standard that the complaint sufficiently notify the defendant of the incident in dispute and afford a *reasonable belief* that the claim has merit.

United States v. Mondragon, 313 F.3d 862, 865 (4th Cir. 2002) (emphasis added) (internal citations, quotation marks, and alterations omitted). While courts to have considered the question are in agreement that the Supplemental Rule E(2)(a) pleading requirement is "heightened," the precise boundaries of such a heightened pleading requirement are not clearly defined.

As one district court explained,

---

[10] The parties dispute whether Supplemental Rule E(2)(a)'s pleading standard is still "heightened" in light of the Supreme Court's holdings in *Twombly* and *Ashcroft v. Iqbal*, 556 U.S. 662 (2009). We need not answer that question here because we conclude that Vitol has failed to carry its pleading burden under either standard.

courts have compared the showing required in a "reasonable grounds" analysis to the more familiar standard of probable cause. *See, e.g., Amstar Corp. v. S/S ALEXANDROS T.*, 664 F.2d 904, 912 (4th Cir. 1981) ("A shipowner challenging the validity of an arrest is constitutionally entitled to a prompt post-arrest hearing in which the plaintiff has the burden of showing probable cause for the arrest"). The Supreme Court, interpreting the phrase "reasonable grounds" as used in a criminal statute, has said that "[t]he terms 'probable cause' as used in the Fourth Amendment and 'reasonable grounds' … are substantial equivalents of the same meaning." *Draper v. United States*, 358 U.S. 307, 311 (1959). Probable cause is less than a preponderance of the evidence; in the criminal context, it has been described as a "fair probability" that the asserted fact is true. *Illinois v. Gates*, 462 U.S. 213, 214 (1983). With this standard in mind, courts in Rule E(4)(f) hearings [—24—] have emphasized that their conclusions are "merely holding that it is likely" that alleged facts are true. *See North of England Protecting and Indem. Ass'n*, 1999 WL 33116416, at *3.

Wajilam Exps. (Singapore) Pte. Ltd. v. ATL Shipping Ltd., 475 F.Supp. 2d 275, 279-80 (S.D.N.Y. 2006).[11]

This Court has only once opined on Supplemental Rule E(2)(a)'s pleading requirement. In *Mondragon*, we expressed our agreement with the majority view, that "[Supplemental] Rule E(2)(a) requires a complaint to allege sufficient facts to support a *reasonable belief* that the property is subject to forfeiture." 313 F.3d at 865 (emphasis added).[12] We went on to explain, however, that "Rule E(2)(a) needs little interpretation. It is plainly written and means precisely what it says." *Id.* (internal quotation marks omitted).

Although Vitol asserts on appeal that the district court erred by applying a "reasonable belief" standard to S&P's motion to vacate, the court unquestionably applied the proper standard in light of *Mondragon*. The district court discussed the "reasonable belief" standard from *Mondragon*, and, as we will discuss in detail below, faithfully applied that requirement. [—25—]

B. Rule 12(b)(6) Standard

We review *de novo* the grant of a Rule 12(b)(6) motion to dismiss for failure to state a claim. *McCorkle v. Bank of Am. Corp.*, 688 F.3d 164, 171 (4th Cir. 2012). To survive a motion to dismiss pursuant to Rule 12(b)(6), Vitol's "[f]actual allegations must be enough to raise a right to relief above the speculative level," thereby "nudg[ing] [its] claims across the line from conceivable to plausible." *Twombly*, 550 U.S. 544, 555, 570 (2007).

The plausibility standard requires a plaintiff to demonstrate more than "a sheer possibility that a defendant has acted unlawfully." [*Ashcroft v. Iqbal*, 556 U.S. 662, 678 (2009)]. It requires the plaintiff to articulate facts, when accepted as true, that "show" that the plaintiff has stated a claim entitling him to relief, i.e., the "plausibility of 'entitlement to relief.'" *Id.* (quoting *Twombly*, 550 U.S. at 557).

To emphasize the Federal Rules' requirements for stating claims that are warranted and therefore form a plausible basis for relief, the Supreme Court has held that a complaint must contain "more than labels and

---

[11] Although *Wajilam Exports* describes a "reasonable grounds" standard, rather than the "reasonable belief" standard noted in our discussion of *Mondragon*, courts appear to use the two terms interchangeably to describe an identical standard for vacating an attachment. *Cf. United States v. Diaz*, 491 F.3d 1074, 1077 (9th Cir. 2007) (noting in the criminal context that "[t]he phrase 'reason to believe' is interchangeable with and conceptually identical to the phrases 'reasonable belief' and 'reasonable grounds for believing'").

[12] *Mondragon* was decided in the context of a civil forfeiture claim. However, the *Mondragon* holding was based in large part on *Riverway Co. v. Spivey Marine and Harbor Service Co.*, 598 F.Supp. 909 (S.D. Ill. 1984), an admiralty *in rem* case.

conclusions, and a formulaic recitation of the elements of a cause of action will not do." *Twombly*, 550 U.S. at 555. To discount such unadorned conclusory allegations, "a court considering a motion to dismiss can choose to begin by identifying pleadings that, because they are no more than conclusions, are not entitled to the assumption of truth." *Iqbal*, [556 U.S. at 679]. This approach recognizes that "naked assertions" of wrongdoing necessitate some "factual enhancement" within the complaint to cross "the line between possibility and plausibility of entitlement to relief." *Twombly*, 550 U.S. at 557 (internal quotation marks omitted). [—26—]

At bottom, determining whether a complaint states on its face a plausible claim for relief and therefore can survive a Rule 12(b)(6) motion will "be a context-specific task that requires the reviewing court to draw on its judicial experience and common sense. But where the well-pleaded facts do not permit the court to infer more than the mere possibility of misconduct, the complaint has alleged— but it has not 'show[n]'— 'that the pleader is entitled to relief,'" as required by Rule 8. *Iqbal*, 55 U.S. at 679 (alteration in original) (citation omitted) (quoting Fed.R.Civ.P. 8(a)(2)).

Francis v. Giacomelli, 588 F.3d 186, 193 (4th Cir. 2009).

C. The Alter Ego Claim

Having described the relevant pleading standards, we turn to the resolution of the merits of Vitol's alter ego claim as pled in the Amended Verified Complaint. "It is well established that an admiralty court can review questions of ... alter ego." *Ost-West-Handel*, 160 F.3d at 174 (citing *Swift & Co. Packers v. Compania Colombiana Del Caribe*, 339 U.S. 684, 689 n. 4 (1950)). "[A] corporate entity is liable for the acts of a separate, related entity only under extraordinary circumstances, commonly referred to as 'piercing the corporate veil.'" *Arctic Ocean Int'l*, 622 F. Supp. 2d at 53 (quoting *Dolco*

Invs., Ltd. v. Moonriver Dev., Ltd., 486 F. Supp. 2d 261, 271 (S.D.N.Y. 2007)). "Although decisions to pierce a corporate veil, exposing those behind the corporation to liability, must be taken reluctantly and cautiously, courts will not hesitate to take such action when justice so requires." *Keffer v. H.K. Porter Co., Inc.*, 872 F.2d 60, 64 (4th Cir. 1989) (citing *In re County Green Ltd. P' ship*, 604 F.2d 289, 292 (4th Cir. 1979)). "[I]n extraordinary cases, such as the corporate form being used for wrongful purposes, courts will pierce the corporate veil and disregard the corporate entity, treating the [—27—] parent corporation and its subsidiary as a single entity." *Corrigan v. U.S. Steel Corp.*, 478 F.3d 718, 724 (6th Cir. 2007).

In *Keffer*, as well as *DeWitt Truck Brokers, Inc. v. W. Ray Flemming Fruit Co.*, 540 F.2d 681 (4th Cir. 1976), we articulated several factors that "guide the determination of whether one entity constitutes the alter ego of another." *Ost-West-Handel*, 160 F.3d at 174. These factors include "gross under-capitalization, insolvency, siphoning of funds, failure to observe corporate formalities and maintain proper corporate records, non-functioning of officers, control by a dominant stockholder, and injustice or fundamental unfairness." *Id.* Other factors properly considered by the district court in this case include intermingling of funds; overlap in ownership, officers, directors, and other personnel; common office space; the degrees of discretion shown by the allegedly dominated corporation; and whether the dealings of the entities are at arm's length. *See Arctic Ocean*, 622 F.Supp. 2d at 53.

At its core, the question of whether to pierce the corporate veil is a fact-intensive inquiry, because "the circumstances necessarily vary according to the circumstances of each case, and every case where the issue is raised is to be regarded as *sui generis* to be decided in accordance with its own underlying facts." *DeWitt Truck Brokers*, 540 F.2d at 684 (internal quotation marks, footnote, and alterations omitted). "Instead of a firm rule, the general principle ... has been that liability is imposed when doing so would achieve an equitable result." *Williamson*, 542

F.3d at 53 (quotation marks omitted). "In applying these factors a court must focus on reality and not form, [on] how the corporation operated and the individual defendant's relationship to that operation." *Ost-West-Handel*, 160 F.3d at 174 (citing *DeWitt*, 540 F.2d at 685) (quotation marks omitted).

Vitol alleged in its Amended Verified Complaint that Capri Marine "made no independent business decisions controlling its principle asset, the ALAMBRA," and that it lacked a busi- [—28—] ness address of its own as "it shared Starlady's address." (J.A. 1129). Further, Vitol made specific allegations that Capri Marine, by its own admission, had no appreciable assets save the ALAMBRA, despite owning unencumbered title to the ALAMBRA and operating it profitably in the years prior to the Oil Spill.

The most significant allegations, however, concern the sale of the ALAMBRA following the Oil Spill in 2001. Vitol specifically alleged that Capri Marine paid Vitol $500,000 in order to lift an injunction restraining its ability to sell the ALAMBRA. Because it lacked other assets, Capri Marine obtained the $500,000 through a loan financed by Trade Maritime in the amount of $1.4 million. Trade Maritime is part of the Kalogiratos Group. At that time, Capri Marine was essentially insolvent (save for its interest in the ALAMBRA) and facing the prospect of considerable liability arising out of the Oil Spill. It thus had little chance of repaying the Trade Maritime loan on its own.

Capri Marine sold the ALAMBRA (its sole asset) in 2001 to what appeared to be a third party, Aurora. Instead, Aurora was also part of the Kalogiratos Group under the control of Gerassimos. The ALAMBRA was later resold at a substantially higher price to a bona fide third party, and the assets of the sale were distributed throughout the Kalogiratos Group including repayment of the loan made by Trade Maritime. The district court concluded that the foregoing allegations were sufficient, for both Supplemental Rule E and Rule 12(b)(6) purposes, to have pled Capri Marine was the alter ego of Gerassimos and his related entities. For purposes of our analysis,

we may assume, without deciding, that the Amended Verified Complaint does adequately plead Capri Marine as the alter ego of Gerassimos.

Even assuming that Capri Marine is an alter ego of Gerassimos, that status does not resolve the issue in the case at bar as to whether alter ego liability can attach to S&P. Rather, [—29—] Vitol must make independent allegations sufficient to avoid dismissal and vacatur that Gerrassimos is the alter ego of S&P. The district court discussed the relevant alter ego allegations as to S&P and Gerassimos in the Amended Verified Complaint and concluded that "more is necessary to establish the degree of actual domination and control essential to prove an alter ego claim." (J.A. 1565). We agree with the district court's holdings both for Supplemental Rule E and Rule 12(b)(6) purposes.

In reviewing the vacatur of attachment under Supplemental Rule E, we look first to the text of that Rule. In doing so, it is clear that S&P could not, without moving for a more definite statement, "frame a responsive pleading." *See* Fed. R. Civ. P. Supp. Adm. R. E(2)(a). This is so because the facts alleged in the Amended Verified Complaint do not give rise to a reasonable belief that Primerose and/or Spartacus are alter egos of Gerassimos or his related entities.

Looking first to allegations concerning the degree to which the Starlady Fleet (unquestionably controlled by Gerassimos) was connected with the Primerose Fleet, we agree with the district court that Vitol's allegations were insufficient to pass the reasonable belief test. Vitol alleged that the Primerose Fleet, including Spartacus (owner of the THOR) was started with funds from the Starlady Fleet, as well as the allegations that Starlady vessels have similar coloration to Primerose vessels, and that Primerose shared offices, phone numbers, and other office facilities with Starlady. Vitol argues that those allegations should be sufficient to establish the alter ego status of S&P, and the district court erred in finding that "more is necessary" for Vitol to demonstrate the interconnectedness of the two shipping fleets.

These allegations of fleet interconnectedness, however, simply do not rise to the level of creating a reasonable belief to support the claim of alter ego. Applying the factors discussed above we conclude that, although Vitol has alleged a [—30—] close business relationship between Kalogiratos-controlled entities and S&P, it has not done enough to allege an alter ego status. At best, Vitol has made allegations with particularity only to support a reasonable belief that the two fleets maintain a close business relationship. Vitol's allegations that the Primerose fleet was started with funds from the Starlady fleet establish little more than that Starlady has invested in Primerose, and not how that event gives Starlady control over Primerose's affairs or establishes any ownership rights. Moreover, allegations that the fleets share similar coloration are not probative of the core question of whether the two entities have disregarded corporate formalities. And while sharing office space may be an indicium of alter ego, we do not believe that shared office space on its own is sufficient to compel a conclusion that Starlady and/or Gerassimos dominated and controlled Primerose.

Vitol has also alleged that Velliades (the alleged owner of Primerose and Spartacus) extended a line of credit to Gerassimos following the sale of the ALAMBRA. The mere extension of a line of credit from one corporate entity to another, however, does not create a reasonable belief of alter ego. Significantly, as the district court noted, the credit line was repaid. In short, that Velliades extended credit to Gerassimos does not tend to show that Velliades's business ventures are dominated or controlled by Gerassimos.

Vitol further alleged that Starlady paid $120,000 into an account held by Seatrade (a non-party owned and managed by Primerose) at Laiki Bank, and on the same day, Seatrade's loan from the same bank was discharged. Again, though, while this allegation is evidence of a close corporate relationship, and perhaps even a failure to

adhere to corporate formalities, it is not evidence that funds were comingled, that Gerassimos "dominates" Seatrade (or indeed, any Primerose- [—31—] affiliated entity), or that the corporate form was in any way materially disregarded.[13]

Vitol also made an allegation that Deep Blue[14] transferred $360,000 to Starlady at the same time as Primerose transferred $10,500 to Starlady. Starlady converted these funds to Euros, then back to dollars, and transferred $306,000 back to Primerose. Vitol alleges that Velliades agreed to assist Gerassimos by transferring the funds temporarily in order to assist Starlady in obtaining favorable tax status under Greek law; but claims that there is no explanation for why Starlady only repaid $306,000 of the $370,500 originally loaned. As the district court explained, however, in light of the fact that Gerassimos owns a 5% interest in Deep Blue, the funds retained by Starlady represent an advance on dividends related to the 5% ownership stake. Again, all that Vitol has pled is that a close relationship exists between the Kalogiratos entities and those controlled by Velliades. But it has effectively alleged nothing more than repaid loans and dividend distributions, which do not establish the type of dominion and control needed to demonstrate alter ego status. Indeed, the specific facts alleged by Vitol simply establish that the two fleets maintain a close business relationship that sometimes results in the disregard of formality. But such allegations alone will not suffice to give rise to a reasonable belief of alter ego status sufficient to invoke the "extraordinary" remedy of piercing the corporate veil. *See Arctic Ocean*, 622 F.Supp. 2d at 53.

The same is true of Vitol's allegation that "Velliades is a [p]uppet of Gerassimos Kalogiratos." (J.A. 1145). This statement, without more, is clearly lacking in the particularity required to satisfy the Supplemental Rule E standard. S&P could not have responded to this bald, conclusory

---

[13] The record does not reflect whether Seatrade repaid to Starlady the $120,000 deposited by Starlady into its account at Laiki Bank.

[14] The Kalogiratos family owns a minority share in Deep Blue, which is managed by Primerose.

assertion [—32—] without moving for a more definite statement. And once again, while Vitol does make certain "factual" allegations, the specific facts that Vitol does allege are not sufficient to support its legal conclusions. Indeed, many of Vitol's allegations never depart the realm of the purely speculative, including the allegation that Velliades cannot be the principal of Primerose because he "had no prior experience in ship management." (J.A. 1146). These speculative allegations simply do not meet the heightened "reasonable belief" standard.[15]

In sum, Vitol has failed to "allege particular facts supporting its alter ego theory of liability to satisfy [Supplemental] Rule E(2)(a)'s heightened pleading standard." *Arctic Ocean*, 622 F. Supp. 2d at 53. In reaching this conclusion we are mindful of the heightened pleading standard of Supplemental Rule E, and again note that courts should be "reluctant[ ]" and "cautious [ ]" when deciding to pierce the corporate veil. *Keffer*, 872 F.2d at 64.

Because Vitol has failed to plead with sufficient specificity that S&P are alter egos of Capri Marine, it has failed to carry its burden to show why the attachment of the THOR Substitute Collateral should not be vacated as the district court held. *See* Fed. R. Civ. P. Adm. Supp. R. E(4)(f) (placing burden on plaintiff "to show why the arrest or attachment should not be vacated'). We therefore conclude that the district court did not abuse its discretion in granting S&P's motion to vacate the attachment. [—33—]

We next turn to the application of the Rule 8 pleading requirements discussed above to determine if Vitol pled allegations in the

---

[15] Vitol does allege that Gerassimos was involved with the financing of the THOR, signing certain mortgage documents on behalf of Spartacus and directing certain loan-related documents to be sent to his attention. While we agree with Vitol that this allegation suggests some degree of cross-collateralization between the entities, we do not agree that Gerassimos' involvement with the THOR's financing makes plausible the otherwise conclusory allegation that he, not Velliades, therefore dominates Primerose and its fleet.

Amended Verified Complaint sufficient to survive Rule 12(b)(6) scrutiny. Indeed, while the Supplemental Rule E reasonable belief standard is not identical to the plausibility standard under Rule 12(b)(6), we find much of the analysis to overlap. For example, the analysis above of Vitol's allegations pertaining to fleet interconnectedness assists and informs our view of the same allegations viewed through the lens of Rule 12(b)(6).

Vitol's allegations that the Primerose Fleet was started with funds from Gerassimos and related entities, and allegations concerning fleet coloration and shared office space, are literally "factual" allegations entitled to a presumption of truth. *See Iqbal*, 556 U.S. at 681. We are not, however, required to accept Vitol's legal conclusions, drawn from those facts, as true. *See Giarratano v. Johnson*, 521 F.3d 298, 302 (4th Cir. 2008) (courts "need not accept the legal conclusions drawn from the facts" stated in the complaint). This is so because, even accepting the well-pleaded facts as true, those facts do not give rise to a plausible allegation of alter ego.

As the district court recognized, taking as true Vitol's allegations of fleet interconnectness, Vitol has at best made a plausible allegation that S&P maintain a close business relationship with Gerassimos and his related entities. There is nothing in the allegations of interconnectness that plausibility suggests the sort of dominion, control, failure to observe corporate formalities, or fundamental unfairness needed to state a claim for alter ego status.

We find the same to be true with respect to Vitol's allegations of comingling of funds. Although Vitol does baldly allege that funds from Primerose were comingled with funds from Starlady, that allegation is conclusory, and not entitled to a presumption of truth. *See Iqbal*, 556 U.S. at 681. With respect to Vitol's allegations concerning the degree to which [—34—] funds were comingled, we once again identify facts in the Amended Verified Complaint that were properly pled: that Velliades extended a credit line to Gerassimos following the sale of the ALAMBRA; that Starlady paid funds to Laki Bank in exchange for discharge of certain loans to Seatrade; and that Deep Blue loaned considerable funds to Starlady, some of which were not repaid.

Again, however, when we apply the alter ego factors discussed *supra* at 27, to these facts, we find that the allegations in the Amended Verified Complaint do not plausibly state an alter ego claim. Indeed, the loans allegedly made between Gerassimos (and related entities) and Velliades (and related entities) were repaid, with the exception of a portion of the loan made by Deep Blue. But Vitol's allegations fail to account for the fact that Gerassimos owned a small share of the interest in Deep Blue, and as the district court explained, the discrepancy between the amount loaned and that repaid was properly attributable to a dividend distribution.

To the extent that these facts show a close business relationship, that allegation falls short of establishing alter ego. And because the loans were largely repaid, we do not agree with Vitol's bald allegation that these transactions represent improper comingling of funds with failure to observe the corporate form. In short, these allegations, in our view, do not contain the "factual enhancement" necessary to cross "the line between *possibility* and *plausibility* of entitlement to relief." *Twombly*, 550 U.S. at 557 (emphasis added) (quotation marks and brackets omitted).

Similarly, the statement that Velliades is a mere puppet of Gerassimos is a bald allegation, couched as fact, that is no more than an unsupported legal conclusion for purposes of Rule 12(b)(6). *See Jordan v. Alt. Res. Corp.*, 458 F.3d 332, 338 (4th Cir. 2006) ("[W]e need not accept the legal conclusions drawn from the facts, and [ ] need not accept as true unwarranted inferences, unreasonable conclusions, or argu- **[—35—]** ments." (internal quotation marks omitted)). As explained above, the factual support for this assertion is simply lacking, and we need not address it further.

Finally, we note that the Amended Verified Complaint is replete with examples of allegations related to whether Primerose is an alter ego of Spartacus and other members of the Primerose fleet. Vitol alleges, for example, that Primerose had "no commercially justifiable reason" to provide funds to secure the release of the THOR in the instant litigation. Besides being a further example of the speculation which we will not accept as true for either Supplemental Rule E or Rule 12(b)(6) purposes, these allegations do little to support Vitol's theory of the case: that Primerose (and its fleet member, i.e., Spartacus) is an alter ego of Gerassimos or the Kalogiratos Group.

In sum, we agree with the district court's holding that the allegations in the Amended Verified Complaint fail to state a claim upon which relief may be granted, and dismissal was therefore warranted pursuant to Rule 12(b)(6). Vitol's allegations are conclusory and contain legal conclusions couched as factual allegations. To the extent that the Amended Verified Complaint does properly allege facts, those facts do not show more than "a sheer possibility that a defendant has acted unlawfully." *See Iqbal*, 556 U.S. at 678. Because "the well-pleaded facts do not permit [this] [C]ourt to infer more than the mere possibility of misconduct, the complaint has alleged— but it has not 'shown'— 'that the pleader is entitled to relief.'" *See id.* at 679. As with the Supplemental Rule E analysis, we conclude the district court did not err in granting S&P's Rule 12(b)(6) motion to dismiss the Amended Verified Complaint.

IV. Conclusion

For the foregoing reasons, we agree that the district court properly exercised admiralty jurisdiction over Vitol's claims. Our review of the merits of Vitol's claim against S&P, how-

[—**36**—] ever, lead us to conclude that dismissal was appropriate pursuant to Rule 12(b)(6), and the district court's *ex parte* order of attachment was properly vacated. We therefore affirm the judgment of the district court.

AFFIRMED

United States Court of Appeals
for the Fourth Circuit

No. 11-2366

VILLAGE OF BALD HEAD ISLAND
vs.
UNITED STATES ARMY CORPS OF ENGINEERS

Appeal from the United States District Court for the
Eastern District of North Carolina

Decided: April 15, 2013

Citation: 714 F.3d 186, 1 Adm. R. 123 (4th Cir. 2013).

Before **NIEMEYER**, **GREGORY**, and **THACKER**, Circuit
Judges.

[—3—] NIEMEYER, Circuit Judge:

The Village of Bald Head Island, a coastal
town in North Carolina, commenced this
action under the Administrative
Procedure Act ("APA") and admiralty
jurisdiction against the U.S. Army Corps of
Engineers to require it, through an order of
specific performance and injunction, to honor
commitments made to the Village and other
North Carolina towns when developing its
plans to widen, deepen, and realign portions of
the Cape Fear River navigation channel. The
Village alleged that when implementing the
project, the Corps failed to honor
commitments to protect the adjacent beaches
against [—4—] the adverse effects of the
project and to restore sand to the beaches, in
violation of the National Environmental Policy
Act, the Coastal Zone Management Act, the
Rivers and Harbors Act, Corps Regulation 33
C.F.R. § 337.10, and contract principles.

The district court dismissed the complaint
for lack of subject-matter jurisdiction,
concluding that the Corps' alleged failure to
implement the project in accordance with its
commitments was not "final agency action"
that was subject to judicial review under the
APA and that it lacked admiralty jurisdiction
over the complaint's contract claims.

We agree with the district court's holding
that the Corps' failure to implement
"commitments" made to the Village during
development of the plans for the project was

not final agency action subject to judicial
review, and we also conclude that the alleged
contracts on which the Village relies for its
contract claims are not maritime contracts
that justify the exercise of admiralty
jurisdiction. Accordingly, we affirm.

I

Since the 1800s, the U.S. Army Corps of
Engineers has maintained a navigation
channel in the Cape Fear River that allows
vessels coming from the Atlantic Ocean to
access the deep-water port in Wilmington,
North Carolina. In the 1980s and 1990s, the
Corps advanced proposals to widen and
deepen the 37-mile channel, and Congress
approved them in the 1986 and 1996 Water
Resources Development Acts. Pub. L. No. 99-
662, § 202(a), 100 Stat. 4082 (1986); Pub. L.
No. 104-303, § 101(a)(23), 110 Stat. 3658
(1996). Shortly thereafter, it combined these
projects into a single project, see Energy and
Water Development Appropriations Act, Pub.
L. No. 105-62, tit. I, 111 Stat. 1320 (1997),
referred to here as the Wilmington Harbor
Project.

In June 1996, the Corps prepared an
Environmental Impact Statement for the
project and scheduled construction to begin
[—5—] in 2000. Before construction began,
however, the Corps discovered an area of rock
at the bottom of the channel that would
require extensive blasting to remove and
learned that the planned extension of the
channel would cut through a substantial
amount of live coral, causing ecological
damage. As a result, it proposed several
revisions to the project, including a
realignment of the channel's entrance closer to
Bald Head Island. It also proposed to dispose
of beach-quality sand dredged during the
project's construction and subsequent
maintenance on the adjacent beaches of Bald
Head Island and Oak Island, two barrier
islands located on either side of the entrance
to the Cape Fear River.

In connection with these proposed
revisions, the Corps issued an Environmental
Assessment in February 2000, evaluating the
revised project's environmental impacts, as

well as its consistency with North Carolina's Coastal Management Plan. The Environmental Assessment included a Sand Management Plan, which described in detail the Corps' plan for depositing dredged beach-quality sand on nearby beaches during construction of the project and predicted the need, after work was complete, to perform "maintenance dredging" every two years. Because a study showed that approximately two-thirds of the sediment at the entrance of the channel came from Bald Head Island and one-third from Oak Island, the Sand Management Plan provided that the dredged beach-quality sand would be placed on Bald Head Island in years two and four following the completion of the project and on Oak Island in year six and that this "disposal cycle" would be followed thereafter.

The Corps also developed the Wilmington Harbor Monitoring Plan, which established a "routine monitoring program" to observe "the response of the adjacent beaches and the shoaling patterns in the entrance channel" and to use the data derived from those observations to make an "initial assessment of the impacts of the sand management plan on the system." The monitoring plan provided that "[a]ny changes in the [—6—] sand management plan ... [would] be fully coordinated with all interested parties prior to implementing any such change."

Both before and after the Corps conducted its Environmental Assessment, the Village of Bald Head Island provided numerous comments to the Corps. The Village contended generally that the Corps' operation and maintenance of the channel in the past had adversely impacted Bald Head Island's shoreline, and it expressed concern that the planned realignment of the channel's entrance closer to the Island, along with the channel's deepening and widening, would exacerbate these effects. The Village informed the Corps that it would oppose the project and consider legal action unless "it received written agreement from the Corps that the project would include sand management and [beach] protection measures or otherwise would be constructed and operated in a manner so as not to adversely impact Bald Head Island or,

if the project caused adverse impacts, the project would be modified and the impacts would be corrected." During this period, as the Village alleges, it entered into negotiations with the Corps and the North Carolina Department of Environment and Natural Resources "in an effort to reach agreement on . . . measures that would protect Bald Head Island or address project impacts," and these negotiations resulted in the issuance of two letters, one from U.S. Army District Engineer Colonel James W. DeLony, dated June 9, 2000, and the other from Donna D. Moffitt, Director of North Carolina's Division of Coastal Management, dated June 15, 2000.

Col. DeLony's letter, which was addressed to the mayors of the Village of Bald Head Island, Caswell Beach, Oak Island, and Holden Beach, stated that it was designed "to bring everyone up to date on the status of our plan to place beach quality sand excavated for the project" on adjacent beaches. After addressing the placement of sand during the construction phase of the project, the letter stated that "the U.S. Army Corps of Engineers will conduct periodic maintenance dredging of the navigation channels" and that "[t]he [—7—] disposal of all beach quality dredged material will be accomplished in accordance with" the Environmental Assessment, its Sand Management Plan, and the Wilmington Harbor Monitoring Plan, reiterating that the disposal would follow the six-year cycle described in those plans. The letter added that the "disposal activities . . . will be at no cost to either community." Finally, DeLony's letter stated that the "Corps will conduct a monitoring program . . . as set out in the Wilmington Harbor Monitoring Plan" and that "[t]he Corps will use this monitoring data to evaluate and adjust the Sand Management Plan, as determined necessary, after coordination with interested parties." In this respect, the letter stated:

> If the Project causes significant adverse effects on adjacent beaches, the Corps and the Sponsor [North Carolina] will respond by adjusting the Sand Management Plan, after consultation with interested parties. If the Project causes significant adverse effects that

cannot be dealt with by modifications to the Sand Management Plan, the Corps and the Sponsor will promptly seek and use their best efforts to implement appropriate corrective measures, such as additional nourishment, subject to consistency review.

The second letter, dated June 15, 2000, from Director Moffitt to Col. DeLony, summarizes the North Carolina Division of Coastal Management's review of the revised project, pursuant to its opportunity to comment on the project's conformance with state policies under the Coastal Zone Management Act, 16 U.S.C. §§ 1451-1466. Moffitt's letter stated:

Based upon our review of the [Environmental Assessment] and the Corps of Engineers' response to comments, we do not disagree with your determination that the proposed construction and changes in harbor maintenance procedures are consistent with [—8—] the North Carolina Coastal Management Program to the maximum practicable, provided that the project is performed according to the [Environmental Assessment] (including the Sand Management Plan and other appendices) and the Corps' responses to comments from the [Environmental Assessment], and to Colonel DeLony's letter of June 9, 2000 (including attachments), and that the conditions below are met.

As relevant here, one of five listed conditions provided:

The placement, timing, costs, and amount of sand to be deposited on Bald Head Island, Caswell Beach, Oak Island, and Holden Beach, both during construction and future maintenance; monitoring; and response to impacts shall be in accordance with Col. DeLony's letter of June 9, 2000 . . . . If the towns, Corps, and project sponsor's representative mutually agree to modifications to the [Sand Management Plan] or Col. DeLony's June 9, 2000

letter, those modifications shall be submitted to the North Carolina Division of Coastal Management for a determination of whether another consistency review is necessary on the modifications.

In August 2000, about six months after the issuance of the Environmental Assessment for the revisions to the project, the Corps issued a Finding of No Significant Impact ("FONSI") (which obviated the need for an Environmental Impact Statement), concluding that the modifications "will not significantly affect the quality of the human environment." The FONSI also stated that the Corps "will comply with the conditions indicated in [Moffitt's] letter."

On September 20, 2000, the Corps formally approved the proposed revisions to the Wilmington Harbor Project, and construction commenced in December 2000. Consistent with [—9—] the plan, beach-quality sand that was dredged during the widening and deepening of the channel was placed on Bald Head Island during the summer of 2001.

Following completion of the project in 2002, the Corps also performed maintenance dredging during the winters of 2004-2005, 2006-2007, and 2008-2009. The sand dredged during the first two of those maintenance operations was placed on Bald Head Island, and the sand from the third was placed on Oak Island. But as the winter of 2010-2011 approached, the Corps informed the Village of Bald Island that the Corps' maintenance for that winter would have to be curtailed for budgetary reasons. It reported that it "ha[d] sufficient funding to dredge a portion of the Channel [that winter], but [did] not have the funding for dredging the portion of the Channel nearest Bald Head Island or for disposing of beach-quality sand onto Bald Head Island beaches."

In response to the Corps' notice, the Village of Bald Island commenced this action against the Corps, several of its officers, and the United States, and the Towns of Caswell Beach and Oak Island subsequently intervened as defendants.[1] The complaint alleged that the Corps had breached its commitments regarding how it would implement the Wilmington Harbor Project, as revised. In particular, it claimed that the Corps had breached (1) a commitment to deposit beach-quality sand from maintenance dredging on the adjacent beaches every two years for the life of the project; (2) a commitment to prevent the project from causing long-term harm to the adjacent beaches; (3) a commitment to adjust the Sand Management Plan if the project caused significant adverse effects to the adjacent beaches; (4) a commitment to take [—10—] additional remedial steps if there were significant adverse effects that could not be dealt with by modifying the Sand Management Plan; and (5) a commitment that the Village would bear no cost for the disposal of beach-quality sand on its beaches. The claims were stated in eight counts, six of which relied on the APA, alleging that the Corps violated the National Environmental Policy Act and its implementing regulations (Count I); the Coastal Zone Management Act (Count II); the Rivers and Harbors Act (Count III); Corps Regulation 33 C.F.R. § 337.10 (Count IV); and contract rights with respect to the commitments stated in the DeLony and Moffitt letters (Counts V and VI). Counts VII and VIII alleged that the DeLony and Moffitt letters constituted "maritime contracts" that the Corps had breached. For relief, the complaint sought declaratory and injunctive relief, including an order of specific performance requiring the Corps to comply with the commitments it had made to the Village and Towns.

On the Corps' motion to dismiss, the district court entered an order, dated November 14, 2011, dismissing the complaint under Federal Rule of Civil Procedure 12(b)(1) for lack of subject-matter jurisdiction. *Village*

---

[1] The Town of Caswell Beach and the Town of Oak Island intervened *as defendants*, but they admitted virtually all of the allegations in the Village's complaint. They apparently chose to join as defendants to claim competing relief. On appeal, however, the Towns support the positions taken by the Village, except with respect to Counts VII and VIII.

of Bald Head Island v. U.S. Army Corps of Eng'rs, 833 F. Supp. 2d 524 (E.D.N.C. 2011). With respect to the Village's APA claims, the court concluded that "[i]mplementation or continued operation of a project [was] not . . . federal agency action," *id.* at 532, and that "[e]ven assuming, *arguendo*, that Plaintiff ha[d] in fact alleged agency action, Plaintiff ha[d] failed to show that any of the alleged agency actions [were] final agency actions that might confer jurisdiction on the Court," *id.* at 531. The court also concluded that the Village did not justify any claim under the provision of the APA that allows a court to compel "agency action that was unlawfully withheld or unreasonably delayed," 5 U.S.C. § 706(1), because none of the project's "documents create[d] an independent duty on the Corps to dredge the Inner Ocean bar according to a particular schedule in order to deposit sand on the neighboring beaches." *Village of Bald Head Island*, 833 F. Supp. 2d at 532. Finally, the [—11—] court determined that it did not have admiralty jurisdiction over the contract claims, concluding that the alleged contracts were not "maritime contracts" that would be subject to admiralty jurisdiction. *Id.* at 534-35.

From the district court's judgment, the Village and intervening Towns filed this appeal.

II

The Village contends that the district court erred in concluding that the Village's APA claims do not challenge a "final agency action" that is subject to judicial review under the APA. It maintains that there are two lenses through which to view the "agency action" at issue in this case. First, as it explains, the Corps' "physical activities in the field"—its implementation of the project by relocating, widening, and deepening the channel without also performing specified maintenance commitments designed to protect the adjacent beaches—constitute "agency action" that is "final" and hence subject to judicial review under the APA. *See* 5 U.S.C. §§ 702, 704. Alternatively, the Village claims that the Corps' failure to perform the beach-protection commitments constitutes a "failure to act," which amounts to the type of agency inaction that is subject to judicial review under the APA. *See id.* § 706(1). The Village admonishes that, without judicial review of such agency action or inaction, federal agencies will be left unaccountable for "implement[ing] a project differently from the plans, promises, and conditions generated during the pre-project environmental review."

The Corps contends that the district court correctly concluded that project implementation is not final agency action within the meaning of the APA. It also contends that the Village has not identified a *discrete* agency action that the Corps was *required to take* but failed to perform, as required for judicial review of an agency's failure to act under the APA. *See Norton v. Southern Utah Wilderness Alliance* ("*SUWA*"), [—12—] 542 U.S. 55, 64 (2004). It argues that allowing "judicial review of the Village's claims would place a burden on courts to manage ongoing agency actions and would eviscerate Congress' carefully crafted scheme for judicial review."

Section 704 of the APA provides that *final agency action* is subject to judicial review, 5 U.S.C. § 704, and "agency action" is defined to "include[ ] the whole or a part of an agency rule, order, license, sanction, relief, or the equivalent or denial thereof, or failure to act," *id.* § 551(13). The term "action" as used in the APA is a term of art that does not include all conduct such as, for example, constructing a building, operating a program, or performing a contract. Rather, the APA's definition of agency action focuses on an agency's *determination* of rights and obligations, *see Bennett v. Spear*, 520 U.S. 154, 177-78 (1997), whether by rule, order, license, sanction, relief, or similar action. The term is similar in concept to the meaning of "final decision" as used in describing the appealability of court orders. *See, e.g.*, 28 U.S.C. § 1291.

In this case, the Corps formally approved the revisions to the Wilmington Harbor Project in September 2000, and the revised project included the Corps' plans on how it would make beneficial use of the sand recovered from periodic maintenance dredging by depositing it on the neighboring beaches.

That *approval* was a "determination" that surely amounted to "agency action." But thereafter, over the course of ten years, the Corps *performed* the work that had been approved in September 2000. The Village does not challenge the *approval* of the project; rather it challenges the Corps' *performance* of it, particularly focusing on a period in 2010. It commenced this action to challenge the adequacy of the performance and to require the Corps to do what it had undertaken to do when approving the project. Essentially, the Village sued the Corps for failing to adequately protect and renourish its beaches. While that alleged failure was a failure to take "action" in its broadest sense, it was not a determination—*i.e.*, a "rule, order, license, sanction, relief, or [—13—] the equivalent"— that is "action" as used in the APA. 5 U.S.C. §551(13).

Moreover, the Corps' performance in maintaining the Wilmington Harbor Project was not action that was circumscribed and discrete. "Agency action" not only has a limited meaning, but it also must be "circumscribed [and] discrete," as those characteristics are inherent in the APA's enumeration of the categories of agency action subject to judicial review—*i.e.*, rule, order, license, sanction, or relief. *SUWA*, 542 U.S. at 62. As the *SUWA* Court explained, limiting judicial review to *discrete* agency action "precludes . . . broad programmatic attack[s]," *id.* at 64, and helps ensure that courts are not injected "into day-to-day agency management," *id.* at 67. By contrast, were a court to review the Corps' performance to determine whether the project here had caused "significant adverse effects on adjacent beaches," whether those adverse effects could be addressed by modifying the Sand Management Plan, and whether they required additional "appropriate corrective measures," it would then be injecting itself into the role of monitoring whether the Corps had complied with vague, undefined corrective measures. The obvious inability for a court to function in such a day-to-day managerial role over agency operations is precisely the reason why the APA limits judicial review to discrete agency actions. *SUWA*, 542 U.S. at 62-64, 66-67.

The Village protests that it *is* challenging agency action that is circumscribed and discrete. It asserts that it is not "challenging a regional or nationwide dredging program for shipping channels" but, instead, the implementation of "a *specific* dredging project at a *specific* coastal site." Yet, by challenging the Corps' ongoing real world physical actions, even at a localized level, the Village is essentially "demand[ing] a general judicial review of the [Corps'] day-to-day operations" in maintaining the channel, the type of review the Supreme Court has explicitly held the APA does not authorize. *Lujan* [—14—] *v. Nat'l Wildlife Fed'n*, 497 U.S. 871, 899 (1990); *see also SUWA*, 542 U.S. at 64, 66-67.

We therefore conclude that the Corps' implementation of the Wilmington Harbor Project, including the ongoing periodic maintenance dredging and resulting nourishment of nearby beaches, does not constitute "agency action" within the meaning of the APA.

Section 704 of the APA *also* requires that "agency action," to be subject to judicial review, be "*final* agency action." 5 U.S.C. § 704 (emphasis added). The Village has not explained how its challenge to the ongoing maintenance of the channel can satisfy this finality requirement.

The Supreme Court has held that "[a]s a general matter, two conditions must be satisfied for agency action to be 'final.'" *Bennett*, 520 U.S. at 177. "First, the action must mark the consummation of the agency's decisionmaking process—it must not be of a merely tentative or interlocutory nature. And second, the action must be one by which rights or obligations have been determined or from which legal consequences will flow." *Id.* at 177-78 (internal quotation marks and citations omitted); *see also Franklin v. Massachusetts*, 505 U.S. 788, 797 (1992) ("The core question is whether the agency has completed its decisionmaking process, and whether the result of that process is one that will directly affect the parties"). Here, the Corps made a *final* determination for purposes of the APA when it announced formal approval of the revised project in

September 2000. That approval, not the Corps' subsequent activities in carrying it out, was the final agency action. *See Bennett*, 520 U.S. at 177-78. Thus, in the context of this case, "project implementation" is neither "agency action" nor "final" agency action subject to judicial review under the APA.

The Village contends, as an alternative argument, that the Corps' "failure to act" consistent with its commitments to [—15—] maintain and protect the beaches adjacent to the channel is subject to judicial review under 5 U.S.C. § 706(1), which provides that a "reviewing court shall . . . compel agency action unlawfully withheld or unreasonably delayed." But, again, the APA's use of the term "agency action" in § 706(1) limits judicial review to discrete determinations of rights and obligations. *See SUWA*, 542 U.S. at 62-63; *Bennett*, 520 U.S. at 177-78. As the *SUWA* Court explained, the term "failure to act" is "properly understood as a failure to take an *agency action*—that is, a failure to take one of the agency actions (including their equivalents) earlier defined in § 551(13)." 542 U.S. at 62. The Court therefore noted that the term "'failure to act' is properly understood to be limited, as are the other items in § 551(13), to a *discrete* action," providing as examples "the failure to promulgate a rule or take some decision by statutory deadline." *Id.* at 63.

Moreover, § 706(1) only authorizes the compulsion of agency action *that is legally required*. *SUWA*, 542 U.S. at 63. In this sense, the Court explained, § 706(1) is like the mandamus remedy, "empower[ing] a court only to compel an agency 'to perform a ministerial or non-discretionary act,' or 'to take action upon a matter, without directing *how* it shall act.'" *Id.* at 64 (quoting Attorney General's Manual on the Administrative Procedure Act 108 (1947)). Thus, it concluded, "a claim under § 706(1) can proceed only where a plaintiff asserts that an agency failed to take a *discrete* agency action that it [was] *required to take*." *Id.*

More telling for the case before us, the *SUWA* Court applied that principle to circumstances similar to those here. The plaintiff there sought to compel the Bureau of

Land Management to comply with certain "commitments" in its land use plans, which stated that a certain area "will be monitored and closed if warranted." *SUWA*, 542 U.S. at 67-68. The Court, however, was unwilling to "conclude that a statement in a plan that [the Bureau] 'will' take this, that, or the other action, is a binding commitment that can be compelled under [—16—] § 706(1)"—"at least absent clear indication of binding commitment in the terms of the plan." *Id.* at 69.

Here, the Village would have us compel the Corps, under § 706(1), to perform "commitments" in DeLony's letter to deposit beach-quality sand on the adjacent beaches every two years for the life of the project. But, as in *SUWA*, the DeLony letter *does not commit* the Corps to do so. Rather, it outlined the *planned* disposal cycle that would follow periodic maintenance dredging "as called for" in the Sand Management Plan, and the Sand Management Plan makes clear that the plan to dredge every two years was the Corps' *projection* as to how often *dredging would be required*. These are hardly binding commitments; rather, they are statements of intent about future performance that are expressly conditioned on unknown conditions and wide-open judgments.

At bottom, we conclude that the Corps' continuing implementation of the Wilmington Harbor Project, as revised, does not constitute final agency action that is subject to judicial review under the APA. And even though "agency action" includes a "failure to act," such agency inaction can only be judicially compelled when it is a discrete "agency action" that the agency was required to take, which is not the type of claim the Village has presented. Accordingly, we affirm the district court's judgment dismissing the Village's APA claims.

III

As to Counts VII and VIII for breach of contract, the Village contends that the DeLony and Moffitt letters created "maritime contracts" that the district court could enforce within its admiralty jurisdiction. In those counts, the Village sought an order of specific performance and other forms of equitable relief. The district court dismissed these counts, concluding that the letters were not *maritime* contracts and [—17—] that the court therefore lacked admiralty jurisdiction over them. *Village of Bald Head Island*, 833 F. Supp. 2d at 534-35.

We agree with the district court. In Count VII, the Village alleged that the DeLony letter of June 9, 2000, "constitute[d] a valid and enforceable express or implied contract between the Village and the Corps" to deposit the spoils of maintenance dredging on adjacent beaches every two years and to take other steps, as necessary, to prevent the project from causing the beaches harm. And in Count VIII, the Village similarly alleged that the Moffitt letter of June 15, 2000, constituted a valid and enforceable contract between the North Carolina Division of Coastal Management and the Corps for the same purposes. We conclude that such contracts—to nourish area beaches with dredged sand and to protect them from further erosion—are not maritime contracts.

The Supreme Court has recognized that the "boundaries of admiralty jurisdiction over contracts" are "conceptual rather than spatial," so that whether a contract qualifies as maritime "depends upon [its] nature and character"—namely, "whether it has reference to maritime service or maritime transactions." *Norfolk S. Ry. Co. v. Kirby*, 543 U.S. 14, 23-24 (2004) (internal quotation marks omitted). In this respect, the Court has explained that the "fundamental interest giving rise to maritime jurisdiction is the protection of maritime *commerce*" and that "[t]he conceptual approach vindicates that interest by focusing [the] inquiry on *whether the principal objective* of a contract is maritime commerce." *Id.* at 25 (second emphasis added) (internal quotation marks omitted).

It is clear that the "principal objective" of the contracts claimed by the Village was not "maritime commerce," but the preservation of area beaches. Indeed, the Village expressly alleged that it "entered into negotiations with the Corps and [the North Carolina Department of Environment and Natural

Resources] in an effort to reach agreement on project conditions or measures that *would protect Bald Head Island or* [—18—] *address project impacts*." (Emphasis added). To be sure, the principal purpose of the Wilmington Harbor Project was to protect maritime commerce by ensuring that vessels could continue to access the port in Wilmington, North Carolina. But the alleged contracts—which were negotiated in response to the project in order to limit its impact on area beaches—were not designed to protect or engage in maritime commerce. Rather, they were sought to serve the recreational and aesthetic interests of the Village, as well as the property interests of property owners in the Village. Because the alleged contracts were not maritime contracts, the Village could not invoke the district court's admiralty jurisdiction.[2]

Moreover, while we conclude that the contracts alleged in Counts VII and VIII were not maritime contracts, we have also concluded, as discussed above in connection with the Village's APA claims, that the negotiations between the Village and the Corps did not result in "binding commitments" that could be contractually enforced. *See ante* at 16. [—19—]

We therefore affirm the district court's judgment dismissing the Village's breach of maritime contract claims for lack of jurisdiction.

AFFIRMED

---

[2] It is also far from clear that the Village could successfully invoke the court's admiralty jurisdiction *only* to achieve equitable relief. Historically, it was understood that admiralty courts could not grant equitable relief. *See Rea v. The Eclipse*, 135 U.S. 599, 608 (1890) (discussing the limited power of admiralty courts). The Supreme Court in 1950, however, recognized that equitable relief may be granted in admiralty. *See Swift & Co. Packers v. Compania Colombiana Del Caribe, S.A.*, 339 U.S. 684, 691-92 (1950) ("We find no restriction upon admiralty by chancery so unrelenting as to bar the grant of any equitable relief even when that relief is subsidiary to issues wholly within admiralty jurisdiction"). Citing this language and Congress' extension of the Federal Rules of Civil Procedure to admiralty cases in 1966, the First Circuit has held that "where equitable relief is otherwise proper under usual principles, it will not be denied on the ground that the court is sitting in admiralty." *Pino v. Protection Maritime Ins. Co.*, 599 F.2d 10, 16 (1st Cir. 1979). Nonetheless, the Court in *Swift & Co. Packers* still held to the proposition that "a court of admiralty will not enforce *an independent equitable claim* merely because it pertains to maritime property." 339 U.S. at 690 (emphasis added). Because of our conclusion that the alleged contracts are not maritime contracts, we need not resolve whether a court exercising admiralty jurisdiction may hear claims seeking only equitable relief.

United States Court of Appeals
for the Fourth Circuit

No. 12-1566

MARINE REPAIR SERVICES, INC.
vs.
FIFER

On Petition for Review of an Order of the Benefits
Review Board (11-0624)

Decided: May 2, 2013

Citation: 717 F.3d 327, 1 Adm. R. 131 (4th Cir. 2013).

Before **WILKINSON, SHEDD,** and **DUNCAN,** Circuit Judges.

[—2—] DUNCAN, Circuit Judge:

Marine Repair Services, Inc. ("Marine") petitions for review of the Decision and Order of the Benefits Review Board ("BRB" or the "Board") awarding permanent partial disability benefits to Marine's former employee, Christopher Fifer, under the Longshore and Harbor Workers' Compensation Act ("LHWCA"). Applying the burden-shifting scheme that governs LHWCA disability claims, the administrative law judge ("ALJ") reviewing Fifer's claim concluded that Marine failed to meet its burden of presenting suitable alternative employment for Fifer. The BRB affirmed. Because the ALJ made findings unsupported by the record and demanded more of Marine than our precedent requires, we grant Marine's petition for review, vacate the Decision and Order of the BRB, and remand for further proceedings consistent with this opinion.

I.

A.

Prior to the events underlying this petition, Fifer earned $1,219 weekly working for Marine as a repairman of large shipping containers, a physically demanding job requiring climbing, bending, and heavy lifting of over fifty pounds. On October 26, 2007, Fifer suffered shoulder, arm, and back injuries in an on-the-job car accident. After the accident, **[—3—]** Marine began paying Fifer temporary total disability benefits while Fifer sought treatment.

Dr. Michael Franchetti became Fifer's primary orthopedist, to whom Fifer complained of back pain which radiated down his legs, as well as back spasms. During his two-year course of treatment, Dr. Franchetti encouraged Fifer to perform physical therapy, prescribed muscle relaxers and painkillers, and reviewed scans of Fifer's spine. He also referred Fifer to another physician for epidural steroid injections. Dr. Franchetti ultimately diagnosed Fifer with chronic lumbosacral strain, sciatica, and disc protrusion and herniation.

Fifer underwent his first functional capacity evaluation ("FCE") in June 2008. In addition to finding that Fifer did "not meet the physical demands of his pre-injury occupation," the evaluator concluded that Fifer should limit himself to jobs within "medium" work parameters, and that he should limit lifting to twenty-five pounds on an occasional basis. J.A. 241. In an attempt to prepare himself to return to Marine, Fifer completed a round of work-hardening from July to September 2008.[1] The work-hardening evaluator released Fifer on September 12, **[—4—]** 2008, ascribing him "full time tolerance[ ] with the lower parameters of heavy work, with limitations in bending and material handling." *Id.* at 263 (the "2008 work-hardening release"). The evaluator instructed Fifer to see Dr. Franchetti on September 15, 2008 for "a full release back to work." Id.

Fifer's September 15 visit to Dr. Franchetti resulted in updated work restrictions (the "September 2008 restrictions"). Dr. Franchetti indicated that Fifer could return "to restricted work status," so long as he performed "[n]o repetitive bending or twisting with [his] back, no lifting more than 55 lbs., no carrying more than 40 lbs., no overhead lifting more than 30 lbs., no lifting more than 30 lbs. frequently,

---

[1] Work-hardening is a rehabilitation process through which injured employees perform tasks that simulate the physical demands of their jobs in an effort to condition them for return to employment.

and no sitting more than 45 minutes without changing positions." J.A. 211. Marine would not employ Fifer while he was subject to the September 2008 restrictions. As a result, Fifer began working at his family's seafood restaurant, where he earned $400 weekly performing odd jobs, errands, and assisting with food preparation. Prior to his work as a longshoreman, Fifer had managed his family's restaurant for two years.

Both parties agree that Fifer reached maximum medical improvement in February 2009. On August 20, 2009, Fifer underwent a second FCE. That evaluation showed reduced lifting ability, as compared to the 2008 FCE, but also indicated that Fifer could sit and stand "frequent[ly]" and walk "const[antly]" [—5—] at a slow pace, improvements from the 2008 FCE. J.A. 371. The evaluator concluded that work in the family restaurant was "consistent with [Fifer's] demonstrated activity tolerances," that Fifer could not return to Marine as a container repairman, and that he should "[m]aintain work activity within the light work parameters." Id. at 373. According to the FCE, "light work" includes jobs that involve occasionally lifting up to twenty pounds and require "walking or standing to a significant degree." Id. at 371.

During an October 2009 deposition in connection with this case, Dr. Franchetti clarified that based on the results of the August 2009 FCE, he would revise his September 2008 restrictions. Specifically, based on the August 2009 FCE, Dr. Franchetti would reduce Fifer's "lifting and carrying weight to 25 pounds," reduce overhead lifting to twenty pounds, and "would recommend no lifting more than about 10 to 15 pounds frequently." J.A. 390 ("the October 2009 restrictions"). Fifer's sitting restriction remained the same: no sitting without changing position for forty-five or more minutes. Dr. Franchetti confirmed that he did not see any problem with Fifer's work in the family restaurant. [—6—]

B.

1.

After Marine discontinued temporary payments in January 2009, Fifer filed this claim for permanent disability benefits under the LHWCA, 33 U.S.C. § 901 et seq. The ALJ conducted a hearing on October 29, 2009.

At the hearing, Fifer and Dr. Franchetti testified that physical limitations prevented Fifer from returning to work as a repairman at Marine.[2] Dr. Franchetti testified that Fifer "has sustained a permanent impairment to his person as a whole, as a result of his lumbar spinal injury," resulting in a "31 percent whole person impairment." J.A. 389.

Marine presented evidence of alternative employment for Fifer in the relevant geographic area. Marine's vocational rehabilitation specialist, Brian Sappington, testified to three labor market studies he had prepared to demonstrate alternative employment. The first two were conducted in December 2008 and relied on Fifer's 2008 work-hardening release, which allowed "[h]eavy duty [work] with limitations." J.A. 276. The first study listed positions as a welder, forklift driver, courier, and security guard; the second included five restaurant management positions with "light duty" physical requirements. [—7—] Sappington's third and final study took Dr. Franchetti's September 2008 restrictions into account. J.A. 359 (noting that Fifer's restrictions were "[u]nlimited standing with restricted lifting per Dr. Franchetti"). That study provided a description of the restaurant manager and assistant manager role from the Dictionary of Occupational Titles ("DOT") and listed six restaurant management positions for which Sappington testified Fifer would be vocationally qualified.

Sappington supplemented the second and third study with his testimony at the hearing before the ALJ. Specifically, upon receiving Dr. Franchetti's October 2009 work restrictions, Sappington had contacted

---

[2] Dr. Franchetti testified by deposition.

employers from the second and third studies and performed site visits to determine whether the restaurant management positions would comport with Fifer's revised lifting restrictions. Sappington testified that he identified two restaurants where a person with a twenty-five pound lifting restriction "would be a candidate" or where "the restaurant would provide reasonable accommodation to someone with Mr. Fifer's background and restrictions," J.A. 156, and two more restaurant positions where employees told Sappington they rarely lifted anything over twenty-five pounds and felt accommodations were possible, *id.* at 157-58, even though the job descriptions for those restaurant posts required an ability to lift more than twenty-five pounds. Sappington identified three [—8—] additional restaurant positions which did not include a minimum lifting requirement, although he was unable to verify actual lifting requirements at those restaurants. Therefore, Sappington concluded that of the seven restaurants he visited, four of them would "definite[ly]" accommodate Fifer's physical limitations. *Id.* at 164. The annual salary for these positions ranged from $28,000 to $40,000. Sappington also testified that the security guard positions listed in the first labor market study, which required "frequent standing and walking," fit within Dr. Franchetti's October 2009 restrictions. J.A. 282.

2.

In an opinion issued on March 28, 2010, the ALJ concluded that Fifer met his burden of establishing a prima facie case of total disability since he could not return to his former position at Marine. The ALJ then assessed whether Marine had rebutted Fifer's showing of disability by demonstrating the availability of suitable alternative employment by comparing Sappington's labor market studies with Fifer's vocational and physical abilities. She found that none of Sappington's studies provided adequate levels of detail regarding the positions' requirements. As such, the ALJ determined that Fifer's job in the family restaurant, where he earns $20,800 annually, represented his wage earning capacity. She awarded

permanent partial disability benefits accordingly. [—9—]

The ALJ credited Fifer's testimony regarding his physical limitations. Fifer testified that he chose to work at his family's restaurant because there, "if I need to take a break and sit down I can sit down and . . . I'm not going to get fired." J.A. 96. While Fifer testified that he can "do everything [at the restaurant] that needs to be done," he has, on at least one occasion, taken a thirty minute break to lay down when he felt a muscle spasm developing in his back. J.A. 96-97. The ALJ also credited the testimony of Fifer's brother, Tracy, who manages the restaurant; Tracy Fifer testified that his brother "has up days and down days" and sometimes "needs to sit down right away" when he arrives to work. J.A. 129. The ALJ also credited the deposition testimony of Dr. Franchetti, who confirmed that Fifer's restaurant work comported with the October 2009 restrictions, which limited Fifer to lifting a maximum of twenty-five pounds.

In rejecting the labor market studies, the ALJ found Marine's first study inconsistent with Fifer's restrictions, as some of the jobs--forklift operator and welder--"require[d] the ability to perform medium or heavy work." *Id.* at 32. The ALJ rejected the security officer positions listed in the first study after finding that Fifer's pain medication regimen would cause him to fail any required drug screenings, precluding employment as a security guard. The ALJ rejected the five light [—10—] duty restaurant management positions in Marine's second study because "Mr. Sappington did not provide a description of the positions, other than by their title," nor did he indicate that he "actually spoke to anyone about the job duties and availability of these positions." *Id.* Finally, although the ALJ recognized that the third study, along with Sappington's testimony, identified four positions where "lifting over 25 pounds was not regularly required of the manager," she faulted that study for failing to "describe[ ] the specific duties of these positions, in particular, whether they require standing for long periods of time, and provide for rest breaks." *Id.* at 33. The ALJ concluded that "Mr. Fifer's credible complaints of pain, his inability to stand for long periods of time, his need for frequent rest breaks, and his regimen of medication" made the restaurant jobs inapplicable "although [the jobs] may accommodate the lifting restrictions." *Id.*

The Board affirmed the ALJ's decision. It concluded that Sappington "did not provide all of the job duties or assess the jobs' suitability in terms of all of claimant's restrictions," and "did not refer to any standard job descriptions." *Id.* at 59. Because Sappington's reports "lack[ed] . . . specific information regarding all the physical duties required of the positions," the ALJ could not determine whether Fifer's need for [—11—] "frequent breaks" and "limit[ations] in the amount of sitting and standing he can do" would be accommodated. *Id.*

The Board issued its final opinion on April 5, 2012. This appeal followed.

II.

On appeal, Marine contends that it met its burden of showing suitable alternative employment for Fifer, and that the ALJ's conclusions are therefore unsupported by substantial evidence.[3]

In determining whether Marine met its burden of showing suitable alternative employment, we review Board decisions for errors of law and "to ascertain whether the Board adhered to its statutorily mandated standard for reviewing the ALJ's factual findings." *Newport News Shipbldg. & Dry Dock Co. v. Riley*, 262 F.3d 227, 231 (4th Cir. 2001). An ALJ's factual findings "'shall be conclusive if supported by substantial evidence in the record considered as a whole.'" *Newport News Shipbldg. & Dry Dock Co. v. Stallings*, 250 F.3d 868, 871 (4th Cir. 2001) (quoting 33 U.S.C. § 921(b)(3)). [—12—]

---

[3] Marine also raises several challenges related to Fifer's attorney's fee award. Attorney's fees are available for successful prosecution of a LHWCA claim. 33 U.S.C. § 928. Because we vacate the Board's Order and remand, we need not address the issue of attorney's fees.

Our assessment of whether the Board complied with that standard comprises "an independent review of the administrative record"; "[l]ike the Board, [we] will uphold the factual findings of the ALJ so long as they are supported by substantial evidence." *Norfolk Shipbldg. & Drydock Corp. v. Faulk*, 228 F.3d 378, 380 (4th Cir. 2000). We consider "substantial evidence" to require "more than a scintilla but less than a preponderance"; it is "such relevant evidence as a reasonable mind might accept as adequate to support a conclusion." *Id.* at 380-81 (internal quotation and citation omitted). We review the ALJ's legal determinations de novo. *Dir., Office of Workers' Comp. Programs v. Newport News Shipbldg. & Dry Dock Co.*, 138 F.3d 134, 141 (4th Cir. 1998).

The Act provides compensation to longshore workers who have experienced on-the-job injuries "for the economic harm suffered as a result of the decreased ability to earn wages." *Norfolk Shipbldg. & Drydock Corp. v. Hord*, 193 F.3d 797, 800 (4th Cir. 1999). LHWCA claims are governed by a burden-shifting scheme; in order to make a successful compensation claim, "a claimant must first establish a prima facie case by demonstrating an inability to return to prior employment due to a work-related injury." *Newport News Shipbldg. & Dry Dock Co. v. Dir., Office of Workers' Comp. Programs*, 315 F.3d 286, 292 (4th Cir. 2002). "If the claimant makes this showing, 'the burden shifts to the [—13—] employer to demonstrate the availability of suitable alternative employment which the claimant is capable of performing.'" *Id.* (citation omitted). If the employer does not itself provide suitable alternative employment, it "'may demonstrate that [such] employment is available to the injured worker in the relevant labor market.'" *Id.* at 293 (citation omitted). If the employer meets this burden, "its obligation to pay disability benefits is either reduced or eliminated, unless the employee shows 'that he diligently but unsuccessfully sought appropriate employment.'" *Id.* (citation omitted).

As Fifer established disability by showing that he is unable to return to his job at

Marine, this case turns on whether Marine has met its burden of showing suitable alternative employment. In particular, Marine contends that it offered evidence of alternative employment more lucrative than Fifer's position at his family's restaurant. A finding of higher-paying alternative employment would increase Fifer's wage-earning capacity and decrease or nullify the disability payments Marine owes Fifer.

We find the ALJ's conclusion that Marine failed to present suitable alternative employment erroneous for two reasons: (1) the ALJ made findings of fact as to Fifer's physical limitations which were unsupported by substantial evidence in the record, and (2), the ALJ faulted Marine for failing to address these [—14—] limitations, imposing a heavier legal burden than our precedent requires.

1.

First, in rejecting Marine's labor market studies, the ALJ emphasized Fifer's "inability to stand for long periods of time," "need for frequent rest breaks," and "regimen of medication," physical limitations unsupported by substantial evidence in the record. J.A. 33. Although we may not disregard the ALJ's findings "'on the basis that other inferences might have been more reasonable,'" *Ceres Marine Terminals, Inc. v. Green*, 656 F.3d 235, 240 (4th Cir. 2011) (citing *Newport News Shipbldg. & Dry Dock Co. v. Tann*, 841 F.2d 540, 543 (4th Cir. 1988)), there must be some evidence in the record to support the findings.

The ALJ's conclusions regarding Fifer's problems standing and need for breaks were unsupported by the evidence in the record. Fifer did not testify that he had trouble standing; instead, he indicated that he needed to take breaks during work-hardening in 2008 (while performing tasks targeted towards returning him to "hard" work parameters) and that he chose to return to his family's restaurant because he knew he could take breaks there without reprimand. On one occasion, he had to lay down to rest his back; his brother testified that sometimes Fifer "needs to sit down right away." *Id.* at 129. While the [—15—] ALJ credited Fifer's

testimony, she also credited the testimony of Dr. Franchetti, who never mentioned standing restrictions or rest break requirements, either in his testimony or in the September 2008 or October 2009 work restrictions. In fact, Dr. Franchetti indicated that Fifer's physical limitations did not bar him from restaurant work. Further, the most recent FCE indicated that Fifer could stand "frequent[ly]" and walk "const[antly]" within light work parameters. J.A. 371.

The ALJ also emphasized Fifer's medication regimen as a barrier to employment, ultimately faulting Marine for failing to address Fifer's medication-related restrictions in its labor market studies. The ALJ indicated that the security guard positions Marine offered would likely require drug tests which Fifer would fail. Nothing in the record, however, indicated that Fifer's medications interfered with his ability to find work. There was no evidence to support the ALJ's conclusion that security guards routinely undergo drug testing, that prescription painkillers cause applicants to fail required drug tests, or that Fifer's regimen would bar Fifer from employment. The ALJ's determination that Fifer could not qualify for the security guard positions because of his medication was thus unsupported by any evidence, much less substantial evidence. [—16—]

2.

Second, the ALJ's emphasis on Fifer's standing, rest break, and medication-related restrictions led her to fault Marine for overlooking them in its labor market studies. The ALJ thus penalized Marine for failing to address restrictions of which it was unaware, imposing too heavy a responsibility under the LHWCA's burden-shifting scheme. This was legal error, for which we vacate the underlying decision and order. *See Universal Mar. Corp. v. Moore*, 126 F.3d 256, 264-65 (4th Cir. 1997) (vacating the BRB's decision and remanding after holding that the ALJ's imposition of too great a burden on the employer to demonstrate suitable alternative employment was an error of law); *Trans-State Dredging v. Benefits Review Board*, 731 F.2d

199, 201 (4th Cir. 1984) (reversing the BRB and remanding after finding that requiring the employer to contact prospective employers to determine whether they would hire someone with the claimant's abilities "place[d] too heavy a burden upon the employer").

We have held that, to meet its burden, "an employer must present evidence that a range of jobs exists which is reasonably available and which the disabled employee is realistically able to secure and perform." *Lentz v. Cottman Co.*, 852 F.2d 129, 131 (4th Cir. 1988). There must be "a reasonable likelihood, given the claimant's age, education, and vocational background that he would be hired if he diligently sought the job[s]" the employer [—17—] presents. *Id.* (quoting *Trans-State Dredging*, 731 F.2d at 201). Demonstrating a single job opening is not enough. *Id.* Once the employer has presented a range of appropriate jobs, however, "the employer need not contact prospective employers to inform them of the qualifications and limitations of the claimant and to determine if they would in fact consider hiring the candidate for their position." *Universal Mar.*, 126 F.3d at 264. Nor must the employer "contact the prospective employers in his survey to obtain their specific job requirements before determining whether the claimant would be qualified for such work." *Id.* Rather, if the employer demonstrates "the availability of specific jobs in a local market," he may rely "on standard occupational descriptions to fill out the qualifications for performing such jobs." *Id.* at 265.

Marine relied on the physical restrictions of which it was aware to present a range of suitable positions for Fifer. Prior to the hearing, Dr. Franchetti never indicated a standing restriction or a rest break requirement; to the contrary, after giving his revised October 2009 restrictions, he indicated that "cooking, deliveries and takeout," as well as managerial work, would comport with Fifer's physical restrictions. J.A. 390. Marine relied on the restrictions *it knew of* to prepare labor market studies, updating those reports as it became aware of revised restrictions. [—18—]

Marine cannot be faulted for failing to account for restrictions which were unannounced prior to the hearing, a conclusion underscored by the ALJ's unfounded findings with respect to Fifer's medication-related restrictions. While the record corroborated the fact that Fifer took medication to manage his pain, neither his nor his treating physician's testimony supports the conclusion that Fifer's medication interfered with his ability to obtain employment. Indeed, as discussed above, nothing in the record indicated that security guards must undergo drug tests to qualify for employment. Faulting Marine for failing to address unfounded restrictions turns the employer's showing of suitable alternative employment into a moving target.

Moreover, the ALJ overstated Marine's burden of presenting suitable alternative employment. The third labor study, at least, described with requisite specificity the responsibilities of a restaurant manager or assistant manager using the DOT. We have expressly approved the use of the DOT's "standard occupational descriptions to fill out the qualifications" of suitable alternative employment in LHWCA cases. *Universal Mar.*, 126 F.3d at 265. In *Universal Maritime*, we explained that we sanction the use of the DOT's occupational descriptions because "the claimant is able to correct any overbreadth in a survey by demonstrating the failure of his good faith effort to secure [—19—] employment" once the burden shifts back to the employee. *Id.* at 264-65. Therefore, the ALJ's rejection of the third labor market study for failing to describe "the specific duties of the[ ] positions" demands more than we require. J.A. 33.

Further, Marine produced at least four alternative positions which the ALJ recognized would "accommodate [Fifer's] lifting restrictions." J.A. 33. Although "the employer need not contact prospective employers to inform them of the qualifications and limitations of the claimant," *Universal Mar.*, 126 F.3d at 264, Sappington communicated Fifer's "physical limitations as [he] understood them" to the potential employers in order to determine whether the jobs were realistically available to Fifer, J.A. 168. Because Dr. Franchetti's lifting and sitting restrictions were the only restrictions of which Marine was aware prior to the hearing, and because Marine presented several suitable positions which the ALJ found comported with those restrictions, we conclude that the ALJ erred in finding that Marine failed to meet its burden under the Act.

Since Marine demonstrated the availability of suitable alternative employment which Fifer is capable of performing, the burden should have shifted to Fifer to prove he could not obtain more lucrative employment despite his diligent effort. We therefore vacate the final Decision and Order of the BRB, and [—20—] remand this matter for further proceedings consistent with this opinion.

III.

For the foregoing reasons, Marine's petition for review is granted, the Decision and Order of the BRB is vacated, and the claim is remanded for further proceedings.

VACATED AND REMANDED

United States Court of Appeals
for the Fourth Circuit

No. 12-4652

UNITED STATES
vs.
SHIBIN

Appeal from the United States District Court for the
Eastern District of Virginia

Decided: July 12, 2013

Citation: 722 F.3d 233, 1 Adm. R. 138 (4th Cir. 2013).

Before **NIEMEYER**, **MOTZ**, and **FLOYD**, Circuit Judges.

[—2—] **NIEMEYER**, Circuit Judge:

On May 8, 2010, Somali pirates seized the German merchant ship the *Marida Marguerite* on the high seas, took hostages, pillaged the ship, looted and tortured its crew, and extorted a $5-million ransom from its owners. Mohammad Saaili Shibin, while not among the pirates who attacked the ship, boarded it after it was taken into Somali waters and conducted the negotiations for the ransom and participated in the torture of the merchant ship's crew as part of the process.

On February 18, 2011, Somali pirates seized the American sailing ship the *Quest* on the high seas. A U.S. Navy ship communicated with the pirates on board in an effort to negotiate the rescue of the ship and its crew of four Americans, but the pirates referred the Navy personnel to Shibin as their negotiator. When the Navy ship thereafter sought to bar the pirates from taking the *Quest* into Somali waters, the pirates killed the four Americans.

Shibin was later located and arrested in Somalia and turned over to the FBI, which flew him to Virginia to stand trial for his participation in the two piracies. A jury convicted him on 15 counts, and he was sentenced to multiple terms of life imprisonment.

On appeal, Shibin contends that the district court erred by refusing (1) to dismiss the piracy charges on the ground that [—3—] Shibin himself did not act on the high seas and therefore the court lacked subject-matter jurisdiction over those charges; (2) to dismiss all counts for lack of personal jurisdiction because Shibin was forcibly seized in Somalia and involuntarily removed to the United States; (3) to dismiss the non-piracy counts involving the *Marida Marguerite* because "universal jurisdiction" did not extend to justify the U.S. government's prosecution of those crimes; and (4) to exclude FBI Agent Kevin Coughlin's testimony about prior statements made to him by a Somali-speaking witness through an interpreter because the interpreter was not present in court.

We conclude that the district court did not err in refusing to dismiss the various counts of the indictment and did not abuse its discretion in admitting Agent Coughlin's testimony. Accordingly, we affirm.

I

The Piracy of the Marida Marguerite

As the *Marida Marguerite* was making way in the Indian Ocean on a trip from India to Antwerp and preparing to join a protected convoy to transit the Gulf of Aden, she was attacked by Somali pirates in a small, high-speed boat. The *Marida Marguerite* was manned by a crew of 22 from Bangladesh, India, and Ukraine, and was carrying a shipment of benzene and castor oil. As the *Marida Marguerite* attempted evasive maneuvers, the [—4—] pirates fired two rocket-propelled grenades at the ship, prompting the ship's captain to surrender. After taking control of the ship in international waters, the pirates, armed with AK-47s, forced the crew to head for Somali waters. While in route, they looted the ship, including the personal valuables of crew members.

The *Marida Marguerite* arrived first at an anchorage near Hafun on the east coast of Somalia, where "a multitude" of other hijacked ships were anchored. At that location, additional pirates boarded the ship with more weapons, including assault weapons, rocket-propelled grenades, and two large stationary machine guns. The ship was then moved to an anchorage off Garaad, a town controlled by pirates, where Shibin boarded the ship. It was ultimately moved to Hobyo, on the southeast coast of Somalia. Shibin remained on board for over 7 months (except for a vacation of 10 to 12 days during the summer) until the ransom was received.

During the period that the ship was held captive, Shibin, who had a high position among the pirates, served principally as the negotiator, using tactics that included the psychological and physical torture of the crew. Ultimately, Shibin was able to extort a $5-million ransom from the ship's owners, and the money was air-dropped at the ship. After the money was confirmed, the pirates released the ship to a waiting U.S. [—5—] frigate, which escorted it to safety. Shibin was among the last of the pirates to disembark.

For a period during the seizure of the *Marida Marguerite* and its crew, Shibin was deposed as the negotiator, and an "investor" took over. For that period, Shibin was demoted to the role of a "regular" or "normal" pirate and carried an AK-47 as he stood guard over the hostages. After a short period of time, however, Shibin was reappointed as the negotiator, and he completed the deal for the $5-million ransom in December 2010.

The Piracy of the Quest

Several months later, on February 18, 2011, as a U.S. sailing vessel, the *Quest*, was making way from India to Oman as part of an international yacht rally, a group of Somali pirates hijacked the ship. The ship was manned by four Americans—its owners Scott and Jean Adams, and their friends Phyllis Macay and Robert Riggle. The pirates, carrying automatic weapons and a rocket-propelled grenade launcher, boarded the *Quest* in the Arabian Sea, roughly 400 miles from Oman and 900 miles from Somalia. The pirates planned to take the ship back to Somalia, where their colleague Shibin would negotiate a ransom.

The U.S. Navy learned of the *Quest's* seizure, and several Navy ships began shadowing it. After Navy personnel were able to establish bridge-to-bridge radio communications with the [—6—] pirates, the pirates told the Navy that they lacked the authority to negotiate and that their job was to capture vessels and hostages and return them to Somalia where their English-speaking negotiator would arrange a ransom. As the pirates and the *Quest* continued towards Somali territorial waters, the Navy asked the pirates for the name and contact information of their negotiator. The pirates told the Navy that the person to contact was Shibin, and they provided the Navy with Shibin's cell phone number. The Navy did not, however, then attempt to call him, for strategic reasons.

By the morning of February 22, 2011, as the *Quest* was nearing Somali waters, Navy personnel advised the pirates that they had to stop. When the pirates did not comply, the Navy attempted to position one of its ships to block the pirates, prompting the pirates to fire a rocket-propelled grenade at the Navy. As the Navy continued to close in, but before it reached the *Quest*, the pirates shot and killed all four Americans on board.

Shibin's Capture

Following the attack on the *Quest*, FBI agents worked to collect evidence of Shibin's involvement in the *Quest* piracy. During the investigation, they learned from German law enforcement authorities about Shibin's possible involvement in [—7—] the hijacking of the *Marida Marguerite*. They also learned from a pirate and from piracy investors that Shibin had planned to invest his share of the *Marida Marguerite* ransom in the *Quest* piracy. Such an investment would entitle him to a return as a portion of the eventual ransom.

On April 4, 2011, "Host Nation Defense Forces" in Somalia, acting in cooperation with the FBI, arrested Shibin in the northern city of Bosasso, in the Puntland region of Somalia. Earlier, they had recovered his cell phone and had turned it over temporarily to the FBI. Within a few hours of Shibin's arrest, two FBI agents arrived in Bosasso to question Shibin while he was still in the Defense Forces' custody. They questioned Shibin three times over the course of three days. Shibin stated that he had used a cell phone with a SIM number matching the phone number that the pirates had given the Navy, but he claimed to have lost the phone several weeks before in a taxi in Zambia. Shibin told the agents that he had operated as the negotiator at one time during the *Marida Marguerite* piracy, for which he had received $30,000. He denied any involvement in the hijacking of the *Quest*, but admitted to conducting internet searches on his phone regarding the *Quest* and its crew simply as a matter of curiosity. He pointed out that he had an "auto-alert" feature on his phone that sent him messages about hijackings in and around Somali waters. [—8—]

With Shibin's permission, the FBI agents searched his luggage, obtaining bank records and other items relevant to the piracies. The bank records showed that Shibin had deposited $37,000 on January 6, 2011, shortly after the payment of the *Marida Marguerite* ransom, and that he had withdrawn $19,952 between January 10 and March 1, 2011.

The cell phone, which Host Nation Defense Forces temporarily turned over to the FBI for its investigation, had the same SIM number that had been provided to the Navy by the pirates on the *Quest*. Shibin's "contacts" list contained entries for several of the investors in the *Quest* piracy. The cell phone revealed that during the time when the *Quest* was in the pirates' custody, one of the *Quest* investors had texted Shibin, asking him to call. Shibin's cell phone was also in frequent contact with various other investors, using both cell phone calls and text messages. On the day that the pirates seized the *Quest*, Shibin received a text message stating, "Sarindaaq captured Americans." Sarindaaq was the leader of the pirates who had physically seized the *Quest*. The cell phone indicated that over the next several days, from February 19 to 21, Shibin conducted internet searches on topics like "Hijacked *S/V Quest* value," "Jean and Scott Adams profile," "address of hijacked *S/V*

Quest owner," and "Jean and Scott Adams telephone number." [—9—]

On April 6, 2011, the Host Nation Defense Forces transferred custody of Shibin to the Bosasso Police Department, and the Bosasso Police in turn transferred custody of Shibin to the FBI. The FBI placed Shibin under arrest for charges related to the *Quest* piracy and transported him to the Oceana Naval Air Station in Virginia Beach, Virginia.

Prosecution

Shibin was initially charged in a three-count indictment for his alleged role in the piracy of the *Quest*. A later superseding indictment, returned on August 17, 2011, added charges relating to the piracy of the *Marida Marguerite*, as well as additional charges relating to the piracy of the *Quest*. Counts 1 through 6, arising from the piracy of the *Marida Marguerite*, charged the following crimes:

1. Piracy under the law of nations, in violation of 18 U.S.C. §§ 1651 and 2;

2. Conspiracy to commit hostage taking, in violation of 18 U.S.C. § 1203(a);

3. Hostage taking, in violation of 18 U.S.C. §§ 1203(a) and 2;

4. Conspiracy to commit violence against maritime navigation, in violation of 18 U.S.C. § 2280(a)(1)(H);

5. Violence against maritime navigation, in violation of 18 U.S.C. §§ 2280(a)(1)(A) and 2; and

6. Use of a firearm during a crime of violence, in violation of 18 U.S.C. §§ 924(c) and 2. [—10—]

Counts 7 through 15, arising from the piracy of the *Quest*, charged the following crimes:

7. Piracy under the law of nations, in violation of 18 U.S.C. §§ 1651 and 2;

8. Conspiracy to commit hostage taking, in violation of 18 U.S.C. § 1203(a);

9. Hostage taking, in violation of 18 U.S.C. §§ 1203(a) and 2;

10. Conspiracy to commit kidnapping, in violation of 18 U.S.C. § 1201(c);

11. Kidnapping, in violation of 18 U.S.C. §§ 1201(a)(2) and 2;

12. Conspiracy to commit violence against maritime navigation, in violation of 18 U.S.C. § 2280(a)(1)(H);

13. Violence against maritime navigation, in violation of 18 U.S.C. §§ 2280(a)(1)(A) and 2;

14. Use of a firearm during a crime of violence, in violation of 18 U.S.C. §§ 924(c) and 2; and

15. Use of a firearm during a crime of violence, in violation of 18 U.S.C. §§ 924(c) and 2.

Shibin filed multiple pretrial motions, including a motion to dismiss the piracy charges in Counts 1 and 7, because the government did not allege that Shibin himself acted on the high seas, and a motion to dismiss all charges for lack of jurisdiction. The district court deferred ruling on the motion to dismiss the piracy charges until hearing evidence at trial and denied the other motions. Shibin renewed all motions to [—11—] dismiss at the close of the government's case and again prior to sentencing, all of which the court denied.

During the course of the trial, which lasted ten days, Shibin called one witness, pirate and family member Mohamud Salad Ali, who was one of the leaders of the *Quest* piracy. While Salad Ali testified that he never personally asked for or formed an agreement with Shibin to be the negotiator for the *Quest*, he acknowledged, on cross examination, that the *Quest* investors could have selected Shibin as the negotiator without his knowledge. Salad

Ali denied having told the FBI during earlier interviews that he had spoken with Shibin before going to sea and had told Shibin that he would call when he had "prey," meaning a captured vessel; that he had told Shibin that he was going to sea to hijack a ship and that Shibin had replied that he was ready to be their translator; and that he had told Shibin that Shibin would be the negotiator.

In rebuttal, the government called FBI Agent Kevin Coughlin, who had participated in the earlier interviews with Salad Ali and had recorded what he had said. Agent Coughlin testified, over Shibin's objection, that Salad Ali had in fact made the statements he denied. Shibin objected because Coughlin reported what an interpreter said, not Salad Ali, and the interpreter was not present to be cross examined. Agent Coughlin explained that he used an FBI Somali linguist to [—12—] translate both his questions and Salad Ali's answers and that Salad Ali did not appear to have any trouble understanding the questions.

The jury convicted Shibin on all counts, and the district court sentenced him to 12 terms of life imprisonment, two of which were to be served consecutively; a consecutive 120-month term of imprisonment; and several concurrent 240-month terms.

This appeal followed.

II

Shibin contends first that he did not "commit the crime of piracy," as charged in Counts 1 and 7, because, "according to statutory text, legislative history, and international law, [he] could only be convicted of aiding and abetting piracy if the government proved that he was on the high seas, and while on the high seas, facilitated piratical acts."

The government observes that there is no dispute that the piracies in this case occurred on the high seas beyond the territorial waters of Somalia, which are generally defined as the waters within 12 nautical miles of the coast. It contends that Shibin is liable as a principal in those piracies, even though he did not personally venture into international waters, because he "intentionally facilitated" and thereby aided and abetted the piracies. The government argues that liability for [—13—] aiding and abetting piracy is not limited to conduct on the high seas, explaining:

That no such limitation is imposed is sensible. Once members of a joint criminal enterprise trigger the universal jurisdiction that applies to piracy on the high seas, both international and domestic law prudently include in the scope of the crime all those persons that worked together to commit it, including those leaders like Shibin who facilitate the crime and without which the crime itself would not be possible.

In Counts 1 and 7, Shibin was charged with committing and aiding and abetting the crime of piracy, in violation of 18 U.S.C. §§1651 and 2. Section 1651 provides:

Whoever, on the high seas, commits the crime of piracy as defined by the law of nations, and is afterwards brought into or found in the United States, shall be imprisoned for life.

18 U.S.C. § 1651. And § 2 provides:

Whoever commits an offense against the United States or aids, abets, counsels, commands, induces or procures its commission, is punishable as a principal.

18 U.S.C. § 2(a).

The district court's jurisdiction over these crimes arises from "universal jurisdiction." Universal jurisdiction is an international law doctrine that recognizes a "narrow and unique exception" to the general requirement that nations have a jurisdictional nexus before punishing extraterritorial conduct committed by non-nationals. *United States v. Hasan*, 747 F. Supp. 2d 599, 608 (E.D. Va. 2010), *aff'd sub nom. United States v. Dire*, 680 F.3d 446 (4th Cir. 2012). It allows any nation [—14—] "jurisdiction to define and prescribe

punishment for certain offenses recognized by the community of nations as a universal concern." *Restatement (Third) of Foreign Relations Law* § 404 (1987). Universal jurisdiction requires "not only substantive agreement as to certain universally condemned behavior but also procedural agreement that universal jurisdiction exists to prosecute a subset of that behavior." *Sosa v. Alvarez-Machain*, 542 U.S. 692, 762 (2004) (Breyer, J., concurring in part and concurring in the judgment). The parties agree that piracy is subject to universal jurisdiction, as pirates are considered *hostis humani generis*, the enemies of all humankind. *See Harmony v. United States*, 43 U.S. (2 How.) 210, 232 (1844).

The issue presented by this appeal is whether Shibin, whose conduct took place in Somalia and in Somalia's territorial waters, may be prosecuted as an aider and abettor of the piracies of the *Marida Marguerite* and the *Quest*, which took place on the high seas. Shibin agrees that if his conduct had indeed taken place on the high seas, he could have been found guilty of aiding and abetting piracy. But in this case he participated in the piracies by conduct which took place only in Somalia and on the *Marida Marguerite* while it was located in Somali territorial waters. The issue thus reduces to a question of whether the conduct of aiding and abetting §1651 piracy must itself take place on the high seas. [—15—]

Section 1651 punishes piracy as that crime is defined by the law of nations *at the time of the piracy*. *See Dire*, 680 F.3d at 469 (noting that "§ 1651 incorporates a definition of piracy that changes with advancements in the law of nations"). In *Dire*, we held that Article 101 of the United Nations Convention on the Law of the Sea ("UNCLOS") accurately articulates the modern international law definition of piracy. *Id.* at 459, 469.*

---

* Although over 160 nations are parties to UNCLOS, making up an "overwhelming majority of the world," the United States has not signed or ratified the Convention because "of its disagreement with the deep seabed regime set out in Part XI of the Convention." *Hasan*, 747 F. Supp.

Article 101 of UNCLOS provides:

Piracy consists of any of the following acts:

(a) any illegal *acts* of violence or detention, or any act of depredation, committed for private ends by the crew or the passengers of a private ship or a private aircraft, and *directed*:

> (i) *on the high seas, against another ship* or aircraft, *or against persons or property on board such ship* or aircraft;

> (ii) against a ship, aircraft, persons or property in a place outside the jurisdiction of any State;

(b) any act of voluntary participation in the operation of a ship or of an aircraft with knowledge of facts making it a pirate ship or aircraft; [—16—]

(c) any *act* of inciting or *of intentionally facilitating an act described in subparagraph (a)* or (b).

UNCLOS art. 101, Dec. 10, 1982, 1833 U.N.T.S. 397, 436 (emphasis added). Thus, as relevant here, Article 101(a) defines piracy to include specified acts "directed on the high seas against another ship . . . or against persons or property on board such ship," and Article 101(c) defines piracy to include any act that "intentionally facilitat[es]" any act described in Article 101(a). The parties agree that the facilitating conduct of Article 101(c) is "functionally equivalent" to aiding and abetting criminal conduct, as proscribed in 18 U.S.C. § 2.

While Shibin's conduct unquestionably amounted to acts that intentionally facilitated Article 101(a) piracies on the high seas, he claims that in order for his facilitating conduct

2d at 619 (citing 1 Thomas J. Schoenbaum, *Admiralty and Maritime Law* § 2–2 (4th ed. 2004)).

to amount to piracy, his conduct must also have been carried out on the high seas. The text, however, hardly provides support for this argument. To the contrary, the better reading suggests that Articles 101(a) and 101(c) address distinct acts that are defined in their respective sections.

Article 101(a), which covers piracies on the high seas, explicitly requires that the specified acts be directed *at ships on the high seas*. But Article 101(c), which defines different piratical acts, independent of the acts described in Article 101(a), is linked to Article 101(a) only to the extent that the [—17—] acts must *facilitate* Article 101(a) acts. Article 101(c) does not limit the facilitating acts to conduct on the high seas. Moreover, there is no conceptual reason why acts facilitating high-seas acts must themselves be carried out on the high seas. The text of Article 101 describes one class of acts involving violence, detention, and depredation of ships on the high seas and another class of acts that facilitate those acts. In this way, Article 101 reaches all the piratical conduct, wherever carried out, so long as the acts specified in Article 101(a) are carried out on the high seas.

We thus hold that conduct violating Article 101(c) does not have to be carried out on the high seas, but it must incite or intentionally facilitate acts committed against ships, persons, and property on the high seas. *See also United States v. Ali*, __ F.3d __, No. 12-3056, slip op. at 12, 20 (D.C. Cir. June 11, 2013) (similarly interpreting Article 101(c) in the course of holding that the liability of an aider and abettor of a § 1651 piracy "is not contingent on his having facilitated these acts while in international waters himself").

Citing UNCLOS Article 86, Shibin argues that we should read a "high-seas" requirement into the definition of the facilitating acts described in Article 101(c). Article 86 provides: "The provisions of this Part [Part VII, "High Seas," which includes Article 101] apply to all parts of the sea that [—18—] are not included in the exclusive economic zone, in the territorial sea or in the internal waters of a State, or in the archipelagic waters of an archipelagic State." UNCLOS art. 86, 1833 U.N.T.S. at 432.

Our reading of Article 101, however, is not inconsistent with Article 86, as Article 101(a) does indeed identify piratical acts as acts against ships *on the high seas.* The subordinated acts of Article 101(c) are also acts of piracy because they facilitate Article 101(a) acts. Moreover, Article 86 serves only as a general introduction, providing context to the provisions that follow. It does not purport to limit the more specific structure and texts contained in Article 101. *See RadLAX Gateway Hotel, LLC v. Amalgamated Bank,* 132 S. Ct. 2065, 2070 (2012) ("[I]t is a commonplace of statutory construction that the specific governs the general" (alteration in original) (quoting *Morales v. Trans World Airlines, Inc.,* 504 U.S. 374, 384 (1992))).

Additionally, Shibin's argument is inconsistent with the interpretation of Article 101 given by various international authorities, including the United Nations Security Council. *Cf. Dire,* 680 F.3d at 469 (looking to a United Nations Security Council resolution to discern that UNCLOS represents "the definition of piracy under the law of nations"). In 2011, the Security Council adopted Resolution 1976, which reaffirmed that [—19—] "international law, as reflected in . . . [UNCLOS], in particular its articles 100, 101 and 105, sets out the legal framework applicable to combating piracy and armed robbery at sea." S.C. Res. 1976, preambular ¶8, U.N. Doc. S/RES/1976 (Apr. 11, 2011). Importantly, the Resolution stressed "the need to investigate and prosecute those who illicitly *finance, plan, organize, or unlawfully profit* from pirate attacks off the coast of Somalia, recognizing that individuals and entities who incite or *intentionally facilitate* an act of piracy are themselves engaging in piracy as defined under international law." *Id.* ¶ 15 (emphasis added). Clearly, those who "finance, plan, organize, or unlawfully profit" from piracy do not do so on the high seas.

Similarly, Security Counsel Resolution 2020, adopted in 2011, recognizes "the need to investigate and prosecute not only suspects captured at sea, *but also anyone who incites or intentionally facilitates piracy operations,* including key figures of criminal networks involved in piracy *who illicitly plan, organize, facilitate, or finance and profit* from such attacks." S.C. Res. 2020, preambular ¶ 5, U.N. Doc. S/RES/2020 (Nov. 22, 2011) (emphasis added).

These sources reflect, without ambiguity, the international viewpoint that piracy committed on the high seas is an act against all nations and all humankind and that persons [—20—] committing those acts on the high seas, *as well as those supporting those acts from anywhere,* may be prosecuted by any nation under international law. *See Ali,* __ F.3d at __, No. 12-3056, slip op. at 20.

Shibin makes a similar argument that he made with respect to UNCLOS to the domestic law provisions of 18 U.S.C. §§ 1651 and 2. Thus, he argues that the "on the high seas" requirement contained in § 1651 means that even those who are charged under § 2 for aiding and abetting a § 1651 piracy must act on the high seas. As he did with Article 101, Shibin seeks to import the high seas locational component of § 1651 into § 2. We believe that this argument fairs no better.

To violate § 1651, a principal must carry out an act of piracy, as defined by the law of nations, *on the high seas.* But Shibin was not prosecuted as a principal; he was prosecuted as an aider and abettor under § 2. Section 2 does not include any locational limitation, just as Article 101(c) of UNCLOS does not contain a locational limitation. Section 2 more broadly punishes conduct that "aids, abets, counsels, commands, induces or procures" commission of "an offense against the United States," including conduct punished in § 1651. 18 U.S.C. § 2(a). And nothing in § 1651 suggests that an aider and abettor must satisfy its locational requirement. [—21—]

It is common in aiding-and-abetting cases for the facilitator to be geographically away from the scene of the crime. For example, to be convicted of aiding and abetting a bank robbery, one need not be inside the bank. *See United States v. Ellis,* 121 F.3d 908, 924 (4th Cir. 1997) ("[O]ne's physical location at the time of the robbery does not preclude the propriety of an aiding and abetting charge"); *United States v. McCaskill*, 676 F.2d 995, 1000 (4th Cir. 1982) (concluding that driver of the getaway car was liable as an aider-and-abettor); *Tarkington v. United States*, 194 F.2d 63, 68 (4th Cir. 1952) ("It is also obvious that there is no merit in the contention that the conviction was invalidated because [the defendant] was not physically present at the bank when the robbery took place"). Similarly, "[o]ne need not be present physically at the time to be guilty as an aider and abettor in an embezzlement." *United States v. Ray*, 688 F.2d 250, 252 (4th Cir. 1982).

Nonetheless, Shibin relies on *United States v. Ali*, 885 F. Supp. 2d 17 (D.D.C. 2012), *rev'd* in relevant part, __ F.3d at __, No. 12-3056, slip op. at 32, to contend that we should read a locational limitation into § 2 based on the Supreme Court's interpretation of the predecessor statute. In *United States v. Palmer*, 16 U.S. (3 Wheat.) 610, 633-34 (1818), the Supreme Court concluded that the piracy provisions of the Crimes Act of 1790 [—22—] did not reach conduct committed by foreign vessels traversing the high seas. To reverse that ruling, Congress revised the offense of general piracy. But in doing so, it did not alter § 10 of the Crimes Act of 1790, which is § 2's predecessor. From this history, Shibin argues that §2 is therefore a municipal statute, applying only to piracy within United States territory. But the tie between *Palmer* and § 2 is not strong enough to validate Shibin's argument. First, the Supreme Court's comments in *Palmer* on § 2's predecessor are dicta. *See Palmer*, 16 U.S. at 629-30. But more importantly, § 2's predecessor was tied to the crimes proscribed by the Crimes Act of 1790 and was narrower than today's § 2. Thus, *Palmer* did not construe the modern aiding-and-abetting liability. We are satisfied to give § 2, in its present form, its natural reading.

Accordingly, we affirm Shibin's piracy convictions in Counts 1 and 7, based on his intentionally facilitating two piracies on the high seas, even though his facilitating conduct took place in Somalia and its territorial waters.

III

Shibin next contends that the indictment should have been dismissed for lack of personal jurisdiction because he was "forcibly seized and removed from [Somalia] by agents of the United States government and was provided no opportunity to [—23—] challenge either his detention or his removal." He argues that the lack of an extradition treaty between Somalia and the United States

> should not be construed to mean one nation's acquiescence to another government's exercise of power over its citizens. The lack of a treaty with Somalia is not permission given by the Somalia government to the United States to enter its country and seize its citizens for arrest, transport, and prosecution.

* * *

> Because the lack of a treaty is not permission or silent acquiescence to foreign governmental seizure of their citizens, the United States must respect Somalia's decision not to enter into an extradition treaty with us and go through official Somali channels to obtain custody of Mr. Shibin -- if Somalia would allow it.

Shibin was initially detained in Bosasso, Somalia, by Host Nation Defense Forces. A few days later, these forces turned him over to the Bosasso Police Department, and the Bosasso Police in turn handed him over to the FBI, which took him to Virginia, where he was "found" for U.S. jurisdictional purposes.

Under the *Ker-Frisbie* doctrine, the manner in which the defendant is captured and brought to court is generally irrelevant to the court's personal jurisdiction over him. *See Ker v. Illinois*, 119 U.S. 436, 444 (1886) ("[S]uch forcible abduction is no sufficient reason why the party should not answer when brought within the jurisdiction of the court which has the right to try him for such an offense, and presents no [—24—] valid objection to his trial in such court"); *Frisbie v. Collins*, 342 U.S.

519, 522 (1952) ("There is nothing in the Constitution that requires a court to permit a guilty person rightfully convicted to escape justice because he was brought to trial against his will"); *see also Kasi v. Angelone*, 300 F.3d 487, 493-95 (4th Cir. 2002).

Shibin argues that the *Ker-Frisbie* doctrine does not apply to him because Somalia and the United States do not have an extradition treaty. He suggests that the absence of a treaty should be taken as Somalia's wish not to have persons extradited and therefore removed involuntarily. But Shibin cites no case law for this theory, and we could find none. Indeed, the existence of an extradition treaty is hardly relevant to the applicability of the doctrine, unless the terms of the treaty explicitly foreclose it.

To be sure, there are fleeting references in the case law to exceptions to the *Ker-Frisbie* doctrine. For instance, in *United States v. Alvarez-Machain*, 504 U.S. 655, 662-70 (1992), the Court analyzed whether a treaty between countries, under which a breach would limit the jurisdiction of a court, prohibited the defendant's abduction. The implication there was that if the treaty so provided, the United States would be bound by the treaty. But the implication was not that the absence of a treaty would limit a court's jurisdiction. [—25—]

More explicitly, in *United States v. Anderson*, 472 F.3d 662, 666 (9th Cir. 2006), the court stated that the *Ker-Frisbie* doctrine does have exceptions that would deprive the court of jurisdiction over an extradited defendant when "(1) the transfer of the defendant violated the applicable extradition treaty, or (2) the United States government engaged in misconduct of the most shocking and outrageous kind to obtain his presence." (Internal quotation marks and citations omitted). Another court observed, however, that the shock-the-conscience exception rests on "shaky ground." *United States v. Best*, 304 F.3d 308, 312-13 (3d Cir. 2002).

Nonetheless, neither of the exceptions suggested in *Anderson* would help Shibin in this case. First, Shibin cites no treaty between Somalia and the United States that could limit a federal court's jurisdiction over him. And second, Shibin has failed to show that the government's conduct in this case was, in any degree, "of the most shocking and outrageous kind." *Anderson*, 472 F.3d at 666 (internal quotation marks omitted).

Factual realities also undermine Shibin's arguments. Although Shibin claims that he should have been allowed some formal process in Somalia, he does not identify what this process might have been. He has identified no extradition treaty or extradition process, and he has pointed to no other established legal process that might have been applicable. [—26—]

At bottom, we conclude that Shibin's presence in the United States, although against his will, satisfied the personal jurisdiction requirements of "brought into" or "found in," as contained in 18 U.S.C. §§ 1651, 1203, and 2280. *See, e.g., United States v. Shi*, 525 F.3d 709, 725 (9th Cir. 2008) (concluding that "the [statutory] requirement that a defendant be 'later found' does not contain the implicit requirement that the defendant's arrival in the United States be voluntary"); *United States v. Rezaq*, 134 F.3d 1121, 1130 (D.C. Cir. 1998) (holding that "found in" does not create a statutory exception to the *Ker-Frisbie* rule); *United States v. Yunis*, 924 F.2d 1086, 1092 (D.C. Cir. 1991) (finding that the statutory term "found in" "does not indicate the voluntariness limitation urged by [the defendant]"). Accordingly, we affirm the district court's ruling denying Shibin's motion to dismiss the indictment for lack of personal jurisdiction based on his being brought into the United States involuntarily.

IV

Shibin next contends that the non-piracy counts related to the *Marida Marguerite*, Counts 2 through 6, must be dismissed because "the universal jurisdiction doctrine did not provide the [district] court with jurisdiction" over those counts. Counts 2 through 6 charge Shibin with the following offenses: [—27—]

Count 2: Conspiracy to commit hostage taking, in violation of 18 U.S.C. § 1203(a);

Count 3: Hostage taking, in violation of 18 U.S.C. §§ 1203(a) and 2;

Count 4: Conspiracy to commit violence against maritime navigation, in violation of 18 U.S.C. §§ 2280(a)(1)(H);

Count 5: Violence against maritime navigation, in violation of 18 U.S.C. §§ 2280(a)(1)(A) and 2; and

Count 6: Use of a firearm during a crime of violence, in violation of 18 U.S.C. §§ 924(c) and 2.

Shibin argues that these crimes do not fit within the small set of crimes that are universally cognizable and therefore subject to prosecution under universal jurisdiction.

The government contends that universal jurisdiction was not invoked for the prosecution of Counts 2 through 6. Rather, "the criminal statutes [themselves] are clear in the extraterritorial scope, and in each case Congress acted pursuant to a constitutional grant of lawmaking power" to extend U.S. jurisdiction over those offenses.

At the outset, we agree that Counts 2 through 6 do not depend on universal jurisdiction. Rather, they rely on the jurisdiction provided by the statutes themselves.

It is well-established that Congress may criminalize extraterritorial conduct. *See, e.g., United States v. Ayesh*, 702 F.3d 162, 166 (4th Cir. 2012) ("'Congress has the authority to apply its laws, including criminal statutes, beyond the **[—28—]** territorial boundaries of the United States'" (quoting *United States v. Dawn*, 129 F.3d 878, 882 (7th Cir. 1997))); *EEOC v. Arabian Am. Oil Co.*, 499 U.S. 244, 248 (1991) ("Both parties concede, as they must, that Congress has the authority to enforce its laws beyond the territorial boundaries of the United States"), *superseded by statute on other grounds*, Civil Rights Act of

1991, Pub. L. No. 102-166, § 109(a), 105 Stat. 1071, 1077.

To be sure, statutes extend extraterritorially only if Congress clearly so provides. *See Morrison v. Nat'l Australia Bank Ltd.*, 130 S. Ct. 2869, 2877-78, 2883 (2010); *see also Kiobel v. Royal Dutch Petroleum Co.*, 133 S. Ct. 1659, 1664-65 (2013) (applying the presumption against extraterritoriality). But when Congress provides a clear indication of extraterritoriality, U.S. jurisdiction is not limited to offenses criminalized under international law nor dependent on universal jurisdiction. *United States v. Yousef*, 327 F.3d 56, 91 (2d Cir. 2003) ("[I]rrespective of whether customary international law provides a basis for jurisdiction over [the defendant] for Counts Twelve thru Nineteen, United States law provides a separate and complete basis for jurisdiction over each of these counts and . . . United States law is not subordinate to customary international law or necessarily **[—29—]** subordinate to treaty-based international law and, in fact, may conflict with both").

In this case, the substantive statutes on which Counts 2 through 6 rest clearly manifest Congress' intent to criminalize conduct that takes place outside the municipal jurisdiction of the United States. Section 1203, on which Counts 2 and 3 are based, criminalizes hostage taking and provides:

(a) Except as provided in subsection (b) of this section, whoever, whether *inside or outside the United States*, [takes hostages], shall be punished by imprisonment for any term of years or for life and, if the death of any person results, shall be punished by death or life imprisonment.

(b)(1) It is not an offense under this section if the conduct required for the offense occurred outside the United States unless–

(A) the offender or the person seized or detained is a national of the United States;

(B) *the offender is found in the United States*; or

(C) the governmental organization sought to be compelled is the Government of the United States.

18 U.S.C. § 1203 (emphasis added). This statute explicitly reaches hostage taking anywhere in the world, so long as the offender ends up in the United States. In this case, Shibin was involved in hostage taking on the *Marida Marguerite* and was later found in Virginia, where he was prosecuted. **[—30—]**

Section 2280, on which Counts 4 and 5 are based, criminalizes maritime violence and includes language similar to that in the hostage taking statute. It provides:

(b) Jurisdiction.— There is jurisdiction over the activity prohibited in subsection (a)–

(1) *in the case of a covered ship*, if–

(A) such activity is committed–

(i) against or on board a ship flying the flag of the United States at the time the prohibited activity is committed;

(ii) in the United States; or

(iii) by a national of the United States or by a stateless person whose habitual residence is in the United States;

(B) during the commission of such activity, a national of the United States is seized, threatened, injured or killed; or

(C) *the offender is later found in the United States after such activity is committed*;

(2) *in the case of a ship navigating* or scheduled to navigate solely within the territorial sea or internal *waters of a country other than the United States, if the offender is later found in the United States after such activity is committed*; and

(3) in the case of any vessel, if such activity is committed in an attempt to compel the United States to do or abstain from doing any act.

18 U.S.C. § 2280(b) (emphasis added). The term "covered ship," as used in § 2280(b), is defined as "a ship that is navigating **[—31—]** or is scheduled to navigate into, through or from waters beyond the outer limit of the territorial sea of a single country or a lateral limit of that country's territorial sea with an adjacent country." 18 U.S.C. § 2280(e). In this case, Shibin was involved in maritime violence against the *Marida Marguerite* in waters other than United States waters and was later found in Virginia, where he was prosecuted.

Finally, § 924(c), on which Count 6 is based, criminalizes the use or possession of a firearm in connection with a crime of violence. It is an ancillary crime that depends on the nature and reach of the underlying crime. Thus, its jurisdictional reach is coextensive with the jurisdiction of the underlying crime. As the statue provides:

[A]ny person who, during and in relation to *any crime of violence* or drug trafficking crime . . . *for which the person may be prosecuted in a court of the United States*, uses or carries a firearm, or who, in furtherance of any such crime, possesses a firearm, shall, in addition to the punishment provided for such crime of violence or drug trafficking crime . . . [be sentenced to an additional term of imprisonment].

18 U.S.C. § 924(c)(1)(A) (emphasis added). Thus, because Shibin could be prosecuted in the United States for hostage taking and maritime violence, he could also be prosecuted under § 924(c) for possessing, using, or carrying a firearm in connection with those crimes. *See United States v. Belfast*, 611 F.3d 783, 814 (11th Cir. 2010) (concluding that § 924(c) applies **[—32—]** extraterritorially because "a statute ancillary to a substantive

offense statute is presumed to have extraterritorial effect if the underlying substantive offense statute is determined to have extraterritorial effect" (internal alterations and quotation marks omitted)); *United States v. Hasan*, 747 F. Supp. 2d 642, 684 (E.D. Va. 2010) (applying § 924(c) extraterritorially), *aff'd sub nom. United States v. Dire*, 680 F.3d 446 (4th Cir. 2012). Thus, as an ancillary crime to underlying crimes that apply extraterritorially, § 924(c) applies coextensively with the underlying crimes.

Congress' power to enact statutes that extend extraterritorially is derived generally from the Define and Punish Clause, U.S. Const. art. I, § 8, cl. 10; the Treaty Power, U.S. Const. art. II, § 2, cl. 2; and the Necessary and Proper Clause, U.S. Const. art. I, § 8, cl. 18.

Thus, § 1203, the hostage-taking statute, is constitutionally valid as the implementation of the International Convention Against the Taking of Hostages, December 17, 1979, T.I.A.S. No. 11,081. *See United States v. Ferreira*, 275 F.3d 1020, 1027-28 (11th Cir. 2001) (concluding that "Congress passed the Hostage Taking Act to implement the International Convention Against the Taking of Hostages" and that it was a valid exercise of congressional authority under [—33—] the Necessary and Proper Clause); *United States v. Lue*, 134 F.3d 79, 81-84 (2d Cir. 1998) (same).

Similarly, § 2280, punishing maritime violence, is constitutionally valid as the implementation of the Convention for the Suppression of Unlawful Acts Against the Safety of Maritime Navigation arts. 7, 11, March 10, 1988, 1678 U.N.T.S. 221. *See United States v. Shi*, 525 F.3d 709, 721 (9th Cir. 2008) ("In order to satisfy this obligation [of the Maritime Safety Convention], it was necessary for the United States to codify the Convention's 'extradite or prosecute' requirement into federal law. Section 2280 accomplishes this task"); *cf. Yousef*, 327 F.3d at 95–96 (discussing a similar provision in the Montreal Convention).

Finally, § 924(c), criminalizing gun use in connection with any crime of violence that can be prosecuted in the United States, is constitutionally valid under the Necessary and Proper Clause in connection with other statutes' implementation of treaties. *See Lue*, 134 F.3d at 84 (relying on *M'Culloch v. Maryland*, 17 U.S. (4 Wheat.) 316 (1819), for the rule that "the 'plainly adapted' standard requires that the effectuating legislation bear a rational relationship to a permissible constitutional end").

At bottom, we reject Shibin's argument that the district court did not have jurisdiction under "universal jurisdiction" [—34—] over the non-piracy counts related to the *Marida Marguerite*, Counts 2 through 6. Universal jurisdiction was irrelevant to the prosecution of those counts, and, we conclude, each of those counts is based on a statute that Congress validly applied to extraterritorial conduct, including Shibin's conduct.

V

Finally, Shibin contends that the district court abused its discretion in admitting into evidence the testimony of FBI Agent Kevin Coughlin, who was called as a witness to rebut testimony given by defense witness Mohamud Salad Ali. Agent Coughlin had conducted pretrial interviews of Salad Ali with the assistance of an FBI Somali linguist, who served as an interpreter. And as the interpreter gave Salad Ali's answers to the questions posed by Agent Coughlin, Coughlin made notes of what Salad Ali said.

During his testimony at trial, Salad Ali denied making some of the statements recorded in Agent Coughlin's notes. After Salad Ali concluded his testimony, the government called Agent Coughlin as a rebuttal witness, and Coughlin testified that Salad Ali did in fact make the statements he denied making. Shibin objected to the testimony because Agent Coughlin was repeating out-of-court statements of an absent declarant—the interpreter—and therefore Coughlin's testimony was inadmissible hearsay. The district court, however, overruled [—35—] the objection. But it pointed out that Shibin could cross examine Agent Coughlin about the use of the interpreter and how the interview was conducted. Shibin now contends that the district court's ruling was an abuse of discretion.

The government argues that Agent Coughlin's testimony was not inadmissible hearsay of the interpreter but rather admissible testimony of prior inconsistent statements made by Salad Ali. *See* Fed. R. Evid. 801(c)(2) (defining hearsay as evidence offered "to prove the truth the matter asserted in the statement"); Fed. R. Evid. 613(b) (providing the procedure for admitting extrinsic evidence of a prior inconsistent statement).

We agree with the government that the district court did not abuse its discretion in admitting Agent Coughlin's testimony about Salad Ali's statements in the interview because they were admitted only as prior inconsistent statements. And the absence in court of the interpreter did not render the statements inadmissible as hearsay because the interpreter was not the declarant, but only a "language conduit." *United States v. Vidacak*, 553 F.3d 344, 352 (4th Cir. 2009) ("[E]xcept in unusual circumstances, an interpreter is no more than a language conduit and therefore his translation does not create an additional level of hearsay" (quoting *United States v. Martinez–Gaytan*, 213 F.3d 890, 892 (5th Cir. 2000) (internal quotation marks omitted)). While interpreted testimony might be unusable [—36—] without the interpreter's presence in a circumstance "where the particular facts of a case cast significant doubt upon the accuracy of a translated confession," *id.*, no such facts were presented in this case. Indeed, Agent Coughlin testified without contradiction that Salad Ali did not have any difficulty understanding the questions.

Shibin also raises for the first time on appeal a challenge under *Crawford*, arguing that the Confrontation Clause required the presence of the interpreter. *See Crawford v. Washington*, 541 U.S. 36, 59 (2004). He argues that "the absence of the interpreter at trial

prevented [him] from being able to challenge by cross-examination, the reliability of the out-of-court statements that the government offered against him." *Crawford*, however, "does not bar the use of testimonial statements for purposes other than establishing the truth of the matter asserted." *United States v. Ayala*, 601 F.3d 256, 272 (4th Cir. 2010) (quoting *Crawford*, 541 U.S. at 60 n.9). Here, the statements were introduced as prior inconsistent statements. The interpreter was nothing more than a language conduit. He translated the statements of Salad Ali and Agent Coughlin, both of whom were subject to cross examination.

Moreover, because we review Shibin's *Crawford* argument for plain error, Shibin must show that the error affected his substantial rights. *See* Fed. R. Crim. P. 52(b); *United States* [—37—] *v. Olano*, 507 U.S. 725, 734-35 (1993). Shibin, however, has made no mention of any substantial rights that were adversely affected. Indeed, Agent Coughlin's rebuttal testimony was not even critical to Shibin's convictions. Shibin admitted his involvement in the ransom negotiations of the *Marida Marguerite*, and his involvement in the *Quest* piracy was established by coconspirator testimony, Shibin's admissions, and the contents of Shibin's cell phone. In addition, Salad Ali himself testified that the investors of the *Quest* piracy could have chosen Shibin to be the negotiator without his knowledge.

In short, we reject Shibin's challenge to the district court's evidentiary ruling.

* * *

For the foregoing reasons, we affirm Shibin's judgments of conviction.

AFFIRMED

United States Court of Appeals
for the Fourth Circuit

No. 12-1888

BUNN

VS.

OLDENDORFF CARRIERS GMBH & CO. KG

Appeal from the United States District Court for the
District of Maryland

Decided: July 17, 2013

Citation: 723 F.3d 454, 1 Adm. R. 151 (4th Cir. 2013).

Before **MOTZ**, **DAVIS**, and **WYNN**, Circuit Judges.

[—2—] **DAVIS**, Circuit Judge:

Defendant-Appellant Oldendorff Carriers GmbH & Co. KG ("Oldendorff") appeals from a judgment entered on a jury verdict under § 5(b) of the Longshore and Harbor Workers' Compensation Act, 33 U.S.C. § 905(b) (the "Act"). The claim arose when the longshoreman, Plaintiff-Appellee Richard Bunn, slipped and fell on Oldendorff's ship, the CHRISTOFFER OLDENDORFF ("the ship"), during loading operations in the Baltimore port. For the following reasons, we reject Oldendorff's challenges and affirm the judgment.

I.

Bunn, who worked for the stevedore, CNX Marine Terminals, Inc. ("CNX"), slipped on ice and injured himself while loading coal onto the ship, a bulk carrier, on February 16, 2007. We set forth the facts in the light most favorable to Bunn, the prevailing party at trial.

CNX shift supervisor Joseph White boarded the ship around 7 p.m. on February 15, 2007, to tell chief officer Andriy Fediv that CNX employees intended "to start[ ] loading that night." J.A. 113–14. Although the ship had been docked "a few days," CNX had been "unable to load [the] vessel" because of "some winter weather." Id. at 113. When White boarded the ship, "[he] noticed that . . . there was ice covered throughout the ship, with the

exception of . . . a pathway back from the gangway to the [—3—] deckhouse." Id. at 114. White "instructed" Fediv, "[W]e need a clear path to the holds to be able to load this vessel." Id. Fediv, who knew "which hatches [the CNX employees] were going to be [loading]," responded "[t]hat [the ship's crew] would salt and sand between the holds." Id. at 115–16.[1]

Based on this conversation, White told longshoreman Christopher Moxey (before the loading operation started) that the ship's crew was "going to treat the ship and make sure it was safe" by "[s]alt[ing] it, sand[ing] it, [and] shovel[ing] it." J.A. 86–88. Hours later, when Moxey and Bunn walked onto the ship, they found the area between the gangway and the deckhouse, and between the starboard rail and hatch number five, "[p]erfectly clear" of ice. Id. at 88–89.

Meanwhile, Bunn had arrived at the terminal at 6 p.m. on February 15, 2007, and began his 12-hour shift an hour later. His job was "to clean the terminal and to spread salt, and to go around and make sure all the equipment . . . was . . . . fueled and running . . . ." J.A. 223. Sometime between midnight and 1 a.m. on February 16, 2007, White approached Bunn to discuss loading the ship. Id. at 30, 224. Specifically, White instructed [—4—] Bunn to work onboard the ship during the night to assist Moxey in the loading operation. Bunn asked:

well, you want me to go now? [White] said no, take your time, finish lunch. He said they're getting the ship ready and we're still finishing up getting the terminal ready.

Id. at 224–25. White told Bunn he would call him or Moxey by radio when the ship was safe to load. Id. at 225.

In due course, Bunn and Moxey "had the instruction that it was okay to go up on the

---

[1] Fediv, the chief officer, testified that the ship's deck was icy but he denied that he and White discussed using salt and sand to treat the ice. Of course, the jury was entitled to reject Fediv's testimony and credit White's, as it did.

ship, the ship was ready," and the two boarded the ship around 1:30 a.m. on February 16, 2007. J.A. 177–78. Bunn testified:

> When we first got up on [the] deck, we could see a clear path to the number five hatch, and looking towards the deckhouse, you could see there was a path made to the deckhouse.

Id. at 178. Bunn and Moxey began loading coal into the number five hatch. *Id.* at 178. During the loading process, coal moves from a silo to a ship loader, *id.* at 121, "a giant crane that hangs over the ship," *id.* at 179.

> It has a boom with a conveyor belt on it that carries the coal. At the end of the boom, it has a spoon that comes down that goes in the hold. It has a spoon that rotates, and that directs the coal.

Id. at 179. Bunn's job was to be on the ship and help guide the coal as it was loaded into the holds.

> Being that the ship loader operator is up in the air, and he sits on one side of the machine, he can't see exactly what we can see when we're close to the hold. So in order to keep everything safe, we have to watch [—5—] his equipment, that he doesn't hit the hatch cover, and also direct him on where's the proper places to put the coal . . . . [T]he only way I see it is if I lean forward over the hold, I can see down in there how the coal is building up.

Id. at 179–80.

After loading the number five hatch, Bunn told Moxey to warm himself in the deckhouse; Bunn walked forward to load the number three hatch, "holding onto the hand rail on the side of the ship," J.A. 180–82, whereupon the accident occurred:

> It was nighttime. It's not much lighting when you get further past the beginning of the ship. At the beginning of the ship,

the deckhouse has lights. But as you get down, the lighting is very poor.

> * * *

> Well, I remember coming off the path, and it felt like I stepped up a little bit. I could tell my surface changed a little.

> I took a couple steps, and the next thing I knew, I had slipped and fell right then, boom; but I caught myself with my knees and my hands when I fell.

> * * *

> Well, then I realized that I kind of hurt myself, so I took my time. Then I figured well, maybe I'm just on a patch of ice that I didn't see and maybe I need to find where this path is.

> So I stood up and I said I'm going to slowly walk, take little steps toward the hold. I still needed to get to the hold . . . . So I started to walk towards the hold, and no more than one, two steps and boom. My feet came out from underneath of me and I landed on my back and my elbow.

Id. at 182–84. [—6—]

After Bunn's fall, Moxey told chief officer Fediv that "the ship was icy forward" and that it needed to be salted. J.A. 90. Fediv responded that "he only had a limited supply of salt." *Id.* at 91. About a half hour later, Moxey loaded coal into hatch number seven. *Id.* at 92. When he returned to hatch number three, he "noticed that it was still icy." *Id.*

At the close of Bunn's case, and again at the conclusion of all the evidence, Oldendorff moved for judgment as a matter of law.[2] The

---

[2] *See* Mot. for J. as a Matter of Law 2, ECF No. 86, *Bunn v. Oldendorff Carriers GmbH & Co. K.G.*, No. 1:10-cv-00255-WMN (D. Md. May 10, 2012). The joint appendix includes neither a complete trial transcript nor excerpts of the oral motions and the district court's reasons for denying them. Accordingly, we infer that information from the

company argued (as it had in seeking summary judgment earlier) that it owed no duty under the Act to warn of the open and obvious danger posed by the presence of ice in the areas where the longshoremen would be working. The district court denied the motions, reasoning that "liability can attach to [a] ship owner" that "voluntarily and affirmatively undertakes to remedy an [otherwise open and obvious] unsafe condition, but fails to do so." *Bunn v. Oldendorff Carriers GmbH & Co. K.G.*, No. WMN-10-255, 2012 WL 2681412, at *1 (D. Md. July 5, 2012). The court noted that, based on White's testimony, the jury could conclude that the ship— on the unquestioned authority to do so [—7—] of the chief officer, Fediv—had "voluntarily assumed the responsibility for salting and sanding the ice in the places where he knew CNX personnel would be working." *Id.* at *2.

The district court also declined to give the following jury instruction, requested by Oldendorff:

In the absence of any agreement, the ship is not responsible for any open and obvious condition.

J.A. 84. The court instructed the jury as follows:

The plaintiff's claims in this case are governed by the law that is set out in what we know as the Longshoreman and Harbor Workers Act. In accord with the law, your basic determination in this case is going to be to decide whether negligence on the part of the operator of the vessel CHRISTOPHER OLDENDORFF caused or directly contributed to the plaintiff's accident on or about February 16, 2007, and the damages claimed to have resulted from that occurrence . . . .

* * *

Negligence, simply stated, is the failure to exercise reasonable care under the existing circumstances.

But once the loading or the unloading of a ship by a stevedoring company has begun, the responsibility for safe working conditions is generally the burden of the terminal or the stevedoring company, in this case, CNX Marine Terminal. A shipowner, Oldendorff Carriers in this case, will only be responsible or liable for injury resulting directly from an unsafe condition on the ship of which it was aware and which it voluntarily agreed and undertook to remedy, but failed to do so.

Id. at 385–87.

The jury found Oldendorff negligent and calculated $1,863,750 in pecuniary and non-pecuniary damages. J.A. 406–07. [—8—] The jury further found, however, that Bunn was also negligent, and that he was 15 percent at fault for the accident. *Id.*

Oldendorff renewed its motion for judgment as a matter of law and moved alternatively for a new trial, arguing that the court had erred in refusing to give an instruction on the "open and obvious" defense. Mot. for J. as a Matter of Law 17, Docket No. 86, *Bunn*, No. 1:10-cv-00255-WMN (D. Md. May 10, 2012). The court denied the post-trial motions, and this timely appeal followed.

II.

Oldendorff raises two principal assignments of error. First, Oldendorff argues that the district court erred in denying the motions for judgment as a matter of law. Second, Oldendorff argues that the district court misinformed the jury about the applicable law, and therefore erred in denying the motion for new trial. We discern no reversible error.[3] [—9—]

---

court's memorandum opinion denying Oldendorff's post-trial motion for judgment as a matter of law.

[3] Oldendorff also argues that the district court erred in denying its motion for summary judgment made at the conclusion of discovery because, as a

A.

Oldendorff first argues that the district court erred in denying its motions for judgment as a matter of law because "[t]he open and obvious nature of the icy deck was established beyond dispute," and Oldendorff had "a responsibility to warn only of hidden dangers." Opening Br. 8, 17.[4] Those assertions are correct statements of the law, as far as they go. The problem for Oldendorff is that its liability does not depend on the duty to warn; rather, as the district court repeatedly (and correctly) indicated, this is a simple case of primary negligence.

1.

Section 5(b) of the Act permits a longshoreman to "seek damages in a third-party negligence action against the owner of the vessel on which he was injured." *Howlett v. Birkdale* [—10—] *Shipping Co., S.A.*, 512 U.S. 92, 96 (1994). The Act does not, however,

---

matter of law, the icy condition of the ship was open and obvious, and therefore Oldendorff had no duty to warn of the danger (the same argument made at and after trial). Although neither party has addressed the propriety of Oldendorff's purported appeal of the summary judgment ruling, it is well settled that we "'will not review, under any standard, the pretrial denial of a motion for summary judgment after a full trial and final judgment on the merits.'" *Varghese v. Honeywell Int'l, Inc.*, 424 F.3d 411, 421 (4th Cir. 2005) (quoting *Chesapeake Paper Prods. Co. v. Stone & Webster Eng'g* (Continued) [—9—] *Corp.*, 51 F.3d 1229, 1237 (4th Cir. 1995)). There is no reason to deviate from that rule here.

[4] Our applicable standard of review in these circumstances is well-settled:

We review the denial of a Rule 50(b) motion de novo, viewing the evidence in the light most favorable to the prevailing party, and will affirm the denial of such a motion unless the jury lacked a legally sufficient evidentiary basis for its verdict. *First Union Commercial Corp. v. GATX Capital Corp.*, 411 F.3d 551, 556 (4th Cir. 2005).

Gregg v. Ham, 678 F.3d 333, 341 (4th Cir. 2012).

"specify the acts or omissions of the vessel that . . . constitute negligence"; rather, "the contours of a vessel's duty to longshoremen [have been] . . . resolved through the application of accepted principles of tort law and the ordinary process of litigation." *Howlett*, 512 U.S. at 97–98 (internal quotation marks omitted). In *Scindia Steam Navigation Co., Ltd. v. De Los Santos* ("*Scindia*"), the Supreme Court "outlined the three general duties shipowners owe to longshoremen." *Id.* at 98 (citing *Scindia*, 451 U.S. 156 (1981)).

The first, which courts have come to call the "turnover duty," relates to the condition of the ship upon the commencement of stevedoring operations. The second duty, applicable once stevedoring operations have begun, provides that a shipowner must exercise reasonable care to prevent injuries to longshoremen in areas that remain under the "active control of the vessel." The third duty, called the "duty to intervene," concerns the vessel's obligations with regard to cargo operations in areas under the principal control of the independent stevedore.

Id. (internal citations omitted) (citing *Scindia*, 451 U.S. at 167–78). Here, only the turnover duty is at issue.

"The turnover duty has two components." *Lincoln v. Reksten Mgmt.*, 354 F.3d 262, 266 (4th Cir. 2003).

The first involves the shipowner's duty with respect to the ship's gear, equipment, tools, and work space that the stevedore will utilize during its operations. The shipowner must "at least [exercise] ordinary care *under the circumstances* to have the ship and its equipment in such condition that an expert and experienced stevedore will be able by the exercise of [—11—] reasonable care to carry on its cargo operations with reasonable safety to persons and property."

Id. (alteration in original) (emphasis added) (quoting *Scindia*, 451 U.S. at 166–67). "As a corollary to this initial turnover duty," the shipowner must

> warn the stevedore of any hazards on the ship or with respect to its equipment that are known to the vessel or should be known to it in the exercise of reasonable care, *that would likely be encountered by the stevedore* in the course of his cargo operations *and that are not known by the stevedore and would not be obvious to or anticipated by him* if reasonably competent in the performance of his work.

Id. (emphasis added) (quoting *Scindia*, 451 U.S. at 167). "The duty to warn attaches only to latent hazards," *id.* (quoting *Howlett*, 512 U.S. at 99–100); "[i]f a defect is open and obvious and the stevedore should be able to conduct its operations around it safely, the shipowner does not violate the duty to warn," *id.*

In denying Oldendorff judgment as a matter of law, the district court reasoned that "[t]he validity of [the] [open and obvious] rule or its applicability to ice on the deck under *general* circumstances [was] never . . . in dispute." *Bunn*, 2012 WL 2681412, at *2 (emphasis added).

> What was in dispute was whether Fediv voluntarily assumed the responsibility for salting and sanding the ice in the places where he knew CNX personnel would be working. [—12—]

Id. The court further reasoned that, "while ice on the deck may [have] be[en] open and obvious, it was not obvious that the ship owner would promise to take care of the hazard, and then not do so." *Id.*

> [W]hen a ship owner voluntarily and affirmatively undertakes to remedy an unsafe condition, but fails to do so, liability can attach to the ship owner.... Thus, there was no question that the central determination regarding liability to be reached at trial was whether Fediv had promised to clear those portions of

the deck where those unloading the vessel would need to traverse.

Id. at *1. Because the jury could reasonably credit White's testimony that Fediv had promised to treat ice leading to and around the cargo holds, the court concluded that the jury could reasonably find Oldendorff liable for affirmatively undertaking, and failing, to remedy the unsafe condition. *Id.* at *2 & n.1. That is, the jury could reasonably find Oldendorff liable for simple negligence.

2.

We find no error in the district court's reasoning. Several other circuits have long held that a shipowner may be liable under the Act for promising, yet failing, to remedy a dangerous condition that injures a longshoreman. *See Lieggi v. Maritime Co. of the Philippines*, 667 F.2d 324, 325–26, 329 (2d Cir. 1981) (affirming a judgment against a shipowner whose agent had "affirmatively undert[aken]," but failed, to remove wire and [—13—] grease spots that caused a longshoreman's injuries because, "by making this affirmative undertaking, the owner [had] eliminated any possible reasonable basis for relying on the stevedore to correct the hazardous condition"); *Bueno v. United States*, 687 F.2d 318, 320–21 (9th Cir. 1983) (finding that a shipowner may be liable for a longshoreman's injury aboard the ship when it "voluntarily undert[akes] to check the safety of the vessel on a regular basis"); *Webster v. M/V Moolchand, Sethia Liners, Ltd.*, 730 F.2d 1035, 1037–38 (5th Cir. 1984) (affirming a jury's finding of liability against a shipowner because "there was evidence that the winch [that injured the longshoreman] was not operating properly, that this was brought to the crew's attention, and that their repair efforts failed").[5]

---

[5] Although some scholars view the relevant duty in *Lieggi* and *Webster* as one of active involvement, not turnover, *see* 1 Thomas J. Schoenbaum & Jessica L. McClellan, *Schoenbaum's Admiralty & Maritime Law* § 7-10 (5th ed. 2012); Kenneth G. Engerrand & Jonathan A. Tweedy, *A Tedious Balance: Third Party Claims Under the Longshore and Harbor Workers' Compensation Act*, 10 Loy. Mar. L.J. 1, 20 (2011), the Supreme Court has

Holding a shipowner liable for promising, but failing, to remedy a dangerous condition comports with "accepted principles of tort law," which inform a shipowner's duties under the Act. [—14—] *Howlett*, 512 U.S. at 97-98.[6] These principles include the general rule that "undertakings can create a duty of care." Dan B. Dobbs, Paul T. Hayden & Ellen M. Bublick, *Dobbs' Law of Torts* § 410 (2d ed. 2012) (noting that "one who voluntarily assumes a duty must then perform that duty with reasonable care"). "An undertaking in this sense is a kind of explicit or implicit promise, or at least a commitment, conveyed in words or in conduct." *Id.* (footnote omitted).

> The general rule is that the defendant is under a duty to perform undertakings made for safety purposes and is liable for physical harm he causes the plaintiff by negligently performing or quitting performance once it has begun.

Id. at § 411. *Accord Dalldorf v. Higgerson-Buchanan, Inc.*, 402 F.2d 419, 422 (4th Cir. 1968) ("[A]nyone who does an affirmative act is under a duty to others to exercise the care of a reasonable man to protect them against an unreasonable risk of harm to them arising out of the act.") (internal quotation marks omitted). Because the credible evidence showed that Fediv promised to treat the ice but failed to do so, the jury reasonably concluded that Fediv had failed to exercise due care.

Holding a shipowner liable for promising, yet failing, to remedy a hazard also comports with a well-settled principle of [—15—] the turnover duty: the scope of that duty depends on the circumstances of each particular case.

See Lincoln, 354 F.3d at 266 (noting that a shipowner must exercise ordinary care "*under the circumstances* to have the ship" in a reasonably safe condition) (emphasis added). When the circumstances include a promise to remedy a dangerous situation, the shipowner may fail to exercise reasonable care if it does not fulfill its promise.[7] Here, the evidence viewed in the light most favorable to Bunn established that Fediv promised to treat the ice, and failed to do so (perhaps because he "had a limited supply of salt," *see supra*, at 6). These circumstances provide a legally sufficient evidentiary basis for holding Oldendorff liable for Bunn's injuries.

3.

Apart from the fact that the jury verdict permissibly rested on a finding of simple negligence, Oldendorff's argument [—16—] that the ice was "open and obvious" conveniently overlooks the fact that the presence of *untreated* ice was assuredly *not* "open and obvious," and betrays the company's misplaced, narrow view of the turnover duty.[8]

---

found that the general principles supporting one duty under the Act may apply to other duties, as well, *Howlett*, 512 U.S. at 102. For the reasons given in text, we can discern no good reason to limit liability arising from a shipowner's breach of a promise to correct a dangerous condition, even one that is otherwise "open and obvious," to the "active involvement" rubric.

[6] Notably, Bunn's complaint alleged negligence for both failing to warn of the untreated ice, and for promising yet failing to treat the ice in the first place. *See* J.A. 13-14 (Compl. ¶¶ 10, 12).

[7] Our colleague in dissent insists that when the circumstances include an open and obvious hazard, the shipowner "has a diminished turnover duty of safe condition." *Post*, at 35 (citing cases from outside the Fourth Circuit). For the reasons stated *infra* in Part II.A.3, however, the untreated ice was neither open nor obvious. Moreover, in none of the cases cited by the dissent did the shipowner expressly promise, and fail, to remedy the hazardous condition. *See, e.g., Pimental v. LTD Can. Pac. Bul*, 965 F.2d 13, 15 (5th Cir. 1992) (observing that the plaintiff had "offered no proof that the[ ] [hazardous] conditions were reported to the vessel crew"), cited *post*, at 35.

[8] Contrary to our dissenting colleague's assertion, Bunn did not concede that the untreated ice that he encountered near hatch number three was open and obvious. *See post*, at 40. Although Bunn asserted in his appellate brief that "the ice-covered condition of the *deck* was open and obvious," Resp. Br. 18 (emphasis added), he maintained that, following Fediv's promise, "the lack of treatment with sand and salt of the ice in the *darkened area where [he] was obliged to work*"-- i.e., the area near hatch number three--"was not open and obvious," *id.* (emphasis added). *See also* Opp'n to Mot. for Summ. J, *Bunn v. Oldendorff Carriers GmbH & Co. K.G.*, No. 1:10-cv-00255-WMN (D. Md. Nov. 18, 2010), ECF No. 27, at 6

That a shipowner *generally* need not warn of open and obvious dangers does not negate the shipowner's duty to exercise ordinary care *under the circumstances* to ensure that the ship is in a reasonably safe condition. *Lincoln*, 354 F.3d at 266 (quoting *Scindia*, 451 U.S. at 166–67). After all, the duty to warn is a mere corollary to the turnover duty, not the sole manner of measuring the reasonableness of a shipowner's actions upon turnover. *See id.* (quoting *Scindia*, 451 U.S. at 167). In other words, failure to warn of a latent hazard is but one way a shipowner may violate its turnover duty; promising, but failing, **[—17—]** to remedy a dangerous condition may also establish a shipowner's failure to exercise ordinary care.

In any case, imposing liability on a shipowner that promises, but fails, to remedy a dangerous condition, and then fails to warn of its own failure, is not inconsistent with our prior cases on the open and obvious rule. Although a shipowner need not warn of hazards that would be "obvious to or anticipated" by a stevedore, *Lincoln*, 354 F.3d at 266 (quoting *Scindia*, 451 U.S. at 166–67), a reasonably competent stevedore has no reason to anticipate a hazard that the shipowner has promised to remedy but fails, without warning, to do so.[9] Here, for instance,

---

("With the assurance by the chief officer that he would make the slippery condition safe, the slippery condition that continued to exist because of the failure on the part of [Oldendorff] to correct same as promised was no longer open and obvious . . . . [U]ntil [Bunn] fell, the fact that [the slippery condition] had not been made safe was neither open nor obvious to [CNX].").

[9] The dissent asserts that "a shipowner can reasonably rely on an expert and experienced stevedore and its expert longshoremen to notice and avoid an open and obvious hazard," regardless of the shipowner's "pre-turnover promise" to remedy the hazard. *Post*, at 38–39. That may well be true when the hazard *remains* open and obvious despite the unfulfilled promise to remove it— imagine, for instance, a longshoreman encountering a large oil slick in bright sunlight—but that is not the case here. Common experience tells us that, unlike a brightly-lit oil slick, ice may not be immediately visible, especially in the dark. And viewing the evidence in the light most favorable to Bunn, the untreated ice he encountered was

the evidence viewed in the light most favorable to **[—18—]** Bunn established that Fediv promised to treat the ice; accordingly, a jury could find that neither CNX (the stevedore) nor Bunn (the longshoreman) had reason to anticipate untreated ice aboard the ship, even though one might otherwise have expected such a hazard following a winter storm.[10]

We are not persuaded by Oldendorff's argument that, regardless of Fediv's promise to treat the ice, the untreated ice remained an open and obvious condition as a matter of law, absolving it of liability, even without Fediv communicating the presence of the untreated ice to the stevedore.[11] **[—19—]**

---

neither open nor obvious. Bunn discovered the ice— at night, in a poorly lit area—only after taking the few steps that led to his fall. Moreover, because Fediv knew where the CNX employees would be working and had promised more than five hours before they commenced work to treat the ice with salt and sand, Bunn had no reason to anticipate a slippery surface near the number three hatch. Thus, the untreated ice was a latent hazard. *See, e.g., Lincoln*, 354 at 266 (describing latent hazards as those that "would not be . . . *anticipated* by" a longshoreman) (emphasis added) (quoting *Scindia*, 451 U.S. at 167).

[10] Indeed, several witnesses testified that shipowners generally bear responsibility for removing ice. *See, e.g.,* Kevin Palmer Test., J.A. 146 (testifying that "[it] would be usual" for a ship's crew to "be scraping the ice off their deck"); White Test., J.A. 115 ("It's [the chief mate's] responsibility, the vessel's responsibility to clear [the ship], to make it safe for stevedores[,] of the ice and the other debris that could be up there.").

[11] It is readily apparent in its briefs and oral argument that Oldendorff feels itself hemmed in by its inability to lay much (if not all) of the blame for Bunn's injury on his employer, CNX. There is some force to Oldendorff's understandable chagrin in this regard. Although Fediv promised to make the work areas safe for the longshoremen loading the coal, White, the CNX shift supervisor, apparently never reboarded the ship to confirm that Fediv had done so before ordering his workers, Bunn and Moxey, to commence operations. But Congress has denied Oldendorff the opportunity it desires. *See Howlett*, 512 U.S. at 97:

Section 5(b) also eliminated the stevedore's obligation, imposed by *Ryan Stevedoring Co. v. Pan-Atlantic S.S. Corp.*, 350 U.S. 124

Moreover, a shipowner is absolved of its duty to warn only if the condition is both open and obvious *and* the stevedore's employee is "able to conduct . . . operations around [the hazard] safely." *Lincoln*, 354 F.3d at 266 (citing *Bonds v. Mortensen & Lange*, 717 F.2d 123, 127-28 (4th Cir. 1983)).[12] The [—20—]

(1956), to indemnify a shipowner, if held liable to a longshoreman, for (Continued) [—19—] breach of the stevedore's express or implied warranty to conduct cargo operations with reasonable safety.

Furthermore, even assuming that Bunn indicated on deposition or otherwise that he expects his employer to furnish a safe place to work, such testimony does not absolve the shipowner of the consequences of its direct primary negligence.

Of course, a *longshoreman's own negligence*, as opposed to the *negligence of his stevedore employer*, may reduce a shipowner's liability. And indeed, as mentioned in text, the jury here found Bunn 15 percent at fault for his injuries. Although Bunn testified that he "noticed [a] pathway" that had been cleared of ice, and "glance[d] around and [saw] ice in other areas," J.A. 226, this testimony does not establish beyond dispute that he knew—before he fell and was injured—that the ice near the number three hatch remained untreated. Indeed, Bunn also testified that he fell almost immediately upon walking toward the hold, *see id.* at 183 (testifying that he took only "a couple steps, and the next thing [he] knew, [he] had slipped and f[allen] right then, boom"). On this record, therefore, even had we been asked to examine the issue (and we have not been asked) we can discern no infirmity in the jury's allocation of fault.

[12] In *Bonds*, we held that the shipowner owed no duty to intervene and stop discharging operations despite a gantry crane's malfunctioning bell, which failed to ring "when the gantry move[d] forward or backward to warn longshoremen and the ship's crew of the gantry's motion." *Bonds*, 717 F.2d at 124. We reasoned that the stevedore and longshoremen "were aware that the bell was not functioning properly" and had not complained; "the malfunctioning bell and ship's design being *obvious and known to all*, the shipowner was entitled to rely on [the stevedore's] judgment as to whether discharge operations could (Continued) [—20—] safely be undertaken." *Id.* at 124, 127-28 & n.4 (emphasis added). The reasoning of *Bonds* is inapplicable when, as here, the shipowner had no reasonable basis for relying on the longshoreman's or stevedore's judgment; neither CNX nor Bunn had reason to expect the untreated ice near hatch

evidence, viewed in the light most favorable to Bunn, showed that Oldendorff breached its duty to warn of the ice near the number three hatch because it was impossible for Bunn to safely navigate around the untreated ice to perform the cargo loading operations. *See, e.g.,* J.A. 92 (Moxey's testimony that the area around hatch number three was so "icy" that it was "unsafe" to complete operations).[13] [—21—]

(We emphasize that our discussion of the duty to warn is merely dictum.)

For all these reasons, we are not persuaded that the "jury lacked a legally sufficient evidentiary basis for its verdict," *Gregg*, 678 F.3d at 341, and, thus, we conclude that the district court did not err in its denial of the motions for judgment as a matter of law.

---

number three after Fediv promised to treat it, and thus, the ice was not "obvious and known to all." *Id.* at 127–28.

[13] Contrary to our dissenting colleague's assertion, *see post*, at 41 n.7, the rule derived from *Bonds* and cited in *Lincoln* is not inconsistent with *Howlett*, which was decided nearly a decade before *Lincoln*. As the dissent recognizes, *see post*, at 33, the duty to warn is a corollary to the turnover duty of safe condition, *Howlett*, 512 U.S. at 98. As such, it is subject to the same governing principles, including the rule that a shipowner's liability depends on whether the stevedore is able "to carry on cargo operations with reasonable safety." *Id.* (internal quotation marks omitted). Indeed, several of our sister circuits—in decisions issued after *Howlett*—have recognized that a shipowner may be liable for failure to warn of even open and obvious hazards. *See, e.g., Hill v. Reederei F. Laesz G.M.B.H., Rostock*, 435 F.3d 404, 409 (3d Cir. 2006) (noting that a shipowner may be liable for not warning of an "open and obvious hazard" if "avoiding the hazard would be impractical for the longshoreman" or "the ship should have known that the longshoremen would confront the hazard"), cited *post*, at 35; *Moore v. Angela MV*, 353 F.3d 376, 381 (5th Cir. 2003) (noting that "a vessel has no duty to warn of dangers that would be obvious to a longshoreman of reasonable competence," unless "the longshoreman's only alternatives to facing the hazard are (Continued) [—21—] unduly impracticable or time-consuming or would force him to leave the job").

4.

Before moving on to consider Oldendorff's second issue on appeal, we feel it appropriate to offer a few respectful responses to our good friend in dissent.

Our colleague laments that

the focus of the parties on the shipowner's promise, rather than the character of the icy conditions, and the alternatives Bunn had in facing those conditions, left the jury with insufficient evidence to find Oldendorff breached its turnover duty.

Post, at 32. But we need not decide whether there was any justification for "the [parties'] focus . . . on the shipowner's promise," *id.*; there clearly was, as the promise was among the circumstances that defined the standard of care. *See Lincoln*, 354 F.2d at 266 (noting that shipowners must exercise ordinary care "under the circumstances"). Moreover, the parties to a [—22—] lawsuit are entitled to frame the issues as each deems best. *See, e.g., Greenlaw v. United States*, 554 U.S. 237, 243 (2008) ("In our adversary system, in both civil and criminal cases, in the first instance and on appeal, we follow the principle of party presentation. That is, we rely on the parties to frame the issues for decision and assign to courts the role of neutral arbiter of matters the parties present . . . . [T]he parties know what is best for them, and are responsible for advancing the facts and arguments entitling them to relief.") (internal quotation marks omitted). The problem for Oldendorff—one from which it cannot be rescued at this stage—is that it has elected to litigate this case *solely* on the theory that it did not breach the *duty to warn*, that is, that Oldendorff owed no duty to warn of untreated ice after having promised, hours before actual turnover of the vessel for loading, to treat the ice and thereby render the areas around and abutting the holds safe. Although we have offered up plenty of *dicta* to question the legal correctness of that assertion, our affirmance of the judgment is based not on the *duty to warn* but on the more general turnover *duty of safe condition*. That is, we conclude that the

district court did not err in treating the breach of Oldendorff's promise, *under the circumstances*, as a failure to exercise reasonable care in executing Oldendorff's more general [—23—] turnover duty. In short, the evidence supported the jury's finding of simple negligence.

Adopting Oldendorff's misguided view that the lawsuit implicates only the duty to warn, the dissent asserts that "the center of [our] disagreement . . . is the question of whether a shipowner's unfulfilled promise to remedy an open and obvious hazard affects its turnover duty." *Post*, at 32. This characterization misses the mark, not only for the reasons articulated above but because it wrongly assumes that the hazard created by the presence of ice on the deck and around the hatches remained precisely the same after Fediv's promise to treat it as it was before he made (and then breached) his promise: perfectly open and obvious. *See, e.g., post*, at 39 (reasoning that "[a]s long as an unremedied hazard *remains open and obvious*, a shipowner's liability . . . is thus extremely limited") (emphasis added). For the reasons stated above, the risk of injury from the untreated ice was decidedly not open and obvious after Fediv made and then breached his promise to treat it. We agree to disagree on that score.[14] [—24—]

Our dissenting colleague insists that a shipowner's turnover duty is narrow, *see, e.g., post*, at 32, 34, and that stevedores and longshoremen bear the primary burden for ensuring safe working conditions for longshoremen, *see, e.g., post* at 36 (observing that "a shipowner can, ordinarily, reasonably rely on the stevedore [and longshoremen] . . .

_____

[14] To put it another way, Oldendorff should have known—after Fediv's promise and failure to treat the ice—that neither Bunn nor his stevedore employer would have expected a longshoreman to encounter the slippery surface near hatch number three. Thus, Oldendorff "should have expected that [Bunn] could not or would not avoid the hazard and conduct cargo operations reasonably safely." *Kirsch v. Plovidba*, 971 F.2d 1026, 1031 (3d (Continued) [—24—] Cir. 1992), *cited in post*, at 39–40. As such, the jury was entitled to find Oldendorff liable based on Fediv's failure to treat the ice as promised. *Id.*

to notice obvious hazards and to take steps consistent with [their] expertise to avoid those hazards where practical to do so") (alterations in original) (quoting *Kirsch v. Plovidba*, 971 F.2d 1026, 1030 (3d Cir. 1992)). Indeed, the dissent suggests that Bunn could have prevented his injury by, *inter alia*, "clear[ing] the ice himself." *Post*, at 42–43. But that, of course, would have required Bunn to know about the untreated ice, which he discovered only upon taking a few steps and immediately falling. Moreover, the evidence at trial overwhelmingly established (and the jury was entitled to find) that the responsibility for removing ice aboard a ship customarily rests with the shipowner. *See supra* n.10. As the dissent concedes, *see post*, at 39, custom, like any other circumstance surrounding an accident, may [—25—] inform a shipowner's duties to longshoremen.[15] And, of course, any negligence on the part of a stevedore—here, CNX, acting through its agent White—does not absolve a shipowner such as Oldendorff of its own duty of care. *See, e.g., Woodruff v. United States*, 710 F.2d 128, 132 n.9 (4th Cir. 1983) (noting that a shipowner "will be liable for the full extent of [a] [longshoreman's] injuries notwithstanding proof of concurrent negligence contributing to the injury on the part of [the stevedore], diminished only by [the longshoreman's] contributory negligence.") (citing *Edmonds v. Compagnie Generale Transatlantique*, 443 U.S. 256 (1979)).

For the reasons set forth, we think to say the turnover duty is "narrow" is to speak descriptively, not prescriptively; we do not believe the Supreme Court has built the kind of impenetrable silos of theories cabining shipowner negligence with the rigidity that the dissent believes exist. If, indeed, that is the import of the rule adopted by the Third, Fifth, and Ninth Circuits, as the dissent's

reliance on their precedents suggests, we choose a different path. [—26—]

In any event, distilled to its essence, the dissent's real concern seems to rest on its unstated belief that the jury should have found Bunn 100 percent at fault rather than merely the 15 percent the jury did find. *See post*, at 39 (suggesting that Bunn "shirk[ed] his duty to act with reasonable care"); *but see supra* n.11. But whether Bunn's failure to exercise reasonable care for his own safety constituted the sole proximate cause of his injuries— the crux of the dissent— is not presented as an issue in this case.

Finally, we confess we find somewhat puzzling the dissent's assertion that the proper outcome is neither affirmance nor judgment for Oldendorff as a matter of law, but rather, "a new trial or other proceedings." *Post*, at 47. Yet our good friend fails to explain what such proceedings would accomplish. Oldendorff has not, for example, challenged the sufficiency of the verdict on the grounds that the district court allowed the jury to consider unreliable, and therefore, inadmissible evidence. *See, e.g., Weisgram v. Marley Co.*, 528 U.S. 440, 443 (2000). Nor has Bunn, as appellee, asked for a new trial if we find the district court erred in denying Oldendorff's motions for judgment as a matter of law. *See* Fed. R. Civ. P. 50(e); *Neely v. Martin K. Elby Constr. Co.*, 386 U.S. 317, 327 (1967) (observing that a plaintiff-appellee may be entitled to a new trial if "[t]he erroneous exclusion of evidence . . . would have [—27—] strengthened his case" or "the trial court itself caused the insufficiency in [the] plaintiff-appellee's case by erroneously placing too high a burden of proof on him at trial"), cited *post*, at 47. The task before us, then, is quite simple, and requires no further proceedings: we need only decide "whether a jury, viewing the evidence in the light most favorable to [Bunn], could have properly reached the conclusion reached by this jury." *Baynard v. Malone*, 268 F.3d 228, 235 (4th Cir. 2001) (internal quotation marks omitted). For the reasons stated above, we conclude that the answer is yes, and affirm the denial of Oldendorff's motions for judgment as a matter of law.

---

[15] The dissent risks oversimplifying the case by suggesting that darkness alone was the hazard giving rise to Bunn's injury. *See post*, at 44–45. As stated above, Oldendorff's liability arose from the *totality* of the circumstances, which included not only the ship's poor lighting, but Fediv's promise to treat the ice, his failure to do so, and the custom of shipowners taking responsibility for removing ice aboard ships.

B.

Finally, Oldendorff argues that the district court erred in denying its motion for a new trial because the court's refusal to give the company's requested "open and obvious instruction deprived the jury of a full and accurate understanding of the law," and "deprived [Oldendorff] of the opportunity to argue effectively the significance of the open and obvious defense." Opening Br. 40–41.

"We review for abuse of discretion a district court's denial of a motion for new trial," and "will not reverse such a decision save in the most exceptional circumstances." *Figg v. Schroeder*, 312 F.3d 625, 641 (4th Cir. 2002) (internal quotation [—28—] marks omitted).[16] Similarly, "[w]e review a trial court's jury instructions for abuse of discretion," keeping in mind that "a trial court has broad discretion in framing its instructions to a jury." *Volvo Trademark Holding Aktiebolaget v. Clark Mach. Co.*, 510 F.3d 474, 484 (4th Cir. 2007). "Instructions will be considered adequate if construed as a whole, and in light of the whole record, they adequately informed the jury of the controlling legal principles without misleading or confusing the jury to the prejudice of the existing party." *King v. McMillan*, 594 F.3d 301, 311 (4th Cir. 2010) (internal quotation marks and brackets omitted). "Even if a jury was erroneously instructed, however, we will not set aside a resulting verdict unless the erroneous instruction *seriously* prejudiced the challenging party's case." *Coll. Loan Corp. v. SLM Corp.*, 396 F.3d 588, 595 (4th Cir. 2005) (emphasis added) (internal quotation marks omitted).

Preliminarily, we hold that Oldendorff has failed to preserve a challenge to the jury instructions, as the company has provided no record of an objection to the district court. *See* Fed. R. Civ. P. 51(c)(1) ("A party who objects to an instruction or the failure to give an instruction must do so on [—29—] the record,

stating distinctly the matter objected to and the grounds for the objection"). When challenging instructions on appeal, a party must "furnish the court of appeals with so much of the record of the proceedings below as is necessary to enable informed appellate review." *Faigin v. Kelly*, 184 F.3d 67, 87 (1st Cir. 1999) (finding that appellant's "fail[ure] to supply a transcript of the Rule 51 sidebar conference" gave rise to a "presumption that none of his challenges to the jury instructions were properly preserved"), *cited in Belk, Inc. v. Meyer Corp.*, U.S., 679 F.3d 146, 154 n.6 (4th Cir. 2012) (finding that appellant had "waived its challenge to any jury instructions" because it had failed, *inter alia*, "to provide a record citation to where it objected to any given or omitted jury instruction"). *See also Maltby v. Winston*, 36 F.3d 548, 560 (7th Cir. 1994) (finding that the appellant had failed to preserve his challenge to jury instructions because "the instruction conference in the district court was not memorialized in the record," and the appellant had not otherwise "ma[d]e a sufficient record").

Here, Oldendorff has provided only its requested instructions, and those that the court ultimately gave the jury. "Importantly, the mere tendering of a proposed instruction will not preserve error for appeal." Kevin F. O'Malley, et al., 1 *Fed. Jury Practice & Instructions* § 7:4 (5th ed. 2012). *See also* [—30—] *City of Richmond, Va. v. Madison Mgmt. Grp., Inc.*, 918 F.2d 438, 453 (4th Cir. 1990) ("Where . . . a party who has violated Rule 51 can point to nothing more than the court's denial of a requested instruction, a reading of Rule 51 loose enough to permit preservation of the point would effectively delete Rule 51 insofar as allegations of error in the failure to give an instruction are concerned.").

In any event, even were we to reach the issue, we would conclude it is meritless. For the reasons stated above, *see supra* Part II.A, the court properly informed the jury that a shipowner may be "liable for injury resulting directly from an unsafe condition on the ship of which it was aware and which it voluntarily agreed and undertook to remedy, but failed to do so." J.A. 387. That a shipowner generally

---

[16] Collapsing all its claims into one, Oldendorff erroneously contends that our standard of review of the denial of its motion for a new trial is de novo. Opening Br. 8-9, 39–41. It is not.

need not warn of an open and obvious hazard does not absolve the shipowner of its more general duty to exercise ordinary care *under the circumstances* to ensure that the ship is in a reasonably safe condition. *Lincoln*, 354 F.3d at 266 (quoting *Scindia*, 451 U.S. at 166–67). Thus, we cannot see how Oldendorff was prejudiced, let alone seriously prejudiced, by the absence of any specific instruction on the open and obvious defense. *Coll. Loan Corp.*, 396 F.3d at 595.

Moreover, Oldendorff's proposed instruction—"In the absence of any agreement, the ship is not responsible for any [—31—] open and obvious condition."—was an incomplete statement of the law in any event. J.A. 84. In fact, a shipowner may still be liable for failing to warn of an open and obvious hazard if a stevedore's employee would not be able to work around the hazard. *Lincoln*, 354 F.3d at 266. Accordingly, we find no abuse of discretion in the district court's denial of the motion for a new trial.

III.

Like ships passing in the night, plaintiff Bunn, the district court, and the jury, on the one hand, understood this case was principally one of simple negligence, whereas on the other hand, Oldendorff has insisted, here to the very end, that it was solely a failure-to-warn case. For the reasons set forth herein, we reject Oldendorff's assertion and therefore affirm the judgment.

AFFIRMED

(Reporter's Note: Dissenting opinion on p. 163).

[—32—] MOTZ, Circuit Judge, dissenting:

With respect, I dissent. In my view, the focus of the parties on the shipowner's promise, rather than the character of the icy conditions, and the alternatives Bunn had in facing those conditions, left the jury with insufficient evidence to find Oldendorff breached its turnover duty.[1]

I.

At the center of my disagreement with the majority is the question of whether a shipowner's unfulfilled promise to remedy an open and obvious hazard affects its turnover duty.

It is well established that § 905(b) of the Longshore and Harbor Workers' Compensation Act imposes upon a shipowner a narrow turnover duty. *See Scindia Steam Navigation Co. v. De Los Santos*, 451 U.S. 156, 166-67 (1981); *Kirksey v. Tonghai Mar.*, 535 F.3d 388, 391 (5th Cir. 2008). This duty "relates to the condition of the ship upon the commencement of stevedoring operations" and "has two components." *Lincoln v. Reksten Mgmt.*, 354 F.3d 262, 266 (4th Cir. 2003). [—33—]

First, a shipowner must exercise "ordinary care *under the circumstances* to have the ship and its equipment in such condition that *an expert and experienced stevedore* will be able by the exercise of *reasonable care* to carry on its cargo operations with *reasonable safety* to persons and property." *Scindia*, 451 U.S. at 166-67 (emphasis added). This duty is known as the turnover duty of safe condition. *See, e.g., Ludwig v. Pan Ocean Shipping Co.*, 941 F.2d 849, 851 (9th Cir. 1991).[2]

As a corollary to the turnover duty of safe condition, a shipowner must also

warn[ ] the stevedore of any hazards on the ship or with respect to its equipment that are known to the vessel or should be known to it in the exercise of reasonable care, that would likely be encountered by the stevedore in the course of his cargo operations and that are not known by the stevedore and would *not be obvious to or anticipated by* him if *reasonably competent* in the performance of his work. [—34—]

Scindia, 451 U.S. at 167 (emphasis added). This duty is known as the turnover duty to warn. *See Howlett v. Birkdale Shipping Co., S.A.*, 512 U.S. 92, 99 (1994).

Thus, § 905(b) imposes on a shipowner duties at turnover that are very narrow. *See Kirsch v. Plovidba*, 971 F.2d 1026, 1029 (3d Cir. 1992) ("[T]he shipowner's duty is only to provide a workplace where skilled longshore workers can operate safely."); *see also Scindia*, 451 U.S. at 170. The turnover duty of safe condition merely requires that a shipowner exercise ordinary care, under the circumstances, to provide an expert and experienced stevedore or longshoreman, who exercises reasonable care, the ability to carry out its operations with reasonable safety. *Scindia*, 451 U.S. at 166-67. The corollary turnover duty to warn requires only that a shipowner exercise ordinary care to provide to a reasonably competent stevedore or longshoreman notice of non-obvious hazards. *Id.* at 167.

---

[1] I agree, for the reasons well stated by the majority, that Oldendorff's appeals of the district court's order denying summary judgment and its jury instructions are not properly before us.

[2] "Although the turnover duty of safe condition is usually framed in terms of stevedores, it is clear that danger to *longshore workers* is an essential part of the inquiry." *Thomas v. Newton Int'l Enters.*, 42 F.3d 1266, 1270 n.4 (9th Cir. 1994) (emphasis original). Turning over a ship upon which an expert stevedore can complete its

operations with reasonable safety necessarily requires turning over a ship upon which the longshoremen—the stevedore's expert employees who actually perform the operations—can complete their duties with reasonable safety. *Id.; accord Kirsch v. Plovidba*, 971 F.2d 1026, 1029-30 (3d Cir. 1992). Hence, when determining whether a shipowner has breached its turnover duty of safe condition, "the focus of the factual inquiry is frequently directed at experienced longshore workers"—not just their expert stevedore employer. *Thomas*, 42 F.3d at 1270 n.4; *accord Kirksey*, 535 F.3d at 396; *Lincoln*, 354 F.3d at 266; *Kirsch*, 971 F.2d at 1029-30.

Indeed, the openness and obviousness of a hazard to a stevedore provides a shipowner with a *complete defense* to a turnover duty to warn claim, no matter how unreasonably dangerous the hazard. *See Kirksey*, 535 F.3d at 393. The majority errs in asserting that a shipowner has a duty to warn a stevedore of even an open and obvious hazard if the stevedore "is [un]able to conduct . . . operations around [the hazard] [—35—] safely." *Ante* at 11, 19-20. In fact, the Supreme Court has explicitly rejected this view of the turnover duty to warn:

> The duty attaches only to latent hazards, defined as hazards that are not known to the stevedore and that would be neither obvious to nor anticipated by a skilled stevedore in the competent performance of its work.

Howlett, 512 U.S. at 105; *see also Ludwig*, 941 F.2d at 851 ("The shipowner had no duty to warn Ludwig [the longshoreman] of the hazard. It was obvious, so its mere presence carried a warning.").

Of course, the openness and obviousness of a hazard does not absolve the shipowner of its turnover duty of safe condition. *See Manuel v. Cameron Offshore Boats, Inc.*, 103 F.3d 31, 34 (5th Cir. 1997); *Kirsch*, 971 F.2d at 1029-30; *Ludwig*, 941 F.2d at 851. But when a hazard is open and obvious, the shipowner has a diminished turnover duty of safe condition. *See, e.g., Kirksey*, 535 F.3d at 395-96; *Hill v. Reederei F. Laeisz G.M.B.H., Rostock*, 435 F.3d 404, 409 (3d Cir. 2006); *Keller v. United States*, 38 F.3d 16, 24 (1st Cir. 1994); *Pimental v. LTD Can. Pac. Bul*, 965 F.2d 13, 16 (5th Cir. 1992); *Ludwig*, 941 F.2d at 851-52.

As the Third Circuit has explained, "a shipowner may be negligent for failing to eliminate an [open and] obvious hazard that it could have eliminated . . . *only* when it should have expected that an expert stevedore [or longshoreman] could not or [—36—] would not avoid the hazard and conduct cargo operations reasonably safely." *Kirsch*, 971 F.2d at 1031 (emphasis added).

This standard recognizes that "a shipowner can, ordinarily, reasonably rely on the stevedore [and longshoremen] . . . to notice obvious hazards and to take steps consistent with [their] expertise to avoid those hazards where practical to do so." *Id.* at 1030; *see also Howlett*, 512 U.S. at 101; *Ludwig*, 941 F.2d at 852.[3] An expert and experienced longshoreman can avoid open and obvious hazards in a number of ways, for example by fixing the hazard himself, *see Albergo v. Hellenic Lines, Inc.*, 658 F.2d 66, 69 (2d Cir. 1981), or completing operations while avoiding the hazard, *see Bjaranson v. Botelho Shipping Corp., Manila*, 873 F.2d 1204, 1208 (9th Cir. 1989); *Morris v. Compagnie Mar. Des Chargeurs Reunis, S.A.*, 832 F.2d 67, 70 (5th Cir. 1987). So long as an expert longshoreman has available such an option, a shipowner cannot be held liable for a breach of its turnover [—37—] duty of safe condition. Rather, the shipowner can reasonably rely on the longshoreman to exercise an alternative option.

II.

The majority largely ignores the above principles. Instead, relying primarily on *Lieggi v. Maritime Co. of Philippines*, 667 F.2d 324 (2d Cir. 1981) and two similar active operations duty cases, the majority holds that "a shipowner may be liable under the Act for promising, yet failing, to remedy a dangerous condition that injures a longshoreman." *Ante* at 12.[4] The case at hand, however, does not

---

[3] The negligence of a stevedore does not bar an injured longshoreman's recovery from a negligent shipowner. *See Woodruff v. United States*, 710 F.2d 128, 131-32 & n.7 (4th Cir. 1983). However, a shipowner breaches its turnover duty of safe condition only when an expert stevedore and its expert longshoremen could not through reasonable care carry on operations with reasonable safety. *See Scindia*, 451 U.S. at 166-67; *Kirsch*, 971 F.2d at 1029. If, through reasonable care, operations could have been completed with reasonable safety, the inquiry ends there, *regardless* of how negligent the stevedore has been.

[4] The active operations duty requires a shipowner after turnover "not to take negligent actions in areas under its control that threaten the longshoremen's safety." *Serbin v. Bora Corp., Ltd.*,

concern the active operations duty. And the logic of the active operations duty does not extend to the turnover duty context.

Contrary to the majority's suggestion, a "stark contrast" exists between the turnover duty and the active operations duty. *See Davis v. Portline Transportes Mar. Internacional*, 16 F.3d 532, 537 (3d Cir. 1994). The turnover duty covers the shipowner's conduct *before* the stevedore's cargo operations have begun, while the active operations duty covers a shipowner's conduct *after* cargo operations have begun in those areas [—38—] remaining *under control of the shipowner. See Scindia*, 451 U.S. at 167; *Davis*, 16 F.3d at 537.

The active operations duty does not rest on whether an expert stevedore and its expert longshoremen could have completed operations with reasonable safety. Instead, that duty rests on whether a shipowner negligently exposes longshoremen to any hazards—even avoidable ones—in areas under the shipowner's control during stevedoring operations. *See Serbin v. Bora Corp., Ltd.*, 96 F.3d 66, 70 (3d Cir. 1996). For this reason, the obviousness of a hazard does not presumptively bar recovery under an active operations duty claim. *Id.* at 75-76; *Pimental*, 965 F.2d at 16.

But the obviousness of a hazard does presumptively bar recovery under a turnover duty claim. *See Kirksey*, 535 F.3d at 395-96; *Kirsch*, 971 F.2d at 1031; *Pimental*, 965 F.2d at 16; *Ludwig*, 941 F.2d at 851-52. And a shipowner's pre-turnover promise to remedy an open and obvious hazard does not itself affect the openness and obviousness of the hazard at turnover. Rather, a shipowner can reasonably rely on an expert stevedore and its expert longshoremen to notice and avoid an open and [—39—] obvious hazard. *See Kirksey*, 535 F.3d at 394; *Kirsch*, 971 F.2d at 1030.[5]

---

96 F.3d 66, 70 (3d Cir. 1996); *see also Scindia*, 451 U.S. at 167.

[5] The case at hand only involves a shipowner's turnover duty regarding *open and obvious* hazards. A shipowner's promise to remedy a hazard that is neither known nor open and obvious may affect the manner in which an expert and experienced

Moreover, a shipowner's promise to remedy a hazard does *not* create a duty actionable under § 905(b). This is so because in the absence of a "contract provision, positive law, or custom to the contrary," all § 905(b) claims must fall under one of the duties identified by the Supreme Court in *Scindia. See* 451 U.S. at 172; *Kirsch*, 971 F.2d at 1031. An expert and experienced longshoreman cannot, by the mere virtue of a shipowner's promise, shirk his duty to act with reasonable care in the face of an open and obvious hazard. Holding otherwise raises a promise to the level of a contract, and impermissibly shifts responsibility for longshoreman safety from stevedore (and the longshoreman himself) to shipowner.

As long as an unremedied hazard remains open and obvious, a shipowner's liability to an injured longshoreman is thus extremely limited. Absent a contract provision, statute, regulation, or custom to the contrary, *Scindia*, 451 U.S. at 172, the shipowner is liable only to the extent "it should have [—40—] expected that an expert stevedore [or longshoreman] could not or would not avoid the hazard and conduct cargo operations reasonably safely," *Kirsch*, 971 F.2d at 1031.

III.

Considering the evidence in the light most favorable to Bunn, and with these legal principles in mind, I cannot agree with the majority's disposition of this appeal.

"[I]n many cases the obviousness of a hazard . . . will be a jury question," *Kirsch*, 971 F.2d at 1033, and if that were the situation here, I would join the majority in sustaining the jury's verdict. But, both before this court and in the district court, Bunn expressly conceded that "the ice-covered condition of the deck was open and obvious." Resp. Br. at 18; *see also Bunn v. Oldendorff Carriers GmbH & Co. K.G.*, No. 1:10-cv-00255-WMN (D. Md. Nov. 18, 2010), ECF No. 27, at

---

stevedore reasonably performs its operations. In short, if a hazard is not open and obvious, a stevedore would have reason to rely on a shipowner's representation that the hazard would be removed.

6. This concession took this important question out of the hands of the jury at trial, and binds us as we consider the proper application of the law on appeal.

Given this concession, the only remaining question is whether the evidence permitted a reasonable jury to conclude that the shipowner, Oldendorff, violated either component of its turnover duty by turning over the ship with open and obvious icy [—41—] conditions. It seems to me that the answer to that question is certainly no.

The parties focus on the turnover duty to warn,[6] and the majority extensively discusses that duty, sometimes suggesting that Oldendorff violated it. *See ante* at 15-23. But the majority ultimately characterizes this discussion as "plenty of *dicta*,"[7] and expressly disavows it as a basis of its holding. The majority explains that its "affirmance of the judgment is based not on the *duty to warn* but

on the more general turnover [—42—] *duty of safe condition*." *Ante* at 22 (emphasis original); *see also ante* at 9 ("[L]iability does not depend on the duty to warn."). This disavowal seems appropriate and inevitable given the clear directive of *Howlett*— that the duty to warn "attaches only to *latent* [*not* obvious] hazards." 512 U.S. at 105 (emphasis added).

However, affirmance on the basis of the turnover duty of safe condition—the sole basis for the majority's holding—is not possible because *no* evidence at trial established a violation of this duty. That is, the jury had insufficient evidence to find that the shipowner, Oldendorff, "should have expected that an expert [longshoreman] could not or would not avoid the hazard [here, icy conditions near hold three] and conduct cargo operations reasonably safely." *Kirsch*, 971 F.2d at 1031.[8]

Indeed, the only relevant evidence presented to the jury on this critical point suggests that an expert longshoreman, in Bunn's position, might have avoided this open and obvious hazard in several ways. He might have avoided the icy condition near [—43—] hold three altogether by loading another hold or undertaking another task. *Cf. Burchett v. Cargill, Inc.*, 48 F.3d 173, 179 (5th Cir. 1995); *Bjaranson*, 873 F.2d at 1208. Alternatively, he might have cleared the ice himself, *see Pimental*, 965 F.2d at 16; *Albergo*, 658 F.2d at 69, or enlisted a crew member to do so, *see Kirsch*, 971 F.2d at 1034. Of course, these options and others may have been unavailable to Bunn, but the record provides no evidence to this effect.

Nor does the record contain any evidence that Bunn was required to finish the job quickly, making him unable to avoid the hazard. *See Teply v. Mobil Oil Corp.*, 859 F.2d 375, 378 (5th Cir. 1988). To the contrary, Bunn's shift supervisor provided unrebutted

---

[6] Contrary to the majority's suggestion, *ante* at 15, 30-31, Bunn deserves as much blame as Oldendorff for focusing on the turnover duty to warn. Both before the district court and on appeal, Bunn did little to prioritize or offer evidence in support of his turnover duty of safe condition claim.

[7] In the course of this dicta, the majority asserts that, although the ice on the ship was open and obvious, the "presence of *untreated* ice was assuredly *not* 'open and obvious.'" *Ante* at 15. *Howlett*, however, cannot be avoided simply by characterizing the ice as "untreated." This is so because, by definition, ice and untreated ice are the *same* hazard. Just as a shipowner's unfulfilled promise to remedy an open and obvious hazard— here icy conditions—does not render the hazard any less open and obvious, so too a shipowner's failure to treat the hazard does not render it any less open and obvious. Whether one frames the hazard in this case as "ice" or "untreated ice," it remains equally open and obvious, and *Howlett* forecloses any turnover duty to warn claim.

Later in its own dicta, the majority relies on dicta in *Lincoln* contending that a shipowner has a duty to warn a stevedore of even open and obvious hazards if the stevedore "is [un]able to conduct . . . operations around [the hazard] safely." *Ante* at 19. But, as noted above, *Howlett* simply does not permit this conclusion. For in *Howlett* the Supreme Court expressly and clearly held that "[t]he duty [to warn] attaches *only* to latent hazards." 512 U.S. at 105 (emphasis added).

[8] The majority, focusing solely on the unfulfilled promise of the shipowner (by Fediv), effectively ignores this most fundamental inquiry into whether an expert longshoreman could have "by the exercise of reasonable care . . . carr[ied] on [his] cargo operations with reasonable safety to persons and property." *Scindia*, 451 U.S. at 166-67.

testimony that if a longshoreman encounters a hazardous condition on a ship "[h]e is empowered to shut the operation down." JA 133. And another longshoreman, Moxey, did shut down operations when the icy conditions around hold three remained hazardous several hours after Bunn's fall. JA 92.[9] [—44—]

Implicit in the majority's holding may be the view that an expert and experienced longshoreman would be unable to distinguish between treated and untreated ice and so have no reason to pursue another option. This may be so, but the record contains no evidence on this point either.

Of course, as the majority notes, Bunn *argues* in his briefs that "the lack of treatment with sand and salt in the area where [he] was obliged to work was not open and obvious." *See, e.g.*, Resp. Br. at 18. No *evidence*, however, supports this argument. Rather, at trial, Bunn himself testified that in well-lit areas of the ship he could distinguish between treated and untreated portions of the deck. JA 178, 226-27. Only in the dark, "very poor[ly]" lit area around hold three was Bunn unable to tell whether the ice had been treated. JA 182-83. Bunn's own testimony therefore supports just one conclusion: that his failure to notice the icy conditions was solely because it was dark, not because treated and untreated ice are indistinguishable. *See* Resp. Br. at 19 (conceding that "Mr. Bunn . . . had testified ... that the darkness in the area around No. 3 hatch prevented [him] from discovering that the ice in that area had not been treated.").

But to the extent that darkness constitutes a hazard, it is assuredly obvious, and easily remedied by an expert longshoreman (or indeed anyone with a flashlight). *See, e.g., Harris v.* [—45—] *Pac.-Gulf Marine, Inc.,* 967 F. Supp. 158, 164-65 (E.D. Va. 1997); *Chapman v. Bizet Shipping, S.A.,* 936 F. Supp. 982, 986 (S.D. Ga. 1996); *Landsem v. Isuzu Motors, Ltd.,* 534 F. Supp. 448, 451 (D. Or. 1982), *aff'd,* 711 F.2d 1064 (9th Cir. 1983) (table). Therefore, darkness provides no basis for a shipowner's liability under its turnover duties. Nor can darkness render an obvious hazard latent. *Cf. Harris,* 967 F. Supp. at 164; *Chapman,* 936 F. Supp. at 986. Otherwise the scope of a shipowner's turnover duties on identically hazardous ships could differ depending solely on the time of day when the turnover occurred.[10]

In response to this record evidence and these legal principles, the majority is left to contend that not just poor lighting but also the unfulfilled promise and a purported custom of shipowners removing onboard ice constitute the *"totality* of the circumstances" that renders Oldendorff liable. *Ante* at 24 n.15 (emphasis in original). But, as explained above, like poor [—46—] lighting, an unfulfilled promise does not render an otherwise obvious hazard latent. *See ante* at 39. And Bunn has *never* even argued that *custom* (rather than the turnover duty) forms the basis for his claim. *See ante* at 43 n.9. Thus, the record provides no support for the view that the totality of these circumstances barred Oldendorff from reasonably relying on an expert longshoreman in Bunn's position to notice and avoid the obvious icy conditions. *See Kirksey,* 535 F.3d at 394; *Kirsch,* 971 F.2d at 1030.[11]

---

[9] Bunn does not argue that a "contract provision, positive law, or custom" forms the basis of his § 905(b) claim. *See Scindia,* 451 U.S. at 172. Indeed, by regulation, it is the duty of the stevedore to "eliminate conditions causing slippery walking and working surfaces in immediate areas used by employees." 29 C.F.R. § 1918.91. Thus, the general principle that a shipowner can reasonably rely on an expert stevedore and its expert longshoremen to notice and avoid an open and obvious hazard applies with full force to this case. *See Kirsch,* 971 F.2d at 1030; *Ludwig,* 941 F.2d at 852.

[10] The regulatory scheme governing stevedoring operations supports the conclusion that natural darkness cannot contribute to the latency of a hazardous condition; for it is the stevedore's—not shipowner's—duty to provide an illuminated workspace for cargo operations, and to provide longshoremen with flashlights or other portable lights. *See* 29 C.F.R. § 1918.2, .92; *see also Scindia,* 451 U.S. at 176 ("The statutory duty of the stevedore under [33 U.S.C.] § 941 to provide a safe place to work has been implemented by the Safety and Health Regulations for Longshoring. 29 CFR §1918.1 *et seq.*").

[11] For, as we explained long ago, a shipowner is "entitled to rely on [a stevedore's] judgment as to

In sum, the record is bereft of evidence that Oldendorff "should have expected that an expert [longshoreman] could not or would not avoid the hazard [here, icy conditions] and conduct cargo operations reasonably safely," *Kirsch*, 971 F.2d at 1031, and contains considerable evidence suggesting the contrary. Accordingly, the jury lacked an evidentiary basis to find that Oldendorff breached its turnover duty of safe condition. [—47—]

IV.

This is a complex case, made only more so by the parties' failure to develop facts concerning the character of the icy conditions and the alternatives Bunn had in facing those conditions. On the one hand, the record does not provide a legally sufficient evidentiary basis from which a jury could find that Oldendorff breached its turnover duty. On the other hand, the record does not clearly foreclose Oldendorff's possible liability for violating its turnover duty. Rather, the record is simply inadequate to allow a jury to resolve—one way or the other—the dispositive legal question in the case: whether "an expert [longshoreman] could not or would not avoid the hazard and conduct cargo operations reasonably safely." *Kirsch*, 971 F.2d at 1031.

The Supreme Court has recognized that in limited circumstances "where the court of appeals sets aside the jury's verdict because the evidence was insufficient to send the case to the jury," as I believe it was here, "it is not so clear that the litigation should be terminated." *Neely v. Martin K. Eby Const. Co.*, 386 U.S. 317, 327 (1967). In my view, this is such a case. Accordingly, I would vacate the judgment of the district court and remand the case for a new trial or other proceedings consistent with this opinion. *See* Fed. R. Civ. P. [—48—] 50(b); *Weisgram v. Marley Co.*, 528 U.S. 440, 451-52 (2000); *Neely*, 386 U.S. at 327-330.

---

whether discharge operations could safely be undertaken." *Bonds v. Mortensen & Lange*, 717 F.2d 123, 127-28 (4th Cir. 1983). There, we reversed a verdict for a longshoreman killed by a crane with a malfunctioning bell on the ground that the hazard was "known to all" and was avoidable. *Id.* We explained that this is "not a situation . . . in which the longshoremen were precluded from performing their tasks except by a means which was inherently dangerous." *Id.* at 127-28 & n.5. That logic would seem to require, at the very least, that in this case we vacate the verdict and remand the case for further proceedings, as I propose.

United States Court of Appeals
for the Fourth Circuit

No. 13-1610

ANGELEX LTD.
vs.
UNITED STATES

Appeal from the United States District Court for the
Eastern District of Virginia

Decided: July 22, 2013

Citation: 723 F.3d 500, 1 Adm. R. 169 (4th Cir. 2013).

Before **KING, FLOYD,** and **THACKER,** Circuit Judges.

[—2—] **THACKER,** Circuit Judge:

The United States of America, the United States Coast Guard, and the United States Customs and Border Protection Agency (collectively, "Respondents" or the "government") appeal the district court's order, which, upon an emergency petition filed in the Eastern District of Virginia, (1) altered the terms of a bond the Coast Guard had fixed for the release of a detained ship that was under investigation; and (2) restricted the types of penalties the government could seek for the ship's potential violations of certain ocean pollution prevention statutes. As explained below, this matter was not subject to review in the district court because the Coast Guard's actions were committed to agency discretion by law. As a result, the district court lacked jurisdiction to consider the petition and we, therefore, reverse and remand for dismissal under Federal Rule of Civil Procedure 12(b)(1).

I.

A.

We begin with the international and domestic legal landscape underlying this matter. The United States is a signatory to MARPOL, which is a multi-national treaty aimed at "achiev[ing] the complete elimination of international pollution of the marine environment by oil and other harmful substances and the minimization of accidental discharge of such [—3—] substances[.]"[1] Protocol of 1978 Relating to the International Convention for the Prevention of Pollution from Ships, Feb. 17, 1978, 1340 U.N.T.S. 61, 128. MARPOL requires member States to prohibit violations of the treaty through domestic laws, and to provide penalties "adequate in severity to discourage violations of [MARPOL]." *Id.* at 186.

In fulfilling its obligations pursuant to MARPOL, Congress enacted the Act to Prevent Pollution from Ships ("APPS"). *See* 33 U.S.C. §§ 1901-15. According to APPS, "the Secretary shall administer and enforce" MARPOL, as well as statutes and regulations designed to preserve the marine environment. *Id.* § 1903(a). The term "Secretary" is defined as "the Secretary of the department in which the Coast Guard is operating." *Id.* §1901(a)(11). At all times relevant to this appeal, the Coast Guard operated under the Department of Homeland Security ("DHS").

The regulations attendant to APPS require, in relevant part, that certain oil-carrying ships must "maintain" an Oil Record Book ("ORB"), and [—4—]

> [e]ntries shall be made in the [ORB] . . . whenever any of the following machinery space operations take place on any ship to which this section applies—(1) Ballasting or cleaning of fuel oil tanks; (2) Discharge of ballast containing an oily mixture or cleaning water from fuel oil tanks; (3) Disposal of oil residue; and (4) Discharge overboard or disposal otherwise of bilge water that has accumulated in machinery spaces.

33 C.F.R. § 151.25(a), (d); *see also United States v. Ionia Mgmt. S.A.,* 555 F.3d 303, 309 (2d Cir. 2009) (holding that "the APPS's requirement that subject ships 'maintain' an

---

[1] The term "MARPOL" refers to two international conventions: the 1973 International Convention for the Prevention of Pollution from Ships, and the Protocol of 1978 Relating to the International Convention for the Prevention of Pollution from Ships.

ORB, 33 C.F.R. § 151.25, mandates that these ships ensure that their ORBs are accurate (or at least not knowingly inaccurate) upon entering the ports or navigable waters of the United States"); *United States v. Jho*, 534 F.3d 398, 403 (5th Cir. 2008) ("[W]e read the requirement that an oil record book be 'maintained' as imposing a duty upon a foreign-flagged vessel to ensure that its oil record book is accurate (or at least not knowingly inaccurate) upon entering the ports of navigable waters of the United States."). A person who knowingly violates APPS or its attendant regulations commits a Class D felony. *See* 33 U.S.C. § 1908(a).

B.

There are two Petitioners in this appeal: the Antonis G. Pappadakis ("Pappadakis" or "the vessel"), an ocean-going bulk cargo carrier, which was built in 1995 and registered in Malta; and Angelex Ltd. ("Angelex"), a company that purchased [—5—] the vessel on March 9, 2007. The vessel is Angelex's sole income-earning asset. Angelex contracted with a third party, Kassian Maritime Navigation Agency, Ltd. ("Kassian"), a Greek company, to serve as the vessel's operator. Kassian also operates several other cargo ships and is not a petitioner in this appeal.[2]

The events giving rise to this action began on April 14, 2013. On that day, the Pappadakis arrived at the Norfolk Southern Terminal in Norfolk, Virginia, and loaded a cargo of coal for delivery to a customer in Brazil. The next day, on April 15, 2013, Coast Guard inspectors conducted a routine Port State Control inspection of the Pappadakis. While Coast Guard personnel were aboard the vessel, a crewmember passed a note to one of the inspectors, which stated that the vessel's oily water separator had been bypassed and

oily bilge water had been discharged overboard. The letter also alleged that this discharge was not reported in the ORB. Upon further inspection, the Coast Guard discovered that the Pappadakis's oily water [—6—] separator was inoperable, the vessel had likely been discharging bilge water overboard, and the ORB was incomplete or falsified, in contravention of MARPOL and APPS.

The Coast Guard referred its findings to the Department of Justice for possible prosecution. It also informed Angelex that the Pappadakis's clearance to depart Norfolk had been withheld, and negotiations for a security agreement between the Coast Guard and counsel for Angelex began.[3]

After a few days, the negotiations stalled with the Coast Guard requiring the posting of a $2.5 million bond, a number of non-monetary obligations intended to ensure the availability and cooperation of the crewmembers and officials, and consent to the United States's continued jurisdiction over the matter. Unable to further negotiate with the Coast Guard, and claiming to be losing money by the day, Angelex and the [—7—] Pappadakis (in rem) then filed an emergency petition on April 25, 2013, in the Eastern District of Virginia, seeking immediate release

---

[2] Kassian was previously prosecuted in 2007 for violating APPS in materially identical circumstances to those presented here. Kassian pleaded guilty, paid a fine of $1 million, and received a sentence of 30 months probation. *See United States v. Kassian Maritime Navigation Agency*, No. 3:07-cr-0048 (M.D. Fla. Aug. 17, 2007), ECF No. 133.

---

[3] APPS provides, as codified as 33 U.S.C. §1908(e),

If any ship subject to the MARPOL Protocol . . . or this chapter, its owner, operator, or person in charge is liable for a fine or civil penalty under this section, or if reasonable cause exists to believe that the ship, its owner, operator, or person in charge may be subject to a fine or civil penalty under this section, the Secretary of the Treasury, upon the request of the Secretary [of the DHS], shall refuse or revoke [departure] clearance . . . . *Clearance may be granted upon the filing of a bond or other surety satisfactory to the Secretary.*

33 U.S.C. § 1908(e) (emphasis supplied).

of the Pappadakis or imposition of an appropriate bond (the "Petition").[4]

Specifically, the Petition asked the court "to fix an amount of security for release of the [Pappadakis]" because (1) the Coast Guard was not authorized and was wrongfully withholding clearance; (2) the vessel was improperly detained; (3) the amount of surety bond being demanded was "unjustified as a matter of fact, law, equity and good conscience and beyond the Coast Guard's authority"; (4) such actions were "causing serious, irreparable harm" to Angelex and the vessel; and (5) the government was improperly making Angelex "act[ ] as the government's proxy in detaining [the crewmembers] for an indefinite and unlimited amount of time, without lawful authority and in violation of their rights to due process of law." J.A. 7. [—8—]

C.

The district court held a hearing on the Petition on May 6, 2013. It recessed court and encouraged the parties to come up with an agreeable bond determination. The parties met for several hours and ultimately reached an agreement of $1.5 million bond and other agreed conditions, subject to approval from the Coast Guard Headquarters in Washington, D.C. ("Headquarters"). But when the court reconvened, the government attorney advised that the settlement had been rejected by Headquarters. According to the district court, that attorney also advised that pursuant to guidance from Headquarters, the Coast Guard "firmly refuses to accept less than the $2.5 million bond it had previously offered." J.A. 629.[5]

---

[4] The Petition, entitled "Emergency Petition and Motion for Release of the Motor Vessel 'Antonis G. Pappadakis,' or alternatively, to Fix an Appropriate Bond Amount for the Immediate Release of the Vessel and to Protect the Rights, Liberties and Freedoms of the Vessel's Crew," is found at J.A. 6-33. (Citations to the "J.A." refer to the contents of the Joint Appendix filed by the parties in this appeal.)

[5] At oral argument, there was dispute amongst the parties as to whether or not negotiations continued beyond the Coast Guard's take it or leave

On May 8, 2013, the district court filed a memorandum opinion, explaining that it possessed subject matter jurisdiction based on the Administrative Procedure Act, 5 U.S.C. §§551, *et seq.* (the "APA"), and federal question jurisdiction, 28 U.S.C. § 1331; or, in the alternative, *in rem* admiralty jurisdiction, 28 U.S.C. § 1333. It then determined that the government had acted unconstitutionally and outside its [—9—] statutory authority by demanding excessive bond for clearance and by insisting that any security agreement include certain non-monetary conditions. *See Angelex Ltd. v. United States*, 2:13-cv-00237 (E.D. Va. May 8, 2013), ECF No. 21 (J.A. 624-39). In a contemporaneous four-page order, the district court set forth new bond conditions. Specifically, the order directed Angelex to post a surety bond in the sum of $1.5 million. The order specified that the government could initiate either civil or criminal proceedings, but not both, and established other bond conditions, including the following:

> [T]he owner will maintain in the Eastern District of Virginia, at the owner's cost and expense, [six named officers and] crew members of said vessel for no greater than one month, and said crew members shall be functionally detained under material witness status so that their deposition may be taken. . . .

> [T]he owner will return, at its cost and expense, Gerasimos Patsalias, Master of said vessel, for either the civil or criminal proceedings (only one or the other) brought against Petitioners under [APPS]. . . .

> [T]he owner agrees to provide Lt. Elizabeth Oliveira, of the United States Coast Guard, with the name, address and telephone number of the hotel or other place where each of said ship's officers and crew members may be located when housed pursuant to the

---

it offer of a $2.5 million bond. Regardless, this debate does not alter our analysis.

conditions of said bond in the Eastern District of Virginia.

Upon the posting of . . . the said bond all parties to this action shall take all actions necessary to immediately release said vessel from arrest and allow it to proceed from this port and issue any and all permits that may be necessary to allow it to proceed out of this port in its trade. **[—10—]**

Id., ECF No. 20 at 2-3 (J.A. 621-22).

On May 9, 2013, the government requested that the district court temporarily stay the order, simultaneously filing a notice of appeal and requesting a stay from this court. The district court denied the stay motion on May 10, 2013. That same day, this court granted a stay that was extended, on May 16, 2013, to encompass the pendency of this appeal. Thereafter, we implemented an expedited briefing schedule and heard argument at the Greenbrier County Courthouse in Lewisburg, West Virginia, on June 25, 2013.[6]

Because the district court's order enjoined the United States to comply with the conditions set forth therein, we possess jurisdiction pursuant to 28 U.S.C. §1292(a)(1). In addition, insofar as the order constitutes the final decision of the district court, we possess jurisdiction pursuant to 28 U.S.C. §1291. **[—11—]**

II.

In this appeal, the government challenges the subject matter jurisdiction of the district court, an issue that we review de novo. *See Dixon v. Coburg Dairy, Inc.*, 369 F.3d 811, 815 (4th Cir. 2003) (en banc).

---

[6] On May 22, 2013, the grand jury in the Eastern District of Virginia indicted Angelex, Kassian, and the vessel's chief engineer, Lambros Katsipis, on multiple charges, including conspiracy to illegally discharge oily water into the sea, presentation of a falsified ORB, and obstruction of justice. *See United States v. Kassian Maritime Navigation Agency, Inc.*, No. 2:13-cr-00070 (E.D. Va. May 22, 2013), ECF No. 12.

III.

The district court asserted jurisdiction over this matter under the APA and pursuant to the court's admiralty jurisdiction. For the following reasons, neither provides the court with the power to review the Coast Guard's actions in this case.

A.

The APA

1.

"Reviewability is a threshold jurisdictional question that must be determined before the merits of the case may be reached." *Sierra Club v. Larson*, 882 F.2d 128, 130 (4th Cir. 1989). The APA "is not a jurisdiction-conferring statute." *Lee v. U.S. Citizenship and Immigration Servs.*, 592 F.3d 612, 619 (4th Cir. 2010) (internal quotation marks omitted). "[T]he jurisdictional source for an action under the APA is the federal question statute," and the APA's judicial provisions provide "a limited cause of action for parties adversely affected by agency action." *Id.* (citations and internal quotation marks omitted). **[—12—]** Because "reviewability is a threshold jurisdictional question," however, we must examine reviewability through the lens of the APA to determine whether the district court properly exercised its jurisdiction. *Larson*, 882 F.2d at 130.

The APA requires a reviewing court to "hold unlawful and set aside agency action, findings, and conclusions found to be . . . arbitrary, capricious, an abuse of discretion, or otherwise not in accordance with law[.]" 5 U.S.C. § 706(2)(A). The APA further provides, "[a]gency action made reviewable by statute and final agency action for which there is no other adequate remedy in a court are subject to judicial review." *Id.* § 704.[7] Of significance here, the APA provides two exceptions to judicial review of agency actions: when

---

[7] "Agency action" is defined as "the whole or part of an agency rule, order, license, sanction, relief, or the equivalent or denial thereof, or failure to act[.]" 5 U.S.C. § 551(13); *see also id.* § 701(b)(2).

"statutes preclude judicial review," or when "agency action is committed to agency discretion by law." *Id.* § 701(a)(2). The government argues that both exceptions apply here, and in any event, there is no "final agency action" of the Coast Guard.

Because the action that occurred in this case is explicitly committed to the discretion of the Coast Guard [—13—] pursuant to APPS, we conclude that this matter was unreviewable, and thus, the district court lacked subject matter jurisdiction.

a.

The idea that courts cannot review actions committed to agency discretion by law was at the forefront of two seminal Supreme Court cases: *Citizens to Preserve Overton Park v. Volpe*, 401 U.S. 402 (1971), and *Heckler v. Chaney*, 470 U.S. 821 (1985). *Volpe* explained that § 701(a)(2) "is a very narrow exception" and "applicable in those rare instances where statutes are drawn in such broad terms that in a given case there is no law to apply." *Volpe*, 401 U.S. at 410. *Heckler* further elucidated, however, that "even where Congress has not affirmatively precluded review, review is not to be had if the statute is drawn so that a court would have no meaningful standard against which to judge the agency's exercise of discretion" and "no judicially manageable standards . . . for judging how and when an agency should exercise its discretion[.]" 470 U.S. at 830.

Our resolution of this matter is further informed by *Speed Mining v. Federal Mine Safety & Health Review Commission*, 528 F.3d 310 (4th Cir. 2008). Speed Mining, an owner-operator of a coal mine in West Virginia, petitioned for review of a decision from the Federal Mine Safety and Health Review Commission, which upheld citations for a crane hoist accident [—14—] that were issued by the Secretary of Labor. Speed Mining argued that, because the accident was caused by independent contractors, the Secretary's decision to cite Speed Mining itself was an abuse of discretion. *See id.* at 311.

This court held,

It is settled law in this and other circuits that the Secretary possesses the discretionary authority to cite owner-operators . . . for safety violations committed by independent contractors. Moreover, there are no manageable standards in the Mine [Safety and Health] Act that enable us to review the Secretary's discretionary exercise of her enforcement authority.

Speed Mining, 528 F.3d at 311. As a result, "the Secretary's discretionary decision to cite [Speed Mining] for the crane hoist accident is 'committed to agency discretion by law,' and therefore unreviewable." *Id.* at 317. Additionally, "[t]he discretionary decision as to which operator to cite for a Mine Act violation rests on a 'complicated balancing of a number of factors which are peculiarly within' the Secretary's expertise[.]" *Id.* at 318.

b.

The circumstances in this case substantially mirror those described by the Supreme Court in *Heckler* and our court in *Speed Mining*. By its Petition, Angelex asserts that the Coast Guard acted "arbitrarily, capriciously, and unreasonably" in detaining the Pappadakis, setting a bond which Angelex cannot post, and demanding a security agreement with terms that are not [—15—] authorized by the operative statute, 33 U.S.C. § 1908(e). J.A. 7. But § 1908(e) grants the Coast Guard broad discretion to deny bond altogether, and it can dictate the terms of any bond that it may accept. *See Giuseppe Bottiglieri Shipping Co. v. United States*, 843 F. Supp. 2d 1241, 1248 (S.D. Ala. 2012) ("Congress did not require the Coast Guard to accept a bond or other surety in any case," or "grant an absolute right to a vessel owner to obtain departure clearance[.]").

Furthermore, the language of § 1908(e) does not provide any "judicially manageable standards" by which to review the Coast Guard's actions. *Heckler*, 470 U.S. at 830. There are no specific guidelines as to when clearance should or should not be granted in APPS, and Congress did not "outline (even in the broadest brushstrokes) the parameters for what form or amount a bond or other surety should take." *Giuseppe*, 843 F. Supp. 2d at 1248. The reasonableness of the Coast Guard's decision cannot be determined pro forma in a vacuum, but only in the context of the standards intended by Congress. As a result, this is a situation where the statute at issue is "'drawn in such broad terms that . . . there is no law to apply.'" *Heckler*, 470 U.S. at 830 (quoting *Volpe*, 401 U.S. at 410); *see also Larson*, 882 F.2d at 132-33 (holding that federal court could not review Federal Highway Administration's (FHWA) decision not to enforce certain provisions of the Highway Beautification Act (HBA), [—16—] explaining, "[t]he relevant question here is whether the HBA provides standards for ascertaining when the FHWA should recommend that formal enforcement proceedings be commenced or when the Secretary is *required* to make a determination of compliance or non-compliance or to institute an enforcement action. As to these points, the statute is silent. Therefore, there is no law to apply and appellant has failed to overcome the presumption of unreviewability.").

2.

Despite these bars to review, the district court nonetheless decided it possessed jurisdiction to review the Coast Guard's bond determination because, even when Congress has committed a specific decision to an agency's discretion by law, "the federal courts retain jurisdiction to review discretionary agency actions for abuse of discretion." J.A. 633 (citing *Elecs. of N.C., Inc. v. Se. Power Admin.*, 774 F.2d 1262, 1267 (4th Cir. 1985); *Littell v. Morton*, 445 F.2d 1207, 1211 (4th Cir. 1971)). But, as the government points out, to adopt this argument would be to "eliminate Section 701(a)(2) from the statute, by providing 'abuse of discretion' review for all discretionary agency decisions, regardless of whether Congress has committed them exclusively to the agency or not." Appellant's Br. 40. In fact, *Heckler* rejected this very argument, explaining that even though the APA sets forth an [—17—] "abuse of discretion" review of agency action in 5 U.S.C. § 706, the § 701(a)(2) exception for actions

committed to agency discretion still applies to "a separate class of cases," as here, in which a statute "is drawn so that a court would have no meaningful standard against which to judge the agency's exercise of discretion." *Heckler*, 470 U.S. at 830.

Angelex asserts, "the very purpose for Angelex's pursuit of judicial intervention—and a significant basis for the District Court's decision—was the Coast Guard's actions beyond its statutory authority and its violation of Angelex's constitutional due process rights." Appellees' Br. 33. Angelex contends that because it raises the "indisputable existence of specific statutory construction issues, various violations of its due process rights, and other constitutional concerns as a result of the Coast Guard's overreaching of its statutory authority," there are clearly "manageable standard[s]" to apply here. *Id.* at 36.

We are cognizant of this court's declaration,

[E]ven where action is committed to absolute agency discretion by law, courts have assumed the power to review allegations that an agency exceeded its legal authority, acted unconstitutionally, or failed to follow its own regulations, but they may not review agency action where the challenge is only to the decision itself.

Elecs. of N.C., 774 F.2d at 1267 (internal quotation marks omitted). Nonetheless, we disagree with Appellees' [—18—] characterization of the Petition as an attack on the statutory authority or constitutionality of the Coast Guard's actions. First, Appellees cannot with a straight face argue that the Coast Guard has acted outside the bounds of §1908(e). Indeed, those bounds are quite limitless. The Coast Guard may demand a low bond, a high bond, or may refuse to grant clearance altogether. *See* 33 U.S.C. § 1908(e) ("Clearance *may* be granted upon the filing of a bond or other surety *satisfactory to the Secretary*." (emphases added)); *see also* 46 U.S.C. § 60105(b) ("[A] vessel that is not a vessel of the United States *shall obtain clearance* from the Secretary before proceeding from a port of place in the United States." (emphasis added)). Further, once the Coast Guard makes its clearance determination, the "Secretary of the Treasury, upon the request of the Secretary [of the DHS], *shall* refuse or revoke [departure] clearance[.]" *Id.* In other words, if the Coast Guard requests that clearance be refused or revoked, it is mandatory that such action occur. In this case, the Coast Guard requested that the Customs and Border Protection ("CBP") withhold the Pappadakis's departure clearance, and the "Customs hold was approved by CBP on April 19, 2013." J.A. 68. This action is specifically permitted in the text of § 1908(e).

Likewise, Angelex's attempt at turning this matter into a constitutional challenge does not make the matter **[—19—]** reviewable and thus, vest the district court with jurisdiction. Specifically, Angelex asserts that the government violated its due process rights by indefinitely detaining the Pappadakis. This attempt at bypassing the reviewability exception in § 701(a)(2) falls flat. As Appellants observed, Angelex's case is "nothing more than a direct review of the specific conditions sought by the Coast Guard in order to allow departure," Appellant's Rep. Br. 8, and we "may not review agency action where the challenge is only to the decision itself," *Elecs. of N.C.*, 774 F.2d at 1267. Furthermore, we reiterate that the Coast Guard's actions are specifically endorsed by the text of § 1908(e). The release of the vessel upon the filing of a bond or other surety is permissive, not mandatory, and is contingent only upon conditions "satisfactory to the Secretary." 33 U.S.C. § 1908(e). In short, the Coast Guard's stringent conformity to §1908(e) simply does not give rise to a reviewable claim.

3.

Finally, APPS contains a built-in safeguard to governmental abuses, which further convinces us that Angelex's Petition is out of place and time. In addition to the criminal and civil penalties that APPS authorizes the United States to seek, APPS provides for compensation for loss or damage as a result of unreasonable detention by the Coast Guard. Section 1904(h) provides, "A ship unreasonably detained or delayed by **[—20—]** the Secretary acting under the authority of this chapter is entitled to compensation for any loss or damage suffered thereby." 33 U.S.C. § 1904(h). This provision is, as the government asserts, an "after-the-fact damages remedy against the United States for unreasonable detention or delay." Appellant's Br. 37. This safeguard gives Appellees a remedy, distinct from the unauthorized injunctive relief they now seek.

For these reasons, the Coast Guard's decisions regarding bond conditions with regard to the Pappadakis are unreviewable, and the district court thereby did not possess subject matter jurisdiction under the APA.

B.

Admiralty Jurisdiction

Judicial review of the Coast Guard's decision on bond and withholding of clearance is likewise unavailable to Angelex under the district court's *in rem* admiralty jurisdiction. The district court determined that the withholding of the Pappadakis for an indefinite period of time, subject to unattainable bond conditions "is tantamount to an arrest of the ship." J.A. 634. Likening such an arrest to a "proper maritime arrest," the district court asserted that the arrest of the vessel *in rem* falls within its admiralty jurisdiction. *Id.*

Pursuant to 28 U.S.C. § 1333(1), district courts have jurisdiction over "[a]ny civil case of admiralty or maritime **[—21—]** jurisdiction[.]" Pursuant to the Supplemental Admiralty and Maritime Claims Rule E, such admiralty jurisdiction "applies to actions in personam with process of maritime attachment and garnishment, *actions in rem*, and petitory, possessory, and partition actions . . . ." Fed. R. Civ. P. Adm. Rule E(1) (emphasis added). An "in rem suit against a vessel is . . . distinctively an admiralty proceeding, and is hence within the exclusive province of the federal courts." *Am. Dredging Co. v. Miller*, 510 U.S. 443, 446-47 (1994).

Appellees unreasonably stretch the law to classify this matter as an *in rem* action. The Coast Guard's withholding of the Pappadakis's departure clearance is not tantamount to an attachment pursuant to a civil action, such as a maritime lien.[8] *See California v. Deep Sea Research, Inc.*, 523 U.S. 491, 501 (1998) (observing that maritime jurisdiction encompasses "maritime causes of action begun and carried on as proceedings in rem, that is, where a vessel or thing is itself treated as the offender and made the defendant by name or description in order to enforce a lien" (internal quotation marks omitted)). The Coast Guard is properly withholding the departure clearance [—22—] pursuant to its authority under § 1908(e), and not pursuant to any rule governing admiralty actions in rem.

Appellees also stretch the facts. They first cite to the Agreement, claiming that the demands therein "insist[ ] upon . . . hav[ing] the surety bond stand in place of the Vessel for the potential criminal fine or civil penalty imposed." Appellees' Br. 43. There is simply no support for this; in fact, the Agreement itself states, "[i]n consideration of the Surety Bonds, the United States agrees not to cause the arrest of the Vessel, nor the arrest, seizure or attachment or any other vessel owned, operated, managed or chartered by the Owner or Operator for the Alleged Violations[.]" J.A. 185.

Appellees then liken the Coast Guard's withholding of clearance to a "functional arrest" that was done in order to "provide the government with the ability to obtain financial security for a potential fine or penalty." Appellees' Br. 43 n.29. In so arguing, Appellees once again twist the facts such that what is actually discretionary action on the part of the Coast Guard under APPS is now considered an offense to the ship itself. Further, the Coast Guard's own regulations provide,

statutes authorizing the Coast Guard to request denial or revocation of CBP clearance are not dependent on, limited in scope by, or equivalent to, the laws and procedures applicable to the assertion of an in rem claim against the vessel. Therefore, applying rules and practices developed with regard to asserting in [—23—] rem claims against vessels under admiralty law is inappropriate and not required.

69 Fed. Reg. 40400-01, 40401 (Jul. 2, 2004). In short, try as they might to make it so, Appellees' argument on this point simply does not fit either the law or the facts.

IV.

Pursuant to the foregoing, we reverse and remand for dismissal of the Petition for lack of subject matter jurisdiction, pursuant to Federal Rule of Civil Procedure 12(b)(1).

REVERSED AND REMANDED

---

[8] "A maritime lien is a special property right in a ship given to a creditor by law as security for a debt or claim," and it attaches "the moment the debt arises." *Dresdner Bank AG v. M/V Olympia Voyager*, 465 F.3d 1267, 1272 (11th Cir. 2006) (internal quotation marks and alterations omitted).

United States Court of Appeals
for the Fourth Circuit

No. 12-1953

TURNER
vs.
UNITED STATES

Appeal from the United States District Court for the
Eastern District of North Carolina

Decided: November 20, 2013

Citation: 736 F.3d 274, 1 Adm. R. 177 (4th Cir. 2013).

Before **MOTZ**, and **DIAZ**, Circuit Judges, and **GIBNEY**,
District Judge, sitting by designation.

[—3—] **GIBNEY**, District Judge:

This case comes before the Court on an appeal of the district court's grant of summary judgment to the defendant, the United States Coast Guard ("USCG"), in a personal injury and wrongful death action. The central issue in the case concerns whether the Coast Guard breached a duty of care in attempting to rescue Susan Turner and her husband, Roger Turner, Jr. Based on the record in this case, we conclude that the Coast Guard is not liable for Ms. Turner's injuries or Mr. Turner's death.

In addition, the case presents questions arising from three subsidiary matters: (1) Ms. Turner demanded sanctions premised on the USCG's alleged deliberate spoliation of evidence; (2) she opposed the district court's decision to grant the USCG permission to file an out-of-time motion for summary judgment, claiming the decision deprived her of due process; and (3) she challenged the propriety of the USCG's responses to Turner's Freedom of Information Act ("FOIA") request. The district court ruled against her on all three issues. We find that the rulings on the issues of spoliation and the timeliness of the motion reflect proper exercises of the district court's discretion and should not be disturbed. We also affirm the district court's ruling that the Coast Guard's response to Ms. Turner's FOIA request satisfied its duty under that Act.

We therefore affirm the judgment of the district court. [—4—]

I.

Susan Turner commenced this action by filing a complaint in which she—in her individual capacity and as administratrix of her husband's estate—brought personal injury and wrongful death claims against the United States and the USCG under the Suits in Admiralty Act ("SIAA"), 46 U.S.C. §§ 30901-30918.

The case arises from a tragic boating incident that occurred in the coastal waters of North Carolina. On the afternoon of July 4, 2007, Ms. Turner and her husband, Roger Turner, Jr. (collectively, the "Turners"), left their home on the Little River on their private 20-foot long motorboat, intending to watch holiday fireworks. Before leaving, Roger Jr. spoke to his father, Roger Sr., telling him that the Turners would be going to one of three possible locations that evening: the Pasquotank River, the Perquimans River, or Mann's Harbor. After leaving home, the Turners decided to travel to a party at the home of a friend, located on the Perquimans River.

The Turners left that affair at around 8:30 p.m. By then, the seas were rough, with waves of three to four feet. The Turners did not wear life jackets. Attempting to move from bow to stern, Ms. Turner fell overboard at approximately 9:00 p.m., nearly one and a half miles offshore. She cried out to her husband, who responded, and turned the boat around to come back for her. Ms. Turner could see the boat but could not see Roger [—5—] Jr. Soon Ms. Turner lost sight of the boat. At some point thereafter, Roger Jr. also entered the water. The Turners' boat stayed afloat, drifting downriver.

When the Turners did not return home by 9:30 p.m., Roger Sr. became concerned. After trying without success to reach the Turners on their cell phones, he called 911 at about 12:25 a.m. That office relayed Roger Sr.'s information to the North Carolina Wildlife Resources Commission ("NC Wildlife") and the

USCG, which returned Roger Sr.'s call at about 1:00 a.m. on July 5.[1] Roger Sr. told the Command Duty Officer that the Turners were overdue in returning home, and that they might be in one of three locations his son had given him earlier that afternoon. He also mentioned that the Turners could be at a fourth location, a friend's cabin of unknown address.

Roger Sr. told the duty officer that the Turners were experienced boaters and strong swimmers. He also told the Coast [—6—] Guard that the Turners' vessel had flares, a VHF radio, cell phones, flotation devices, an anchor, and food and water. Upon receipt of this information, the USCG decided that, due to the number of potential locations and the current deployment of search assets on a confirmed emergency mission (a missing jet ski), the USCG would not initiate an active search for the Turners' overdue boat at that time. Instead, the duty officer informed Roger Sr. that the USCG would begin making radio calls and would inquire with local marinas later that morning.

NC Wildlife contacted the USCG in regards to Roger Sr.'s call. The USCG told NC Wildlife that it would request assistance from NC Wildlife if necessary, but that due to the size of the area in which the Turners might be located and the nature of the call (an overdue boat manned by two experienced boaters and swimmers), the USCG did not intend to initiate a search and rescue operation at that time.

---

[1] The log for the Turner case in the CG's Marine Information for Safety and Law Enforcement (MISLE) system contains an entry corresponding with the time of 9:58 p.m. on July 4, 2007, stating: "Response resource requested." The resource requested, "UTL-212051," was a 21-foot utility boat stationed at the USCG's Elizabeth City Air Station. The USCG later explained this entry was a "placeholder" created by the watch-stander, and unrelated to any actual call. The watch-stander testified that he chose this time randomly. The record contains no evidence that the USCG tried to rescue the Turners as early as 9:58 p.m., or that the USCG even had any information concerning the Turners at that time.

At approximately 1:00 a.m., a USCG helicopter that had been searching for the overdue jet ski left that operation to return to Elizabeth City to refuel, traveling on a flight path that led up the Pasquotank River. The USCG ordered that helicopter, as it traveled up the Pasquotank, to look for the Turners' boat, an activity that did not require the helicopter to deviate from its flight path. The crew did not see the Turners' boat while en route to Elizabeth City. [—7—]

Later that morning, the USCG conducted a series of preliminary and extended communication searches ("PRECOMS" and "EXCOMS," respectively). These operations, in effect information-gathering activities, included call-outs to the Turners' boat, an "Urgent Marine Information Broadcast" requesting other boaters to contact the USCG with any information, and calls and visits to marinas where the Turners might have decided to tie up. The USCG concluded their PRECOM and EXCOM searches at approximately 8:40 a.m. on July 5.

Shortly before 8:00 a.m., the USCG dispatched a 21-foot utility boat from the Oregon Inlet Coast Guard Station. That craft launched at approximately 9:15 a.m. and began searching the area of Mann's Harbor, one of the four places that Roger Sr. gave as a possible location of the Turners. Meanwhile, the host of the party the Turners had attended on July 4, aware of their failure to return home, began retracing the Turners' likely return route up the Perquimans River. He discovered the Turners' boat, beached and empty, at approximately 9:00 a.m. Upon learning of this discovery, the USCG reclassified the incident from a "possible overdue" to an "overdue distress" case, and launched an air and sea search for the Turners. From the morning of July 5 through the evening of July 6, the USCG deployed twelve manned search and rescue boats and planes, and searched 173 square nautical miles. The USCG utilized the [—8—] Turners' boat's GPS when performing their search. The USCG suspended its search activities on July 6 at 7 p.m.

During the night of July 4 and into the morning of July 5, Ms. Turner tread water for nearly 12 hours, surviving by clinging to crab pot buoys. She came ashore at about 9:20 a.m. on July 5. The USCG, despite the extensive search efforts described above, did not find Roger Jr.; his body washed ashore two days later. The medical examiner listed Roger Jr.'s cause of death as drowning but could not identity a precise time of death.

II.

We review a district court's decision granting summary judgment *de novo,* applying the same legal standards as the district court and viewing all facts and reasonable inferences therefrom in the light most favorable to the nonmoving party, here the Turners. *T-Mobile Ne. LLC v. City Council of Newport News,* 674 F.3d 380, 384-85 (4th Cir. 2012). Summary judgment is appropriate "if the movant shows that there is no genuine dispute as to any material fact and the movant is entitled to judgment as a matter of law." Fed. R. Civ. P. 56(a). [—9—]

Ms. Turner's claim arises under admiralty law.[2] In the arena of tort law, general maritime law mirrors many principles of traditional negligence law. *See McMellon v. United States,* 338 F.3d 287, 298 (4th Cir. 2003) (*McMellon I*), *vacated en banc on other grounds,* 387 F.3d 329 (4th Cir. 2004). Ms. Turner bears the burden of establishing that the USCG owed her and her late husband an identifiable duty, that the USCG breached that duty, and that the USCG's breach of duty proximately caused harm to the Turners. *Id.*

---

[2] Ordinarily, the USCG enjoys sovereign immunity in its activities. The SIAA provides a limited waiver of sovereign immunity. *See Sagan v. United States,* 342 F.3d 493, 497 (6th Cir. 2003). Even with the waiver of immunity, the USCG cannot be held liable for injuries arising from the performance of discretionary functions. *See McMellon v. United States,* 387 F.3d 329, 338 (4th Cir. 2004) (*McMellon II*). The parties devote a considerable portion of their briefs to the issue of sovereign immunity, but we need not consider this issue because we find that the USCG did not violate the relevant standard of care in any action taken or decision made.

Ms. Turner's attempt to establish a prima facie case falls short on several fronts.

The USCG's enabling statute, 14 U.S.C. §88, authorizes the USCG to undertake rescue efforts, but does not impose any affirmative duty to commence such rescue operations. *See Hurd v. United States,* 34 F. App'x 77, 81 (4th Cir. 2002) (collecting cases). But, "once the Coast Guard undertakes a rescue [—10—] operation, it must act with reasonable care."[3] *Sagan,* 342 F.3d at 498 (citing *Patentas v. United States,* 687 F.2d 707 (3d Cir. 1982)). "Its actions are judged according to the so-called 'Good Samaritan' doctrine." *Id.* "Under this doctrine, a defendant [becomes] liable for breach of a duty voluntarily assumed by affirmative conduct, even when that assumption of duty was gratuitous." *Id.* (citing *Indian Towing Co. v. United States,* 350 U.S. 61 (1955)); *see also, Thames Shipyard & Repair Co. v. United States,* 350 F.3d 247, 261 (1st Cir. 2003); *Frank v. United States,* 250 F.2d 178, 180 (3d Cir. 1957).

The Good Samaritan doctrine, however, sets a high bar to impose liability on a rescuer. The evidence must show that the rescuer failed to exercise reasonable care in a way that worsened the position of the victim. *See Sagan,* 342 F.3d at 498 (citing *Myers v. United States,* 17 F.3d 890, 903 (6th Cir. 1994)). "There are two ways in which a rescuer can worsen the position of the subject of the rescue. The first is by increasing the risk of harm to the person in distress. The second is to induce reliance, either by the subject or other [—11—] potential rescuers, on the rescuer's efforts." *Hurd,* 34 F. App'x at 84 (internal citations omitted); *see also,* Restatement (Second) of Torts §§ 323, 324A, 327. The test is whether "the risk was increased over what it would have been had

---

[3] Because the USCG has no duty to rescue, the law imposes no standard of care until an attempted rescue commences. The parties devoted much effort below, and considerable effort in this Court, arguing over when the USCG's attempted rescue began. Because we find that the USCG did not violate the operative standard of care at any time, we need not address the issue of when the formal rescue attempt began.

the defendant not engaged in the undertaking at all." *Sagan*, 342 F.3d at 498.

The Turners have not shown that the USCG's actions worsened their position. Whatever happened to the Turners, the Coast Guard did not "increase the risk of harm" that confronted the unfortunate couple. In fact, the USCG did not intervene in their situation at all until their boat was discovered grounded, so it could hardly have worsened their position. Indeed, the thrust of the plaintiff's case is that the USCG should have done something to alleviate the Turners' predicament sooner. As we noted above, the USCG was under no obligation to do so. *Cf. Hurd*, 34 F. App'x at 81.

Nor did the USCG's actions worsen the Turners' position by inducing reliance on the part of either the Turners or a third party. Obviously, the Turners themselves never spoke with the Coast Guard, and so could not have relied on representations by the USCG.

Recognizing this problem, Ms. Turner points to the discussion between a USCG command duty officer and an official from NC Wildlife as evidence that the latter relied on the [—12—] USCG's rescue efforts and so was dissuaded from commencing its own rescue effort. The record does not support this claim. The USCG did *not* represent to NC Wildlife that it would undertake a rescue operation. In fact, the duty officer expressly told NC Wildlife that the USCG was *not* preparing to launch search and rescue operations. A NC Wildlife official testified that his agency also would not have launched a search and rescue operation at that time, *regardless* of the USCG's actions, because of both the dearth of actionable information and the prevailing weather conditions.

In short, the USCG neither increased the danger facing the Turners nor induced reliance on the part of either the Turners or a third party. Accordingly, Ms. Turner cannot prove the USCG breached its duty to the Turners,[4] and the district court properly

entered summary judgment on the Turners' tort claims.

III.

The district court properly denied Ms. Turner's motion for sanctions based on spoliation. Spoliation is a rule of [—13—] evidence, and the decision to impose sanctions for violations is one "'administered at the discretion of the trial court'" and governed by federal law. *Hodge v. Wal-Mart Stores, Inc.*, 360 F.3d 446, 450 (4th Cir. 2004) (quoting *Vodusek v. Bayliner Marine Corp.*, 71 F.3d 148, 155 (4th Cir. 1995)). When reviewing a district court's ruling on a plaintiff's request for a spoliation inference, even on a grant of summary judgment, we have held that the district court's ruling "must stand unless it was an abuse of the district court's 'broad discretion'" in this regard." *Id.* (citing *Cole v. Keller Indus., Inc.*, 132 F.3d 1044, 1046-47 (4th Cir. 1998)). Ms. Turner, as the party disputing the district court's ruling, bears the burden of establishing spoliation. *See id.* at 453.

A party seeking sanctions based on the spoliation of evidence must establish, inter alia, that the alleged spoliator had a duty to preserve material evidence. This duty arises "not only during litigation but also extends to that period before the litigation when a party reasonably should know that the evidence may be relevant to anticipated litigation." *Silvestri v. Gen. Motors Corp.*, 271 F.3d 583, 591 (4th Cir. 2001). Generally, it is the filing of a lawsuit that triggers the duty to preserve evidence. *Victor Stanley, Inc. v. Creative Pipe, Inc.*, 269 F.R.D. 497, 522 (D. Md. 2010). Moreover, spoliation does not result merely from the "negligent loss or destruction [—14—] of evidence." *Vodusek*, 71 F.3d at 156. Rather, the alleged destroyer must have known that the evidence was relevant to some issue in the anticipated case, and thereafter willfully engaged in conduct resulting in the evidence's loss or destruction. *See id.* Although

---

[4] An additional problem exists for Ms. Turner as administratrix of her husband's estate. The evidence does not establish when Mr. Turner died.

Roger Jr. could well have been dead before the USCG even had a chance to try to rescue him. Given this gap in the plaintiff's evidence, the Coast Guard could not have been held liable for Roger Jr.'s unfortunate death.

the conduct must be intentional, the party seeking sanctions need not prove bad faith. *Id.*

Here, Ms. Turner says the USCG wrongfully destroyed audio recordings of telephone calls to the Coast Guard by recycling them and recording over them. The plaintiff, however, did nothing to trigger a duty to preserve evidence on the part of the USCG. She did not send the USCG a document preservation letter, or any other correspondence threatening litigation. After learning that Roger Jr. had gone overboard the night of July 4, the USCG specifically reviewed the voice recordings for that night the very next morning and discovered nothing. The action of recycling the voice recordings was standard operating procedure for the USCG. Without a warning of future litigation or reason to believe that voice recordings devoid of a rescue call would be relevant in any event, the Coast Guard had no reason to change its standard routine. Ms. Turner has not established that the USCG had a duty to preserve the audio [—15—] recordings, so the district court's decision not to award sanctions is clearly correct.[5]

IV.

We review a grant of summary judgment in a FOIA claim *de novo. Hunton & Williams v. U.S. Dep't of Justice,* 590 F.3d 272, 276-76 (4th Cir. 2010). In this case, the plaintiff sought certain documents from the USCG. The Coast Guard produced all documents responsive to the request, but Ms. Turner argues that the USCG must have other, additional records responsive to her request.

A valid FOIA claim requires three components: the agency must have (1) improperly (2) withheld (3) agency records. *Kissinger v. Reporters Comm. for Freedom of the Press,* 445 U.S. 136, 150 (1980). "[D]istrict courts typically dispose of FOIA cases on summary judgment before a plaintiff can

conduct discovery." *Rugiero v. U.S. Dep't of Justice,* 257 F.3d 534, 544 (6th Cir. 2001).

Here, the district court concluded that the USCG conducted a proper and reasonable search for records in response to the [—16—] Turner's FOIA request, and determined that the USCG had provided the Turners with all such documents in its possession. The USCG stated it did not withhold any responsive documents, and Ms. Turner advanced no evidence to refute this contention.

The FOIA imposes limited duties on federal agencies. "[FOIA] does not obligate agencies to create or retain documents; it only obligates them to provide access to those which it in fact has created and retained." *Kissinger,* 445 U.S. at 152. To this end, courts have held that FOIA does not provide a remedy for "destruction of documents." *See Inman v. Comm'r,* 871 F. Supp. 1275, 1277 (E.D. Cal. 1994) ("The destruction of documents in the normal course of an agency's business is not relevant to whether or not the agency has complied with a FOIA request.").

Recognizing the limitations of the FOIA, Ms. Turner argues that the USCG's failure to retain voice tapes and emails should stand as proof that the USCG's *search* for such responsive documents was inadequate. This is illogical and incorrect. The lack of responsive documents does not signal a failure to search. The USCG's diligence in this case is underscored by its [—17—] candid admission that it had recorded over its tape of phone calls from the night of the accident.[6]

---

[5] Ms. Turner also attempts to state a tort claim for spoliation. Spoliation of evidence, standing alone, does not constitute a basis for a civil action under either federal or admiralty law. *See Silvestri,* 271 F.3d at 590.

[6] On appeal, Ms. Turner emphasizes the USCG's failure to search for a duplicate set of tapes that may have existed at the USCG's District 5 Command Center in Virginia. The USCG reported that it found no responsive recordings based on a search for electronic recordings only at its Atlantic Beach facility in North Carolina. The latter facility coordinated the USCG's efforts with respect to the Turners. The FOIA officer did not search District 5, nor did the Coast Guard initially disclose the possible existence of a duplicate set of tapes at that location. Nonetheless, the district court's grant of summary judgment was proper because the FOIA officer had a reasoned explanation for not searching the Virginia Command Center, and FOIA does not require duplicative searches. *See Rein v. U.S.*

FOIA required that the USCG satisfy its duty of production by producing the responsive documents in the USCG's possession at the time of Ms. Turner's FOIA request. The USCG did so. The district court appropriately granted summary judgment to the USCG on this claim.

V.

Ms. Turner argues the district court deprived her of due process by permitting the USCG to file its summary judgment motion more than twelve months after the deadline for filing dispositive motions. We review a district court's decisions pertaining to the management of its own docket under an abuse of discretion standard. *Marryshow v. Flynn*, 986 F.2d 689, 693 (4th Cir. 1993). [—18—]

The de facto extension of time to file the motion lay within the sound discretion of the district court, and we see no reason to disturb the court's action. The district court gave Ms. Turner the opportunity to file a brief in opposition to the USCG's motion for summary judgment, and Ms. Turner did so. Her due process rights were not violated.[7]

VI.

For the reasons stated above, we affirm the judgment of the district court.

AFFIRMED

Patent & Trademark Office, 553 F.3d 353, 358 (4th Cir. 2009).

[7] Ms. Turner also contends that the district court erred when it denied a joint motion for a court-hosted settlement conference. The decision to conduct a settlement conference pertains, again, to the district court's management of its own docket. Ms. Turner cannot show that the district court abused its discretion in this matter.

United States Court of Appeals for the Fifth Circuit

United States Court of Appeals
for the Fifth Circuit

No. 12-30378

SMITH MARITIME, INC.
vs.
L/B KAITLYN EYMARD

Appeal from the United States District Court for the
Western District of Louisiana

Decided: January 3, 2013

Citation: 710 F.3d 560, 1 Adm. R. 184 (5ᵗʰ Cir. 2013).

Before **DAVIS, JONES,** and **SMITH,** Circuit Judges.

[—1—] PER CURIAM:

In this dispute between the owner of two liftboats, Associated Gas & Oil Company, Limited ("Associated"), and Tram Shipyards, Incorporated ("Tram"), a shipyard which performed work on the liftboats, the issue is whether the economic loss rule of *East River Steamship Corp. v. Transamerica Delaval, Inc.*, [—2—] 476 U.S. 858 (1986), precludes claims by the vessel owner Associated for economic loss resulting from the negligence of Tram. We find that *East River* and its progeny clearly apply to these facts, barring recovery to Associated under a products liability or other tort theory and limiting its recovery to its contractual remedies.

I.

On or about February 16, 2010, Associated purchased two self-elevating liftboats, the L/B KAITLYN EYMARD ("KAITLYN") and L/B NICOLE EYMARD ("NICOLE"), from Offshore Marine, Inc. ("OMI"), pursuant to an Asset Purchase Agreement. Under the Asset Purchase Agreement, OMI agreed to provide certain spare parts, and to provide and install additional living quarters and accessories on the two vessels. Since OMI does not own a shipyard, and thus could not install the additional living quarters and accessories on the liftboats itself, OMI used its sister corporation, Tram Shipyards, Inc. ("Tram"), to purchase the materials and perform the

installation of the additional living quarters and accessories. In the course of installing the additional living quarters on the NICOLE, Tram cut, extended, and re-welded the crane boom cradle stanchion of the hydraulic pedestal crane mounted aboard the NICOLE.

Associated modified these liftboats to perform work in Nigeria under a contract Associated had recently won. This required Associated to ship the vessels from Louisiana to Nigeria. As the flotilla transporting the liftboats to Nigeria encountered rough seas, the stanchion snapped at the site of the weld, causing the crane boom on the NICOLE to swing wildly and crash into the additional living quarters, causing damage. As a result of this damage, the flotilla had to be diverted to St. Thomas, British Virgin Islands, for evaluation of the damage. After recommencing the voyage, further rough seas exacerbated the damage, and the flotilla diverted to Trinidad and ultimately returned to [—3—] Amelia, Louisiana for repairs, where the vessels were located at the time of the filing of the instant suit.

Associated alleged in its Counterclaim against Tram that the damage from the swinging crane, the resulting diversions from the planned route for evaluation of the damage, and the ultimate failure of the liftboats to reach Nigeria to perform the work for which Associated purchased the liftboats, are all a direct result of the negligence of Tram in (1) unilaterally deciding to cut and re-weld the crane boom cradle stanchion aboard the NICOLE; (2) re-welding the crane boom cradle stanchion with such inferior workmanship that the weld could not withstand the stresses of mere rough seas; and (3) failing to have the weld inspected or certified to ensure its structural soundness, integrity, and ability to survive rough sea conditions. Furthermore, the delays during, and ultimate failure of, the transport of the vessels to Nigeria, as directly caused by the negligence of Tram, caused Associated to suffer a crippling loss of profits because the liftboats were not performing the work for which they were purchased and were not generating income for Associated during the lengthy repair process in Louisiana.

After other parties in this suit settled, Tram filed a motion for summary judgment claiming that despite any factual dispute, the economic loss rule of *East River* precluded Associated from recovering economic losses against Tram. The district court granted Tram's motion and dismissed Associated's counterclaim. Associated appeals.

II.

The disposition of this case depends on whether the facts require application of the rule announced by the Supreme Court in *East River*. In *East River*, a shipbuilder contracted with the defendant Delaval to design, manufacture and supervise the installation of turbines in four supertankers it was building. 476 U.S. at 859. After the ships were put into service under a [—4—] charter to the plaintiffs, the turbines on all four ships malfunctioned due to design and manufacturing defects. Only the turbines were damaged as a result of the defects. *Id.* at 860-61. The Supreme Court held that a manufacturer in a commercial relationship has no duty under either a negligence or strict products-liability theory to prevent a product from injuring itself. *Id.* at 871. Thus the charterer could not recover for damage to the turbines or resulting economic losses from Delaval.

East River has been extended to claims brought against a provider of professional services (construction supervision) provided to a vessel manufacturer, *Employers Ins. of Wausau v. Suwannee River Spa Lines, Inc.*, 866 F.2d 752 (5th Cir. 1989), and a repairer of a vessel, *Nathaniel Shipping, Inc. v. General Elect. Co.*, 920 F.2d 1256 (5th Cir. 1991)(*Nathaniel Shipping I*). In *Wausau*, plaintiff chemical company entered into a contract with a naval architectural firm and a ship manufacturer for the construction of a vessel to be used to ship its chemicals. 866 F.2d at 756. On its second voyage, the vessel's tug section broke loose from the barge section and sank. *Id.* The plaintiff filed suit alleging that the vessel was unseaworthy on delivery. *Id.* at 757. This court precluded "recovery in maritime tort for purely economic loss stemming from the negligent performance of a contract for professional services where those services are rendered as part of the construction of a vessel." *Id.* at 755. Plaintiffs were therefore limited to their contractual remedies. *Id.*

In *Nathaniel Shipping I*, the plaintiff shipowner Nathaniel Shipping contracted with a shipyard, Louisiana Gulf Shipyards (LGS) to replace a damaged thrust block. 920 F.2d at 1258. LGS contracted with defendant General Electric to drill holes for the new thrust block. *Id.* Nathaniel Shipping's suit alleged that General Electric negligently drilled the holes and sought economic damages allegedly caused by the negligence. *Id.* Even though the shipowner was not in contractual privity with General Electric, who provided [—5—] repair services rather than construction or manufacture of a vessel, this court held that the *East River* economic loss rule precluded the shipowner's recovery against General Electric. *Id.* at 1264-65. In *Nathaniel Shipping, Inc. v. General Elec. Co.*, 932 F.2d 366 (5th Cir. 1991)(*Nathaniel Shipping II*) (on petition for rehearing), this court declined to find a distinction between services for the manufacture of a new vessel and services related to the repair of an existing vessel. "Such a distinction would be inconsistent with our reasoning in *Wausau*. The public policy concerns underpinning tort duties are not present here, and the parties are capable of defining satisfactory performance and allocating the risk of defective performance in their contract." *Id.* at 368, n.3.

Associated argues that this case does not fall within the rule of *East River* and the other cases discussed above because it involves, not a vessel's manufacture or repair, but the modification of a vessel. We see this as a distinction without a difference insofar as the applicability of the *East River* rule is concerned. In the Asset Purchase Agreement with OMI, Associated purchased two vessels with living quarters installed. Associated took the Purchased Assets (which is defined as the Vessels and the Living Quarters (Additional Equipment) "as is, where is"). Associated's complaint, like those in *East River* and the other cases described above, is that it did not receive the benefit of its bargain because the quality of the product did not meet its expectations. As the Supreme Court stated in *East River*, "Damage to a product itself it most naturally understood as a warranty claim. Such damage means simply that the product has not met the customer's expectations, or, in other words, that the customer has received 'insufficient product value.'" 476 U.S. at 872. Such claims are best governed by contract law and the law of warranty - not tort.

Associated also argues that the living quarters that were added to the liftboats and damaged by Tram's alleged negligence are "other property" so the vessel did not damage 'itself' and its claims are not subject to the *East River* [—6—] rule. This argument requires us to define "other property" for this purpose. In *Shipco 2295, Inc. v. Avondale Shipyards, Inc.*, the plaintiff brought tort claims against the manufacturer of several vessels for alleged design defects in the propellers and hull brackets and brought claims against the supplier of the vessels' steering systems for alleged defects. 825 F.2d 925, 926 (5th Cir. 1987). The plaintiffs argued that defects in certain components of each vessel caused damage to unrelated components in the same vessel. *Id*. at 928. They argued that the resulting damage was damage to "other property" and that *East River* recognizes a purchaser's right to recover economic losses resulting from damage to the product in tort when the defect in the product causes damage to other property. *Id*. To determine "what is the product?" this court looked to the object of the contract or bargain that governs the rights of the parties. *Id*. This court found that *East River* barred plaintiff's claims against the manufacturer and against the supplier because the "object of the contract" was the completed vessel and not the component parts of the vessel. *Id*.

Associated argues that the living quarters are "other property" because the purchase from OMI set a separate price for that component. The Asset Purchase Agreement in this case does set separate prices for the vessel and the added living quarters.[1]

---

[1] The relevant provisions of the contract follow:

However, the Asset Purchase Agreement also combines the [—7—] Vessels and other components including the Living Quarters / Additional Equipment as the "Purchased Assets."

1.1 <u>Purchase and Sale of Assets</u>, At the Closing, Seller will sell, convey, transfer, assign, and deliver to Buyer (i) the **Vessels** together with their engines, tackle, winches, cranes, fuel on board, cordage, general outfit, electronic and navigation equipment, radio installations, appurtenances, appliances, inventory, spare parts, stores, tools and provisions on board each of the Vessels; (ii) all Permits (to the extent transferable) relating to the Vessels transferred; (iii) all business records relating exclusively to the Vessels (the "Records"); (iv) any technical or regulatory documentation already aboard the Vessels, including classification certificates, loadline certificates, radio licenses, operating manuals, vessel logs and preventative maintenance manuals (collectively, the "Vessel Documentation"); and (v) all drawings and intellectual property related to each of the Vessels (the "Intellectual Property"). The assets described in the foregoing clauses (i) through (v) are hereinafter collectively referred to, together with the **Additional**

WHEREAS, Seller desires to sell to Buyer, and Buyer desires to acquire from Seller, the Vessels as defined herein, for a total purchase price for the Vessels of Thirty-Five Million Two Hundred Thousand and No/100 United States Dollars ($35,200,000.00 USD) on the terms and conditions specified herein;

WHEREAS, In addition to the Vessels, Buyer has agreed to purchase from Seller additional equipment, specifically Living Quarters and Accessories as detailed on the ProForma Invoice attached hereto as Exhibit "A" and incorporated herein by reference (hereinafter "**Additional Equipment**"), for an additional Seven Hundred Twenty Seven Thousand Nine Hundred Twenty Seven and No/100 United States Dollars ($727,927.00);

Equipment, as the **"Purchased Assets."**
(emphasis added)

The Asset Purchase Agreement defines the "Purchased Assets", which are the object of the contract as subject to the warranty. In para. 3.4, the Purchased Assets are conveyed "as is, where is." Accordingly, the Living Quarters are not "other property" for purposes of this analysis and Associated cannot avoid application of the rule from *East River*.

III.

The crane boom cradle stanchion and the living quarters that were damaged were integral parts of the vessel as it was sold to Associated. The economic losses Associated suffered as a result of the damage are not recoverable [—8—] under tort theories from Tram. Under *East River*, the plaintiff is relegated to its rights under the contract. The district court properly dismissed Associated's claims on summary judgment. AFFIRMED.

United States Court of Appeals
for the Fifth Circuit

No. 12-30280

INTERNATIONAL MARINE, L.L.C.,
VS.
DELTA TOWING, L.L.C.

Appeal from the United States District Court for the
Eastern District of Louisiana

Decided: January 8, 2013

Citation: 704 F.3d 350, 1 Adm. R. 188 (5ᵗʰ Cir. 2013).

Before **STEWART**, Chief Judge, **KING**, and **OWEN**,
Circuit Judges.

[—1—] **STEWART**, Chief Judge:

The district court entered an order declaring enforceable under general maritime law a liquidated damages provision in a contract between Defendant-Appellee Delta Towing, L.L.C. and Plaintiffs-Appellants International Marine, L.L.C. and International Offshore Services, L.L.C. Upon Plaintiffs' motion, the district court certified the order as a final judgment pursuant to Federal Rule of Civil Procedure 54(b), and Plaintiffs now appeals. We AFFIRM. [—2—]

I. BACKGROUND

A. Negotiations Lead to Vessel Sales Agreement

On September 8, 2006, International Marine, L.L.C.[1] entered into a Vessel Sales Agreement ("VSA") with Delta Towing, L.L.C. ("Delta") wherein International purchased two tugboats from Delta for $4 million. The companies' agreement was preceded by several months of negotiations between International's president, Stephen Williams, and counsel, Peter Rouse, and the treasurer of Delta's parent company, Darren Vorst. Throughout the negotiations, Williams was

---

[1] International Offshore Services, L.L.C. served as International Marine, L.L.C.'s guarantor in the subsequently signed Vessel Sales Agreement. Collectively, we refer to both companies as "International."

clear that the vessels were for "in house" use and would not be used to compete with Delta. Delta initially declined to sell the vessels because it intended to use them to grow its business, but ultimately agreed to sell them subject to its standard non-compete language.

The signed VSA includes a liquidated damages provision ("LD Provision") that, *inter alia*, provided for a $250,000 payment for, *inter alia*, each violation of the non-competition clause. This figure had been the subject of significant negotiations between Rouse and Delta, and its magnitude had dropped significantly over several rounds of negotiations, from a starting figure of $4 million per violation.

B. Liquidated Damages and Related Provisions

The VSA contains two relevant contract provisions. The first, Paragraph 11F, is a non-competition clause between International (Buyer) and Delta (Seller), which reads as follows:

F. <u>Covenant Regarding Name/Use of Vessels/Hiring of Crews</u>. . . . Buyer represents that it is purchasing the Vessels for use with Buyer's owned or chartered equipment in support of Buyer's internal operations. [—3—] Inasmuch, Buyer covenants and agrees that **neither it nor any of its affiliated companies will charter out or enter into towing contracts or otherwise utilize or permit anyone else to utilize the Vessels for hire** (collectively "Charters Out") in the inland or offshore waters of the U.S. Gulf of Mexico . . . (the "Covered Trade") for a period of five (5) years from the date of this Agreement (the "Covered Term")…. Notwithstanding the foregoing, **in the event Buyer or its affiliated companies wish to Charter Out either or both of the Vessels in the Covered Trade during all or part of the Covered Term, Buyer shall be obligated to time charter the applicable Vessels to Seller for Seller to enter into Charters Out** with customers acceptable to Seller….

VSA ¶ 11F (emphasis added). Thus, in the event International decided to compete with Delta for third-party charters, it was first obligated to notify Delta and give it the option of operating charters itself. If Delta chose to operate the charter, it would remit ninety percent of the gross charter fee to International. If Delta was unable to secure charter customers for the vessels within a reasonable period of time, International was permitted to operate its own charters and would remit ten percent of the charter fee to Delta. Additionally, the charter hire rate charged to customers had to be reasonably agreeable to both Delta and International.

The VSA's LD Provision, Paragraph 11G, reads as follows:

> G. <u>Liquidated Damages</u>. The consideration for the provisions in paragraph 11F and this paragraph 11G is that the above Purchase Price is below the fair market price of the Vessels at the time of sale and other good and valuable consideration the receipt and sufficiency of which is hereby acknowledged and confessed. **In the event Buyer or its affiliated companies or other subsequent owner, manager, or charter of the Vessels violates any of the covenants and agreements in paragraph 11F, Buyer shall pay to [—4—] Seller as liquidated damages, and not as a penalty, the greater of (i) the sum of Two Hundred Fifty Thousand and no/100 Dollars ($250,000.00) per incident or occurrence or (ii) if applicable the gross amount of revenue earned in violation of such covenant and agreement with respect of the incident or occurrence in question**. . . . All liquidated damages shall be payable within 30 days of notice of the violation. It is understood that the **resultant damages of any such breach of the covenants and agreements contained in paragraph 11F would be difficult to ascertain with certainty but that the amount stipulated herein is a good faith reasonable estimate of the damages Seller would suffer**. . . . In no event shall any party or the affiliated companies thereof or the respective shareholders, officers, directors, employees, agents, or representatives thereof circumvent or attempt to circumvent the provisions of paragraph 11F or this paragraph 11G by any means, direct or indirect.

VSA ¶ 11G (emphasis added).

C. Delta Discovers Breach of VSA ¶ 11F

In July 2008, Delta notified International that it had become aware that the vessels had been chartered without Delta's knowledge in violation of the VSA. International responded in late November 2008 by remitting a check for $53,293.33, which it claimed was the extent of the "owed commissions." Delta refused to accept the check as the full amount owed and requested material backing up International's figure. In early 2009, while conducting an audit with one of Delta's employees, International discovered that it owed Delta an additional $37,657, which it remitted in another check. Delta refused to negotiate this check as well, and later sent a demand letter for the liquidated damages amount multiplied by the alleged thirty-six charters that breached the [—5—] VSA, which totaled $9 million. International has conceded it breached the contract by operating twenty-seven charters.

D. International Seeks Declaratory Judgment

In December 2009, Delta sued International in Texas state court for breaching the VSA, including for failing to timely remit multiple charter payments. The VSA's forum selection clause mandates the parties resolve their dispute in the United States District Court for the Eastern District of Louisiana. Therefore, International filed the instant suit, seeking a declaratory judgment that it had not breached the VSA and that the LD Provision was an unenforceable penalty as a matter of law. Delta counterclaimed for breach of contract, seeking enforcement of the LD Provision. Judge McNamara was assigned to the case. The parties engaged in discovery, including conducting depositions.

On March 11, 2011, in a detailed and well-reasoned Order and Reasons,[2] Judge McNamara granted Delta's motion for summary judgment in part and denied International's motion, finding the LD Provision was enforceable. The McNamara Order declined to resolve the issue of damages. Subsequently, Judge McNamara retired, and the case was reassigned to Judge Fallon. International then filed a Motion to Vacate pursuant to Federal Rule of Civil Procedure 60(b) and a Motion to Reconsider based on additional testimony obtained from Delta's former damages expert and Chief Operating Officer, Barry Matherne, who had left Delta since his previous deposition. On February 13, 2012, the district court denied International's motion in its entirety and reaffirmed that the LD Provision was enforceable.[3] The Fallon Order specifically declined to revisit the merits of the McNamara Order, and instead focused on whether the new [—6—] Matherne deposition changed the analysis as to whether the LD Provision was enforceable. The Fallon Order concluded that it did not.

International then moved for Judge Fallon to certify the judgment as final or for interlocutory appeal. On March 16, 2012, Judge Fallon certified the Fallon Order as a final judgment pursuant to Federal Rule of Civil Procedure 54(b). International timely appealed.[4]

---

[2] Hereinafter, we will refer to this order as the "McNamara Order."

[3] Hereinafter, we will refer to this order as the "Fallon Order."

[4] Delta briefly asserts that International has not properly appealed the McNamara and Fallon Orders. Although Delta does not press this argument, we are "obligated to examine the basis for our jurisdiction, *sua sponte*, if necessary." *In re Cortez*, 457 F.3d 448, 453 (5th Cir. 2006) (citation and internal quotation marks omitted). We have determined that we have jurisdiction over this appeal.

Additionally, the VSA states that it is governed according to general maritime law and Louisiana law, if applicable. Judge McNamara determined the LD Provision was subject to general maritime law, a determination the parties have not appealed. (*Reporter's note: misnumbered in the original opinion as Footnote 3*).

II. DISCUSSION

At its core, International's argument is that both the McNamara and Fallon Orders erred when they held the LD Provision was enforceable. International raises several specific points of error in the Orders, including improper consideration of the parties' negotiating capacities and the application of an improper standard of review.

We review a grant of summary judgment de novo, applying the same standard as the district court. *QT Trading, L.P. v. M/V Saga Morus*, 641 F.3d 105, 108 (5th Cir. 2011) (citation omitted). Summary judgment is appropriate when "there is no genuine dispute as to any material fact and the movant is entitled to judgment as a matter of law." Fed. R. Civ. P. 56(a). "Factual controversies are construed in the light most favorable to the nonmovant, but only if both parties have introduced evidence showing that an actual controversy exists." *QT Trading*, 641 F.3d at 108 (citation and internal quotation marks omitted). We review the district court's judgment, and our analysis need not be based solely on the district court's stated reasons. *See Cambridge Integrated* [—7—] *Servs. Grp., Inc. v. Concentra Integrated Servs., Inc.*, 697 F.3d 248, 253 (5th Cir. 2012) (citation and internal quotation marks omitted) ("We are not limited to the district court's reasons for its grant of summary judgment and may affirm the district court's summary judgment on any ground raised below and supported by the record.").

The interpretation of maritime contract terms is a matter of law we review de novo. *One Beacon Ins. Co. v. Crowley Marine Servs., Inc.*, 648 F.3d 258, 262 (5th Cir. 2011). When interpreting maritime contracts, federal admiralty law rather than state law applies. *See Har-Win, Inc. v. Consol. Grain & Barge Co.*, 794 F.2d 985, 987 (5th Cir. 1986) (collecting citations). Whether a liquidated damages clause is a penalty is a question of law. *Louis Dreyfus Corp. v. 27,946 Long Tons of Corn*, 830 F.2d 1321, 1331 (5th Cir. 1987) (citation omitted). The burden of proving that a liquidated damages clause is a penalty is on the party urging for it to be viewed as a penalty. *Farmers Exp. Co. v. M/V Georgis Prois*, 799 F.2d 159, 162 (5th Cir. 1986) (citation omitted).

A. Applicable Law

In interpreting liquidated damages clauses in maritime contracts, we apply the *Restatement (Second) of Contracts* Section 356 comment b (the "Restatement") to determine whether such a clause is "so unreasonably large as to be a penalty." We have explained the comment's two-part test as follows:

> The first factor is the anticipated or actual loss caused by the breach. The amount fixed is reasonable if it approximates the actual loss that has resulted from a particular breach, even though it may not approximate the loss that might have been anticipated under other possible situations, *or* if the breach approximates the loss anticipated at the time of making the contract, even though it does not approximate the actual loss. The second factor is the difficulty of proof of loss. The greater the difficulty of proof of loss, the more flexibility [—8—] is allowed in approximating the anticipated or actual harm.

Farmers Exp., 799 F.2d at 162 (citations omitted).

Our circuit precedent in the context of maritime liquidated damages is limited to two cases: *Farmers Export*, 799 F.2d 159, and *Louis Dreyfus*, 830 F.2d 1321. Both concern liquidated damages that attached when a vessel overstayed its timeslot at a berth. In *Farmers Export*, we upheld a $5,000 per hour liquidated damages charge as reasonable and not a penalty. 799 F.2d at 165. In reaching this conclusion, we noted that while "the reasonableness of the damages [is] a question of law, in making that determination we rely on the findings of fact of the district court." *Id.* at 164. We therefore viewed as persuasive the district court's factual findings that $5,000 was a reasonable forecast of the grain facility owner's damages. *Id.* at 165. To reach that conclusion, the district court considered expert

testimony about actual damage estimates and the charges levied by other grain elevators. *Id.* at 164.

In *Louis Dreyfus*, we refused to enforce a liquidated damages clause that assessed a $30,000 per day liquidated damages charge to a ship that failed to vacate its loading berth. 830 F.3d at 1332. We stated that the "district court was entitled to find" that the charge, which was based on a "reasonable preestimate of" the damages that would accrue in a full calendar day, "is excessive when the vessel occupies the berth for a much shorter time." *Id.*

B. Analysis

Our review of the record shows that Delta's concerns about competition—and International's assurances that it would not compete with Delta—were critical in the negotiations that led to the sale of the vessels, and they underpin the LD Provision. This conclusion anchors our analysis of the Restatement's factors. [—9—]

Pursuant to our precedent, we first examine the second Restatement factor "because the more difficult it is to prove damages, the more leeway the court allows in determining whether the liquidated damages are reasonably related to anticipated damages." *Farmers Exp.*, 799 F.2d at 162. Contrary to International's assertions, the damage that would accrue from International's breach of VSA Paragraph 11F was not just the ten-percent fee International owed when it chartered out the vessels. Instead, and more importantly, it was also Delta's inability to prevent competition, leading to the potential loss of customers, business opportunities and market share due to International's failure to notify Delta of its intent to compete.

International does not dispute the difficulty in estimating damages before a non-competition clause is breached. We have previously recognized that it is difficult to calculate the damage that results when a covenant not to compete is breached. *See Blase Indus. Corp. v. Anorad Corp.*, 442 F.3d 235,

238 (5th Cir. 2006) ("[C]ovenants not to compete often include a liquidated damages provision to avoid the difficulty of calculating damages."). The McNamara Order considered testimony about the difficulty of estimating damages *ex ante*, and we agree with its conclusion that these damages are difficult to prove. Therefore, we have—and the district courts properly had—"more leeway" in determining whether the LD Provision is reasonably related to anticipated damages. *Farmers Exp.*, 799 F.2d at 162.

In reaching its decision as to the first Restatement factor, which assesses the reasonableness of the LD Provision, the McNamara Order assessed the expert testimony as to potential charter contracts that Delta could have obtained and the typical charter fee at which the vessels had been hired out before they were sold. The testimony showed that there was variability in the length of charter contracts, but that a single contract could last for as long as several years. The testimony also showed that day rates for charters in late 2006 and [—10—] 2007 could range up to several thousand dollars. Thus, a single charter contract could reasonably generate substantial revenue equal to or in excess of the LD Provision. Moreover, as the McNamara Order noted, "International Marine has presented no evidence suggesting that [Delta's] concerns regarding loss of market share, future customers or future business were unreasonable or unrelated to [Delta's] anticipated loss." R. at 3742. We follow *Farmers Export* in finding persuasive the district court's careful factual findings as to whether the LD Provision was a reasonable forecast of damages. Adopting the language of the McNamara Order, we hold that "[l]ooking at the contract at the time it was made, *ex ante* breach, this court cannot bicker with the $250,000 per occurrence forecast."[5] R. at 3746.

International has not met its burden to prove that the LD Provision was a penalty. We thus hold that the district court properly held the LD Provision enforceable.[6]

III. CONCLUSION

For the foregoing reasons, we AFFIRM the district court's judgment.

---

[5] International places considerable emphasis on the total amount of liquidated damages Delta has claimed. Notwithstanding the Fallon Order's express reservation of the damages issue for trial, we note that the total damages claimed are so large because International breached the non-competition provision at least twenty-seven times. We are loath to find the LD Provision unenforceable merely because International adopted a pattern of disregarding its contractual obligations. *(Reporter's note: misnumbered as Footnote 4 in the original opinion).*

[6] Because we have determined the district courts' judgment was correct, we need not reach International's arguments related to the district courts' allegedly improper reasoning and standard of review. We also decline to decide whether the Restatement's "extreme case" language applies to this situation. *See* Restatement (Second) of Contracts § 356 comment b ("If, to take an extreme case, it is clear that no loss at all has occurred, a provision fixing a substantial sum as damages is unenforceable."). Matherne's testimony that he was unaware of any damage to Delta's competitive position as a result of International's breaches is more probative of the difficulty of proving such damages than of whether damage actually occurred. *(Reporter's note: misnumbered as Footnote 5 in the original opinion).*

United States Court of Appeals
for the Fifth Circuit

No. 12-30136

CENTER FOR BIOLOGICAL DIVERSITY, INC.
vs.
BP AMERICA PRODUCTION CO.

Appeal from the United States District Court for the
Eastern District of Louisiana

Decided: January 9, 2013

Citation: 704 F.3d 413, 1 Adm. R. 193 (5th Cir. 2013).

Before **STEWART,** Chief Judge, and **KING,** and **OWEN,**
Circuit Judges.

[—1—] **KING,** Circuit Judge:

This appeal arises from the multi-district litigation spawned from the disaster on the *Deepwater Horizon* drilling rig and the resulting massive oil spill that occurred at the Macondo well site in the Gulf of Mexico. Plaintiff Center for Biological Diversity appeals from the district court's dismissal of its action brought under the citizen-suit provisions of the Clean Water Act ("CWA"), 33 U.S.C. § 1365(a)(1), the Comprehensive Environmental Response, Compensation, and Liability Act ("CERCLA"), 42 U.S.C. § 9659(a), and the Emergency Planning and Community Right-to-Know Act ("EPCRA"), 42 U.S.C. [—2—] § 11046(a). The district court dismissed the suit for lack of standing, mootness, and failure to state a claim for relief. We agree that most of the plaintiff's claims for relief have become moot because the Macondo well has been capped and sealed. We conclude that, at least on the current record, the EPCRA claim remains viable. We therefore AFFIRM IN PART and REVERSE IN PART the district court's judgment.

I. FACTUAL AND PROCEDURAL BACKGROUND

Plaintiff Center for Biological Diversity ("the Center") is a non-profit environmental organization with over 40,000 members, including over 3,500 members living in the Gulf of Mexico region. Defendants BP, P.L.C. and its corporate subsidiaries BP America Production Co. and BP Exploration & Production, Inc. (collectively "BP") conduct exploration and drilling operations in the Gulf of Mexico. As part of those operations, BP leased the mobile offshore drilling unit known as *Deepwater Horizon* from Defendants Transocean, Ltd. and its subsidiary companies in order to drill the Macondo well, which is located on the sea floor at Mississippi Canyon Block 252.

On April 20, 2010, an explosion on *Deepwater Horizon* tragically killed eleven people and accompanied an oil spill that caused an environmental disaster of immense proportion. Millions of gallons of oil spewed from the well site over the course of several months as the defendants and government authorities sought to stop it.

In the face of an extensive oil spill, federal law directs the President to ensure the effective and immediate removal of the oil in accordance with a National Contingency Plan and to direct all federal, state and private actions in that regard. *See* 33 U.S.C. §1321(c)(1)(A), (2)(A). Consistent with the National Contingency Plan, the President must also create a National Response System, which establishes multiple levels of federal contingency plans for addressing a discharge of oil and hazardous substances. 33 U.S.C. §1321(j); *see also* 40 C.F.R. [—3—] § 300.210. Pursuant to these plans, a Federal On-Scene Coordinator ("FOSC") will direct and coordinate all efforts at the scene of the discharge. 40 C.F.R. § 300.120(a). When a discharge occurs in a coastal zone of the United States, the Coast Guard provides the FOSC, and if the spill is especially complex the Coast Guard can name a National Incident Commander to assume the role of the FOSC. *See* 40 C.F.R. §§ 300.120(a)(1), 300.5, 300.323.

In the case of the *Deepwater Horizon* disaster, the federal government's response to the spill involved monumental efforts. Almost 50,000 people, including over 17,000 National Guard members, and over 4,000 vessels were deployed in the Gulf of Mexico and the coastal region. Federal oversight of the matter spanned multiple governmental agencies, with the President dispatching to the Gulf region the Secretaries of the Interior and Homeland Security, the Administrator of the EPA, the President's Assistant for Energy and Climate Change Policy, and the Administrator of NOAA. BP participated in the response activities at the direction of the federal authorities to stop the oil spill. On July 15, 2010, a permanent cap was put in place at the well site to halt the flow of oil. On September 19, 2010, the National Incident Commander announced that a relief well had been completed, which effectively "killed" the Macondo well.

Meanwhile, as the response efforts were ongoing, the Center filed suit against BP and Transocean on June 18, 2010, alleging that the defendants violated CWA because of the discharged oil and toxic pollutants from the ruptured well. In August 2010, the Center filed a second action against BP and Transocean asserting additional claims under CWA, CERCLA, and EPCRA. The Center asserted the following counts of statutory violations: discharge of pollutants, in violation of CWA, 33 U.S.C. § 1311 (Count 1); discharge of oil and hazardous substances, in violation of CWA, 33 U.S.C. § 1321 (Count 2); discharge of toxic pollutants, in violation of CWA, 33 U.S.C. § 1317 (Count 3); discharge of pollutants, in violation of national standards of performance for [—4—] offshore drilling operations under CWA, 33 U.S.C. § 1316 (Count 4); gross negligence or willful misconduct pursuant to CWA, 33 U.S.C. §1321(b)(7)(D) (Count 5); failure to report to the National Response Center the release of hazardous substances, in violation of CERCLA, 42 U.S.C. § 9603(a) (Count 6); and failure to report the release of hazardous substances to the emergency coordinator for the local emergency planning committee, in violation of EPCRA, 42 U.S.C. § 11004 (Count 7).

In its prayer for relief, the Center sought the following: (1) a declaratory judgment that the defendants had violated, continued to violate, or were reasonably likely to continue to violate CWA, CERCLA, and EPCRA; (2) an injunction enjoining the defendants from operating their offshore facility in a manner that would result in further violation of CWA, CERCLA, and EPCRA, specifically from discharging any further pollutants or from releasing any hazardous substance without full and complete reporting under CERCLA and EPCRA, and requiring full and complete reporting for hazardous substances already released; (3) an order that the defendants divulge the complete list and amounts of toxic pollutants contained in the oil and other releases from the *Deepwater Horizon* rig and well; (4) civil penalties pursuant to CWA, CERCLA, and EPCRA; (5) an order authorizing the Center to sample any discharge of pollutants from the well for a period of ten years; (6) an order requiring the defendants to provide the Center with copies of all reports and other documents that defendants submit to regulatory authorities for a period of five years; and (7) an injunction requiring the defendants to pay the cost of any environmental restoration or remediation deemed necessary by the district court.

The Multidistrict Litigation ("MDL") Panel transferred the Center's complaints to MDL-2179 in the Eastern District of Louisiana (Judge Barbier). The MDL case before Judge Barbier consists of hundreds of cases, with over 100,000 individual claimants, all in connection with the *Deepwater Horizon* [—5—] disaster. In order to manage this complex litigation, the district court issued Pretrial Order No. 11 establishing several "pleading bundles" into each of which claims of similar nature would be placed for the purpose of filing a master complaint, answers, and any Rule 12 motions. The Center's complaints were placed into Pleading Bundle D1, which was for claims by private parties for injunctive relief and provided as follows:

D. Injunctive and Regulatory Claims. These claims brought by private parties challenging regulatory action or authority and/or seeking injunctive relief will each be pled pursuant to Master Complaints as delineated below, and will include the following types of claims.

D1. Claims Against Private Parties. These claims will be pled separately and uniformly in a Master Complaint.

For purposes of answering or otherwise responding to the complaints in Pleading Bundle D1, the allegations and prayers for relief contained in the Master Complaint were deemed to amend and supersede allegations and claims contained in the pre-existing individual complaints. The Center's individual complaints were not eliminated, however, but rather were stayed until further order of the court.

Consistent with the pretrial order, the D1 plaintiffs, including the Center, filed a Master Complaint that was in most respects similar to the Center's individual complaints. The D1 Master Complaint alleged the same violations of CWA, CERCLA, and EPCRA that had been alleged in the Center's complaints, as well as additional claims under the Endangered Species Act ("ESA"), state law, and general maritime law.[1] The Master Complaint also sought essentially the same declaratory and injunctive relief that was sought in the Center's [—6—] individual complaints. Unlike the Center's individual complaints, however, the D1 Master Complaint contained no prayer for civil penalties.

The district court's Pretrial Order No. 11 provided that civil penalties requested in separate suits by governmental entities were to be placed in Pleading Bundle C. The order also provided that civil penalties would not be included in any other pleading bundles or master complaints. In Pretrial Order No. 25, the district court later clarified that "[a]ny case currently pending in the MDL that does not fall within pleading bundles A or C is deemed to fall within one or more of the following: Pleading Bundle B1, Pleading Bundle B3, and/or pleading Bundle D1, as may be applicable." The Center's civil penalty claims did not fall within Pleading Bundles A or C, and the Center unsuccessfully moved on three occasions in the district court to have all of its claims moved into Pleading Bundle C.

---

[1] The district court's resolution of the claims under ESA, state law, and general maritime law are not part of the instant appeal.

BP and Transocean separately moved to dismiss the D1 Master Complaint pursuant to Federal Rules of Civil Procedure 12(b)(1) and 12(b)(6). The district court conducted a hearing, during which it also considered motions to dismiss other pleading bundles. The district court granted the motions to dismiss the D1 Master Complaint, finding that (1) the D1 plaintiffs lacked standing because their alleged injuries were not redressable by a favorable decision, (2) the D1 claims were moot, and (3) the D1 claims were not actionable because the defendants were not "in violation" of the alleged statutes.

The court took judicial notice that the Macondo well had been capped on July 15, 2010, thereby stopping the uncontrolled flow of oil, and that the well had been permanently killed on September 19, 2010, when a relief well was used to pump cement into the Macondo well. The court reasoned, therefore, that the D1 plaintiffs' claims were not redressable for two reasons. First, an injunction would be useless because there was no longer an ongoing release from the well, and there was no viable offshore facility from which any release could possibly [—7—] occur. Second, because cleanup activities were ongoing under the direction of the National Incident Commander, the FOSC, and the Unified Area Command, any order from the court would implicate parties not before the court, and the plaintiffs could not show that an order would resolve any potential deficiency in the cleanup effort. The court further held that the plaintiffs lacked standing to bring their failure-to-report claim under EPCRA "[i]n light of the fact that there is no on-going release of oil and that data regarding the spill and its cleanup are easily accessible."

Similarly, the court held that the claims for injunctive relief were moot. The court reasoned that because the Macondo well was dead and no longer discharging oil, an injunction could not provide meaningful relief in terms of stopping discharges that had already ceased. The court further noted that because Pretrial Order No. 11 had limited the D1 Master Complaint to injunctive relief, the D1 plaintiffs were not seeking the kind of civil penalties that otherwise might prevent mootness.

Finally, the court held that CWA, CERCLA, and EPCRA require plaintiffs to show a reasonable likelihood of an ongoing violation in order to have an actionable claim. But because there was no longer a viable facility from which a release could occur, there was no reasonable possibility for a future release and no ongoing violation. The district court dismissed the D1 Master Complaint in its entirety.

Following the district court's written order, the Center filed an unopposed motion for clarification pursuant to Federal Rule of Civil Procedure 59(e), asking that the district court make explicit that the order dismissing the D1 Master Complaint was a final judgment that also dismissed the Center's underlying individual complaints. Any confusion about the finality of the judgment with respect to the Center presumably existed because the district court's order had adjudicated only claims for injunctive relief and did not mention the Center's [—8—] individual claims for civil penalties. Indeed, the Center's motion advised that the Plaintiffs' Steering Committee ("PSC") believed the court's order was not a final judgment under Federal Rule of Civil Procedure 54(b) but that the PSC did not oppose such a designation by the district court.

Thereafter, the Center filed a Notice of Non-Opposition, indicating that no party had opposed the motion for clarification. The Center again asked the district court to enter a final judgment. Approximately two months after filing the Notice of Non-Opposition, the Center filed a renewed motion for clarification, which had been temporarily withdrawn, yet again asking that an explicit final judgment be entered within 30 days. When the district court did not enter such an order, the Center's counsel wrote a letter to the district court further raising the issue of a final judgment. Counsel asked that the court enter a final judgment in order to "allow the Center to exercise its right of appeal in this matter." Counsel stated that "[w]ithout an entry of final judgment, the Center is in the untenable position of not being able to participate in the ongoing MDL while also not being clear that it is able to appeal the Court's ruling." None of the Center's pleadings or correspondence suggested or requested that any of the Center's claims would remain live following entry of the final judgment.

The district court then entered a final judgment "for the reasons stated in the Court's Order Dismissing the Bundle D1 Master Complaint . . . as that Order relates to [the Center's individual complaints]." The Center now appeals.

II. STANDARD OF REVIEW

A district court's dismissal for lack of subject matter jurisdiction pursuant to Rule 12(b)(1) or for failure to state a claim pursuant to Rule 12(b)(6) is reviewed de novo. *Ballew v. Cont'l Airlines, Inc.*, 668 F.3d 777, 781 (5th Cir. 2012); *Turner v. Pleasant*, 663 F.3d 770, 775 (5th Cir. 2011). Legal questions relating to standing and mootness are also reviewed de novo. *Envtl.* [—9—] *Conservation Org. v. City of Dallas*, 529 F.3d 519, 524 (5th Cir. 2008); *Ctr. for Individual Freedom v. Carmouche*, 449 F.3d 655, 659 (5th Cir. 2006).

III. STATUTORY PROVISIONS

The CWA was intended "to restore and maintain the chemical, physical, and biological integrity of the Nation's waters." 33 U.S.C. § 1251(a). As a general matter, its provisions prohibit the unauthorized discharge of pollutants, including oil and other hazardous substances, into the waters of the United States, and set standards for evaluating discharges from various sources. *See* 33 U.S.C. §§ 1311, 1316, 1317, 1321. The CWA authorizes citizen suits to obtain injunctions and civil penalties, "payable to the United States Treasury, against any person found to be in violation of 'an effluent standard or limitation' under the Act." *Envtl. Conservation Org.*, 529 F.3d at 526 (quoting 33 U.S.C. § 1365(a)). The district court has jurisdiction to enforce such effluent standard or limitation regardless of the amount in controversy. § 1365(a).

CERCLA and EPCRA require, *inter alia*, that discharges of certain pollutants and hazardous substances be reported to the National Response Center, *see* 42 U.S.C. §9603(a) (CERCLA), or to state and local emergency planning personnel. *See* 42 U.S.C. § 11004(b)(1) (EPCRA). Both statutes authorize citizen suits to enforce their requirements and also permit both injunctive relief and civil penalties. *See* 42 U.S.C. §§9659(a), (c) (CERCLA), 11046(a), (c) (EPCRA). Pursuant to CERCLA, the district court may "order such action as may be necessary to correct the violation." § 9659(c).

IV. DISCUSSION

The Center challenges the district court's dismissal of its claims, contending that the court failed to accept the well-pleaded facts of its complaint as true. It contends that the court improperly found that injunctive relief would be moot because the Center alleged that the defendants were reasonably likely to continue to discharge pollutants from the well site. According to the Center, [—10—] because jurisdiction is determined at the time of filing the complaint, and the complaint alleged that there were continuing discharges of pollutants, it set forth plausible claims for relief. The Center further argues that the district court erroneously focused on the claim for injunctive relief enjoining the defendants from operating the offshore facility in violation of CWA, CERCLA, and EPCRA, while ignoring the Center's other claims. It contends that because all of its claims for relief are redressable by the district court, it has standing and the suit should be reinstated.

Upon review of the briefs, the applicable law, and the record in this case, we conclude that the district court correctly dismissed most of the Center's claims as moot. But before considering mootness with respect to the Center's individual claims and prayers for relief, we first consider the district court's taking of judicial notice that the Macondo well was capped in July 2010 and killed in September 2010, which was of central importance to the court's decision.

A. Judicial notice

Pursuant to Federal Rule of Evidence 201, a court is "entitled to take judicial notice of adjudicative facts from reliable sources 'whose accuracy cannot reasonably be questioned.'" *Sosebee v. Steadfast Ins. Co.*, No. 11-31134, 2012 WL 5914081, at *14 n.1 (5th Cir. Nov. 27, 2012) (quoting FED. R. EVID. 201(b)). A district court's application of judicial notice under Rule 201 is reviewed for an abuse of discretion. *Funk v. Stryker Corp.*, 631 F.3d 777, 783 (5th Cir. 2011).

Here, the district court noted at the hearing on the defendants' motions to dismiss the D1 Master Complaint that the Macondo well was dead. The court did not, either at the oral hearing or in its written decision, indicate the source or sources upon which the court relied for this information. Nevertheless, the record bears out the district court's statement. [—11—]

For example, on September 19, 2010, National Incident Commander Admiral Thad Allen issued a formal announcement that, due to BP's completion of the relief well and cementing, the Macondo well was "effectively dead" and "poses no continuing threat to the Gulf of Mexico." Admiral Allen indicated that the relief well was completed by BP under the direction and authority of the federal government's science and engineering teams, and that the well's killing had been confirmed by the Department of the Interior's Bureau of Ocean Energy Management. Furthermore, on September 28, 2010, the Federal On-Scene Coordinator, Rear Admiral Paul Zukunft, also stated that the well had been killed on September 19, 2010, and that there had been no new oil introduced since July 15.

The Center argues that the district court was bound to accept the well-pleaded facts of the complaint concerning alleged future discharges from the well, essentially contending that the court improperly took judicial notice of the well's closing. The district court was not bound by the pleadings in order to decide the Rule 12(b)(1) motion, however; rather, it was empowered to make factual findings that were determinative of jurisdiction. *Williamson v. Tucker*, 645 F.2d 404, 413 (5th Cir. 1981).

The Center further complains that it requested prior notice of any facts to be judicially noticed but received no advance warning. Ordinarily, a party should be given notice that the court intends to judicially notice facts and, when appropriate, should be given an opportunity for discovery germane to a jurisdictional dispute implicated by the noticed facts. *See id.* at 414; *see also* FED. R. EVID. 201(e). We are not persuaded, however, that the district court's procedure was erroneous under the circumstances of this case.

The court's taking of judicial notice before notifying a party is not alone improper, as the rule specifically contemplates such a possibility but allows the party an opportunity to be heard if the party so requests. *See* FED. R. EVID. [—12—] 201(e) ("If the court takes judicial notice before notifying a party, the party, on request, is still entitled to be heard."). Here, the Center had notice from the defendants' motions to dismiss that the court was being asked to take judicial notice. BP specifically argued that the capping and killing of the well were judicially noticeable facts and that the Center's claims were moot because the well was dead. The Center therefore had an opportunity to be heard and actually did—albeit minimally—respond to BP in its opposition. *Cf. In re Eckstein Marine Serv., L.L.C.*, 672 F.3d 310, 316 (5th Cir. 2012) (holding that defendant's pleadings gave adequate notice to plaintiff that defendant was challenging the district court's jurisdiction under Rule 12(b)(1)); *see also Amadasu v. The Christ Hosp.*, 514 F.3d 504, 508 (6th Cir. 2008) (noting that Rule 201(e) "does not require 'under all circumstances, a formal hearing'" and finding no error because the plaintiff had an opportunity to be heard on judicial notice by filing objections to the magistrate judge's report and recommendations (quoting *Am. Stores Co. v. Comm'r of Internal Revenue*, 170 F.3d 1267, 1271 (10th Cir. 1999))). At the hearing on the motions to dismiss, the district court then asked the Center what evidence it had that the well was not indeed dead. The Center did

not indicate that it had at that time any evidence to refute that fact, nor did it state that discovery was necessary.[2]

More importantly, even after the district court took judicial notice in its written decision, the Center could have moved for reconsideration or a further hearing but it did not do so. *See MacMillan Bloedel Ltd. v. Flintkote Co.*, 760 F.2d 580, 587 (5th Cir. 1985) (holding that party "did not properly challenge the [—13—] district court's procedure, for there is nothing in the record to indicate that it filed a motion after the district court took notice seeking an opportunity to be heard concerning the propriety of taking judicial notice"); *see also* 21B CHARLES ALAN WRIGHT & KENNETH W. GRAHAM, JR., FEDERAL PRACTICE AND PROCEDURE § 5109 (2d ed. 2005) ("[T]he party must request a retrospective hearing in order to preserve the error for appeal."). The Center fails to show even on appeal that a different result could have been obtained through discovery. The Center points to allegations and evidence that there may have been some minimal additional discharges from the well site after the well was capped on July 15, 2010, but it fails to show or even argue that there were discharges after the well was killed in September 2010. Instead, the Center concedes in its brief that the completion of the relief well in September 2010 was the only way to effectively kill the well. We therefore see no reason to believe that the Center would have been able to make different or more persuasive arguments in opposition to the judicial notice had it been given additional notice or an opportunity for discovery.

---

[2] The Center's written opposition requested an opportunity to conduct discovery only if the court took judicial notice of any facts, but when the district court asked about evidence at the hearing, the Center apparently changed tracks and argued only that the court could still order injunctive relief in the form of appropriate cleanup measures. The Center indicated that at some unspecified future time hearings could be held and "experts" could educate the court, but it did not indicate a need for, nor did it request, immediate discovery on the well's status or continued discharge of pollutants from the site.

Moreover, our conclusion is informed by the atypical circumstances of this case. As part of the MDL, the district court was receiving regular status updates about the situation in the Gulf and was kept apprised of the well's condition and the ongoing efforts to shut it down. It is clear that the Government, which was in charge of the situation, acted to force BP to stop the discharge, kill the well, and abandon the site. Under all of the above circumstances, we conclude that there was no error in the district court's taking of judicial notice of the well's status. Therefore, we must next consider whether the district court, after taking judicial notice, correctly concluded that the Center's individual claims are moot.

B. Mootness

Federal court jurisdiction under Article III of the Constitution is limited to "cases" and "controversies." U.S. CONST. art. III, § 2, cl. 1; *see City of Los Angeles v. Lyons*, 461 U.S. 95, 101 (1983). In order to have standing to assert [—14—] federal jurisdiction, a plaintiff "must have suffered, or be threatened with, an actual injury traceable to the defendant and likely to be redressed by a favorable judicial decision." *Spencer v. Kemna*, 523 U.S. 1, 7 (1998) (internal quotation marks and citation omitted). A plaintiff that has sufficiently alleged an injury or a threatened injury to invoke federal jurisdiction may nevertheless lose the ability to maintain the suit. *See Envtl. Conservation Org.*, 529 F.3d at 526 ("[D]evelopments subsequent to the filing of a citizen suit may moot the citizen's case."). "[A]ny set of circumstances that eliminates actual controversy after the commencement of a lawsuit renders that action moot." *Ctr. for Individual Freedom*, 449 F.3d at 661.

"[M]ootness can be described as 'the doctrine of standing set in a time frame: The requisite personal interest that must exist at the commencement of the litigation (standing) must continue throughout its existence (mootness).'" *Friends of the Earth, Inc. v. Laidlaw Envtl. Servs. (TOC), Inc.*, 528 U.S. 167, 189 (2000) (citation omitted); *see also Spencer*, 523 U.S. at 7 ("This case-or-controvesy requirement subsists through all stages of federal judicial proceedings.")

(internal quotation marks and citation omitted). "If a case has been rendered moot, a federal court has no constitutional authority to resolve the issues that it presents." *Envtl. Conservation Org.*, 529 F.3d at 525. Mootness applies when intervening circumstances render the court no longer capable of providing meaningful relief to the plaintiff. *See Harris v. City of Houston*, 151 F.3d 186, 189 (5th Cir. 1998); *see also Pac. Ins. Co. v. Gen. Dev. Corp.*, 28 F.3d 1093, 1096 (11th Cir. 1994).

As noted above, the district court held that the Center's case became moot after BP successfully killed the Macondo well because that event meant that any injunctive order to cease the discharge would be useless. The Center argues that the court's reasoning was flawed because under the stringent test for mootness there must be absolutely no possibility for recurrence of the alleged violations. [—15—] It points out that it alleged that the defendants were reasonably likely to continue to violate the environmental statutes. In cases dealing with alleged polluters it is often appropriate to place a "heavy" burden on defendants to prove that "it is *absolutely clear* that the allegedly wrongful behavior could not reasonably be expected to recur." *Gwaltney of Smithfield, Ltd. v. Chesapeake Bay Found., Inc.*, 484 U.S. 49, 66 (1987) (internal quotation marks and citations omitted). This standard "protects plaintiffs from defendants who seek to evade sanction by predictable protestations of repentance and reform" after a lawsuit is filed but who then continue their unlawful conduct upon dismissal of the suit. *Id.* at 67 (internal quotation marks and citation omitted).

We have explained, however, that this standard applies when a defendant's *voluntary* conduct is claimed to have mooted the plaintiff's suit. *Envtl. Conservation Org.*, 529 F.3d at 527. For example, we explained that this standard would be necessary if an alleged polluter asserted that CWA claims became moot when it "*voluntarily* hired the requisite number of compliance and monitoring staff or *voluntarily* set aside funds for supplemental environmental projects" because otherwise "there would no impediment to the [polluter's] laying off the new hires or reallocating the funds" after the suit is dismissed. *Id.* In other words, when a defendant has taken voluntary measures to stop a statutory violation because it is facing litigation but could otherwise revert to the offending conduct once litigation has ended, the defendant must bear the heavy burden of showing the impossibility of that result in order to prove mootness.

In this case, however, the defendants did not act voluntarily in a feigned effort to comply with the environmental statutes and stave off litigation. The killing of the Macondo well occurred at the insistence of the federal government acting pursuant to the extraordinary powers granted to the President to oversee and direct the emergency response to the oil spill. By all accounts in the record before us, the well site is now effectively dead. This is not the typical case where [—16—] defendants may claim repentance and reform through voluntary action only to revert to their old ways upon dismissal of the suit. We therefore must analyze mootness by asking whether the citizen-suit plaintiff has proven "that there is a realistic prospect that the violations alleged in its complaint will continue notwithstanding" government-mandated corrective action. *Id.* at 528. If not, the case is moot. As we have previously explained, this "realistic prospect" standard is consistent with "Congress's intent that citizen suits 'supplement rather than . . . supplant government action.'" *Id.* (citation omitted). We therefore turn now to the Center's individual claims for relief.

1. *Injunctive relief to stop violating CWA, CERCLA, and EPCRA*

The Center first requested declaratory and injunctive relief declaring that the defendants violated CWA, CERCLA, and EPCRA, and enjoining them from operating the offshore facility in a manner that would result in further violations. As the district court found, however, the record shows that the Macondo well has been effectively killed and cemented shut, and there is no offshore facility at the site being operated by the defendants. Therefore, because there is no realistic prospect that further discharges will occur, there can be no meaningful relief granted by an injunctive order enjoining the defendants from operating the site in violation of CWA, CERCLA, and EPCRA. The district court correctly held that this claim is moot. *See Harris*, 151 F.3d at 189 ("[A] request for injunctive relief generally becomes moot upon the happening of the event sought to be enjoined."); *see also Gwaltney*, 484 U.S. at 66 (the mootness doctrine "prevent[s] the maintenance of suit when there is no reasonable expectation that the wrong will be repeated") (citations and quotation marks omitted); *cf. S.F. BayKeeper, Inc. v. Tosco Corp.*, 309 F.3d 1153, 1160 (9th Cir. 2002) (suggesting [—17—] that complete dismantling of a polluting facility could result in mootness of civil penalty claims).[3]

---

[3] The Center suggests that the case is not moot because BP retains its National Pollutant Discharge Elimination System ("NPDES") permit and could return to the well site. In support, the Center cites *San Francisco BayKeeper* and *Puerto Rico Campers' Association v. Puerto Rico Aqueduct and Sewer Authority*, 219 F. Supp. 2d 201 (D.P.R. 2002). In both of those cases, however, the alleged polluting facility was still in operation; therefore, the possibility for future violations to recur was entirely reasonable even though the unlawful discharges had ceased from the specific source. *See S.F. BayKeeper*, 309 F.3d at 1160 (holding that even though defendant had sold the facility and was no longer operating it, claims were not moot because facility was still operating and civil penalties imposed on defendant could also have deterrent effect on new or future owners); *Puerto Rico Campers' Ass'n*, 219 F. Supp. 2d at 220 (holding that claim was not moot even though source of effluent had been sealed because defendant was still operating the facility, retained its NPDES permit, and was actually diverting effluent from that facility to another facility). In this case, it is undisputed that there is no facility operating at the Macondo well site and that the relief well, which was completed under the supervision and approval of the federal government, was the only way to kill the well. *See also Friends of the Earth*, 528 U.S. at 193 (recognizing that defendant's closure of its facility could moot the case but noting that disputed issues of fact remained). We are not persuaded that the speculative possibility that BP could some day return to this site, after the tremendous time, energy, and manpower expended to close it, saves

The Center argues that its claims for civil penalties keep the case alive and preclude a finding of mootness. The Center's individual complaints requested civil penalties of up to $4,300 per barrel or $37,500 per day of violation pursuant to CWA, and up to $37,500 per day of violation for each hazardous substance not reported under CERCLA and EPCRA. It is true that the potential deterrent effect of civil penalties may in some cases prevent mootness even where injunctive relief has become moot. *See Friends of the Earth*, 528 U.S. at 185–86; *Envtl. Conservation Org.*, 529 F.3d at 530; *see also Powell v. McCormack*, 395 U.S. 486, 496 n.8 (1969) ("Where several forms of relief are requested and one of these requests subsequently becomes moot, the Court has still considered the remaining requests."). The Center's civil penalty claims do not save its complaint, however, because the Center abandoned those claims when it sought a final judgment from the district court for purposes of appeal. **[—18—]**

As noted above, the district court's Pretrial Order No. 11 placed the Center's complaints into Pleading Bundle D1. The district court's order dismissing the D1 Master Complaint did not address civil penalties, however. The district court's opinion noted that the D1 pleading bundle was limited to injunctive claims. In an action involving multiple claims, a judgment that fails to resolve all of a party's claims is not a final appealable order. *See* FED. R. CIV. P. 54(b) ("[A]ny order or other decision, however designated, that adjudicates fewer than all the claims or the rights and liabilities of fewer than all the parties does not end the action as to any of the claims or parties."); *Thompson v. Betts*, 754 F.2d 1243, 1245 & n.1 (5th Cir. 1985). When the Center sought a final judgment for purposes of appeal, it even stated the position of the Plaintiffs' Steering Committee that a final order had not been entered. Yet, the Center took no action to ensure that its civil penalty claims remained live. For example, it could have asked for a certification of final judgment for purposes of an interlocutory appeal. *See* 28

the Center's current claims from a finding of mootness.

U.S.C. § 1292(b); FED. R. CIV. P. 54(b). Instead, it sought an immediate final judgment ordering that its individual complaints be dismissed in their entirety along with the D1 Master Complaint.

The Center acted at its own peril and may not now complain when the district court did what it asked the court to do. *See United States v. Baytank (Houston), Inc.*, 934 F.2d 599, 606 (5th Cir. 1991) ("A party generally may not invite error and then complain thereof."). Indeed, the Center apparently acted strategically in order to pursue its appeal to this court. As the Seventh Circuit has explained, however, "if plaintiff loses on A and abandons B in order to make the judgment final and thus obtain immediate review, the court will consider A, but B is lost forever." *Fairley v. Andrews*, 578 F.3d 518, 522 (7th Cir. 2009). We conclude, therefore, that the Center abandoned its civil penalty claims in order to obtain a final appealable judgment, and those claims may not now prevent a finding that the adjudicated claims in the complaint are moot. **[—19—]**

2. *Authorization to sample discharge*

The Center next requested as relief an order authorizing it to sample or arrange for sampling of any discharge of pollutants from the well for a period of ten years after the defendants come into compliance with CWA, CERCLA, and EPCRA. Because the well site is now dead there is no reasonable prospect for continued discharges, and thus nothing to sample. This claim for relief is therefore moot for the same reasons that the request for injunctive relief discussed above is moot.

3. *Copies of reports*

Next, the Center sought an order requiring the defendants to provide, for a period of five years, copies of all reports that the defendants submit to regulatory authorities. This requested relief "cannot conceivably remedy any past wrong but is aimed at deterring" future statutory violations. *Steel Co. v. Citizens for a Better Env't*, 523 U.S. 83, 108 (1998). In *Steel Company*, the Supreme Court considered a similar request for relief under

EPCRA and found it insufficient to confer Article III standing. *See id.* The Court reasoned that in order for such requested relief to provide the basis for Article III standing, there must be the prospect for continuing violations. *See id.* ("If respondent had alleged a continuing violation or the imminence of a future violation, the injunctive relief requested would remedy that alleged harm."). Here, the Center did allege in its individual complaints that the defendants were likely to continue violating EPCRA by failing to report future discharges from the well site. But as already noted, the district court correctly noticed that the well has been killed and there is no competent record evidence of continued discharges from the site. Therefore, on the facts of this case, the issue of standing is not implicated, but because there is no longer a basis for the Center to seek copies of the defendants' future reports, the requested relief has become moot. [—20—]

4. *Reporting under CERCLA and EPCRA for substances already released*

The Center further sought injunctive relief ordering the defendants to provide a complete reporting in accordance with CERCLA and EPCRA "for all hazardous substances already released." The Center alleged first that the defendants' failure to report the substances released violated Section 103 of CERCLA, 42 U.S.C. § 9603(a). That provision states, in relevant part, that the owner of an offshore facility "shall, as soon as he has knowledge of any release . . . of a hazardous substance from such . . . facility in quantities equal to or greater than those determined pursuant to section 9602 of this title, immediately notify the National Response Center . . . of such release." *See also* 40 C.F.R. § 302.6. The purpose of CERCLA's reporting requirement is to ensure "the Government's ability to move quickly to check the spread of a hazardous release." *United States v. Laughlin*, 10 F.3d 961, 966 (2d Cir. 1993) (internal quotation marks and citation omitted). It is undisputed that BP notified the National Response Center of the explosion on *Deepwater Horizon* and the oil spill soon after they occurred, which

resulted in an immediate governmental response. The Center's allegations and request for relief with respect to § 9603(a) are therefore moot.[4] *See Harris*, 151 F.3d at 189.

The Center's complaint further alleged that the defendants did not report the types and quantities of pollutants released in the spill, which the Center contends was required by EPCRA, 42 U.S.C. § 11004. The district court held that the Center lacked standing to bring its EPCRA claim because it was [—21—] "unclear how the data collected under EPCRA can remedy the injury alleged by Plaintiffs." We conclude that the district court's conclusion was incorrect.

Pursuant to EPCRA, the owner or operator of a facility is required to provide notice of a release of certain extremely hazardous substances or substances covered under CERCLA to the "emergency coordinator for the local emergency planning committees . . . for any area likely to be affected by the release and to the State emergency planning commission of any State likely to be affected by the release." 42 U.S.C. § 11004(a), (b)(1). The purpose of the EPCRA framework is "to inform the public about the presence of hazardous and toxic chemicals, and to provide for emergency response in the event of [a] health-threatening release." *Steel Co.*, 523 U.S. at 86; *see also* 42 U.S.C. § 11023(h). Like CERCLA, EPCRA thus ensures that appropriate government authorities are informed about the release of hazardous substances, but EPCRA also ensures that the public is given access to important health-related information.

---

[4] The defendants make an alternative argument that the Center's CERCLA claim fails on the merits because of the so-called "petroleum exclusion," which excludes "petroleum, including crude oil or any fraction thereof" from the definition of hazardous substances to be reported under CERCLA. *See* 42 U.S.C. §§ 9601(14), 9603(a); *Wilshire Westwood Assocs. v. Atl. Richfield Corp.*, 881 F.2d 801, 805 (9th Cir. 1989). We do not decide the question in light of our conclusion about mootness, and the fact that the district court made no findings with respect to the petroleum exclusion.

The defendants argue that EPCRA requires no particular form of notice that a release has occurred, and they assert that the information the Center seeks about the oil spill is readily available on various government web sites. They contend, therefore, that the Center's claim is moot because it has been overtaken by the presence of information, including health and safety information, available on the Internet. The defendants' argument essentially challenges the redressability of the Center's claimed injury, but we are not persuaded.

Under EPCRA, the initial notice to state and local emergency planners may be oral and given by "telephone, radio, or in person." 42 U.S.C. § 11004(b)(1). But the owner or operator must also provide *written* emergency followup notice "[a]s soon as practicable after a release." § 11004(c); *see* 40 C.F.R. § 355.41. Both the initial notice and the written followup emergency notice are required to include, *inter alia*, the name and estimated quantity of any [—22—] substance involved in the release, the medium or media into which the release occurred, any known or anticipated acute or chronic health risks associated with the release, and precautions to take as a result of the release. § 11004(b), (c); *see also* 40 C.F.R. §§ 355.11, 355.40. The written notices must be maintained by the state emergency response commission and must be made available to members of the general public. *See* §§ 11001(a), 11044(a). The statute specifically authorizes "any person" to commence an action against an owner or operator for failing to submit the written emergency followup notice. § 11046(a)(1)(A)(i).

The Center provided affidavits from its members averring that they had been exposed to substances emanating from the disaster either through direct physical contact in the Gulf and on the shore or through contact with fish and other wildlife. Those members averred that they were concerned about breathing air or ingesting water exposed to the substances and wanted to know what types of substances were involved in the *Deepwater Horizon* release so that they could assess the possible health effects of the exposure. At least one member specifically averred that he had not seen any reports from BP documenting the substances that were released in the spill despite his search for such reports. This is the kind of concrete informational injury that the statute was designed to redress. *See FEC v. Akins*, 524 U.S. 11, 21 (1998) ("[A] plaintiff suffers an 'injury in fact' when the plaintiff fails to obtain information which must be publicly disclosed pursuant to a statute."); *see also Sierra Club, Inc. v. Tyson Foods, Inc.*, 299 F. Supp. 2d 693, 703–06 (W.D. Ky. 2003) (holding that denial of right to be informed of releases from defendant's facility afforded plaintiff standing to assert EPCRA claim for failure to report release of chemicals).

BP suggests in its brief that the Center's informational injury claim is moot because there is no continuing discharge from the well, and it cites the Supreme Court's decision in *Steel Company*. In that case, the Court did hold [—23—] that the plaintiff could not maintain its EPCRA suit based solely on past violations of the statute. *See Steel Co.*, 523 U.S. at 109. But in that case, the defendant had complied with EPCRA's reporting requirements before the plaintiff filed suit, and the issue was whether the plaintiff could sue for a violation based on the untimely reporting. *See id.* at 88. The Court held that the plaintiff lacked standing because the requested relief would not redress its claimed injury by remedying past wrongs. *See id.* at 105–09. Here, however, BP has never claimed that it has at any time complied with EPCRA's reporting requirement for a written notice. The Center's suit specifically sought relief based on a release of substances that had already occurred but remained unreported under EPCRA, namely the spill from the ruptured well. The defendants' failure to submit the required written emergency notice is thus a continuing violation of EPCRA's provisions. An order from the district court that the defendants comply with EPCRA's reporting requirement for that release could therefore redress the Center's claimed informational injury.

The defendants' insistence that the claim is moot because information about the spill is already publicly available is unavailing, at least on the current record. First, the claim that information about the disaster may be found by hunting on the Internet ignores the fact that EPCRA places an affirmative statutory duty on the owner or operator of the facility to report the information. Second, it ignores the EPCRA requirement that reports provided by owners or operators be maintained by state emergency planning authorities and be made available to the public at a designated location. *See* 42 U.S.C. §§ 11001(a), 11044(a). The obvious advantage of this requirement is to have vital health information available in one easily accessible place. Finally, although the defendants claim that the information is otherwise readily available, their citation to several government web sites is unconvincing. Our review of those web sites reveals a voluminous amount of information about the spill and the [—24—] Government's response, but the specific information required by EPCRA is not immediately apparent.[5] To be sure, the district court held that "data regarding the spill and its cleanup are easily accessible," but it cited no sources of information and made no findings as to where the information specifically required by EPCRA may be found. If the information required by EPCRA's reporting provisions may indeed be easily located from alternate sources, it may be that a further order from the district court would provide no meaningful relief to the Center and its members. Such a conclusion, although not affecting the Center's standing, might render the claim moot. *See Harris*, 151 F.3d at 189. But we are simply unable to decide that question on this record, and the case therefore must be remanded to the district court for further proceedings.

5. *Remediation*

Finally, the Center also sought injunctive relief ordering the defendants to remove the pollutants from the water and affected coastal areas, and to pay the costs of any environmental restoration or remediation that the court deemed necessary and proper. The district court held that because cleanup efforts by the defendants and by agencies from the federal government's Unified Area Command were already underway in the Gulf of Mexico there was no further relief that it could order. The court further reasoned that it could not second-guess the Government's remediation decisions. We agree with the district court.

The question when assessing whether a case is moot is whether *any* effective relief can be granted. *See Vieux Carre Prop. Owners, Residents & Assocs., Inc. v. Brown*, 948 F.2d 1436, 1446 (5th Cir. 1991). The Center argues here that the district court erroneously dismissed its claim for an injunction addressing remediation because a full remedial plan for the Gulf was not yet in [—25—] place. It asserts that the district court should not have dismissed the complaint on the basis of the Government's cleanup efforts before the Center could develop its own proposed remediation plan. But the Center offers nothing more than speculative and conclusory assertions about remediation efforts and the existence of "vast amounts of oil" still in the Gulf rather than a coherent assertion of what effective relief could be ordered by the district court. The Center does not dispute that cleanup efforts are and have been ongoing in the Gulf, and it identifies no deficiency in those efforts. Instead, the Center would have the district court oversee remediation without identifying why or how it should do so.[6] As noted above, the Executive Branch is charged with the responsibility to oversee the cleanup. *See* 33 U.S.C. §1321(c)(1)(A), (2)(A). Because those efforts

---

[5] Some of the web pages cited in the defendants' briefs lead to links to documents comprising thousands of pages of information. We do not think that the intent of EPCRA is met by requiring the public to search for a needle in a cyberspace haystack.

[6] The Center asserts that the D1 plaintiffs raised concerns about the nature of the cleanup efforts in the district court, but it cites without further discussion to the master complaint and to its opposition to the motions to dismiss. The problem with this argument is two-fold. First, an appellant may not incorporate by reference arguments made in the district court. *See Turner v. Quarterman*, 481 F.3d 292, 295 n.1 (5th Cir. 2007). Second, the arguments to which the Center refers concerned only whether the government cleanup efforts would resolve the D1 plaintiffs' ESA and state law trespass claims, but those claims are not before us.

have been ongoing, and absent a clear reason from the Center to find them deficient, we see no error in the district court's conclusion that it could grant no further relief to the plaintiff beyond what is already being done. *See, e.g., 87th St. Owners Corp. v. Carnegie Hill-87th St. Corp.*, 251 F. Supp. 2d 1215, 1219 (S.D.N.Y. 2002) (declining to order injunctive remedial relief for oil spill because "plaintiff has been unable to describe a single action that defendant could be ordered to take to reduce or eliminate any risk its past actions may have caused, that is not already being undertaken by [the state environmental agency]"). The Center asserts that it sought injunctive relief beyond that which any government actor has already undertaken, but it cites only to its general prayers for relief in the complaint, which we have already [—26—] discussed above. We conclude that the district court properly dismissed this claim as moot.

C. Case management

The Center also challenges the district court's case management of the MDL, specifically the district court's use of pleading bundles and the separation of the Center's claims for injunctive relief and civil penalties. The Center argues that the district court's failure to place its civil penalty claims into a pleading bundle (1) was contrary to the citizen-suit provisions of CWA, CERCLA, and EPCRA, which permit federal courts to impose both injunctive relief and civil penalties, and (2) resulted in a *de facto* dismissal of those claims.

A district court's decisions relating to case management are reviewed for an abuse of discretion. *See Pierce v. Underwood*, 487 U.S. 552, 558 n.1 (1988); *In re Air Crash Disaster at Fla. Everglades on Dec. 29, 1972*, 549 F.2d 1006, 1013 (5th Cir. 1977). "The trial court's managerial power is especially strong and flexible in matters of consolidation." *In re Air Crash Disaster*, 549 F.2d at 1013; *see also* MANUAL FOR COMPLEX LITIGATION (FOURTH) §10.1 (2004) ("Although not without limits, the court's express and inherent powers enable the judge to exercise extensive supervision and control of litigation."). The Federal Rules of Civil Procedure specifically contemplate

that in complex matters the district court may adopt "special procedures for managing potentially difficult or protracted actions that may involve complex issues, multiple parties, difficult legal questions, or unusual proof problems." FED. R. CIV. P. 16(c)(2)(L). Moreover, the district court is empowered to order separate trials of any "claim, counterclaim, crossclaim, third-party claim, or particular issue." FED. R. CIV. P. 16(c)(2)(M); *see also* FED. R. CIV. P. 42(b).

To say the least, the instant case presents an exceedingly complex matter, consisting of hundreds of individual cases and tens of thousands of claimants. In the face of this daunting litigation, and given the "broad grant of authority" [—27—] to the district court, we perceive no error in those aspects of the court's management of the MDL that are involved in this case. *In re Air Crash Disaster*, 549 F.2d at 1013. The decision to create pleading bundles or to separate claims for relief was well within the district court's discretion. This managerial framework did not cause a *de facto* dismissal of the Center's civil penalty claims. Rather, as noted above, those claims were dismissed at the Center's own insistence by demanding a final judgment for purposes of appeal. We therefore find no merit in the Center's challenge to the district court's case management orders.

V. CONCLUSION

For the reasons stated above, we conclude, with one exception, that the district court did not err by dismissing the Center's claims as moot. We further conclude that, on the present state of the record, the Center has standing to assert its claim for relief based on the defendants' alleged failure to comply with the reporting requirements of EPCRA, and that the EPCRA claim is not moot. We therefore AFFIRM IN PART and REVERSE IN PART the district court's judgment and REMAND the case for further proceedings. Each party shall bear its own costs.

United States Court of Appeals
for the Fifth Circuit

No. 12-20150

BARKER

vs.

HERCULES OFFSHORE, INC.

Appeals from the United States District Court for the Southern District of Texas

Decided: February 1, 2013
Revised: March 20, 2013

Citation: 713 F.3d 208, 1 Adm. R. 206 (5th Cir. 2013).

Before **HIGGINBOTHAM, CLEMENT,** and **HAYNES,** Circuit Judges.

[—1—] **CLEMENT,** Circuit Judge:[1]

After watching his friend and co-worker die as a result of an accident on a jack-up rig attached to the Outer Continental Shelf ("OCS"), Francis Barker filed suit in Texas state court seeking relief under general maritime law, the Longshore and Harbor Workers' Compensation Act ("LHWCA"), and Texas tort law. The District Court for the Southern District of Texas denied Barker's [—2—] motion for remand and granted summary judgment to Defendants Hall-Houston and Hercules Offshore under Texas law or, in the alternative, under general maritime law. On appeal Barker challenges both the denial of the remand motion and the grant of summary judgment. For the following reasons, we AFFIRM.

FACTS AND PROCEEDINGS

Hall-Houston Exploration II is the owner of a federal mineral lease located on the Outer Continental Shelf off the coast of Texas and outside of Texas state waters. In January 2008, Hall-Houston contracted with Hercules Offshore to obtain a mobile offshore jack-up drilling unit or drilling rig, known as the Hercules 251, to drill offshore oil and gas wells including the well at issue in this case.

Hall-Houston also contracted with Frank's Casing to run a 60 inch casing over the well before drilling commenced.

On January 27, 2008, Barker, a welder employed by Frank's, was performing work onboard the Hercules 251 rig in preparation for running the casing over the well. At the time of the incident the drilling rig was in the "jacked-up" position, meaning that its hull and work deck were lifted completely out of the water. The legs of the rig extended downward through the water into the seabed which provided the means of support. In order to drive the casing over the well, Frank's employees had to enlarge a hole in the pollution pan, which sat about six feet below the rig's floor. Unbeknownst to the Frank's crew, the pollution pan was not welded to the rig structure as is customary in the standard jack-up configuration, but instead was held in place by straps that were in turn welded to the structure. Barker and his long-time friend Frank Broussard were told to, and did, cut the straps supporting the pan, causing the pan to fall 100 feet into the ocean. Frank Broussard was standing on the pollution pan when it fell, and although he was initially able to hang on to a beam for support, he lost his grip and fell into the ocean, striking another beam [—3—] on the way down. When the incident occurred Barker was standing about two feet from the pan with his back turned. Although he did not see the incident itself, he turned around in time to witness his friend fall to his death.

Barker filed suit against Hercules and Hall-Houston ("Defendants") in Texas state court. Although Barker admits he was not physically injured in the incident, he claims to have suffered severe emotional distress from witnessing his friend's death. He also alleges various physical injuries resulting from that emotional injury.

Barker alleged three causes of action in his original petition. He sought general, special, and punitive damages for negligence, gross negligence, and wanton disregard for his safety and that of Broussard under general maritime law or, in the alternative, under 33 U.S.C. § 905(b) of the Longshore and Harbor Workers' Compensation Act. He also sought

---

[1] Judge Haynes concurs in this opinion except for section I.b., which she does not join.

general, special, and punitive damages under Texas tort law to the extent that Texas tort law supplemented or supplanted general maritime law.

Defendants removed this action to the Southern District of Texas under the jurisdictional grant contained in the Outer Continental Shelf Lands Act ("OCSLA"). The district court denied Barker's motion to remand and granted summary judgment to Defendants, holding that Barker could not recover under either Texas law or maritime law. On appeal, Barker challenges the district court's decisions with respect to both his motion to remand and the Defendants' motion for summary judgment.

STANDARD OF REVIEW

This court reviews decisions denying remand *de novo*. *Maguno v. Prudential Prop.&Cas. Ins. Co.*, 276 F.3d 720, 722 (5th Cir. 2002). On a motion to remand, "[t]he removing party bears the burden of showing that federal jurisdiction exists and that removal was proper." *Id.* at 723. "Any ambiguities [—4—] are construed against removal because the removal statute should be strictly construed in favor of remand." *Id.*

"This court reviews a district court's grant of summary judgment *de novo*, applying the same standards as the district court." *Greater Houston Small Taxicab Co. Owners Ass'n v. City of Houston*, 660 F.3d 235, 238 (5th Cir. 2011). "Summary judgment is warranted if the pleadings, the discovery and disclosure materials on file, and any affidavits show there is no genuine [dispute] as to any material fact and that the movant is entitled to judgment as a matter of law." *Id.* (alteration in original).

DISCUSSION

I. Motion to Remand

The district court held, and Defendants maintain on appeal, that Barker's suit was properly removed to federal court because the Outer Continental Shelf Lands Act provides federal subject matter jurisdiction over this action pursuant to 43 U.S.C. § 1349(b)(1). Barker concedes that OCSLA provides original federal subject matter jurisdiction as required for removal under 28 U.S.C. §1441(a), but nevertheless argues that removal was improper because maritime law provides the rule of decision, and therefore this action can only be removed if no defendant is a resident of the state where the suit is brought. *See* 28 U.S.C. § 1441(b) (2011).[2] For the following reasons, we hold that removal of this action was proper.

a. Background and application of OCSLA

When it was passed in 1953, the purpose of OCSLA was to allocate to the federal government "jurisdiction, control, and power of disposition" over "the subsoil and seabed of the Outer Continental Shelf."[3] 43 U.S.C. §1332(1). [—5—] OCSLA asserts exclusive federal question jurisdiction over the OCS by specifically extending "[t]he Constitution and laws and civil and political jurisdiction of the United States . . . [to the OCS] and all installations and other devices permanently or temporarily attached to the seabed . . . for the purpose of exploring for, developing, or producing resources therefrom." *Id.* §1333(a)(1); *accord id.* §1349(b)(1); *see also Recar v. CNG Producing Co.*, 853 F.2d 367, 370 (5th Cir. 1988) (acknowledging that "OCSLA invests [a] district court with original federal question jurisdiction."). The jurisdictional grant in OCSLA is broad, covering a "wide range of activity occurring beyond the territorial waters of the states." *Texaco Exploration & Prod., Inc. v. AmClyde Engineered Prods. Co.*, 448 F.3d 760, 768 (5th Cir. 2006) *amended on reh'g*, 453 F.3d 652 (5th Cir. 2006) (quoting *Demette v. Falcon Drilling Co.*, 280 F.3d 492, 495 (5th Cir. 2002), *overruled on other grounds by Grand Isle Shipyard v. Seacor Marine, LLC*, 589 F.3d 778 (5th Cir. 2009) (en banc)).

---

[2] This is the version of the statute that was in effect when this suit was removed.

[3] The Outer Continental Shelf consists of the seabed and natural resources underlying the coastal waters greater than three geographical miles from the coastline. *See* [—5—] 43 U.S.C. §§1301(a), 1331(a).

A plaintiff does not need to expressly invoke OCSLA in order for it to apply. *Amoco Prod. Co. v. Sea Robin Pipeline Co.*, 844 F.2d 1202, 1205 (5th Cir. 1988) ("In determining federal court jurisdiction, we need not traverse the Serbonian Bog of the well pleaded complaint rule because § 23 of OCSLA expressly invests jurisdiction in the United States District Courts." (citation omitted)). To determine whether a cause of action arises under OCSLA, the Fifth Circuit applies a but-for test, asking whether: (1) the facts underlying the complaint occurred on the proper situs; (2) the plaintiff's employment furthered mineral development on the OCS; and (3) the plaintiff's injury would not have occurred but for his employment. *See Demette*, 280 F.3d at 496; *Recar*, 853 F.2d at 369. There is no dispute that these requirements are satisfied on the present record. [—6—]

OCSLA covers, among other situs, a device "permanently or temporarily attached to the seabed [of the OCS] . . . for the purpose of exploring for, developing, or producing resources therefrom." 43 U.S.C. § 1333(a)(1)). A jack-up rig attached to the Outer Continental Shelf (like the one at issue in this case) qualifies as such a device. *Demette*, 280 F.3d at 498. Accordingly, the jack-up rig is a proper OCSLA situs for the purpose of this tort action. *See Grand Isle*, 589 F.3d at 784-85.

By his own admission Barker's employment on the jack-up rig was directly related to the development of minerals or other natural resources on the OCS. *See Tenn. Gas Pipeline v. Houston Cas. Ins. Co.*, 87 F.3d 150, 154-55 (5th Cir. 1996). Furthermore, it is clear that but for his employment, Barker would not have been involved in the incident forming the basis of this suit. *See id.* at 155. Therefore, as the parties both acknowledge, this action arises under OCSLA.

b. Choice of law under OCSLA

The more difficult question in this appeal is whether federal, state, or maritime law provides the substantive rule of decision for Barker's OCSLA claim. For the reasons explained below, the panel chooses not to decide this issue because the result is the same regardless of which law is applied.

Although my colleagues do not join this section of the opinion discussing choice of law under OCSLA, I write separately to offer my thoughts on an area that has given rise to varying conclusions over the last few years. OCSLA provides a federal cause of action for incidents arising on the OCS, and also extends federal substantive law to cover these incidents. 43 U.S.C. § 1333(a)(1); *Hufnagel v. Omega Serv. Indus., Inc.*, 182 F.3d 340, 349 (5th Cir. 1999). The Act borrows from state law to fill any gaps in federal law "[t]o the extent that [state law is] applicable and not inconsistent with this subchapter or with other Federal laws and regulations." 43 U.S.C. § 1333(a)(2)(A). However, when maritime law applies of its own force (meaning that a court could otherwise have [—7—] admiralty jurisdiction over the claim), it displaces not only state law, but any federal law that might have applied to the action. *Union Tex. Petroleum Corp. v. PLT Eng'g, Inc.*, 895 F.2d 1043, 1047 (5th Cir. 1990).

As courts in this circuit have acknowledged, the application of maritime law under OCSLA was not explicitly contemplated by its framers. Rather, the application of maritime law under OCSLA is the result of both our long-standing maritime precedent, as well as gaps within the OCSLA statute itself. As one court has noted:

> The legislative history of [OCSLA] clearly shows that Congress intended to preempt the application of maritime law to activities on platforms on the OCS. Unfortunately . . . the statute itself does not say this. . . . Therefore, in this Circuit, federal law as defined by OCSLA does not apply if maritime law applies "of its own force."

Walsh v. Seagull Energy Corp., 836 F. Supp. 411, 415-16 (S.D. Tex. 1993) (citing *Rodrigue v. Aetna Cas. & Sur. Co.*, 395 U.S. 352, 363-66 (1969) and *Smith v. Penrod Drilling Corp.*, 960 F.2d 456, 459 (5th Cir. 1992), *overruled on other grounds by Grand Isle*, 589 F.3d 778)). This circuit has explicitly recognized the tension between congressional intent and the application of maritime law under OCSLA:

[W]e note that our caselaw arguably conflicts with OCSLA. As explained in *Rodrigue*, Congress intended that, after the passage of OCSLA, the oil and gas exploration industries would be governed by state law. Several of our cases recognize Congress's intention to limit the application of maritime law in oil and gas industry cases. *See Matte* [*v. Zapata Offshore Co.*], 784 F.2d [628,] 630 [(5th Cir. 1986)]; *Thurmond v. Delta Well Surveyors*, 836 F.2d 952, 954-55 (5th Cir. 1988); *Union Texas Petroleum*, 895 F.2d at 1048-49. The Supreme Court has criticized our "expansive" view of maritime employment in *Herb's Welding v. Gray*, 470 U.S. 414, 422-23 (1985). Only our en banc court, however, can consider whether our expansive view of maritime *contracts* similarly should be narrowed. [—8—]

Smith, 960 F.2d at 460 (emphasis in original). Although the application of maritime law under OCSLA may be contrary to the intention of Congress, we are bound by our precedent to apply maritime law as the substantive rule of decision where it otherwise applies "of its own force." *Union Tex. Petroleum*, 895 F.2d at 1047. It is to this question that I now turn.

In order for maritime law to apply to an OCSLA tort action such as this one, there must be both a "maritime situs and a connection to traditional maritime activity." *Hufnagel*, 182 F.3d at 351. The Supreme Court has repeatedly emphasized the importance of this two-factor test in tort actions, as distinguished from a mere "locality rule." In *Executive Jet Aviation, Inc. v. City of Cleveland, Ohio*, the Supreme Court recognized that:

[T]here has existed over the years a judicial, legislative, and scholarly recognition that, in determining whether there is admiralty jurisdiction over a particular tort or class of torts, reliance on the relationship of the wrong

to traditional maritime activity is often more sensible and more consonant with the purposes of maritime law than is a purely mechanical application of the locality test.

409 U.S. 249, 261 (1972). This holding was extended to all maritime torts by *Foremost Insurance Co. v. Richardson*, after the Supreme Court took note of "the theoretical and practical problems inherent in . . . applying the traditional locality rule." 457 U.S. 668, 673-74 (1982). In *Sisson v. Ruby*, the Court emphasized that the two-part test should be applied broadly, looking to "the general features of the type of incident involved to determine whether such an incident is likely to disrupt commercial activity." 497 U.S. 358, 363 (1990). And in *Jerome B. Grubart, Inc., v. Great Lakes Dredge & Dock Co.*, the Supreme Court officially adopted the two-prong test we use today, noting that, "[a]fter *Sisson* . . . a party seeking to invoke federal admiralty jurisdiction . . . over a tort [—9—] claim must satisfy conditions both of location and of connection with maritime activity." 513 U.S. 527, 534 (1995).

To satisfy the first prong of this test, a plaintiff must show that the tort at issue either "occurred on navigable water," or if the injury is suffered on land, that it was "caused by a vessel on navigable water." *Id.* In this circuit, jack-up drilling platforms (like the one at issue in this suit) are considered vessels under maritime law. *Demette*, 280 F.3d 498 n.18 (collecting cases); *Smith*, 960 F.2d at 460; *but see Rodrigue*, 395 U.S. at 360 (holding that fixed drilling platforms "were islands, albeit artificial ones. . . . [and that] drilling platforms are not within admiralty jurisdiction."). Even though the first prong of this test is satisfied, however, maritime law will not apply unless this suit also involves a "connection to traditional maritime activity." *Hufnagel*, 182 F.3d at 351; *accord Exec. Jet*, 409 U.S. at 261 (emphasizing the importance of this second factor).

To satisfy the second prong of the maritime requirement, a plaintiff must show that the incident caused a "potentially disruptive impact on maritime commerce," and that "the general character of the activity giving rise to the incident shows a substantial relationship to traditional maritime activity." *Great Lakes*, 513 U.S. at 534 (citations and internal quotation marks omitted). Barker makes no serious allegation that any part of the incident, or any of Defendants' failures, affected the jack-up rig's movement across water or affected the movement of any other ships. This tort arose in the ordinary course of offshore drilling, when the vessel was attached to the seabed and not scheduled for travel. In the absence of an explanation as to why a single worker injury upon a jacked-down vessel has a potentially disruptive impact on maritime commerce, I would not find the first part of the connection inquiry satisfied.

The second part of the connection test looks to whether the "tortfeasor's activity . . . on navigable waters is so closely related to activity traditionally subject to admiralty law that the reasons for applying special admiralty rules [—10—] would apply in the suit at hand." *Great Lakes*, 513 U.S. at 539-40. In applying this test, courts look generally to the activity giving rise to the instant suit. *Sisson*, 497 U.S. at 365 ("[W]e need not ascertain the precise cause of the [incident] to determine what 'activity' Sisson was engaged in; rather, the relevant activity was the storage and maintenance of a vessel at a marina on navigable waters."). The activity giving rise to this suit was installing casing in furtherance of oil and gas drilling on the Outer Continental Shelf. So classified, I would hold that the general character of this suit does not bear a substantial relationship to traditional maritime activity.[4]

---

[4] Although this circuit has varied in the level of generality used in classifying tort actions, *see, e.g., Strong v. B.P. Exploration&Prod., Inc.,* 440 F.3d 665, 669-70 (5th Cir. 2006), the Supreme Court has cautioned against looking narrowly at the specific cause of the harm in applying this test, as that would require courts to "decide . . . the merits of the causation issue to answer the legally and analytically antecedent jurisdictional question." *Sisson*, 497 U.S. at 365.

The Supreme Court has stated in no uncertain terms that "exploration and development of the Continental Shelf are not themselves maritime commerce," *Herb's Welding*, 470 U.S. at 425, and activities upon "drilling platforms [are] not even suggestive of traditional maritime affairs." *Id.* at 422. Although this circuit had previously adopted a different view, the Supreme Court in *Herb's Welding* rejected the Fifth Circuit's view that "offshore drilling is maritime commerce," finding that position to be "untenable," in light of the LHWCA and other congressional dictates. *Id.* at 421; *see id* at 421-24 (expressly rejecting the "Fifth Circuit's expansive view of maritime employment.").

Furthermore, even if traditional maritime principles would lead to a conclusion that events which occur on *jack-up* rigs are maritime in nature, we are bound to look to the intention of Congress when interpreting which law applies under OCSLA. *See Rodrigue*, 395 U.S. at 361 ("Even if the admiralty law would have applied to the deaths occurring in these cases under traditional [—11—] principles, the legislative history shows that Congress did not intend that result."). This circuit has already acknowledged the tension between congressional intent and the application of maritime law under OCSLA. However, as noted by Judge DeMoss in his dissenting opinion in *Demette*, we must be particularly mindful of Congress's 1978 amendment to OCSLA, which expanded the reach of OCSLA from "fixed structures" to "all installations and other devices permanently or *temporarily* attached to the seabed." 43 U.S.C. § 1333(a)(1) (emphasis added). This amendment "made clear that Federal law [as opposed to maritime law] is to be applicable to all activities *on all devices* in contact with the seabed for exploration, development, and production" of resources, *Demette*, 280 F.3d at 507 (DeMoss, J., dissenting) (emphasis added) (quoting H.R. Rep. No. 95-590 (1978)), including devices such as jack-up drilling rigs.

I certainly do not disagree that, under our current precedent, incidents which occur on jack-up rigs may bear a substantial relationship to traditional maritime activity when they arise out of or implicate the rig's movement across water. Thus, for example, incidents on jack-up rigs docked at marinas may be classified as maritime in nature, even when those rigs are engaged for the purpose of offshore drilling. *Coats v. Penrod Drilling Corp.*, 61 F.3d 1113, 1119 (5th Cir. 1995) (en banc) (holding that worker injuries in the course of repair and maintenance "can have a disruptive impact on maritime commerce by stalling or delaying the primary activity of the vessel."); *see also Sisson*, 497 U.S. at 362, 367 (noting that "docking a vessel at a marina on a navigable waterway is a common, if not indispensable, maritime activity," and that a fire upon such a vessel could "spread to nearby commercial vessels or make the marina inaccessible to such vessels." (citation omitted)). This circuit also recognizes that maritime law applies to incidents arising from "repair or maintenance work [—12—] [performed from a vessel] on a navigable waterway," *Great Lakes*, 513 U.S. at 540, including work upon jack-up drilling rigs.

However, our case law reflects that incidents which occur *as a result* of offshore drilling are, for the reasons stated above, generally not maritime in nature. *See Texaco Exploration & Prod., Inc. v. AmClyde Engineered Products Co., Inc.*, 448 F.3d 760, 771 *amended on reh'g on different grounds*, 453 F.3d 652 (5th Cir. 2006) ("Texaco's complaint . . . arises not from traditionally maritime activities but from the development of the resources of the Outer Continental Shelf . . . [t]o the extent that maritime activities surround the construction work underlying the complaint, any connection to maritime law is eclipsed by the construction's connection to the development of the Outer Continental Shelf"); *Hufnagel*, 182 F.3d at 352 ("Construction work on fixed offshore platforms bears no significant relation to traditional maritime activity"); *Thibodeaux v. Grasso Prod. Mgmt. Inc.*, 370 F.3d 486, 493 (5th Cir. 2004) ("Both this court and the Supreme Court have expressed the opinion that work commonly performed on oil production platforms is not maritime in nature"); *accord Sohyde Drilling & Marine Co. v. Coastal States Gas Producing Co.*, 644 F.3d 1132, 1136-38 (5th Cir. 1981); *In re Dearborn*

Marine Serv., Inc., 499 F.2d 263, 272-73 (5th Cir. 1974); *Dozier v. Rowan Drilling Co.*, 397 F. Supp. 2d 837, 850 (S.D. Tex. 2005).[5] [—13—]

Navigating this precedent I would conclude that, when determining whether maritime law applies under the second part of the connection inquiry, this court should look to whether the act which gave rise to the incident in question—in this case, replacing casing over a well—was in furtherance of the non-maritime activity of offshore oil exploration and drilling, or whether it was related to repair and maintenance of a jack-up drilling rig for the purpose of enabling the rig

---

[5] Despite Barker's allegations to the contrary, contract cases with similar fact patterns are not binding on whether this tort action is maritime in nature, since tort and contract cases apply different tests to determine whether maritime law applies. *Dozier*, 397 F. Supp. 2d at 849 (citing *Hufnagel*, 182 F.3d at 351 and *Great Lakes*, 513 U.S. at 534); *accord Grand Isle*, 589 F.3d 778. We also note that some such cases are of limited precedential value after the Supreme Court's decision in *Herb's Welding, supra*. As this court noted in *Smith v. Penrod Drilling*:

> After *Herb's Welding*, our cases that propound the maritime nature of offshore drilling-related contracts have been limited to their facts. *See Union Texas Petroleum*, 895 F.2d at 1049; *Lewis* [*v. Glendel Drilling Co.*], 898 F.2d [1083,] 1086 [(5th Cir. 1990)]. In each new case, a panel of this court must comb through a bewildering array of cases that rely upon inconsistent reasoning in the hope of finding an identical fact situation. Absent en banc reconciliation, [—13—] cases thus are decided on what seems to be a random factual basis. *See Lewis*, 898 F.2d at 1084 ("[B]ecause of an apparently contradictory line of cases in our circuit and the uncertain policy underpinning our result, the appellant would justly ask 'why?'".)

960 F.2d at 461. We need not delve into the weeds of our contract-based case law here. Although some of this confusion was clarified by our en banc court in *Grand Isle*, 589 F.3d 778, it is worth noting that the difficulty in reconciling our precedent with the Supreme Court's dictate regarding the non-maritime nature of oil and gas drilling is not limited to maritime torts.

to move across water. I recognize that courts in this circuit have not always followed this test with respect to incidents occurring on jack-up drilling rigs. However, I consider this test to be a faithful application of both Supreme Court precedent—which is structured to divorce the location of the activity from the nature of the activity itself—as well as our own case law. *See Laredo Offshore Constructors, Inc. v. Hunt Oil Co.*, 754 F.2d 1223, 1230 (5th Cir. 1985) ("[I]n the context of oil and gas exploration on the Outer Continental Shelf, admiralty jurisdiction and maritime law will only apply if the case has a sufficient maritime nexus wholly apart from the situs of the relevant structure in navigable waters."); *accord Union Tex. Petroleum*, 895 F.2d at 1048 ("[T]he principal obligation of PLT and the subcontractors was to build the gathering line and connect it to the platform and the transmission line. These activities are not traditionally maritime. Rather they are the subjects of oil and gas exploration and production."); *Dozier*, 397 F. Supp. 2d at 850. [—14—]

Barker and Broussard's work on the jack-up rig likely falls into the first category. Installing casing is part and parcel of the larger activity of exploring, developing, and producing resources from the Outer Continental Shelf, and not, as Barker maintains, of a "general character [that has a] substantial relationship to traditional maritime activity." *Great Lakes*, 513 U.S. at 534 (citations and internal quotation marks omitted). Instead, the purpose of installing the casing was to permit the jack-up rig and its crew to begin drilling for oil, an activity that could have just as easily been done, and is done, on land. *Cf. Herb's Welding*, 470 U.S. at 425 (noting that "[t]here is nothing inherently maritime about [building and maintaining pipelines]. The[se tasks] are also performed on land, and their nature is not significantly altered by the marine environment, particularly since exploration and development of the Continental Shelf are not themselves maritime commerce").

Therefore the general character of this incident appears to be nonmaritime in nature. *See Sisson*, 497 U.S. at 363.

c. Removal of an OCSLA action

In this case and others, however, the question of whether maritime law applies is not always conclusively answered at the removal stage of a lawsuit. There may be insufficient factual development at that time to determine either the cause of the incident or the general character of the activity giving rise to it. With this in mind, we note that we need not definitively determine whether maritime or Texas law applies to this lawsuit, because under either theory, removal was proper.

Although we do not decide whether maritime law applies to this suit, we acknowledge that when maritime law applies under OCSLA, maritime law will displace the application of federal law and any supplemental state law. *Tenn. Gas*, 87 F.3d at 154 ("While OCSLA was intended to apply to the full range of disputes that might occur on the OCS, it was not intended to displace general [—15—] maritime law."); *Smith*, 960 F.2d at 459 ("When an event occurs on an OCSLA situs but also is governed by maritime law, maritime law controls."). This overlap has caused some confusion among courts considering removal of OCSLA claims in which maritime law provides the substantive rule of decision, because even though federal courts have original jurisdiction over maritime claims under 28 U.S.C. § 1333, they do not have removal jurisdiction over maritime cases which are brought in state court. *Romero v. Int'l Terminal Operating Co.*, 358 U.S. 354, 377-79 (1959). Instead, such lawsuits are exempt from removal by the "saving-to-suitors" clause of the jurisdictional statute governing admiralty claims, *see id.*, and therefore may only be removed when original jurisdiction is based on another jurisdictional grant, such as diversity of citizenship. *In re Dutile*, 935 F.2d 61, 63 (5th Cir. 1991).

The question before this court is whether maritime law, when it provides the substantive rule of decision under OCSLA, abrogates OCSLA's grant of federal question jurisdiction and prohibits removal of an action filed in state court absent complete diversity. Two previous panels of this circuit have recognized the "conundrum" posed by the removal of OCSLA claims when general maritime law provides the substantive law of decision. However, both panels declined to rule on this issue, instead finding the cases removable on other grounds. *Hufnagel*, 182 F.3d at 351 (holding that the claim at issue was non-maritime in nature); *Tenn. Gas*, 87 F.3d at 156 (holding that "removal is consistent with the second sentence of §1441(b), if not the first").

In the absence of guidance from this court, district courts have fallen on both sides of this issue. Some district courts have held that when maritime law applies to an OCSLA claim, maritime law will deprive that suit of original federal question jurisdiction under §1441(a). *See, e.g., Courts v. Accu-Coat Servs., Inc.*, 948 F. Supp. 592, 595 (W.D. La. 1996) ("There is no concrete evidence that Congress intended to supersede the language of §1441 or have the [—16—] federal courts ignore the parties' citizenship when it granted broad jurisdiction under the OCSLA. . . . Based on the foregoing, the Court finds that independent federal question jurisdiction does not exist."); *Walsh*, 836 F. Supp. at 417 ("[T]he *sole* question for this Court is a choice of law question: whether Walsh's claim of 'negligence' against the operator of a drilling vessel on the OCS is necessarily an action 'arising under' the laws of the United States, or simply one arising under the general maritime law. Because the answer is the latter, Walsh has not pled a cause on which Seagull may base removal."); *Fogleman v. Tidewater Barges, Inc.*, 747 F. Supp. 348, 355-56 (E.D. La. 1990) ("The only possible . . . basis upon which the defendants would have this Court exercise jurisdiction is under OCSLA. However . . . in the instant case, OCSLA cannot be a basis for federal question removal because the case necessarily has a maritime character.").

Other district courts, however, have recognized that "the question of subject matter jurisdiction is entirely independent of choice of law analysis." *Broussard v. John E. Graham & Sons*, 798 F. Supp. 370, 373 (M.D. La. 1992). As this circuit has acknowledged, "the decision to apply maritime law . . . has

nothing to do with whether or not a federal court has jurisdiction." *Dahlen v. Gulf Crews, Inc.*, 281 F.3d 487, 492 (5th Cir. 2002). Rather, "[t]he sole question . . . is whether OCSLA invests [a court] with original federal jurisdiction . . . [and t]he fact that [a] case may be governed by the substantive principles of general maritime law does not dictate remand." *Fallon v. Oxy USA, Inc.*, No. 2049, 2000 WL 1285397, at *3 (E.D. La. Sept. 12, 2000).

We find the second line of cases to more accurately describe the case law in this circuit. Maritime law, when it applies under OCSLA, displaces federal law only as to the substantive law of decision and has no effect on the removal of an OCSLA action. *See Dahlen*, 281 F.3d at 492. As will be explained below, we base this holding on reasoning from three previous panels of this court, as well as a straightforward reading of the OCLSA statute. [—17—]

As a primary matter, this court has emphasized that "the saving to suitors" clause under general maritime law "does not guarantee [plaintiffs] a nonfederal *forum*, or limit the right of defendants to remove such actions to federal court where there exists some basis for federal jurisdiction other than admiralty." *Tenn. Gas*, 87 F.3d at 153 (emphasis in original). Instead, removal of maritime cases is permissible as long as there is an independent basis for federal jurisdiction. *See id.* Second, federal courts retain their original federal question jurisdiction under OCSLA even when maritime law eventually provides the substantive rule of decision. *Recar*, 853 F.2d at 369 (holding that a federal court "may well have both admiralty jurisdiction under the general maritime law and federal question jurisdiction by virtue of OCSLA."). This means that maritime law will not supplant OCSLA's grant of federal question jurisdiction, but that both maritime jurisdiction and OCSLA jurisdiction may exist side-by-side. Third, following this precedent, we have recognized that OCSLA provides a "basis for federal jurisdiction other than admiralty," which may permit removal even when maritime law provides the substantive rule of decision. *See, e.g, Morris v. T.E. Marine Corp.*, 344 F.3d 439, 444 (5th Cir. 2003); *Dahlen*, 281 F.3d at 492.[6] Therefore, the application of maritime law does not displace OCSLA's grant of federal question jurisdiction.

This conclusion is bolstered by the structure of OCSLA itself. Because OCSLA's jurisdictional provisions are independent from the sections outlining the applicable law, "the application of the law selected by the choice-of-law analysis [was not intended to] affect the independent basis for federal jurisdiction conferred by the OCSLA." Kenneth G. Engerrand, *Primer of [—18—] Remedies on the Outer Continental Shelf*, 4 LOYOLA MAR. L.J. 19, 25 (2005); *see also* 43 U.S.C. §§1333(a)(1)-(2). Instead, choice of law and the evaluation of subject-matter jurisdiction under OCSLA involve two distinct inquiries. *See generally Morrison v. Nat'l Austl. Bank Ltd.*, 130 S. Ct. 2869, 2877 (2010); *Hartford Fire Ins. Co. v. California*, 509 U.S. 764, 812 (1993) (Scalia, J., dissenting) (discussing the distinction between federal subject matter jurisdiction and choice of law). More importantly, however, OCSLA *explicitly provides* that district courts have federal question jurisdiction over claims occurring on the Outer Continental Shelf. 43 U.S.C. §1333(a)(1). Thus, even though maritime cases are exempted by statute from original question jurisdiction under § 1441(a), *Romero*, 358 U.S. at 377-79, OCSLA statutorily restores federal question jurisdiction over these claims even when they apply maritime law as the substantive law of decision.

The reasoning employed by the district courts in *Courts*, *Walsh*, and *Fogelman* is not necessarily to the contrary. These cases primarily rely on the cases of *Smith v. Penrod Drilling* and *Laredo Offshore Constructors v.*

Hunt Oil, where we stated that "where admiralty and OCSLA jurisdiction overlap, the case is governed by maritime law." *Laredo*, 754 F.2d at 1229; *accord Smith*, 960 F.2d at 459. However, in *Laredo*, the court rejected petitioner's claim that admiralty law should apply to the action, holding that "the case is governed solely by the OCSLA and the [state] law incorporated by reference thereunder." *Laredo*, 754 F.2d at 1229. And in *Smith*, the only question presented to the panel was whether maritime law provided the substantive rule of decision, not whether removal was proper. 960 F.2d at 459-61. Thus, neither *Laredo* nor *Smith* stands for the proposition that maritime law will displace OCLSA's explicit grant of federal question jurisdiction to bar removal where it applies.

Furthermore, to the extent that we can reconcile our precedent with the legislative history of OCSLA, we must recognize that "[g]iven the national [—19—] interests that prompted Congress to pass OCSLA and grant broad jurisdiction under 43 U.S.C. § 1349, Congress arguably intended to vest the federal courts with the power to hear any case involving the OCS, even on removal, without regard to citizenship." *Tenn. Gas.*, 87 F.3d at 156. Following this understanding, we hold today that the application of maritime law as the rule of decision does not displace OCSLA's grant of federal question jurisdiction; 28 U.S.C. § 1331 provides original federal question jurisdiction over this claim because it "aris[es] under the . . . laws of the United States;" *Recar*, 853 F.2d at 370, and therefore removal of this action was proper regardless of the citizenship of the parties. *See* 28 U.S.C. §1441(b) (2011) (holding that [a]ny civil action of which the district courts have original jurisdiction founded on a claim or right arising under the . . . laws of the United States shall be removable without regard to the citizenship or residence of the parties.").

d. The effect of the parties' citizenship on removal

Although OCSLA provides courts with original federal question jurisdiction under §1331, Barker nevertheless argues that this suit was improperly removed because

---

6 Both *Morris* and *Dahlen* are ultimately distinguishable from this case, although both cases permitted removal. In *Morris* the Defendant was not a citizen of the state in which the action was brought, so there was no question as to whether 28 U.S.C. § 1441(b) barred removal, a matter which will be discussed below. In *Dahlen* maritime law was found not to apply. However, the dictates of both cases provide strong support for our holding today.

Defendants are citizens of the state in which the action was brought. In other words, Barker urges this court to hold that when maritime law provides the substantive rule of decision under OCSLA, the "home-state defendant" rule must also be satisfied before an action may be removed. *See* 28 U.S.C. §1441(b) (2011); *see also* 28 U.S.C. §1441(b)(2). Barker's suggestion is contrary to both the letter and spirit of the removal statute, especially as it has been recently clarified by Congress.

At the time that this action was removed, the federal removal statute provided that:

> Any civil action of which the district courts have original jurisdiction founded on a claim or right arising under the Constitution, treaties or laws of the United States shall be removable without regard to the citizenship or residence of the parties. *Any other such action* [—20—] shall be removable only if none of the parties in interest properly joined and served as defendants is a citizen of the State in which such action is brought.

28 U.S.C. § 1441(b) (2011) (emphasis added). Barker contends that although original federal question jurisdiction is present in this action, this is not a case in which original jurisdiction is "founded on a claim or right arising under the . . . laws of the United States," because maritime law provides the substantive rule of decision. He argues that this claim instead falls into the category of "any other such action" in which removal is only proper if "none of the . . . defendants is a citizen of the State in which such action is brought." *Id.*

For Barker's argument to be successful, the phrase "any other such action" must apply not only to diversity actions, but also to certain actions over which district courts would have had original jurisdiction under § 1441(a), but for which jurisdiction is not "founded on a claim or right arising under the laws of the United States." The only type of jurisdiction that could arguably satisfy that standard in this case is admiralty jurisdiction. *See Dutile*,

935 F.2d at 63 (noting that the words of the arising under statute "do not extend, and could not reasonably be interpreted to extend, to cases of admiralty and maritime jurisdiction." (quoting *Romero*, 358 U.S. at 378)).[7] Federal question jurisdiction is not implicated by the second sentence of § 1441(b) because federal question jurisdiction is, simply put, founded on a claim or right "arising . . . under the laws . . . of the United States," 28 U.S.C. § 1331, and therefore expressly excluded from application of the home-state defendant rule.[8] [—21—]

However, admiralty jurisdiction is not present in this suit because Barker filed in state court, therefore invoking the saving-to-

---

[7] Note that "[t]he practical effect of these provisions is to prevent the removal of admiralty claims pursuant to § 1441(a) unless there is complete diversity of citizenship. . . . [and thus a] defendant who desires to remove a maritime action from state court to federal court must establish diversity jurisdiction." *Dutile*, 935 F.2d at 63.

[8] Previous panels of this court have contemplated, but not held, that OCSLA claims applying maritime law are not removable absent satisfaction of the home-state defendant rule. *See, e.g., Morris*, 344 F.3d at 444; *Hufnagel*, 182 F.3d at 350. Following this [—21—] precedent, some have argued that although such claims "aris[e] under the . . . laws of the United States" by virtue of OCSLA's jurisdictional grant, they are not "*founded . . . on* the laws of the United States," when maritime law provides the substantive rule of decision. However, the relevant inquiry is not necessarily whether the cause of action is founded on the laws of the United States, but whether "*original jurisdiction* [is] founded on a claim or right arising under the . . . laws of the United States." § 1441(b) (2011). *See, e.g., Tenn. Gas*, 87 F.3d at 153 (noting that "maritime claims do not 'aris[e] under the . . . laws of the United States' for purposes of federal question *and* removal jurisdiction." (quoting 28 U.S.C. § 1441(b) (2011)) (emphasis added)); *accord Dutile*, 935 F.2d at 62-63. Pursuant to our holding today, federal courts have original jurisdiction over OCSLA claims because they "aris[e] under the . . . laws of the United States," 28 U.S.C. § 1441(b) (2011); *see also Recar*, 853 F.2d at 370, and this jurisdictional grant is not superseded by maritime law, even when maritime law provides the substantive rule of decision. Accordingly, we find that the parties need not satisfy the home-state defendant rule in order to remove this OCSLA action.

suitors exception to original admiralty jurisdiction. *See* 28 U.S.C. § 1333; *Romero*, 358 U.S. at 378. Instead, for the reasons discussed above, jurisdiction in this suit is premised on—and only on—federal question jurisdiction under OCSLA. Because federal question jurisdiction is present under OCSLA, and because we hold today that maritime law does not supplant that grant of federal question jurisdiction, it follows that this action is removable "without regard to the citizenship or residence of the parties" under §1441(b) (2011).

This interpretation is especially persuasive in light of Congress's recent clarification of 28 U.S.C. § 1441(b). Instead of the amorphous dictate that *"[a]ny other such action* shall be removable only if none of the ... defendants is a citizen of the State in which such action is brought," the statute now explicitly specifies that a "civil action otherwise removable *solely on the basis of [diversity jurisdiction]* may not be removed if any of the ... defendants is a citizen of the State in which such action is brought." § 1441(b)(2) (emphasis added); *accord* H.R. REP. NO. 112-10 (explaining that the updated version is a clarification, as opposed to an amendment, of the original statute). Thus, it is clear that the citizenship requirement in § 1441(b) only applies when a case is removed on the [—22—] basis of diversity jurisdiction. Although cases invoking admiralty jurisdiction under 28 U.S.C. § 1333 may require complete diversity prior to removal, *Dutile*, 935 F.2d at 63, the same is not true for OCSLA claims in which maritime law provides the substantive rule of decision, because these claims are removable under federal original question jurisdiction for the reasons discussed above.

This holding is also consistent with the purpose of § 1441(b). There is no reason why, in the absence of a requirement of diversity jurisdiction, removal should be limited based on the citizenship of a defendant. OCSLA provides that defendants anywhere are entitled to a federal forum for their claims, not because of a risk that they might be "home-towned" but out of a concern for a uniform application of the law governing the OCS. *See* Engerrand, *Primer of Remedies on the Outer*

Continental Shelf. Accordingly, Defendants' removal of this suit was proper, and the district court's order denying remand is AFFIRMED.

II. Summary Judgment

Because we have not decided whether Texas or maritime law applies to this dispute, we can only affirm the district court's grant of summary judgment if there is no genuine issue of material fact under either theory. For the reasons stated below, we find that there is none.

a. Texas law

As a primary matter, Barker's cause of action against Hall-Houston for negligence is barred by Chapter 95 of the Texas Civil Practices and Remedies Code, which limits the liability of property owners in personal injury actions brought by independent contractors when the claims "arise[ ] from the condition or use of an improvement to real property where the contractor or subcontractor constructs, repairs, renovates, or modifies the improvement." TEX. CIV. PRAC. & REM. CODE § 95.002. When a contractor or subcontractor files a suit against a property owner for negligence, the property owner will not be liable unless the plaintiff can satisfy both conditions of Section 95.003, which require the plaintiff [—23—] to show that the property owner (1) exercised or retained "some control over the manner in which the work is performed" and (2) had "actual knowledge of the danger or condition resulting in personal injury, death, or property damage," yet "failed to adequately warn" of that danger. *Id.* §95.003; *see also Francis v. Coastal Oil & Gas Corp.*, 130 S.W.3d 76, 84 (Tex. App.—Houston [1st Dist.] 2003, no pet.).

It is undisputed that Hall-Houston was the owner of the mineral lease at issue, and that the well on which Barker and Broussard were working constituted an "improvement" to this property, sufficient to trigger application of Chapter 95. *Francis*, 130 S.W.3d at 84. Barker presented no evidence that Hall-Houston either exercised control over his work, or had actual knowledge of any dangerous condition on the rig, as required by the statute. Barker did not have a direct contract with Hall-Houston at the time of the accident, and the mere presence of a representative on site to observe an independent contractor's work does not evidence control. *Koch Ref. Co. v. Chapa*, 11 S.W.3d 153, 157 (Tex. 1999). Accordingly, Barker's negligence claims against Hall-Houston are barred by the Texas Civil Practices and Remedies Code.

As to Barker's claims against both defendants, Barker cannot recover for negligent infliction of emotional distress because Texas does not recognize a cause of action under this theory. *Twyman v. Twyman*, 855 S.W.2d 619, 621 (Tex. 1993). Nor can Barker recover under a theory of bystander recovery, as Texas courts have limited this cause of action to incidents involving close family members. *Rodriguez v. Motor Express, Inc.*, 909 S.W.2d 521, 525 (Tex. App.—Corpus Christie 1995) *rev'd on other grounds*, 925 S.W.2d 638 (Tex. 1996). Therefore, Barker cannot sustain a claim under Texas law against either Defendant.

b. Maritime law [—24—]

Because Barker does not allege that he suffered any physical injury as a direct result of the incident, he may only recover under maritime law if he can show that (a) the "zone of danger" theory applies to allow recovery for purely emotional injuries in non-Jones Act cases, and (b) he satisfies the requirements of that theory.

Under maritime law, a bystander cannot recover merely for witnessing harm to another where the bystander suffered no harm or threat of harm. *Gaston v. Flowers Transp.*, 866 F.2d 816, 818-20 (5th Cir. 1989). However, this court has left open "the question whether a [bystander] may recover for purely emotional injuries under a zone of danger theory" at maritime law. *Plaisance v. Texaco, Inc.*, 966 F.2d 166, 169 (5th Cir. 1992) (en banc); *accord Consol. Rail Corp. v. Gottshall*, 512 U.S. 532, 557 (1994) (adopting this theory in Jones Act cases). Although some circuits have adopted the zone of danger test

for non-Jones Act maritime claims, *Chan v. Soc'y Expeditions, Inc.*, 39 F.3d 1398 (9th Cir. 1994); *see also Chaparro v. Carnival Corp.*, 693 F.3d 1333, 1338 (11th Cir. 2012) (per curiam) (noting that "but federal maritime law has adopted Gottshall's application of the 'zone of danger' test"), this circuit and others have "yet to recognize recovery under the zone of danger rule" for general maritime claims. *Genie-Lyn Ltd. v. Del. Marine Operators, Inc.*, No. 50, 2006 WL 42169, at *24 n.36 (W.D. La. Jan. 3, 2006) (quoting *Ainsworth v. Penrod Drilling Corp.*, 972 F.2d 546, 548 (5th Cir. 1992)).

We need not decide today whether the zone of danger theory applies to non-Jones act maritime claims, because even if it were to apply, Barker could not satisfy the requirements of that theory as a matter of law. We agree with the district court that Barker was not in "immediate risk of physical harm" as required by the theory, *Gottshall*, 512 U.S. at 548, because at the time of the incident he was standing two feet away from the opening in the rig's drill floor. Barker specifically testified that he was sanding "on solid ground [which] was [—25—] not going to fall," and by the time the pan fell, Barker was "out of the dangerous position where something could have happened . . . if the pan had been cut." In fact, Barker had his back turned to the opening at the time of the incident, and only became aware of it after he heard a noise behind him. Barker further testified that his initial "reaction was not that [he] was scared that [he] was going to fall," but that he should make sure that his co-workers were safe. Because Barker does not allege any facts which would place him in immediate risk of physical harm, the zone of danger theory is inapplicable. *See id.* at 548.

c. LHWCA

If Texas law applies to this action, Barker cannot maintain a cause of action under the LHWCA, as that statute only applies where maritime law applies. *May v. Transworld Drilling Co.*, 786 F.2d 1261, 1264 (5th Cir. 1986). If maritime law applies to this action, then the LHWCA is incorporated through OCSLA and may be actionable under the provisions of that Act. 43 U.S.C. § 1333(b). However, Barker is not entitled to recover under LHWCA for the same reason that he cannot recover under the bystander rule under general maritime law. *See Dierker v. Gypsum Transp., Ltd.* 606 F. Supp. 566, 567-69 (E.D. La. 1985) (discussing the non-recoverability of bystander injuries under LHWCA). Therefore, for the reasons stated above, Barker cannot maintain a cause of action under the LHWCA, and summary judgment for the Defendants on all counts is AFFIRMED.

CONCLUSION

This suit was properly removed to federal court under OCSLA's grant of original federal question jurisdiction, regardless of whether maritime law provides the substantive rule of decision, and regardless of the citizenship of the parties. Because Barker cannot show a genuine issue of material fact with respect to his claims under either Texas or maritime law, the district court's [—26—] orders denying remand and granting summary judgment to Defendants are AFFIRMED.

(Reporter's Note: Dissenting opinion on p. 219).

[—27—] **HIGGINBOTHAM**, Circuit Judge, dissenting:

I write separately because I find it clear that maritime law applies to Barker's action against Hercules Offshore and Hall-Houston. As such, my analysis of both the motion to remand and the motion for summary judgment differs from that proposed by the majority.

I. CHOICE OF LAW

Judge Clement's concurrence expresses doubt as to whether maritime law applies to Barker's action, concluding that even though a jack-up rig is a vessel, "the general character of the incident appears to be non-maritime in nature." Although Judge Clement does not "definitively determine" whether maritime law or Texas law applies to this lawsuit, because under either theory it contends removal was proper, I respond to the uncertainty her approach brings to settled law.

At the outset, we do agree on the basic premises surrounding the choice of law analysis, and those principles are well-established by this Circuit's precedent: Even when the OCSLA's choice of law provision applies, adjacent state law does not apply as surrogate federal law if maritime law applies of its own force.[1] And, in order for maritime law to apply of its own force, there must be both a maritime location and a connection to a traditional maritime activity.[2] Specifically, as explained by the Supreme Court in *Jerome B. Grubart, Inc. v. Great Lakes Dredge & Dock Co.*, the following test should be used to determine whether maritime law applies: [—28—]

A court applying the location test must determine whether the tort occurred on navigable water or whether injury suffered on land was caused by a vessel on navigable water. The connection test raises two issues. A court, first, must "assess the general features of the type of incident involved" to determine whether the incident has "a potentially disruptive impact on maritime commerce." Second, a court must determine whether "the general character" of the "activity giving rise to the incident" shows a "substantial relationship to traditional maritime activity."[3]

I find that test satisfied in this case.

The location test is easily satisfied here because the alleged tort occurred on navigable water. My main departure from Judge Clement's concurrence comes in its analysis of the second prong of the *Grubart* test— whether the claim has a connection with maritime activity.

Under the first prong of the connection inquiry, we ask whether the incident has "a potentially disruptive impact on maritime commerce."[4] In answering that question, we look "to potential effects, not to the 'particular facts of the incident' . . . focus[ing] not on the specific facts at hand but on whether the 'general features' of the incident were 'likely to disrupt commercial activity.'"[5] Importantly, in conducting its analysis, the *Grubart* Court looked to "the 'general features' of the *incident* at issue," not at the activity being undertaken at the time of the accident.[6] Thus, although Barker and Broussard were running casing over a well, the relevant "incident" upon which the disruption analysis should be conducted is the fall of the pollution pan from the jack-up rig (a vessel). "So characterized, there is little question that this is the kind of incident [—29—] that has a 'potentially disruptive impact on maritime commerce.'"[7] As we explained in *Coats v. Pernod Drilling Corp.*, a case involving an injury to a worker on a jack-up rig, "worker injuries . . . can have

---

[1] *Union Tex. Petroleum Corp. v. PLT Eng'g, Inc.*, 895 F.2d 1043, 1047 (5th Cir. 1990).

[2] *Jerome B. Grubart, Inc. v. Great Lakes Dredge & Dock Co.*, 513 U.S. 527, 534 (1995); *Foremost Ins. Co. v. Richardson*, 457 U.S. 668, 673-74 (1982); *Hufnagel v. Omega Serv. Indus., Inc.*, 182 F.3d 340, 351 (5th Cir. 1999).

[3] *Grubart*, 513 U.S. at 534 (quoting *Sisson v. Ruby*, 497 U.S. 358, 363–65 (1990)).

[4] *Id.* (quoting *Sisson*, 497 U.S. at 364 n.2).

[5] *Id.* at 538 (quoting *Sisson*, 497 U.S. at 363).

[6] *Id.* (quoting *Sisson*, 497 U.S. at 363).

[7] *Id.* at 539.

a disruptive impact on maritime commerce by stalling or delaying the primary activity of a vessel."[8]

I realize that *Coats* involved an injury sustained while repairing and maintaining a jack-up rig that was located in port, while this case involves an injury sustained while conducting casing operations on a jack-up rig with its legs extended into the seabed of the outer Continental Shelf. But that distinction does not undermine our rationale for finding a potentially disruptive impact in *Coats*—that "worker injuries . . . can have a disruptive impact on maritime commerce by stalling or delaying the primary activity on the vessel."[9] That reasoning rests not on the particular task the worker is completing at the time of his injury but instead on the delay in vessel operations inherent in dealing with a worker's injury or death. I find support for that reading in the Supreme Court's articulation of the "potentially disruptive impact on maritime commerce" standard in *Sisson v. Ruby*.[10] That case involved a fire on a noncommercial vessel docked at a marina on a navigable waterway. The Supreme Court found that "such a fire has a potentially disruptive impact on maritime commerce, as it can spread to nearby commercial vessels or make the marina inaccessible to such vessels."[11] After so finding, the Supreme Court clarified that the "potentially disruptive impact" inquiry does not "turn on the particular facts of the incident in this case, such as the source of the fire or the specific location of [—30—] the yacht at the marina, that may have rendered the fire . . . more or less likely to disrupt commercial activity."[12]

Moreover, it is immaterial whether the accident in this case actually caused such a delay in maritime commerce. As the Supreme Court explained in *Sisson*, the inquiry focuses on whether the incident had a *potentially* disruptive impact on maritime commerce:

We determine the potential impact of a given type of incident by examining its general character. The jurisdictional inquiry does not turn on the *actual* effect on maritime commerce of the fire . . . . Rather, a court must assess the general features of the type of incident involved to determine whether such an incident is likely to disrupt commercial activity.[13]

Thus, I would find that the incident here had a "potentially disruptive impact on maritime commerce," satisfying the first prong of *Grubart*'s connection inquiry.[14]

Turning to the second prong of the connection inquiry, we "must determine whether 'the general character' of the 'activity giving rise to the incident' shows a 'substantial relationship to traditional maritime activity.'"[15] This inquiry turns on "whether a tortfeasor's activity, commercial or uncommercial, on navigable waters is so closely related to activity traditionally subject to admiralty law that the reasons for applying special admiralty rules would apply in the suit at [—31—] hand."[16] In his complaint, Barker alleges that the Defendants failed to provide a safe workplace aboard the Hercules 251—a vessel. This Court has previously explained that "failing to provide a safe workplace aboard a vessel is a maritime tort," even when the work the plaintiff is performing is non-maritime in nature.[17] Because vessel maintenance is a traditional maritime activity, I would find the tortfeasors' activity bears a substantial relationship to a

---

[8] 61 F.3d 1113, 1119 (5th Cir. 1995) (en banc).

[9] *Id.*

[10] 497 U.S. 358 (1990).

[11] *Id.* at 362.

[12] *Id.* at 363.

---

[13] *Id.* (emphasis in original).

[14] Judge Clement's concurrence seems to rely on the fact that offshore drilling is not maritime commerce. However, it finds support for that proposition in statements dealing with offshore drilling from a fixed platform. That analysis does not rebut the argument that accidents on jack-up drilling rigs (vessels) have a potentially disruptive impact on maritime commerce even if the jack-up rig is engaged in offshore drilling at the time of the accident.

[15] *Grubart*, 513 U.S. at 534 (quoting *Sisson*, 497 U.S. at 364–65).

[16] *Id.* at 539–40.

[17] *Strong v. B.P. Exploration & Prod., Inc.*, 440 F.3d 665, 669 (5th Cir. 2006).

traditional maritime activity. That conclusion is only bolstered by the fact that this tort occurred aboard a vessel, and "[p]roviding compensation for shipboard injuries is a traditional function of the admiralty laws."[18]

Because the *Grubart* test is clearly satisfied in this case, I would find that Barker has alleged a maritime tort. It is equally clear to me that Barker's action against the vessel and the vessel-owner is cognizable under §905(b) of the LHWCA. In § 905(b), Congress preserved the longshoremen's right to recover against the vessel-owner for negligence.[19] Because the OCSLA, specifically 43 [—32—] U.S.C. § 1333(b), makes the LHWCA applicable to Barker,[20] section 905(b) by its terms preserves his action against the vessel and vessel-owner.[21]

---

[18] *Coats*, 61 F.3d at 1119 (citing *Sisson*, 497 U.S. at 368–75 (Scalia, J., concurring) (arguing that all vessel-related torts fall within the admiralty jurisdiction)); *see Grubart*, 513 U.S. at 542–43 ("Grubart makes an additional claim that *Sisson* is being given too expansive a reading. If the activity at issue here is considered maritime related, it argues, then virtually 'every activity involving a vessel on navigable waters' would be 'a traditional maritime activity sufficient to invoke maritime jurisdiction.' But this is not fatal criticism. This Court has not proposed any radical alteration of the traditional criteria for invoking admiralty jurisdiction in tort cases, but has simply followed the lead of the lower federal courts in rejecting a location rule so rigid as to extend admiralty to a case involving an airplane, not a vessel, engaged in an activity far removed from anything traditionally maritime . . . . Although we agree with petitioners that these cases do not say that every tort involving a vessel on navigable waters falls within the scope of admiralty jurisdiction no matter what, they do show that ordinarily that will be so.").

[19] *Scindia Navigation Co. v. Santos*, 451 U.S. 156, 165 (1981).

[20] 43 U.S.C. § 1333(b); *see Demette v. Falcon Drilling Co.*, 280 F.3d 492, 497–98 (5th Cir. 2002), overruled on other grounds, *Grand Isle Shipyard v. Seacor Marine, LLC*, 589 F.3d 778 (5th Cir. 2002) (en banc); *Lormand v. Int'l Mooring & Maine*, 845 F.2d 536, 541 (5th Cir. 1987).

[21] *See Lormand*, 845 F.2d at 541; *Longmine v. Sea Drilling Corp.*, 610 F.3d 1342, 1347–52 (5th Cir. 1980).

II. MOTION TO REMAND

At the time the action was removed to federal court, the federal removal statute provided in relevant part:

(a) Except as otherwise provided by Act of Congress, any civil action brought in a State court of which the district courts of the United States have original jurisdiction, may be removed by the defendant or the defendants, to the district court of the United States for the district and division embracing the place where such action is pending. For purposes of removal under this chapter, the citizenship of defendants sued under fictitious names shall be disregarded.

(b) Any civil action of which the district courts have original jurisdiction founded on a claim or right arising under the Constitution, treaties or laws of the United States shall be removable without regard to the citizenship or residence of the parties. Any other such action shall be removable only if none of the parties in interest properly joined and served as defendants is a citizen of the State in which such action is brought.[22]

Thus, for removal to be proper, § 1441(a) required that the federal district courts have original jurisdiction over the action. Then, for certain cases, § 1441(b) imposed the additional requirement that "none of the . . . defendants is a citizen of the State in which [the] action [was] brought" (the "forum-defendant requirement"). I find removal proper here because Barker's action is one "of [—33—] which the district courts of the United States have original jurisdiction" by virtue of the OCSLA's grant of original jurisdiction. Moreover, § 1441(b)'s forum-defendant requirement is inapplicable because the case was not removed on the basis of diversity jurisdiction.

---

[22] 28 U.S.C. § 1441(a), (b).

A. Section 1441(a)

The Defendants removed this action to the Southern District of Texas based on the OCSLA's grant of original jurisdiction. Specifically, 43 U.S.C. § 1349(b)(1) provides that "the district courts of the United States shall have jurisdiction of cases and controversies arising out of, or in connection with, . . . any operation conducted on the outer Continental Shelf which involves exploration, development, or production of the minerals, of the subsoil and seabed of the outer Continental Shelf."[23]

Although maritime law applies to Barker's action, and federal courts do not have removal jurisdiction over maritime cases which are brought in state court,[24] this Circuit allows removal of a claim governed by maritime law if the claim falls within the OCSLA's grant of original jurisdiction.[25] In those cases, the OCSLA provides an independent basis of jurisdiction to make otherwise non-removable maritime claims removable.

Here, it is undisputed that the federal district courts have original jurisdiction over this action based on § 1349(b)(1) because the case arises out of an operation conducted on the outer Continental Shelf which involves development of the minerals of the subsoil and seabed of the outer Continental [—34—] Shelf.[26] Although the OCSLA does not define the term "operation," this Court has explained that the term "refers to the doing of some physical act."[27] 43 U.S.C. § 1331 defines "development" to mean "those activities which take place following discovery of minerals in

paying quantities, including . . . drilling . . . for the purpose of ultimately producing the minerals discovered."[28] The Hercules 251 was in the process of drilling on the outer Continental Shelf at the time of the accident, and Barker and Broussard were "preparing the rig's drill floor substructure to run casing," such that they were undertaking an operation involving development of minerals of the subsoil and seabed of the outer Continental Shelf. We have employed a but-for test to decide whether a dispute "aris[es] out of or in connection with" an operation, thus granting federal subject matter jurisdiction.[29] Because Barker would not have been injured but for the work he was performing on the Hercules 251, his action "aris[es] out of or in connection with" an operation on the outer Continental Shelf which involves development of minerals. Thus, his action is "a civil action . . . of which the district courts of the United States have original jurisdiction" and was properly removed by the Defendants under § 1441(a).

B. Section 1441(b)

I interpret § 1441(b)'s forum-defendant requirement as only applying to cases removed on the basis of diversity jurisdiction. Because this case was [—35—] removed on the basis of the OCSLA's independent grant of federal jurisdiction, the forum-defendant requirement does not limit its removal.

As part of the Federal Courts Jurisdiction and Venue Clarification Act of 2011, Congress amended § 1441(b) to clarify that the forum-defendant requirement only applies to actions removed on the basis of diversity jurisdiction. The statute now explicitly states: "A civil action otherwise removable on the basis of jurisdiction under section 1332(a) of this title may not be removed if any of the parties in interest properly joined and served as defendant is a citizen of the State in which such action is brought."[30] The House Report accompanying the amendment explains: "Proposed paragraph 1441(b)(2) restates the

---

[23] 43 U.S.C. § 1349(b)(1).

[24] *Romero v. Int'l Terminal Operating Co.*, 358 U.S. 354, 377–79 (1959). Similarly, a § 905(b) action does not arise under a federal statute for purposes of federal question jurisdiction. *Richendollar v. Diamond M*, 819 F.2d 124 (5th Cir. 1987).

[25] *Morris v. T.E. Marine Corp.*, 344 F.3d 439, 444 (5th Cir. 2003); *Tennessee Gas Pipeline v. Hous. Cas. Ins.*, 87 F.3d 150, 153–55 (5th Cir. 1996).

[26] Indeed the district court below found that the case calls [sic] within the OCSLA's jurisdictional grant, and the parties do not dispute that finding.

[27] *Amoco Prod. Co. v. Sea Robin Pipeline Co.*, 844 F.2d 1202, 1207 (5th Cir. 1988).

---

[28] 43 U.S.C. § 1331(l).

[29] *See, e.g., Tenn. Gas Pipeline*, 87 F.3d at 155; *Recar v. GNG Producing Co.*, 853 F.2d 367, 369 (5th Cir. 1988).

[30] 28 U.S.C. § 1441(b)(2).

substance of the last sentence of current subsection 1441(b), which relates only to diversity."[31] Based on that explanation, I view the amendment as a clarification that Congress, when it enacted § 1441(b), only intended the forum-defendant requirement to apply to cases in which removal was based on diversity; Congress did not intend the limitation to apply in other cases.[32]

Moreover, this interpretation of § 1441(b) as only applying the forum defendant requirement to actions removed on the basis of diversity jurisdiction is consistent with the purpose of both the OCSLA's jurisdictional grant and the forum-defendant requirement. "Absent diversity . . . it simply does not make any [—36—] sense to make removal of a saving-clause case turn on whether one of the defendants is a citizen of the forum state. The fortuity of citizenship is totally irrelevant to the policy factors germane to the removal question under discussion."[33] As this Court has previously explained, "[g]iven the national interests that prompted Congress to pass OCSLA and grant broad jurisdiction under 43 U.S.C. § 1349, Congress arguably intended to vest the federal courts with the power to hear any case involving the OCS, even on removal, without regard to citizenship."[34]

In sum, I find removal proper here because the OCSLA provides an independent basis of federal jurisdiction to make otherwise non-removable maritime claims removable, and section 1441(b)'s forum-defendant requirement does not limit removal because the case was not removed on the basis of diversity jurisdiction.

III. MOTION FOR SUMMARY JUDGMENT

I disagree with the majority opinion's conclusion that summary judgment was proper under maritime law. To my eyes, a genuine issue of material fact exists as to whether Barker was in the zone of danger at the time of the accident, and as such I would reverse the district court's grant of summary judgment in favor of the Defendants and remand for further proceedings on the merits.

To be clear, this Circuit has not yet decided whether a plaintiff may recover under maritime law for emotional injury claims based on the "zone of danger" theory. It is true, as the majority opinion explains, that "a bystander [cannot] recover for merely witnessing harm to another where the plaintiff [—37—] suffered no harm or threat of harm."[35] However, this Circuit has explicitly "[left] open[ ] the question [of] whether a plaintiff may recover for purely emotional injuries under a zone of danger theory."[36] Based on the Supreme Court's recent decision in *Consolidated Rail Corp. v. Gottshall* and other Circuits interpretations of that decision, I would hold that the zone of danger theory applies in maritime cases. In *Gottshall*, the Supreme Court held that a plaintiff who brings a Jones Act claim for emotional injury unaccompanied by a physical injury may recover under a zone of danger theory.[37] Barker urges that after *Gottshall*, claims for

---

[31] H.R. REP. NO. 112-10, at 12 (2011).

[32] I realize Congress provided that the amendment only applies to actions commenced on or after the expiration of the 30-day period beginning on the date of enactment (December 7, 2011). Federal Courts Jurisdiction and Venue Clarification Act of 2011, Pub. L. 112-63, § 105, 125 Stat. 758 (2011). Congress also explained that "an action or prosecution commenced in State court and removed to Federal court shall be deemed to commence the date the action or prosecution was commenced, within the meaning of State law, in State court." *Id.* Because Barker filed his action in state court on January 27, 2010, the pre-amendment version of § 1441 applies. Despite the fact that the amendment to § 1441(b) does not apply retroactively, I believe that it illuminates a key aspect of congressional intent that is helpful in interpreting the applicability of § 1441(b)'s forum-defendant requirement.

[33] C. Wright, A. Miller, & E. Cooper, 14A Federal Practice & Procedure § 3674.

[34] *Tenn. Gas*, 87 F.3d at 156.

---

[35] *Plaisance v. Texaco*, 966 F.2d 166, 169 (5th Cir. 1992) (en banc) (citing *Gaston v. Flowers Transp.*, 866 F.2d 816 (5th Cir. 1989)).

[36] *Id.*

[37] *Consol. Rail Corp. v. Gottshall*, 512 U.S. 532 (1994). To be clear, although *Gottshall* involved claims under FELA, because the Jones Act incorporates FELA, decisions in FELA cases are applicable to cases brought under the Jones Act.

negligent infliction of emotional distress unaccompanied by physical injury are compensable under maritime law as long as the plaintiff was within the zone of danger. I agree. Although *Gottshall* did not explicitly hold that the zone of danger theory applies in non-Jones Act maritime cases for negligent infliction of emotional distress, at least two other Circuits have held that the *Gottshall* test, which allows plaintiffs "to recover for injuries—physical and emotional—caused by the negligent conduct of their employers that threatens them imminently with physical impact,"[38] applies in the maritime law context.[39] I would join them. [—38—]

Under the zone of danger theory, summary judgment in favor of the Defendants was not proper. Contrary to the conclusion reached by the majority opinion, the evidence before the district court on summary judgment created a genuine issue of material fact as to whether Barker was threatened imminently with physical impact. Barker testified that he was standing a mere two feet from the hole when the pan fell, and that he feared he was going to fall into the hole himself. Looking at the accident, we must ask what a reasonable trier of fact might conclude. With that cast of sight, this was a man standing two feet from certain death with no protective harness, stunned at witnessing his friend cling to a beam then fall to his death. An involuntary reach out and he, too, would have died. This is the stuff of a live trial, not a paper review. He was at least arguably within the zone of danger, and the final determination of that issue should have been left with the jury.

IV.

Today, Judge Clement brings uncertainty to the law applicable to accidents occurring on jack-up rigs. To these eyes her approach defies our precedent. Clarity of the metric in the law of the sea and its relations is especially prized as it is so much the law of insurance—define the rules and the underwriter can assess the risk and cost its distribution. I would hold that Barker has alleged a maritime tort and has created a genuine issue of material fact as to whether he was in the zone of danger at the time of the accident and reverse and remand.

---

[38] *Id.* at 566.

[39] *See Chaparro v. Carnival Corp.*, 693 F.3d 1333, 1338 (11th Cir. 2012) (per curiam) (explaining that "federal maritime law has adopted *Gottshall*'s application of the 'zone of danger' test"); *Stacy v. Rederiet Otto Danielsen*, 609 F.3d 1033, 1035 (9th Cir. 2010) (explaining in a maritime case that "[t]he federal standard for the negligent infliction of emotional distress is provided by *Consolidated Railway Corp. v. Gottshall*").

United States Court of Appeals for the Fifth Circuit

No. 12-30780

IN RE BERTUCCI CONTRACTING CO.

Appeal from the United States District Court for the Eastern District of Louisiana

Decided: March 22, 2013

Citation: 712 F.3d 245, 1 Adm. R. 225 (5th Cir. 2013).

Before **DAVIS, GRAVES,** and **HIGGINSON,** Circuit Judges.

[—1—] **GRAVES,** Circuit Judge:

This appeal arises out of a maritime accident in which a vessel owned by Bertucci Contracting Co. hit the Leo Kerner bridge in Louisiana. Appellants are residents of an affected community arguing that they suffered damages as a [—2—] result of the accident. The district court dismissed Appellants' claims, holding that recovery was barred by circuit precedent. We affirm.

I. Factual and Procedural Background

On May 31, 2011, the vessel JULIE MARIE, owned by Bertucci Contracting Co., LLC ("Bertucci"), allided with the Leo Kerner Bridge ("the bridge"). The bridge, owned by the State of Louisiana, spans the Intracoastal Waterway in Louisiana and links the communities of Lafitte and Barataria. As a result of the accident, the bridge sustained damage that prevented its use by pedestrians and vehicles and was closed for several days for repairs.

In June 2011, Bertucci filed a complaint-in-limitation under the Limitation of Liability Act, 46 U.S.C. §§ 30501 et seq., concerning the accident in the Eastern District of Louisiana. Numerous claimants filed answers in Bertucci's limitation proceeding, including Appellants. Despite the district court's order that no claims relating to the accident be filed outside the limitation proceeding, Carol Steele filed a separate class action suit on behalf of residents of Barataria, seeking to recover damages resulting from the closure of the bridge. In their class action complaint, Appellants outlined their damages resulting from the bridge closure as including loss of use of property, loss of income and revenue due to restricted access to their homes and businesses, and damages due to inconvenience. The district court consolidated the class action proceeding with Bertucci's limitation proceeding.

Bertucci filed a motion to dismiss Appellants' claims pursuant to Federal Rule of Civil Procedure 12(b)(6). On April 18, 2012, the district court granted Bertucci's motion to dismiss Appellants' claims in both the limitation proceeding and in the class action. The district court held that in maritime negligence cases, recovery for economic damages is barred unless a plaintiff sustains physical damage to a proprietary interest, relying on *State of Louisiana ex rel Guste v. M/V TESTBANK,* 752 F.2d 1019 (5th Cir. 1985) (en banc). The district [—3—] court then found that Appellants had not stated facts that could plausibly state a claim for physical damage to any property they own, as required for recovery under the *Testbank* rule. Appellants appeal the dismissal of their claims.

II. Discussion

Recovery by Appellants in this case is barred by Supreme Court and circuit precedent. Our en banc opinion in *Testbank* reviewed and reaffirmed the "prevailing" maritime rule that "denie[s] a plaintiff recovery for economic loss if that loss resulted from physical damage to property in which he had no proprietary interest." 752 F.2d at 1022; *see Robins Dry Dock v. Flint,* 275 U.S. 303, 308-09 (1927). Since *Testbank,* this court has consistently applied the rule limiting recovery in maritime cases to plaintiffs who sustain physical damage to a proprietary interest. *See, e.g., In re Taira Lynn Marine Ltd. No. 5, LLC,* 444 F.3d 371, 377 (5th Cir. 2006); *Reserve Mooring Inc. v. Am. Commercial Barge Line, LLC,* 251 F.3d 1069, 1071 (5th Cir. 2001); *IMTT-Gretna v. Robert E. Lee SS,* 993 F.2d 1193, 1194 (5th Cir. 1993). We have stated that "[i]t is unmistakable that the law of this circuit does not allow recovery of purely economic claims absent physical injury to a proprietary interest in a maritime negligence suit." *Taira Lynn*, 444 F.3d at 377.

Appellants argue that the *Testbank* rule should not bar recovery here because they are not maritime actors and have no connection to traditional maritime activity. Appellants assert that their claims may be heard in federal court pursuant to maritime jurisdiction, but the substantive law that should apply is not the *Testbank* maritime rule, but Louisiana law.

Appellants' attempts to distinguish *Testbank* and its progeny are not persuasive. Appellants put forth no principled distinction between themselves and similarly situated parties who have been consistently denied recovery under the *Testbank* rule. Parties who have been denied recovery under this rule include lessees with contractual rights to use docks and bridges near the water [—4—] who lost use of that property due to a maritime tort, *see IMTT-Gretna*, 993 F.2d at 1194; *Louisville & Nashville R.R. Co. v. M/V BAYOU LACOMBE*, 597 F.2d 469, 474 (5th Cir. 1979), and local businesses engaged in a variety of commercial activities near the water who lost business and money due to a maritime tort that damaged a bridge, *Taira Lynn*, 444 F.3d at 378-79. Yet Appellants argue that dozens of private property owners residing near a damaged bridge, who suffered no physical damage to their property, are different and can recover. Appellants essentially argue that because they are not engaged in any maritime activity, they are more remote than the parties denied recovery in cases like *Taira Lynn*, *IMTT-Gretna*, and *Testbank,* and are in fact so remote from the maritime accident and maritime activity that the *Testbank* limitation and established maritime principles should cease to apply. This distinction is antithetical to the *Testbank* rule's purpose to create "a pragmatic limitation ... upon the tort doctrine of foreseeability." *Testbank*, 752 F.2d at 1023.

Appellants' argument that recovery under state law is available even if maritime law bars recovery is foreclosed by circuit precedent and by principles of maritime law. We have clearly held that "state law does not supply an alternative remedy to [a claimant] when its claim was already denied in its proper maritime jurisdiction." *IMTT-Gretna*, 993 F.2d at 1195; *see Taira Lynn*, 444 F.3d at 380. The claims at issue arise from an alleged tort by a vessel on a navigable waterway and are thus properly within the maritime jurisdiction of the federal courts. *See, e.g, Testbank*, 752 F.2d at 1031; *Jerome B. Grubart, Inc. v. Great Lakes Dredge & Dock Co.*, 513 U.S. 527, 542-43 (1995). "Maritime law specifically denies recovery to non proprietors for economic damages. To allow state law to supply a remedy when one is denied in admiralty would serve only to circumvent the maritime law's jurisdiction." *IMTT-Gretna*, 993 F.2d at 1195; *Taira Lynn*, 444 F.3d at 380. Appellants' appeal to *Erie v. Tompkins*, 304 U.S. 64 (1938), is misplaced. As the *Testbank* court explained, "While our maritime [—5—] decisions are informed by common law developments in the state courts, there is no requirement, as in diversity cases, that state law be adopted. Indeed the federal interest in protecting maritime commerce is often best served by the establishment of uniform rules of conduct . . . ." *Testbank*, 752 F.2d at 1032; *see IMTT-Gretna*, 993 F.2d at 1195. Accepting Appellants' argument for an exception to the *Testbank* rule would subject a maritime tortfeasor on navigable waters to more extensive liability when a tort has economic effects in a state that allows for economic damages absent physical injury. This is precisely the kind of non-uniformity that maritime law seeks to prevent. *See Testbank*, 752 F.2d at 1031-32.

Appellants alternatively argue that even if *Testbank* is not distinguishable, the district court erred in dismissing their claims because some of the claimants might have suffered physical injuries. In resolving this question, we accept "all well-pleaded facts as true, viewing them in the light most favorable to the plaintiff." *In re Katrina Canal Breaches Litig.*, 495 F.3d 191, 205 (5th Cir. 2007) (internal quotation marks omitted). However, as they recognize, to survive a Rule 12(b)(6) motion to dismiss, Appellants must plead "enough facts to state a claim to relief that is plausible on its face." *Bell Atl. Corp. v.*

Twombly, 550 U.S. 544, 570 (2007). Appellants clearly have not met this standard. While Appellants assert that the bridge damage and closing interfered with the use of their property, interference with access is not physical damage. *See Reserve Mooring*, 251 F.3d at 1071-72 (holding that a barge sinking and blocking a mooring facility was not physical damage). On appeal, Appellants do not point to any facts that might plausibly state a claim for physical damages of any kind. The only specific facts referenced on appeal concern Carol Steele's increased medical expenses resulting from the restricted access to her home. The district court thus correctly dismissed the claims [—6—] because Appellants have alleged no facts, even if construed liberally, that plausibly state a claim for physical damages.

III. Conclusion

For the above-stated reasons, we AFFIRM the district court's dismissal of Appellants' claims in the limitation proceeding and in the class action.

United States Court of Appeals
for the Fifth Circuit

No. 11-60057

NEW ORLEANS DEPOT SERVICES, INC.
vs.
DIRECTOR, OFFICE OF WORKERS' COMPENSATION
PROGRAMS

Appeal from the Benefits Review Board

Decided: April 29, 2013

Citation: 718 F.3d 384, 1 Adm. R. 228 (5ᵗʰ Cir. 2013).

Before **STEWART**, Chief Judge, and **KING, JOLLY, DAVIS, JONES, SMITH, DENNIS, CLEMENT, PRADO, OWEN, ELROD, SOUTHWICK, HAYNES, GRAVES**, and **HIGGINSON**, Circuit Judges.

[—1—] DAVIS, Circuit Judge:

In this case, we review the determination of the Benefits Review Board ("BRB") that the claimant, Juan Zepeda, was entitled to compensation benefits under the Longshore and Harbor Workers' Compensation Act ("LHWCA" or "the Act"), from Petitioner New Orleans Depot Services, Inc. ("NODSI").

In particular, the BRB found that the claimant's employment activities with NODSI took place in an area or location "adjoining" navigable waters [—2—] "customarily used by an employer in loading [or] unloading . . . a vessel"[1] and therefore NODSI's facility met the situs requirement of the Act. We conclude that because the NODSI facility where Mr. Zepeda worked did not border on navigable waters, it was not a covered situs and Mr.

Zepeda is entitled to no benefits under the Act from Petitioner NODSI. We therefore vacate the award of the BRB as against NODSI and remand for further proceedings.

I. Facts

The claimant, Mr. Zepeda, filed a claim for LHWCA benefits against one of his prior employers, New Orleans Marine Contractors ("NOMC"), to recover benefits for his hearing loss due to continuous exposure to loud noises. As a defense, NOMC contended that NODSI was a subsequent maritime employer and that NODSI rather than NOMC was therefore the responsible party.[2] The issue then presented to the Administrative Law Judge ("ALJ") and BRB was whether NODSI was responsible as a subsequent employer for benefits under the LHWCA. NOMC then, in effect, prosecuted Mr. Zepeda's claim against NODSI so that NOMC would avoid its liability to him.

Following his employment with NOMC, Mr. Zepeda was employed by the Petitioner, NODSI, at its "Chef Yard" facility on the Chef Menteur Highway in New Orleans. NODSI and its employees were engaged in the repair, [—3—] maintenance, and storage of shipping containers and chassis.[3] Some of the containers had been used to transport ocean cargo. NODSI had more than one facility, but the Chef Yard facility is the only facility relevant to this appeal. The Chef Yard, with access to the Chef Menteur Highway and rail transportation, can best be described as a small industrial park. The Chef Yard is located approximately 300 yards from the Intracoastal Canal and is surrounded by a carwash, a radiator shop, an automobile repair shop, a bottling company, and a

---

[1] 33 U.S.C. § 903(a) provides:

[C]ompensation shall be payable under this chapter in respect of disability or death of an employee, but only if the disability or death results from an injury occurring upon the navigable waters of the United States (including any adjoining pier, wharf, dry dock, terminal, building way, marine railway, or other adjoining area customarily used by an employer in loading, unloading, repairing, dismantling, or building a vessel).

---

[2] "When the disability arises from an 'occupational injury' incurred while working for different employers, the last employer who exposes the claimant to the injury-causing condition may be responsible for all of the benefits." FRANK L. MARAIST ET AL., ADMIRALTY IN A NUTSHELL 291 (6th ed. 2010) (citing *Avondale Indus., Inc. v. DOWCP*, 977 F.2d 186 (5th Cir. 1992)).

[3] A chassis is what we ordinarily consider the trailer portion of the 18-wheeler unit on which shipping containers are loaded and transported by truck.

company that manufactures boxes. The bottling company's facility is located between the Intracoastal Waterway and the Chef Yard.

NODSI employees worked only within NODSI's facility as they repaired or performed maintenance on containers and chassis. They had no access to the Intracoastal Canal and all of the equipment NODSI serviced was delivered to the Chef Yard by truck. Once NODSI completed repairs to the equipment, it was picked up by truck or rail, and no containers were loaded with cargo while in NODSI's custody.

II. Procedural Background

The ALJ, after conducting a hearing in this case, found that some of the containers repaired and maintained by NODSI employees had been used for marine transportation and off-loaded at the port of New Orleans. Representatives of Evergreen, NODSI's customer, also stated that at least some of the containers would be returned to service as marine containers. The ALJ concluded that the NODSI Chef Yard employees' work repairing ocean containers was "a process which was a significant maritime activity" necessary to loading and unloading cargo. In addition, the ALJ concluded that the location of the NODSI Chef Yard located some 300 yards from the Intracoastal Canal [—4—] satisfied the situs requirement that the injury occur in an area "adjoining navigable waters." Also, the ALJ found that the repair work and maintenance Mr. Zepeda performed on these containers was closely related to loading or unloading vessels and constituted "maritime employment" which satisfied the status test under the Act.

The BRB affirmed the ALJ's order and a divided panel of this court affirmed the BRB. We then voted this case en banc, primarily to consider the BRB's determination that Mr. Zepeda was injured in an area "adjoining navigable waters" so as to satisfy the Act's situs test.

III. Standard of Review

Because the LHWCA situs inquiry requires the application of a statutory standard to case-specific facts, it is ordinarily a mixed question of law and fact. However, where, as in this case, the facts are not in dispute, "[LHWCA] coverage is an issue of statutory construction and legislative intent," and should be reviewed as a pure question of law. *See DOWCP v. Perini North River Associates*, 459 U.S. 297, 300, 305 (1983). We therefore review the BRB's determination of coverage under the LHWCA in this case *de novo*. *Equitable Equip. Co. v. DOWCP*, 191 F.3d 630, 631 (5th Cir. 1999) (citation omitted).

IV. Analysis

A.

Before turning to the merits of this appeal, we first consider a preliminary objection the Respondent raises. The Director argues that NODSI has waived the argument that Mr. Zepeda failed to establish that he met the situs requirement of the Act—*i.e.*, that his injury occurred in an area "adjoining navigable waters"—by failing to raise it before the BRB or the panel of this court that heard the appeal. Specifically, the Director argues that NODSI cannot [—5—] argue that this en banc Court should adopt a new interpretation of "adjoining" when it failed to make the argument before two previous tribunals.

Generally, we do not consider issues on appeal that were not presented and argued before the lower court. *See Lampton v. Diaz*, 639 F.3d 223, 227 n.14 (5th Cir. 2011). "The waiver rule exists to prevent an appellate court from '[analyzing] the facts of a particular [issue] without the benefit of a full record or lower court determination.'" *Id.*[4] In its opening brief to the panel of this court that initially heard the appeal, NODSI only

---

[4] (Alterations in original) (quoting 19 JAMES W. MOORE ET AL., MOORE'S FEDERAL PRACTICE § 205.05[1], at 205–57 (3d ed. 2011) (quoting *Yee v. City of Escondido*, 503 U.S. 519, 538 (1992))).

challenged the functional component[5] of the situs requirement and acknowledged that our caselaw foreclosed consideration of the geographic component.[6] However, this is not a case in which a party has wholly ignored a major issue. The issue of LHWCA situs has been contested throughout the case's history, with the proper application of "adjoining area" being squarely addressed by both the ALJ and the BRB. NODSI's recognition of the fact that it was bound by this Court's current interpretation of "adjoining" does not deprive us of the right to visit the issue.

Moreover, a well-settled discretionary exception to the waiver rule exists where a disputed issue concerns "a pure question of law." *Texas v. United States*, 730 F.2d 339, 358 n.35 (5th Cir. 1984); *see also Atl. Mut. Ins. Co. v. Truck Ins. Exch.*, 797 F.2d 1288, 1293 (5th Cir. 1986). In this case, the ALJ, after a full hearing, resolved the factual disputes presented by the parties. At the hearing, witnesses testified about the nature of the industrial park where NODSI's operations were conducted, the nature of NODSI's work, and the relationship of [—6—] the work to maritime activities. The evidence was undisputed that NODSI's Chef Yard is located about 300 yards from the Intracoastal Canal, and that a bottling plant is located on the tract of land between the Canal and NODSI's yard.

Because the legal issue of whether the location of the claimant's injury "adjoined" navigable waters was presented to the ALJ and the facts involving this issue were fully litigated before the ALJ, we are left with a pure question of law to decide. Moreover, every party was provided an adequate opportunity to brief and argue the issue before the en banc court. Therefore, notwithstanding NODSI's failure to challenge our governing precedent before the BRB or our panel, we exercise our discretion to decide this legal issue: whether, under these undisputed facts, claimant was injured in an area adjoining navigable waters so as to satisfy the LHWCA situs requirement. We now turn to the merits of the appeal.

B.

Before 1972, coverage under the LHWCA was provided only if the injury occurred on navigable waters. This "situs" requirement was strictly enforced.[7] However, by its nature, loading and unloading a vessel required a longshoreman to continuously go from ship to wharf and back again, and a longshoreman might work part of the day aboard the ship and the rest of the day on the pier.[8] Similar movement by workers from vessel to dock also occurred in vessel repair work. When Congress made extensive amendments to the Act in 1972, it expressed [—7—] concern about longshoremen walking in and out of coverage and, to meet this concern, broadened coverage by amending LHWCA § 903(a).[9]

Congress made another change in the 1972 amendments by adding a status requirement, thus limiting LHWCA coverage to traditional maritime occupations. This was accomplished by defining a covered "employee" as "any person engaged in maritime employment, including any longshoreman or other person engaged in longshoring operations, and any harbor-worker including a ship repairman, shipbuilder, and ship-breaker." 33 U.S.C. §902(3).

---

[5] The injury must occur in an area "customarily used by an employer in loading, unloading, repairing, dismantling, or building a vessel." *See* 33 U.S.C. § 903(a).

[6] The injury must occur "upon the navigable waters of the United States . . . or other adjoining area." *See* 33 U.S.C. § 903(a).

[7] *See, e.g., Victory Carriers, Inc. v. Law*, 404 U.S. 202, 209–12 (1971) (longshoreman injured on pier while operating cargo forklift not in covered situs); *Nacirema Operating Co. v. Johnson*, 396 U.S. 212, 223 (1969) (longshoremen injured on pier while attaching cargo to ship's cranes not in covered situs).

[8] *See Ne. Marine Terminal Co. v. Caputo*, 432 U.S. 249, 272–74 (1977).

[9] Section 903 was amended, in part, to provide compensation "if the disability or death results from an injury occurring upon the navigable waters of the United States (including any adjoining pier, wharf . . . *or other adjoining area customarily used by an employer in loading, unloading, repairing, dismantling, or building a vessel*)." 33 U.S.C. §903(a) (emphasis added).

The Supreme Court has made it clear that "situs" and "status" are separate, independent elements and that a claimant must establish both elements to recover benefits.[10]

C.

The LHWCA only extends coverage to "injur[ies] occurring upon the navigable waters of the United States (including any adjoining pier, wharf . . . or *other adjoining area* customarily used by an employer in loading, unloading, repairing, dismantling, or building a vessel)." 33 U.S.C. § 903(a) (emphasis added).

Most courts addressing this issue understand that an "other adjoining area" must satisfy two distinct situs components: (1) a geographic component (the area must adjoin navigable waters) and (2) a functional component (the area must be "customarily used by an employer in loading [or] unloading . . . a [—8—] vessel").[11] We took this case en banc primarily to decide whether the claimant was injured in an area "adjoining" navigable waters.

In 1980, our en banc court interpreted the geographic component of situs in *Texports Stevedore Co. v. Winchester*, 632 F.2d 504 (5th Cir. 1980) (en banc). In that case, Mr. Winchester was injured when he fell in his employer's gear room. He and others at that facility were engaged in repairing and maintaining gear used by longshoremen in loading and unloading vessels. The gear room in question was located five blocks from the gate of the nearest Houston port dock. In holding that the employee met the situs

requirement and was entitled to benefits, the court stated:

> Although "adjoin" can be defined as "contiguous to" or "to border upon," it also is defined as "to be close to" or "to be near." "Adjoining" can mean "neighboring." To instill in the term its broader meanings is in keeping with the spirit of the congressional purposes. So long as the site is close to or in the vicinity of navigable waters, or in a neighboring area, an employee's injury can come within the LHWA. To require absolute contiguity would be to reenact the hard lines that caused longshoremen to move continually in and out of coverage.

Id. at 514 (footnotes omitted).

The *Winchester* court stressed the desirability of avoiding any hard line for defining what is "adjoining." Rather, "[t]he situs requirement compels a factual determination that cannot be hedged by the labels placed on an area." *Id.* at 513. "The best way to effectuate the congressional purposes is to determine the situs question by looking at all the circumstances." *Id.* Other than these vague instructions, the court provided little guidance to other courts or future litigants on how to determine from "the circumstances" whether a claimant satisfies the [—9—] situs test. This is apparent from the court's statement: "[O]uter limits of the maritime area will not be extended to extremes. We would not extend coverage in this case to downtown Houston. The site must have some nexus with the waterfront."[12] *Id.* at 514. The court then concluded that the injured employee was within a situs protected by the

---

[10] *See Herb's Welding, Inc. v. Gray*, 470 U.S. 414, 415–16 (1985); *P.C. Pfeiffer Co. v. Ford*, 444 U.S. 69, 73–74 (1979); *see also King v. Universal Elec. Constr.*, 799 F.2d 1073, 1073–74 (5th Cir. 1986); *Valladolid v. Pac. Operations Offshore, LLP*, 604 F.3d 1126, 1140 (9th Cir. 2010); *Jonathan Corp. v. Brickhouse*, 142 F.3d 217, 220 (4th Cir. 1998).

[11] *See, e.g., Coastal Prod. Servs. Inc. v. Hudson*, 555 F.3d 426, 432 (5th Cir. 2009); *Sidwell v. Express Container Servs., Inc.*, 71 F.3d 1134, 1139 (4th Cir. 1995); *Hurston v. DOWCP*, 989 F.2d 1547, 1549 (9th Cir. 1993).

---

[12] At oral argument, we learned that the port of Houston is approximately 5 miles from downtown Houston. Counsel for the Director was unable to tell us how the claimant or the employer would determine—short of trial—whether, in *Winchester*, if the injury had occurred 1 mile or 2 miles from the port of Houston, the claimant would have been injured in an area adjoining navigable waters.

LHWCA. *Id.* at 516. We have followed the *Winchester* analysis in a number of cases.[13]

Our sister circuits have taken varying positions on the interpretation of "other adjoining areas."

In *Brady-Hamilton Stevedore Co. v. Herron*, 568 F.2d 137, 139 (9th Cir. 1978), an employee was injured while unloading steel plates from a truck parked at the employer's gear locker, located some 2,600 feet north of the Columbia River and outside the entrance gate of the port of Longview. The Ninth Circuit concluded:

> [T]he phrase "adjoining area" should be read to describe a functional relationship that does not in all cases depend upon physical contiguity. Consideration should be given to the following factors, among others, in determining whether or not a site is an "adjoining area" under section 903(a): the particular suitability of the site for the maritime uses referred to in the statute; whether adjoining properties are devoted primarily to uses in maritime commerce; the proximity of the site to the waterway; and whether the site is as close to the waterway as is feasible given all of the circumstances in the case. [—10—]

Id. at 141.[14]

In *Sea-Land Service, Inc. v. DOWCP*, 540 F.2d 629 (3d Cir. 1976), an employee was using a truck to move cargo that had been unloaded from a vessel to a building, so it could be further transported to a more permanent location. The employee was injured on a public street in an area outside the terminal that was not under the employer's control. *Id.* at 632. The court held that the restriction on coverage to an "other adjoining area" did not preclude coverage to this employee. The court found situs had been established and stated, "[t]he key is the functional relationship of the employee's activity to maritime transportation, as distinguished from such land-based activities as trucking, railroading or warehousing."[15] *Id.* at 638.

In contrast, the Fourth Circuit has taken a much different approach—an approach that adheres more faithfully to the plain language of the statute. In *Sidwell v. Express Container Services, Inc.*, 71 F.3d 1134 (4th Cir. 1995), the facts were almost identical to the facts in the instant case. The plaintiff was a shipping container mechanic who sought to recover benefits under the Act after he was injured while repairing a container. *Id.* at 1135. His injury occurred at his employer's facility located approximately .8 miles from the closest ship terminal in an area with diverse, non-maritime commercial and residential facilities. *Id.* [—11—]

In deciding whether the employer's container repair facility was an "adjoining area," the Fourth Circuit recognized that the Supreme Court had not defined the term, but that the Third, Fifth, and Ninth Circuits had each adopted expansive, yet differing approaches. *Id.* at 1136–37. After reviewing these cases, the *Sidwell* court stated, "Because none of these proffered tests even purports to

---

[13] *See Coastal Prod. Servs. Inc.*, 555 F.3d at 432–37; *Reynolds v. Ingalls Shipbuilding Div., Litton Sys., Inc.*, 788 F.2d 264, 272 (5th Cir. 1986), *overruled on other grounds by Stewart v. Dutra Const. Co.*, 543 U.S. 481, 496 (2005); *Alford v. Am. Bridge Div. U.S. Steel Corp.*, 642 F.2d 807, 814 (5th Cir. 1981), *vacated in part on reh'g*, 655 F.2d 86.

[14] In *Cunningham v. DOWCP*, 377 F.3d 98, 101 (1st Cir. 2004), the First Circuit considered coverage for an injury to a pipe fitter who worked at the manufacturing facility of his employer located some 3.5 miles from the employer's shipyards where pipe units were installed on ships. The court held that it had not determined a methodology for approaching the question of "adjoining area," but assumed the correctness of the Ninth Circuit's broad approach because it was clear that LHWCA coverage was foreclosed in any case. *Id.* at 105.

[15] The Supreme Court, in *Northeast Marine*, criticized this opinion when it stated: "The [Third] Circuit appears to have essentially discarded the situs test, holding that only '(an) employment nexus (status) with marine activity is (necessary)' and that the situs of the maritime employee at the time of injury is irrelevant." 432 U.S. at 278 n.40 (quoting *Sea-Land Servs., Inc.*, 540 F.2d at 638) (citations omitted).

follow the language of the statute—indeed, for the most part they all openly disavow the statutory text—we decline to adopt any of these tests." *Id.* at 1138. The court held:

> The plain language of the LHWCA requires that covered situses actually "adjoin" navigable waters, not . . . that they merely be in "the general geographic proximity" of the waterfront. Because Congress did not specify a more technical definition of the word "adjoining" (if that is even possible), we must accord that word its ordinary meaning, as, incidentally, the legislative history confirms Congress intended. To be sure, dictionaries do include "neighboring" and "in the vicinity of" as possible definitions of "adjoining," but such is not the ordinary meaning of the word; rather, the ordinary meaning of "adjoin" is "to lie next to," to "be in contact with," to "abut upon," or to be "touching or bounding at some point."

Id. (footnotes omitted) (citations omitted).

The *Sidwell* court found support for its interpretation from the House Report on the 1972 amendments: "The bill also expands the coverage of this Act to cover injuries occurring in the *contiguous* dock area related to longshore and ship repair work."[16]

Responding to the argument that the word "adjoining" should be given a broad meaning so as to accommodate Congress's concerns about workers moving in and out of coverage, the *Sidwell* court stated:

> The LHWCA was enacted to address a specific problem, and the actual language that Congress chose does just that. The problem, as we have explained, was that longshorem[e]n loading and [—12—] unloading ships walked in and out of LHWCA coverage as they walked the gangplank from ship to shore. In response, Congress extended coverage to both navigable waters and

> "the adjoining land area," S. Rep. 92-1125, 92d Cong., 2d Sess. 13 (1972), so that the longshoremen at both ends of the gangplank would be covered equally by the LHWCA. As the Supreme Court has repeatedly stated, "Congress intended that a worker's eligibility for federal benefits would not depend upon whether he was injured while walking down a gangway or while taking his first step onto the land", *P.C. Pfeiffer,* 444 U.S. at 75; rather, coverage would extend to "the waterfront areas where the overall loading and unloading process occurs." *Northeast Marine,* 432 U.S. at 272; *see also Herb's Welding,* 470 U.S. at 423 (explaining that Congress expanded coverage to include "rather large *shoreside* areas" (emphasis added)). The definition we adopt today ensures coverage for all maritime employees injured in the waterfront areas where the loading, unloading, and repair of vessels occurs, as Congress plainly intended and as the Supreme Court has directed.

Id. at 1140.

The court made clear that its literal definition of adjoining could not be circumvented by a broad interpretation of "area."

> Thus, an "other adjoining area" as to which coverage extends must be *like* a "pier," "wharf," "dry dock," "terminal," "building way," or "marine railway." Each of these enumerated "areas" is a discrete structure or facility, the very *raison d'etre* of which is its use in connection with navigable waters. Therefore, in order for an area to constitute an "other area" under the statute, it must be a discrete shoreside structure or facility.

Id. at 1139 (emphasis in original) (footnote omitted).

The court also indicated that it is the parcel of land underlying the employer's facility that must adjoin navigable waters, not

---

[16] S. Rep. No.92-1125, 92d Cong., 2d Sess. 2 (1972) (emphasis added).

the particular part of that parcel upon which a claimant is injured. The court quoted our language in *Alabama Dry Dock & Shipbuilding Co. v. Kininess* to demonstrate this point:

> [The back lot upon which a crane was located by which claimant was injured was somewhere] from 150 to 2,000 feet from the water's [—13—] edge. In any event, the physical distance is not decisive here. The test is whether the situs is within a contiguous shipbuilding area which adjoins the water. Alabama Dry Dock's shipyard adjoins the water. The lot was part of the shipyard, and was not separated from the waters by facilities not used for shipbuilding.

Id. at 1140 n.11 (alteration in original) (quoting *Ala. Dry Dock*, 554 F.2d 176, 178 (5th Cir. 1977)).

Finally, the *Sidwell* court determined that Congress further restricted the definition of "situs" by requiring the area to be: "customarily used by an employer in loading, unloading, repairing, dismantling, or building a vessel." 33 U.S.C. § 903(a). An "other adjoining area" seeking coverage as an LHWCA-covered situs must therefore satisfy both a geographic and a functional component. The court criticized other circuit courts such as the Third Circuit *Sea-Land* court, which suggested that the functional component (an area customarily used for designated maritime purposes) should be dispositive of the situs inquiry. The court stated:

> This language, however, is a *further* restriction upon "other adjoining areas"—implying that there are areas adjoining navigable waters that nonetheless do not meet the situs requirement because they are not customarily so used—not an implicit elimination of the requirement that the area first be adjoining navigable waters.[17] In any event, reading the

language in the manner proposed by the Director collapses the separate status and situs requirements into a single inquiry into status, in contravention of the Supreme Court's injunctions in *Herb's Welding* and *P.C. Pfeiffer* that we not read the status and situs requirements as one and the same.

Sidwell, 71 F.3d at 1139–40 n.10 (citations omitted). [—14—]

In response to *Sidwell*'s reasoning, the Director has advanced two primary arguments for avoiding the plain meaning of "adjoining." First, the Director argues that a broad definition of "adjoin" furthers the congressional goal of preventing longshoremen from walking in and out of coverage. By reading "adjoining" broadly, longshoremen would less frequently exit and enter the perimeters of LHWCA coverage. However, as the *Sidwell* court explained, Congress's primary concern was that longshoremen constantly walked the gangplank between the ship and the dock so that the worker injured on the dock was not covered under the LHWCA and his co-worker injured on the ship was covered. This loss of coverage when a longshoreman crossed the ship's gangplank was the inequity Congress sought to cure.[18]

Moreover, by adopting a situs requirement, Congress obviously recognized that a longshoreman could still leave and re-enter the geographic bounds of LHWCA coverage. As the Court in *Herb's Welding* stated: "[T]here will always be a boundary to coverage, and there will always be people who cross it during their employment. If that phenomenon was enough to require coverage, the Act would have to reach much further

---

17 We disagree with *Winchester*'s holding that even an injury that occurred in a facility that did not border on navigable waters nevertheless satisfied the situs test if the "area" was customarily

used for loading and unloading or some other designated maritime purpose. *See Winchester*, 632 F.2d at 515.

18 *See P.C. Pfeiffer Co.*, 444 U.S. at 75 ("By enlarging the covered situs . . . , Congress intended that a worker's eligibility for federal benefits would not depend on whether he was injured while walking down a gangway or while taking his first step onto the land."); *see also Chesapeake & Ohio Ry. Co. v. Schwalb*, 493 U.S. 40, 46 (1989).

than anyone argues that it does or should." 470 U.S. at 426–27 (citation omitted).

The Director also argues that as a compensation statute, the LHWCA should be construed liberally in favor of coverage. *See Ne. Marine*, 432 U.S. at 268. However, the first rule of statutory construction is that we may not ignore the plain language of a statute. *See Matter of Appletree Markets, Inc.*, 19 F.3d 969, 974 (5th Cir. 1994) ("[T]o ignore the plain language of the statute would be to substitute improperly our own policy predilections for the express intent of [—15—] Congress."). The LHWCA dictates that a covered situs actually adjoin navigable waters, and we may not ignore this limitation.

V. Conclusion

For the reasons stated above, we adopt the *Sidwell* definition of "adjoining" navigable water to mean "border on" or "be contiguous with" navigable waters.[19] We, therefore, overrule the contrary definition and analysis of *Winchester* and its progeny inconsistent with this opinion. We adopt this definition primarily because it is more faithful to the plain language of the statute. We are also influenced by the fact that the vague definition of "adjoining" we adopted thirty years ago in *Winchester* provides litigants and courts, in cases such as this one, with little guidance in determining whether coverage is provided by the Act.[20] More than perhaps any other statutory scheme, a worker's compensation statute should be "geared toward a nonlitigious, speedy, sure resolution of the compensation claims of injured workers." *Winchester*, 632 F.2d at 518 (Tjoflat, J., dissenting). One could hardly imagine an area where predictability is more important.

Applying the *Sidwell* definition of "adjoining" to the instant case, there is no dispute that the Chef Yard where Mr. Zepeda's injury occurred did not adjoin navigable waters. Because the Chef Yard did not border upon and was not contiguous with navigable waters, it is not an LHWCA-covered situs.[21] [—16—]

For these reasons we VACATE the award of the BRB against NODSI and REMAND for further proceedings as necessary against the alternate employer, New Orleans Marine Contractors.

VACATED AND REMANDED.

(Reporter's note: Concurring opinion on p. 236).

---

[19] *See also* Bryan Garner, Garner's Dictionary of Legal Usage 25 (3d ed. 2011) ("Etymologically, *adjoining* means 'directly abutting; contiguous' . . . .").

[20] Also, as demonstrated by this case, our former vague definition of "adjoining area" makes it difficult for an employer to know whether it should purchase insurance coverage for injuries under the Act.

[21] Because we determine that the Act's situs requirement is not satisfied in this case, we need not address the question of whether Mr. Zepeda's employment activities would satisfy the Act's status requirement.

[—17—] CLEMENT, Circuit Judge, with whom JOLLY, JONES, SMITH, PRADO, OWEN, and ELROD, Circuit Judges, join, concurring:

I fully concur in the majority's formulation of the situs inquiry, finding it to be a faithful application of the plain text of the LHWCA. I write separately to explain why the status requirement is not met in this case, even under the generous precedent established by this circuit and the Supreme Court.

This en banc decision to return the situs inquiry to its textual roots will certainly impose a natural limitation on the status of employees who are eligible under the LHWCA. But both Congress and the Supreme Court have acknowledged that the situs and status inquiries are separate and distinct, and that a claimant must establish both before he can recover under the LHWCA. *See, e.g.*, 33 U.S.C. §§ 903(a), 902(3); *Herb's Welding, Inc. v. Gray*, 470 U.S. 414, 415–16 (1985). It is important to clarify the status test to ensure that this circuit's application of the LHWCA as a whole remains true to its proper purpose. As the status inquiry provides an alternative ground to vacate the decision of the Benefits Review Board, this discussion is not dictum. *U.S. v. Potts*, 644 F.3d 233, 237 n.3 (5th Cir. 2011) (explaining that an alternative holding is binding precedent).[1]

I. Controlling Precedent

An individual located on a proper situs will qualify as a covered employee under the LHWCA only if he is also "engaged in maritime employment." 33 U.S.C. § 902(3). This statute provides that, for example, "any longshoreman or other person engaged in longshoring operations, and any harbor-worker including a ship repairman, shipbuilder, and ship-breaker," has the status of a maritime employee. *Id.* The Supreme Court has acknowledged that the Act also [—18—] extends to cover workers other than those in the delineated occupations, *Chesapeake & Ohio Ry. Co. v. Schwalb*, 493 U.S. 40, 45 (1989), as long as the worker is "engaged in loading, unloading, repairing, or building a vessel." *P.C. Pfeiffer Co. v. Ford*, 444 U.S. 69, 79 (1979) (quoting S. Rep. No. 92-1125 (1972) and H.R.Rep. No. 92-1441 (1972)).

As acknowledged in *Chesapeake & Ohio Railway Co. v. Schwalb*, "the maritime employment requirement as applied to land-based work other than longshoring and the other occupations named in § 902(3) is an occupational test focusing on loading and unloading. Those not involved in those functions do not have the benefit of the Act." 493 U.S. at 46 (citing *Herb's Welding*, 470 U.S. at 424). In the context of the LHWCA, loading and unloading includes those tasks incident to the process of "handling of cargo as it moves between sea and land transportation," *Ne. Marine Terminal Co., Inc. v. Caputo*, 432 U.S. 249, 267, 273–74 (1977), because such tasks are of the sort traditionally performed by longshoremen, *see Ford*, 444 U.S. at 74, 81–82. Thus, "land-based activity occurring within the § 903 situs will be deemed maritime . . . if it is an *integral* or *essential* part of loading or unloading a vessel," viewed from the position of a longshoreman or harborworker. *Schwalb*, 493 U.S. at 45 (emphasis added). Maritime employment does not extend to workers "beyond those actually involved in moving cargo between ship and land transportation." *Herb's Welding*, 470 U.S. at 424.

In *Schwalb*, the Supreme Court recognized that "employees who are injured while maintaining or repairing equipment essential to the loading or unloading process," in addition to longshoremen who physically handle cargo, are covered by the LHWCA. 493 U.S. at 47. It premised this conclusion on the fact that the process of loading and unloading vessels would stop if the machinery used by the longshoremen became broken, clogged, or fouled. An individual who either fixed that machinery or ensured that such a breakdown [—19—] did not occur was "just as vital to and an integral part of the loading process as the operator of the equipment," *id.*, sufficient to trigger application of the LHWCA.

---

[1] Prior to this en banc decision, the situs inquiry was often used to bolster and provide context for the status inquiry. The change in the nature of the situs inquiry provides an additional reason to clarify the proper formulation of the status inquiry.

This circuit applied a version of this test in *Hullinghorst Indus., Inc. v. Carroll*, 650 F.2d 750, 754–58 (5th Cir. 1981), to hold that a carpenter injured while building scaffolding beneath a pier was a maritime employee for purposes of the LHWCA. Although the carpenter had no direct involvement in loading or unloading, his scaffolding work "was an integral step in a maritime project of the type that could be performed by a typical harborworker," and "directly furthered . . . the loading and unloading of ships" by enabling the owner of the pier to perform its core longshoring operations. *Id.* at 756. Because a loading company would have otherwise had to provide for the repair of its piers, an employee engaged in that activity was covered under the LHWCA even if he was employed as an independent contractor. *See id.* at 757–58.

II. Discussion

Juan Zepeda was not involved in the process of moving cargo between ship and land transportation. His task was to repair empty containers, some of which may have been used in maritime shipping. The now-vacated panel opinion nevertheless concluded that, because containers themselves are "integral" or "essential" to the loading process, the repair of such containers triggered application of the LHWCA. *See Schwalb*, 493 U.S. at 45 ("[L]and-based activity occurring within the § 903 situs will be deemed maritime only if it is an integral or essential part of loading or unloading a vessel.").

Although this conclusion is not an unreasonable interpretation of "integral" and "essential" as those words are understood on their own, the panel opinion as a whole divorces *Schwalb* and its predecessors from their roots. *Schwalb* stands for the proposition that employees who repair equipment used by longshoremen to load or unload vessels are just as essential to the loading [—20—] process as the individuals who load or unload the cargo, because the actual process, once begun, would be arrested in the absence of their contributions. *See id.* at 48 (noting the "determinative consideration" was that the "ship loading process could not continue" in the absence of the repair). Because these

workers repair the tools and instrumentalities that longshoremen rely on to execute their tasks, they are "engaged in the type of duties that longshoremen perform in transferring goods between ship and land transportation," *Ford*, 444 U.S. at 81, and covered by the LHWCA.

On its own terms and against the backdrop of *Caputo*, *Ford*, and *Herb's Welding*, *Schwalb* does not create a rule under which *all* employees who repair *any* equipment that *may* be used in the loading process are similarly integral. If this were the inquiry, it would only be a short step to the conclusion that a manufacturer of shoes or walkie talkies should be covered, because, arguably, the modern loading process cannot be accomplished without those items. But the LHWCA does not provide a but-for test for determining coverage. Instead, the statute looks to the customary maritime functions of dockworkers, albeit without an eye toward who is actually performing those functions. *See Schwalb*, 493 U.S. at 46; *Ford*, 444 U.S. at 81–82; *Caputo*, 432 U.S. at 273–74. With this understanding, the proper question when defining the status of an employee under the LHWCA is whether the task that the employee engages in is the type of customary maritime work that a dockworker or longshoreman would have to perform in order to successfully transfer cargo between ship and land transportation. *See Ford*, 444 U.S. at 81.

This inquiry distinguishes tasks necessary to execute a loading process from the perspective of a longshoreman—such as repair of a longshoreman's tools and facilities—from tasks that are only tangentially connected to the loading process. Construed broadly, the first category may capture a person whose sole responsibility is to sweep clear a loading ramp. It may even include [—21—] someone who repairs broken dollies in between loading jobs. But it does not include, for example, a manufacturer of cardboard boxes. The way that cargo arrives at port may determine how the loading and unloading process is executed, but nothing about the production of the container is the customary job of a harborworker or longshoreman.[2]

Although container repair is not customarily the task of longshoremen, courts have recognized that container repair satisfies the status test in some instances. For example, the Eleventh Circuit has held that container repair is "integral" or "essential" to the loading process when it "consist[s] of making . . . outbound, loaded chassis road worthy" and when, "[w]ithout the essential maintenance necessary to make the outbound rigs road worthy, the unloading process would stop indefinitely at the Port Authority." *Atl. Container Serv., Inc. v. Coleman*, 904 F.2d 611, 613, 618 (11th Cir. 1990). In other words, container repair satisfies the status inquiry when it is one step in the direct chain of unloading a ship, and when "the maintenance men would [halt] the entire loading process" if they were not available for the repair. *Sea-Land Serv., Inc. v. Rock*, 953 F.2d 56, 67 (3d Cir. 1992) (citing *Coloma v. Dir., Office of Workers' Comp. Programs*, 897 F.2d 394, 400 (9th Cir. 1990)); *accord Schwalb*, 493 U.S. at 48 ("The determinative consideration is that the ship loading process could not continue unless the retarder that Goode worked on was operating properly. It is notable that the loading actually was stopped while Goode made the repairs and that one of his supervisors apparently expressed the desire that Goode hurry up so that the loading could continue."); *Sidwell v. Va. Int'l Terminals, Inc.*, 372 F.3d 238, 243 (4th Cir. 2004) ("This standard makes the capacity to interrupt ongoing longshoring activities paramount.").
[—22—]

However, container repair does not satisfy this standard when it is not of the sort that is, or would have been, traditionally performed by longshoremen or harborworkers. Zepeda's work—the repair of empty containers that were neither headed for delivery nor toward a ship for transport, and indeed may well have been destined for a truck or train rather than

a vessel—is clearly of this second character. This was not an instance in which the containers came off of a ship needing repair, and Zepeda was on hand to perform such repairs essential or necessary to ensure that the containers made it to their final destination. Nothing about Zepeda's work was done with the purpose of assisting a longshoreman or harborworker execute his task, and nothing about the maritime nature of the location at which Zepeda worked, even if it was to be considered a proper situs, was functionally related to his repair work. In short, Zepeda's work was not "essential" or "integral" to a longshoreman's task of loading or unloading a vessel, because nothing about Zepeda's work was part of the process of "moving cargo between ship and land transportation." *Herb's Welding*, 470 U.S. at 424.

III. Conclusion

The LHWCA is to be "liberally construed in conformance with its purpose, and in a way which avoids harsh and incongruous results." *Caputo*, 432 U.S. at 266 (quoting *Voris v. Eikel*, 346 U.S. 328, 333 (1953)). But incongruity is a two-sided inquiry. Zepeda, an individual who never loaded or unloaded a vessel, never assisted anyone else load or unload a vessel, and never witnessed a vessel being loaded or unloaded, is "a far cry from the paradigmatic longshoreman who walked in and out of coverage during his workday and spent substantial amounts of his time 'on navigable waters.'" *Herb's Welding*, 470 U.S. at 427 n.13. Constructing the status inquiry so as to include Zepeda would make application of the Act unwieldy as to those who should be covered, and create a lack of uniformity between individuals such as Zepeda and similarly situated nonmaritime employees who are limited to state compensation schemes. Under the [—23—] precedent defining status established by this circuit and the Supreme Court, I would hold that Zepeda was not a maritime employee for purposes of the LHWCA while employed by NODSI.

(Reporter's Note: Concurring opinion on p. 239).

---

[2] So stated, this distinction also avoids the red herring argument that what is "integral" to the loading or unloading process depends on the size and financial capabilities of the entity supplying that product or service.

[—24—] HIGGINSON, Circuit Judge, concurring in the judgment:

Farsightedly or fortuitously, Congress in 1972 amended the Longshore and Harbor Workers' Compensation Act (Longshore Act), 33 U.S.C. §§ 901–50, legislation that this Court applied in *Textports Stevedore Co. v. Winchester*, 632 F.2d 504 (5th Cir. 1980) (en banc), setting forth a two-part rule that extended benefits coverage to injuries not just on navigable waters, but also at specific "adjoining" facilities ("pier, wharf, dry dock, terminal, building way, marine railway"), as well as any "other adjoining area customarily used by an employer in loading, unloading, repairing, dismantling, or building a vessel." 33 U.S.C. § 903(a). Congress sought to be comprehensive of common shipping facilities, such as piers, docks, and wharfs, as well as other "adjoining" property *provided that* the property is "used by an employer in loading, unloading, repairing, dismantling, or building a vessel." *Id.* Not to restrict coverage to nomenclature, Congress in § 903(a) extended coverage to "other adjoining areas," but again, only if such areas are used for *vessel-related* activities.

In my view, this necessity of proximity to a navigable waterway as well as with the functional requirement that the area is "customarily used for loading, unloading, repairing . . . *a vessel*" (emphasis added), requires reversal in the case before us because the Chef Yard area was not used to load or unload or repair *vessels*. Its use, like many current and under-construction container terminals (some even named "inland ports") was container repair, storage, and transshipment by ground, air, or sea. These container yards do exist to support port, air, and rail gateways, but they have emerged since Congress' amendments to the Longshore Act and we cannot declare that just because of their recent essentiality, they have become areas that load, unload or repair vessels.

This short plain language analysis necessitates reversal in this case because the Benefits Review Board, utilizing dicta from our decision in *Coastal Production Services, Inc. v. Hudson*, 555 F.3d 426 (5th Cir. 2009), that Longshore [—25—] Act coverage could extend beyond vessel work to more general work "associated with items used as part of the loading process," *id.* at 434, goes beyond Congress' legislation and its purpose, indeed, beyond the reality of cargo shipping prevalent fifty years ago. It may be that Congress will determine that containers have become the functional equivalent of vessel-loading equipment, like cranes, or are becoming even the functional equivalent of the holds of vessels themselves. But I do not think that we enlarge the commonsense meaning of the word "vessel" ourselves.

Consequently, I would reverse the Benefits Review Board decision and clarify that the clause "associated with items used as part of the loading process" in *Hudson* cannot be understood to expand Longshore Act coverage beyond areas that operate to load and repair vessels to areas that operate to store and repair the cargo containers that go onto vessels and trains and trucks.

Deciding this case on the word "vessel," I would not reach whether we would answer differently what the word "adjoin" meant to Congress half a century ago. Contemporaneous with that syntactical choice, our court, then also sitting en banc, gave its reasoned answer, not withholding Longshore Act coverage when the area of injury was a dock equipment room that, unlike two other gear rooms, was not "on the docks" abutting the water because "the docks had insufficient space for an additional gear room," so it had to be located five blocks away. *Winchester*, 632 F.2d at 507.

I would not disturb our decision in *Winchester* because it is time-settled, *cf. Dickerson v. United States*, 530 U.S. 428 (2000); because it was authored by a majority of judges who were contemporaries with the statute they were interpreting; because that decision, defining "adjoin" as adjacent, is as faithful to Congress' literal instruction as the majority's decision today assigning a strict contiguity meaning; and because the rule propounded by Congress, applied by us in *Winchester*, announced a layered approach which has proven fair and [—26—] workable over fifty years of change that always will be the circumstance of longshoreman work.

Even etymologically, I do not think we are in a position to say there is certainty that "adjoin" means contiguousness, not adjacency. Shakespeare spoke of the hills "adjoining" Alexandria. From the standpoint of persons, industry, and legislators, unbroken contiguity to navigable water is impractical for reasons that our court identified in *Winchester* and that are even more pressing today: land abutting water is finite and expensive, yet ship size and cargo capacity, total shipping volume, and loading and offloading equipment are ever-increasing. *See Winchester*, 632 F.2d at 513–14.

Neither the record in this case, nor in any case drawn to our attention, suggests that Congress' layered approach, applied in *Winchester*, has proven unworkable.[1] Indeed, if impracticality or uncertainty or injustice has occurred, Congress would receive and test that proposition in hearings and tighten the interpretation of § 903(a) that we have applied for almost half a century. But no reference to a proposal for legislative action has been drawn to our attention. By contrast, this court in *Winchester*, at the time presiding over port, shipping and longshoreman activity from Florida to Texas, pointed out that a strict abutment rule could exacerbate the very gangplank benefits coverage problem Congress sought to alleviate. 632 F.2d at 514–15. Employers could relocate obvious longshoreman's work across a property break. This in fact was the circumstance in *Winchester*, compelled not by a desire to withhold benefits but simply because there was no more dock space. *Id.* at 507.[2] [—27—]

---

[1] During oral argument, the *Hudson* case was identified as proof of unpredictability. But in *Hudson*, there was no contiguity problem because the platform where the injury occurred was located entirely at sea. *See* 555 F.3d at 428.

[2] Unsurprisingly, during oral argument to us, the answer candidly was given that rescinding *Winchester* would mean coverage would cease. There is no reason to criticize or call into question that answer. A property break could mean substantial cost savings which would [—27—] be sensible, though the rule behind it would not be.

For the above reasons, I concur in the judgment of the court.

(Reporter's Note: Dissenting opinion on p. 241).

[—28—] STEWART, Chief Judge, dissenting, joined by **DENNIS** and **GRAVES,** Circuit Judges:

Over thirty years ago, our en banc court confronted the same issue we confront today: how to interpret the geographic component of the situs test in the Longshore and Harbor Workers' Compensation Act ("LHWCA" or "the Act") and specifically, how to define "adjoining area" under the Act.[1] *Texports Stevedore Co. v. Winchester*, 632 F.2d 504 (5th Cir. 1980) (en banc), *cert denied*, 452 U.S. 905 (1981). The *Winchester* majority adopted a broad definition of "adjoining area" that was in keeping with the plain meaning of the words, as well as "the spirit of the congressional purposes." *Id.* at 514. The decades since *Winchester* was decided have revealed no catastrophic consequences of that decision. Nonetheless, the majority now overrules this precedent and adopts the Fourth Circuit's more restrictive definition of "adjoining area," thereby enhancing an existing circuit split. As I find no compelling reason to alter the LHWCA legal landscape in this circuit, I respectfully dissent.

I.

To support its adoption of the Fourth Circuit's test, *Sidwell v. Express Container Servs., Inc.*, 71 F.3d 1134 (4th Cir. 1995), the majority advances two arguments critical of *Winchester*: (1) the court provided only vague instructions as to how to analyze the totality of the circumstances; and (2) that the court's interpretation of "adjoining area" is not faithful to the plain language of the LHWCA. I address each argument in turn. [—29—]

A.

The majority criticizes *Winchester* for dispensing "vague instructions [that] provided

little guidance to other courts or future litigants on how to determine from 'the circumstances' whether a claimant satisfies the situs test." Slip Op. at 7. However, in the thirty-three years since it was passed, *Winchester* has not proven to be overly vague or unworkable. Indeed, the standard is clear enough that since 1980, there have been only nine cases in this circuit where the meaning of "adjoining area" was contested. Moreover, few of these cases challenged the application of *Winchester* to land-based operations. *Coastal Prod. Servs., Inc. v. Hudson*, 555 F.3d 426 (5th Cir. 2009) (deciding that fixed loading platform was a maritime situs); *Thibodeaux v. Grasso Prod. Mgmt. Inc.*, 370 F.3d 486 (5th Cir. 2004) (holding that a fixed oil production platform was not a covered situs); *Boomtown Belle Casino v. Bazor*, 313 F.3d 300 (5th Cir. 2002) (holding that floating casino was not a covered situs); *E. J. Fields Mach. Works Inc v. Guidry*, 54 F. App'x 793 (5th Cir. 2002) (per curiam) (unpublished) (affirming LHWCA situs status for job shop specializing in the repair and construction of marine parts where shop was one-hundred feet from river and located in area customarily used for maritime activity); *Mobil Mining & Minerals v. Nixson*, 209 F.3d 719 (5th Cir. 2000) (per curiam) (unpublished) (holding injury at premises adjacent to the Houston Ship Channel occurred on a covered situs); *Sisson v. Davis & Sons, Inc.*, 131 F.3d 555 (5th Cir. 1998) (per curiam) (holding that injury in a parking lot did not occur on a covered situs); *Universal Fabricators, Inc. v. Smith*, 878 F.2d 843 (5th Cir. 1989) (upholding ALJ's situs determination where employer's yard adjoined navigable waters); *Reynolds v. Ingalls Shipbldg. Div., Litton Sys., Inc.*, 788 F.2d 264 (5th Cir. 1986) (discussing coverage for seaman injured at sea); *Alford v. Am. Bridge Div., U.S. Steel Corp.*, 642 F.2d 807 (5th Cir. Apr. 1981), *modified in part*, 668 F.2d 791 (5th Cir. Sept. 1981) (holding employer's location on the Sabine River fell within [—30—] the situs requirement). Additionally, Petitioners have presented no industry reports, data, hearings, or related information to support any alleged negative effects *Winchester* has had on the maritime industry.

---

[1] Under the Act, compensation is owed for the disability or death of an employee where the injury causing such death or disability occurs "upon the navigable waters of the United States (including any adjoining pier, wharf, dry dock, terminal, building way, marine railway, or *other adjoining area* customarily used by an employer in loading, unloading, repairing, dismantling, or building a vessel)." 33 U.S.C. § 903(a) (emphasis added).

In the absence of any compelling evidence of *Winchester*'s dysfunction or change in the maritime industry, I decline to join the majority in overruling well-reasoned precedent of this en banc court that involves carefully-considered statutory interpretation. "[S]*tare decisis* in respect to statutory interpretation has 'special force,' for 'Congress remains free to alter what we have done.'" *John R. Sand & Gravel Co. v. United States*, 552 U.S. 130, 139 (2008) (quoting *Patterson v. McLean Credit Union*, 491 U.S. 164, 172-73 (1989)).

B.

The majority also reasons that the Fourth Circuit's interpretation of "adjoining area" is more faithful to the plain language of the statute. The *Winchester* Court observed that "adjoin" could be defined as "contiguous to or to border upon," as well as "to be close to or to be near." 632 F.2d at 514 (citation and internal quotation marks omitted). The *Winchester* court chose to adopt the second set of definitions in accordance with its interpretation of congressional intent. *Id.* In repudiating this interpretation, the majority here cites with approval *Sidwell*'s comment that while "dictionaries do include 'neighboring' and 'in the vicinity of' as possible definitions of 'adjoining,' . . . such is not the ordinary meaning of the word." 71 F.3d 1134, 1138.

Webster's Third New International Dictionary defines "adjoining" as "touching or bounding at some point or on some line: near in space." Webster's Third New Int'l Dictionary 27 (1993). Other dictionaries define adjoining similarly—that is, with more than one definition, one of which does not require contiguity. *See, e.g.,* Am. Heritage Dictionary of the English Language 22 (1992) ("neighboring; contiguous"); *but see* Black's Law Dictionary 62 (1968) ("The word in its etymological sense means touching or contiguous, as distinguished from [—31—] lying near to or adjacent."). The majority refuses to construe "adjoining area" liberally because "the first rule of statutory construction is that we may not ignore the plain language of the statute." However, this argument does not recognize the multiple ordinary meanings of "adjoining" nor the ambiguity intrinsic in defining how far from shore an "adjacent *area*" extends. Such ambiguities as these may be resolved by applying canons of statutory interpretation, including an analysis of legislative history. *See Perrone v. Gen. Motors Acceptance Corp.*, 232 F.3d 433, 440 (5th Cir. 2000).

Accordingly, the *Winchester* court reasonably—and properly, in my opinion—sought to resolve the issue by looking to congressional intent and Supreme Court precedent. *See, e.g., Winchester*, 632 F.2d at 514-15; *see also Ne. Marine Terminal Co. v. Caputo*, 432 U.S. 249, 261-65 (1977) (describing expansion of LHWCA coverage under 1972 amendments). The *Winchester* court's broad reading of the complete clause,"adjoining area," also was consistent with "[o]ne of the primary motivations for Congress' decision to extend [LHWCA] coverage shoreward," which was the "recognition that the advent of modern cargo-handling techniques had moved much of the longshoreman's work off the vessel and onto land." *Caputo*, 432 U.S. at 269-70. Attendant to this recognition is the practical reality that the amount of land contiguous to the water is limited. Consider the following scenario: A company maintains three gear rooms, all of which are supervised by the same shop foreman. Two of those gear rooms are on the docks, but the third is located a few blocks away from the docks because there was insufficient space for an additional gear room on the docks, and the company could find no space closer to the docks.[2] Under the majority's [—32—] strict interpretation of the

---

[2] This is the factual background presented by *Winchester*, 632 F.2d at 506-07. *See also Parker v. Dir., Office of Workers' Comp. Programs*, 75 F.3d 929 (4th Cir. 1996), *rejected on other grounds by Ingalls Shipbldg., Inc. v. Dir., Office of Workers' Comp. Programs*, 519 U.S. 248 (1997) (concluding facility was not a covered situs where state had terminated employer's lease for part of the terminal, forcing employer to locate part of its facility one mile from [—32—] navigable waters, even though maritime employees traveled between the terminal facility and the off-site facility).

Act, a worker injured in the gear room on the docks will be covered under the LHWCA, but an identical worker injured under the same circumstances at the off-dock location will not be covered. While I acknowledge that "there will always be a boundary to coverage," *Herb's Welding, Inc. v. Gray*, 470 U.S. 414, 426-27 (1985), I am not convinced Congress intended this type of "harsh and incongruous" result. *Caputo*, 432 U.S. at 268 (citation and internal quotation marks omitted).

Moreover, as Petitioner conceded at oral argument, adopting a narrow definition of "adjoining area" would allow maritime employers to circumvent LHWCA coverage by purchasing land with a narrow gap separating it from the water. *See, e.g., Walker v. Metro Mach. Corp.*, 50 F. App'x 104 (4th Cir. 2002) (per curiam) (unpublished) (declining to disturb ALJ's decision finding facility was not a covered situs because employer's waterfront facility was divided into two areas separated by a fenced-off path owned by the city, and employee was injured in area not contiguous to navigable waters).

II.

Although the majority discusses the circuit split that exists between the Fourth and Ninth Circuits[3], it fails to observe the extent to which the Fourth Circuit's test is an outlier among circuits that have addressed this issue. No other circuit has adopted *Sidwell*'s restrictive test. Instead, the trend is to adopt a more expansive view of coverage. *See Consolidation Coal Co. v. Benefits Review Bd.*, 629 F.3d 322, 330-31 (3d Cir. 2010) (adopting a liberal reading of "adjoining area" after looking to *Winchester* and the Ninth Circuit, and specifically rejecting the *Sidwell* approach); *Cunningham v. Dir., Office of* [—33—] *Workers' Comp. Programs*, 377 F.3d 98, 105 (1st Cir. 2004) (assuming without deciding that ALJ and Benefits Review Board were correct to apply Ninth Circuit's approach); *Garvey Grain Co. v. Dir., Office of Workers' Comp. Programs*, 639 F.2d 366, 369-71 (7th Cir. 1981) (applying a "liberal" test

---

[3] *Brady-Hamilton Stevedore Co. v. Herron*, 568 F.2d 137, 139 (9th Cir. 1978).

following *Caputo*). Additionally, the majority's decision creates a split with the Eleventh Circuit, which continues to apply *Winchester*. *See, e.g., Ramos v. Dir., OWCP*, 486 F. App'x 775 (11th Cir. 2012) (per curiam) (unpublished). Given the importance of maintaining uniformity in maritime law, I disagree with the majority's decision to move away from the more liberal interpretation favored by the majority of circuits that have addressed the issue.

III.

As I also disagree with Judge Clement's concurrence, I briefly address the key difficulties with her separate opinion.

In addition to the situs requirement already discussed, an injured claimant must also satisfy the status requirement. *See* 33 U.S.C. § 902(3) ("The term 'employee' means any person engaged in maritime employment, including any longshoreman or other person engaged in longshoring operations, and any harbor-worker including a ship repairman, shipbuilder, and ship-breaker . . . ."). The Act does not define "maritime employment," but the Supreme Court has explained that "employees who are injured while maintaining or repairing equipment essential to the loading or unloading process are covered by the Act. . . . Someone who repairs or maintains a piece of loading equipment is just as vital to and an integral part of the loading process as the operator of the equipment." *Chesapeake & Ohio Ry. Co. v. Schwalb*, 493 U.S. 40, 47 (1989).

The concurrence argues that "container repair is not customarily the task of longshoremen . . . ." Concurrence Slip Op. at 5. Respectfully, I disagree. While this statement may have been true many years ago, it does not acknowledge the changes in the maritime industry in the twentieth century that [—34—] were reflected in the 1972 amendments to the LHWCA and subsequent Supreme Court precedent. As the Supreme Court recognized thirty-five years ago, "the container is the modern substitute for the hold of the vessel." *Caputo*, 432 U.S. at 270. Moreover, I find it persuasive that the

Benefits Review Board decided over thirty years ago that container repair mechanics are engaged in maritime employment. *See, e.g., Cabezas*, 11 Ben. Rev. Bd. Serv. (MB) 279 (1979), *Parker*, 8 Ben. Rev. Bd. Serv. (MB) 321 (1978).

The concurrence then distinguishes between two types of container repair: (1) repair that is "one step in the direct chain of unloading a ship and when 'the maintenance men would [halt] the entire loading process' if they were not available for the repair" and (2) repair "not of the sort that is, or would have been, traditionally performed by longshoremen or harborworkers." Concurrence Slip Op. at 5-6. I find this distinction problematic. The concurrence does not lay out a clear test for this distinction but relies on four characteristics of Zepeda's work to find that he falls into the second category—the containers Zepeda repaired were (1) empty, (2) not headed for delivery, (3) not headed toward a ship for transport, and (4) "may well have been destined for a truck or train rather than a vessel." Concurrence Slip Op. at 6. The concurrence has cited no authority, nor am I aware of any such authority, that would support the adoption of tests requiring a quantitative assessment of a container's contents or a requirement that each individual container an employee works on be tracked from its origin to its ultimate destination. Furthermore, the concurrence's assertions contradict the ALJ's findings, which are "conclusive if supported by substantial evidence in the record considered as a whole." 33 U.S.C. § 921(b)(3). The ALJ found, based on the weight of the evidence, that Zepeda worked on Evergreen marine containers while he was a NODSI employee. There is substantial evidence in the record to support this conclusion, including testimony that (1) some of the Evergreen containers repaired by [—35—] NODSI were used for marine transportation; (2) some of the containers were offloaded at the Port of New Orleans; (3) it was common for empty containers to be loaded onto and unloaded from ships; (4) NODSI initially only serviced Evergreen containers and was required under Evergreen's labor contract to hire unionized maritime workers who were the only workers

permitted to work on marine containers; and (5) when Zepeda began working for NODSI, he was a unionized maritime worker. Repair of marine containers lies within the scope of maritime employment, and the proper functioning of these containers, including maintenance and repair when damage is discovered, is essential to the loading and unloading process. "It is irrelevant that an employee's contribution to the loading process is not continuous or that repair or maintenance is not always needed." *Schwalb*, 493 U.S. at 47.

Finally, the concurrence appears to disregard the need for companies to engage in maintenance and repair before the container condition becomes so degraded as to render it unusable and a physical impediment to the loading or unloading process. The Supreme Court recognized the necessity of continuously maintaining equipment with the goal toward preventing machinery breakage. *See id.* ("When machinery breaks down or becomes clogged or fouled because of the lack of cleaning, the loading process stops until the difficulty is cured."). Thus, an individual who *prevents* that stoppage is covered under the LHWCA because his work is integral to maintaining a smooth loading and unloading process. The concurrence turns this objective—to prevent stoppages in loading and unloading—on its head by essentially requiring the process to stop before an employee's work is integral. Certainly, if Evergreen repaired none of their containers until they were so broken as to spill cargo during the loading or unloading process, that process would stop. That Evergreen has made the prudent business decision to prevent such occurrences should not deprive its contracted workers of LHWCA coverage. [—36—]

IV.

The *Winchester* en banc court adopted an approach that gave effect to each part of the statute, relied on definitions of the statutory terms that are consistent with congressional intent, and abided by the Supreme Court's guidance to take an expansive view of the post-1972 coverage provisions. Beyond Petitioner's obvious disenchantment with the

ALJ's granting relief to Zepeda, I see no reason to overrule our precedent. Similarly, the ALJ's finding that Zepeda was a covered maritime worker was well supported by precedent. For the reasons above, I am satisfied that no changes to the maritime industry or other societal forces compel the conclusion that our precedent as to situs should be overturned or that we should construct a new test for determining status.

United States Court of Appeals
for the Fifth Circuit

No. 12-20228

INSURANCE CO. OF THE STATE OF PA.
VS.
DIRECTOR, OFFICE OF WORKERS' COMPENSATION
PROGRAMS

Appeal from the United States District Court for the
Southern District of Texas

Decided: February 15, 2013
Revised: May 13, 2013

Citation: 713 F.3d 779, 1 Adm. R. 246 (5th Cir. 2013).

Before **KING**, **SOUTHWICK** and **GRAVES**, Circuit
Judges.

[—1—] PER CURIAM:

Plaintiffs-Appellants appeal from the district court's judgment affirming a decision of the Benefits Review Board that affirmed an Administrative Law Judge's decision awarding temporary total disability and medical benefits to Defendant-Appellant Glen Vickers. For the reasons that follow, we reverse the Board's decision, vacate the award for Vicker's polyneuropathy, and remand to the ALJ for a determination of whether Vickers's polyneuropathy naturally or unavoidably resulted from the work-related arm injury cited in his claim. **[—2—]**

I. FACTS AND PROCEDURAL HISTORY

Defendant-Appellee Glen Vickers is a former employee of Plaintiff-Appellant Service Employees International, Inc. ("SEI"). While Vickers was working for SEI in Iraq as a logistics coordinator, his left arm was severely injured in a tank fuel adapter explosion on August 14, 2004. Eleven days later, Vickers traveled to Texas and had surgery on his left arm performed by Dr. Roger Sessions, an orthopedic surgeon. Vickers was released to full duty in December 2004, and he returned to Iraq that January. In April or May 2005, Vickers developed a gastrointestinal illness that lasted four or five days. He returned to Texas in August 2005 and saw Dr. Roger

Sessions for another operation on his arm—a carpal tunnel syndrome release.

Around November and December 2005, Vickers began to experience numbness, stinging, tingling, and pain in areas other than his left arm: mainly his right arm and shoulder, both of his legs, and his neck. On the basis of an EMG, Vickers was referred to Dr. Joseph Vaughan, a neurophysiologist, who diagnosed him with an autoimmune disorder known as chronic inflammatory demyelinating polyneuropathy ("CIDP").[1]

On December 21, 2006, Vickers filed a claim for compensation seeking permanent total disability benefits from SEI and its insurance carrier, Plaintiff-Appellant Insurance Company of the State of Pennsylvania (collectively "Plaintiffs"), under the Longshore and Harbor Workers' Compensation Act ("LHWCA"), 33 U.S.C. §901, *et seq.*, as amended and extended by the Defense **[—3—]** Base Act ("DBA"), 42 U.S.C. §1651, *et seq.* Specifically, Vickers's claim sought compensation for Vickers's arm injury and for injuries to "other parts of [his] body, [and] other related problems associated with [his] injury and working conditions in Iraq."

The Administrative Law Judge ("ALJ") awarded Vickers temporary total disability benefits for the injury to his arm and for his CIDP. The ALJ invoked the 33 U.S.C. § 920(a)

---

[1] Also called "chronic inflammatory demyelinating polyradiculoneuropathy," CIDP is a rare, acquired, immune-mediated inflammatory disorder of the peripheral nervous system. The disease is believed to be caused by immune cells—which normally protect the body from foreign infection—attacking the body's nerves. Affected nerves fail to respond to stimuli, causing pain, progressive muscle weakness, tingling, and numbness. *See All About CIDP*, GBS/CIDP Foundation International, http://www.gbs-cidp.org/home/cidp/cidp; *Chronic Inflammatory Demyelinating Polyneuropathy (CIDP) Information Page*, Nat'l Inst. of Neurological Disorders & Stroke, http://www.ninds.nih.gov/disorders/cidp/cidp.htm.

presumption (the "Section 20(a) presumption") that Vickers's CIDP was work-related based on Dr. Vaughan's testimony that Vickers's gastritis, in conjunction with the surgeries for his work-related arm injury, could have precipitated his CIDP. The ALJ found that the opinion of one Dr. Maudlin—who reviewed Vickers's conditions based upon documents that Plaintiffs provided—was sufficient to rebut the presumption that the arm injury caused Vickers's polyneuropathy. However, the ALJ also found that Dr. Maudlin did not address the effect of Vickers's gastritis or his surgeries on the development of his CIDP, and thus, that the Section 20(a) presumption linking this condition to his employment was not rebutted.

Plaintiffs appealed to the Benefits Review Board ("BRB"), and sought reversal on the grounds that the ALJ erred in finding the evidence sufficient to invoke the Section 20(a) presumption as to Vickers's CIDP and in finding the evidence insufficient to establish rebuttal of the presumption. TheBRB affirmed the ALJ's decision. Plaintiffs then filed a motion for reconsideration, arguing that our decision in *Amerada Hess Corp. v. Dir., OWCP*, 543 F.3d 755 (5th Cir. 2008), which was decided after the BRB's decision, mandated reversal of the ALJ's decision. The BRB found *Amerada Hess* distinguishable from this case because the claim Vickers filed included the "sequelae of the arm injury." In summary, the BRB's analysis consisted of the following steps: first, the BRB made the legal determination that employers are liable for sequelae resulting from the original injury alleged in the claim filed; second, it found that Vickers [—4—] made a claim for sequelae, including his CIDP, by claiming injuries to "other parts of [his] body, [and] other related problems associated with [his] injury and working conditions in Iraq"; and third, it determined that the ALJ properly applied the presumption to conditions "that were part of the claim filed," including Vickers's CIDP, in light of Dr. Vaughan's testimony that Vickers's "disabling CIDP could have been precipitated by his initial arm injury or the subsequent surgeries therefore." Thus, it denied the motion for rehearing.

Plaintiffs timely filed a notice of appeal in the district court, challenging the benefits granted to Vickers for his CIDP, and asking it to reverse the BRB's decision as to this alleged claim. On February 29, 2012, the district court denied Plaintiffs' request for reversal and affirmed the BRB's decision.

Plaintiffs timely appealed to this court raising four issues concerning the benefits awarded to Vickers for his CIDP. First, Plaintiffs contend that the ALJ erred by not applying the *Amerada Hess* standard and correspondingly, by applying the Section 20(a) presumption to Vickers's CIDP, which, Plaintiffs claim, is a secondary condition to which the presumption does not apply. Second, Plaintiffs argue that the inclusion of a catch-all clause in Vickers's claim for compensation did not convert potential allegations of illness or secondary conditions (such as his CIDP) into primary claims subject to the Section 20(a) presumption. Third, Plaintiffs argue that the ALJ erred in finding that Vickers established a prima facie case through Dr. Vaughan's testimony, because Dr. Vaughan did not pinpoint the cause of Vickers's gastritis and polyneuropathy. Finally, Plaintiffs argue that the ALJ erred in finding that they did not offer substantial evidence to rebut Vickers's prima facie case, even though, they maintain, the record contains expert testimony that Vickers's CIDP was not related to his working conditions in Iraq. [—5—]

II. STANDARD OF REVIEW

In an appeal of a claim under the LHWCA as extended by the DBA, we review the decisions of the BRB to determine whether it adhered to the proper scope of review: namely, "whether the ALJ's findings of fact are supported by substantial evidence and are consistent with the law." *Gulf Best Elec., Inc. v. Methe*, 396 F.3d 601, 603 (5th Cir. 2004). Under the LHWCA, the BRB must uphold the factual findings of the ALJ if they are rational and supported by substantial evidence in the record taken as a whole. 33 U.S.C. § 921(b)(3); *Gulf Best*, 396 F.3d at 603. Substantial evidence is "that relevant evidence—more than a scintilla but less than a preponderance—that would cause a reasonable person to accept the fact finding." *Coastal Prod. Servs., Inc. v. Hudson*, 555 F.3d 426, 430 (5th Cir. 2009). As the factfinder, the ALJ is exclusively entitled to assess the weight of the evidence and credibility of witnesses. *Ceres Gulf, Inc. v. Dir., OWCP*, 683 F.3d 225, 228 (5th Cir. 2012) (citations omitted); *see Mendoza v. Marine Pers. Co.*, 46 F.3d 498, 500-01 (5th Cir. 1995) (citing *Mijangos v. Avondale Shipyards*, 948 F.2d 941, 945 (5th Cir. 1991) (holding that the BRB may not reweigh evidence or make its own credibility determinations)). We review the BRB's legal conclusions de novo. *Tarver v. Bo-Mac Contractors, Inc.*, 384 F.3d 180, 181 (5th Cir. 2004). Moreover, we accord no deference to the district court's conclusion as to whether the record supports the administrative determination. *H.B. Zachry Co. v. Quinones*, 206 F.3d 474, 477 (5th Cir. 2000).

III. DISCUSSION

Plaintiffs contend that the BRB erred in affirming the ALJ's decision as to Vickers's CIDP because the ALJ's findings with respect to this illness were unsupported by substantial evidence and inconsistent with the law. Plaintiffs raise four issues concerning Vickers's CIDP: (1) whether the ALJ's application of the Section 20(a) presumption to Vickers's CIDP was proper; (2) whether CIDP was properly included in Vickers's claim for compensation; (3) whether [—6—] Vickers made a prima facie case that his CIDP was a work-related injury; and (4) whether Plaintiffs presented substantial evidence in rebuttal of the presumption. We address the first and second issues together, and do the same for the third and fourth.

A. Section 20(a) Presumption

1. Relevant LHWCA Provisions

The LHWCA provides that "compensation shall be payable under this chapter in respect of disability . . . of an employee, but only if the disability . . . results from an injury occurring" at a covered situs. 33 U.S.C. § 903(a). "Disability" is defined, in relevant part, as an "incapacity because of injury." 33 U.S.C.

§902(10). And "injury" is defined as an "accidental injury or death arising out of and in the course of employment, and such occupational disease or infection as arises naturally out of such employment or as naturally or unavoidably results from such accidental injury . . . ." 33 U.S.C. § 902(2). The Supreme Court has determined that the phrases "arising out of" and "in the course of" are separate requirements for establishing an injury: "the former refers to injury causation; the latter refers to the time, place, and circumstances of the injury." *See U.S. Indus./Fed. Sheet Metal, Inc. v. Dir., OWCP*, 455 U.S. 608, 615, (1982) (hereinafter *U.S. Industries*). "Not only must the injury have been caused by the employment, it also must have arisen during the employment." *Id.* To make a claim for compensation under the LHWCA, an injured employee "must timely file a claim with the Deputy Commissioner" that gives notice of the injury and contains "a statement of the time, place, nature, and cause of the injury." *Id.* (quoting 33 U.S.C. §912(b)).

The LHWCA also specifies the order of proof in compensation cases. Section 20(a) of the Act provides: "[in] any proceeding for the enforcement of a claim for compensation under this chapter it shall be presumed, in the absence of substantial evidence to the contrary . . . [t]hat the claim comes within the [—7—] provisions of this chapter." 33 U.S.C. §920(a). To invoke the presumption, a claimant must offer a prima facie case that he (1) suffered a "harm," and (2) a workplace condition "could have caused, aggravated, or accelerated" the harm. *Conoco, Inc., v. Dir., OWCP*, 194 F.3d 684, 687 (5th Cir. 1999). If the claimant establishes a prima facie case, "the burden shifts to the employer to rebut it through facts—not mere speculation—that the harm was not work-related." *Id.* at 687-88. If the employer rebuts the presumption, it drops out of the case, and the ALJ must weigh the totality of the evidence to determine whether the injury arose out of the claimant's employment. *Del Vecchio v. Bowers*, 296 U.S. 280, 286-87 (1935); *see also U.S. Indus.*, 455 U.S. at 612 n.6 (noting that it seems fair to assume that the Section 20(a) presumption is of the same nature as the presumption created under Section 20(d) of the LHWCA, as construed in *Del Vecchio*); *Amerada Hess*, 543 F.3d at 761. Throughout this burden-shifting process, the claimant retains the burden of persuasion.

2. Amerada Hess

The ALJ applied the Section 20(a) presumption to Vickers's CIDP. In affirming the ALJ's decision, the BRB also found the presumption applicable. Plaintiffs argue that the BRB erred in affirming the ALJ's decision because Vickers's CIDP was not included in his claim, and at most was a secondary injury to which the Section 20(a) presumption does not apply under the reasoning in *Amerada Hess*. 543 F.3d at 761-62.

In *Amerada Hess*, the claimant sought benefits for a heart condition that allegedly resulted from treatment—steroid use and surgery—for work-related back and groin injuries. *Id.* at 758-59. The ALJ invoked the Section 20(a) presumption, found that the employer did not rebut the presumption, and awarded compensation and medical benefits related to claimant's heart condition. *Id.* at 759. The BRB affirmed, holding that if the claimant's heart [—8—] problems arose as a consequence of the steroid injections he received as treatment for his work injury, then his heart problems were work-related. *Id.*

We reversed the BRB's decision in that case for reasons that mirror the issues Plaintiffs now raise on appeal. First, we found that the ALJ and BRB erred in applying the Section 20(a) presumption to claimant's alleged heart condition because it was not part of his original claim, which was for his back and groin injury. *Id.* at 761 (noting that the presumption applies to the claim) (citing *U.S. Indus.*, 455 U.S. at 613). Second, we decided that the Section 20(a) presumption did not apply to claimant's heart condition because it was a secondary injury to which the presumption did not apply:

In sum, we hold that the statute does not support a presumption that any medical condition that an injured

claimant suffers after a work-related injury is caused by the work-related injury. Furthermore, not all "secondary" injuries are covered under the LHWCA simply because the claimant demonstrates a subsequent harm that could have stemmed from the covered injury. Instead, to receive benefits under the LHWCA for a subsequent injury, the claimant must present substantial evidence that the secondary condition "naturally or unavoidably" resulted from the first covered injury, as is required by the statute.

Id. at 763 (citation omitted). As discussed, Plaintiffs argue that Vickers did not refer to his CIDP in his claim, and that his CIDP is at most a secondary injury subject to the "naturally or unavoidably" causation standard we articulated in *Amerada Hess*. Since these issues are related, we address them together.

3. Analysis

Vickers's claim requested compensation for his arm injury of August 14, 2004, and for "other related problems associated with [this] injury and working conditions in Iraq." Plaintiffs argue that this catch-all clause did not convert potential allegations of illness or secondary conditions (such as his CIDP) into primary claims subject to the Section 20(a) presumption. We agree. [—9—]

The Supreme Court has stated clearly that the Section 20(a) presumption applies to the claim. *U.S. Indus.*, 455 U.S. at 612-13. In addition, the Court has stated that "[a] prima facie 'claim for compensation,' to which the statutory presumption refers, must at least allege an injury that arose in the course of employment as well as out of employment." *Id.* at 615. In other words, "the presumption cannot apply to a claim that has never been made." *Id.* at 614. Rather, the claim must contain "a statement of the time, place, nature, and cause of the injury." *Id* at 613. A general reference to a nonspecific injury or illness will not suffice:

This statement must be more than a mere declaration that the employee has received an injury or is suffering from an illness that is related to his employment; it must contain enough details about the nature and extent of the injury or disease to allow the employer to conduct a prompt and complete investigation of the claim so that no prejudice will ensue.

Id. at 613 n.6 (internal quotations and citation omitted). Although the Act's pleading requirements have some flexibility, "there is a point beyond which the sweeping-aside of 'technicalities' cannot go." *Id.* at 613 n.7. And in this case, Vickers's claim went beyond that threshold.

Vickers's claim for "other . . . problems associated with [his arm] injury and working conditions in Iraq" is exactly the sort of vague declaration that the Supreme Court in *U.S. Industries* deemed insufficient to constitute a "claim" to which the Section 20(a) presumption applies. Although Defendants maintain that this case is distinguishable from *U.S. Industries* in that the claimant in that case filed a claim for a specific injury, and did not leave open the possibility that the claim could include other, related injuries, this reasoning is unpersuasive. The conclusion that the vague allegations in that claim should not receive the statutory presumption was not contingent on the claimant's failure to allege a catch-all category of injury. Indeed, trying to differentiate these cases on this [—10—] basis requires circular reasoning (i.e., the catch-all statement in Vickers's claim is unproblematic because the claim in *U.S. Industries* did not involve a catch-all statement). *U.S. Industries* is apposite, and pursuant to the Court's reasoning therein, Vickers did not assert a primary claim for gastrointestinal symptoms or CIDP to which the Section 20(a) presumption applies.

Because the Section 20(a) presumption does not apply to Vickers's CIDP, the BRB and ALJ erred in applying it to that illness. Since Vickers's CIDP allegedly resulted from an autoimmune response owing to some combination of the gastritis he contracted in Iraq and the surgeries for his arm, they should have applied the more stringent "naturally or unavoidably" causation standard

used to assess whether secondary conditions are eligible for benefits. *See Amerada Hess*, 543 F.3d at 763. In *Amerada Hess*, we echoed the determination in *U.S. Industries* that the Section 20(a) presumption applies only to injuries specifically referenced in the claim. *Id.* at 761-62. Moreover *Amerada Hess* held that where the alleged injury does not arise "out of and in the course of" employment, it is a secondary injury subject to the "naturally or unavoidably" standard. *Id.* at 763. As we explained in *Amerada Hess*, the LHWCA "does not support a presumption that any medical condition that an injured claimant suffers after a work-related injury is caused by the work-related injury," and "not all 'secondary' injuries are covered under the LHWCA simply because the claimant demonstrates a subsequent harm that could have stemmed from the covered injury." *Id.* Rather, "to receive benefits under the LHWCA for a subsequent injury, the claimant must present substantial evidence that the secondary condition 'naturally or unavoidably' resulted from the first covered injury, as is required by the statute." *Id.*

Just as the claimant in *Amerada Hess* failed to reference a work-related injury in his claim, Vickers's description of "other related problems" was insufficient to trigger the Section 20(a) presumption. And just as in *Amerada* [—11—] *Hess*, where the claimant's heart problem was deemed "secondary," Vickers's CIDP is properly understood as a secondary injury because it allegedly arose from an autoimmune response to the surgeries related to his work-related arm injury referenced in the claim and the gastritis he allegedly contracted due to working conditions in Iraq. Accordingly, we hold that Vickers's CIDP is subject to the causation standard for secondary injuries. *Id.* at 761-62. In order to recover for his CIDP, Vickers must "present substantial evidence" that it "'naturally or unavoidably' resulted from the first covered injury"—namely, his arm injury. *Id.* at 763. Whether his CIDP "naturally or unavoidably" resulted from his work-related arm injury is a question for the ALJ to decide on remand.

B. Prima Facie Case and Rebuttal

Because the preceding analysis forms the basis for our judgment, we do not need to address the final two issues that Plaintiffs have raised: that the ALJ erred in finding that Vickers established a prima facie case through Dr. Vaughan's testimony, and that the ALJ erred in finding that Plaintiffs did not present substantial evidence in rebuttal concerning Vickers's prima facie case. These issues involve the application of the Section 20(a) presumption, which does not apply to Vickers's CIDP for the reasons discussed.

IV. CONCLUSION

For the reasons provided, we REVERSE the BRB's decision and order, VACATE the ALJ's award of temporary total disability benefits for Vickers's CIDP, and REMAND to the ALJ for a determination of whether his CIDP naturally or unavoidably resulted from his work-related arm injury.

[—12—] GRAVES, Circuit Judge, concurring.:

I agree with the majority that *Amerada Hess* mandates reversal. Nevertheless, I believe the *Amerada Hess* majority erred in finding that the presumption created by §20(a) of the LHWCA is inapplicable to a "secondary" injury or an injury not expressly listed on the original claim form. In that connection, I find Judge Reavley's concurrence persuasive. *See Amerada Hess Corp. v. Dir., OWCP*, 543 F.3d 755, 764-66 (5th Cir. 2008) (Reavley, J., concurring) (noting that, for purposes of the § 20(a) presumption, because worker's injury listed on original claim form arose out of his employment, "any injury resulting from treatment for that injury should also be presumed to have arisen out of the employment and the primary injury.").

United States Court of Appeals
for the Fifth Circuit

No. 12-30474

MIKE HOOKS DREDGING CO.
VS.
MARQUETTE TRANSPORT. GULF-INLAND, L.L.C.

Appeal from the United States District Court for the
Eastern District of Louisiana

Decided: May 21, 2013

Citation: 716 F.3d 886, 1 Adm. R. 252 (5th Cir. 2013).

Before JOLLY, GARZA, and OWEN, Circuit Judges.

[—1—] JOLLY, Circuit Judge:

This admiralty appeal challenges the district court's finding of liability arising from an allision in the Gulf Intracoastal Waterway ("ICW"). The dredge [—2—] MIKE HOOKS[1] was operating in the ICW under its contract with the Army Corps of Engineers when it was struck by a passing vessel, the PAT MCDANIEL,[2] while the dredge was moored on the bank of the narrow Wax Lake intersection undergoing repairs. We agree with the district court and hold that the MIKE HOOKS violated Inland Navigation Rule 9 ("INR 9") by mooring in a narrow channel; and that the violation triggered the rule of *The Pennsylvania*, 86 U.S. (19 Wall.) 125 (1873), shifting the burden of proving causation to the dredge. Because Hooks failed to rebut the presumption of causation by demonstrating that the dredge was not a cause of the allision,[3] we AFFIRM the district court's judgment holding Hooks partially liable.

The district court apportioned liability for the allision among three parties: (1) Hooks

(the MIKE HOOKS) was found 70 percent liable; (2) Eckstein (the PAT MCDANIEL) was found 30 percent liable; and (3) the Tommie Vizier Towing Company ("Vizier"), owner of the CAP'N TOMMIE VIZIER JR., was found "50 percent liable for Hooks's claims against Eckstein." The court's order further stated that "Eckstein is liable for a total of 15 percent of the damages and Vizier is liable for a total of 15 percent of the damages." We find that the district court committed no error in finding Hooks 70 percent liable and thus AFFIRM the allocation of fault.

I.

The MIKE HOOKS was moored on the north bank of the ICW near the intersection with the Wax Lake outlet undergoing repairs at the time of the [—3—] allision. The PAT MCDANIEL, along with its six barges, allided with the stationary dredge. Hooks was operating the dredge in the ICW under a contract with the Army Corps of Engineers for the purpose of completing various dredging projects in the ICW. The contract required Hooks to "provide one 1200hp towboat to serve as picket boat to assist passing traffic and/or to assist the dredge." This provision applied when the dredge was going to be at certain project locations known to be dangerous. The Wax Lake intersection was one such location. At the time of the allision, Hooks had hired the CAP'N TOMMIE VIZIER JR. to serve as the dredge's picket boat.

Around 1:35 a.m. on May 31, 2008, the MIKE HOOKS arrived at the project location near the Wax Lake intersection and began setting up near the middle of the channel in anticipation of beginning operations. The Wax Lake intersection is prone to dangerous currents and eddies. Indeed, at 2:15 a.m., a vessel ran aground on the south bank, which the picket boat helped free. And, between 3:50 and 4:20 a.m., two other vessels came "within inches from hitting the dredge." Then, around 4:20 a.m., a tow, the SARAH D, collided with the MIKE HOOKS, causing a starboard-side hole. The MIKE HOOKS subsequently was moved to the northwest corner of the Wax Lake intersection, and the crew began making

---

[1] The MIKE HOOKS was owned and operated by Mike Hooks Dredging Company, Inc. ("Hooks").

[2] The PAT MCDANIEL was owned and operated by Eckstein Marine Services, Inc. ("Eckstein"). Eckstein was the predecessor of Marquette Transportation Gulf-Inland, LLC.

[3] Black's Law Dictionary defines "allision" as: "The contact of a vessel with a stationary object such as an anchored vessel or a pier." BLACK'S LAW DICTIONARY 88 (9th ed. 2009).

repairs.[4] Evidence did not conclusively establish the width of the channel where the MIKE HOOKS moored, but it was between 400 and 800 feet.

Despite the near misses with other vessels and the actual collision with the SARAH D, the MIKE HOOKS captain did not inform the approaching PAT MCDANIEL about the earlier incidents.[5] And, due to high water and existing [—4—] weather conditions, there was a stronger-than-normal current on May 31. Based on the current, in order for vessels successfully to navigate the Wax Lake intersection, they had first to steer toward the north bank so that when the current pushed them south they would not run aground on the south bank. The MIKE HOOKS's position thus caused westbound vessels, like the PAT MCDANIEL, to steer directly at the dredge to navigate the Wax Lake intersection.

Around 9:15 a.m., the PAT MCDANIEL allided with the dredge. The allision occurred during daylight, and visibility was good. The PAT MCDANIEL captain was aware of the relevant weather and current conditions when he decided to cross the Wax Lake intersection, but he remained unaware of the early morning incidents involving the MIKE HOOKS—evidence showed that there was very little, if any, communication among the MIKE HOOKS, the PAT MCDANIEL, and the picket boat. The PAT MCDANIEL captain testified that he misjudged the current and ultimately allided with the MIKE HOOKS.

The picket boat also played a role in the allision. The contract provision requiring Hooks to employ a picket boat to assist passing traffic meant that the picket boat physically had to assist the PAT MCDANIEL

in avoiding the MIKE HOOKS.[6] In addition, Hooks knew that the picket boat would not physically assist passing traffic before the MIKE HOOKS was moved to the Wax Lake intersection. An earlier collision at a different location with another vessel had resulted in a discussion between the MIKE HOOKS and the picket boat about the need to aid passing vessels. The picket boat captain stated that he would communicate with passing traffic, but would not physically assist them. With [—5—] the knowledge that the picket boat would not provide physical assistance, the MIKE HOOKS nonetheless proceeded on to the Wax Lake intersection.

Hooks filed suit in admiralty in the Eastern District of Louisiana against a number of parties. With respect to Eckstein, Hooks alleged that the PAT MCDANIEL was in violation of a number of INRs and thus at fault. Eckstein counterclaimed alleging both statutory and INR violations by Hooks, and further brought third-party claims against Vizier pursuant to Federal Rule of Civil Procedure 14(c), arguing that Vizier was responsible for all of Hooks's claims against Eckstein. After a bench trial, the district court found all three parties partially liable. Only Hooks has appealed.

II.

"The standard of review for a bench trial is well established: findings of fact are reviewed for clear error and legal issues are reviewed *de novo*." *Mid- South Towing Co. v. Exmar Lux*, 418 F.3d 526, 531 (5th Cir. 2005) (quoting *Kona Tech Corp. v. S. Pac. Transp. Co.*, 225 F.3d 595, 601 (5th Cir. 2000)) (internal quotation marks omitted). Findings of fact are clearly erroneous only when a review of the record leaves a "definite and firm conviction that a mistake has been made." *Stolt Achievement v. Dredge B.E. Lindholm*, 447 F.3d 360, 363 (5th Cir. 2006). "If the district court's account of the evidence is plausible in light of the record, this [c]ourt may not reverse, even though convinced that had it

---

[4] Trial testimony indicated that the dredge was basically on the bank, dropping its spuds around two feet in order to anchor.

[5] The only contact between the MIKE HOOKS and the PAT MCDANIEL appears to have been the formation of an agreement for the PAT MCDANIEL to "pass on the two whistles." Testimony established that this phrase refers to a starboard passing agreement.

[6] At trial, Hooks took the position that physical assistance was not required under the contract, but this contention was not supported by any of the testimony, including from its own witnesses.

been sitting as the trier of fact, it would have weighed the evidence differently." *Id.* at 363-64.

III.

A.

We will first turn our attention to Hooks's argument that the district court erred in applying *The Pennsylvania* presumption against the MIKE HOOKS. The rule of *The Pennsylvania* has its origin in a seminal admiralty case, in which the Supreme Court established the burden-shifting presumption for causation [—6—] when a vessel "at the time of a collision is in actual violation of a statutory rule intended to prevent collisions." 86 U.S. (19 Wall.) 125, 136 (1873). "In such a case the burden rests upon the ship of showing not merely that her fault might not have been one of the causes, or that it probably was not, *but that it could not have been.*" *Id.* (emphasis added); *see also Tokio Marine & Fire Ins. Co. v. FLORA MV*, 235 F.3d 963, 966 (5th Cir. 2001). "The rule thus creates a presumption that one who violates a regulation intended to prevent collisions will be deemed responsible." *Tokio Marine*, 235 F.3d at 966. The presumption, however, is rebuttable and "applies only to violations of statutes that delineate a clear legal duty." *Id.*

B.

We agree with the district court that INR 9(g) establishes such a clear legal duty. The regulation expressly prohibits vessels from anchoring in narrow channels, except in exceptional circumstances. Given the facts of the instant case, which we shall shortly discuss, we hold that the district court did not clearly err in applying *The Pennsylvania* rule against Hooks. Furthermore, because Hooks failed to show "that [the MIKE HOOKS] could not have been" a cause of the allision, Hooks did not rebut the presumption of causation. *The Pennsylvania*, 86 U.S. (19 Wall.) at 136. Accordingly, based on these findings, the district court thus did not err in holding Hooks partially liable as a result.

Originally enacted by Congress,[7] the INRs established the "rules of the road" for proper navigation based on long-standing principles and were intended to prevent collisions in inland waterways. Indeed, the INRs "apply to all vessels upon the inland waters of the United States." 33 C.F.R. § 83.01(a) (INR 1). INR 9 sets forth the rules for vessels operating in narrow channels. 33 C.F.R. § [—7—] 83.09. Subsection (g) states, "Avoidance of anchoring in narrow channels. Every vessel shall, if the circumstances of the case admit, avoid anchoring in a narrow channel." *Id.*; *see also* 33 C.F.R. 83.02(b) (Rule 2) ("In construing and complying with these Rules due regard shall be had to all dangers of navigation and collision and to any special circumstances, including the limitations of the vessels involved, which may make a departure from these Rules necessary to avoid immediate danger."). As part of the INR's overall scheme to manage the risk of collisions, INR 9(g) plainly imparts a clear legal duty on vessels to avoid mooring in narrow channels absent special circumstances. Violation of such a regulation is sufficient to trigger the rule of *The Pennsylvania*.

Although the INRs do not define "narrow channel," we have held that the term generally includes bodies of water that are less than 1,000 feet in width. *See Marine Transp. Lines v. M/V TAKO INVADER*, 37 F.3d 1138, 1142-43 (5th Cir. 1994) (noting that "the determination of what is a 'narrow channel' is a mixed question of law and fact"). Here, the Wax Lake intersection admittedly was less than 1,000 feet wide, and the district court made specific factual findings regarding the dangers associated with the intersection, including the existence of high water conditions, strong currents and eddies, and high winds. The district court thus did not clearly err in finding that the area where the MIKE HOOKS moored was a narrow channel. Hooks, however, raises two arguments as to

---

[7] The Inland Navigational Rules Act of 1980, Pub. L. No. 96-591, which codified the INRs at 33 U.S.C. §§ 2001-2038, was repealed in 2010. The current rules subsequently were promulgated as Part 83 of Title 33 of the Code of Federal Regulations.

why the district court erred in finding that the MIKE HOOKS was in violation of INR 9(g).

(1)

Initially, Hooks asserts that INR 9(g) is inapplicable unless the vessel first is found to be an obstruction of navigation. Hooks bases its argument primarily on *Self Towing, Inc. v. Brown Marine Services*, 837 F.2d 1501 (11th Cir. 1988), [—8—] in which the Eleventh Circuit evaluated the statutory predecessor to INR 9(g)[8] and held that, "The touchstone for a violation under [INR 9(g) and other statutory provisions] is that the offending vessel obstructed the passage of another vessel." *Id.* at 1504. The court's interpretation, however, was in large part premised on a Senate Report, which stated that "Rule 9(g) . . . is essentially an embodiment of existing law," before quoting the text of Rivers and Harbors Act § 409. S. Rep. No. 96-979 ("Section 409 of the title 33, U.S.C. states: it shall not be lawful to tie up or anchor barges or other craft in navigable channels in such a manner as to prevent or obstruct the passage of other vessels or craft."); *see also Self Towing*, 837 F.2d at 1504 n.6. We find *Self Towing* unpersuasive and decline to adopt its interpretation of INR 9(g).

In determining that INR 9(g) required an antecedent finding that a vessel was an obstruction of navigation in order for the rule to be violated, *Self Towing* departed from the plain wording of the statute. As noted above, INR 9(g) states only that: "Every vessel shall, if the circumstances of the case admit, avoid anchoring in a narrow channel." 33 C.F.R. §83.09(g). "[O]ur inquiry begins with the statutory text, and ends there as well if the text is unambiguous." *E.g., BedRoc Ltd. v. United States*, 541 U.S. 176, 183 (2004); *In re Amy Unknown*, 701 F.3d 749, 760 (5th Cir. 2012) (en banc) ("Where 'the words of a statute are unambiguous, then, this first canon is also the last: judicial inquiry is complete.'" (quoting *Conn. Nat'l Bank v. Germain*, 503 U.S. 249, 254 (1992)) (internal quotation marks omitted)).

INR 9(g) is unambiguous. The rule ("shall . . . avoid") expressly prohibits vessels from anchoring in narrow channels, subject only to the exception where circumstances do not permit alternative action. And, whether circumstances excuse an otherwise clear violation of INR 9(g) obviously turns on the facts and [—9—] must be resolved on a case-by-case basis. Although INR 9(g) violations may likely occur when one of the vessels arguably was an obstruction to navigation, INR 9(g) certainly does not mandate the district court to first adjudge the moored vessel to be an obstruction. Indeed, nothing in INR 9 suggests an obstruction requirement. The MIKE HOOKS therefore violated INR 9(g) unless the prior incident with the SARAH D qualified as a circumstance excepting the dredge from the general rule.

(2)

We thus turn to Hooks's second argument that the district court clearly erred in finding that the MIKE HOOKS could have been moved to an alternative mooring location. In short, Hooks argues that the starboard-side hole in the dredge was a sufficient factual condition to allow it to anchor in the narrow Wax Lake intersection. Hooks's argument essentially is based on our decision in *Crescent Towing & Salvage Co. v. CHIOS BEAUTY MV*, 610 F.3d 263 (5th Cir. 2010), in which we noted that the decisions of imperiled parties are entitled to deference. *See id.* at 267-68. We stated that, "It has long been the law that errors in judgment committed by a vessel put in sudden peril through no fault of her own are to be leniently judged. . . . Courts are not supposed to second guess parties in peril and expect from them the most precise judgments." *Id.* at 267 (alteration in original) (citation omitted). *Crescent Towing*, however, involved a challenge to the appropriate negligence standard of care, with the vessel arguing that the district court should have applied the *in extremis* standard. *Id.* at 268. No such argument is raised in the instant case.[9] And, although we recognize the general

---

[8] The text of the statute and the current regulation are identical.

[9] Indeed, Hooks's decision to proceed to the Wax Lake intersection with a picket boat that it knew would not physically assist passing traffic may

proposition that imperiled parties should not be second-guessed by courts, the district court carefully reviewed the evidence [—10—] with respect to the situation the MIKE HOOKS faced following the SARAH D collision.

Substantial testimony was offered regarding the dangerous weather and current conditions in the Wax Lake intersection, and the amount of damage caused to the dredge by the SARAH D collision. Witnesses testified that "[i]t was high water season at the time of the allision," and that "the Wax Lake intersection has strong currents and eddies which are stronger during high water season and in windy conditions." Evidence showed that Hooks was aware of these conditions, which caused "passing vessels [to] actively steer toward the north," directly towards the moored dredge. As to the damage suffered by the MIKE HOOKS, Ricky Domengue, the captain of the MIKE HOOKS, testified that there was a "crack above the water level of the dredge," but "there was no imminent danger of it sinking." Despite Hooks's assertion that the MIKE HOOKS was in serious peril, the evidence supports the district court's conclusion that the dredge was not in an emergency situation that excused its violation of INR 9(g). The district court thus did not commit clear error in finding that the dredge could have been moved to an alternative location without a high risk of additional damage.

(3)

In connection with its argument that the district court clearly erred in its finding relating to the availability of alternative mooring locations, Hooks also contends that the district court erred by relying on the testimony of David Scruton, Eckstein's marine navigation expert. At trial, Hooks objected that Scruton was not qualified to be an expert witness because he had never operated a boat in the ICW, he was not licensed to "operate a vessel under the U.S. Coast Guard Rules of the Road," and he was not licensed to do

anything in the United States. The district court overruled the objection. [—11—]

Challenges to the admission of an individual as an expert witness under *Daubert v. Merrell Dow Pharmaceuticals, Inc.*, 509 U.S. 579 (1993), are reviewed for an abuse of discretion. *Kumho Tire Co. v. Carmichael*, 526 U.S. 137, 142 (1999). Scruton testified that he was licensed in the United Kingdom and worked under similar circumstances in Europe, Africa, and the Far East; he had over forty years of maritime experience. Although Scruton did not have practical experience concerning the ICW, Hooks has not demonstrated that the district court abused its discretion in admitting Scruton as an expert witness given his extensive experience with maritime navigation.

Moreover, Scruton's testimony regarding alternative mooring locations was based on a chart of the Wax Lake intersection that had already been admitted into evidence.[10] He identified several mooring basins nearby in which the MIKE HOOKS could have moored and been outside of the narrow channel. Scruton further testified that, based on his experience, it would not have taken long to move the dredge to one of the mooring basins. And, he stated that moving the dredge out of the dangerous Wax Lake intersection was the prudent thing to do in the situation.

After careful consideration of all relevant testimony, the district court concluded that, although the MIKE HOOKS was damaged in the SARAH D incident, the damage was not so extensive that it excused the MIKE HOOKS's decision to moor in a narrow channel in violation of INR 9(g). We cannot say that the district court clearly erred in reaching its conclusion. The MIKE HOOKS violated INR 9(g); *The Pennsylvania* rule thus applied; and Hooks failed to show that the dredge could not have been a cause of the allision. The district court therefore properly found Hooks partially liable. [—12—]

---

deprive the MIKE HOOKS of the deference described in *Crescent Towing*.

---

[10] At trial, Hooks did not object to the specific testimony regarding other potential mooring locations.

IV.

Having concluded that the district court did not err in finding Hooks liable, we turn now to the district court's apportionment of liability among Hooks, Eckstein, and Vizier. We review the district court's apportionment of fault for clear error. *Tokio Marine*, 235 F.3d at 970.

Hooks argues that, "It is a misapplication of the law to give Eckstein a 50% credit for Vizier's fault when the comparative fault findings in the [district court opinion] as to Eckstein and Vizier are clear and concise." The district court order initially stated that Hooks was 70 percent liable and Eckstein 30 percent liable. The district court further found, however, that Vizier "is 50 percent liable for Hooks's claims against Eckstein. Accordingly, Eckstein is liable for a total of 15 percent of the damages and Vizier is liable for a total of 15 percent of the damages."

Hooks's arguments under Federal Rule of Civil Procedure 14(c) are meritless. Rule 14(c)(1) expressly provides that the third-party defendant, Vizier, may be liable to either the plaintiff, Hooks, or the third-party plaintiff, Eckstein. Here, the district court held Vizier liable for 50 percent of the claims against Eckstein. Hooks has not demonstrated, nor cited any caselaw showing, why such an apportionment of fault is not supported under Rule 14(c), and such an apportionment is not otherwise clearly erroneous. We thus affirm the district court's order finding Hooks 70 percent at fault.

V.

For the reasons stated above, the district court's judgment of liability with respect to Hooks is, in all respects,

AFFIRMED.

United States Court of Appeals
for the Fifth Circuit

No. 11-31030

IN RE SETTOON TOWING, L.L.C.

Appeal from the United States District Court for the
Eastern District of Louisiana

Decided: June 18, 2013

Citation: 720 F.3d 268, 1 Adm. R. 258 (5th Cir. 2013).

Before **STEWART**, Chief Judge, and **GARZA** and
ELROD, Circuit Judges.

[—2—] **GARZA**, Circuit Judge:

This appeal arises out of an allision between the M/V CATHY M. SETTOON (the "CATHY"), a vessel owned by Settoon Towing, L.L.C. ("Settoon"), and an oil well. Settoon appeals the district court's grant of summary judgment in favor of New York Marine and General Insurance Company ("NYMAGIC"), Federal Insurance Company ("Federal"), and St. Paul Fire & Marine Insurance Company ("St. Paul") (together, the "umbrella insurers"), concluding the umbrella insurers are not liable to Settoon for damages resulting from the allision. State National Insurance Company ("SNIC") cross-appeals the district court's grant of summary judgment in favor of Settoon, finding SNIC liable to Settoon for damages and prejudgment interest resulting from the allision. We AFFIRM the district court's judgment in all respects except for the calculation of prejudgment interest. We REVERSE and REMAND for calculation of prejudgment interest in a manner consistent with this opinion. [—3—]

I

On January, 20, 2007, the CATHY struck an oil well in Bayou Perot, Louisiana, causing damage to the wellhead and uncontrolled discharge of oil into the water. The captain of the CATHY did not report the allision to the United States Coast Guard or to Settoon. The next day, the captain of the M/V CHERYL SETTOON, another vessel owned by Settoon, saw the oil spill as it passed by the allision site and reported the spill to the Coast Guard and Settoon's management. The Coast Guard conducted an investigation, and the captain of the CATHY initially denied involvement. When the Coast Guard confronted him with a reconstruction of the allision from the CATHY's tracking system on February 23, 2007, thirty-four days after the allision, the captain of the CATHY admitted involvement. Settoon notified its insurers of the event on February 26, 2007, thirty-seven days after the allision.

Three insurance policies belonging to Settoon are at issue in this litigation, all of which provide excess insurance coverage over Settoon's underlying primary policies. SNIC insures the first layer bumbershoot policy ("Bumbershoot 1"), which provides the first $4,000,000 of excess coverage. SNIC sent Settoon a binder for this policy on November 8, 2006, listing the underlying insurance policies and indicating the policy included a "Pollution Liability" endorsement. The binder included a "Conditions" section that stated, "Warranted copies of all underlying policies scheduled in item 5, received within 60 days of attachment." We interpret this as a requirement that Settoon send SNIC the full texts of its underlying policies. The "Conditions" section also stated, "All coverages scheduled to remain in force for the entire term . . . ." The binder stated the insurance policy was effective from November 2, 2006 to November 2, 2007. [—4—]

On December 13, 2006, SNIC contacted Settoon stating several items were needed to issue the policy, including copies of the underlying policies and the premium payment. On December 28, 2006, SNIC contacted Settoon stating SNIC received the premium payment but still required the underlying policies, among other items. On January 10, 2007, SNIC contacted Settoon again stating it required the underlying policies to issue the insurance policy. On January 23, 2007, three days after the allision, SNIC contacted Settoon again stating it needed the underlying policies to issue the insurance policy. On February 7, 2007, SNIC contacted Settoon again stating it needed the underlying policies to issue the policy. SNIC received all the underlying policies by March 1, 2007, and sent Settoon the Bumbershoot 1 policy on March 2, 2007.

Bumbershoot 1 begins by defining the general scope of the agreement in Section I-A, titled "Coverage." In relevant part, the Coverage section reads:

The Policy shall indemnify the Insured . . . for the following . . . :

1) All Protection and Indemnity risks covered by the underlying Protection and Indemnity Insurance . . . .

2) . . . marine collision liabilities . . . .

3) All other sums which the Insured shall become legally liable to pay as damages on account of . . . b. property damage . . . .

Section III of Bumbershoot 1 is titled "Exclusions." In relevant part, the Exclusions section reads: "This insurance does not apply to . . . xi. Any liability for, or any loss, damage, injury or expense caused by, resulting from or incurred by reason of: . . . f. pollution liability." One of the endorsements attached to the policy is titled "Pollution Liability," which reads:

This endorsement forms a part of the policy to which it is attached. . . . [—5—]

Exclusion xi.f. "Pollution Liability" of this policy shall not apply, however, provided that the Insured establishes that all of the following conditions have been met:

. . .

C) The discharge, dispersal, release or escape became known to the Insured within 72 hours after its commencement.

D) The discharge, dispersal, release or escape was reported in writing to these underwriters within 21

days after having become known to the Insured.

. . .

Coverage, if any, provided by the endorsement will:

A) Apply only if such coverage is also provided in the underlying insurance(s) . . . .

. . .

Such coverage, however, shall only apply excess of valid and collectible underlying insurance.

All other terms and conditions remaining unaltered.

NYMAGIC insures the second bumbershoot policy ("Bumbershoot 2"), which provides $5,000,000 over Bumbershoot 1. The first section under the heading "Insuring Agreement" in Bumbershoot 2 is titled "Coverage" and reads in pertinent part:

This Policy is to indemnify the "Assured" in respect of the following . . .

(a) All Protection and Indemnity risks....

(b) . . . Collision . . . Liabilit[y] . . . .

(c) All other sums which the "Assured" shall become legally liable to pay . . . in respect of claims made against the "Assured" for damages . . . on account of . . . "Property Damage" .... [—6—]

Under the heading "Exclusions" Bumbershoot 2 states:

This Policy Shall Not Apply: –

1. To any claim directly or indirectly in consequence of the actual or potential discharge, dispersal, release, or escape of smoke, vapors, soot, fumes, acids, alkalis, petroleum products or derivatives, liquids or gases, waste materials, sewerage or other toxic

chemicals, irritants, contaminants or pollutants into or upon land, atmosphere or any watercourse or body of water.

Under the heading "Conditions" Bumbershoot 2 lists, among other conditions, the following:

9. NOTICE OF OCCURRENCE: Whenever the "Assured" has information from which the "Assured" may reasonably conclude that an "occurrence" covered hereunder involved injuries or damages which, in the event that the "Assured" should be held liable, is likely to involve this policy, notice shall be sent as soon as practicable to the Company, provided, however, that failure to notify the Company of any "occurrence" which at the time of its happening did not appear to involve this Policy, but which, at a later date, would appear to give rise to claims hereunder, shall not prejudice such claims.

Endorsement #8, attached to Bumbershoot 2 and titled "Follow-Form Pollution Endorsement (Sudden & Accidental Limitation)," further explains the pollution exclusion and provides a buyback. The endorsement states in relevant part:

I. ABSOLUTE POLLUTION EXCLUSION

(A) In consideration of the premium charged, it is hereby agreed that this policy shall not apply to any liability for . . . "property damage" . . . arising out of the . . . "release" of "pollutants" into . . . any watercourse, water supply, reservoir or body of water.

It is further agreed that the intent and effect of this exclusion is to delete from any and all coverage's afforded by this policy any "occurrence", claim, suit, cause of action, liability, settlement, [—7—] judgment, defense costs or expenses in any way arising out of such "release" . . . .

. . .

II. SUDDEN AND ACCIDENTAL BUYBACK

(A) It is hereby agreed that the above Absolute Exclusion shall not apply provided that the Named Assured establishes that all of the following conditions have been met:

. . .

(4) The occurrence became known to the assured within 72 hours after its commencement.

(5) The occurrence was reported in writing to those underwriters within 30 days after having become known to the assured.

. . .

ALL OTHER TERMS AND CONDITIONS REMAINING UNCHANGED.

NYMAGIC, Federal, and St. Paul insure the third bumbershoot policy ("Bumbershoot 3"), which provides $40,000,000 over Bumbershoot 2. The second section under the heading "Excess Bumbershoot Liability" in Bumbershoot 3 is titled "Coverage" and reads in pertinent part:

The company hereby agrees, subject to the limitations, terms and conditions hereinafter mentioned, to indemnify the Assured in respect of the following:

A. All Protection and Indemnity risks of whatsoever nature covered by the underlying Bumbershoot policies.

B. . . . Collision Liabilities . . . .

C. All other sums which the Assured shall become legally liable to pay . . . in respect of claims made against the Assured for damages of whatsoever nature, on account of: [—8—]

. . .

2) Property Damage . . . .

The fourth section under the "Excess Bumbershoot Liability" heading is titled "Conditions" and lists, among other conditions, the following "Notice of Occurrence" condition:

> Whenever the Assured has information from which the Assured may reasonably conclude that an occurrence covered hereunder involved injuries or damages which, in the event that the Assured should be held liable, is likely to involve this policy, notice shall be sent to the Company as soon as practicable, provided, however, that failure to notify the Company of any occurrence which at the time of its happening did not appear to involve this Policy, but which, at a later date, would appear to give rise to claims hereunder, shall not prejudice such claims.

Endorsement #8 attached to Bumbershoot 3 is exactly the same as Endorsement #8 attached to Bumbershoot 2, containing the same "ABSOLUTE POLLUTION EXCLUSION" and "SUDDEN AND ACCIDENTAL BUYBACK" provisions as reproduced in relevant part above.

The insurers sought a declaratory judgment that they are not liable for the losses arising out of the allision because Settoon did not meet the requirements in the endorsements, which would have provided the pollution liability excluded by the pollution exclusions. The parties filed cross-motions for partial summary judgment. The district court made three holdings: 1) the umbrella insurers are not liable on the Bumbershoot 2 and Bumbershoot 3 policies because Settoon did not comply with the 72-hour knowledge and 30-day notice provisions in the buybacks; 2) SNIC is liable on the Bumbershoot 1 policy because it delayed delivery of the policy to Settoon; and 3) SNIC is liable for prejudgment interest beginning on the date Settoon made judicial demand. [—9—]

II

We review grants of summary judgment de novo, applying the same standards as the district court. *Burge v. Parish of St. Tammany*, 187 F.3d 452, 464 (5th Cir. 1999). "[T]he party moving for summary judgment must 'demonstrate the absence of a genuine issue of material fact . . . .'" *Little v. Liquid Air Corp.*, 37 F.3d 1069, 1075 (5th Cir. 1994) (quoting *Celotex Corp. v. Catrett*, 477 U.S. 317, 323 (1986)). "An issue is 'genuine' if the evidence is sufficient for a reasonable jury to return a verdict for the nonmoving party." *Hamilton v. Segue Software, Inc.*, 232 F.3d 473, 477 (5th Cir. 2000) (per curiam) (citing *Anderson v. Liberty Lobby, Inc.*, 477 U.S. 242, 248 (1986)). A fact issue is "material" if its resolution could affect the outcome of the action. *Hamilton*, 232 F.3d at 477 (citing *Anderson*, 477 U.S. at 248). When reviewing summary judgment decisions, we construe all facts and inferences in the light most favorable to the non-moving party. *Cooper Tire & Rubber Co. v. Farese*, 423 F.3d 446, 454 (5th Cir. 2005).

We review interpretations of insurance policies de novo. *Old Republic Ins. Co. v. Comprehensive Health Care Assocs., Inc.*, 2 F.3d 105, 107 (5th Cir. 1993). Likewise, we review interpretations of state law de novo, *Bayou Steel Corp. v. Nat'l Union Fire Ins. Co. of Pittsburgh, Pa.*, 642 F.3d 506, 509 (5th Cir. 2011), "resolving questions of Louisiana law the way the Louisiana Supreme Court would interpret the statute based upon prior precedent, legislation, and relevant commentary." *Commerce & Indus. Ins. Co. v. Grinnell Corp.*, 280 F.3d 566, 570 (5th Cir. 2002) (internal quotation marks omitted). [—10—]

III

Settoon asserts the umbrella insurers are liable despite Settoon's failure to provide them notice within 30 days. To provide the pollution liability excluded by the pollution exclusion, Bumbershoot 2 and Bumbershoot 3 require the following condition be met in the pollution endorsement: "(5) The occurrence was reported in writing to those underwriters within 30 days after having become known to the assured." Settoon asserts its non-compliance with the 30-day notice provision is not cause for barring liability for three reasons: 1) the insurers must, but cannot, show they were prejudiced by the delay; 2) when the 30-day notice provision is read alongside the general "Notice of Occurrence" provision in the Bumbershoot 3 policy, it is clear that delays beyond 30 days are permitted when the insured does not immediately realize the occurrence gives rise to a claim; and 3) Louisiana's doctrine of impossibility excuses Settoon's failure to provide notice within 30 days. Settoon is mistaken on all three counts; the umbrella insurers are not liable because Settoon failed to provide notice within 30 days.

A

First, Settoon asserts the insurers are required to, but cannot, show prejudice from the delay. The parties rely on Texas law a great deal in debating whether the insurers must show prejudice resulting from the late notice. This case arises under Louisiana law, so Texas law is informative but not controlling. In interpreting Texas law, we have drawn a distinction between "occurrence" policies, where "any notice requirement is subsidiary to the event that triggers coverage," and "claims-made" policies, where "notice itself constitutes the event that triggers coverage," in deciding whether the insurer is required to show [—11—] prejudice as a result of late notice. *See Matador Petroleum Corp. v. St. Paul Surplus Lines Ins. Co.*, 174 F.3d 653, 658–59 (5th Cir. 1999). *Matador* involved a 30-day notice provision in a pollution buyback very similar to the one at issue here, and we held, "The nature of St. Paul's and Matador's bargain . . . resembles the nature of the bargain underlying a 'claims-made' policy. Accordingly, we see no reason to apply a prejudice requirement and not to hold the parties to the specific terms of their bargain." *Id.* at 659; *see also Certain Underwriters at Lloyd's London v. C.A. Turner Constr. Co.*, 112 F.3d 184, 189 (5th Cir. 1997) (interpreting Texas law to require strict compliance with notice provision in pollution endorsement where pollution exclusion was clear). In a pair of decisions after *Matador*, the

Texas Supreme Court held that even in claims-made policies, insurers must show prejudice to defeat liability where the insured does not comply with a notice provision that is a condition precedent in the main body of the policy. *Fin. Indus. Corp. v. XL Specialty Ins. Co.*, 285 S.W.3d 877, 879 (Tex. 2009); *Prodigy Commc'ns Corp. v. Agric. Excess & Surplus Ins. Co.*, 288 S.W.3d 374, 375 (Tex. 2009). Those cases applied Texas law and did not address notice provisions in endorsements.

Only one Louisiana case has addressed the interpretation of notice provisions in exceptions to exclusions under Louisiana law, but then only tangentially. *Smith v. Reliance Ins. Co. of Il.*, 807 So. 2d 1010, 1023 (La. Ct. App. 2002) (Daley, J., concurring). The concurring opinion contrasted the position of the insurer in that case, which cited *Matador* for the proposition that notice requirements in buyback endorsements must be strictly construed, with the position of the insured, which asserted Louisiana law, unlike the Texas law holding in *Matador*, requires a showing of prejudice. *Id.* The concurring opinion [—12—] explicitly recognized Louisiana law does not squarely answer the question: "This unresolved question of law, whether to strictly apply the notice requirements of a Limited Buy Back Endorsement, is an issue upon which the trial court has not yet ruled. This [is an] open question of law . . . ." *Id.*

In Louisiana, an insurer is not liable where a claims-made policy requires notice within the policy period but notice is not given until after the policy period. *Hood v. Cotter*, 5 So. 3d 819, 824–25, 830 (La. 2008). The notice provision in the main body of the policy "provides the scope of coverage bargained for by defendant." *Id.* at 829; *see also Vitto v. Davis*, 23 So. 3d 1048, 1053 (La. Ct. App. 2009) (holding requirement of notice within policy period in the main body of the policy controls scope of coverage by insurer even though injured third party bringing suit could not have known of claim within policy period because of wrongdoing of insured). *Hood* reasoned, "[T]he purpose of the claims-made-and-reported requirement is to ease problems in determining when a claim is made or whether an insured should have known a claim was going to be made." *Hood*, 5 So. 3d at 827 (citing *Livingston Parish Sch. Bd. v. Fireman's Fund Am. Ins. Co.*, 282 So. 2d 478 (La. 1973)).

In an earlier case interpreting Louisiana law, this circuit held where "immediate notice" is an express condition precedent to coverage in the main body of the policy, "failure to comply with the provision precludes coverage" and "prejudice need not enter the calculation." *Joslyn Mfg. Co. v. Liberty Mut. Ins. Co.*, 30 F.3d 630, 633–634 (5th Cir. 1994). Where policy holders are "consumers unlikely to be conversant with all the fine print of their policies," strict adherence to notice provisions that are conditions precedent is not as important as when "both parties are sophisticated businesses, which are expected to be [—13—] conversant with the terms of their contracts." *Id.* at 634 (citing *MGIC Indem. Corp. v. Cent. Bank of Monroe, La.*, 838 F.2d 1382, 1387 (5th Cir. 1988)); *see also Jackson v. State Farm Mut. Auto. Ins. Co.*, 29 So. 2d 177, 179 (La. 1946) (holding delayed-notice cases must balance equities, including prejudice and discovery of injury, in case where injured party was ordinary consumer). On the other hand, where notice is *not* a condition precedent to coverage, an "insurer cannot deny coverage merely because its insured failed to give notice of loss as soon as practicable" without a showing of prejudice. *Peavey Co. v. M/V ANPA*, 971 F.2d 1168, 1172 (5th Cir. 1992). Louisiana case law does not directly address whether, to deny recovery, an insurer must show prejudice resulting from an insured's non-compliance with a condition precedent in an endorsement that requires notice within a set time period after an occurrence. *See Smith*, 807 So. 2d at 1023 (Daley, J., concurring).

Whether a notice provision is a "condition precedent" to recovery depends on the language of the policy; we have held that "the words 'condition precedent' mean exactly what they say, and failure to comply with this provision preclude[s] recovery, regardless of whether prejudice [is] shown." *Gulf Island, IV v. Blue Streak Marine, Inc.*, 940 F.2d 948, 955 (5th Cir. 1991) (citing *MGIC*, 838 F.2d at

1385–86). *Gulf Island, IV* went on to state that certain language short of the exact phrase "condition precedent" may not be sufficient to make a notice requirement a condition precedent to recovery:

> The Lloyd's policy requires notice only when the assured "may reasonably conclude" that a covered occurrence has taken place. This language falls short of the express condition precedent language that we held in *MGIC* and *Auster Oil* [*& Gas, Inc. v. Stream*, 891 F.2d 570 (5th Cir. 1990)] was necessary to make giving notice a condition precedent to recovery. [—14—]

Gulf Island, IV, 940 F.2d at 956.

Turning to the insurance contracts at issue, we hold the umbrella insurers are not liable to Settoon regardless of prejudice to the umbrella insurers. First, it is clear that the notice condition in the endorsement is a "condition precedent" despite not using the precise phrase "condition precedent." The buyback clearly indicates the notice provision is a condition precedent to recovery under the endorsement. The absolute pollution exclusion states, "It is . . . agreed that the intent and effect of this exclusion is to delete from any and all coverage's . . . any . . . claim . . . in any way arising out of [pollution]." The buyback states, "It is hereby agreed that the above Absolute Exclusion shall not apply provided that the Named Assured established that all of the following conditions have been met . . . ." Settoon must "establish" that the "conditions" have been met in order for the absolute pollution exclusion not to apply. Short of the exact phrase "condition precedent," there is almost no stronger language that could establish a "condition precedent" to recovery. Further, Settoon is a sophisticated business, not an ordinary consumer. *Cf. Joslyn Mfg.*, 30 F.3d at 633–34. Therefore, we analyze the notice provision in the buyback as a condition precedent directed at a sophisticated business.

The bargain here "delete[s] from any and all coverage[]" pollution liability unless the insured gives notice within 30 days of the occurrence. Pollution liability is not stripped away because of a violation of the notice provision; rather, non-compliance prevents the exception to the exclusion from taking effect in the first instance, meaning the pollution exclusion remains in effect. In Louisiana a violation of a provision mandating notice within the policy period allows the insurer to avoid liability, *Hood*, 5 So. 3d at 824–25, because the notice [—15—] provision determines the scope of coverage bargained for, *Vitto*, 23 So. 3d at 1053. Here, the notice provision in the buyback reflects the allocation of risk the parties bargained for. Therefore, holding the umbrella insurers liable where the conditions of the buyback were not met would alter the terms of the parties' bargain. Because Settoon did not comply with the 30-day notice provision, which is a condition precedent to recovery under the buyback, the umbrella insurers are not liable under the Bumbershoot 2 and Bumbershoot 3 policies.

B

Second, Settoon points out that although the 30-day notice provision is present as a condition in the pollution endorsement, the notice provision in the bodies of the main Bumbershoot 2 and Bumbershoot 3 policies requires notice "as soon as practicable" and provides that "failure to notify the Company of any occurrence which at the time of its happening did not appear to involve this Policy, but which, at a later date, would appear to give rise to claims hereunder, shall not prejudice such claims." Settoon asserts this notice provision in the main body of the policy must be given effect because the endorsement includes a clause stating, "All other terms and conditions remaining unchanged" and does not include a ranking clause that would have given precedence to provisions of the endorsement over provisions of the main body of the policy. By reading the two provisions together, Settoon maintains delays of notice beyond 30 days are permitted because the occurrence "did not appear to involve this Policy" until the captain of the CATHY confessed his vessel's involvement in the allision. The umbrella insurers respond that the "Notice of Occurrence" provision does not apply to claims under endorsements, but

rather only to claims under the main body of the policy, because it speaks of occurrences "covered hereunder." [—16—]

Where an insurance policy is clear, we do not engage in further interpretation beyond the plain meaning of the words. *See* LA. CIV. CODE art. 2046 ("When the words of a contract are clear and explicit and lead to no absurd consequences, no further interpretation may be made in search of the parties' intent."); *La. Ins. Guar. Ass'n v. Interstate Fire & Cas. Co.*, 630 So. 2d 759, 763 (La. 1994) ("The parties' intent as reflected by the words in the policy determine the extent of coverage." (citing *Trinity Indus., Inc. v. Ins. Co. of North America*, 916 F.2d 267, 269 (5th Cir. 1990))). Where a policy's words are subject to different interpretations, we resolve ambiguities in favor of the insured. *Coleman v. Sch. Bd. of Richland Parish*, 418 F.3d 511, 517–18 (5th Cir. 2005).

Additionally, we read each insurance policy as a whole. *Id.* at 517. "[E]ndorsements affixed to a policy of insurance are to be construed in connection with the printed provisions of the policy and the entire agreement harmonized, if possible, but in the event of irreconcilable conflict, the endorsement or rider prevails." *Zurich Ins. Co. v. Bouler*, 198 So. 2d 129, 131 (La. Ct. App. 1967); *see also Smith v. Burton*, 928 So. 2d 74, 79 (La. Ct. App. 2005) ("Documents evidencing the complete contract, such as binders and riders, when executed together for that purpose, must be read together."). In contract interpretation in the context of insurance policies, "the specific controls the general." *Smith*, 928 So. 2d at 79.

Here, under Louisiana law primacy is given to the endorsement over the main body of the policy. *See Zurich Ins. Co.*, 198 So. 2d at 131. That is, the liability provisions of the policy do not encompass pollution liability until the conditions of the endorsement are met. The absolute pollution exclusion specifically states, "It is . . . agreed that the intent and effect of this exclusion is [—17—] to delete from any and all coverage's afforded by this policy any . . . claim . . . in any way arising out of [pollution]." The buyback then states this language will not apply "provided that" notice is given within 30 days. Therefore, even assuming without deciding that Settoon complied with the notice requirement in the main body of the policy, the absolute pollution exclusion remains in effect because Settoon did not meet the notice condition in the buyback.

C

Third, Settoon asserts Louisiana's doctrine of impossibility excuses its noncompliance with the 30-day notice provision. It is true that under Louisiana law, an insurer cannot impose a *penal reduction* in benefits for failure to comply with a notice provision. *Mansour v. State ex rel. State Emps. Grp. Benefits Program*, 694 So. 2d 1096, 1100 (La. Ct. App. 1997) (holding insurer liable despite insured's non-compliance with 72-hour notice provision where insurer could not show prejudice and where insured could not comply with notice provision because of condition insured against, which was a heart attack); *see also Hayward v. Carolina Ins. Co.*, 51 So. 2d 405, 407 (La. Ct. App. 1951) (holding insurer cannot rely on failure to serve prompt notice when insured gave notice immediately after discovery of claim and in absence of fraud or prejudice to insurer). This case law, however, is not an application of the doctrine of impossibility, which is codified as follows: "An obligor is not liable for his failure to perform when it is caused by a fortuitous event that makes performance impossible." LA. CIV. CODE art. 1873. The doctrine applies to failures to perform *obligations*. *Id.* An insured party is not contractually obliged to satisfy conditions precedent, so the doctrine of impossibility is inapplicable. Therefore, [—18—] we hold the doctrine of impossibility does not excuse Settoon's failure to provide notice within 30 days.

D

The umbrella insurers are not liable to Settoon because Settoon failed to comply with the 30-day notice provision in the buyback. Therefore, we need not reach the issue of whether Settoon complied with the 72-hour knowledge provision. The district court did not err in holding the umbrella insurers are not liable to Settoon.

IV

The district court held SNIC cannot rely on the specific terms in the Bumbershoot 1 buyback because SNIC delayed delivery of the policy in violation of LOUISIANA REVISED STATUTES Annotated § 22:873(A) (2012), which, subject to payment of the premium, requires insurers to deliver policies within a reasonable period of time after issuance. SNIC did not give Settoon the policy until months after Settoon's premium payment. Therefore, the district court held SNIC liable to Settoon on the Bumbershoot 1 policy. On cross-appeal, SNIC asserts the terms of the policy are applicable for two reasons: 1) SNIC did not "issue" the policy when it sent the binder, so the delivery obligations of § 22:873(A) do not apply; and 2) delayed delivery in violation of §22:873(A) does not free Settoon from the policy terms if Settoon was not prejudiced by a lack of knowledge of the terms, and Settoon was not prejudiced. Because delayed delivery in violation of § 22:873(A) prevents SNIC from relying on the exclusions in the policy and the conditions precedent of the exceptions to the exclusions, whether or not the delay caused prejudice to Settoon, we hold SNIC is liable to Settoon. [—19—]

A

"We may affirm the district court's judgment on any basis supported by the record," *United States v. Roussel*, 705 F.3d 184, 195 (5th Cir. 2013); however, "[t]he general rule of this court is that arguments not raised before the district court are waived and will not be considered on appeal." *Celanese Corp. v. Martin K. Eby Constr. Co., Inc.*, 620 F.3d 529, 531 (5th Cir. 2010). SNIC did not argue before the district court that §22:873(A) does not apply to its delay in delivering the policy because SNIC did not "issue" the policy until Settoon sent the underlying policies. Rather, SNIC's primary argument before the district court was that it *complied* with the statute by delivering the binder that stated the effective date of the policy was November 2, 2006.

Admittedly, in one paragraph of its summary judgment motion SNIC contended the only reason the policy did not "issue" until March 2, 2007 was that Settoon delayed in delivering the underlying policies. It is clear from the context of the brief that SNIC did not mean to argue in this paragraph that §22:873(A) did not apply because SNIC did not "issue" the policy for purposes of the statute's delivery requirement; rather, SNIC used this paragraph to argue Settoon should not be advantaged by its own delay in sending the underlying policies. SNIC maintained throughout its summary judgment motion that it delivered the policy in compliance with § 22:873(A) by delivering the binder. Thus, the district court did not have an opportunity to decide whether § 22:873(A) was applicable on SNIC's "issuance" theory because Settoon and SNIC disputed only whether SNIC's delivery of the binder sufficed for compliance with the statute's delivery requirement. *See Celanese Corp.*, 620 F.3d at 531. Accordingly, SNIC waived its assertion that § 22:873(A)'s delivery [—20—] requirement is inapplicable because it did not "issue" the policy until after Settoon sent the underlying policies.

B

SNIC asserts the terms of Bumbershoot 1 are applicable because the delayed delivery of the policy did not prejudice Settoon, as Settoon had knowledge of the terms regardless of the delivery timing. Settoon asserts prejudice is not a relevant factor under Louisiana law and, in any event, Settoon was in fact prejudiced because it could not have known of Bumbershoot 1's specific terms. Louisiana statutory law provides:

> Subject to the insurer's requirements as to payment of premium, every policy shall be delivered to the insured or to the person entitled thereto within a reasonable period of time after its issuance.

LA. REV. STAT. Ann. § 22:873(A) (2012).

In *Louisiana Maintenance Services, Inc. v. Certain Underwriters at Lloyd's of London*, 616 So. 2d 1250 (La. 1993), the Louisiana Supreme Court held an insurer could not rely on an exclusion to deny recovery where the insurer violated § 22:873(A) by failing to deliver the policy and where the insured "reasonably assumed that its liability . . . was covered." *Id.* at 1253. *Louisiana Maintenance Services* did not explicitly state whether it relied on both grounds in denying the insurer the right to rely on the exclusion, but it strongly suggested the statutory violation was enough standing alone. *Id.* ("Insurance policy exclusions are not valid unless clearly communicated to the insured. . . . Since Lloyd's failed to comply with the statutory requirement of delivery, it could not rely on its policy exclusions."). The Louisiana Supreme Court did, however, explain that the insured reasonably thought the insurer covered the claim (because of the specific needs of the insured) and concluded the insurer acted in [—21—] an arbitrary and capricious manner. *Id.* The Court explained the statute "require[s] that an insured be informed of a policy's contents. Notice of any exclusionary provisions is essential because the insured will otherwise assume the desired coverage exists." *Id.* at 1252.[1]

A Louisiana appellate court relied on *Louisiana Maintenance Services* in holding an insurer did not violate § 22:873(A) when it delivered the policy to the *association* it insured but not to each *individual* within the association. *Naquin v. Fortson*, 774 So. 2d

---

[1] A Louisiana appellate court applying *Louisiana Maintenance Services* held an insurer did not violate § 22:873(A) where it delivered the policy after the event giving rise to the claim but within a reasonable time period (two months) and where the insured had knowledge of the relevant exclusion. *MacLaff, Inc. v. Arch Ins. Co.*, 978 So. 2d 482, 488–89 (La. Ct. App. 2008). The Louisiana Supreme Court vacated that opinion on appeal, however, in an opinion that reads in its entirety, "There exist genuine issues of material fact that require a trial on the merits. The decision of the court of appeal and the trial court are vacated. The case is remanded to the trial court for further proceedings." *MacLaff, Inc. v. Arch Ins. Co.*, 996 So. 2d 1080, 1080–81 (La. 2008). Because the basis for the Louisiana Supreme Court's decision is opaque, we do not rely on the appellate court opinion, any part of which could be an incorrect espousal of Louisiana law.

1277, 1280 (La. Ct. App. 2000). *Naquin* held delivery to the association complied with the statute and also relied on the fact that "the principles underlying the delivery requirement were met in this case; that is, [the insured] was clearly aware that automobile liability coverage was excluded under the [insurer's] policy." *Id.* The statutory compliance alone, however, seems to have been enough to allow the insurer to rely on the exclusion. *Id.* at 1279 ("If an insurer fails to comply with the statutory requirement of delivery, it cannot rely on its policy exclusions." (citing *La. Maint. Servs.*, 616 So. 2d at 1253)).

We hold a finding of prejudice is not required to disallow reliance on the policy terms and endorsement provisions. *Louisiana Maintenance Services* [—22—] indicates delayed delivery in violation of § 22:873(A) is enough to prevent SNIC from relying on the pollution exclusion in the main body of the policy regardless of prejudice to Settoon. *See La. Maint. Servs.*, 616 So. 2d at 1253 ("Since [the insurer] failed to comply with the statutory requirement of delivery, it could not rely on its policy exclusions."). The Louisiana Supreme Court's explanation of the purpose of § 22:873(A) was not essential to its holding; rather, what was essential was the violation of the statute. *Id.* at 1252–53; *see also Naquin*, 774 So. 2d at 1279–80. Therefore, under Louisiana law an insurer cannot take advantage of favorable policy terms where it delayed delivery of the policy after the insured payed the premium. *La. Maint. Servs.*, 616 So. 2d at 1253. Moreover, even if Settoon could have known of the pollution exclusion, it could not have known of the specific terms of the pollution buyback endorsement prior to receiving the policy and endorsements. SNIC cannot rely on the pollution exclusion or specific terms of the buyback because it delayed delivery of the policy and endorsements to Settoon after Settoon paid the premium. The district court did not err in holding SNIC is liable to Settoon.

V

SNIC asserts that even if it is liable to Settoon, it is not liable for prejudgment interest because federal maritime law, not Louisiana law, controls. Further, SNIC asserts that if it is liable for prejudgment interest, the interest should be calculated from the date Settoon paid for the allision, not from the date of judicial demand. SNIC is incorrect in its first assertion: SNIC is liable for prejudgment interest because Louisiana law controls. SNIC is correct, however, in its second assertion: prejudgment interest should be calculated from the date Settoon paid for the allision. [—23—]

A

SNIC is liable for prejudgment interest because Louisiana law applies over federal maritime law. This circuit created a three-part instructive test for determining whether federal maritime or state law controls a disputed issue in *Albany Ins. Co. v. Anh Thi Kieu*, 927 F.2d 882, 886–87 (5th Cir. 1991). The three factors are: "(1) whether the federal maritime rule constitutes entrenched federal precedent; (2) whether the state has a substantial and legitimate interest in the application of its law; (3) whether the state's rule is materially different from the federal maritime rule." *Id.* at 886 (internal quotation marks and citations omitted).

The first prong of the three-factor test asks whether federal law is entrenched. *Id.* "In the absence of preexisting entrenched federal maritime law . . . [t]he application of unfamiliar federal maritime rules engenders undesirable uncertainty among maritime actors." *Id.* at 888. In order to determine whether federal law was entrenched, *Anh Thi Kieu* analyzed our circuit precedent and concluded that although the language in our precedent *recognized* the federal law at issue in that case, it did not have to *apply* the federal law, so the federal law was not entrenched. *Id.* at 888–89. The same conclusion is warranted here.

Where a primary and excess policy are drafted together in a "carefully dovetailed, integrated program in which each [insurer] had significant interests at stake," this circuit has held under maritime law the excess insurer is liable for prejudgment interest on the amount owed by the primary insurer that exceeds the primary policy's limit. *Alcoa S.S. Co. v. Charles Ferran & Co.*, 443 F.2d 250, 255 (5th Cir. 1971). *Alcoa Steamship* specifically held, "But we do not make this as a choice of law for general (or Louisiana) application." *Id.* Rather, [—24—] *Alcoa Steamship* limited the holding to the carefully crafted insurance plan, where "[o]bviously what was in mind was what has occurred here—a Court holding that despite the fixed ceiling of [a certain amount], the law requires payment of interest thereon." *Id.* at 256. In the context where both the primary and excess insurer were liable to the insured, the court required the excess insurer to pay any prejudgment interest beyond the limits of the primary insurance policy. *Id.* This circuit relied on *Alcoa Steamship* fifteen years later to hold, "[A] marine insurer is not liable for interest in excess of its policy limits unless language in the policy so provides." *Ryan Walsh Stevedoring Co. v. James Marine Servs., Inc.*, 792 F.2d 489, 493 (5th Cir. 1986).

Ryan Walsh and *Alcoa Steamship* addressed situations where both primary and excess insurers were liable, and held the excess insurers were liable for prejudgment interest beyond the limits of the primary insurers. *Ryan Walsh*, 792 F.2d at 493; *Alcoa S.S.*, 443 F.2d at 256. Whether the primary or excess insurer was held liable, the insured received prejudgment interest as contemplated in the drafting of the policies.[2] Our precedent has not applied the *Alcoa Steamship* rule where no insurer would be liable for prejudgment interest. Therefore, the *Alcoa Steamship* rule is not entrenched federal maritime law in this context, where there is no excess insurance liability beyond Bumbershoot 1.

The second *Anh Thi Kieu* factor asks whether Louisiana has a substantial interest exceeding the interest of maritime law. *Anh Thi Kieu*, 927 F.2d at 886. *Anh Thi Kieu* explained a state has "a substantial and

legitimate interest" if "the local state interest materially exceeds the comparative maritime concerns in the [—25—] controversy." *Id.* at 887 (emphasis removed). There, we held "Texas has a material interest in ensuring that marine insurance underwriters do not invalidate the insurance protection of Texas citizens on the basis of misrepresentations that were neither willfully or intentionally asserted." *Id.* at 887–88. Similarly, here Louisiana has an interest in compensating insured parties with prejudgment interest when insurers wrongfully deny recovery, especially where insurers violate Louisiana statutory law—in this case §22:873(A) governing delivery of insurance policies.

The third *Anh Thi Kieu* factor asks whether there is a material difference between state and federal law. *Anh Thi Kieu*, 927 F.2d at 886. "[A]pplication of state law inconsistent with the core principles of maritime law would defeat the reasonably settled expectations of maritime actors. . . . [S]tate law should not be applied unless it bears a reasonable similarity to the federal maritime practice." *Id.* at 887 (internal quotation marks and citations omitted). Unlike the federal law of *Alcoa Steamship* and *Ryan Walsh*, the Louisiana courts have held primary and excess insurers are liable for prejudgment interest on their portion of liability, even if the interest *exceeds policy limits*. *Moon v. City of Baton Rouge*, 522 So. 2d 117, 127 (La. Ct. App. 1987) ("[The requirement to pay prejudgment interest] applies to primary as well as excess insurers, making each liable for the interest attributable to their proportionate share of the total judgment."). This is a difference from federal law. *See Ryan Walsh*, 792 F.2d at 493. This is not, however, a case where "application of state law inconsistent with the core principles of maritime law would defeat the reasonably settled expectations of maritime actors" because Louisiana "law shares the concern of federal maritime law" that insurers should be liable for prejudgment interest, [—26—] even if the allocation of that interest is different. *Anh Thi Kieu*, 927 F.2d at 887. Therefore, this factor adds little weight to SNIC's assertions, especially when weighed against the other two factors. As a result, the

---

[2] One Eleventh Circuit case that dealt with only one insurance policy relied on *Alcoa Steamship* and *Ryan Walsh* to disallow prejudgment interest beyond the policy's limit. *Steelmet, Inc. v. Caribe Towing Corp.*, 842 F.2d 1237, 1244 (11th Cir. 1988).

Anh Thi Kieu factors lead us to conclude Louisiana law should be applied to the issue of prejudgment interest. Accordingly, SNIC is liable to Settoon for prejudgment interest.

B

SNIC is correct to assert the interest should be calculated from the date Settoon paid out its obligations rather than the date Settoon made judicial demand. As the above analysis indicates, Louisiana law is applicable to liability for prejudgment interest. *See* Part V.A. *supra*. Under Louisiana law, interest is calculated from the date of judicial demand only for "*ex delicto*" damages. LA. REV. STAT. Ann. § 13:4203. Louisiana law distinguishes between "*ex delicto*" and "*ex contractu*" damages:

> The Louisiana Court of Appeals explained that "the classical distinction between 'damages *ex contractu*' and 'damages *ex delicto*' is that the former flow from the breach of a special obligation contractually assumed by the obligor, whereas the latter flow from the violation of a general duty owed to all persons."

Amoco Prod. Co. v. Tex. Meridian Res. Exploration Inc., 180 F.3d 664, 672 (5th Cir. 1999) (alterations removed) (quoting *Davis v. LeBlanc*, 149 So. 2d 252, 254 (La. Ct. App. 1963)).

Here, the insurance obligations are "*ex contractu*" because they "flow from the breach of a special obligation contractually assumed by the obligor." *Davis*, 149 So. 2d at 254. SNIC's obligation is contractual, arising out of SNIC's agreement to pay Settoon for Settoon's liability for damage to third parties; SNIC's obligation does not arise out of a general duty SNIC owes all persons or [—27—] out of its agreement to pay Settoon for damage to Settoon (even though the underlying incident with the third party was a tort). "The general rule in Louisiana is that legal interest runs from the due date of the obligation in question." *Am. Cyanamid Co. v. Elec. Indus., Inc.*, 630 F.2d 1123, 1129 (5th Cir. Unit A 1980). In this case the obligation was due on

the date Settoon paid for the damage from the allision, which is the date Settoon suffered the insured-against loss because it lost the funds it paid to third parties. *See Arceneaux v. Amstar Corp.*, 969 So. 2d 755, 785 (La. Ct. App. 2007) (holding insurer liable to insured for prejudgment interest on amount insured paid in settlement to third parties from date insured paid third parties, not from date of judicial demand). The outcome may be different were SNIC providing recovery for damage to Settoon resulting from an accident or a tort caused by a third party because in that case the damage to Settoon would arise at the time of the accident or tort. That is not our case. *Cf. id.* (". . . [The insured] argues that this is a tort suit in which [the insurer] was joined as a direct defendant; thus, interest on an award against [the insurer] is due from the date of judicial demand. . . . This argument . . . overlooks that the present dispute is solely a contractual dispute between [the insured] and [the insurer]."). Accordingly, SNIC is liable for prejudgment interest from the date Settoon paid third parties for the damage caused by the allision because that is when SNIC's obligation arose.

VI

For these reasons, we AFFIRM the district court's judgment in all respects except for the calculation of prejudgment interest. We REVERSE and REMAND for calculation of prejudgment interest in a manner consistent with this opinion.

United States Court of Appeals
for the Fifth Circuit

No. 12-31102

DUVAL

VS.

NORTHERN ASSURANCE CO. OF AMERICA

Appeal from the United States District Court for the
Western District of Louisiana

Decided: July 5, 2013

Citation: 722 F.3d 300, 1 Adm. R. 270 (5th Cir. 2013).

Before **STEWART**, Chief Judge, and **HIGGINBOTHAM**
and **JONES**, Circuit Judges.

[—1—] **HIGGINBOTHAM**, Circuit Judge:

This appeal turns on whether third-party insurers can enforce a master services agreement's defense, indemnification, and insurance obligations. We conclude that those obligations run between the two parties to the master services agreement and thus are not enforceable by the insurers. [—2—]

I.

BHP Billiton Petroleum Deepwater, Inc. ("BHP") is an energy exploration company. Prior to its bankruptcy filing, Deep Marine Technology, Inc. ("Deep Marine") was an oilfield service company that owned and operated vessels to support offshore construction. Effective April 18, 2006, BHP and Deep Marine entered into a Master Services Agreement ("MSA"), pursuant to which Deep Marine agreed to provide construction support vessels to BHP. The MSA contained reciprocal indemnity obligations and required the parties to support their respective indemnity obligations with liability insurance, self-insurance, or a combination thereof. In addition, the MSA contained a choice of law clause, stipulating that general maritime law governs interpretation of the MSA and, to the extent general maritime law is not applicable, Texas law applies.

Glen Duval ("Duval"), an employee of Wood Group/Deepwater Specialists, Inc. (another BHP contractor), claims to have suffered injuries during an offshore personnel basket transfer from a vessel owned by Deep Marine to a tension-leg platform owned by BHP. On April 8, 2008, he filed suit against Deep Marine, alleging that the negligence of Deep Marine's personnel aboard the vessel caused his injuries. In an amended complaint, he also asserted a claim against Dolphin Services, L.L.C., the employer of the allegedly negligent crane operator. Duval did not, and has not, alleged that BHP has any liability for his injuries. On April 25, 2008, Deep Marine sought defense, additional insured status, and indemnity from BHP under the MSA, and it tendered the defense of Duval's claims to BHP. BHP accepted tender on May 14, 2008.

On December 4, 2009, Deep Marine filed for Chapter 11 bankruptcy in the Southern District of Texas, and Duval's suit was automatically stayed. On September 10, 2010, the bankruptcy court entered an order permitting Duval to proceed with his case against Deep Marine's insurers, but permanently enjoining him from "enforcing, levying, attaching, collecting, or otherwise recovering in any matter or by any means" against Deep Marine or its estate. Pursuant to [—3—] that order, the district court reopened the case. On January 4, 2012, Duval amended his complaint to name Northern Assurance Company of America and Markel American Insurance Company ("Underwriters"), the protection and indemnity insurers of Deep Marine, as additional defendants under Louisiana's Direct Action Statute.[1] On February 7, 2012, Underwriters filed a third-party complaint against BHP, seeking to be "fully protected, defended, indemnified, held harmless and provided insurance coverage" by BHP in accordance with the MSA and purporting to tender BHP to Duval under Federal Rule of Civil Procedure 14(c).

Underwriters and BHP filed cross-motions for summary judgment, each disputing whether Underwriters could enforce BHP's contractual insurance, defense, and indemnity obligations to Deep Marine after Deep Marine's bankruptcy discharge. Following a

---

[1] LA. REV. STAT. ANN. § 22:1269.

hearing with oral argument, the district court granted BHP's motion for summary judgment, denied Underwriters' motion for summary judgment, and dismissed the action with prejudice.[2] Underwriters timely appealed.[3] We have subject matter jurisdiction pursuant to 28 U.S.C. § 1292(a)(3), which provides for interlocutory appeal from a district court's order "determining the rights and liabilities of the parties to admiralty cases."[4]

II. [—4—]

We review a district court's order granting summary judgment *de novo*, applying the same standards as the district court.[5] "Summary judgment is warranted if the pleadings, the discovery and disclosure materials on file, and any affidavits show that there is no genuine [dispute] as to any material fact and that the movant is entitled to judgment as a matter of law."[6] When parties file cross-motions for summary judgment, "we review each party's motion independently, viewing the evidence and inferences in the light most favorable to the nonmoving party."[7]

"Interpretation of the terms of a contract, including an indemnity clause, is a matter of law, reviewable *de novo* on appeal."[8] "[T]he obligation to indemnify is to be strictly construed,"[9] and "a court should not construe an indemnity clause to impose liability for a loss neither expressly within its terms nor of

such a character that the parties probably intended to exclude the loss."[10]

III.

The parties dispute whether the MSA requires BHP to protect, defend, indemnify, and hold harmless Underwriters against Duval's claim. We conclude that it does not and therefore affirm the district court's grant of summary judgment in favor of BHP. To be clear, the parties agree that the MSA required [—5—] BHP to protect, defend, indemnify, release and hold harmless Deep Marine against Duval's claim. Specifically, the MSA provided:

> Company [BHP] shall protect, defend, indemnify, release, and hold harmless Contractor Group from and against any and all claims arising out of, resulting from or in connection with the provision of the Goods and/or Services pursuant to this Contract for:
>
> (I) any injury, death, or illness suffered by any person in Company Group; and
>
> (II) any damage to or loss of any equipment, materials, vessels, or other property of any member of Company Group . . . .

The parties defined "Contractor Group" to include the Contractor (Deep Marine); its subsidiaries, affiliates, contractors, and subcontractors; and the "agents, representatives, servants, directors, officers, assigns, managers, members, shareholders, owners, employees and invitees of all of the foregoing." It defined "Company Group" to include BHP, as well as its subsidiaries, affiliates, contractors, and subcontractors, and employees "of all of the foregoing." Finally, the MSA defined "claims" to include "all claims losses, demands, causes of action, suits, proceedings, fines, penalties, judgments, obligations and liabilities of every kind and

---

[2] The district court did not issue a written opinion.

[3] Duval did not appeal the district court's judgment.

[4] 28 U.S.C. § 1292(a)(3).

[5] *Greater Hous. Small Taxicab Co. Owners Ass'n v. City of Hous.*, 660 F.3d 235, 238 (5th Cir. 2011).

[6] *Id.* (quoting *DePree*, 588 F.3d at 286) (alteration in original).

[7] *Ford Motor Co. v. Tex. Dept. of Transp.*, 264 F.3d 493, 498 (5th Cir. 2001).

[8] *Kemp v. Gulf Oil Corp.*, 745 F.2d 921, 924 (5th Cir. 1984).

[9] *Foreman v. Exxon Corp.*, 770 F.2d 490, 497 n.12 (5th Cir. 1985) (internal quotations and citations omitted).

[10] *Kemp*, 745 F.2d at 924 (quoting *Corbitt v. Diamond M. Drilling Co.*, 654 F.2d 329, 333 (5th Cir. 1981)); *see Hardy v. Gulf Oil Corp.*, 949 F.2d 826, 834 (5th Cir. 1992); *Foreman*, 770 F.2d at 497 n.12.

character." Thus, Duval's claim against Deep Marine fell within the scope of BHP's indemnification obligation because it was a personal injury claim asserted by a person in Company Group (an employee of a BHP contractor) against a member of Contractor Group (Deep Marine). But the same is not true of Duval's claim against Underwriters. Under the plain language of the MSA, BHP's indemnification and defense obligations only ran to members of the "Contractor Group." The parties could have included the Contractor's insurers within the definition of "Contractor Group," as parties in other cases have done,[11] [—6—] but they did not do so. In turn, BHP owes no duty to Underwriters, and we find Underwriters' arguments to the contrary unpersuasive.

Underwriters argue that BHP waived any potential defenses to its contractual obligations by accepting Deep Marine's tender of Duval's claim and defending Deep Marine in the matter. But waiver is simply inapplicable here. Even though BHP accepted Deep Marine's tender of Duval's claim, it never indicated it had any obligation to Underwriters. Instead, its defense arises out of an unknowable change in factual circumstances—specifically Deep Marine's discharge in bankruptcy, the bankruptcy court's order permanently enjoining Duval from proceeding against Deep Marine, and Underwriters' subsequent claim against BHP.

Underwriters also make four substantive arguments in favor of their interpretation of the MSA. First, Underwriters attack BHP's characterization of the MSA as an indemnity agreement requiring that Deep Marine make payment to Duval before BHP's indemnification obligation becomes enforceable.[12] They argue that the MSA requires BHP to indemnify Deep Marine against liability, so BHP's indemnification obligation becomes enforceable once Deep Marine's liability is established, not when Deep Marine eventually makes payment on that liability.[13] Underwriters point out that, under Louisiana's Direct Action Statute, Deep Marine must be found liable in [—7—] order for Underwriters to be held liable.[14] Therefore, they contend, even though Deep Marine will never pay damages to Duval, BHP's indemnification obligation will become enforceable once liability is established. But even assuming *arguendo* that the MSA requires indemnification against liability and that Deep Marine will eventually be held liable, Underwriters still cannot prevail because BHP's indemnification obligation— whatever its scope—runs only to Deep Marine.

Second, Underwriters contend that summary judgment in favor of BHP was improper because, upon their payment of any judgment or settlement to Duval, they will become subrogated to all of Deep Marine's rights, including its rights against BHP under the MSA. This argument also fails to persuade. Assuming *arguendo* that payment by Underwriters would give rise to subrogation, Underwriters would nevertheless have no claim against BHP because "a subrogee can obtain no greater rights than its subrogor had."[15] Deep Marine would not, and

---

[11] *See, e.g., Mid-Continent Cas. Co. v. Swift Energy Co.*, 206 F.3d 487, 494 (5th Cir. 2000); *Magee v. Ensco Offshore Co.*, No. 11-1351, 2012 WL 1825274, at *3 (E.D. La. May 18, 2012); *BJ Serv's Co., USA v. Thompson*, No. 6:08-510, 2010 WL 2024725, at *6 (W.D. La. May 14, 2010).

[12] Underwriters also attack BHP's general characterization of the MSA as an indemnity agreement. They contend that an indemnity agreement must contain a pre-payment provision, requiring payment of claims by the indemnitee, and argue that because the MSA contains no language requiring pre-payment of claims by Deep Marine, it is not an indemnity agreement. We disagree. The cases Underwriters rely on to argue that an indemnity agreement requires pre-payment are insurance cases in which the policies at issue were characterized as indemnity policies because they required pre-payment as a prerequisite to the insurer's liability. The MSA does not purport to be a liability insurance policy, and Underwriters cite no authority indicating that the MSA's indemnification language should be interpreted to require anything other than indemnification as it is typically understood.

[13] *See* 42 C.J.S. § 27, § 28.

[14] *See Descant v. Adm'rs of Tulane Educ. Fund*, 639 So. 2d 246, 249 (La. 1994).

[15] *Complaint of Admiral Towing & Barge Co.*, 767 F.2d 243, 250 (5th Cir. 1985).

could not, incur any loss in the Duval action, so Underwriters could not seek indemnification from BHP. And, because BHP has agreed to continue providing Deep Marine with a nominal defense, Underwriters would not have a breach of contract claim against BHP.

Third, Underwriters argue that BHP agreed to become Deep Marine's primary insurer against liability to members of Company Group. They point to the MSA's requirements (1) that BHP support its indemnification obligations with self-insurance, a liability insurance policy, or a combination thereof and (2) that the insurance coverage BHP obtains name Deep Marine as an additional insured and serve as primary insurance, without the right of contribution from any insurance policies maintained by Deep Marine. We find the argument inapplicable here because BHP chose to self-insure for claims under $1 million [—8—] and the parties agree that Duval's claim is not for more than $1 million. We conclude that the additional insured and primary insurance requirements do not apply to BHP's self-insurance. For one, the MSA focuses on "insurance coverage" and "policies of insurance" when describing both the additional insured and primary insurance requirements, leading us to believe that those requirements only apply when BHP chooses to support its indemnity obligation with a liability insurance policy. When a company self-insures, by contrast, "there is no contract with an insurance company."[16] We find further support for our reading in Texas case law. In *Hertz Corp. v. Robineau*, the Texas Court of Appeals explained that "the term 'self-insurance' is a misnomer" because "in effect, a self-insurer does not provide *insurance* at all."[17] It went on to make clear that a self-insurer does not "assume[ ] all the duties and burdens of an insurer," unless the parties have expressly contracted for "liability coverage."[18] "To say that a self-insurer will pay the same judgments and in the same amounts as insurance company would have

had to pay is one thing; while it is obvious that to assume all the obligations that exist under a [liability policy] is quite another thing."[19] We therefore conclude that the additional insured and primary insurance requirements do not apply to BHP's self-insurance.

Fourth, Underwriters argue that because "discharge of the debtor does not affect the liability of any other entity on, or the property of any other entity for, such debt,"[20] we should enforce BHP's contractual obligations. Otherwise, they contend, BHP will receive a windfall. This argument, too, misses the point. It is true that Deep Marine's bankruptcy does not affect the liability of any other [—9—] entity, such as Underwriters, to Duval. But Duval has not alleged that BHP has any potential liability for his claims. That makes sense because BHP's only obligation is an indemnification obligation to Deep Marine; unlike Underwriters, it has no secondary liability to injured tort victims, like Duval.

Before concluding, we pause briefly to address Underwriters' contention that they could tender BHP directly to Duval under Federal Rule of Civil Procedure 14(c). Such tender was improper because Duval has no claim against BHP. The MSA only obligates BHP to indemnify members of the "Contractor Group." As an employee of Wood Group (a BHP contractor), Duval is only a member of "Company Group," not "Contractor Group," so BHP's contractual obligations do not run to him. And, even if they did, because no claims have been asserted against Duval, BHP would have no obligation to indemnify and defend him.[21] Moreover, as we have previously explained, Underwriters did not agree to act as the primary insurer of Deep Marine against Duval's claim, so Duval could not bring suit directly against BHP under Louisiana's Direct Action Statute.

---

[16] BLACK'S LAW DICTIONARY 819 (8th ed. 2004).

[17] 6 S.W.3d 332, 336 (Tex. Ct. App. 1999) (emphasis in original).

[18] *Id.*

---

[19] *Id.* (internal quotations omitted).

[20] 11 U.S.C. § 524(e).

[21] It is worth noting that Duval neither opposed BHP's motion for summary judgment (which expressly sought dismissal of the tendered claim) nor appealed the district court's dismissal of the tendered claim.

IV.

For the reasons set forth above, we AFFIRM the judgment of the district court.

United States Court of Appeals
for the Fifth Circuit

No. 12-30041

BOUDREAUX
vs.
TRANSOCEAN DEEPWATER, INC.

Appeal from the United States District Court for the
Eastern District of Louisiana

Decided: July 12, 2013

Citation: 721 F.3d 723, 1 Adm. R. 275 (5th Cir. 2013).

Before **HIGGINBOTHAM, CLEMENT,** and **HAYNES**,
Circuit Judges.

[—1—] HIGGINBOTHAM, Circuit Judge:

Our prior opinion is vacated and withdrawn, and this opinion is substituted in its place.[1] This case presents the question of whether a Jones Act employer who successfully establishes a defense to liability for further maintenance and cure under *McCorpen v. Central Gulf Steamship Corp.*[2] is [—2—] thereby automatically entitled to restitution for benefits already paid. The district court answered in the affirmative, creating a right of action never before recognized in maritime law. We reverse and render.

I.

Wallace Boudreaux began working for Transocean Deepwater, Inc. ("Transocean") in January 2005. He failed to disclose serious back problems in Transocean's pre-employment medical questionnaire, affirmatively answering "no" to several inquiries regarding any history of back trouble. Less than five months after his hire, Boudreaux claimed that he had injured his back while servicing equipment. As a consequence, Transocean paid the seaman maintenance and cure for nearly five years.

In April 2008, Boudreaux filed suit against Transocean, alleging a right to further maintenance and cure, seeking punitive damages for Transocean's alleged mishandling of past benefits, and asserting claims for Jones Act negligence and unseaworthiness. During discovery, Transocean obtained evidence of Boudreaux's pre-employment history of back problems. Transocean filed an unopposed motion for partial summary judgment on Boudreaux's claim for further benefits, invoking *McCorpen* as a defense to maintenance and cure liability. Under *McCorpen*, a vessel owner's obligation to pay maintenance and cure to an injured seaman terminates upon proof that the seaman, in procuring his employment, "intentionally" and "willfully" concealed a material medical condition causally linked to the injury later sustained.[3]

The district court granted Transocean's unopposed motion. Thereafter, Transocean filed a counterclaim to recover the maintenance and cure payments it had already made to Boudreaux. Transocean moved for summary judgment [—3—] on the counterclaim, contending that its successful *McCorpen* defense automatically established its right to restitution under general maritime law. Prior to the district court's ruling on the motion, Transocean and Boudreaux reached a bracketed settlement that resolved Boudreaux's Jones Act negligence and unseaworthiness claims and left for decision only the viability of Transocean's proposed counterclaim for restitution. Under the settlement, Boudreaux was entitled to a lesser sum of money if the court recognized the counterclaim and a greater sum if it did not.

Though Transocean acknowledged that its restitution-via-*McCorpen* theory was novel, it urged the district court to fashion a new maritime right of action based on state law principles of fraud and unjust enrichment. In a thoughtful opinion, the district court agreed and awarded summary judgment to Transocean on its counterclaim, albeit without

---

[1] No member of this panel nor judge in regular active service on the court having requested that the court be polled on Rehearing En Banc (FED. R. APP. P. and 5th CIR. R. 35) the Petition for Rehearing En Banc is DENIED.

[2] 396 F.2d 547 (5th Cir. 1968).

[3] 396 F.2d at 549; *Johnson v. Cenac Towing Inc.*, 544 F.3d 296, 301 (5th Cir. 2008).

accepting Transocean's state-law theories. Boudreaux appeals.

II.

In light of the parties' bracketed settlement, this case turns on the purely legal question of whether a Jones Act employer who has paid maintenance and cure to a seaman injured in its employ is, upon successfully establishing a *McCorpen* defense to further liability, automatically entitled to a judgment against the seaman for benefits already paid. Transocean made a strategic decision not to litigate this case on its facts; rather, it asks this Court to hold that *any* employer who establishes a *McCorpen* defense is automatically entitled to restitution. We decline the invitation.

We begin with an overarching reality: the First Congress, convening in New York, created the federal district courts primarily in service of the maritime law, thereby continuing the British law of the sea. Under that comprehensive [—4—] body of jurisprudence, whose origins trace back to the middle ages, a seaman injured in his employ enjoys a right to maintenance and cure—a small daily stipend to pay for food, lodging, and basic medical care.[4] The right is intrinsic to the employment relationship and essentially unqualified: it cannot not be contracted away by the seaman,[5] does not depend on the fault of the employer,[6] and is

not reduced for the seaman's contributory negligence.[7]

To be sure, it has always been the rule that a seaman can lose the right to maintenance and cure through gross misconduct. Traditionally, this exception was narrowly confined to "injuries or illnesses resulting from extreme drunkenness, brawls or the contraction of venereal disease."[8] In *McCorpen*, this Court clarified that the exception includes instances where a seaman procures his employment by "intentionally" and "fraudulently" concealing a material medical condition causally related to the injury later sustained.[9] The requisite quantum of proof under *McCorpen* is the same as that for fraud claims. But [—5—] *McCorpen* never addressed the issue of restitution for benefits already paid.[10] Indeed, *McCorpen* itself is in tension with *Still v. Norfolk & Western Railway Co.*,[11] in which Justice Black clarified that a worker's fraud in procuring his employment does not vitiate the employment relationship, allowing him to maintain a suit for damages under the Federal Employers' Liability Act.[12] Courts including ours have since recognized that *Still*'s logic and congressionally rooted paternal policy applies

---

[4] 1 THOMAS SCHOENBAUM, ADMIRALTY AND MARITIME LAW § 6-28 (5th ed. 2012); *see also Calmar S.S. Corp. v. Taylor*, 303 U.S. 525, 528 (1938) ("The maintenance exacted is comparable to that to which the seaman is entitled while at sea, and 'cure' is care, including nursing and medical attention during such period as the duty continues.").

[5] *Terrebonne v. K-Sea Transp. Corp.*, 477 F.3d 271, 279 (5th Cir. 2007) ("[M]aintenance and cure is an intrinsic part of the employment relationship, separate from the actual employment contract. . . . [it] cannot be contracted away.").

[6] *Calmar*, 303 U.S. at 527 ("The duty, which arises from the contract of employment, does not rest upon negligence or culpability on the part of the owner or master.").

[7] *Chelentis v. Luckenbach S.S. Co.*, 247 U.S. 372, 379 (1918).

[8] 1B BENEDICT ON ADMIRALTY § 45 (Matthew Bender ed. 2012).

[9] *McCorpen*, 396 F.2d at 549. One of the earliest published cases to develop a *McCorpen*-esque defense to maintenance and cure liability is the Third Circuit's decision in *Lindquist v. Dilkes*. See 127 F.2d 21, 22–23 (3d Cir. 1941).

[10] *See McCorpen*, 396 F.2d at 549; *see also Patterson v. Allseas USA*, 145 F. App'x 969, 970 (5th Cir. 2005) ("The issue of whether a shipowner may affirmatively recover maintenance and cure payments it makes to a seaman if the shipowner makes these payments before learning of the seaman's conduct was not before the court in *McCorpen* . . . we decline to decide this difficult *res nova* issue on this record.").

[11] 368 U.S. 35 (1961).

[12] *See id.* at 45 ("[T]he status of employees who become such through other kinds of fraud . . . must be recognized for purposes of suits under the Act. And this conclusion is not affected by the fact that an employee's misrepresentation may have, as is urged here, contributed to the injury or even to the accident upon which his action is based.").

with equal force to seamen.[13] Yet if the seaman's dishonesty does not terminate his status as seaman or his damages remedy, the right to maintenance and cure ought be an *a fortiori* case; after all, it is an essential part of the employment relationship—a down payment on damages that allows the seaman to subsist and pay for basic medical expenses in the [—6—] immediate aftermath of his injury.[14] Though the viability of the *McCorpen* defense cannot seriously be questioned at this late hour, Transocean's novel attempt to extend the defense into an affirmative right of recovery finds virtually no support, and we are not inclined to accede.[15]

---

[13] *See, e.g., Johnson*, 544 F.3d at 301–02 ("The Supreme Court's decision in *Still* makes clear that a seaman . . . is not barred from suit under the Jones Act because he conceals a material fact in applying for employment." (citations omitted) (internal quotation marks omitted)); *Brown v. Parker Drilling Offshore Corp.*, 410 F.3d 166, 178 (5th Cir. 2005) ("The Supreme Court has effectively foreclosed any argument that misrepresentations in an application for employment might void the necessary employment relation.") (quoting *Reed v. Iowa Marine & Repair Corp.*, 143 F.R.D. 648, 651 (E.D. La. 1992)); *Omar v. Sea-Land Serv., Inc.*, 813 F.2d 986, 989–90 (9th Cir. 1987) ("Maintenance and cure . . . derives from a seaman's employment on a vessel . . . . The remedial nature of the Jones Act and maritime law requires a less technical, contractual definition of 'employee' than Sealand asks us to use.") (citing *Still*, 368 U.S. at 45)).

[14] *See Fitzgerald v. U.S. Lines Co.*, 374 U.S. 16, 18 (1963) ("[R]emedies for negligence, unseaworthiness, and maintenance and cure . . . serve the same purpose of indemnifying a seaman for damages caused by injury, depend in large part upon the same evidence, and involve some identical elements of recovery.").

[15] In *Vitcovich v. Ocean Rover O.N.*, an unpublished memorandum decision, the Ninth Circuit sanctioned a restitution-via-*McCorpen* counterclaim; however, the decision is devoid of analysis. *See* 1997 WL 21205 (9th Cir. 1997). Courts that have meaningfully engaged with the proposed counterclaim's broader implications for maritime practice have rejected *Vitcovich*. *See Dolmo v. Galliano Tugs, Inc.*, 2011 WL 6817824, at *2 (E.D. La. 2011), *aff'd* 479 F. App'x 656 (5th Cir. 2012); *Hardison v. Abdon Callais Offshore, LLC*, 2012 WL 2878636, at *7 (E.D. La. 2012); *Am. River Transp. Co. v. Benson*, 2012 WL 5936535, at *5 (N.D. Ill. 2012); *Cotton v. Delta Queen Steamboat Co., Inc.*, 36 So. 3d 262 (La. Ct. App. 2010).

The district court's concern with the egregious facts here is understandable, but the sweeping counterclaim it endorses would mark a significant retreat from our hoary charge to safeguard the well-being of seamen.[16] Already, even without fraud, an employer may offset any Jones Act damages recovered by the seaman to the extent they duplicate maintenance and cure previously paid.[17] This, if the employer "show[s] that the damages assessed against it have in fact and in actuality been previously covered."[18] As a fully developed Jones Act damages model duplicates, "in fact and in actuality," past payments for maintenance and cure, it is not clear that the current regime affords a dishonest seaman anything more than the sums to which he is already [—7—] entitled under *Still*—unless the damages recovery is insufficient to absorb the prior payments.[19] Yet we are urged to strike a new balance and allow an employer who establishes a *McCorpen* defense to automatically recover prior payments, without requiring the employer to prove duplication and regardless

---

[16] *See Karim v. Finch Shipping Co. Ltd.*, 374 F.3d 302, 310 (5th Cir. 2004) ("[T]he protection of seamen was one of the principal reasons for the development of admiralty as a distinct branch of law." (citation omitted)).

[17] *See Wood v. Diamond M Drilling Co.*, 691 F.2d 1165, 1171 (5th Cir. 1982).

[18] *Id.* at 1171 (internal quotation marks omitted).

[19] We have recognized that cure payments are inherently duplicative of a Jones Act damages award for past medical expenses. *Brister v. A.W.I., Inc.*, 946 F.2d 350, 361 (5th Cir. 1991). Maintenance payments also duplicate a lesser-included portion of a Jones Act recovery, as they compensate the seaman for the loss of fringe benefits (food and lodging) he would have enjoyed aboard the vessel had he not been injured. *See, e.g., Williams v. Reading & Bates Drilling Co.*, 750 F.2d 487, 490 (5th Cir. 1985) (holding that a Jones Act damages award for lost compensation includes both wages and fringe benefits); *see also Averett v. Diamond Offshore Drilling Servs., Inc.*, 980 F. Supp. 855, 859 (E.D. La. 1997) ("[The seaman] has already received wages plus fringe benefits which included the food and lodging as part of his general damage award under the Jones Act and General Maritime Law. Thus, he is not entitled to recover this item under his maintenance and cure remedy.").

of the outcome of the primary suit. In cases where no damages are recovered, or the award is insufficient to offset the seaman's restitution liability, the employer would gain an affirmative judgment against the seaman. Although most likely uncollectible, the judgment would stand as a serious impediment to the seaman's economic recovery, and its threat would have a powerful *in terrorem* effect in settlement negotiations. The high-low settlement confected by the parties in this case evidences this effect, hinging on whether the risk factor of affirmative recovery will be allowed by this Court.

Transocean asks us to weigh again conflicting values—of protecting seamen from the dangers of the sea, and employers from dishonesty. But the existing regime hardly leaves employers powerless in the face of seaman fraud. Contrary to Transocean's suggestion, an employer is entitled to investigate a claim for maintenance and cure before tendering any payments to the seaman—without subjecting itself to liability for compensatory or punitive damages.[20] [—8—] If the employer finds any "causal link" between the seaman's present injury and a concealed prexisting disability, it can bring suit under *McCorpen* and terminate its obligation to pay—even if the seaman's on-the-job accident (and the employer's negligence) contributed to the injury. And to the extent that the employer has already paid benefits, it is entitled to recoup them when there are damages to offset. In our view, this scheme achieves a fair reconciliation between protecting seamen in the wake of debilitating on-the-job injury and ensuring that shipowners can protect themselves from liability for sums attributable to concealed preexisting injuries. The scheme has held its

own for decades and we are not so bold as to now claim a new view—one that the hundreds before us have either overlooked or rejected.

Today, we merely render explicit what has been implicit for many years: that once a shipowner pays maintenance and cure to the injured seaman, the payments can be recovered only by offset against the seaman's damages award—not by an independent suit seeking affirmative recovery. The case for exercising our extraordinary power to create a new right of action has not been made. There is only the change of advocates and judges, by definition irrelevant to the settling force of past jurisprudence—always prized but a treasure in matters maritime. This against the cold reality that the sea has become no less dangerous, and the seaman no less essential to maritime commerce.

III.

We REVERSE the district court's order awarding summary judgment to Transocean on its counterclaim and RENDER judgment for Boudreaux.

(Reporter's Note: Concurring opinion on p. 279).

---

[20] *See Morales v. Garijak, Inc.*, 829 F.2d 1355, 1358 (5th Cir. 1987) ("Upon receiving a claim for maintenance and cure, the shipowner need not immediately commence payments; he is entitled to investigate and require corroboration of the claim. . . . A shipowner who is in [—8—] fact liable for maintenance and cure, but who has been reasonable in denying liability, may be held liable only for the maintenance and cure[,] [not compensatory or punitive damages].").

[—9—] **CLEMENT,** Circuit Judge, concurring in the judgment.

Transocean asks us to recognize a counterclaim for restitution upon a successful establishment of a *McCorpen* defense. While I believe that such a counterclaim is possible under maritime law and general equitable principles, *see Pizani v. M/V Cotton Blossom*, 669 F.2d 1084, 1089 (5th Cir. 1982) ("A court of admiralty is, as to all matters falling within its jurisdiction, a court of equity." (quoting *The David Pratt*, 7 Fed. Cas. 22, 24 (D. Me. 1839)), the majority has expressed concern about recognizing this counterclaim wholesale with little in terms of caselaw to guide us.[1] Given the lack of precedent on this issue, the majority does not see this case as the ideal vehicle for evaluating the proposed counterclaim because it does not present sufficient information on the practical effect the claim would have on a seaman.

Although I concur in the judgment—if not the discussion of *Still v. Norfolk & Western Railway Co.*—I would recognize (not inconsistently with the majority opinion) that an employer may assert a counterclaim for maintenance and cure as a set-off to Jones Act damages when restitution will not result in an undue adverse impact on the seaman, and when maintenance and cure is not entirely duplicative of Jones Act damages. *Cf. Colburn v. Bunge Towing, Inc.*, 883 F.2d [—10—] 372, 378 (5th Cir. 1989).[2] I see nothing in our caselaw at variance with this conclusion, and believe that it is necessary, especially in the wake of *Atlantic Sounding Co. v. Townsend*, 557 U.S. 404 (2009), for this court to be able to continue to promote the "combined object of encouraging marine commerce and assuring the well-being of seamen." *Aguilar v. Standard Oil Co.*, 318 U.S. 724, 727 (1943).

---

[1] *But see Souviney v. John E. Graham & Sons*, No. 93-0479, 1994 WL 416643, at *5 (S.D. Ala. 1994) (unpublished) ("Because plaintiff intentionally concealed material facts about the very back injury for which he now seeks recovery against the defendant . . . as a matter of law, plaintiff is not entitled to receive maintenance and cure benefits. To the extent that such benefits have been paid by the defendant, the defendant is entitled to recover the amount of those benefits by way of judgment against the plaintiff."); *Quiming v. Int'l Pac. Enters., Ltd.*, 773 F. Supp. 230, 235-37 (D. Haw. 1990) (granting a counterclaim for $30,000 of maintenance and cure after defendants established that the plaintiff was never legally entitled to receive the benefits); *see also Bergeria v. Marine Carriers, Inc.*, 341 F. Supp. 1153, 1154-56 (E.D. Pa. 1972) ("In addition to our finding that [a] counterclaim [for improperly paid maintenance and cure] is cognizable within the maritime jurisdiction, it must also be allowed as a contractual set-off.").

[2] This is the result Boudreaux and Transocean sought by way of their bracketed settlement agreement. On the facts of this case, I would find recovery permissible.

United States Court of Appeals
for the Fifth Circuit

No. 12-30230

IN RE DEEPWATER HORIZON

RANGER INS., LTD.
vs.
TRANSOCEAN OFFSHORE DEEPWATER DRILLING,
INC.

Appeal from the United States District Court for the
Eastern District of Louisiana

Decided: August 29, 2013

Citation: 728 F.3d 491, 1 Adm. R. 280 (5th Cir. 2013).

Before **JOLLY, BENAVIDES,** and **HIGGINSON,** Circuit
Judges.

[—2—] **JOLLY,** Circuit Judge:

The original opinion in this case was filed on March 1, 2013.[1] Because this case involves important and determinative questions of Texas law as to which there is no controlling Texas Supreme Court precedent, the panel, upon the petition for rehearing, unanimously withdraws the previous opinion and substitutes the following certified questions to the Supreme Court of Texas.

CERTIFICATION FROM THE UNITED STATES COURT OF APPEALS FOR THE FIFTH CIRCUIT TO THE SUPREME COURT OF TEXAS, PURSUANT TO THE TEXAS CONSTITUTION ART. 5 § 3-C AND TEXAS RULE OF APPELLATE PROCEDURE 58.1. [—3—]

TO THE SUPREME COURT OF TEXAS AND THE HONORABLE JUSTICES THEREOF:

I. Style of the Case: Parties and Counsel

The style of the case is In re: Deepwater Horizon: Ranger Insurance, Limited, Plaintiff–Appellee v. Transocean Offshore Deepwater Drilling, Incorporated; Transocean Holdings, L.L.C.; Transocean Deepwater, Incorporated; Triton Asset Leasing GMBH, Intervenor Plaintiffs–Appellees v. BP P.L.C.; BP Exploration & Production, Incorporated; BP American Production Company; BP Corporation North America, Incorporated; BP Company North America, Incorporated; BP Products North America, Incorporated; BP America, Incorporated; BP Holdings North America, Limited Defendants–Intervenor Defendants–Appellants; Certain Underwriters at Lloyd's London, Plaintiff–Appellee, Transocean Offshore Deepwater Drilling, Incorporated; Transocean Holdings, L.L.C.; Transocean Deepwater, Incorporated; Triton Asset Leasing GMBH, Intervenor Plaintiffs–Appellees v. BP P.L.C.; BP Exploration & Production, Incorporated; BP America Production Company; BP Corporation North America, Incorporated; BP Company North America, Incorporated; BP Products North America, Incorporated; BP America, Incorporated; BP Holdings North America, Limited, Defendants–Intervenor Defendants–Appellants. This is Case No. 12-30230, in the United States Court of Appeals for the Fifth Circuit, on appeal from the judgment of the United States District Court for the Eastern District of Louisiana. Federal jurisdiction is premised upon 28 U.S.C. § 1333.

The names of all the parties to the case, each of whom is represented by counsel, and the respective names, addresses, and telephone numbers of their counsel, are as follows:

• Ranger Insurance, Limited, plaintiff in the district court and appellee in this court, represented by Michael John Maloney of Maloney, Martin & [—4—] Associates, Suite 100, 3401 Allen Parkway, Houston, TX 77019-0000, Tel. 713-759-1600;

• Transocean Offshore Deepwater Drilling, Incorporated; Transocean Holdings, L.L.C.; Transocean Deepwater, Incorporated; and Triton Asset Leasing GMBH, intervenor-plaintiffs in the district court and appellees in this court, represented by Steven Lynn Roberts, of Sutherland Asbill & Brennan, L.L.P., Suite 3700, 1001 Fannin Street, Houston, TX 77002-6760, Tel. 713-470-6192;

---

[1] *In re Deepwater Horizon,* 710 F.3d 338 (5th Cir. 2013).

- BP, P.L.C.; BP Exploration & Production, Incorporated; BP American Production Company; BP Corporation North America, Incorporated; BP Company North America, Incorporated; BP Products North America, Incorporated; BP America, Incorporated; BP Holdings North America Limited, defendants and defendant-intervenors in the district court and appellants in this court, represented by David B. Goodwin of Covington & Burling, L.L.P., 35th Floor, 1 Front Street, San Francisco, CA 94111-5356, Tel. 415-591-6000; and

- Certain Underwriters at Lloyds London, plaintiff in the district court and appellee in this court, represented by Richard N. Dicharry of Phelps Dunbar, L.L.P., Suite 2000, 365 Canal Street, 1 Canal Place, New Orleans, LA 70130, Tel. 504-556-1311.

II. Statement of the Case

Transocean Holdings, Inc. ("Transocean") owned the *Deepwater Horizon*, a semi-submersible, mobile offshore drilling unit. In April 2010, the *Deepwater Horizon* sank into the Gulf of Mexico after burning for two days following an onboard explosion ("Incident" or "*Deepwater Horizon* Incident"). At the time of the Incident, the *Deepwater Horizon* was engaged in exploratory drilling activities at the Macondo Well under a Drilling Contract between the Appellant BP American Production Company's (together with its affiliates, "BP") [—5—] predecessor and Transocean's predecessor. This Contract required Transocean to maintain certain minimum insurance coverages for the benefit of BP. The extent to which these policies covered BP's pollution-related liabilities arising from the *Deepwater Horizon* Incident is the subject of this appeal.

The Insurance Contracts

Transocean held insurance policies with a primary liability insurer, Ranger Insurance Ltd. ("Ranger"), as well as several excess liability insurers led by London market syndicates ("Excess Insurers;" together with Ranger, "Insurers"). Transocean's insurance policy with Ranger provided at least $50 million of general liability coverage, and its policies with the Excess Insurers formed four layers of excess coverage directly above the Ranger Policy that provided at least $700 million of additional general liability coverage. The Ranger and Excess Policies contain materially identical provisions.[2] The Policy terms that are important to this case are "Insured" and "Insured Contract." The Policies define "Insured" as including the Named Insured, other parties, and

> (c) any person or entity to whom the "Insured" is obliged by any oral or written "Insured Contract" (including contracts which are in agreement but have not been formally concluded in writing) entered into before any relevant "Occurrence", to provide insurance such as is afforded by this Policy . . . .

The Policies define "Insured Contract" as follows:

> The words "Insured Contract", whenever used in this Policy, shall mean any written or oral contract or agreement entered into by the "Insured" (including contracts which are in agreement but have not been formally concluded in writing) and pertaining to business under which the "Insured" assumes the tort liability of another party to pay for "Bodily Injury", "Property Damage", "Personal Injury" or "Advertising Injury" to a "Third Party" or organization. [—6—] Tort Liability means a liability that would be imposed by law in the absence of any contract or agreement.[3]

---

[2] As the district court noted (and the Insurers have not disputed), this similarity allows the court to treat all of the Insurers as one for purposes of analysis in this case.

[3] The Policies contain further provisions addressing other insureds. Endorsement 1 provides a general condition that additional insureds are automatically included where required by written contract. Condition D.1 to Section I coverage limits the coverage of additional insureds: Transocean has the privilege to name additional insureds only to the extent as is required under contract or agreement.

The Drilling Contract

The Drilling Contract defines BP's and Transocean's obligations to one another, separately identifying the liabilities each party assumes. Article 20 of the Contract is a singular provision that imposes upon Transocean an insurance requirement:

20.1 INSURANCE

Without limiting the indemnity obligations or liabilities of CONTRACTOR [Transocean] or its insurer, at all times during the term of this CONTRACT, CONTRACTOR **shall maintain insurance covering the operations to be performed under this CONTRACT as set forth in Exhibit C.**

(Emphasis added.) Exhibit C to the Drilling Contract is titled "Insurance Requirements" and establishes the types and minimum level of coverage that Transocean is obligated to maintain. This Exhibit provides that Transocean shall carry all insurance at its own expense and that the policies "shall be endorsed to provide that there will be no recourse against [BP] for payment of premium." Further, Exhibit C states:

[BP], its subsidiaries and affiliated companies, co-owners, and joint venturers, if any, and their employees, officers and agents **shall be named as additional insureds in each of [Transocean's] policies, except Workers' Compensation for liabilities assumed by [Transocean] under the terms of this Contract.**

(Emphasis added.)

The Procedural History [—7—]

Following the Incident, BP notified the Insurers of its *Deepwater Horizon*-related losses. The Excess Insurers and Ranger each filed a one-count declaratory judgment action against BP.[4] The Insurers' complaints are substantively identical—both request a declaration that the Insurers have "no additional-insured obligation to BP with respect to pollution claims against BP for oil emanating from BP's well" as a result of the *Deepwater Horizon* Incident. The Insurers acknowledge that "the [D]rilling Contract requires additional insured protection in favor of certain BP entities." Thus, all parties concede that the Drilling Contract is an "insured contract" under the policies and that the policies provide some insurance coverage to BP as an additional insured. The issue in contention is the scope of BP's insurance coverage.

In July 2011, BP moved for judgment on the pleadings, under Rule 12(c) of the Federal Rules of Civil Procedure, against the Insurers. Relying upon Texas and Fifth Circuit precedent as developed in *Evanston Ins. Co. v. ATOFINA Petrochems., Inc.*, 256 S.W.3d 660 (Tex. 2008), and in *Aubris Resources LP v. St. Paul Fire & Marine Ins. Co.*, 566 F.3d 483 (5th Cir. 2009), BP argued (1) it was an "additional insured" under the insurance policies at issue and (2) the insurance policies alone—and not the indemnities detailed in the Drilling Contract—govern the scope of BP's coverage rights as an "additional insured."[5]

The district court found *ATOFINA* and *Aubris* are distinguishable from the case at hand and denied BP's Rule 12(c) motion in November 2011. In [—8—] particular, the court read Transocean's insurance obligation in Exhibit C to the Drilling Contract to be to name BP as an "additional insured[] in each of [Transocean's] policies . . . for liabilities assumed by [Transocean] under the terms of the contract." That is, the district court found BP's proffered reading of this clause unreasonable, and read the clause as if there

---

[4] In February 2011, the Judicial Panel on Multidistrict Litigation transferred both cases to the United States District Court for the Eastern District of Louisiana for coordinated pretrial proceedings with the other *Deepwater Horizon*-related litigation pending in that court. In March 2011, Transocean moved for leave to intervene in the consolidated actions, which motion the court granted.

[5] BP argues this motion did not require a determination of any rights or obligations of BP or Transocean to one another under any provisions of the Drilling Contract.

were a comma following the phrase "except Workers' Compensation;" this reading rendered those three words their own discrete carve out from liability. Reasoning further that this interpretation required Transocean to name BP as an insured only for liabilities Transocean explicitly assumed under the contract, the court then looked to Article 24 of the Drilling Contract to conclude that BP was not covered under Transocean's policy for the pollution-related liabilities deriving from the *Deepwater Horizon* Incident (as the spill originated below the surface of the water).[6]

Following further submissions of the parties, the district court then entered a partial final judgment on the Insurers' complaints under Rule 54(b). [—9—] Effective March 1, 2012, the court held "by its terms, the Court's Order and Reasons [on BP's motion for judgment on the pleadings] not only denied BP's motion but also granted

---

[6] With respect to pollution-related liabilities, Article 24.1 of the Contract provides:

CONTRACTOR [Transocean] shall assume full responsibility for and shall protect, release, defend, indemnify, and hold COMPANY [BP] and its joint owners harmless from and against any loss, damage, expense, claim, fine, penalty, demand, or liability **for pollution or contamination**, including control and removal thereof, **originating on or above the surface of the land or water**, from spills, leaks, or discharges of fuels, lubricants, motor oils, pipe dope, paints, solvents, ballast, air emissions, bilge sludge, garbage, or any other liquid or solid whatsoever in possession and control of CONTRACTOR . . . .

(Emphasis added.) Article 24.2 then provides:

COMPANY [BP] shall assume full responsibility for and shall protect, release, defend, indemnify, and hold CONTRACTOR [Transocean] harmless from and against any loss, damage, expense, claim, fine, penalty, demand, or liability **for pollution or contamination**, including control and removal thereof, **arising out of or connected with operations under this CONTRACT hereunder and not assumed by CONTRACTOR in Article 24.1 above** . . . .

(Emphasis added.)

judgment on the pleadings against [BP] and in favor of the Plaintiff Insurers on the Plaintiff Insurers' complaints."[7] BP timely appealed. A unanimous panel of this court initially reversed the district court's judgment. *In re Deepwater Horizon*, 710 F.3d 338 (5th Cir. 2013). The Insurers and Transocean petitioned for rehearing, and we withdrew that ruling to certify the following question to the Texas Supreme Court.

III. Legal Issues

BP appeals the district court's conclusion that it is not entitled to coverage under the policies, because Transocean was only required to name BP as an additional insured as to the risks Transocean assumed in the indemnities provisions of the Drilling Contract.

A.

The first issue is the scope of BP's coverage as an additional insured, and whether the umbrella policy itself determines the extent of coverage, or the indemnity clauses in the Drilling Contract effectively limit BP's coverage.

In 2008, the Texas Supreme Court addressed "whether a commercial umbrella insurance policy that was purchased to secure the insured's indemnity obligation in a service contract with a third party also provides direct liability coverage for the third party." *ATOFINA*, 256 S.W.3d at 662. Both the appellants and the appellees agree this case is instructive, but they proffer different applications of its holding to the facts of the case at issue. Uncertainty regarding the outcome under *ATOFINA* ultimately triggered this certification. [—10—]

In *ATOFINA*, ATOFINA owned an oil refinery at which it hired Triple S to perform maintenance functions. *Id.* at 662. ATOFINA

---

[7] In its brief, BP notes that this partial final judgment was entered in favor of the Insurers "and Transocean" and argues that Transocean is not a proper party to this order. BP's Rule 12(c) motion was directed only to the Insurers' complaints and claims—not against Transocean.

and Triple S entered a services contract which stipulated that ATOFINA was to be named an additional insured in each of Triple S's policies. Specifically, this provision stated:

> [ATOFINA], its parents, subsidiaries and affiliated companies, and their respective employees, officers and agents shall be named as additional insured in each of [Triple S's] policies, except Workers' Compensation; however, such extension of coverage shall not apply with respect to any obligations for which [ATOFINA] has specifically agreed to indemnify [Triple S].[8]

After a Triple S employee drowned while servicing the ATOFINA refinery, his estate sued ATOFINA and Triple S for wrongful death. *Id.* at 663. Triple S's insurer, Evanston, and ATOFINA disagreed over who was required to pay for the litigation; ATOFINA contended it was an additional insured and thus covered, while Evanston argued ATOFINA's agreement to indemnify Triple S for ATOFINA's sole negligence precluded coverage. *Id.*

The Texas Supreme Court began by noting that ATOFINA sought coverage from Evanston on the basis that it was Triple S's additional insured—and had not sought indemnity directly from Triple S. *Id.* at 663-64. The court next looked to Section III.B.6 of the policy, which defined who is an insured as

> A person or organization for whom you have agreed to provide insurance as is afforded by this policy; but that person or organization is an insured only with respect to operations performed by you

or on your behalf, or facilities owned or used by you. [—11—]

Id. at 664. Because, by its own terms, this Section covered ATOFINA "with respect to operations performed by" Triple S, the court found this Section provided ATOFINA direct coverage even for its sole negligence.[9] *Id.* at 667. The court reached this conclusion, in part, because it found "it . . . unmistakable that the agreement in this case to extend *direct* insured status to ATOFINA as an additional insured is separate and independent from ATOFINA's agreement to forego *contractual* indemnity for its own negligence."[10] *Id.* at 670.

In this appeal, BP focuses upon the *ATOFINA* court's statement that, "[i]nstead of looking, as the court of appeals did, to the indemnity agreement in the service contract to determine the scope of coverage, we base our decision on the terms of the umbrella insurance policy itself." 256 S.W.3d at 664. And it further highlights that, as in *ATOFINA*, it is seeking insurance coverage from the Insurers, not indemnification from Transocean, and that the umbrella policy itself does not limit coverage for additional insureds.[11] Because the additional insured provision and the indemnities provisions in the Drilling Contract are separate and independent, because the Policy provides coverage to additional insureds "such as is afforded by this Policy," and because Transocean would be covered for the injuries at issue, BP contends it, too, is entitled to coverage.

---

[8] Petitioner's Br. on the Merits, *Evanston Ins. Co. v. ATOFINA Petrochemicals, Inc.*, 256 S.W.3d 660 (Tex. 2008) (No. 03-0647), 2004 WL 1047377, at *4. Triple S also agreed to indemnify ATOFINA from all personal injuries and property losses sustained during the performance of the contract, "except to the extent that any such loss is attributable to the concurrent or sole negligence, misconduct, or strict liability of [ATOFINA]." 256 S.W.3d at 662.

[9] Moreover, the court stated that "had the parties intended to insure ATOFINA for vicarious liability only, 'language clearly embodying that intention was available.'" *Id.* at 666 (citing *McIntosh v. Scottsdale Ins. Co.*, 992 F.2d 251, 255 (10th Cir. 1993)).

[10] The court further "disapprove[d] of the view that this kind of additional insured requirement fails to establish a separate and independent obligation for insuring liability." 256 S.W.3d at 670.

[11] For example, that policy does not say coverage for additional insureds is "limited to the liabilities assumed by the Named Insured in the agreement between the Named Insured and Additional Insured."

The Insurers and Transocean, to the contrary, highlight the differences between the additional insured provisions at issue in *ATOFINA* and here. The *ATOFINA* clause, they proffer, imposed a broad requirement to list ATOFINA [—12—] as an additional insured, whereas the analogous clause in the Drilling Contract creates a far more limited obligation, namely, to name BP as an additional insured only for liabilities Transocean specifically assumed in the contract. Furthermore, they contend that this language renders the additional insured provision inextricable from the indemnities provisions of the Drilling Contract; unlike in *ATOFINA*, the additional insured requirement is not separate and independent. They argue further the umbrella policy requires an "Insured Contract" exist between the named insured and the third party, while in *ATOFINA* no contract was required. In combination, the appellees contend, these factors allow the court to consider the indemnities clauses in the Drilling Contract in discerning the extent to which BP is covered as an additional insured.

Because there are potentially important distinctions between the facts of the instant case and *ATOFINA*, the outcome is not entirely clear.

B.

In the event the court must consider whether the Drilling Contract imposes limitations upon BP's coverage as an additional insured, an issue then arises of how to interpret the additional insured provision of that Contract. The parties offer competing interpretations, and which party prevails may depend upon whether the doctrine of *contra proferentem* applies.

Texas law has consistently held that, if an insurance coverage provision is susceptible to more than one reasonable interpretation, the court must interpret that provision in favor of the insured, so long as that interpretation is reasonable. *Nat'l Union Fire Ins. Co. of Pittsburgh, Pa. v. Hudson Energy Co.*, 811 S.W.2d 552, 555 (Tex. 1991). The court must do so even if the insurer's interpretation is

more reasonable than the insured's—"[i]n particular, exceptions or limitations on liability are strictly construed against the insurer and in favor of the insured," *id.*, and "[a]n intent to exclude coverage must be expressed in [—13—] clear and unambiguous language." *ATOFINA*, 256 S.W.3d at 668, 668 n.27 (citing *Hudson Energy*, 811 S.W.2d at 555); *see also Certain Underwriters at Lloyds, London v. Law*, 570 F.3d 574, 577 (5th Cir. 2009) ("If . . . ambiguity is found, the contractual language will be 'liberally' construed in favor of the insured." (citing *Barnett v. Aetna Life Ins. Co.*, 723 S.W.2d 663, 666 (Tex. 1987))).

This rule favoring the insured derives, in part, from the "special relationship between insurers and insureds arising from the parties' unequal bargaining power." *Balandran v. Safeco Ins. Co. of America*, 972 S.W.2d 738, 741 n.1 (Tex. 1998). This aspect of the rule's foundation hearkens to the doctrine of *contra proferentem*, which construes any ambiguities against the drafter, and the "sophisticated insured" exception, which may apply when the policy is in some way negotiable (i.e., it is not a contract of adhesion) and the insured is as capable as the insurer of interpreting the contract.

The Texas Supreme Court has never recognized a sophisticated insured exception to the general rule of interpreting insurance coverage clauses, nor has it ever indicated *contra proferentem* would not apply in construing these clauses. *See, e.g., ATOFINA*, 256 S.W.3d at 668 (stating the traditional rule construing coverage clauses in favor of the insured). Given that Texas has long recognized its rules regarding interpretation of insurance coverage clauses are partially derivative of the unequal bargaining power typical in many negotiations over insurance contracts, however, it is possible that such an exception may be deemed appropriate in a case like this, where all the parties involved are highly capable contractors.[12] On the one

---

[12] One federal district court in Texas has found that the sophisticated insured exception might apply under Texas law, given the right circumstances. *Vought Aircraft Indus., Inc. v.*

hand, the facts here indicate Insurers were not involved in drafting the Drilling Contract, and thus construing ambiguities in that contract against them might be inappropriate. But on the other, the [—14—] Insurers were involved in drafting the umbrella policy language at issue, and the failure of that policy language to limit coverage in underlying "Insured Contracts" to the liabilities assumed by the named insured in those contracts is part of what ails the Insurers now.

C.

Each party contends that its interpretation and application of *ATOFINA* better advances the goals of Texas insurance law and is more aligned with the intent of the parties. Their arguments illuminate the magnitude and wide ramifications, both throughout the oil and gas industry and for insurance law, of this case. Where state law governs such an issue, these policy factors are better gauged by the state high court than by a federal court.

IV. Questions Certified

For the reasons discussed above, we hereby certify the following determinative questions of Texas law to the Supreme Court of Texas.

1. Whether *Evanston Ins. Co. v. ATOFINA Petrochems., Inc.*, 256 S.W.3d 660 (Tex. 2008), compels a finding that BP is covered for the damages at issue, because the language of the umbrella policies alone determines the extent of BP's coverage as an additional insured if, and so long as, the additional insured and indemnity provisions of the Drilling Contract are "separate and independent"?

2. Whether the doctrine of *contra proferentem* applies to the interpretation of the insurance coverage provision of the Drilling Contract under the *ATOFINA* case,

256 S.W.3d at 668, given the facts of this case?

We disclaim any intention or desire that the Supreme Court of Texas confine its reply to the precise form or scope of the questions certified.

Falvey Cargo Underwriting, Ltd., 729 F. Supp. 2d 814, 824-25 (N.D. Tex. 2010).

United States Court of Appeals
for the Fifth Circuit

No. 13-30315

IN RE DEEPWATER HORIZON

LAKE EUGENIE LAND & DEV., INC.
vs.
BP EXPLORATION & PROD., INC.

Appeal from the United States District Court for the
Eastern District of Louisiana

Decided: October 2, 2013
Revised: November 5, 2013

Citation: 732 F.3d 326, 1 Adm. R. 287 (5th Cir. 2013).

Before **DENNIS, CLEMENT,** and **SOUTHWICK,** Circuit
Judges.

[—3—] **CLEMENT,** Circuit Judge:

BP Exploration & Production, Inc. ("BP")
appeals the district court's decision
upholding the Claims Administrator's
interpretation of the settlement agreement
between it and the class of parties injured in
the *Deepwater Horizon* oil spill. BP also
appeals the district court's dismissal of its
action for breach of contract against the
Administrator and denial of its motion for a
preliminary injunction. We affirm the district
court's dismissal of BP's suit against the
Claims Administrator. We reverse the district
court's denial of BP's motion for a preliminary
injunction and the district court's order
affirming the Administrator's interpretation of
the Settlement and remand to the district
court for further consideration.

FACTS AND PROCEEDINGS

BP leased the *Deepwater Horizon* drilling
platform from Transocean to drill its Macondo
prospect off the Louisiana coast. On April 20,
2010, the exploratory well Transocean was
drilling blew out. After the initial explosion
and during the ensuing fire, the platform
sank, causing millions of barrels of oil [—4—]
to spill into the Gulf of Mexico. Eleven
workers died; sixteen more were injured.
Litigation followed.

The Judicial Panel on Multidistrict
Litigation centralized the non-securities
federal lawsuits in the District Court for the
Eastern District of Louisiana. BP, as lessor of
the rig, was named as a defendant in most of
these suits.

BP waived its statutory limit of liability
and committed to pay all legitimate claims,
even those in excess of the $75 million liability
cap under the Oil Pollution Act, 33 U.S.C.
§2704(a)(3). BP initially established its own
claims process and later funded the claims
process administered by the Gulf Coast
Claims Facility ("GCCF") to begin paying out
claims immediately instead of at the
conclusion of litigation. Over approximately
18 months, the company paid out more than
$6.3 billion to individuals and businesses with
spill-related losses.

BP began negotiating a class settlement in
February 2011. In March 2012, the district
court granted the parties' request to
implement a process to transfer claims from
the GCCF to a court-supervised program that
the parties agreed to in principle. The court
appointed Patrick Juneau as Claims
Administrator of this program. The parties
filed notice of their proposed settlement (the
"Settlement") in April 2012, to which the
district court gave preliminary approval in
May and directed to begin processing claims
in June.

Businesses' claims for economic loss are
one type of claim covered by the Settlement.
Under the class definition, business economic
loss ("BEL") claimants must have conducted
commercial activities in the Gulf Coast region
[—5—] during the relevant period.[1] In order
to qualify as a class member, BEL claimants
also must have suffered loss of income,
earnings, or profits as a result of the
Deepwater Horizon accident. This category of
economic damage to a business is fully

---

[1] Business claimants must have owned,
operated, or leased property, or conducted certain
business activities within Louisiana, Mississippi,
Alabama, and certain coastal counties in eastern
Texas and Western Florida, as well as specified
adjacent Gulf waters and bays between April 20,
2010 and April 16, 2012.

described in the attached Exhibit 4, which includes requirements for documenting losses (Exhibit 4A) and establishing causation (Exhibit 4B), as well as the compensation scheme (Exhibit 4C).

After a BEL claimant provides the documentation needed to submit a claim and evidence required that the oil spill caused its losses, the claimant is entitled to compensation for the difference between its actual profit "during a defined post-spill period in 2010 [and] the profit that the claimant might have expected to earn in the comparable post-spill period of 2010." This amount includes "the reduction in Variable Profit," defined as "any reduction in profit between the 2010 Compensation Period selected by the claimant and the comparable months of the Benchmark Period." The post-spill Compensation Period "is selected by the Claimant to include three or more consecutive months between May and December 2010." It is compared to a pre-spill baseline, the "Benchmark Period," of the claimant's choosing: either 2009, the average of 2008-2009, or the average of 2007-2009. Variable Profit "is calculated for both the Benchmark Period and the Compensation Period as follows:

1. Sum the monthly revenue over the period.
2. Subtract the corresponding variable expenses from revenue over the same time period." [—6—]

As early as September 28, 2012, BP raised concerns about the varied accounting methods claimants used in the ordinary course of their record-keeping and the ways in which erroneously-stated expenses could cause erroneous variable profit calculations. The district court held the final fairness hearing on November 8 and granted final approval on December 21, 2012.

On December 5, 2012, BP requested that the Administrator convene a Claims Administration Panel to consider "the issue of the assignment of revenue to the proper months for purposes of the BEL causation framework and the proper matching of

revenue and corresponding expenses for purposes of the BEL compensation framework."[2] BP asked to meet with the Administrator, Class Counsel, and the accounting vendors to discuss this issue, followed by a formal Panel, if necessary.

On December 16, Class Counsel requested a Policy Announcement addressing the issue. After reviewing both parties' written submissions, the Administrator issued a Policy Announcement on January 15, 2013. He stated that, for both calculation of Variable Profit and purposes of causation, he would "typically consider both revenues and expenses in the periods in which those revenues and expenses were recorded at the time," and would "not typically re-allocate such revenues or expenses to different periods," but would "however, reserve the right to adjust the financial statements in certain circumstances, including but not limited to, inconsistent basis of accounting between benchmark and compensation periods, errors in previously recorded transactions and flawed [—7—] or inconsistent treatment of accounting estimates." The Administrator later explained that he did not believe he was authorized "to carve out specific types of claims for additional analysis as BP had proposed."

BP was not satisfied with the Policy Announcement. BP alleged that the Administrator's misinterpretation of the Settlement resulted in awards of hundreds of millions of dollars to BEL claimants with inflated losses or no losses at all. The parties convened a Claims Administration Panel. When the panel failed to reach a unanimous agreement, they presented the matter to the district court for resolution. Before the district court, BP contested the Administrator's interpretation of the meaning of several of the Settlement's terms: "revenue," "expenses,"

---

[2] As specified in the Settlement, a Claims Administration Panel is the first step in resolving a disagreement over how the Administrator is administering the Settlement Program. If the Panel, composed of the Administrator and representatives from each party, cannot reach a unanimous decision, the issue is "referred to the Court for resolution."

"corresponding," and "comparable." According to the company, revenue and expenses have generally accepted definitions among economists and accountants that do not permit the Administrator to calculate a BEL claimant's Variable Profit based only on cash receipts or cash disbursements. Rather, a claimant's expenses must be "matched" to corresponding revenue. In addition, the Settlement's requirement that the Administrator measure the difference between Variable Profit in the Compensation Period and the "comparable months of the Benchmark Period" requires that the Administrator compare Variable Profit in comparable months—in other words, when a claimant engaged in similar conduct—not necessarily the "same" months.

On January 30, the district court affirmed the Administrator's Policy Announcement. The district court acknowledged that the Administrator's interpretation "may sometimes cause apparent anomalies (in either direction) in claim determinations." But it noted that this consequence "appears to be the result of the objective, straight-forward mechanisms set forth in the Settlement." [—8—] It found that "BP's proposed remedy does not appear to be based on any generally accepted accounting principle, and might only result in adding another level of complexity and subjective analysis to the BEL calculation."

BP filed a motion to reconsider, and the district court issued a written ruling on March 5 upholding the Administrator's interpretation and denying BP's motion. The district court reasoned that "[n]owhere does the Agreement state or indicate that revenue and expenses must be 'matched' or revenues 'smoothed,' nor does it state that one should inquire into when revenue was 'earned.'" The district court held that revenues and expenses need not be matched and that "the same months of the Compensation Period are to be compared with the months in the Benchmark Period" rather than "months where the claimant engaged in comparable activity."

In response to the district court's order, BP filed a breach of contract claim against the Administrator and an emergency motion for a preliminary injunction to enjoin the Administrator from implementing the Settlement in accordance with the March 5 order and instead to require the Administrator to implement BP's proposed interpretation. The Administrator filed a motion to dismiss BP's breach of contract claim, arguing that BP failed to state a claim. The district court granted the motion, concluding that the Administrator could not breach the Settlement by interpreting and implementing the agreement in compliance with the district court's order. It also denied BP's request for injunctive relief.

BP appeals the district court's March 5 order affirming the Administrator's interpretation of the Settlement, its order granting the Administrator's motion to dismiss, and its order denying a preliminary injunction.

STANDARD OF REVIEW [—9—]

A district court's interpretation of a settlement agreement is a question of law, which we review de novo. *Waterfowl L.L.C. v. United States*, 473 F.3d 135, 141 (5th Cir. 2006).[3] For a denial of a preliminary

---

[3] We have jurisdiction over BP's appeal of the district court's March 5 order under the collateral order doctrine. The order conclusively determined the interpretation dispute, which is completely separate from the merits of BP's liability for the oil spill, and it will be effectively unreviewable on appeal from final judgment because, at that point, the improper awards will have been distributed to potentially thousands of claimants and BP will have no practical way of recovering these funds should it prevail. *See Walker v. U.S. Dep't of Hous. & Urban Dev.*, 99 F.3d 761, 766-67 (5th Cir. 1996).

Moreover, the procedures for resolving disputes concerning the Administrator's administration of the Settlement specify that a disagreement is "referred to the Court for resolution" if it is not resolved by the Claims Administration Panel. Based on its use throughout the Settlement, the term "the Court" appears to refer to the district court. Such an interpretation of the parties' agreement would render the district court's ruling final. However, the parties clearly intended a broader interpretation of the term—one that retained their right to appeal to this court—as

injunction, a "district court's findings of fact 'are subject to a clearly-erroneous standard of review,' while conclusions of law 'are subject to broad review and will be reversed if incorrect.'" *Janvey v. Alguire*, 647 F.3d 585, 591-92 (5th Cir. 2011) (citations omitted).

DISCUSSION

BP argues that the district court disregarded the plain text of the Settlement by interpreting it to permit recovery of fictitious and inflated losses. It contends that this misinterpretation also leads to absurd results and contravenes the purpose of the Settlement, which BP characterizes as "compensat[ing] for actual lost profits rather than . . . provid[ing] unjustifiable windfalls to uninjured claimants."

I. Artificial Claims

We repeat the relevant language of Exhibit 4C: [—10—]

Variable Profit: This is calculated for both the Benchmark Period and the Compensation Period as follows:

1. Sum the monthly revenue over the period.
2. Subtract the corresponding variable expenses from revenue over the same time period.

BP contends that the district court's interpretation of "revenue" and "expenses" for the purposes of Exhibit 4C does not comport with the accepted economic and accounting meanings of those terms. It also argues that "corresponding" necessarily implies matching variable expenses to the revenues with which they are properly associated. Accordingly, BP argues the district court erred in concluding that "revenue" and "corresponding variable expenses" refer only to "cash received" and "cash disbursed" in the relevant period. We will explain why this language in Exhibit 4C cannot be interpreted so that it always means cash received and cash disbursed. We leave

---

shown by BP's appeal and Class Counsel's failure to object.

open for remand whether it ever has that meaning.

To understand our interpretation of variable profit, we start with a discussion of some accounting concepts that are fundamental in understanding the meaning of the agreement.

A. *Revenue and Expense Recognition Principles*

The purpose of financial record-keeping is to provide businesses with accurate and reliable information upon which to make decisions. Principles of revenue and expense recognition vary based upon accounting judgment, regulatory or transactional requirements, or even internal management preferences. While an imperfect presentation of the broad array of accounting [—11—] methods in the business world at-large, a delineation might be fairly made between cash and accrual accounting. Depending on which of these methods a business chooses, the terms "revenue" and "expenses" take on widely variant meanings.

Typically, only very small and fledgling businesses keep their primary financial records in accordance with cash accounting principles. *See* CPA Societies' Amicus Brief at 7-8 ("some small enterprises . . . use a strict or modified cash-basis approach"). That is, they recognize revenue when cash from a given transaction is received and expenses when cash is paid. *Id.* at 11-12. Class Counsel urged in a December 2012 memorandum: "[w]hen a business keeps its books on a cash-basis, revenue is earned during the month of receipt, irrespective of when the contract was entered or services were performed." It argued further that "[t]he 'corresponding variable expenses' associated with monthly revenue are the expenses that are expended or incurred during the ... months in question." These statements are consistent only with revenue and expense recognition principles of cash accounting. Cash accounting can be useful for many enterprises as a method of analyzing periodic cash needs, but this use is largely unrelated to the concepts of "revenue" and "expenses."

On the other hand, accrual accounting has as a fundamental principle the recognition of revenue when the entity becomes entitled to receive payment, as opposed to when the payment is actually received. *See Statement of Financial Accounting Concepts No. 6*, Fin. Accounting Standards Bd., ¶ 139. Expenses that can be readily traced to the recognized revenues are themselves recognized [—12—] at the same time as those revenues. *Id.* at ¶146.[4] This correlation gives business decision-makers a real-time view of the net economic value of a transaction in the period most relevant to its overall economic significance. *Id.* at ¶ 140. This is sometimes referred to as "matching" revenues and expenses, but in any case this procedure is a fundamental aspect of day-to-day record-keeping on the accrual-basis. *See id.* at ¶ 144, 146.

BP argues extensively in its brief that these revenue and expense recognition principles were to apply to Exhibit 4C computations. Class Counsel argues that the agreement's language does not, in fact, permit such an interpretation because the settlement does not state that revenues and expenses must be matched or that revenues must be recognized according to any objective standard.

Business and Economic Loss ("BEL") claimants in the agreement are a broad spectrum of businesses throughout the Gulf region. Some claimants ("cash-basis claimants") will present cash-basis records because this is how they contemporaneously record their financial activities. Others ("accrual-basis claimants") will present accrual-basis records for the same reason. For many of the BEL claimants who are the focus of this appeal, their contemporaneously recorded financial records, absent mere bookkeeping errors, will contain "matched" revenues and expenses before they even submit their claims. In a [—13—] December 2012 Memorandum, BP acknowledged that many claims presented data that "sufficiently match" revenue and expenses. This is because they apply the accrual accounting recognition and matching principles BP advances here as a matter of their ordinary record-keeping. On the other hand, cash-basis claimants might present records that are not so matched.

The March 5 Order apparently adopted Class Counsel's interpretation of Exhibit 4C, holding that revenue and expenses referred only to cash payments and disbursements. The practical effect of this ruling is unclear in light of the different recognition principles under different accounting methods. We now turn to a more focused discussion of the district court's decision.

B. Accrual-basis Claimants

Exhibit 4C directs the Administrator to "[s]um the monthly revenue over the period," and then "[s]ubtract the corresponding variable expenses from revenue over the same time period." In the March 5 order, the district court appears to have interpreted "revenue" as "cash received" and "expenses" as "cash disbursed," without reference to whether the holding was to apply to all claims or just those from cash-basis claimants. The order derives from a series of events that we briefly trace.

In December 2012, following unsuccessful attempts to raise the issue since September, BP requested a formal policy statement from the Administrator on matching. The Administrator responded by soliciting responses from BP and Class Counsel to help him make his policy determination. In the December 2012 memorandum to the Administrator, mentioned briefly above, Class Counsel urged an interpretation which could easily be read to interpret revenues and [—14—] expenses under Exhibit 4C by their cash accounting meanings. Counsel also explicitly stated that "corresponding variable

---

[4] It should be noted that even those expenses that cannot be directly traced to certain revenues are often allocated over multiple time periods, even if the cash outlay occurs all at once. For example, a large advertising purchase may occur by a single cash payment, but the purchased advertising time or space may be utilized in multiple future periods. As such, the expense is recognized incrementally over those relevant future periods. *See Statement of Financial Accounting Concepts No. 6*, ¶ 147. Nonetheless, these are not often thought of as "variable" expenses.

expenses" should be cash paid out during those periods, also a statement consistent only with cash accounting. Class Counsel's Memorandum was not clear whether its proposal applied to both cash and accrual records, despite discussing both. BP responded with its December 2012 memorandum, also referenced above, by explicitly rejecting Class Counsel's interpretation of "corresponding variable expenses," restating its insistence that the agreement requires matching, and presenting alternative frameworks for industries it thought were most problematic. The dissent treats this argument as an effort to modify the agreement. That conclusion seems too facile. The process for resolving disputes between the Administrator and BP was to be collaborative and cooperative. Consequently, it is not clear to us that BP was attempting to rewrite the agreement as much as it was attempting to resolve apparent anomalies without derailing the entirety of the claims process.

In his January 15, 2013 Policy Statement, the Administrator stated, in relevant part:

In performing these calculations, the Claims Administrator will typically consider both revenues and expenses in the periods in which those revenues and expenses were recorded at the time. The Claims Administrator will not typically re-allocate such revenues or expenses to different periods.

Given that "revenues" and "expenses" take on different meanings in the context of cash or accrual accounting, this statement is ambiguous at best as to how exactly the Administrator is processing accrual-basis claims. Further, this Policy Statement apparently rejects BP's proposal and adopts, at least in part, Class Counsel's interpretation. [—15—]

As we understand the district court's March 5 order, it interpreted "corresponding" to mean that any cash disbursed within a given month should be deemed to "correspond" to cash received in that month, simply by virtue of the fact that the cash flowed in and out in the same month. This is consistent with

Class Counsel's December 2012 memorandum. At one point, the district court said it agreed with Class Counsel as to the method of identifying revenue and expenses, though it is not entirely clear to what aspect of Class Counsel's argument the court was referring. The district court determined that "in the same time period" would be deprived of meaning if "corresponding" were interpreted to connect expenses to the revenues with which they are directly related. The district court echoed Class Counsel's December 2012 memorandum, holding that "matching" would require the Administrator to look outside the claimant's chosen Benchmark and Compensation periods. Finally, the district court's only discussion of cash or accrual-basis regarded whether one or the other was required under Exhibit 4A's documentation requirements. The court said there was no such requirement, and the parties agree that claimants may submit documents using either method.

In light of the proposals and rulings we just discussed, we consider it possible (though unlikely) that the district court was holding that the cash-in, cash-out interpretation applied to all claims, including those supported by accrual accounting. If so, then the inherent matching that occurs as a matter of course would be undone. Regardless of whether Exhibit 4C *requires* matching when it has not been undertaken in the ordinary course of record-keeping, it cannot be said to permit ignoring sufficiently matched data from accrual-basis [—16—] claimants. We conclude it would be error if the district court was stating that already-matched revenue and expenses could be ignored.

The Administrator has not made clear whether he is ignoring already-matched revenues and expenses in the manner the district court's interpretation appears to suggest. BP, though, has not explicitly complained to us that he is doing so. Implicit in this silence is that accrual-based claims continue to be processed using the inherently matched revenue and expense figures. BP acknowledged, in its own December 2012 Memorandum, that "[m]any types of Business Economic Loss claims . . . sufficiently match revenue and corresponding variable expenses, and as a result, [the Settlement] is properly applying" Exhibit 4C." This would likely be the case with most accrual-basis claimants. We see no reason for the Administrator to be doing this, but there are a few contrary indications. Class Counsel's December 2012 Memorandum, the January 15, 2013 Policy Statement, and the March 5 order do not offer any assurance that the Administrator is not applying the cash-in, cash-out interpretation to claims that are presented with matched revenues and expenses.

The district court on remand should make certain that this is not occurring. The Administrator on remand should be able quickly to dispel any doubts about the handling of accrual-basis claims. We expect the dissent is correct that this is not occurring, but we wish to be assured of that point. Once that is done, the more serious work of the remand can commence. We explain that beginning in the next section.

C. Cash-basis Claimants [—17—]

Neither the Policy Statement nor the Order make any reference to the recognition principles discussed above. The district court's interpretation gives little weight to the terms "corresponding" and "variable," and the parties apparently agree that matching is required[5] and occurring with respect to the vast majority of accrual-basis claims. For these reasons, BP's argument that matching applies to all claims warrants significant further consideration.

As noted above, the district court held that the words "corresponding" and "in the same time period" must be read to mean that expenses correspond to the time period in

which they were recorded and further that "expenses" means "cash paid." The court did not qualify its interpretation to state that this was not true of accrual-basis claimants, or to explain why one form of claims would be matched but not others. The district court's interpretation would fit the language of Exhibit 4C better if the agreement had said this about the Benchmark and Compensation Periods:

1. Sum the monthly revenue over the period.
2. Sum the expenses over the same time period, and subtract.

Instead, step 2 says this: "Subtract the corresponding variable expenses from revenue over the same time period."

Had the words "corresponding" and "variable" been omitted, the district court's explanation would not be so difficult to accept, economic incoherence notwithstanding. The difficulty is that subtracting temporally-related revenues and expenses recorded by cash-basis claimants would not result in numbers that [—18—] could fairly be said to represent actual economic losses or lost "variable profits." It is difficult to understand why some claimants would be compensated for lost "variable profits," while others would be compensated for negative cash flows, based solely on how claimants maintained their financial records. Though in our view the agreement fails to provide absolutely clear direction on processing claims based on cash-basis records, we conclude that the district court's holding too quickly dismissed the concept of matching, and did not deal with the inconsistent results the court's interpretation gives to claims presented on an accrual-basis and those on a cash-basis.

We suggest a more consistent interpretation of Exhibit 4C, one that fits both accrual- and cash-basis claims, is as follows. Such parol evidence as would assist the district court in deciding if this is correct can be presented on remand. After the heading "Variable Profit," Exhibit 4C reads "This is calculated for both the Benchmark Period and the Compensation Period." Then, part 1

---

[5] As to accrual-basis claimants, matching is "required" in the sense that claimants are not permitted to present statements which contain inconsistent methodologies. This means that if a claimant's records are already matched, it must submit them in that form. Furthermore, accrual-basis claimants are not allowed to adjust their records to the cash-basis, though the reverse is permitted. *See* October 8, 2012, Policy Statement on the matter.

references a "period," which seems reasonably to refer either to the Benchmark or to the Compensation designations set out immediately above, depending on which one is being calculated. Part 2 is where the "corresponding" expenses are subtracted from revenues "over the same time period." This reasonably could be interpreted to mean that the expenses to be subtracted must be those that "correspond" to the revenue earned and that the "same time period" refers to the Benchmark period on the one hand, and to the Compensation period on the other, whichever is being calculated. In other words, sum the monthly revenue over the [Benchmark or Compensation] period and then subtract *corresponding* expenses over the same [Benchmark or Compensation] time period. Such an [—19—] interpretation seems amply supported by the language of Exhibit 4C and much more consistent with general accounting and economic norms.

Weight to such an interpretation comes from the fact that the agreement cannot be read to permit ignoring "sufficiently-matched" revenue and expenses from accrual-basis claimants. The fact that Exhibit 4C requires processing of claims supported by sufficiently-matched, accrual-basis accounting should inform but does not necessarily control how cash-basis claims are to be analyzed. In any case, it does not appear to us that the district court gave real meaning to "corresponding" and "variable" when interpreting Exhibit 4C. It also did not articulate a basis to distinguish between determining actual economic losses for those claimants whose records were maintained on an accrual-basis, but abandoning that purpose when cash-basis claims were presented, with such a distinction being supported by exactly the same words in Exhibit 4C.

BP has been arguing at least since September 2012 that treating cash-basis claims by their own terms, that is, treating cash inflows and outflows as revenues and expenses, violates the express language of the agreement. As we understand its contention, BP argues that Exhibit 4C represents an agreement on a specific accounting methodology, based loosely on accrual accounting revenue and expense recognition principles. Central to this argument is that the term "corresponding variable expenses," the detailed computation instructions, the detailed expense classifications, and extensive documentation requirements would be largely superfluous if all claims, but especially cash-basis ones, were meant to be treated on their own terms.

As discussed above, the district court held that "corresponding" referred to a temporal connection between cash inflows and outflows. That is, cash [—20—] receipts and payments corresponded to one another because they flow in and out during a given month. In a literal sense, this is true. But cash accounting, by nature, ignores any significance that might be related to the timing of cash receipts and payments, beyond mere cash flow concerns. *See* CPA Societies' Amicus Brief at 7-8. Because cash accounting does not inherently recognize relationships between cash flows and their underlying transactions, the term "corresponding variable expenses" reasonably could imply an accrual-style framework inherent in Exhibit 4C.

BP argues that the detailed expense classifications and adjustments outlined in Exhibit 4C as well as the requirement of annual and tax financial statements in addition to monthly profit-and-loss statements in Exhibit 4A indicate that claims are to be adjusted to "match" revenue and expenses and then provide for the records necessary to doing. Exhibit 4A lists numerous documents a claimant must submit to make a claim. These documents presumably would allow accountants fairly, if at times imperfectly, to "match" revenues and expenses if such were required.

Class Counsel and the Administrator argue that BP fully agreed during negotiations in 2012 to the district court's March 2013 interpretation in order to achieve "global peace," and that it should not now be permitted to extract itself from its bargain. This analysis persuaded the dissent, which argues that BP's purpose here is to modify the agreement to require conversion of cash-basis claimants' records to the accrual-basis, even though it specifically agreed that such was not required. Our analysis finds different meaning in what was agreed. The difference is between what claimants had to present—either cash-basis or accrual-basis claims—and what the Administrator thereafter was to do. At least [—21—] as to claims presented on an accrual-basis, not only did BP not assent to ignoring the need for matching revenues with expenses, it clearly insisted on it. In December 2012, the parties seemingly agreed that properly matched claims led to fair and proper results. We do not agree that the record of negotiations supports that BP was oblivious until quite recently to the desirability of matching; the record actually supports that both parties agreed all along that properly-matched accrual-basis claims should not be disturbed and indeed should not be converted to cash-basis claims precisely because of the risk of artificially-inflated or entirely fictitious losses.

The record creates a different perplexity, namely, why would parties who agree as to the propriety of matching for one set of claims reject it for other claims? Our doubt is particularly strong due to the fact that only matching provides a realistic chance of achieving the ostensible goal of the settlement of compensating claimants for real losses. Furthermore, the only support for not matching seems to derive from the conclusion that cash-basis claimants' own books are not matched. It hardly seems conclusive to us that a claimant's idiosyncratically-maintained records dictate the way Exhibit 4C is applied to a claim, especially if Exhibit 4C is supposed to be an objective formula.

Class Counsel and the Administrator argue that significant parol evidence, including e-mails where BP counsel appears to accept the occasional false positive, shows BP's acquiescence. One form of a false positive discussed during negotiations would arise from the agreement to assume factual causation. Under Exhibit 4B, causation is generally assumed if economic loss can properly be shown. BP did agree that alternative causes of losses were irrelevant if the financial figures supported that a loss occurred. The false positives BP criticizes

[—22—] now are based on loss calculations produced under the district court's cash-in, cash-out approach. The approach could lead to false positives or false negatives, though negatives presumably would not lead to claims. In either event, the issue is whether it is permissible to allow the often economically meaningless temporal coinciding of cash received and paid to determine the value of a claim. BP never acquiesced to a cash accounting interpretation of "revenue" and "expenses" for *all* claims, *i.e.*, not for accrual-based ones. It has argued consistently that the formula was intended to compensate for real economic losses, not artificial losses that appear only from the timing of cash flows.

The dissent concludes that the course of dealing outlined above, beginning with the September 28 correspondence between BP and the Administrator, shows that BP missed its opportunity to raise these objections. Much has been made of an October 2 conference call, where the concerns BP raised on September 28 were to be resolved. During that call, according to a number of affidavits, BP asked about the treatment of certain cash-basis claims and apparently left assured that they need not fear the way the Administrator was proceeding. The dissent cites the affidavit of Charles Hacker, partner in the Price Waterhouse accounting firm. He states that he told BP that accountants were not converting cash-basis claims to accrual-basis for the purposes of the agreement. According to the dissent, BP's apparent silence at that moment shows their assent to treatment of cash-basis claims by their own terms. We do not find the dissent's interpretation of the limited factual matter from the October 2 conference call conclusive. Hacker also asserted that "[w]ith respect to irregularly received revenue, the accountants' practice was to follow up with claimants to better understand significant outliers . . . the accountants were not [—23—] auditing claimants' financial information but . . . were performing certain procedures to analyze the accuracy, validity, and authenticity of outlier items."

Perhaps whatever was specifically said in the October 2 conference call indicated to BP that the accountants were making Exhibit 4C calculations in accordance with the interpretation it advances here. Thus, BP would have agreed to finalizing the agreement. That possibility would support that BP thought the agreement was functioning properly, and then raised these issues later when BP came to believe that something was amiss.

After all the other arguments are considered, it remains of significance that the interpretation urged by the Administrator is completely disconnected from any reasonable understanding of calculation of damages. In interpreting a settlement, surely some weight has to be given to what damages recoverable in civil litigation actually are. If clear words in a settlement require the use of randomly associated numbers for calculating damages, even if there is little likelihood that, after subtracting one of those numbers from the other, the remainder will in fact show anything relevant to damages, then so be it. We do not perceive such clarity here.

Given the record before us, we cannot determine with an adequate level of certainty whether a matching principle should apply to all claims. Even with the interpretation we outlined above, it is not wholly clear that the words "corresponding" and "variable" unequivocally imply matching. Given the divergent effects of differing recognition principles, we hold that Exhibit 4C is ambiguous as to whether claims that are not based on matched revenues and expenditures are to be matched for Exhibit 4C purposes. We have not discovered whether, before the agreement was signed, the parties discussed the divergent [—24—] effects of cash- and accrual-basis accounting records on the Exhibit 4C formula. Furthermore, neither the January 15, 2013 Policy Statement nor the March 5 order mentions the inherent but crucial differences in these recognition principles. Instead, we remand to the district court to develop a more complete factual record regarding the meaning of Exhibit 4C or other relevant parts of the agreement and make relevant findings. The Administrator needs to assure the court that he is not ignoring already-matched accrual-basis accounting records.

We remand because the district court did not acknowledge the requirement of matching that is foundational for accrual-basis claims and it did not then explain why it was interpreting the same Exhibit 4C language that leads to matching for accrual-based claims as not requiring the matching of cash-basis claims. This is particularly questionable when the agreement contains not only the terms "corresponding" and "variable," but extensive documentation requirements which would allow claims administration accountants to process claims in accordance with economic reality.

D. "Comparable" Periods

BP further argues that "comparable" months of the Benchmark and Compensation period refer to months in which comparable activities took place. We find nothing in the record to support that interpretation.

The district court held that "comparable" refers to the same calendar months in both the Benchmark and Compensation period. We do not disturb this holding for two reasons. First, we conclude that this is the most natural reading of the word "comparable" in the context of the agreement. The agreement allows the claimant to pick as few as three months or as much as an [—25—] average of nine months over three calendar years. This, along with the word "comparable," clearly indicate that the Benchmark and Compensation periods were referring to months of the same name, without any complex analysis of what type of business activities took place within those months. Second, we conclude that our holding as to cash and accrual-basis claimants will resolve some of the issues BP claims results from the district court's interpretation of "comparable."

BP's primary concern seems to be the uneven cash flows of certain types of businesses. We accept this possibility, but we see nothing in the agreement that provides a basis for BP's interpretation. Despite the potential existence of this kind of distortion, the parties may not have considered it, agreed to ignore it, or failed for other reasons to provide clearly for this eventuality. The district court was correct that BP's proposed interpretation is not what the parties agreed.

II. "Fictitious" claims

BP alleges not only that the Administrator's interpretation of the disputed terms inflates awards to legitimate BEL claimants, but also that the interpretation results in awards to BEL claimants who admittedly either have suffered no loss at all or have suffered losses that were not caused by the oil spill. Such claimants would have no colorable legal claim. *See Richardson v. United States*, 468 U.S. 317, 326 n.6 (1984) (defining a "colorable claim" as one with "some possible validity"). Absent a loss, a claimant has suffered no injury. Unless a claimant can colorably assert a loss, it lacks standing. *See Lujan v. Defenders of Wildlife*, 504 U.S. 555, 560 (1992) (noting that an injury is a [—26—] required element of constitutional standing); *Jobe v. ATR Mktg., Inc.*, 87 F.3d 751, 753 (5th Cir. 1996) ("[T]he conventional tort elements in a negligence action are duty, breach of duty, proximate causation and injury."). Similarly, if a claimant has suffered a loss, but it has no colorable claim that the loss was caused by the spill, it also lacks standing and cannot state a claim. It lacks standing because it cannot allege "a causal connection" between its loss and the spill. *Lujan*, 504 U.S. at 560. Its injury is not "fairly traceable to the challenged action of the defendant;" rather, it is "the result of the independent action of some third party not before the court." *Id.* (citation, quotation marks, and alteration omitted). Moreover, it cannot state a claim because it is unable to plead the causation element of a negligence cause of action. *See Jobe*, 87 F.3d at 753. Therefore, such non-colorable claims do not constitute Article III cases or controversies and are not founded on any substantive right.[6]

The Supreme Court has cautioned that "Rule 23's requirements must be interpreted in keeping with Article III constraints, and with the Rules Enabling Act, which instructs that rules of procedure 'shall not abridge, enlarge or modify any substantive right.'"[7] *Amchem Products, Inc. v. Windsor*, 521 U.S. 591, 613 [—27—] (1997) (quoting 28 U.S.C. §2072(b)); *see also id.* (quoting Fed. R. Civ. P. 82's mandate that "rules shall not be construed to extend . . . the [subject-matter] jurisdiction of the United States district courts" (alterations in original)); *Sullivan v. DB Investments, Inc.*, 667 F.3d 273, 343 (3d Cir. 2011) (Jordan, J. dissenting) ("Rule 23 . . . is designed to efficiently handle claims recognized by law, not to create new claims."); *Broussard v. Meineke Disc. Muffler Shops, Inc.*, 155 F.3d 331, 345 (4th Cir. 1998) ("It is axiomatic that the procedural device of Rule 23 cannot be allowed to expand the substance of the claims of class members."); *cf. Cimino v. Raymark Indus., Inc.*, 151 F.3d 297, 312 (5th Cir. 1998) (concluding that the Rules Enabling Act mandates that "use of Rule 23(b)(3) ...

---

[6] The dissent contends that it is hornbook law that standing is never an issue in the class action context so long as one class representative has standing. While the hornbook quoted does refer to a narrow use of the word standing, the same material also concedes that courts use the term in a broader

context to address Article III constraints such as actual injury and traceability as well as Rule 23 requirements such as typicality and commonality. WILLIAM B. RUBINSTEIN, NEWBERG ON CLASS ACTIONS 2:1, 2:5 (5th ed.). This analysis utilizes this broader meaning of the term, validated by other auspicious courts with access to the hornbooks. *Amchem Products, Inc. v. Windsor*, 521 U.S. 591, 612 (1997) (referring to a class issue of uninjured plaintiffs as concerning "standing," even when some of the named plaintiffs in the case had actual injuries).

[7] The Supreme Court in *Amchem* considered the approval of a global settlement class in the asbestos litigation that consisted of individuals injured by asbestos and those who had [—27—] been exposed to asbestos but not yet injured. *Amchem*, 521 U.S. at 597. Although concluding that the class could not be certified because it did not meet the requirements of Rule 23, the Court noted that, "[i]f certification issues were genuinely in doubt, however, the jurisdictional issues [concerning the ripeness of the exposure-only class members' claims] would loom larger." *Id.* at 613 n.15. The Court directed attention to Judge Wellford's concurrence in the court below that argued that there could be no standing for uninjured plaintiffs and emphasized again the importance of limitations imposed by Article III and the Rules Enabling Act. *Id.* at 611-13.

does not alter the required elements which must be found to impose liability and fix damages (or the burden of proof thereon) or the identity of the substantive law . . . which determines such elements).[8] By including claimants [—28—] in the class definition that lack colorable claims, a court disregards this warning. It ignores the standing requirement of Article III and creates a substantive right where none existed before. Allowing recovery from the settlement fund by those who have no case and cannot state a claim, the court acts *ultra vires*.

"To avoid dismissal based on a lack of standing, the court must be able to find that both the class and the representatives have suffered some injury requiring court intervention. The class must therefore be defined in such a way that anyone within it would have standing." *Denney v. Deutsche Bank AG*, 443 F.3d 253, 264 (2d Cir. 2006) (internal citations and quotation marks omitted). "In order to state a class action claim upon which relief can be granted, there must be alleged at the minimum (1) a reasonably defined class of plaintiffs, (2) all of who have suffered a constitutional or statutory violation (3) inflicted by the defendants." *Adashunas v. Negley*, 626 F.2d

---

[8] In addition, "[Rule 23's predominance] inquiry trains on the legal or factual questions that qualify each class member's case as a *genuine controversy*." *Amchem*, 521 U.S. at 623 (emphasis added). Thus, an interpretation of the Settlement that defines the class to include claimants who "have suffered no actual injury from [BP's] allegedly [tortious acts] on the basis of a much smaller group of [claimants] who have sustained such injury" also may call into question whether the settlement class satisfies the predominance test for certification. *Karvaly v. eBay, Inc.*, 245 F.R.D. 71, 85 (E.D.N.Y. 2007); *see also Sullivan*, 667 F.3d at 343-47 (Jordan, J. dissenting) (pointing out that including "putative class members who do not even have an arguable cause of action under applicable law" in the class definition also calls the related requirement of commonality into doubt, because it "requires plaintiffs to show that the elements of their claim are capable of proof at trial through evidence that is common to the [—28—] class rather than individual to its members" and, "for plaintiffs who lack any claim, there are certainly no elements of a claim that are capable of proof, either common or individual" (citation and quotation marks omitted)).

600, 603 (7th Cir. 1980) (affirming the denial of a plaintiff class). A claimant "must actually have a legal claim before getting in line for a legal recovery. When objections are raised that persuasively demonstrate that a portion of a proposed class does not have any such claim, courts of law are obliged to follow the law." *Sullivan*, 667 F.3d at 347 (Jordan, J. dissenting); *see In re Chicken Antitrust Litig. Am. Poultry*, 669 F.2d 228, 238 (5th Cir. Unit B 1982) ("Of course, had indirect purchasers been completely without any colorable legal claims against defendants, it would have been an abuse of the court's discretion to allow them to share in the settlement fund."); *see also In re Agent Orange Prod. Liab. Litig. MDL No. 381*, 818 F.2d 179, 184 (2d Cir. 1987) (approving a settlement distribution plan to class [—29—] members who had "stated 'colorable legal claims against defendants'" because their claims "d[id] not entirely disregard traditional tort principles of causation" (citation omitted)). *But see Sullivan*, 667 F.3d at 310 ("[W]ere we to mandate that a class include only those alleging 'colorable' claims, we would effectively rule out the ability of a defendant to achieve 'global peace.'").

There is a distinction here between whether a claim is colorable and whether it is meritorious. A plaintiff's claim is colorable if he can *allege* standing and the elements necessary to state a claim on which relief can be granted—whether or not his claim is ultimately meritorious—whether he can *prove* his case. *See Sullivan*, 667 F.3d at 340 (3d Cir. 2011) (Jordan, J. dissenting) (explaining that the problem with the class "is not that it may include people with marginal or dubious claims" but that it "includes people who have no legal claim whatsoever" as is "clear on the face of the [applicable] statutory and decisional law"). Class settlements certainly can encompass unmeritorious claims, because such claims, successful or not, are based on existing substantive rights. Class settlements, however, cannot create new rights and then settle claims brought under them. *See id.* (dissenting because "the Majority has endorsed the fabrication of substantive rights where none before existed"); *see also Messner v. Northshore Univ. HealthSystem*, 669 F.3d 802, 824 (7th Cir. 2012).[9] **[—30—]**

It makes no difference that a defendant may bargain for global peace by agreeing to allow claimants with no colorable legal claim to recover from the settlement fund. A class settlement is not a private agreement between the parties. It is a creature of Rule 23, which authorizes its use to resolve the legal claims of a class "only with the court's approval." FED. R. CIV. P. 23(e); *see also Amchem*, 521 U.S. at 620 (explaining in a related circumstance that the specifications of Rule 23 designed to "block[] unwarranted or overbroad class definitions . . . demand undiluted, even heightened, [judicial] attention in the settlement context"). In granting approval, the court must, as always, adhere to the precepts of Article III and the Rules Enabling Act.[10] While a "welcome byproduct" of deciding cases or controversies on a class-wide basis, the goal of global peace does not trump Article III or federal law. *Sullivan*, 667 F.3d at 355-56 (Jordan, J. dissenting). Courts do not have the authority to create a cause of action (and their

---

[9] "At first glance, it would seem that Northshore is arguing . . . that certification must be denied because plaintiffs' proposed class contains members whose claims will fail on the merits. In actuality, however, Northshore is arguing that the class for which certification is requested is fatally overbroad because it contains members who could not have been harmed by any post-merger price increases ... This distinction is critical for class certification purposes. As explained above, if a proposed class consists largely (or entirely, for that matter) of members who are ultimately shown to have suffered no harm, that may not mean that the class was improperly certified but only that the class failed to meet its burden of proof on the **[—30—]** merits. If, however, a class is defined so broadly as to include a great number of members who for some reason could not have been harmed by the defendant's allegedly unlawful conduct, the class is defined too broadly to permit certification." *Id.* (citations omitted).

[10] This is particularly true here, as the district court, in its order approving the Settlement, "retain[ed] continuing and exclusive jurisdiction to interpret, implement, administer and enforce the Settlement Agreement, in accordance with its terms, and to implement and complete the claims administration and distribution process, in accordance with the Settlement Agreement."

corresponding subject-matter jurisdiction over it) and then give peace with regard to that cause of action.[11] **[—31—]**

Turning to the present case, the district court had no authority to approve the settlement of a class that included members that had not sustained losses at all, or had sustained losses unrelated to the oil spill, as BP alleges. If the Administrator is interpreting the Settlement to include such claimants, the Settlement is unlawful. Should BP's proposed interpretation of the Settlement exclude putative class members with no colorable legal claim, the district court should have rendered the Settlement lawful by adopting that interpretation, as long as the interpretation is reasonable and effective. *See Harvey v. Joyce*, 199 F.3d 790, 794 (5th Cir. 2000) ("A court must strive to reach an interpretation which gives a reasonable, lawful, and effective meaning to all the terms of an agreement.").

Moreover, if BP's counsel did negotiate a Settlement that included payouts to businesses whose losses were not caused by the oil spill, agreeing to pay a client's funds to claimants that concede that they have no causally related injury is counterintuitive and contradictory to common tenets of both tort and contract law—and to common sense. The

---

[11] The dissent critiques as "unworkable" an approach that would require that class members have a colorable claim because it would require some analysis of harm at the certification stage. The Supreme Court in *Wal-Mart Stores, Inc. v. Dukes*, 131 S. Ct. 2541 (2011) clarified that "Rule 23 does not set forth a mere pleading standard . . . certification is proper only if the trial court is satisfied, after a rigorous analysis, that the prerequisites of Rule 23(a) have been satisfied . . . . Frequently that rigorous analysis will entail some overlap with the merits of the plaintiff's underlying claim. That cannot be helped . . . . Nor is there **[—31—]** anything unusual about that consequence: The necessity of touching aspects of the merits in order to resolve preliminary matters, e.g., jurisdiction and venue, is a familiar feature of litigation." *Id.* at 2251-52 (internal citations and quotation marks omitted). Preliminary matters such as whether broad swaths of the proposed class would have standing are no more difficult to ascertain.

fact that these claimants cannot show causation translates to a Settlement that lacks valid consideration. Why would BP pay to resolve claims that cannot be plead? The myth of "global peace" through payment of *admittedly* non-spill-related claims is a legal nullity that cannot remedy this deficiency. There is no need to secure peace with those with [—32—] whom one is not at war. Total lack of consideration for non-recoverable claims would call into question the validity of the Settlement Agreement.

The class settlement cases the dissent cites to the contrary all involved classes that suffered actual economic loss that resulted from the conduct of the party agreeing to the settlement. In *Sullivan*, direct and indirect purchasers of diamonds settled a class action suit against the operator of a diamond cartel for violations of federal and state antitrust laws. 667 F.3d at 285-293. The *Sullivan* majority pointed out that while considering predominance, "commonality is informed by the defendant's conduct as to all class members and any *resulting* injuries common to all class members." *Id.* at 297 (emphasis added). Both the majority and the dissent recognized "that, well yes, there must be some limiting feature of the class and that feature is injury; class members must have been injured by De Beers's unlawful conduct." *Id.* at 343 (Jordan, J. dissenting). In *Sullivan*, the majority and the dissent sparred over whether or not this financial injury was legally cognizable, because the settlement proposed to settle claims in all 50 states whether or not the states had causes of action for these kinds of injury. What the *Sullivan* majority never approved was a class that consisted of people who had never purchased diamonds at all and thus suffered no losses. In *In re American International Group, Inc. Securities Litigation*, 689 F.3d 229 (2d Cir. 2012), three public pension funds sought class certification to settle a securities fraud claim against an issuer for violations of federal securities fraud that led to losses in their portfolios. *Id.* at 232-37. "All plaintiffs here claim injury that by reason of defendants' conduct . . . has caused a common and measurable form of economic damage." *Id.* at 240 (quoting *Sullivan*, 667 F.3d at 338 (Scirica, J., concurring)).

Similarly, this case did not involve class [—33—] approval of people who had never invested in the stock market and therefore never could have experienced traceable loss.[12] Surely, these cases do not stand for the proposition that there is no judicial role to ensure that class definitions comply with statutory and constitutional strictures.

These issues are important in this case, and not just in future cases, because these legal principles further undermine an interpretation of the Settlement Agreement that includes businesses without colorable legal claims. Such an interpretation could imperil a final approval of the settlement and can be considered in evaluating the correct interpretation of possible ambiguities in this agreement.

III. Preliminary Injunction

"It takes time to decide a case on appeal. Sometimes a little; sometimes a lot. No court can make time stand still while it considers an appeal . . . and if a court takes the time it needs, the court's decision may in some cases come too late for the party seeking review." *Nken v. Holder*, 556 U.S. 418, 421 (2009) (internal quotations and citations omitted). Despite the generally deferential standard accorded to a district court's denial of a preliminary injunction, "a decision grounded on erroneous legal principles is reviewed de novo." *Byrum v. Landreth*, 566 F.3d 442, 445 (5th Cir. 2009). [—34—]

BP moved for a preliminary injunction and a stay pending appeal, arguing that the

---

[12] The dissent also cites to *Kohen v. Pacific Investment Management Company LLC*, 571 F.3d 672 (7th Cir. 2009). In *Kohen*, buyers of short positions in ten-year Treasury notes filed suit against an investment firm which had taken long positions, seeking sums lost when the firm allegedly cornered the market in violation of the Commodity Exchange Act. 571 F.3d at 674-77. *Kohen* was not a settlement class action and did not raise causation concerns. "If PIMCO is found to have cornered the market . . . then each member of the class will have to submit a claim for the damages it sustained *as a result of* the corner." *Id.* at 676 (internal citations omitted) (emphasis added).

continued distribution of its assets under a potentially improper reading of the Agreement was causing it irreparable harm. The district court denied the motions from the bench and in a subsequent minute entry. The court believed that BP was asking it to enjoin an interpretation of the Settlement Agreement that the court itself had ordered on March 5. As such, the court viewed it as a request for reconsideration of an issue the court had considered.

"As to each element of the district court's preliminary-injunction analysis, the district court's findings of fact 'are subject to a clearly-erroneous standard of review,' while conclusions of law 'are subject to broad review and will be reversed if incorrect.'" *Janvey v. Alguire*, 647 F.3d 585, 591-92 (5th Cir. 2011) (citations and quotation omitted).

The conclusions the district court made here were conclusions of law. Contract interpretation, such as the meaning of the Settlement Agreement, is a question of law. *Becker v. Tidewater, Inc.*, 586 F.3d 358, 369 (5th Cir. 2009). Proper claimants under a class are a question of law. *Wal-Mart Stores, Inc.*, 131 S. Ct. at 2550-51. For this reason, errors in conclusions of law are subject to broad review and will be reversed if incorrect. The errors in conclusions of law involved are laid out in the preceding sections of this opinion. Because of these, the preliminary injunction should be granted while the judicial process takes its course.

The traditional four-factor test for a stay pending appeal is typically used to analyze requests for a preliminary injunction.[13] However, "where there is a [—35—] serious

legal question involved and the balance of the equities heavily favors a stay . . . the movant only needs to present a substantial case on the merits." *Weingarten Realty Investors v. Miller*, 661 F.3d 904, 910 (5th Cir. 2011). This case is one of the largest and most novel class actions in American history. As such, significant legal questions are involved that will affect the course of class action law in this country going forward, and the class action as a suitable vehicle for the resolution of conflict for businesses and litigants.

The balance of equities favors a tailored stay. The interests of individuals who may be reaping windfall recoveries because of an inappropriate interpretation of the Settlement Agreement and those who could never have recovered in individual suits for failure to show causation are outweighed by the potential loss to a company and its public shareholders of hundreds of millions of dollars of unrecoverable awards. A stay tailored so that those who experienced actual injury traceable to loss from the Deepwater Horizon accident continue to receive recovery but those who did not do not receive their payments until this case is fully heard and decided through the judicial process weighs in favor of BP. We therefore REVERSE the denial of the preliminary injunction[14] and instruct the district court to expeditiously craft a narrowly-tailored [—36—] injunction that allows the time necessary for deliberate reconsideration of these significant issues on remand.

---

[13] "Four factors must be considered by this Court in determining whether to stay the district court's order under Fed. R. App. P. 8. These are (1) whether the movant has made a showing of likelihood of success on the merits, (2) whether the movant has made a showing [—35—] of irreparable injury if the stay is not granted, (3) whether the granting of the stay would substantially harm the other parties, and (4) whether the granting of the stay would serve the public interest." *United States v. Baylor Univ. Med. Ctr.*, 711 F.2d 38, 39 (5th Cir. 1983).

[14] By way of example, BP's proposed tailored injunction read as follows: "The Claims Administrator and Settlement Program are ENJOINED from issuing or paying to claimants in the agriculture, construction, professional services, real estate, wholesale trade, manufacturing, and retail trade industries any determinations for business economic loss claims under the Economic and Property Damages Settlement Agreement ("Settlement Agreement"). The North American Industry Classification System ("NAICS") codes for these specified industries are all codes starting with 11 (except 114111, 114112, 114119, and 114210), 23, 31 (except 311711 and 311712), 32, 33, 42 (except 424460), 44, 45, 53, or 54."

CONCLUSION

We AFFIRM the district court's dismissal of BP's suit against the Claims Administrator. We REVERSE the district court's order affirming the Administrator's interpretation of the Settlement and denial of a preliminary injunction and REMAND to the district court for further consideration while retaining jurisdiction.

[—37—] SOUTHWICK, Circuit Judge, concurring:

I concur in Part I of the opinion, which analyzes why we are vacating and remanding for further consideration of the interpretation of Exhibit 4C of the Settlement Agreement. I also agree, as stated in Part III, that the district court should enter a narrowly tailored and potentially brief stay to allow the purposes of the remand to be realized. I do not join the broader Rule 23 analysis that appears in Part II. The discussion is logical in finding that constitutional infirmities would exist if certain corrections are not made to the interpretation of Exhibit 4C. There is, though, no briefing on the constitutional issues that are addressed. I am concerned that those observations imply— though they may well not be intended to go that far—an invalidity to the Settlement Agreement's causation framework, which no one challenges. I would not make the pronouncements that appear in Part II. Instead, I would defer the issue and allow the parties on remand to give it the attention it deserves.

The Settlement Agreement resolved two separate issues by, in effect, combining them. One concerned loss *causation*, and the other loss *measurement*. If a BEL claimant could prove an economic loss, properly measured, that proof substituted for evidence of causation. Improper measurement of losses under Exhibit 4C might compensate claimants without actual losses. That potential raises the causation question in the sense that a party who suffered no loss regardless of cause certainly did not have a loss caused by the oil spill. Even so, the parties agreed by Exhibit 4B's causation framework to ignore

alternative explanations for actual losses that occurred to claimants during the proper time [—38—] period. The agreement simplified the claims process by making proof of loss a substitute for proof of factual causation.

The question of loss measurement is clearly before us. BP argues almost exclusively that the Administrator and the district court misinterpreted the formula for measurement of business and economic losses that appears in Exhibit 4C. Part I of the panel opinion identifies the crucial question for remand: should matching be required for *all* claims when it is clearly required for many? I agree to remand with instructions to reconsider the interpretation of Exhibit 4C for unmatched claims in light of the necessity of revenue and expense matching to realistic measurement of economic loss.

Part II of the opinion elaborates on a causation issue under Rule 23, which affects the class definitions. As noted already, causation was addressed by the parties in Exhibit 4B of the Settlement Agreement. BEL claimants within a defined geographic region closest to the Gulf do not need to present any evidence of factual causation. The same is true of BEL claimants in certain sensitive industries, such as seafood processors, regardless of geographic location. For those groups of BEL claimants, a mathematical loss as calculated under Exhibit 4C is compensated without any proof of the cause of the loss. BEL claimants operating further from the Gulf must show a mathematical loss under Exhibit 4C, subject to a requirement that the loss meet a certain percentage threshold, and must also provide documentation that the claimant lost revenues from certain classes of customers. As the last alternative to other forms of evidence, these more distant claimants could offer evidence of factual causation.

Thus, Exhibit 4B of the Settlement Agreement allowed causation to be supported simply by loss calculations under Exhibit 4C rather than by requiring [—39—] the claimant to prove that the loss had any factual relationship to BP's actions. No one on appeal is challenging Exhibit 4B. BP is arguing that the erroneous variable profit decision endangers class certification by potentially allowing parties not harmed by BP's actions to recover from the settlement fund. That potential arises from miscalculating loss. Other than by the challenge to the application of the method of showing loss, BP has not argued that the Settlement Agreement is defective under Rule 23.

Given that we are remanding so that the interpretation of variable profit will be reconsidered, it is not apparent that we should reach any fundamental Rule 23 concerns at this time. I agree that parts of the analysis have been briefed. For example, if the methods of computing losses do not, at least for a large number of claimants, determine in any reasonable fashion whether a financial loss actually occurred, there are significant Rule 23 problems in the incoherence of the calculation method. Because proof of loss largely substitutes for proof of causation, to allow the means of showing loss to become disconnected from economic realities threatens to distort entry into the class and is a defect under Rule 23. There is no evidence yet presented that BP ever agreed to this. Because the Rule 23 problem BP raises is confined to the measurement of loss and not to questions of standing of claimants who cannot show their losses were caused by BP's actions, I would not at this time suggest there is a fundamental Rule 23 defect in the Settlement Agreement.

I do not minimize the concern about recognizing limitations for Rule 23. The opinion correctly notes that class actions are not meant to be vessels for achieving "global peace" by creating substantive rights that would not otherwise exist. *See Amchem Products, Inc. v. Windsor*, 521 U.S. 591, 612-13 (1997). I **[—40—]** would only have identified the relevant principles and authorities, then remanded for such consideration as the parties and the district court bring to the issue of causation as they address the measurement of loss.

(Reporter's Note: Concurring opinion in part, and dissenting opinion in part on p. 304).

[—41—] DENNIS, Circuit Judge, concurring in part and dissenting in part:

This case arises out of BP's proposal to the Administrator that he modify the consent decree and settlement agreement, or his interpretation of them, to provide that the Administrator must convert a claimant's cash-method accounting data into the accrual-method data proposed by BP before using the data to calculate the business economic loss of the claimant. The Administrator rejected BP's proposal and the district court affirmed the Administrator's decision. BP appealed to this court. The majority, instead of addressing the only question presented, whether conversion of cash-method data into accrual-method data is or should be required, declares the record confusing, intuits a different issue, whether the Administrator has been converting accrual-method data into cash-method data before processing claims, and remands for the district court to determine whether the Administrator has done so.

In my view, we should affirm the district court's judgment for the reasons assigned hereinafter. Moreover, the remand is unnecessary because the record clearly reflects that the dispute between the Administrator and BP is only about whether the Administrator must convert a claimant's cash-method data into BP's proposed accrual-method data before calculating a claimant's business economic loss. BP does not contend that the Administrator is mishandling claimants' accrual-method data claims.

In this opinion, I first explain why this appellate court must uphold the district court's judgments affirming the Administrator's rejection of BP's actions to force him to modify, or to revise his interpretation of, the district court's consent decree incorporating the parties' settlement agreement. Second, I explain how the majority misunderstands the record, sails past the only issue on [—42—] appeal, and unnecessarily and prematurely remands the case to the district court. Finally, I respectfully disagree with Judge Clement's separate opinion, which expounds on class-action-law issues that are not presented to this panel but to a different three-judge panel scheduled to hear that appeal in November and which purports to instruct the district court to issue an injunction pursuant to her class-action-law declarations.

I.

Having failed to convince the Administrator to modify the terms of the district court's consent decree, which approves and adopts the parties' settlement agreement, or to persuade the district court to reverse the Administrator's decision, BP appeals to this court. Because BP agreed to the settlement and, in fact, actively sought the district court's approval and adoption of it in its consent decree, BP cannot seek to modify the consent decree unless it demonstrates that there has been a significant change in circumstances or the law that warrants a revision of the decree by the district court. BP appears to acknowledge that it failed to carry this burden below, for it now argues that the parties' settlement agreement incorporated in the district court's consent decree has always required the Administrator to convert a claimant's cash-method data into BP's proposed accrual-method data before calculating a claimant's business economic loss. However, the Supreme Court, in *United States v. Armour & Co.*, 402 U.S. 673 (1971), and its progeny, has explained that a consent decree must be interpreted within its "four corners" and that an appellate court cannot add to or subtract from the consent decree or interpret it according to what the court thinks is the purpose of the agreement. This court, applying the four corners of [—43—] *Armour*, must find that the decree does not contain the conversion and matching requirements that BP asks us read into it.

A.

I start by reviewing background that highlights the true issue on these appeals. In this case, the settlement agreement and consent decree resolved all claims for business economic losses against BP resulting from the 2010 explosion and oil spill of the BP Deepwater Horizon rig. The settlement establishes formulas by which the

Administrator is authorized to identify eligible claimants, calculate their business economic losses, and pay their claims. BP agreed to fund the settlement program without ceiling or limit (other than those limits inherent in the formulas for calculating loss) with respect to the amount that the Administrator may award to business-economic-loss claimants. Class counsel sought and obtained the district court's certification of a settlement-only class, and, in exchange, BP received a class- and region-wide release from liability for spill-related business-economic-loss claims.[1]

The Administrator began identifying, calculating, and paying business economic-loss claims in May 2012 and continued to do so without any objection from the parties relating to his calculations or otherwise.[2] On September 28, 2012, BP requested a discussion regarding how the Administrator calculated [—44—] compensation with respect to business-economic-loss claimants that maintain their books using cash-basis accounting principles. On October 2, 2012, Charles R. Hacker, an accountant employed by the settlement program, participated in a conference call with the Administrator's staff and the parties to answer BP's questions. During the call, Mr. Hacker stated that "the Settlement Agreement does not specify a prescribed accounting methodology" and that "a claimant's accounting method needed to be applied on a consistent basis," in other words, that the Administrator and his team would consider revenue and expenses as they were

booked by the claimant. R. 18336-37.[3] In other words, Mr. Hacker told the conference call participants that claims submitted with data from a claimant's books using cash-method accounting would be accepted by the settlement program so long as the claimant utilized that accounting practice consistently. See R. 18336-37. After the call, BP made no objection, did not file a complaint, or ask for an administrative panel hearing on the matters discussed.

On November 8, 2012, the district court conducted a hearing on final approval of the parties' class action and settlement agreement. By this time, the settlement program had received over 79,000 completed claims and authorized payment in excess of $1.3 billion. At the hearing, BP supported final approval [—45—] of the settlement and, with class counsel, rebutted the objections of certain objectors. In fact, mere weeks after BP was told on the October 2, 2012 conference call that the Administrator and his accountants were accepting and processing claims based on claimants' cash-method accounting data, BP informed the court that, "[t]he settlement is working as we anticipated and as we negotiated." R. 8251. BP did not argue at the hearing, or in any filings submitted in connection with the hearing, that it had any objection or disagreement regarding the Administrator's use of claimants' cash-method accounting data to calculate the claimants' business economic losses. On December 21, 2012, the district court granted final approval of the settlement agreement and adopted it in

---

[1] The settlement also entitled BP to walk away from the parties' agreement prior to final approval if too many plaintiffs opted out. BP never availed itself of this right, instead actively seeking the district court's final approval.

[2] On May 2, 2012, the parties entered into a settlement agreement that was preliminarily approved by the district court. In its preliminary-approval order, the court ordered the Administrator to commence the settlement program under the terms of the settlement agreement. The substance, terms, and conditions of the May 2, 2012 preliminary settlement agreement are identical to those that the district court finally approved and made part of its consent decree on December 21, 2012.

[3] The majority thus omits significant parts of Mr. Hacker's affidavit. A complete and accurate reading of his affidavit makes clear that the Administrator and his team were using the data provided by each claimant from its business records, regardless of whether it had been kept by cash-method or accrual-method accounting. Moreover, the fragment that the majority does quote demonstrates that the settlement program would "follow up with claimants to better understand significant outliers" and "analyze the accuracy, validity and authenticity of outlier items." R. 18336. It would have been unreasonable for BP to have taken from this any representation that "the accountants were making Exhibit 4C calculations in accordance with the interpretations [BP] advances here." Ante, at 23.

its consent decree. In short, BP did not complain or object to the court in respect to the consent decree or ask for any provision that would allow it to change the decree after it became final.

It was not until December 5, 2012, almost a month after the final-approval hearing, that BP first expressed its concern to the Administrator that his use of claimants' cash-method data, particularly in connection with construction and professional-services firms' claims, might, according to BP, result in overcompensation of those claimants. *See* R. 18325. Several days later, on December 11, 2012, BP sent a follow-up email to the Administrator's special counsel, raising a number of questions and posing several hypotheticals involving claims by construction, professional-services, and agriculture-industry claimants. R. 18372-74. In particular, BP asked, "[i]f financial data submitted by a claimant does not accurately assign revenue to the months in which it was earned" (which, according to BP, occurs with cash basis accounting), "what steps do you take to obtain financial data that accurately reflects the earning of [—46—] revenue by month?" R. 18372. Days later, on December 16, 2012, class counsel responded by asking the Administrator to issue a policy statement providing that, "[w]hen a business keeps its books on a cash basis, revenue is earned during the month of receipt, irrespective of when the contract was entered or services were performed." R. 18381.

BP's next move, on the 8th or 9th of January 2013, was to seek to have the Administrator modify the settlement's formula for compensating business economic loss or revise his interpretation of that formula.[4] In a lengthy memorandum, BP

expressed its opinion, based on its reading in isolation the terms "revenue," "earned," "corresponding," and "comparable," that the settlement requires the Administrator, before calculating business economic loss, to convert the books of *all* claimants using cash-basis accounting to accrual-basis accounting, displaying revenue in the months earned and matching it with the expenses that produced it, regardless of when the expenses may have been incurred. BP, however, in an attachment to its memorandum labeled "Tab 1," proposed a compromise: "In a good faith effort to implement the [business economic-loss] framework, BP proposes a simple[] and workable approach for each industry [construction, agriculture, and professional services] that is claimant-friendly and requires limited *additional* effort by the Settlement Program." R. 18399 (emphasis added). BP then proceeded to set forth its proposed modifications to the business-economic-loss compensation formula for [—47—] claimants from the concerned industries. For construction claims, for instance, BP proposed the following:

Alignment of revenue and corresponding variable expenses can be substantially improved in two steps:

First, determine the ratio of claimant's annual revenue to annual variable expenses for 2010 and each of the Benchmark Period years.

Second, match revenue to corresponding variable expenses by multiplying (i) variable expenses reported for a given month and (ii) the ratio of revenue to variable costs calculated on an annual basis.

Last, adjustments should be made for irregular or extraordinary cost entries that can appear in monthly financial statements. . . .

After undertaking these steps, the variable profit calculation in Step 1 of the [business-economic-loss] compensation formula and the revenue calculations of the causation formula

---

[4] It is unclear from the record whether this response from BP was sent on January 8 or 9 of 2013. BP proposed these modifications as part of its response to the December 16, 2012 request for a policy statement, which, according to an email from the Administrator's special counsel establishing a briefing schedule, was due on January 8, 2012. *See* R. 18388. However, in a later piece of correspondence from BP, the company refers to its January 9, 2012 response. *See* R. 18402.

can proceed as usual with the Settlement Program selecting the Compensation Period months and Benchmark Period year(s) that maximize the claimant's award.

R. 18399-400. Following this section, BP's Tab 1 sets forth similar detailed changes and additions with respect to farming firms' claims that it describes as a "proposed approach to improving the alignment of revenue to corresponding expenses for farm claims [that] generally tracks the two-step approach proposed . . . for construction firm claims." R. 18400. Finally, BP's Tab 1 outlines its proposals with respect to professional services firms, including a detailed "proposed approach to align revenue to corresponding expenses for professional services firms [that also] generally tracks the two-step approach proposed . . . for construction and farming claims." R. 18401. [—48—]

Having reviewed the parties' submissions, the Administrator, on January 15, 2013, issued a policy statement stating that, in performing the calculations under the business-economic-loss framework, he would typically consider both revenue and expenses in the periods in which the revenues and expenses were recorded at the time and would not typically reallocate such revenue or expenses to different periods, but he would reserve the right to adjust financial statements in certain circumstances, including but not limited to, inconsistent basis of accounting between the Benchmark and Compensation Periods, errors in previously recorded transactions, and flawed or inconsistent treatment of accounting estimates. R. 18327-28. Importantly, the Administrator's special counsel, in the cover letter transmitting the policy statement, made clear that the Administrator "d[id] not view it within his authority to carve out specific types of claims in the fashion" proposed by BP. R. 18326. BP appealed to the district court, complaining of the Administrator's refusal to either modify the settlement decree or revise his interpretation of the compensation formula so as to bring about the same result as a modification. The district court, however, upheld the decision of the Administrator,

ruling that BP's proposed modification would both conflict with the terms of the parties' agreement and add substantive provisions thereto that had not been agreed to by the parties or approved of by the court during the final-approval hearing in which BP could have complained but did not. BP has now appealed to this court.

B.

Because BP has not satisfied its heavy burden of showing that a change in circumstances or law warranted the modifications it sought, the district court correctly affirmed the Administrator's decision rejecting BP's argument and [—49—] actions to modify the agreement to which the parties had agreed and which the district court had approved and adopted in its consent decree.

A party seeking to modify the substance of a district court's consent decree bears a heavy burden of establishing that revision of the decree is justified. *See Rufo v. Inmates of Suffolk Cnty. Jail*, 502 U.S. 367, 383 (1992). In *Rufo*, the Supreme Court explained that,

> [a]lthough . . . a district court should exercise flexibility in considering requests for modification of a[] . . . consent decree, it does not follow that a modification will be warranted in all circumstances. Rule 60(b)(5) provides that a party may obtain relief from a court order when "it is no longer equitable that the judgment should have prospective application," not when it is no longer convenient to live with the terms of a consent decree. Accordingly, a party seeking modification of a consent decree bears the burden of establishing that a significant change in circumstances warrants revision of the decree.

Id.[5] Further, the Court said that, "[a] party seeking modification of a consent decree may

---

[5] *Rufo* articulated these principles in the context of institutional-reform consent decrees. *See id.* However, the same principles apply to all consent decrees. *See, e.g., Alexis Lichine & Cie v. Sacha A. Lichine Estate Selections, Ltd.*, 45 F.3d 582, 586

meet its initial burden by showing either a *significant* change either in factual conditions or in law." *Id.* at 384 (emphasis added). "Ordinarily, however, modification should not be granted where a party relies upon events that actually were anticipated at the time it entered into a decree." *Id.* at 385 (citing *Twelve John Does v. District of Columbia*, 861 F.2d 295, 298-99 (D.C. Cir. 1988), and *Ruiz v. Lynaugh*, 811 F.2d 856, 862-63 (5th Cir. 1987)). But, "[i]f it is clear that a party anticipated changing conditions that would make [—50—] performance of the decree more onerous but nevertheless agreed to the decree, that party would have to satisfy a heavy burden to convince a court that it agreed to the decree in good faith, made a reasonable effort to comply with the decree, and should be relieved of the undertaking under Rule 60(b)." *Id.*

BP has failed to demonstrate that there has been a significant change either in circumstances or in the law since it entered into—and, in fact, affirmatively sought adoption of—the consent decree approving and incorporating the settlement agreement. As the record reflects, BP was fully aware that it would be required to pay claims by firms in the construction, agriculture, and professional-services industries that were supported by these businesses' cash-basis accounting data and yet, nevertheless, BP agreed to the settlement and actively sought the district court's approval of the eventual consent decree. Accordingly, it is this court's clear duty to affirm the district court's judgment rejecting BP's attempts to force the Administrator to modify the consent decree and the parties' settlement simply because it is no longer convenient for BP to live with the terms to which it agreed.

C.

In its appeals to this court, BP conveniently forgets that it sought to have the Administrator modify the settlement agreement's formula for calculating business economic loss by adding the detailed

provisions that it proposed in Tab 1, attached to its January 2013 memorandum. Now, BP argues, belied by its attempt to have the Administrator modify the settlement decree, that the parties intended all along to require the Administrator to convert each claimant's cash-basis data to accrual-basis data by restating revenue in the month in which it was earned and matching it to the expenses that generated it, regardless of [—51—] when the expenses were incurred. The words of the district court's consent decree, and the settlement agreement approved therein, however, do not support BP's proposed interpretation.

In reviewing a district court's consent decree, our primary rule of interpretation is the "four corners" doctrine, under which the decree is construed according to its terms, not on the basis of "what might satisfy the purpose of one of the parties to it." *See United States v. Armour & Co.*, 402 U.S. 673, 682 (1971). In addition, certain "aids to construction" commonly employed in construing contracts may be referenced. *See United States v. ITT Continental Baking Co.*, 420 U.S. 223, 238 (1972). "Such aids include the circumstances surrounding the formation of the consent order, any technical meaning words used may have had to the parties, and any other documents expressly incorporated in the decree." *Id.* In so doing, we must not strain the decree's precise terms or impose other terms in an attempt to reconcile the decree with our own conception of its purpose. *See Armour*, 402 U.S. at 681-82. A consent decree is the product of negotiation between the parties and embodies a compromise struck among various factors, including the parties' competing goals and the time, expense, and risk of litigation. *See id.* at 681. In this way, "the decree itself cannot be said to have a purpose; rather the parties have purposes, generally opposed to each other, and the resultant decree embodies as much of those opposing purposes as the respective parties have the bargaining power and skill to achieve." *Id.* at 681-82.[6] By consenting to a

_____

(1st Cir. 1995) ("While *Rufo* was a case involving institutional reform, we do not read it as being confined in principle to such cases.").

[6] In this regard, the majority does what *Armour* directs us not to do, *viz.*, the majority defines the "purpose" of the settlement agreement from outside sources and then uses that "purpose" to interpret

decree, the parties have [—52—] waived their rights under the Due Process Clause to litigate the issues raised by a complaint. *Id.* at 682. A court should not later modify the decree by interposing terms not agreed to by the parties or not included in the language of the decree. *See id.*; *see also United States v. Atl. Ref. Co.*, 360 U.S. 19, 23 (1959); *Hughes v. United States*, 342 U.S. 353, 357 (1952).

Exhibit 4C of the settlement and consent decree, which is the pertinent subject of these appeals, details the compensation framework for business economic loss.[7] By its terms, the framework "compares the actual profit of a business during a defined post-spill period in 2010 to the profit that the claimant might have expected to earn in the comparable post-spill period of 2010." R. 4277. The framework includes two steps. Step one, which is at issue here, "[c]ompensates claimants for any reduction in profit between the 2010 Compensation Period selected by the claimant and the comparable months of the Benchmark Period" and "reflects the reduction in Variable Profit (which reflects the claimant's revenue less its variable costs) over this period." R. 4277. Step two, which is not at issue in these appeals, is intended to "[c]ompensate[] claimants for incremental profits or losses the claimant might have been expected to generate in the absence of the spill relative to sales from the Benchmark Period." R. 4277. [—53—]

With regard to step one, the Compensation Period is "selected by the claimant and may

include three or more consecutive months between May and December 2010" (in other words, several months shortly after the oil spill began). R. 4277. The "Benchmark Period" is "the pre-[spill] period which claimant chooses as the baseline for measuring its historical financial performance"; for the Benchmark Period, "the claimant can select among the following . . . [p]eriods: 2009; the average of 2008–2009; or the average of 2007–2009, provided that the range of years selected by the claimant will be utilized for all Benchmark Period purposes." R. 4277. Variable Profit is then defined as follows:

> **Variable Profit**: This is calculated for both the Benchmark Period and the Compensation Period as follows:
>
> 1. Sum the monthly revenue over the period.
>
> 2. Subtract the corresponding variable expenses from revenue over the same time period.

R. 4277. Having defined the relevant terms, the settlement finally prescribes "Step 1 Compensation" as follows: "Step 1 of the compensation calculation is determined as the difference in Variable Profit between the 2010 Compensation Period selected by the claimant and the Variable Profit over the comparable months of the Benchmark Period." R. 4277.

The majority states, and I agree, that the settlement permits a business economic-loss claimant to select a comparison interval as short as three months (or as long as eight months). That is, claimants may choose income from any three consecutive months between May and December of 2010 to compare with income in a Benchmark Period of the same three to eight months in 2009, the average of 2008–2009, or the average of 2007–2009. This flexibility to choose a [—54—] shorter comparison interval allows a claimant to take advantage of the natural variability in revenue over the course of a given year. Claimants may choose a three-month period in which their income was particularly bad in 2010, or particularly good in the Benchmark Period, and exclude from the calculation other

---

the consent decree. Nothing within the four corners of the consent decree indicates that the overriding purpose of the agreement, as the majority assumes, was [—52—] to perfectly match revenue to the expenses that generated it. *See Ante*, at 21.

[7] "The Settlement recognizes six categories of damage: (1) specified types of economic loss for businesses and individuals, (2) specified types of real property damage (coastal, wetlands, and real property sales damage), (3) Vessel of Opportunity Charter Payment, (4) Vessel Physical Damage, (5) Subsistence Damage, and (6) the Seafood Compensation Program." *In re Oil Spill by Oil Rig Deepwater Horizon in Gulf of Mexico, on April 20, 2010*, 910 F. Supp. 2d 891, 903 (E.D. La. 2012). Categories of damage other than business economic loss are not at issue in these appeals.

months in which their 2010 income might have actually been quite good. The text of the settlement illustrates this feature (and others involving the settlement's causation framework) with three examples as follows:

Scenario 1:

1) Claimant selected the months of May–July 2010 for the purpose of determining causation, and the claimant, using these months, meets the causation test for the Benchmark period years of 2009, 2008–2009 and 2007–2009;

2) In determining Compensation, Claimant would be allowed to select the months of August through November 2010 as compared to the months of August through November in either 2009, 2008–2009 or 2007–2009 as the Benchmark years—whichever provides the highest compensation.

Scenario 2:

1) Claimant selected the months of October–December 2010 for the purpose of determining causation and the claimant, using these months, meets the causation test for the Benchmark period years of 2009, 2008–2009;

2) In determining compensation, Claimant could select the months of May–September 2010 as compared to the months of May–September in either 2009 or 2008–2009—whichever provides the highest compensation.

Scenario 3: [—55—]

1) Claimant selected the months of June–August 2010 for the purpose of determining causation and the claimant, using these months, meets the causation test for the Benchmark period year of 2009. In

addition, Claimant selected the months of August–October 2010 for the purpose of determining causation, and the claimant, using these months, meets the causation test for the Benchmark period years of 2007–2009;

2) In determining compensation, Claimant could select the months of May–December 2010 as compared to the months of May–December in either 2009 or 2007–2009—whichever provides the highest compensation.

R. 4283. Consequently, if this court were to interpret the settlement agreement to require the Administrator to convert each claimant's cash-method data into accrual-method data showing monthly revenue as earned matched with the expenses that generated it regardless of when the revenue and expenses were recorded on the claimant's books, we necessarily would be violating *Armour*'s four-corners rule: BP's proposed conversion and matching requirements, which would require the Administrator to restate the months in which claimants recorded their revenue and expenses, are not contained within the four corners of the decree and settlement. And, for the reasons already stated, we, in effect, would be modifying the terms of the consent decree without BP having satisfied its burden of showing a significant change in circumstances or law justifying that modification. Such a modification of the settlement decree would conflict with the clear examples in the settlement agreement and would require the Administrator go outside and perhaps far beyond the Compensation and Benchmark Periods selected by the claimant to trace the generative expenses to match with revenue earned in those periods. Further, even if such a [—56—] reconstruction of the claimant's business history were possible, it would likely differ markedly from the cash-method claimant's records kept in 2009 and the first quarter of 2010 when the claimant had no inkling that an oil spill affecting his business would occur on April 20, 2010. The effect of our so interpreting the settlement agreement could be devastating to many claimants who are unable to translate or reconstruct their cash-basis data into revenue matched to the expenses that generated it under BP's proposed conversion and ultra matching requirements. Moreover, forced conversion of all cash-basis data into accrual-basis data would discriminate against the remaining cash-basis claimants by either thwarting their claims entirely or treating their claims less favorably than the cash-basis claims already resolved.

The plain wording of the settlement agreement read as a whole and with all of its supporting documents permits claimants to support their business-economic-loss claims using their own business records and does not require that these records be kept in any particular form. In fact, BP, jointly with class counsel, told the district court that "[t]he documents required to support Business Economic loss claims . . . are the documents that businesses either keep in the ordinary course or that may readily be prepared from a business's books and records." R. 8558 (jointly proposed findings of fact and conclusions of law filed in the district court by BP and class counsel in support of final approval); *see also In re Oil Spill by Oil Rig Deepwater Horizon in Gulf of Mexico, on April 20, 2010*, 910 F. Supp. 2d 891, 904 (E.D. La. 2012) (same) (final-approval order); CPA Societies' Amicus Br. at 1-14. This is the way the district court interpreted the settlement agreement and consent decree in its March 5, 2013 order upholding the Administrator's rejection of BP's attempt to modify the [—57—] parties' agreement or change the Administrator's interpretation of it. R. 12550 ("[T]he documentation provisions contained within Exhibit 4A make it clear that the Program's analysis is to be based on revenue and expenses during the relevant periods chosen by the claimant, *as reflected in historical business records*. . . . Exhibit 4A does not require that accounting occur on an 'accrual' basis, as opposed to a 'cash' basis.") (emphasis added). In other words, a claimant may support its claim with data recorded using cash-basis accounting if it has consistently used that method in the ordinary course of its

business.[8] Further, the claimant may use records kept using accrual-basis accounting if that is what it has consistently applied in the ordinary course of its business. Likewise, the settlement does not instruct the Administrator to refrain from accepting and relying on claims supported by a claimant's own business records, whether cash basis or accrual basis, so long as the claimant's books have been consistently kept on the same method and in the ordinary course of business. Most important, the settlement nowhere instructs the Administrator to restate or convert a claimant's claim submitted using cash-basis accounting data into accrual-basis accounting data, showing revenue only in the months in which it was earned, and matching the monthly earned revenue with the expenses that generated it, regardless of when the expenses were made or incurred.[9] Simply [—58—] stated, none of the terms, conditions, and qualifications that BP proposes and argues for are stated or contained within the four corners of the consent decree and settlement agreement.

For these reasons, I respectfully conclude that the majority has unintentionally fallen into legal error by not recognizing that the

---

[8] For that matter, the federal government accepts, for tax purposes, submissions supported using a business's data recorded using cash-basis accounting so long as such accounting has consistently been used in the ordinary course of business. *See* 26 U.S.C. §446(a) ("Taxable income shall be computed under the method of accounting on the basis of which the taxpayer regularly computes his income in keeping his books.").

[9] The April 18, 2012 version of the settlement contained a requirement that accounting professionals seeking reimbursement for their services certify that they submitted their reimbursement request "in compliance with generally accepted accounting principles" ("GAAP"), a requirement which was subsequently removed from the May, 2 2012 version that [—58—] was approved by the district court. *Compare* R. 2445 (April 18, 2012 version), *with* R. 3955 (May 2, 2012 version). BP knew how to insist that claims abide by GAAP but failed to do so, suggesting that it understood that claims could be submitted based on documents prepared using cash-method accounting. *See* CPA Societies' Amicus Br. at 6.

four-corners rule of *Armour* and other teachings by the Supreme Court require that the district court's consent decree containing the settlement agreement be interpreted as written; that this appellate court may not add to or subtract from the district court's consent decree; that likewise we must not strain the decree's precise terms or impose other terms in an attempt to reconcile the decree with our own conception of its purpose; and that the district court's interpretation of its own consent decree was correct and should be affirmed. *See Armour*, 402 U.S. at 682; *see also United States v. Atl. Ref. Co.*, 360 U.S. 19, 23 (1959); *Hughes v. United States*, 342 U.S. 353, 357 (1952); *Walker v. U.S. Dep't of Hous. & Urban Dev.*, 912 F.2d 819, 825 (5th Cir. 1990) ("Nor are courts at liberty to redraft the obligations commanded by the decree absent consent of the parties.").

II.

I respectfully disagree with the majority's reversal of the district court's decision and its remand of the case to the district court to determine whether the Administrator has been converting claims submitted with accrual-method accounting data into cash-method supported claims and processing them on that basis. The majority itself concedes that this scenario is "unlikely" and that BP [—59—] has not explicitly asserted this. *Ante*, at 15. That BP has not so argued in these appeals makes the majority's *sua sponte* raising of the issue highly irregular and contrary to our normal rule of addressing on appeal only the issues raised and argued by the appellant. Furthermore, careful inspection of the record in this case demonstrates that the majority's intuited scenario is not just unlikely; the record demonstrates that it is plainly not the case.

Neither BP nor class counsel has ever questioned whether the Administrator was properly applying Exhibit 4C's compensation requirements to use claimants' accrual-method accounting data to calculate and pay business-economic-loss claims. On December 5, 2012, BP expressed concern to the Administrator that he was overcompensating claimants by using their cash-method data in

his calculations. On December 11, 2012, BP sent a follow-up email to the Administrator's special counsel asking, if financial data submitted by a claimant does not accurately assign revenue to the months in which it was earned, what steps would the Administrator take to obtain financial data that accurately reflect the earning of revenue by month. R. 18372. On December 16, 2012, class counsel responded by asking the Administrator to issue a policy statement providing that, "[w]hen a business keeps its books on a cash basis, revenue is earned during the month of receipt, irrespective of when the contract was entered or services were performed." R. 18381. On January 8 or 9, 2013, BP demanded that the Administrator revise his interpretation of the Exhibit 4C formula so as to require him to convert the books of *all* claimants using cash-basis accounting to accrual-basis accounting or to modify the formula to do so for construction, farming, and professional-services firms using cash-method accounting. The Administrator's refusal to do so and his January 15, 2013 policy [—60—] statement, stating that he "will typically consider both revenues and expenses in the periods in which those revenues and expenses were recorded at the time" and that he lacked authority to change the settlement agreement by carving out exceptions for certain categories of claimants, led directly to BP's appeal to the district court to reverse the Administrator's decision. Thus, nothing in the communications between the parties and the Administrator indicates that their dispute involved the conversion of accrual-based accounting data to cash-based accounting data. The district court affirmed the decision of the Administrator rejecting BP's demand that the Administrator either (a) interpret the settlement agreement to require the conversion of all claimants' cash-method accounting data to a particular kind of accrual-method data prior to calculating the claimants' business economic loss or (b) modify the settlement agreement in that way with respect to construction, farming, professional-services claims based on cash-method accounting data.

Consequently, the majority's notion that Administrator has ever converted any claimant's accrual-method accounting data to cash-method data has no support in the record or the briefs in this case. The majority's precipitous reversal of the district court's judgment and remand for unnecessary proceedings is erroneous and quite unfortunate for everyone concerned in this case.

III.

A.

I now turn to the discussion in the majority opinion of so-called "fictitious" claims (part II of the opinion), which is now supported by the vote of one judge. Like Judge Southwick, I do not join this section of the opinion and I respectfully dissent from it as well. These appeals arise from a dispute regarding BP's [—61—] proposed modification or reinterpretation of the settlement agreement's text; a separate appeal addressing the district court's certification of this class action and acceptance of the settlement agreement has been docketed and calendared for oral argument on November 4, 2013 before a different panel of judges. *See In re Deepwater Horizon Appeals of the Economic and Property Damage Class Action Settlement*, No. 12-31155 (5th Cir. filed Nov. 19, 2012). The parties have not argued those certification and acceptance issues to this panel, and we may not properly decide them or pronounce upon them.

Judge Clement begins her discussion by expressing concern regarding whether the plaintiff class members have "colorable legal claims" which she defines as an "[ability] to plead" the elements of a claim. *See ante*, at 26; *see also ante*, at 29 (stating that a claim is "colorable" if the plaintiff "can *allege* standing and the elements necessary to state a claim on which relief can be granted"). I do not understand what that concern has to do with this case. Here, the district court held, in an opinion to which Judge Clement makes no reference, that "the class representatives— *like all class members*—allege economic and/or property damage stemming directly from the *Deepwater Horizon* spill." *In re Oil Spill by Oil Rig Deepwater Horizon in Gulf of Mexico, on April 20, 2010*, 910 F. Supp. 2d at 915

(emphasis added). And the district court went on to say that, under the class definitions, "persons with marginal or potentially worthless claims . . . [are] excluded." *Id.* at 917; *see also id.* at 917 (stating that the "class in this case consists exclusively of individuals and businesses that have already suffered economic loss"). Nobody has appealed from this finding that the class members here allege losses stemming directly from BP's conduct. Judge Clement's dicta are divorced from the facts and issues in this case. [—62—]

Turning, very briefly, to Judge Clement's legal pronouncements, I must say that I respectfully disagree with her statement that a court cannot allow a single person lacking a "colorable claim" against a class-action defendant to recover compensation in a class-action settlement because to do so would "ignore[] the standing requirement of Article III and create[] a substantive right where none existed before." *Ante,* at 27-28. This analysis confuses the relevant legal principles, is not supported by any law from our circuit or others, and would cause our circuit to split with at least three of our sister circuits if it were binding. First, although Judge Clement leans heavily on a dissenting opinion in the Third Circuit's *Sullivan* case, that dissent was joined by only a single other judge and its analysis was squarely rejected by the seven-judge majority. *See Sullivan v. DB Invs., Inc.*, 667 F.3d 273, 305 (3d Cir. 2011) (en banc); *see also Rodriguez v. Nat'l City Bank*, No. 11-8079, 2013 WL 4046385, at *4 (3d Cir. Aug. 12, 2013) (Jordan, J.) ("*Sullivan* instructed that assessing whether individual class members have viable claims is inappropriate in the context of reviewing a proposed settlement class."). Second, although Judge Clement cites a decades-old Seventh Circuit decision, *see ante*, at 28, a more recent decision from that circuit rejects her analysis in no uncertain terms:

[The class-action defendant] argues that before certifying a class the district judge was required to determine which class members had suffered damages. But putting the cart before the horse in that way would vitiate the economies of class action procedure; in effect the trial would precede the certification. It is true that injury is a prerequisite to standing. But as long as one member of a certified class has a plausible claim to have suffered damages, the requirement of standing is satisfied. [—63—]

Kohen v. Pac. Inv. Mgmt. Co. LLC, 571 F.3d 672, 676 (7th Cir. 2009). And third, the analysis also conflicts with the Second Circuit's. *See In re Am. Int'l Grp., Inc. Sec. Litig.*, 689 F.3d 229, 243-44 (2d Cir. 2012).

And, for the reasons explained at length in *Sullivan*, requiring a district court to ensure that every class-action settlement beneficiary has a "colorable" cause of action against the defendant is unworkable in practice. Should the district court require that every settlement beneficiary file a separate complaint consisting of individual allegations and that BP file separate motions to dismiss each of the complaints? I do not think it wise to mandate such an unwieldy and expensive undertaking when the parties settled precisely to avoid that sort of costly litigation. *See* Fed. R. Civ. P. 1 (the civil procedure rules "should be construed and administered to secure the just, speedy, and inexpensive determination of every action and proceeding"). Nor do I see how it is required by existing law.[10]

Lastly, Judge Clement's theory rests on a false premise: the idea that every individual who benefits from a class-action settlement must or is deemed to have an independent cause of action against the class-action defendant. I do not think that is the case. In a simple non-class-action lawsuit between a single [—64—] plaintiff and a single defendant, I am not aware of any rule that would prohibit the litigants from reaching a settlement in which the defendant agrees to make payment not to the plaintiff he has allegedly wronged but rather to, say, a favored charity instead. Should that happen, neither the law nor common sense presumes that the charity has an independent cause of action against the defendant. *See, e.g., King v. Emp'rs Nat'l Ins. Co.*, 928 F.2d 1438, 1442 (5th Cir. 1991) (discussing third-party beneficiaries to settlement agreements). This basic principle seems no less applicable in the class-action context and to apply with no less force whether the settlement benefits a charity, one or more specifically enumerated individuals or entities, or a class of individuals or entities as defined by whatever characteristics the negotiating parties choose. *See id.* at 1442 ("In fact, there is no requirement that the third-party beneficiary even be specifically named in the contract."); *Montana v. United States*, 124 F.3d 1269, 1273 (Fed. Cir. 1997) ("The intended beneficiary need not be specifically or individually identified in the contract, but must fall within a class clearly intended to be benefitted thereby."). In short, whether a settlement agreement arises in the class-action context or not, there seems to me no requirement that every beneficiary of the agreement have a "colorable" cause of action against the defendant.[11]

A fundamental flaw in Judge Clement's analysis is that it conflates and fails to distinguish between, on the one hand, the legal requirements for *certifying a class, see ante,* at 27-28 (arguing that courts act unlawfully "[b]y including claimants in the class definition that lack colorable claims"), and, on [—65—] the other hand, those for *approving and enforcing a settlement agreement* in the class-action context, *see ante,* at 31 (arguing that a class-action settlement

---

[10] I certainly do not see how it is required by the law of standing. It is hornbook law that, "[i]n class action cases, the standing inquiry focuses on the class representatives. The class representatives must have individual standing in order to sue. . . . [T]he representative need not prove that each member of the class has standing." WILLIAM B. RUBENSTEIN, NEWBERG ON CLASS ACTIONS § 2:1 (5th ed.) (collecting cases in omitted footnotes); *see, e.g., Kohen*, 571 F.3d at 676 ("It is true that injury is a prerequisite to standing. But as long as one member of a certified class has a plausible claim to have suffered damages, the requirement of standing is satisfied."); *Denney v. Deutsche Bank AG*, 443 F.3d 253, 263 (2d Cir. 2006) ("We do not require that each member of a class submit evidence of personal standing.").

[11] This is not to say that the parties here intended to benefit third parties lacking viable causes of action; rather, the point is that there is no legal reason to inquire into whether the settlement benefits persons lacking viable causes of action.

"is unlawful" and cannot be approved if it grants compensation to businesses "that had not sustained losses"), assuming without explication that the former are coterminous with the latter. However, the distinction should not be elided: whether or not it is true that Rule 23 or another provision of law is violated by maintaining a class action including class members lacking "colorable" claims—one legal issue—it does not follow either way that the court's approval or enforcement of a settlement that benefits persons without "colorable" claims violates any law—a distinct legal issue. *See, e.g., Denney v. Deutsche Bank AG*, 443 F.3d 253, 268-76 (2d Cir. 2006) (addressing separately the class certification and settlement approval issues); *cf. Messner v. Northshore Univ. HealthSystem*, 669 F.3d 802, 824 (7th Cir. 2012) ("[The class-action defendant] argu[es] that the class for which certification is requested is fatally overbroad because it contains members who could not have been harmed by any post-merger price increases .... This [issue] is critical *for class certification purposes*.") (emphasis added). Without embracing either of Judge Clement's propositions, because neither are presented to this panel for decision, any discussion of them will not be furthered by conflating one for the other as she does here.

B.

BP twice sought a preliminary injunction from the district court and was twice denied. Thereafter, BP sought both a stay pending appeal and a preliminary injunction from this court, which were also denied. I see no reason to reverse any of these decisions. The majority opinion, however, purports to reverse the district court's denial of a preliminary injunction and appears to [—66—] "instruct the district court to expeditiously craft a narrowly-tailored injunction" that allows the claims of "those who experienced actual injury traceable to loss from the Deepwater Horizon accident" to proceed while staying the claims of "those who did not." *Ante*, at 35-36. Because the majority opinion's instruction to the district court regarding the injunction appears to be based on Judge Clement's separate opinion concerning class-action law, that

instruction does not appear to be based on a majority vote of this panel. Moreover, for the same reasons I discussed in the foregoing sections of this opinion, this appellate court may not modify the terms and conditions of the district court's consent decree or order the district court to do so; and this court cannot use material outside of the four corners of the consent decree to reinterpret that decree. Consequently, it would be clear legal error for this court to assume that it has jurisdiction and authority to impose on the Administrator the requirement that, in addition to identifying a claimant as eligible and entitled to compensation for business economic loss under the consent decree encompassing the parties' settlement agreement, he must also find independently that the claimant is not one of "those who [did not] experience[] actual injury traceable to loss from the Deepwater Horizon accident" before paying the claim. Such an injunction would be broader than the alleged purpose of the remand and tantamount to modifying the consent decree for the benefit of one of the parties, BP, without that party carrying its burden to show a change in circumstances or law that warrants changing the decree; or else to interpreting the consent decree based on material or purposes not stated within the four corners of the consent decree. [—67—]

CONCLUSION

For these reasons, I concur in the majority's affirmance of the district court's dismissal of BP's suit against the Administrator for failure to state a claim under Rule 12(b)(6) but I respectfully dissent from the majority opinion in all other respects.

United States Court of Appeals
for the Fifth Circuit

No. 12-30714

MCBRIDE
vs.
ESTIS WELL SERVICE, L.L.C.***

Appeal from the United States District Court for the
Western District of Louisiana

Decided: October 2, 2013

***Petition for rehearing en banc granted on Feb. 24, 2014.

Citation: 731 F.3d 505, 1 Adm. R. 316 (5th Cir. 2013)

Before STEWART, Chief Judge, and BARKSDALE and
HIGGINSON, Circuit Judges.

[—2—] HIGGINSON, Circuit Judge:

The principal question presented by this case is whether seamen may recover punitive damages for their employer's willful and wanton breach of the general maritime law duty to provide a seaworthy vessel. Answering in the affirmative, we REVERSE and REMAND for further proceedings.

FACTS AND PROCEEDINGS

The consolidated cases arise out of an accident aboard Estis Rig 23, a barge supporting a truck-mounted drilling rig operating in Bayou Sorrell, a navigable waterway in Iberville Parish, Louisiana. As crew members were attempting to straighten the monkey board—the catwalk extending from the derrick—which had twisted the previous night, the derrick pipe shifted, causing the rig and truck to topple over. One crew member, Skye Sonnier, was fatally pinned between the derrick and mud tank, and three others, Saul Touchet, Brian Suire, and Joshua Bourque, have alleged injuries. At the time of the incident, Estis Well Service, L.L.C. ("Estis") owned and operated Rig 23, and employed Sonnier, Touchet, Suire, and Bourque (collectively, the "crew members").

Haleigh McBride, individually, on behalf of Sonnier's minor child, and as administratrix of Sonnier's estate, filed suit against Estis,

stating causes of action for unseaworthiness under general maritime law and negligence under the Jones Act and seeking compensatory as well as "punitive and/or exemplary" [—3—] damages.[1] The other crew members filed separate actions against Estis alleging the same causes of action and requesting the same relief. Upon the crew members' motion, the cases were consolidated into a single action over which a Magistrate Judge presided with the parties' consent.[2] Estis moved to dismiss the claims for punitive damages, arguing that punitive damages are not an available remedy for unseaworthiness or Jones Act negligence as a matter of law. Treating it as a motion for judgment on the pleadings under Federal Rule of Civil Procedure 12(c), the Magistrate Judge granted the motion, and correspondingly entered judgment dismissing all claims for punitive damages. Recognizing that the issues presented were "the subject of national debate with no clear consensus," the court granted plaintiffs' motion to certify the judgment for immediate appeal under 28 U.S.C. § 1292(b). This interlocutory appeal followed.

STANDARD OF REVIEW

Whether punitive damages are an available remedy under maritime law is a question of law reviewed de novo. *See Atl. Sounding Co., Inc. v. Townsend*, 496 F.3d 1282, 1284 (11th Cir. 2007) (citations omitted), *aff'd*, 557 U.S. 404 (2009).

BACKGROUND

I. Sources of maritime law

There are two primary sources of federal maritime law: common law developed by

---

[1] "Punitive damages" and "exemplary damages" are synonymous. They reflect two principal purposes of such damages: to *punish* the wrongdoer and thereby make an *example* of him in the hopes that doing so will deter him and others from wrongdoing. David W. Robertson, *Punitive Damages in American Maritime Law*, 28 J. Mar. L. & Com. 73, 82–83 (1997). For ease of reference, we refer to all such damages as "punitive damages."

[2] In March 2012, Bourque settled his claims against Estis.

federal courts exercising the maritime authority conferred on them by the Admiralty Clause of the Constitution ("general maritime law"), and statutory law enacted by Congress exercising its authority under the Admiralty [—4—] Clause and the Commerce Clause ("statutory maritime law"). *See* U.S. CONST. art. III, § 2, cl. 1 (extending the judicial power of the United States "to all [c]ases of admiralty and maritime [j]urisdiction"); *Romero v. Int'l Terminal Operating Co.*, 358 U.S. 354, 360–61 (1959) (explaining that the Admiralty Clause "empowered the federal courts in their exercise of the admiralty and maritime jurisdiction which had been conferred on them, to draw on the substantive law 'inherent in the admiralty and maritime jurisdiction,' [ ] to continue the development of this law within constitutional limits[,]" and "empowered Congress to revise and supplement the maritime law within the limits of the Constitution") (citation omitted).[3]

II. Causes of action under maritime law

Traditionally, general maritime law afforded ill and injured seamen two causes of action against shipowners and employers. If a seaman became ill or injured while in the service of the ship, the seaman's employer and the ship's owner owed the seaman room and board ("maintenance") and medical care ("cure") without regard to fault, and, if not provided, the seaman had a claim against them for "maintenance and cure." If a seaman was injured by a ship's operational unfitness, the seaman had a cause of action for "unseaworthiness." General maritime law did not provide seamen with a separate cause of action for personal injury resulting from employer negligence, *The Osceola*, 189 U.S. 158, 175 (1903), nor did it permit wrongful death or survival claims on behalf of seamen killed during the course of their employment, *The Harrisburg*, 119 U.S. 199, 204–14 (1886),

---

[3] For a discussion of the division of maritime rulemaking authority between Congress and the federal courts, see David W. Robertson, *Our High Court of Admiralty and Its Sometimes Peculiar Relationship With Congress*, 55 St. Louis U. L.J. 491, 494–513 (2011).

overruled by Moragne v. States Marine Lines, Inc., 398 U.S. 375 (1970). [—5—]

To remedy those perceived gaps in general maritime law, which, until then, had been filled by a patchwork of state wrongful death statutes,[4] Congress in 1920 enacted the Jones Act and the Death on the High Seas Act ("DOHSA"), which created causes of action for employer negligence in navigable waters and on the high seas, respectively, and authorized survival and wrongful death remedies. *See* 46 U.S.C. § 688 (1920) (codified as amended at 46 U.S.C. § 30104 (2006));[5] 46 U.S.C. §§ 761–68 (1920) (codified as amended at 46 U.S.C. §§30301–08 (2006)).[6] The Supreme Court has since recognized a parallel cause of action under general maritime law for employer negligence resulting in injury or death. *See*

---

[4] "These statutes were often unwieldy and not designed to accommodate maritime claims; moreover, because they varied from state to state, the representatives of similarly situated deceased seamen might be awarded widely varying sums based on the fortuity of whether the accident occurred within or without the three-mile limit and, if it were within that limit, based on the laws of the particular state where the casualty occurred." *Ivy v. Security Barge Lines, Inc.*, 606 F.2d 524, 527 (5th Cir. 1979).

[5] The Jones Act provides, in pertinent part:

> A seaman injured in the course of employment or, if the seaman dies from the injury, the personal representative of the seaman may elect to bring a civil action at law, with the right of trial by jury, against the employer. Laws of the United States regulating recovery for personal injury to, or death of, a railway employee apply to an action under this section.

46 U.S.C. § 30104.

[6] DOHSA provides, in pertinent part:

> When the death of an individual is caused by wrongful act, neglect, or default occurring on the high seas beyond 3 nautical miles from the shore of the United States, the personal representative of the decedent may bring a civil action in admiralty against the person or vessel responsible. The action shall be for the exclusive benefit of the decedent's spouse, parent, child, or dependent relative.

46 U.S.C. § 30302.

Norfolk Shipbuilding & Drydock Corp. v. Garris, 532 U.S. 811, 818–20 (2001) (citing *Moragne*, 398 U.S. at 409).

III. Punitive damages under maritime law [—6—]

"Historically, punitive damages," though not always designated as such,[7] "have been available and awarded in general maritime actions." *Townsend*, 557 U.S. at 407; *see also id.* at 414 (citing as examples of early punitive damages awards *The City of Carlisle*, 39 F. 807, 817 (D. Or. 1889) (adding $1,000 to plaintiff's damages award for "gross neglect and cruel maltreatment"), and *The Troop*, 118 F. 769, 770–771, 773 (D. Wash. 1902) (concluding that $4,000 was a reasonable award because the captain's "failure to observe the dictates of humanity" and obtain prompt medical care for an injured seaman constituted a "monstrous wrong")). In the early nineteenth century, Justice Story spoke of maritime punitive damages as "the proper punishment which belongs to [ ] lawless misconduct." *The Amiable Nancy*, 16 U.S. (3 Wheat.) 546, 558 (1818).

Over the next century and a half, the availability of punitive damages for unseaworthiness claims arising under general maritime law was largely unquestioned. In *Complaint of Merry Shipping, Inc.*, 650 F.2d 622, 623 (5th Cir. Unit B Jul. 1981), our court confirmed the prevailing view that "punitive damages may be recovered under general maritime law upon a showing of willful and wanton misconduct by the shipowner in the creation or maintenance of unseaworthy conditions." Our court based its holding on the historical availability of punitive damages under general maritime law, the public policy interests in punishing willful violators of

maritime law and deterring them from committing future violations, and the uniformity of contemporary courts on the issue. *Id.* at 624–26.[8] After *Merry Shipping*, the Ninth and Eleventh Circuits followed suit. [—7—] *See Evich v. Morris*, 819 F.2d 256, 258 (9th Cir. 1987) ("Punitive damages are available under general maritime law for claims of unseaworthiness.") (citations omitted); *Self v. Great Lakes Dredge & Dock Co.*, 832 F.2d 1540, 1550 (11th Cir. 1987) ("Punitive damages should be available in cases where the shipowner willfully violated the duty to maintain a safe and seaworthy ship . . . .").

In *Miles v. Melrose*, 882 F.2d 976, 989 (5th Cir. 1989) (citations omitted), we reiterated that "[p]unitive damages are recoverable under the general maritime law 'upon a showing of willful and wanton misconduct by the shipowner' in failing to provide a seaworthy vessel[,]" but held, for the first time, that loss of society damages were not available to nondependent parents in a general maritime cause of action for the wrongful death of a Jones Act seaman.[9]

---

[7] *See Townsend*, 557 U.S. at 414 n.3 (citing awards of punitive damages in early maritime cases and pointing out that "[a]lthough these cases do not refer to 'punitive' or 'exemplary' damages, scholars have characterized the awards authorized by these decisions as such"); Robertson, *Punitive Damages in American Maritime Law*, *supra*, at 88 (noting that eighteenth and nineteenth century maritime courts used a variety of terms to designate damages intended to punish and deter).

[8] At the time *Merry Shipping* was decided, the Second and Sixth Circuits had held that punitive damages were available in unseaworthiness actions, and no circuit court had ruled [—7—] otherwise. *See In re Marine Sulphur Queen*, 460 F.2d 89, 105 (2d Cir. 1972) (noting, in the unseaworthiness context, that "the award of punitive damages is discretionary with the trial court[,]" and "[a] condition precedent to awarding them is a showing by the plaintiffs that the defendant was guilty of gross negligence, or actual malice or criminal indifference which is the equivalent of reckless and wanton misconduct") (citations omitted); *U.S. Steel Corp. v. Fuhrman*, 407 F.2d 1143, 1148 (6th Cir. 1969) (noting that punitive damages are recoverable against a ship owner for the actions of a master if "the owner authorized or ratified the acts of the master" or "the owner was reckless in employing him") (citations omitted).

[9] A "Jones Act seaman" is "a master or member of a crew of any vessel," *Stewart v. Dutra Const. Co.*, 543 U.S. 481, 488 (2005) (internal quotation marks omitted) (citations omitted), as distinguished from a "*Sieracki* seaman," which refers to a longshoreman or harborworker who is injured on a vessel while performing traditional work of a seaman and, by virtue of *Seas Shipping*

Judge Rubin, speaking for the court, was guided by the "twin aims of maritime law": "achieving uniformity in the exercise of admiralty jurisdiction and providing special solicitude to seamen." *Id.* at 987. It would be anomalous, the court reasoned, if a wrongful death claimant were permitted to recover for loss of society damages under general maritime law even though the claimant was barred from recovering such damages under statutory maritime law. *Id.* at 987–88. And the goal of providing special solicitude to seamen, the wards of [—8—] admiralty, "would not be furthered in any meaningful way by allowing nondependent parents to recover for loss of society." *Id.* at 988; *see also id.* ("Admiralty cannot provide the parents solicitude at a voyage's outset when their right to recover for loss of society is dependent on the fortuity that the deaths occur in territorial waters and are caused by unseaworthiness." (quoting *Sistrunk v. Circle Bar Drilling Co.*, 770 F.2d 455, 460 (5th Cir. 1985)) (emphases omitted).

The Supreme Court affirmed in a decision most significant for its announcement of a new age of maritime law:

We no longer live in an era when seamen and their loved ones must look primarily to the courts as a source of substantive legal protection from injury and death; Congress and the States have legislated extensively in these areas. In this era, an admiralty court should look primarily to these legislative enactments for policy guidance. We may supplement these statutory remedies where doing so would achieve the uniform vindication of such policies consistent with our constitutional mandate, but we must also keep strictly within the limits imposed by Congress. Congress retains superior authority in these matters, and an admiralty court must be vigilant not to overstep the well-considered boundaries imposed by

---

Co. v. Sieracki, 328 U.S. 85 (1946), may bring a claim for unseaworthiness, *Burks v. Am. River Transp. Co.*, 679 F.2d 69, 71, 71 n.1 (5th Cir. 1982), *abrogated on other grounds by Lozman v. City of Riviera Beach, Fla.*, 133 S. Ct. 735 (2013).

federal legislation. These statutes both direct and delimit our actions.

Miles v. Apex Marine Corp. ("Miles"), 498 U.S. 19, 27 (1990); *see also id.* at 36 ("We sail in occupied waters. Maritime tort law is now dominated by federal statute, and we are not free to expand remedies at will simply because it might work to the benefit of seamen and those dependent upon them."). Analyzing the issue presented with this guiding principle in mind, the Court reasoned that because DOHSA, by its terms, limits damages recovery to "pecuniary loss," *id.* at 31 (citation omitted), and the same limitation had been incorporated into the Jones Act, *id.* at 32,[10] non-pecuniary damages, such as loss of society damages, [—9—] should not be recoverable in a parallel cause of action for the wrongful death of a Jones Act seaman under general maritime law, *id.* at 33. "It would be inconsistent with our place in the constitutional scheme," the Court in *Miles* concluded, "were we to sanction more expansive remedies in a judicially created cause of action in which liability is without fault than Congress has allowed in cases of death resulting from negligence." *Id.* at 32–33.

Miles addressed the availability of loss of society damages to non-seamen under general maritime law, not punitive damages, but the general principle appearing to underlie its analysis—that if a category of damages is unavailable under a maritime cause of action established by statute, it is similarly unavailable for a parallel claim brought under general maritime law—began to be extended by lower courts to cover punitive damages

---

[10] This pecuniary-loss limitation arose out of the Jones Act's incorporation of the remedial provisions of the Federal Employers' Liability Act ("FELA"), 46 U.S.C. § 30104 [—9—] ("Laws of the United States regulating recovery for personal injury to, or death of, a railway employee apply to an action under this section."), which, at the time the Jones Act was enacted, had been interpreted by the Supreme Court to limit recovery to compensation for "pecuniary" damages, *Mich. Cent. R.R. Co. v. Vreeland*, 227 U.S. 59, 68 (1913) ("[FELA limits] liability [to] the loss and damage sustained by relatives dependent upon the decedent. It is therefore a liability for the pecuniary damage resulting to them, and for that only.").

claims by seamen. *See, e.g., Miller v. Am. President Lines, Ltd.*, 989 F.2d 1450, 1454–59 (6th Cir. 1993).

Similarly applying the *"Miles* uniformity principle," as it came to be known, our court, sitting en banc, held that *Miles* "effectively overruled" *Merry Shipping*, concluding that "punitive damages [are not] available in cases of willful nonpayment of maintenance and cure under the general maritime law." *Guevara v. Maritime Overseas Corp.*, 59 F.3d 1496, 1513 (5th Cir. 1995) (en banc), *abrogated by Atl. Sounding Co. v. Townsend*, 557 U.S. 404 (2009). The court reasoned that because punitive damages, which are "rightfully classified as non-pecuniary," are not an available remedy for personal injury to a seaman under the Jones Act, they likewise are not an available remedy for personal injury to a seaman, including injury resulting from a maintenance and cure [—10—] violation, under the general maritime law. *Id.* at 1506–07, 1510–12.[11] The court in *Guevara* did not address the availability, post-*Miles*, of punitive damages in unseaworthiness actions; it restricted its discussion to the availability of such damages in the maintenance and cure context. *Id.* at 1499. But it was perceived by some to "portend[] the disappearance of punitive damages from the entire body of maritime law." Robertson, *Punitive Damages in American Maritime Law, supra*, at 154 (collecting cases).

Momentum in that direction was sea-tossed by *Atlantic Sounding Co., Inc. v. Townsend*, 557 U.S. 404, 424 (2009), which explicitly abrogated *Guevara* and restored the availability of punitive damages for maintenance and cure claims under general maritime law. The Supreme Court reasoned that "punitive damages have long been an accepted remedy under general maritime law," including for egregious maintenance and cure violations, and concluded, contrary to *Guevara*, that "nothing in the Jones Act altered this understanding." *Id.* at 424. The Jones Act, the Court reminded, "created a statutory cause of action for negligence, but it did not eliminate pre-existing remedies available to seamen for the separate common-law cause of action based on a seaman's right to maintenance and cure." *Id.* at 415–16. "Its purpose was to enlarge [seamen's] protection, not to narrow it." *Id.* at 417 (citations omitted). Indeed, the Court noted, the Jones Act specifically preserved the seaman's right to "elect" between the remedies provided by the Jones Act and those recoverable under pre-existing general maritime law; "[i]f the Jones Act had been the only remaining remedy [—11—] available to injured seamen, there would have been no election to make." *Id.* at 416. As further evidence that punitive damages "remain[ed] available in maintenance and cure actions after the [Jones] Act's passage," the Court pointed out that in *Vaughan v. Atkinson*, 369 U.S. 527, 529–31 (1962), it "permitted the recovery of attorneys' fees [as a punitive sanction] for the 'callous' and 'willful and persistent' refusal to pay maintenance and cure." *Townsend*, 557 U.S. at 417.

The Supreme Court clarified that its interpretation of *Miles* did *not* represent an " 'abrup[t]' change of course." *Id.* at 422 n.8, 418–22. Rather, the Court explained, reliance on the *Miles* uniformity principle to bar punitive damages recovery under general maritime causes of action would read *Miles* "far too broad[ly]." *Id.* at 418–19. *Miles*, which addressed loss of society damages in maritime wrongful death actions, presented an issue of a different nature than the one presented in *Townsend*, which addressed punitive damages in the maintenance and cure setting:

> Unlike the situation presented in *Miles*, both the general maritime cause of action (maintenance and cure) and the remedy (punitive damages) were well

---

[11] The court in *Guevara* went on to hold, in addition, that punitive damages are not available for the willful and wanton refusal to pay maintenance and cure even when personal injury does not result. *Id.* at 1512. The court noted that it was not constrained by the *Miles* uniformity principle in its second inquiry because there was no overlap between statutory and general maritime law: neither the Jones Act nor DOHSA, as does the general maritime law, provides for a cause of action for maintenance and cure not resulting in personal injury. *Id.* The court nevertheless exercised its maritime authority to bar punitive damages in such actions as a matter of policy. *Id.* at 1513.

established before the passage of the Jones Act. Also unlike the facts presented by *Miles*, the Jones Act does not address maintenance and cure or its remedy. It is therefore possible to adhere to the traditional understanding of maritime actions and remedies without abridging or violating the Jones Act; unlike wrongful-death actions, this traditional understanding is not a matter to which "Congress has spoken directly." Indeed, the *Miles* Court itself acknowledged that "[t]he Jones Act evinces no general hostility to recovery under maritime law," and noted that statutory remedy limitations "would not necessarily deter us, if recovery . . . were more consistent with the general principles of maritime tort law." The availability of punitive damages for maintenance and cure actions is entirely faithful to these "general principles of maritime tort law," and no statute casts doubt on their availability under general maritime law. [—12—]

Id. at 420–21 (citations omitted). Thus, it concluded more generally, "[t]he laudable quest for uniformity in admiralty does not require the narrowing of available damages to the lowest common denominator approved by Congress for distinct causes of action." *Id.* at 424.[12]

---

[12] This shift from *Miles* to *Townsend* was foreshadowed in *Exxon Shipping Co. v. Baker*, 554 U.S. 471 (2008), which presented the issue of whether the Clean Water Act ("CWA") implicitly preempted maritime causes of action by fishermen, Alaska Natives, and others with property rights in the resources of the ocean. 554 U.S. at 484–89. The Court concluded that the CWA did not preempt plaintiffs' claims, reasoning: "we find it too hard to conclude that a statute expressly geared to protecting 'water,' 'shorelines,' and 'natural resources' was intended to eliminate *sub silentio* oil companies' common law duties to refrain from injuring the bodies and livelihoods of private individuals." *Id.* at 488–89. In so ruling, the Court sounded a different tune on statutory displacement of general maritime law:

To be sure, "Congress retains superior authority in these matters," and "[i]n this era, an admiralty court should look primarily

DISCUSSION

The crux of this dispute lies in the parties' competing theories of statutory displacement of general maritime law.

The crew members read *Miles* and *Townsend* as providing, narrowly, that federal courts, in exercising their maritime lawmaking authority, cannot authorize a more expansive remedy for a general maritime cause of action than exists for a parallel statutory maritime cause of action if, at the time the statutory cause of action or remedy was enacted, the parallel cause of action or remedy did not exist under general maritime law. Applying that principle, they urge that punitive damages remain available as a remedy for the general maritime law cause of action for unseaworthiness because, like maintenance and [—13—] cure, unseaworthiness was established as a cause of action before the passage of the Jones Act, courts traditionally awarded punitive damages under general maritime law, and the Jones Act does not address unseaworthiness or purport to limit its remedies.

Estis reads those cases as providing, more broadly, that where claimants seek redress for a type of harm compensable under both general and statutory maritime law, they are limited in their recovery to the class of damages authorized by the Jones Act and DOHSA. That is, punitive damages are available only where there is no remedial overlap between general and statutory

---

to these legislative enactments for policy guidance." *Miles v. Apex Marine Corp.*, 498 U.S. 19, 27 (1990). But we may not slough off our responsibilities for common law remedies because Congress has not made a first move, and the absence of federal legislation constraining punitive damages does not imply a congressional decision that there should be no quantified rule.

Id. at 508 n.21 (citation omitted). This sentiment was echoed in *Townsend*: "Although 'Congress . . . is free to say this much and no more,' *Miles*, 498 U.S., at 24, 111 S. Ct. 317 (internal quotation marks omitted), we will not attribute words to Congress that it has not written." *Townsend*, 557 U.S. at 424.

maritime claims. In its view, punitive damages were available in *Townsend*, but not *Miles*, because the *Miles* plaintiffs sought redress for physical injury and wrongful death, harms compensable under both general and statutory maritime law, whereas the *Townsend* plaintiffs sought redress for harm caused by wrongful deprivation of maintenance and cure that did not result in physical injury, a type of harm compensable under general maritime law but not under statutory maritime law, which does not separately provide for a cause of action for maintenance and cure or a remedy for its deprivation. Applying that reasoning here, Estis argues that because the crew members seek redress for wrongful death and personal injuries arising from a maritime accident—types of harm compensable under both general and statutory maritime law—and punitive damages are not available under statutory maritime law, punitive damages are not available in the present action.

To the extent that its focus is on the case's factual setting and not the specific cause of action alleged, Estis's proposed test for determining whether the *Miles* uniformity principle limits the damages recoverable in a maritime case mirrors the one previously adopted by the en banc court in *Guevara*:

> In order to decide whether (and how) *Miles* applies to a case, a court must first evaluate the factual setting of the case and determine [—14—] what statutory remedial measures, if any, apply in that context. If the situation is covered by a statute like the Jones Act or DOHSA, and the statute informs and limits the available damages, the statute directs and delimits the recovery available under the general maritime law as well.

59 F.3d at 1506 (emphasis omitted). Estis highlights this congruity and argues that although *Guevara*'s holding that punitive damages are unavailable in actions for maintenance and cure was overruled by *Townsend*, its guidance on how to apply the *Miles* uniformity principle remains intact.

We disagree. *Townsend* abrogated *Guevara*'s holding because of *Guevara*'s interpretation of *Miles*, not in spite of it. The petitioners in *Townsend* urged the Supreme Court to adopt the factual setting approach of *Guevara*, but the Court in *Townsend* declared that reading was "far too broad." 557 U.S. at 419. That approach, the Court went on, "would give greater pre-emptive effect to the Act than is required by its text, *Miles*, or any of this Court's other decisions interpreting the statute." *Id.* at 424–25. Indeed, the Court noted, it had already rejected that view in *Norfolk Shipbuilding & Drydock Corp. v. Garris*, 532 U.S. 811, 818 (2001), an intervening case holding that a wrongful death remedy is available under general maritime law for the death of a harborworker attributable to negligence, even though "neither the Jones Act (which applies only to seamen) nor DOHSA (which does not cover territorial waters) provided such a remedy." *Townsend*, 557 U.S. at 421 (citations omitted). The broader point made in *Townsend*, which we heed today, is that "[t]he laudable quest for uniformity in admiralty does not require the narrowing of available damages to the lowest common denominator approved by Congress for distinct causes of action." *Id.* at 424.

To give effect to that principle, *Townsend* established a straightforward rule going forward: if a general maritime law cause of action and remedy were established before the passage of the Jones Act, and the Jones Act did not address [—15—] that cause of action or remedy, then that remedy remains available under that cause of action unless and until Congress intercedes.[13] Estis does not

---

[13] *Id.* at 414–15 ("The settled legal principles discussed above establish three points central to resolving this case. First, punitive damages have long been available at common law. Second, the common-law tradition of punitive damages extends to maritime claims. And third, there is no evidence that claims for maintenance and cure were excluded from this general admiralty rule. Instead, the pre-Jones Act evidence indicates that punitive damages remain available for such claims under the appropriate factual circumstances. As a result, respondent is entitled to pursue punitive damages unless Congress has enacted legislation departing from this common-law understanding. As explained below, it has not.") (footnote omitted); *id.* at 420

dispute that the rule's premises are satisfied in this case: the cause of action (unseaworthiness) and the remedy (punitive damages) were both established before the passage of the Jones Act, and that statute did not address unseaworthiness or its remedies.[14] Seeking to avoid the conclusion that follows, Estis attempts to distinguish *Townsend* in two ways.

Estis first attempts to distinguish *Townsend* on the ground that it involved a maintenance and cure claim, as opposed to an unseaworthiness claim. It is true that unseaworthiness claims are more closely related to negligence claims than they are to maintenance and cure claims. But as we noted in *Guevara*—the [—16—] primary case upon which Estis relies—the displacement analysis for unseaworthiness claims is "wholly applicable to maintenance and cure cases as well." *Guevara*, 59 F.3d at 1504. Indeed, if the decisive paragraph in *Townsend* were

---

("Unlike the situation presented in *Miles*, both the general maritime cause of action (maintenance and cure) and the remedy (punitive damages) were well established before the passage of the Jones Act. Also unlike the facts presented by *Miles*, the Jones Act does not address maintenance and cure or its remedy. It is therefore possible to adhere to the traditional understanding of maritime actions and remedies without abridging or violating the Jones Act.") (citations and footnote omitted); *id.* at 424 ("Because punitive damages have long been an accepted remedy under general maritime law, and because nothing in the Jones Act altered this understanding, such damages for the willful and wanton disregard of the maintenance and cure obligation should remain available in the appropriate case as a matter of general maritime law.").

[14] Additionally, we note that Estis does not ask us to bar punitive damages in unseaworthiness cases as a matter of policy. *E.g.*, *Guevara*, 59 F.3d at 1512–13. Accordingly, we will not reach this issue. *See United States v. Delgado*, 672 F.3d 320, 329 n.6 (5th Cir. 2012) (citations omitted); *see also Townsend*, 557 U.S. at 424 n.11 ("Although this Court has recognized that it may change maritime law in its operation as an admiralty court, petitioners have not asked the Court to do so in this case or pointed to any serious anomalies, with respect to the Jones Act or otherwise, that our holding may create. . . . We do not decide th[is] issue[ ].") (citation omitted).

amended by replacing "maintenance and cure" with "unseaworthiness," it would retain its persuasive force:

> Unlike the situation presented in *Miles*, both the general maritime cause of action ([unseaworthiness]) and the remedy (punitive damages) were well established before the passage of the Jones Act. Also unlike the facts presented by *Miles*, the Jones Act does not address [unseaworthiness] or its remedy. It is therefore possible to adhere to the traditional understanding of maritime actions and remedies without abridging or violating the Jones Act; unlike wrongful-death actions, this traditional understanding is not a matter to which "Congress has spoken directly." Indeed, the *Miles* Court itself acknowledged that "[t]he Jones Act evinces no general hostility to recovery under maritime law," and noted that statutory remedy limitations "would not necessarily deter us, if recovery . . . were more consistent with the general principles of maritime tort law." The availability of punitive damages for [unseaworthiness] actions is entirely faithful to these "general principles of maritime tort law," and no statute casts doubt on their availability under general maritime law.

Townsend, 557 U.S. at 420–21 (citations omitted).

Estis argues also that the "chronological" framework announced in *Townsend* is inapt because of the evolution of claims of unseaworthiness. Unlike maintenance and cure, which has remained unchanged in substance for centuries, the claim of unseaworthiness has evolved over the years. Although it was well established before the passage of the Jones Act, it did not become a strict liability claim until 1944, *Mahnich v. Southern S.S. Co.*, 321 U.S. 96, 100 (1944), and was not available to seamen killed during the course of their employment until 1970, *Moragne*, 398 U.S. at 409.

We agree that this case differs from *Townsend* in that respect. That is, punitive damages for the willful violation of the duty to provide maintenance [—17—] and cure appear to have been available, if sparingly awarded, during the pre-Jones Act era. *See Townsend*, 557 U.S. at 414 (citing *The City of Carlisle*, 39 F. at 809, 817 and *The Troop*, 118 F. at 770–71, 773). It is less clear whether punitive damages were awarded for unseaworthiness violations during that period. The parties do not brief this point. This distinction, if factually supported, would change the inquiry: the question would not be whether the Jones Act was intended to displace existing remedies, but whether it was meant to foreclose future remedies. But the outcome would be the same.

Our task is not to reconstruct maritime law as it existed in 1920, but to assess whether Congress, in passing the Jones Act and DOHSA, intended to displace pre-existing maritime remedies or foreclose them going forward. *See Townsend*, 557 U.S. at 419–25. Let us assume for the sake of argument that maritime courts during the pre-Jones Act era had taken no position on the propriety of punitive damages in unseaworthiness actions; that Congress in 1920 was painting on a blank canvas. Had Congress "spoken directly" on the matter, then we would follow its guidance. *Townsend*, 557 U.S. at 420–21; *Miles*, 498 U.S. at 27, 32–33. But the Jones Act does not mention unseaworthiness or its remedies. 46 U.S.C. § 30104. And "a remedial omission in the Jones Act is not evidence of considered congressional policymaking that should command our adherence in analogous contexts." *Am. Export Lines, Inc. v. Alvez*, 446 U.S. 274, 283–84 (1980); *see also id.* at 282 ("Nor do we read the Jones Act as sweeping aside general maritime law remedies."). Similarly, "no intention appears that [DOHSA] ha[d] the effect of foreclosing any nonstatutory federal remedies that might be found appropriate to effectuate the policies of general maritime law." *Moragne*, 398 U.S. at 400. Given that "the absence of federal legislation constraining punitive damages does not imply a congressional decision that there should be no quantified rule," *Baker*, 554 U.S. at 508 n.21, it follows that the matter

remained open after the Jones Act and DOHSA. We resolved it in [—18—] *Merry Shipping* when we held that punitive damages were an appropriate remedy to effectuate the policies of general maritime law, a view shared then and since by other circuit courts.

Estis goes on to argue that allowing seamen to recover punitive damages under general maritime law would create a number of anomalies. Though one acknowledged function of maritime courts is to reconcile anomalies that present themselves in the law, *e.g.*, *Moragne*, 398 U.S. at 395–409 (overruling *The Harrisburg*, 119 U.S. at 205 to remedy three maritime law anomalies), we perceive no anomalies arising from our holding.

Estis argues that our decision would allow plaintiffs to circumvent the pecuniary damages limitation in the Jones Act by pleading a claim for unseaworthiness. This is not an anomaly, as the Supreme Court has highlighted; it is a traditional feature of maritime law designed to protect seamen, the wards of admiralty.[15] By design, seamen have always had the "right to choose among overlapping statutory and common-law remedies" for their injuries. *Townsend*, 557 U.S. at 423 (citation omitted); *see also Cortes v. Baltimore Insular Lines*, 287 U.S. 367, 374–75 (1932) (A seaman's "cause of action for personal injury created by the [Jones Act] may have overlapped his cause of action for breach of the maritime duty of maintenance and cure, just as it may have overlapped his cause of action for injury caused through an unseaworthy ship. In such circumstances it was his privilege, in so far as the causes of action covered the same ground, to sue indifferently on any one of them.") (citations omitted); *Hlodan v. Ohio Barge Line, Inc.*, 611

---

[15] Seamen have long been characterized as "wards of admiralty" deserving special protection under maritime law. *See, e.g., Townsend*, 557 U.S. at 417 (noting that seamen are "peculiarly the wards of admiralty"); *Robertson v. Baldwin*, 165 U.S. 275, 287 (1897) ("The ancient characterization of seamen as 'wards of admiralty' is even more accurate now than it was formerly."); *see also* David W. Robertson, *Punitive Damages in U.S. Maritime Law: Miles, Baker, and* Townsend, 70 LA. L. REV. 463, 485 n.147 (2010) (collecting cases).

F.2d 71, 75 (5th [—19—] Cir. 1980) ("[A] Jones Act claim may be joined with a wrongful death claim for nonpecuniary damages based on general maritime law, where the incident does not arise on the high seas, and that nonpecuniary damages may be recovered under the unseaworthiness claim.") (citations omitted). That a violation of the unseaworthiness duty "may also give rise to a Jones Act claim is significant only in that it requires admiralty courts to ensure against double recovery." *Townsend*, 557 U.S. at 423 n.10 (citation omitted).

Estis argues, similarly, that it would be anomalous for the law to allow different remedies for what amounts to the same cause of action. Though they are similar, Jones Act negligence and unseaworthiness are "separate and distinct" claims with different elements and standards of causation. *Chisholm v. Sabine Towing & Transp. Co., Inc.*, 679 F.2d 60, 62 (5th Cir. 1982) (citation omitted); *Ferrara v. A. & V. Fishing, Inc.*, 99 F.3d 449, 452 (1st Cir. 1996). It is true that plaintiffs often bring claims for both causes of action, and that the same act that results in liability for one will often result in liability for the other. But that is a common feature of the law.

Finally, Estis argues that it would make little sense to permit the recovery of punitive damages for unseaworthiness, which imposes liability without regard to fault, while denying such relief on a Jones Act claim, which requires a finding of negligence. *See Merry Shipping*, 650 F.2d at 626. This argument overlooks that punitive damages recovery always requires a finding of willful and wanton conduct, whether the cause of action is for maintenance and cure or unseaworthiness. *See id.* Punitive damages differ in that way from other types of non-pecuniary damages, such as the loss of society damages addressed in *Miles*. In light of that distinction, we previously have rejected this argument against allowing punitive damages recovery under general maritime law. *Id.* ("It does not follow . . . that if punitive damages are not allowed under the Jones Act, they should also not be allowed under general maritime law [because] recovery [—20—] of punitive

damages is restricted to where there is willful and wanton misconduct, reflecting a reckless disregard for the safety of the crew, a much higher standard of culpability than that required for Jones Act liability."). The central concern of *Miles*—that it would be inappropriate to "sanction more expansive remedies in a judicially created cause of action in which liability is without fault than Congress has allowed in cases of death resulting from negligence"—thus, is not present here. 498 U.S. at 32–33.

CONCLUSION

Like maintenance and cure, unseaworthiness was established as a general maritime claim before the passage of the Jones Act, punitive damages were available under general maritime law, and the Jones Act does not address unseaworthiness or limit its remedies. We conclude, therefore, that punitive damages remain available to seamen as a remedy for the general maritime law claim of unseaworthiness. *See Townsend*, 557 U.S. 404.[16] We REVERSE and REMAND for further proceedings.*****

*(Reporter's Note: On February 24, 2014, the U.S. Fifth Circuit ordered that this case be reheard en banc, with oral argument, on a date thereafter to be fixed.)***

---

[16] Having so concluded, we decline to revisit whether punitive damages are available to seamen bringing claims for negligence under the Jones Act. *See id.* at 424 n.12 (declining to decide whether punitive damages are available to a seaman in a cause of action for negligence under the Jones Act after ruling that such damages are available to a seaman in a cause of action for maintenance and cure).

United States Court of Appeals
for the Fifth Circuit

No. 12-60289

BPU MANAGEMENT, INC.
VS.
DIRECTOR, OFFICE OF WORKERS'
COMPENSATION PROGRAMS

Petition for Review of an Order of the Benefits
Review Board

Decided: October 8, 2013
Revised: October 10, 2013

Citation: 732 F.3d 457, 1 Adm. R. 326 (5th Cir. 2013).

Before **DAVIS** and **JONES**, Circuit Judges, and **MILAZZO**, District Judge of the Eastern District of Louisiana, sitting by designation.

[—1—] DAVIS, Circuit Judge:

Petitioner BPU Management Inc./Sherwin Alumina Co. ("Sherwin") employed Respondent David Martin ("Martin") as a dockworker at its waterside ore processing facility. When Martin was injured in one of the facility's underground ore transport tunnels, the Benefits Review Board ("BRB") ordered Sherwin to pay Martin benefits under the Longshore and Harbor Workers' Compensation Act ("LHWCA" or "the Act"). Because we conclude that the [—2—] underground transport tunnel where Martin was injured is not used in the vessel-unloading process, Martin's injury did not occur on a LHWCA-covered situs. We therefore GRANT Sherwin's Petition for Review of the BRB's decision, and REMAND to the BRB to dismiss Martin's claim.

I.

Sherwin operates an alumina processing facility on the Texas Gulf Coast, the primary purpose of which is the production of industrial alumina from raw bauxite.[1] Like many industrial production sites, Sherwin's alumina facility is situated along a navigable waterway so that vessels can easily unload feedstock materials and load finished product.

Because Sherwin's facility includes both its manufacturing and its loading/unloading operations. Bauxite unloaded from ships is moved directly into the alumina production process. Sherwin's operation begins when raw bauxite is unloaded from vessels at docks in Sherwin's deep water port using an "overhead conveyor system." The overhead conveyor system carries the bauxite over a street and fence separating the dock area from the alumina processing facility. There the conveyor deposits the bauxite into one of several dozen "bins" located in a large covered storage area. The bauxite remains in the storage area until it is needed; this varies from a few weeks to a period of years. Once a particular grade of bauxite is selected for alumina extraction, a small gate located in the floor beneath the appropriate bin or pile is opened to drain the bauxite into a large, underground "reclaim system." There the bauxite is mechanically sifted through a "screw feeder," which breaks down the bauxite into smaller pieces and deposits it on the "reclaim conveyor belt." From there, the reclaim conveyor belt transports and drops the bauxite onto the "cross-tunnel conveyor." In turn, the cross-tunnel conveyor transports the selected bauxite to [—3—] the "rod mill," where it is further pulverized as part of the manufacturing process.[2] In the course of conveyor belt transport, bauxite often spills off the cross-tunnel conveyor onto the floor and must occasionally be shoveled back onto the conveyor.

From 1997 to 2006, Sherwin employed David Martin as a dockworker. Though Martin's primary duty was to ensure that ships were properly docked and loaded or unloaded, he ordinarily spent several hours each month cleaning the cross-tunnel of debris. On February 15, 2006, Martin was in the cross-tunnel shoveling fallen bauxite back onto the conveyor when he injured his lower back.

Martin was allegedly unable to return to his job with Sherwin and filed a claim seeking

---

[1] Bauxite is the principal ore of aluminum.

[2] Once the manufacturing process is completed, the alumina is sent by a separate series of conveyor belts to alumina silos, then to the dock, and finally to a loading tower.

benefits under the LHWCA. At the benefits hearing, the ALJ concluded that the cross-tunnel where Martin was injured is a LHWCA-covered situs because it is "linked to buildings where vessels were loaded and unloaded." As such, the ALJ found that Sherwin was responsible to Martin for benefits under the LHWCA.

Sherwin appealed the ALJ's order to the BRB, arguing that the cross-tunnel is not a LHWCA-covered situs. However, the BRB rejected Sherwin's argument, reasoning that the cross-tunnel has a substantial nexus with the bauxite-unloading process. Because the cross-tunnel is underneath the storage area, which adjoins and has a "functional relationship with navigable waters," the BRB concluded that it is a LHWCA-covered situs. Accordingly, the BRB affirmed the ALJ's decision, and Sherwin now petitions for review.

II. [—4—]

We conduct a de novo review of the BRB's legal conclusions.[3] The question of LHWCA situs is ordinarily a mixed question of law and fact.[4] "However, where, as in this case, the facts are not in dispute, '[LHWCA] coverage is an issue of statutory construction and legislative intent,' and should be reviewed as a pure question of law."[5]

III.

The sole question we must decide in this case is whether the cross-tunnel where Martin was injured is a covered situs under the LHWCA.

The LHWCA extends coverage to employees only if their injury occurred on a covered situs. This situs is defined in 33 U.S.C. § 903(a), and extends coverage to "injur[ies] occurring upon the navigable waters of the United States (including any

adjoining pier, wharf, dry dock, terminal, building way, marine railway, or other adjoining area customarily used by an employer in loading, unloading, repairing, dismantling, or building a vessel)." In the instant case, Martin's injury did not occur on navigable waters or in one of the LHWCA's enumerated areas. Therefore, Martin's injury only satisfies the situs requirement if he shows his injury occurred in an "other adjoining area customarily used by an employer in loading [or] unloading . . . a vessel."[6]

In a recent en banc decision of this court, *New Orleans Depot Services, Inc. v. DOWCP*, we explained precisely what the LHWCA's other-adjoining-area situs provision requires: "[A]n 'other adjoining area' must satisfy two distinct situs components: (1) a geographic component (the area must adjoin navigable [—5—] waters) and (2) a functional component (the area must be 'customarily used by an employer in loading [or] unloading . . . a vessel')."[7]

A.

Turning first to the geographic component of the situs test, the LHWCA only covers injuries in an area which "adjoins" navigable waters.[8] In *New Orleans Depot*, we specifically rejected a broad definition of "adjoins" and found that the word should be given its ordinary meaning: "contiguous with" or "abutting upon."[9] Therefore, an area is only adjoining navigable waters—and within the reach of the LHWCA—if it borders on or is contiguous with navigable waters.[10] Here, the employer's entire facility including the location where Martin was injured adjoins navigable water. Martin has therefore satisfied the geographic prong of the situs test.

---

[3] *Andrepont v. Murphy Exploration & Prod. Co.*, 566 F.3d 415, 417 (5th Cir. 2009).

[4] *New Orleans Depot Servs., Inc. v. DOWCP*, 718 F.3d 384, 387 (5th Cir. 2013) (en banc).

[5] *Id.* (quoting *DOWCP v. Perini North River Assocs.*, 459 U.S. 297, 300, 305 (1983)).

[6] *See id.* It is undisputed that Sherwin's facility is not used for "repairing, dismantling, or building a vessel." *See* 33 U.S.C. § 903(a).

[7] 718 F.3d at 389–90 (quoting 33 U.S.C. §903(a)).

[8] *See* 33 U.S.C. § 903(a).

[9] *See* 718 F.3d at 390–94.

[10] *Id.*

B.

Proceeding to the functional prong, the situs of Martin's injury is only a LHWCA-covered "other adjoining area" if it is "customarily used" for unloading vessels.[11] To satisfy the situs inquiry's functional prong, the site of the injury need not be "exclusively" or "predominantly" used for unloading—only customarily.[12] Moreover, we look to the general purpose of the area rather [—6—] than requiring "every square inch of an area" to be used for a maritime activity.[13]

In the instant case, the BRB concluded that the cross-tunnel where Martin suffered his injury is used in the unloading process and therefore has a functional relationship with navigable waters. According to the BRB, the surface storage buildings above the cross-tunnel are connected to the docks by conveyor belts and are therefore a part of Sherwin's unloading process. Because the storage buildings are used in unloading bauxite and do not house manufacturing facilities, the BRB reasoned that the cross-tunnels beneath the buildings are necessarily involved in the unloading process.

However, the BRB's analysis mischaracterizes the nature of the cross-tunnels and their connection to the unloading process. Specifically, the fact that surface-level storage buildings are connected to the unloading process does not automatically render everything above and below the buildings a part of the unloading process. Such a generalization ignores the operational realities of a sophisticated multi-tier facility and arbitrarily attributes to one distinct area the functions of another. Moreover, the correct question is not whether Sherwin's cross-tunnels are used for manufacturing, but whether the cross-tunnels are customarily used for unloading a vessel. If the tunnels are not used for unloading a vessel, then Martin's injury did not occur in a LHWCA-covered situs.

As this court has previously recognized, "the primary purpose of . . . loading and unloading [is] to get cargo on or off the [vessel]."[14] Moreover, [—7—] the mere act of loading, unloading, moving, or transporting something is not enough: "Nothing intrinsic in any of these activities establishes their maritime nature, rather it is that they are undertaken with respect to a ship or vessel."[15] Thus, "the essential elements of unloading a vessel" are "taking cargo out of the hold, moving it away from the ship's side, and carrying it immediately to a storage or holding area."[16] Although maritime unloading necessarily requires some nexus with a vessel, the Supreme Court has rejected a definition of unloading which stops the moment a vessel's cargo is unloaded onto the dock.[17]

Several courts have considered the extent to which an activity is part of the vessel-unloading process. In *Chesapeake & Ohio Ry. Co. v. Schwalb*, the Supreme Court determined that where a conveyor belt is used to load coal onto a ship, employees who clean up fallen coal beneath the conveyor are involved in the unloading process.[18] Because the unloading operations would soon cease if the loading area was not maintained, the Court reasoned that such employees are "essential to the loading . . . process."[19]

---

[11] *See* 33 U.S.C. § 903(a). No one alleges that Sherwin's facility is used for any of the LHWCA's other enumerated activities: vessel loading, repair, construction, or dismantling.

[12] *See Coastal Prod. Servs., Inc. v. Hudson*, 555 F.3d 426, 435 (5th Cir. 2009).

[13] *See id.* The LHWCA situs inquiry is not "a game of hopscotch" in which "[t]he bathrooms in an otherwise 'adjoining area' would not be covered, [or the] pavement that although clearly within the area, had not been walked on by stevedores loading and unloading a vessel."

[14] *Owens v. SeaRiver Maritime, Inc.*, 272 F.3d 698, 704 (5th Cir. 2001).

[15] *Fontenot v. AWI, Inc.*, 923 F.2d 1127, 1131 (5th Cir. 1991). *See also Herb's Welding, Inc. v. Gray*, 470 U.S. 414, 424 (1985) ("We have never read 'maritime employment' to extend so far beyond those *actually involved* in moving cargo between ship and land transportation.") (emphasis added).

[16] *Northeast Marine Terminal Co., Inc. v. Caputo*, 432 U.S. 249, 267 (1977).

[17] *See id.* at 266–67.

[18] 493 U.S. 40, 47 (1989).

[19] *Id.*

Martin argues that *Schwalb* controls here, but the facts of the instant case are distinguishable from *Schwalb* because as we explain below, Martin was not injured while participating in unloading a vessel or conduct essential to that activity. At least two decisions from other circuits involving facts similar to the [—8—] instant case demonstrate why *Schwalb* does not control. The Eleventh Circuit, in *Bianco v. Georgia Pacific Corp.*, found that the portions of a large riverside industrial gypsum facility used for bagging gypsum and slicing sheetrock were not related to the facility's vessel-unloading activities.[20] *Bianco* involved a multi-stage process for unloading and production comparable to the instant case.[21] First, raw gypsum was unloaded from the ship by a conveyor belt into a hopper.[22] Then, a second conveyer belt carried the gypsum to a Transfer House, where it proceeded to a third conveyor belt to be poured into a rock shed.[23] The gypsum would remain in storage inside the rock shed until it was needed for the production of sheet-rock or gypcrete.[24] When it was needed for production, the gypsum would be "crushed, screened, [and] baked" before it was sent to a production department.[25] The employee suffered two injuries in the sheet-rock production department of the facility.[26] The court held that, it was inappropriate to find that the employer's entire facility was an "adjoining area," irrespective of the activities occurring in different areas. The court reasoned that it "would effectively be writing out of the statute the requirement that the adjoining area be 'customarily used by an employer in loading, unloading, repairing, dismantling, or building a vessel.'"[27] [—9—]

Another case, perhaps even closer to the facts of today's case, the Eighth Circuit considered whether part of an industrial coal-loading facility—whose entire purpose was to load coal onto vessels—was customarily used in the loading process.[28] Specifically, an employee sought LHWCA benefits after being injured in an area that temporarily stored loaded coal cars before they were released down an incline to the ship-loading conveyor.[29] The employee's job duties were limited to placing the cars in the Barney Yard and setting their handbrakes to secure them in place.[30] After the cars were secured, a separate crew would release them to be sent down an incline where the coal was loaded.[31] Reasoning that the loading process did not begin until the coal cars were identified and released towards the area where coal was physically loaded, the court concluded that the car storage area was not customarily used in the loading process.[32]

The Supreme Court has not provided a firm definition of unloading in this context, but its decision in *P.C. Pfeiffer Co. v. Ford* provides the most guidance.[33] Specifically, the *P.C. Pfeiffer* Court was concerned with whether two workers were involved in unloading vessels and thereby engaged in "maritime employment."[34] The Court reasoned that the traditional longshoreman's job was only to "transfer[] goods between ship and land transportation," the Court concluded that anyone participating in this unloading [—10—] process was engaged in maritime employment.[35] In determining the point at which the unloading process had been completed, the Court's line was clear: the LHWCA covers all of the unloading activities in the chain of transferring cargo from vessel to land transport, but it does not cover the activities of a person whose "responsibility is only to pick up stored cargo for further trans-shipment."[36] The employees in *Pfieffer* were both injured while preparing cargo for further

---

[20] 304 F.3d 1053, 1058 (11th Cir. 2002).
[21] *See id.* at 1053.
[22] *Id.*
[23] *Id.*
[24] *Id.*
[25] *Id.*
[26] *Id.*
[27] *Id.* at 1060 (internal citations omitted).

[28] *See In re Norfolk Southern Ry. Co.*, 592 F.3d 907, 914 (8th Cir. 2010).
[29] *Id.*
[30] *Id.* at 910.
[31] *Id.* at 914.
[32] *See id.*
[33] 444 U.S. 69, 79–80 (1979).
[34] *Id.* at 77–82.
[35] *Id.* at 80–82.
[36] *Id.* at 83.

transport.[37] The first employee, Diverson Ford, injured a finger on his left hand as he fastened military vehicles onto railroad flatcars for land shipment; the second employee, Will Bryant, was injured while unloading a bale of cotton into a pier warehouse, where it would later be moved out of the warehouse to a ship for transportation.[38] The Court held that both men were injured before the cargo had been surrendered for land transport—before the unloading process had been completed.

The *P.C. Pfeiffer* Court's rationale suggests a clear rule in the usual case where cargo is unloaded for ultimate shipment over land: Vessel-unloading includes the transfer of cargo from ship to shore only until it is surrendered for land transport. Because a shoreside industrial facility such as Sherwin's does not utilize any land transport, we must determine what part of Sherwin's bauxite intake process is the appropriate analog for the surrender of cargo to land transport.

We read *Pfeiffer* to hold that the surrender of cargo for land transport marks the end of the maritime unloading process because it is the point where [—11—] the longshoreman's duty to unload and move the cargo ceases.[39] Not coincidentally, the point of surrender is also the point at which the receiving party takes responsibility for the cargo.[40] In the instant case, the point at which Sherwin's dock employees cease moving bauxite and deposit it for another "party" to retrieve is when the bauxite is delivered into the storage area. Once the ore is deposited into storage, it is Sherwin's engineering employees who manage and control the bauxite's further movement. Because Sherwin's dock employees no longer exercise control over bauxite in storage, the delivery of bauxite into storage is the functional equivalent of the surrender of cargo for land transport.

The operational layout of Sherwin's bauxite processing system reinforces the conclusion that the vessel-unloading process is complete long before bauxite reaches the cross-tunnels. Although incoming bauxite is deposited on top of the bauxite stockpiles, bauxite used in production is extracted from the *bottom* of the stockpiles. Therefore, because Sherwin stockpiles bauxite for periods of months and years, it would be inaccurate to describe this stored bauxite as a mere step in the vessel-unloading process. Also relevant is the fact that the alumina manufacturing process begins—which would suggest any vessel-unloading is finished—the instant bauxite is funneled from the stockpiles into the reclaim system. In fact, bauxite only enters the cross-tunnel where Martin was injured after it sits in a long-term storage stockpile, migrates to the bottom of its respective ore pile, is specifically selected by Sherwin's process engineers for production, is crushed in the screw feeder, and is finally transported towards the [—12—] metal-extraction facility. Ore at this stage is clearly no longer being "unloaded" from a vessel in any sense of the word.[41]

Martin responds by insisting that shoveling ore debris in the cross-tunnel is part of unloading because it is "essential to the [un]loading . . . process."[42] Specifically, Martin contends that if the cross-tunnel area was not routinely cleaned of debris, the cross-tunnel would theoretically fill up with ore, the conveyor would have to be shut down, the stockpile areas would eventually fill up, and no more ore could be unloaded from vessels. While unloading does embrace those activities on which the unloading process directly depends—such as cleaning the unloading area and maintaining the unloading equipment—this is not one of those areas. The record

---

[37] *Id*. at 71–72.

[38] *Id*.

[39] *See id*. at 79–84.

[40] *See id*.

---

[41] *See Sidwell v. Va. Int'l Terminals, Inc.*, 372 F.3d 238, 244 (4th Cir. 2004) ("The LHWCA requires a direct and immediate role in the loading or unloading process."); *see also Bianco*, 304 F.3d at 1058 ("'Here, the . . . production plant was not an 'area' used either exclusively, or even customarily, for a maritime purpose or for significant maritime activity."); *In re Norfolk Southern Ry. Co.*, 592 F.3d 901. Note also that because a longshoreman involved in unloading ore at Sherwin's dock is not required to enter and exit the cross-tunnels, the LHWCA's concern for shifting coverage does not apply here.

[42] *See Schwalb*, 493 U.S. at 47.

indicates that an extraordinary amount of additional bauxite could be deposited in outdoor storage before unloading would have to cease.[43] Cleaning an area so far removed from any unloading operations is not "integral to the unloading process."[44]

Because the delivery of shipped cargo into Sherwin's storage area is the functional equivalent of surrendering the cargo to a receiving land carrier, we conclude that this is where the vessel-unloading process ends. Thus, we hold [—13—] that Sherwin's underground cross-tunnels are not customarily used for unloading vessels and do not satisfy the LHWCA's functional prong. Accordingly, Martin fails to satisfy the LHWCA's situs test.

IV.

For the reasons stated above, the Petition for Review is granted and the case is remanded to the BRB to enter an order dismissing Martin's claim for benefits under the LHWCA.

PETITION GRANTED and REMANDED.

---

[43] Specifically, uncontradicted testimony established that Sherwin's additional storage areas could accommodate more than a million tons of bauxite ore, while those storage areas only contained about a quarter of a million tons of ore at the time of the formal hearing.

[44] *See Schwalb*, 493 U.S. at 47.

United States Court of Appeals
for the Fifth Circuit

No. 12-31222

DELAHOUSSAYE
vs.
PERFORMANCE ENERGY SERVICES, L.L.C.

Appeal from the United States District Court for the
Eastern District of Louisiana

Decided: October 24, 2013

Citation: 734 F.3d 389, 1 Adm. R. 332 (5th Cir. 2013).

Before **JOLLY, JONES,** and **BARKSDALE,** Circuit
Judges.

[—1—] **JONES,** Circuit Judge:

Appellant Scott Joseph Delahoussaye sued several parties, including Cross-Appellants Performance Energy Services, L.L.C. ("Performance") and One Beacon Insurance Company ("One Beacon"),[1] for damages stemming from personal injury that Delahoussaye sustained while working on a fixed platform located in the Gulf of Mexico. After the other parties settled, the suit proceeded to a bench trial, and the district court found Performance 15% at fault for the [—2—] accident that caused Delahoussaye's injury and awarded Delahoussaye, *inter alia*, $200,000 in general damages. On appeal, Delahoussaye challenges the district court's allocation of fault, while Performance challenges the amount of general damages that the district court awarded Delahoussaye as well as the court's ruling that Performance employee Shalico Andow was not a "borrowed employee" of another contractor or the platform owner. We AFFIRM the judgment allocating liability, but because the award of general damages is excessive as a matter of law, we VACATE and REMAND the general damages award and order REMITTITUR.

---

[1] Cross-Appellants Performance and One Beacon will be referred to collectively as "Performance" unless specified otherwise.

BACKGROUND

Pisces Energy, LLC ("Pisces") is the owner of the Mustang Island 739-A Platform ("Platform") located in the Gulf of Mexico off the coast of Texas. In August 2009, Pisces retained several independent contractors to perform work-over recompletion on the Platform, including Crescent Drilling Foreman, Inc. ("Crescent"), which provided Richard John Boutte as an on-site consultant for the project; Performance, for which Andow worked as a crane operator; and Warrior Energy Services, LLC ("Warrior"), which supplied a crew to perform coiled tubing work and other operations on the Platform. Delahoussaye worked on the Platform as part of the Warrior crew.

On August 22, in order to create more room on the Platform, Boutte decided to backload some equipment from the Platform onto an adjacent vessel. Boutte instructed Delahoussaye to serve as a flagman on the vessel as Andow operated a crane to lower the equipment from the Platform onto the vessel's deck. When Andow first attempted the lift, he could not see the vessel from his vantage point on the crane. Andow stopped the lift and asked that the vessel be moved farther from the Platform so that he could see the vessel more clearly. However, Boutte stated that he wanted to carry on with the blind lift and would act as signalman, relaying directions to Andow on how to move the [—3—] load. The blind lift proceeded with Boutte standing by the Platform handrail, signaling Andow. At some point during the lift Boutte walked away from the handrail but continued to give Andow the signal to lower the load onto the vessel. Andow could see that Boutte did not have a clear view and had lost visual contact with the load for thirty to forty-five seconds. Andow, however, continued to follow Boutte's hand signals to lower the load. As the load descended, it hit other equipment on the deck of the vessel and jarred a handrail free. The handrail struck Delahoussaye on the head and shoulder; he was thrown approximately twenty feet and knocked unconscious for a few moments. After the accident, Delahoussaye was treated for chronic pain and diagnosed with degenerative disk disease, a back injury at L5-S1, an annular tear, and foraminal stenosis.

Delahoussaye filed suit against Pisces and eventually added Crescent, Boutte, Performance, and Performance's liability insurer, One Beacon, as defendants. After the summary judgment phase of litigation, Delahoussaye settled with Pisces, Crescent, and Boutte. The matter proceeded to a bench trial, and the district court found that Boutte (i.e., Crescent) was 85% at fault in causing Delahoussaye's injuries, and Andow (i.e., Performance) was 15% at fault. The court also awarded Delahoussaye $786,824.66 in damages, including $200,000 in general damages, which made Performance, as Andow's employer, liable to Delahoussaye for $118,023.69 of the total amount. Delahoussaye and Performance both timely appealed the judgment.

STANDARD OF REVIEW

When reviewing a bench trial, this court reviews findings of fact for clear error and legal issues *de novo*. *Water Craft Mgmt. LLC v. Mercury Marine*, 457 F.3d 484, 488 (5th Cir. 2006). Factual findings are clearly erroneous if "(1) the findings are without substantial evidence to support them, (2) the court misapprehended the effect of the evidence, and (3) although there is evidence [—4—] which if credible would be substantial, the force and effect of the testimony, considered as a whole, convinces the court that the findings are so against the preponderance of credible testimony that they do not reflect or represent the truth and right of the case." *Id.* To reverse for clear error, this court must have "a definite and firm conviction that a mistake has been committed." *Canal Barge Co. Inc. v. Torco Oil Co.*, 220 F.3d 370, 375 (5th Cir. 2000).

DISCUSSION

I. Allocation of Fault

According to Delahoussaye, the evidence shows that Andow was more culpable for Delahoussaye's injuries than Boutte, and, therefore, Andow should be 85% at fault, whereas Boutte's allocation should be only

15%. A district court's allocation of fault is reviewed for clear error. *McCuller v. Nautical Ventures, L.L.C.*, 434 F. App'x 408, 415 (5th Cir. 2011). "Where there are two permissible views of the evidence, the factfinder's choice between them cannot be clearly erroneous." *In re Cardinal Servs., Inc.*, 304 F. App'x 247, 251 (5th Cir. 2008) (internal quotation marks omitted) (quoting *Anderson v. Bessemer City*, 470 U.S. 564, 573-74, 105 S. Ct. 1504, 84 L. Ed. 2d 518 (1985)).

Delahoussaye's expert testified at trial that once a crane operator is given a signal from a signalman, the crane operator is generally responsible for completing that task until a different signal is given. It is undisputed that Boutte gave Andow no other signal than the come-down signal until after the accident occurred. Delahoussaye's expert also testified that the accident occurred because Boutte left his position on the Platform and continued to signal Andow without actually seeing where the load was going. Performance's expert similarly testified that the accident was caused because of the hand signals that Boutte gave Andow. He stated that Andow was to assume that Boutte knew it was safe to lower the load and continue following Boutte's come-down signal until Boutte directed otherwise because it could be dangerous for [—5—] a crane operator to stop his load without his signalman instructing him to do so. Furthermore, a certified rigger and eyewitness to the accident testified at trial that when a signal is given to a crane operator, the crane operator is expected to follow that signal. In light of the evidence presented at trial, it was not implausible for the court to find that Boutte, as the designated signalman for the blind lift, was significantly more at fault for Delahoussaye's injuries than was Andow. Because the district court took a permissible view of the evidence in finding Andow only 15% at fault, we will not alter its determination.

II. The Borrowed Employee Doctrine

In an effort to exonerate itself from fault, Performance argues that the district court erred when it found that Andow was not a borrowed employee of Pisces, Crescent, or

Boutte at the time of Delahoussaye's accident. "[A]n employer will be liable through respondeat superior for negligence of an employee he has 'borrowed[.]'" *Gaudet v. Exxon Corp.*, 562 F.2d 351, 355 (5th Cir. 1977). The borrowed employee doctrine "is the functional rule that places the risk of a worker's injury on his actual rather than his nominal employer." *Baker v. Raymond Int'l, Inc.*, 656 F.2d 173, 178 (5th Cir. 1981). Whether Andow was a borrowed employee is a question of law, though in some cases factual disputes must be resolved before the district court can make this determination. *See Billizon v. Conoco, Inc.*, 993 F.2d 104, 105 (5th Cir. 1993).

There is no indication in the record that Performance argued before the district court that Andow was a borrowed employee of Pisces. In the district court, Performance contended that Crescent or Boutte were borrowing employers, and the court ruled against Performance. "It is the unwavering rule in this Circuit that issues raised for the first time on appeal are reviewed only for plain error." *McCann v. Tex. City Refining, Inc.*, 984 F.2d 667, 673 (5th Cir. 1993). Under the plain error standard, this court may correct "a plain [—6—] forfeited error affecting substantial rights if the error seriously affects the fairness, integrity or public reputation of judicial proceedings." *Douglass v. United Servs. Auto. Ass'n*, 79 F.3d 1415, 1424 (5th Cir. 1996) (en banc) (superseded by statute on other grounds). Performance does not assert that its failure to raise the defense concerning Pisces in the trial court warrants reversal under the plain error standard, nor is there evidence suggesting that Performance's error seriously affects judicial fairness, integrity, or public reputation. Perhaps recognizing this deficiency, Performance has failed to clearly assert on appeal who was Andow's borrowing employer. Instead, as admitted by its counsel during oral argument, Performance simply urges this court to hold that Andow was a borrowed employee of somebody—anybody—other than Performance. This tactic of "throwing everything at the wall to see what sticks" is not the basis upon which a party

successfully invokes the borrowed employee doctrine.

Where multiple contractors are named as defendants, a plaintiff can be the borrowed employee of only one. That defense, if accepted, exonerates the borrowing employer from liability. While liberal pleading rules would have allowed Performance to assert the defense alternatively against the other defendants, those defendants had to be placed on notice of the assertion in order to prepare for trial and engage in settlement discussions. Performance cannot, for the first time on appeal, re-order its defenses in an attempt to overcome the district court's adverse holding. Because Performance's newly minted strategy fails to show that borrowed employee status should be applied in the instant case, the district court's holding that Andow was not a borrowed employee is affirmed. [—7—]

III. General Damages

Neither party disputes the district court's factual findings with regard to Delahoussaye's injuries and post-accident medical treatment. Rather, Performance contends that those findings do not support the general damages award of $200,000. A district court's award of damages is a finding of fact, which we will reverse only for clear error. *Moore v. M/V ANGELA*, 353 F.3d 376, 384 (5th Cir. 2003). This court has stated that "[a]n award is excessive only if it is greater than the maximum amount the trier of fact could properly have awarded," *id.*, and that the "maximum recovery rule" for applying remittitur only becomes operative if the award at issue exceeds 133% of the highest previous recovery for a factually similar case in the relevant jurisdiction. *Lebron v. U.S.*, 279 F.3d 321, 326 (5th Cir. 2002). Because the facts of every case are different, prior damage awards from other cases are not always controlling, *id.*, and excessiveness is determined by reviewing a case on its own facts, *Moore*, 353 F.3d at 384.

The district court found that Delahoussaye sustained a back injury at L5-S1 as a result of the August 22, 2009, accident, which will require future visits with his physician, periodic doses of medication, and perhaps periodic stints of physical therapy. However, the court also acknowledged that several hours of surveillance footage show Delahoussaye performing various tasks, including picking up ice chests, squatting with a bag of dog food on his shoulder, jumping in and out of a truck bed, lifting and carrying equipment, bending, dancing, and running up and down steps. The district court pointed out that during the course of the surveillance, Delahoussaye was not noted to wince, guard, limp, or make any other outward expressions of pain or discomfort. Accordingly, the district court found that Delahoussaye exaggerated his complaints of pain and was not a candidate for L5-S1 fusion, despite the recommendation of Delahoussaye's orthopedic surgeon. Moreover, [—8—] the district court found that Delahoussaye can return to work in a low-sedentary type position and that his back injury has not significantly affected his relationship with his son.

Although Delahoussaye insists that this case is similar to other Louisiana cases where courts have held that general damage awards higher than $200,000 are not excessive, all of the cases upon which he relies are pointedly dissimilar from this case in that either (1) Delahoussaye's injuries do not rise to the level of the other plaintiffs', or (2) the credibility of the other plaintiffs was not seriously undermined by surveillance video showing performance of daily activities without any indication of pain.[2] The most factually similar

case to Delahoussaye's is *Bazile v. Chevron USA, Inc.*, where the Western District of Louisiana awarded $65,000 in general damages to a plaintiff who was injured while descending his bunk in the housing area of an oil platform on which he worked. No. 10-0050, slip op., 2013 WL 1288698 at *1 (W.D. La. March 27, 2013). In *Bazile*, the plaintiff suffered from a central and right side herniated disc at the L4-5 level that caused significant stenosis, as well as associated changes at L5-S1 and L3-4. *Id.* at *3. The plaintiff was not able to return to offshore work following his accident, and although the [—9—] treating physician believed that the plaintiff was a surgical candidate, surgery was too risky because of the plaintiff's weight and high blood pressure. *Id.* Based upon the plaintiff's medical information, the district court concluded that $65,000 was an appropriate general damages award. *Id.* at *6. In reaching this conclusion, the district court referenced three Louisiana Court of Appeal cases that found general damage awards ranging from $40,000 to $100,000 were appropriate based on facts similar to the ones at hand.[3]

In light of these authorities, a general damages award of $65,000 is much closer to what Louisiana courts would award

---

[2] *See e.g., Brock v. Singleton*, 65 So.3d 649 (La. Ct. App. 2011) ($590,000 in general damages to plaintiff injured in truck accident who suffered from pain in his leg, shoulder, fingers, back, foot, toes, head, arm, and hand; had to wear a corset and take medication for pain; would undergo major back surgery; was depressed and suffered from a diminished sexual relationship with his wife); *Cox v. Shelter Ins. Co.*, 34 So.3d 398 (La. Ct. App. 2010) ($250,000 in general damages to plaintiff injured in multi-vehicle accident who suffered from protruding disc in back that would never heal on its own; experienced pain when sitting or standing for long periods of time, severe headaches, and problems picking up her children or lifting any heavy weight; was facing a serious surgery; and video surveillance showed that she was in pain when going about her daily activities); *Desselle v.*

LaFleur, 865 So. 2d 954 (La. Ct. App. 2004) ($350,000 in general damages to plaintiff injured in car accident who suffered from cervical problems and joint dysfunction; would require annual dental visits for the rest of her life to treat temporomandibular joint dysfunction; was credible with respect to her pain complaints; and surgery was recommended).

[3] *See Raimondo v. Hayes*, 30 So.3d 1177 (La. Ct. App. 2010) ($65,000 in general damages to plaintiff who suffered multiple disc injuries and would continue to experience chronic pain throughout her life); *Gradnigo v. La. Farm Bureau Cas. Ins. Co.*, 6 So.3d 367 (La. Ct. App. 2009) ($40,000 in general damages to plaintiff who suffered from mild disc herniations, bone spurs, and a lumbar bulging disc and faced the possibility of future surgery); *Coutee v. Global Marine Drilling Co.*, 895 So. 2d 631 (La. Ct. App. 2005) ($100,000 in general damages to plaintiff who suffered from multiple levels of degenerative disc disease, a herniated disc, myofascial pain syndrome, major episodic depression, and chronic pain syndrome) *rev'd on other grounds*, 924 So. 2d 112 (La. 2006).

Delahoussaye based on the facts of this case. Because $200,000 is more than 133% of $65,000, the district court's award of general damages is excessive as a matter of law. We remit the general damage portion of Delahoussaye's award to $86,450—that is, 133% of $65,000—unless he elects to have a new trial on general damages. *Eiland v. Westinghouse Elec. Corp.*, 58 F.3d 176, 183 (5th Cir. 1995) ("[T]his circuit's case law provides for remittitur if the award is excessive, and new trial on damages alone if the plaintiff declines the remitted award.").

CONCLUSION

For the foregoing reasons, the judgment of the district court is AFFIRMED with respect to liability issues. However, we VACATE and REMAND to the district court the award of general damages and order a REMITTITUR to $86,450 unless Delahoussaye elects to have a new trial on [—10—] general damages alone. Additionally, the district court's judgment is REFORMED to include Performance's undisputed liability insurer, One Beacon, which the district court mistakenly omitted from judgment. Judgment AFFIRMED in part, VACATED and REMANDED in part with instructions, REFORMED in part.

United States Court of Appeals for the Fifth Circuit

No. 12-60222

ISLAND OPERATING CO.
vs.
DIRECTOR, OFFICE OF WORKER'S COMPENSATION PROGRAMS

Petition for Review from an Administrative Decision of the Benefits Review Board

Decided: December 20, 2013

Citation: 738 F.3d 663, 1 Adm. R. 337 (5th Cir. 2013).

Before DeMOSS, OWEN, and HAYNES, Circuit Judges, Chief Judge.

[—1—] OWEN, Circuit Judge:

Island Operating Company and its carrier, the Louisiana Workers' Compensation Corporation (collectively, Island) have petitioned this court to review a modification of a benefits award under the Longshore and Harbor Workers' Compensation Act (LHWC Act). Island asks that we reverse the modified decision because the original judgment was not eligible for modification or alternatively, because the facts do not support the modification. We affirm. [—2—]

I

In January 2006, Martin B. Taylor, Jr. (Taylor) was working offshore for Island on an oil production platform when his right knee popped as he was crossing the deck. Over the next month, Island sent Taylor to two different physicians and an orthopaedic surgeon, all of whom pronounced that he would progress back to full-time work. It was during this time that Taylor began to experience pain in his left knee as well. Taylor performed light duty work for Island until late May when his employment was terminated. Following his termination, Taylor continued to experience pain in both knees so he consulted another orthopaedic surgeon, Dr. John Fairbanks, who performed surgery on Taylor's knees. Despite the surgery, Taylor continued to suffer from pain in both knees.

In May 2006, Taylor filed a claim for benefits under the LHWC Act. The administrative law judge (ALJ) initially denied the claim, finding that Taylor's condition had been caused by preexisting arthritis and not a traumatic workrelated incident. The Benefits Review Board (BRB) reversed and remanded, explaining that proof of a traumatic injury was unnecessary because preexisting conditions that are aggravated by a claimant's work are covered by the LHWC Act. The ALJ then awarded Taylor temporary partial disability benefits and temporary total disability benefits for two periods prior to September 16, 2006—the date at which the ALJ determined Taylor's condition had reached "maximum medical improvement" (MMI). The ALJ explained that except for the period from August 9, 2006 to September 16, 2006 when Dr. Fairbanks took Taylor off work, Taylor was not completely disabled because Island had established that suitable alternative employment was available.

In January 2010—within the mandated one-year period—Taylor filed a modification application to seek benefits for permanent partial disability. The issues are whether, and to what extent, Taylor's knees were impaired after [—3—] reaching MMI on September 16, 2006. Taylor submitted reports from two physicians, Dr. Fairbanks and Dr. Murphy, which both found that Taylor had a 25-percent permanent disability in each knee. On this basis, the ALJ granted Taylor's modification petition. Though Island argued—and the ALJ acknowledged—that "the impairment ratings used as evidence . . . to establish his modification were arguably available at the time of the original hearing," the ALJ concluded that "a modification can be granted based upon previously available evidence." Therefore, the ALJ modified the previous judgment to include permanent partial disability benefits commensurate with a 25-percent impairment of each knee to commence on September 16, 2006.

Island appealed this decision to the BRB, which affirmed. Explaining that the modification provision was intended to replace finality with accuracy, it held that the ALJ had properly modified the award based on a mistake, despite the fact that the evidence Taylor presented in support was available prior to the initial hearing. Island now files a petition for review.

II

We review appeals from BRB decisions to correct errors of law and to determine whether the BRB properly deferred to the ALJ's factfinding.[1] Because the BRB's conclusion that the ALJ correctly applied § 22 to reopen Taylor's claim is a question of law, it is subject to this court's de novo review.[2]

As to disputed issues of fact, like the BRB, "[w]e may not substitute our judgment for that of the ALJ, nor reweigh or reappraise the evidence, but may only determine whether evidence exists to support the ALJ's findings."[3] Accordingly, we examine "whether the BRB properly concluded that the ALJ's [—4—] factual findings were supported by substantial evidence on the record as a whole."[4] Substantial evidence is that which "provides a substantial basis of fact from which the fact in issue can be reasonably inferred."[5] The BRB and this court will not disturb an ALJ's factual findings unless reasonable minds would not accept the findings as "adequate to support a conclusion."[6]

III

Island first argues that Taylor's claim was never eligible for modification because he never satisfied the legal predicate necessary to invoke this action. Island argues in the alternative that even if reopening the claim

was appropriate, the modification decision was not supported by the facts. We address each challenge in turn.

A

The threshold issue is whether Taylor has established sufficient grounds to invoke a modification of a prior judgment under the LHWC Act.[7] Section 22 of the Act provides, in relevant part:

> Upon his own initiative, or upon the application of any party in interest . . . on the ground of a change in conditions or because of a mistake in a determination of fact by the [ALJ],[8] the [ALJ] may, at any time prior to one year after the date of the last payment of compensation, whether or not a compensation order has been issued, or at any time prior to one year after the rejection of a claim, review a compensation case . . . [—5—] [and] issue a new compensation order which may terminate, continue, reinstate, increase, or decrease such compensation, or award compensation.[9]

By its terms, the statute provides two avenues for modification of a prior judgment: (1) a change in conditions, or (2) a mistake in a determination of fact by the ALJ. The sole basis of this petition concerns what constitutes "a mistake in a determination of fact" such that a prior judgment is eligible for modification.

Island urges that a mistake of fact can serve as grounds for modification only if it is based on completely new and previously unattainable evidence. To hold otherwise, it argues, would permit claimants to relitigate claims under the guise of § 22, which would compromise judicial finality. Because the testimony of both physicians was available at

---

[1] *Ceres Marine Terminal v. Hinton*, 243 F.3d 222, 224 (5th Cir. 2001).

[2] *Pool Co. v. Cooper*, 274 F.3d 173, 177 (5th Cir. 2001).

[3] *SGS Control Servs. v. Dir., Office of Worker's Comp. Programs, U.S. Dep't of Labor*, 86 F.3d 438, 440 (5th Cir. 1996).

[4] *Pool*, 274 F.3d at 178 (internal quotation marks omitted).

[5] *Avondale Indus., Inc. v. Dir., Office of Workers' Comp. Programs*, 977 F.2d 186, 189 (5th Cir. 1992) (internal quotation marks omitted).

[6] *Id.* (internal quotation marks omitted).

[7] 33 U.S.C. §§ 901-950.

[8] While § 22 under the Act specifically refers to the "deputy commissioner," the 1972 Amendments transferred the hearing functions formerly exercised by those officials to administrative law judges. *Id.* § 919(d).

[9] *Id.* § 922.

the time of Taylor's original hearing, Island asserts that this evidence cannot support a mistake and therefore, that modification of the judgment is not available.

The Supreme Court, however, has expressly permitted modification under these circumstances. In *Banks v. Chicago Grain Trimmers Ass'n*,[10] the Court concluded that the language "a mistake in a determination of fact" was intended to have a broad scope.[11] In *Banks*, a death-benefits claim was initially denied because the survivor-claimant had failed to prove a causal connection between the worker's fatal fall at home and a work-connected injury.[12] Several months later, the survivor filed a second claim after discovering an eyewitness to a work-connected injury suffered by the decedent on the same day as his fall.[13] While the court of appeals held this second claim was barred by res judicata, the Court [—6—] held that the purpose of the amendment to § 22 was to displace finality "in order to render justice under the act."[14] The Court held that the second claim, challenging the factual finding that the decedent's fall did not result from a work-related injury, came within the scope of § 22.[15]

Significantly, the Court did not discuss whether the survivor-claimant could have discovered the eyewitness before the first hearing. Rather, it upheld the modification award because "nothing in [§ 22's] legislative history [ ] support[ed] the [ ] argument that a 'determination of fact' means only some determinations of fact and not others."[16] Therefore, a "determination of fact" could include facts which may have been known to the claimant since the "purpose of this amendment was to broaden the grounds on which [an ALJ] can modify an award."[17]

The Court revisited § 22 in *O'Keeffe v. Aerojet-General Shipyards, Inc.*,[18] in which a disability claim was initially denied for failure to prove that the condition was work-related.[19] Based on the testimony of two physicians, the claimant reopened his case under § 22 to show that contrary to the initial determination, his condition had "been materially aggravated and hastened by the circumstances of [his] employment."[20] The lower court denied modification because without "new" evidence, § 22 did not permit an ALJ "to receive [—7—] additional but cumulative evidence and change his mind."[21] The Court, however, upheld the modification award because "[n]either the wording of [§ 22] nor its legislative history supports this narrowly technical and impractical construction."[22] "[O]n its face, the section permits a reopening within one year because of a mistake in a determination of fact," and "[t]here is *no limitation* to particular factual errors, or to cases involving *new* evidence."[23]

Island asserts, however, that even if § 22 was intended to favor justice over finality, the Court's interpretation ignores finality altogether. Despite the one-year limitations period, a claimant can theoretically create endless litigation by continuously moving to modify an award within a year of the previous modification. While we acknowledge Island's concerns, the remedy lies with Congress and not with this court. In *Metropolitan Stevedore Co. v. Rambo*,[24] the petitioner similarly argued that to equate a change in wage-earning capacity to a "change in conditions" under § 22 would "flood" courts with litigation "because parties [would] request modification every time an employee's wages change[d] or the economy [took] a turn."[25] But the Court held that such an argument was "better directed at Congress" rather "than at the

---

[10] 390 U.S. 459 (1968).

[11] *Banks*, 390 U.S. at 464.

[12] *Id.* at 460.

[13] *Id.* at 461.

[14] *See id.* at 461, 464 (internal quotation marks omitted).

[15] *Id.* at 465.

[16] *Id.*

[17] *Id.* at 464 (internal quotation marks omitted).

[18] 404 U.S. 254 (1971) (per curiam).

[19] *O'Keeffe*, 404 U.S. at 254.

[20] *Id.* (internal quotation marks omitted).

[21] *Id.* at 255 (internal quotation marks omitted).

[22] *Id.* (internal quotation marks omitted).

[23] *Id.* (emphasis added) (internal quotation marks omitted).

[24] 515 U.S. 291 (1995).

[25] *Rambo*, 515 U.S. at 300.

courts."[26] Likewise, any narrowing of the mistake-modification language must be enacted through legislative channels. [—8—]

In sum, both *Banks* and *O'Keeffe* clearly establish that contrary to Island's position, mistakes of fact are not limited to newly discovered and previously unattainable evidence. Therefore, we affirm the BRB's decision on this basis.

B

Island next argues that even if Taylor presented a legally sufficient claim to reopen his award, the facts do not support the modification he received. As noted earlier, this court does not reweigh or reappraise evidence but only determines whether evidence exists to support the ALJ's findings.[27] Here, the ALJ granted modification on the basis of testimony from two different physicians who had examined Taylor and reviewed his medical records. Both physicians concurred that Taylor had a 25-percent impairment rating in both knees. Accordingly, there was evidence to support the ALJ's finding, and the BRB correctly affirmed the modification of Taylor's award to include permanent partial benefits.[28]

* * *

For the foregoing reasons, the BRB's decision is AFFIRMED.

---

[26] *Id.*

[27] *Supra* notes 3-6 and accompanying text.

[28] *See SGS Control Servs. v. Dir., Office of Worker's Comp. Programs, U.S. Dep't of Labor*, 86 F.3d 438, 443-44 (5th Cir. 1996) (affirming the grant of permanent disability benefits because the ALJ had substantial factual evidence to support its conclusion).

United States Court of Appeals
for the Fifth Circuit

No. 12-30965

VENABLE
VS.
LOUISIANA WORKERS' COMPENSATION CORP.

Appeal from the United States District Court for the
Eastern District of Louisiana

Decided: December 30, 2013

Citation: 740 F.3d 937, 1 Adm. R. 341 (5th Cir. 2013).

Before SMITH, PRADO, and ELROD, Circuit Judges.

[—1—] SMITH, Circuit Judge:

Timothy and Julia Venable appeal a summary judgment in favor of the Louisiana Workers' Compensation Corporation ("LWCC"), which cross-appeals the denial of its motion to dismiss for want of subject-matter jurisdiction. Because the district court lacked subject-matter jurisdiction, we reverse the [—2—] summary judgment and render a judgment of dismissal.

I.

While employed by Greene's Energy Company, LLC ("Greene's"), Timothy Venable suffered a heart attack at work in Louisiana waters aboard the Stingray drilling barge, which was owned and operated by Hillcorp Energy Company ("Hillcorp"). LWCC, Greene's insurance carrier for purposes of the Longshore and Harbor Workers' Compensation Act ("LHWCA"), immediately began providing Venable medical and indemnity benefits pursuant to that act.

The Venables sued Hillcorp for negligence in federal court, alleging that an unreasonable delay in obtaining medical care had resulted in further harm.[1] After extensive pre-trial litigation related to the issue of indemnity, the parties participated in a settlement conference. Although LWCC was not yet a party, its representative was present.[2] Hillcorp and the Venables tentatively agreed to settle for $350,000. The Venables contend that, during the settlement conference, the representative for LWCC expressed that LWCC would consent to the proposed amount. The district court conditionally dismissed the Venables' claim based on the understanding that it had been settled.

After the settlement conference, however, LWCC refused to sign the [—3—] LS-33 form that the Venables' counsel had forwarded to LWCC's attorney. At some point after the settlement conference, LWCC learned that Venable would likely need a heart transplant, meaning that LWCC would be left liable for significant future exposure even with the settlement of third-party claims.

Because LWCC refused to sign, the district court vacated the conditional dismissal. The Venables then joined LWCC as a party to enforce LWCC's purported consent to the settlement, asking the court to order LWCC to execute the LS-33 form and otherwise to approve the third-party settlement with Hillcorp. In the alternative, the Venables requested the court to find that LWCC had waived § 933(g)'s written-approval requirement by consenting to the settlement, such that no written approval was required. LWCC moved to dismiss for lack of subject-matter jurisdiction, but the court determined that the waivability of the § 933(g) written-

---

[1] The district court found that it had admiralty and maritime jurisdiction.

[2] Under the LHWCA, Venable would forfeit any future benefit from LWCC if he settled his claims against Hillcorp without receiving written approval of the settlement from LWCC on a Department of Labor-issued form, as required by statute. *See* 33 U.S.C. § 933(g)(1) (2012) ("If the person entitled to compensation . . . enters into a settlement with a third person . . . for an amount less than the compensation to which the person . . . would be entitled under this chapter, the employer shall be liable for compensation as determined under subsection (f) of this section only if written approval of the settlement is obtained from the employer and the employer's carrier, before the settlement is executed, and by the person entitled to compensation . . . . The approval shall be made on a form provided by the Secretary and shall be filed in the office of the deputy commissioner within thirty days after the settlement is entered into.").

approval requirement raised a substantial federal issue that conferred federal-question jurisdiction.

The Venables then moved for partial summary judgment. In turn, LWCC filed a cross-motion for summary judgment, contending that the written approval requirement of § 933(g) is not waivable, and even if it can be waived, the conduct of LWCC's representative did not constitute a waiver. The district court granted summary judgment for LWCC and dismissed the complaint with prejudice, holding that LWCC's decision to withhold consent on the settlement was a proper exercise of its power under the LHWCA. The Venables appeal that order, and LWCC cross-appeals the denial of its motion to dismiss for lack of jurisdiction.

II.

We review a ruling on subject-matter jurisdiction *de novo*. *See PCI Transp., Inc. v. Fort Worth & W. R.R. Co.*, 418 F.3d 535, 540 (5th Cir. 2005) (quoting *Hoskins v. Bekins Van Lines*, 343 F.3d 769, 772 (5th Cir. 2003)). "As [—4—] a court of limited jurisdiction, a federal court must affirmatively ascertain subject-matter jurisdiction before adjudicating a suit."[3] A district court should dismiss where "it appears certain that the plaintiff cannot prove a plausible set of facts that establish subject-matter jurisdiction."[4] The plaintiff has the burden of establishing jurisdiction.[5]

The district court incorrectly found that it had federal-question jurisdiction under 28 U.S.C. § 1331. Because the federal issue raised does not satisfy the well-pleaded-complaint rule, the court lacked such jurisdiction.

Section 1331 vests lower federal courts with jurisdiction over "all civil actions arising under the Constitution, laws, or treaties of the United States." An action can arise under federal law for purposes of § 1331 in two ways: In a well-pleaded complaint (1) the party has asserted a federal cause of action, *see Am. Well Works Co. v. Layne & Bowler Co.*, 241 U.S. 257, 260 (1916), or (2) the party has asserted a state cause-of-action claim that "necessarily raise[s] a stated federal issue, actually disputed and substantial, which a federal forum may entertain without disturbing any congressionally approved balance of federal and state judicial responsibilities," *see Grable & Sons Metal Prods., Inc. v. Darue Eng'g & Mfg.*, 545 U.S. 308, 314 (2005).

First, the Venables have not asserted any federal cause of action against LWCC and instead only point to state causes of action in their amended [—5—] complaint.[6] The Venables cannot rely on § 933, which does not create a private cause of action.[7]

---

[3] *Sawyer v. Wright*, 471 F. App'x 260, 261 (5th Cir.) (per curiam), *cert. denied*, 133 S. Ct. 615 (2012); *see also Ashcroft v. Iqbal*, 556 U.S. 662, 671 (2009).

[4] *Castro v. United States*, 560 F.3d 381, 386 (5th Cir. 2009), *vacated on other grounds*, 608 F.3d 266 (5th Cir. 2010).

[5] *Ramming v. United States*, 281 F.3d 158, 161 (5th Cir. 2001) ("The burden of proof for a Rule 12(b)(1) motion to dismiss is on the party asserting jurisdiction. Accordingly, the plaintiff constantly bears the burden of proof that jurisdiction does in fact exist." (citations omitted)).

[6] The amended complaint includes the following counts: (1) "LWCC should be ordered to execute the LS-33 or judgment should be entered providing that written consent to the settlement is unnecessary"; (2) "The parties to this litigation detrimentally relied on the assurances of LWCC that the amount and other terms of the settlement being negotiated would be approved by LWCC and its consent would be given"; (3) intentional misrepresentation; (4) making impossible a condition of the settlement; and (5) abuse of rights. During oral argument, the Venables' counsel indicated that he was relying on federal common law. In his view, one "could supplement or inform the district court's discretion by using analogous situations under state law." Therefore, counsel "gave [the district court] concepts in Louisiana law that would be helpful to inform [the court of its] discretion." Counsel, however, acknowledged that his pleadings had not mentioned this reliance on federal common law. Moreover, this theory of federal-question jurisdiction does not appear in the briefing, so it is waived. *See United States v. Thibodeaux*, 211 F.3d 910, 912 (5th Cir. 2000).

[7] *See McLaurin v. Noble Drilling (U.S.) Inc.*, 529 F.3d 285, 291–92 (5th Cir. 2008) ("Importantly, §933 recognizes that a covered employee may have

Because state law, and not federal law, creates the causes of action at issue, we turn to *Grable*, 545 U.S. at 314, under which a federal court can exercise federal-question jurisdiction over a state-law claim if (1) the state-law claim raises a substantial federal issue; (2) the parties actually dispute the federal issue; and (3) exercising jurisdiction over the particular category of cases will not disturb any "congressionally approved balance of federal and state judicial responsibilities." The district court found it had subject-matter jurisdiction because it determined that the state-law claims satisfied *Grable*.[8]

A federal court can exercise jurisdiction only where the case satisfies the well-pleaded-complaint rule, according to which, to assess whether the case arises under federal law, the court must look only to "what necessarily appears [—6—] in the plaintiff's statement of his own claim . . . unaided by anything alleged in anticipation of avoidance of defenses which it is thought the defendant may interpose." *Taylor v. Anderson*, 234 U.S. 74, 75–76 (1914). Federal courts lack jurisdiction "over a case in which the complaint presents a state-law cause of action, but also asserts that federal law deprives the defendant of a defense he may raise, or that a federal defense the defendant may raise is not sufficient to defeat the claim." *Franchise Tax Bd. of State of Cal. v. Constr. Laborers Vacation Trust for S. Cal.*, 463 U.S. 1, 10 (1983) (citations omitted).

Furthermore, although the parties may ultimately litigate a federal issue in their case, that fact does not "show that the suit, that is, the plaintiff's original cause of action, arises under the Constitution" or the laws of the United States. *See Louisville & Nashville*

R.R. Co. v. Mottley, 211 U.S. 149, 152 (1908). "[A] right or immunity created by the Constitution or laws of the United States must be an element, and an essential one, of the plaintiff's cause of action." *Gully v. First Nat'l Bank in Meridian*, 299 U.S. 109, 112 (1936).

The federal issue the district court relied upon—whether a party can waive the written-consent requirement under § 933—anticipates LWCC's prospective defense. That issue would otherwise come up in litigation in the following hypothetical situation: First, without obtaining LWCC's written consent, the Venables entered into the settlement agreement with Hillcorp. In response, LWCC terminated benefits. After that, the Venables sought judicial intervention to have the benefits reinstated. At that point, LWCC would argue that the Venables had not complied with § 933's written-consent requirements. The Venables would then reply as they have here (and would urge, among other reasons) that LWCC had waived § 933's requirements). In line with this hypothetical, the district court's assessment demonstrates that the Venables [—7—] raised this federal issue in anticipation of LWCC's defense.[9]

Furthermore, none of the Venables' claims requires proving a federal issue as an element of the claim. To the extent they have asserted valid Louisiana claims, the Venables have not shown that those state-law claims require proving a substantial federal issue. Certainly, none of them would require proving that LWCC had waived § 933's written-consent requirement.

Even assuming *arguendo* the district court was correct that the issue of waiver under §933 raises a substantial federal issue for purposes of *Grable*, the well-pleaded-complaint rule forecloses federal-question

---

tort remedies against third parties under federal or state law. Section 933 preserves and codifies a maritime worker's common law right to pursue a negligence claim against a third party that is not the employer or a coworker; it does not create a cause of action nor establish a third party's liability for negligence." (citations omitted)).

[8] In its order, the district court noted that it was "persuaded that the proper interpretation of the settlement provision of the LHWCA presents a substantial question of federal law whose resolution is crucial to the state law claims at issue."

[9] The district court's order notes, "If a § 933(g) is enforced as written then Plaintiffs cannot prevail on their state law claims because the LHWCA will necessarily control and preempt any state law to the contrary." If § 933(g)'s written-consent requirement would necessarily preempt any contrary state law, LWCC would raise this issue as an affirmative defense.

jurisdiction. We therefore do not need to address whether the § 933 written-consent requirement poses a "substantial" federal issue.

III.

We still must examine whether the Venables have established any other basis for federal jurisdiction. As a threshold matter, they do not posit that § 933 itself vests federal-court jurisdiction over their claims. Instead, they offer a myriad of other theories to demonstrate that the district court had subject-matter jurisdiction: (1) diversity jurisdiction under 28 U.S.C. § 1332; (2) supplemental jurisdiction under 28 U.S.C. §1367; (3) admiralty and maritime jurisdiction under 28 U.S.C. § 1333; and (4) jurisdiction under the district court's "inherent power to enforce [] settlement[s]."

As to the first theory, § 1332 requires "the matter in controversy [to] exceed[] the sum or value of $75,000, exclusive of interest and costs, and [be] [—8—] between . . . citizens of different States . . . ."[10] Both the Venables and LWCC, however, are citizens of Louisiana.

As to the second theory, § 1367 "grants supplemental jurisdiction over other claims that do not independently come within the jurisdiction of the district court but form part of the same Article III 'case or controversy.'" *State Nat'l Ins. Co. v. Yates*, 391 F.3d 577, 579 (5th Cir. 2004). "[I]n any civil action of which [a] district court [has] original jurisdiction, [that] court[] shall have supplemental jurisdiction over all other claims that are so related to claims in the action . . . that they form part of the same case or controversy. . . ." 28 U.S.C. § 1367(a) (2012).[11] A claim forms part of the same case or controversy if the "claim[is] so related to the original claims

that [it] derive[s] from a common nucleus of operative fact." *Bella v. Davis*, 531 F. App'x 457, 459 (5th Cir. 2013) (per curiam).

The claims the Venables assert against LWCC in their amended complaint do not derive from the same nucleus of operative facts as does their negligence claim against Hillcorp. LWCC's potential waiver of § 933(g)'s written-consent requirement occasioned by its conduct during and after a settlement conference depends on facts that are completely different from those related to any torts committed by Hillcorp years before. The district court therefore could not have exercised supplemental jurisdiction over the claims the Venables bring against LWCC.

As to the third theory, § 1333 vests exclusive federal jurisdiction involving "[a]ny civil case of admiralty or maritime jurisdiction, saving to suitors in [—9—] all cases all other remedies to which they are otherwise entitled." 28 U.S.C. § 1333 (2012). "[A] party seeking to invoke federal admiralty jurisdiction pursuant to 28 U.S.C. § 1333(1) over a tort claim must satisfy conditions both of location and of connection with maritime activity." *Jerome B. Grubart, Inc. v. Great Lakes Dredge & Dock Co.*, 513 U.S. 527, 534 (1995). The locality test assesses "whether the tort occurred on navigable water or whether injury suffered on land was caused by a vessel on navigable water." *Id.* The connection test requires two showings:

> A court, first, must assess the general features of the type of incident involved, to determine whether the incident has a potentially disruptive impact on maritime commerce. Second, a court must determine whether the general character of the activity giving rise to the incident shows a substantial relationship to traditional maritime activity.

Id. (citations and internal quotation marks omitted).

---

[10] 28 U.S.C. § 1332 (2012); *see also Mumfrey v. CVS Pharmacy, Inc.*, 719 F.3d 392, 397 (5th Cir. 2013).

[11] Even if the claim falls within § 1367(a), the exceptions specified in § 1367(b) and (c) may apply. Because § 1367(a) does not apply, however, we do not need to determine whether an exception nevertheless precludes jurisdiction.

The Venables' claims against LWCC do not satisfy the locality test.[12] The Venables conflate the district court's jurisdiction over their negligence claim—the basis of which appears to have occurred on navigable water—with the claims they assert against LWCC. They allege that LWCC committed various state-law torts by its conduct during or after the settlement conference. But none of that conduct occurred on navigable waters, nor were these alleged torts caused by a vessel on navigable water.[13] Therefore, the Venables cannot claim admiralty jurisdiction as the basis for subject-matter jurisdiction.

As to their fourth and final theory, the Venables assert that the district [—10—] court could exercise jurisdiction over these claims by its "inherent power to enforce [] settlement[s]." They appear to suggest that the court could exercise its ancillary-enforcement jurisdiction as a basis for subject-matter jurisdiction.

In *Kokkonen v. Guardian Life Insurance Co. of America*, 511 U.S. 375 (1994), the Court explained when a federal court can retain jurisdiction over a settlement agreement by exercising this ancillary enforcement jurisdiction. There, Guardian Life Insurance Company ("Guardian") terminated Kokkonen's general agency agreement, prompting Kokkonen to sue in state court, whereupon Guardian removed to federal court. *See id.* at 376. Before jury deliberations, "the parties arrived at an oral agreement settling all claims and counterclaims, the substance of which they recited, on the record, before the District Judge in chambers." *Id.* Although the judge was aware of the settlement, the dismissal order made no reference to the settlement agreement. *Id.* at 377. Thereafter, the parties disagreed as to Kokkonen's obligation to return certain files, and Guardian moved to enforce the agreement. *Id.*

In determining whether a federal court could exercise its inherent jurisdiction, the *Kokkonen* Court first explained that state law governs the enforcement of contracts, including settlement agreements that result in the dismissal of federal suits. *See id.* at 378. The Court therefore held that an action to enforce a settlement agreement "is more than just a continuation or renewal of the dismissed suit, and hence requires its own basis for jurisdiction." *Id.*

Having established that federal courts require an independent jurisdictional basis to enforcement settlement agreements, the Court then described two general situations in which a federal court can exercise independent "ancillary jurisdiction": "(1) to permit disposition by a single court of claims that are, in varying respects and degrees, factually interdependent; and (2) to enable a court to function successfully, that is, to manage its proceedings, vindicate its authority, and effectuate its decrees." *Id.* at 379–80 (citations omitted). As [—11—] was the case in *Kokkonen*, the first basis does not generally apply in the instant context because the terms of a settlement agreement usually will not be "factually interdependent" with the claims underlying the original lawsuit.[14] The Court further noted that the second basis did not apply to the circumstances we face here because (1) the district court, in its order, had not expressly retained jurisdiction over the settlement agreement, and (2) the order did not incorporate the settlement agreement.[15]

---

[14] *Kokkonen*, 511 U.S. at 380 ("[T]he facts underlying respondent's dismissed claim for breach of agency agreement and those underlying its claim for breach of settlement agreement have nothing to do with each other; it would neither be necessary nor even particularly efficient that they be adjudicated together.").

[15] *Id.* at 381 ("The situation would be quite different if the parties' obligation to comply with the terms of the settlement agreement had been made part of the order of dismissal—either by separate provision (such as a provision 'retaining jurisdiction' over the settlement agreement) or by incorporating the terms of the settlement agreement in the order. In that event, a breach of the agreement would be a violation of the order, and ancillary jurisdiction to enforce the agreement would therefore exist.").

---

[12] We therefore do not need to address whether the Venables' claims satisfy the connection test.

[13] *See Miller v. Griffin-Alexander Drilling Co.*, 873 F.2d 809, 812 (5th Cir. 1989) ("We see no reason for expanding admiralty jurisdiction to cases with such scant involvement of maritime locations.").

Applying *Kokkonen*, we likewise require one of those two showings for a district court to exercise ancillary jurisdiction in enforcing a settlement agreement.[16] The Venables do not have a settlement agreement that they seek to enforce but instead want a federal court to compel LWCC to consent to their tentative agreement with Hillcorp. Under *Kokkonen*, a district court cannot exercise ancillary jurisdiction to compel a third party's consent to a proposed, but not final, settlement agreement; none of the slew of cases cited by the [—12—] Venables suggests as much.[17] Therefore, they have not demonstrated that the district court could exercise ancillary jurisdiction.

Because the district court lacked subject-matter jurisdiction over the state claims the Venables brought against LWCC, we need not decide whether the court correctly determined that LWCC's decision to withhold consent on the settlement was a proper exercise of its power under the LHWCA. The summary judgment is REVERSED, and a judgment of dismissal for want of jurisdiction is RENDERED.

---

[16] *See, e.g., Hospitality House, Inc. v. Gilbert*, 298 F.3d 424, 430–31 (5th Cir. 2002); *Woolwine Ford Lincoln Mercury v. Consol. Fin. Res., Inc.*, No. 00-60314, 245 F.3d 791 (table), 2000 WL 1910184, at *2 (5th Cir. Dec. 27, 2000) (per curiam) (unpublished). *See generally* Andrew S. Hanen & Jeffrey M. Benton, *The Enforceability of Settlement Agreements*, 40 THE ADVOC. (TEX.) 69, 70 (2007) ("It is clear after *Kokkonen* . . . that a party wishing to preserve a district court's jurisdiction over a settlement agreement can only do so in one of two ways: (1) through an express retention of jurisdiction by the court or (2) by incorporation of the settlement agreement into the judgment.").

[17] The Venables principally rely on *Bell v. Schexnayder*, 36 F.3d 447 (5th Cir. 1994), decided shortly after *Kokkonen*. In *Bell*, however, the parties had entered into a settlement agreement, and the district court's order expressly retained jurisdiction over the settlement agreement. *See id.* at 449 ("On October 14, the court signed a sixty day order of dismissal. The order states that the court, 'having been advised by counsel for the parties that the above action has been settled,' was dismissing the case 'without prejudice to the right, upon good cause shown within sixty (60) days, to reopen it if settlement is not consummated and seek summary judgment enforcing the compromise.'"). *Bell* does not apply where the parties have not entered into a settlement agreement.

United States Court of Appeals for the Sixth Circuit

United States Court of Appeals
for the Sixth Circuit

Nos. 11-3723

WILLIAMSON

vs.

RECOVERY LIMITED PARTNERSHIP

Appeal from the United States District Court for the
Southern District of Ohio

Decided: October 2, 2013

Citation: 731 F.3d 608, 1 Adm. R. 348 (6th Cir. 2013).

Before **BOGGS** and **SUHRHEINRICH**, Circuit Judges;
and **MURPHY**, United States District Judge for the
Eastern District of Michigan, sitting by designation.

[—2—] **BOGGS**, Circuit Judge:

This appeal is the latest skirmish in the legal battle over the treasures recovered from the of the 19th-century steamship *S.S. Central America*, a battle that has spanned three decades and numerous courts. Dubbed the "Ship of Gold,"[1] the *Central America* sank in the Atlantic Ocean in September 1857, taking over 400 passengers and many tons of gold with her. Her wreckage was discovered over 130 years later by a group of explorers led by Thomas Thompson, in what remains one of the most significant finds in maritime history. One jurist described the feat as "a paradigm of American initiative, ingenuity, and determination."[2]

Ominously, the same jurist opened his opinion with words that are equally fitting: "*Quid non mortalia pectora cogis, Auri sacra fames!*"[3] The individuals who dedicated their time and talent to the recovery of the *Central America* have not seen a dime of their promised share of the spoils; Thompson is a fugitive from the law, actively pursued by

United States Marshals; and the vast wealth representing the ship's golden cargo is as lost today as it was before September 1988.

The instant consolidated appeal concerns a suit brought by a group of plaintiffs who assisted Thompson in locating the wreckage of the *Central America*. All signed non-disclosure agreements with Thompson, through his business entities, promising to hold his projects and ideas in confidence in exchange for a percentage of the net recovery of the *Central America*. All claim to have upheld their respective ends of the bargain, yet none have received payment. The business entities respond by asserting a [—3—] two-year statute of limitations for actions in salvage and three counterclaims. The district court rejected the business entities' time-bar argument and granted summary judgment against all of their counterclaims. The defendants took an interlocutory appeal of that decision. During the pendency of that appeal, the district court granted a motion for prejudgment attachment and an injunction against one of the business entities and Thompson, forbidding them from divesting certain assets. The two defendants took an interlocutory appeal of that order as well. We consolidated the two appeals.

This appeal requires us to resolve several complex questions of federal jurisdiction and admiralty law. We must first decide which issues we have jurisdiction to hear. In response to the parties' jurisdictional motions in the two appeals, we will assert jurisdiction over the time-bar issue, all of the entity defendants' counterclaims, and the injunction defendants' appeal of the attachment and injunction order insofar as the district court issued a preliminary injunction. As to other issues, we refuse to entertain the appeal for want of jurisdiction.

We must then turn to the substantive issues over which we have jurisdiction. We must first determine whether or not the plaintiffs' action is time barred. We hold that the time bar does not apply. Next, we must address the district court's grant of summary judgment against the entity defendants' counterclaims. As the entity defendants have

---

[1] *See generally* GARY KINDER, SHIP OF GOLD IN THE DEEP BLUE SEA: THE HISTORY AND DISCOVERY OF THE WORLD'S RICHEST SHIPWRECK (1998).

[2] *Columbus–Am. Discovery Grp. v. Atl. Mutual Ins. Co. [CADG II]*, 56 F.3d 556, 576 (4th Cir. 1995) (Hall, J.).

[3] "To what cannot you compel the hearts of men, O cursed lust for gold!" *Id.* at 561 (quoting Virgil, *Aeneid*, Bk. III 56).

failed to raise an issue of fact material to the disposition of the case, we affirm the district court's order. Finally, we must assess whether or not the district court abused its discretion in granting a preliminary injunction against Thompson and one of the business entities. We hold that it did not. For the reasons discussed in detail below, we affirm the district court in full as to all issues over which we have jurisdiction.

I

A

The tale of the last days of the *S.S. Central America* has been retold many times by many courts throughout the many years of litigation in this case. None, however, [—4—] match the excellence of the narrative given by the late Judge Donald Russell of the Fourth Circuit:

The year 1857 is justly famous in American history for its many notable events. Among these was the beginning of a fairly serious financial decline, the aptly named Panic of 1857. Associated with the Panic, and another reason why the year is so famous, is one of the worst disasters in American maritime history, the sinking of the S.S. CENTRAL AMERICA.

The CENTRAL AMERICA was a black-hulled, coal-fired, three-decked, three-masted sidewheeler with a cruising speed of eleven knots. Built in 1852, and launched the following year, she carried passengers, mail, and cargo between Aspinwall, Colombia (on the Caribbean side of the isthmus of Panama), and New York City, with a stopover in Havana. Most, if not all, of her passengers were headed to or from California, the route being one leg of the then quickest way between the west coast and the eastern seaboard-from California to the Pacific side of the isthmus of Panama aboard a steamship, across the isthmus on the Panama Railroad, and then from Aspinwall to New York aboard another steamship. Owned by the U.S. Mail and Steamship

Company and originally named the S.S. GEORGE LAW (until June 1857), the CENTRAL AMERICA completed forty-three voyages between Panama and New York in her four years of operation. During this period, the California gold rush was in full swing, and it has been said that the ship carried one-third of all gold shipped at that time from California to New York.

In August of 1857, over four hundred passengers and approximately $1,600,000 (1857 value) in gold (exclusive of passenger gold) left San Francisco for Panama aboard the S.S. SONORA. Many of the passengers were prospectors who had become rich and were returning home, either for good or to visit. Also on board were California Judge Alonzo Castle Monson, who resigned from the bench after losing his house and all his money in a famous poker game, and Mrs. Virginia Birch, a.k.a. "the notorious Jenny French," a former dance hall girl well known in San Francisco. As for the gold, it was being shipped by California merchants, bankers, and express companies, including Levi Straus and Wells Fargo, to New York banks, the banks wanting specie to stave off the effects of the financial downturn.

The travellers and the cargo reached Panama without incident, and they crossed the isthmus by rail. On September 3, over six hundred people came aboard the CENTRAL AMERICA, as well as $1,219,189 of the gold shipped on the SONORA, the remainder being shipped to England aboard a different vessel. The CENTRAL AMERICA first headed for Havana, which was reached on September 7. There, the ship [—5—] lay over for a night, and some of the passengers debarked to catch another vessel for New Orleans. On September 8, under clear skies, the CENTRAL AMERICA left Havana for New York, carrying approximately 580 persons and her golden treasure.

On the second day out of Havana, the weather changed and a mighty storm came up. What the passengers and crew could not know was that they were headed directly into the teeth of a ferocious hurricane. As the storm worsened around the CENTRAL AMERICA, a leak developed and soon water was rushing into the boat. The water extinguished the fires in the ship's boilers, and this in turn caused the ship's pumping system to fail. All able male passengers began a systematic bailing of water out of the ship, but it was to no avail; after thirty frantic hours, the boiler fires would still not light and the water level continued to rise.

Knowing the situation was hopeless, Captain William Lewis Herndon managed to hail a passing ship, the brig MARINE, and one hundred persons, including all but one of the women and children aboard, were safely transferred to the other ship. Time and conditions would not allow for any more transfers, however, and shortly after 8 p.m. on September 12, the CENTRAL AMERICA began making its quick descent to the bottom of the ocean.

After being flung into the sea, many of the men managed to come to the top and float there, desperately holding onto any buoyant material available. Six to nine hours after the sinking, fifty of these men were rescued by the Norwegian bark ELLEN. Earlier, a small bird had thrice circled the ELLEN and flown directly into the face of the ship's captain. Taking this as a sign, the captain changed his course to follow from whence the bird had come, and in so doing discovered the fifty floating survivors. Three other men were also rescued when, nine days later and 450 miles away, a ship spotted their lifeboat, which had been riding the Gulf Stream.

In all, 153 persons were rescued, while approximately 425 lost their lives. Also lost were hundreds of bags of mail and

the $1,219,189 in gold. At the time, there were rumors that other commercial shipments of gold were aboard, but these were quickly discounted. It is true, though, that a significant amount, probably several hundred thousand dollars worth (1857 valuation), of passenger gold was lost. Many passengers had with them their earnings from several years' labor in the California gold fields. Some kept this gold on their person, while others carried it in carpetbags or trunks. Also, passenger gold could have been checked with the ship's purser, although these records were lost with the ship. Captain Thomas W. Badger is one example of a passenger carrying gold, he having lost $17,500 of it stored in a carpetbag. Also, the newspapers reporting the disaster contained vivid accounts of men [—6—] flinging down their hard earned treasure in disgust upon realizing their impending doom.

Needless to say, for the next several weeks newspapers around the country devoted much space to the disaster which befell the CENTRAL AMERICA. While people mourned the over four hundred persons who had valiantly lost their lives, they also feared that the loss of such a large amount of specie would exacerbate the country's already serious financial situation. The commercial shipments of gold had been insured, though, and the insurance underwriters began advertising in the newspapers that they would pay off their commitments upon the proper proofs being presented. Approximately one-third of the treasure had been underwritten by New York insurers while the rest was underwritten in London. Without doubt, most, if not all, of the claims were promptly paid off by the underwriters.

Under applicable law, then and now, once the underwriters paid the claims made upon them by the owners of the gold, the treasure became theirs. Thus, less than two weeks after the disaster, the underwriters began negotiating with the Boston Submarine Armor Company about possibly raising the ship and her cargo. Also, on June 28, 1858, two of the underwriters (Atlantic Mutual Insurance Company and Sun Mutual Insurance Company) contracted with Brutus de Villeroi, a Frenchman then living in Pennsylvania, to salvage the gold. The contract states that de Villeroi, "by means of his Invention of a Submarine boat" and at his own expense, would raise the treasure and receive a salvage award of seventy-five percent. At this time, though, no one was quite sure where the boat had gone down, or in how deep of water. At first, some estimated the ship was in only twenty-eight fathoms of water (168 feet), when in fact it was over 8,000 feet below the surface. As would be expected, nothing came of the salvage attempts in the late 1850s, and the issue, and the gold, would lie dormant for over a hundred and twenty years.

Columbus–Am. Discovery Grp. v. Atl. Mutual Ins. Co. [*CADG I*], 974 F.2d 450, 455–57 (4th Cir. 1992).

B

Advances in sonar-search and deep-sea-recovery technology brought renewed interest in locating the *Central America* in the late 1970s and 1980s. Thomas Thompson incorporated the Columbus–America Discovery Group in order to lead the efforts to recover the ship and her golden payload. Through a related business entity, Recovery Limited Partnership, Thompson began soliciting investors to back his venture and [—7—] assembling a crew to help him locate the *Central America*. Relevant to this matter, Thompson executed two documents with each employee—an employment contract and a non-disclosure agreement. The employment contracts were fairly standard, promising a modest daily wage in exchange for services rendered. The non-disclosure agreements, on the other hand, were far more valuable. In exchange for maintaining the secrecy of Thompson's operations, theories, work

product, and the like, each employee was to receive a share of the "net recovery" of the venture. In addition to employing the crew, Recovery Limited rented a side-scan sonar from plaintiff International Deep Sea Survey, Inc. Again, the parties executed a lease agreement and a separate non-disclosure agreement.

Thompson and his colleagues located the *Central America* in September 1988 off the coast of South Carolina. Using a submersible robot invented by Columbus–America, they began removing millions of dollars in gold coins, ingots, and bars from the wreckage. As one might expect, however, the discovery of such a vast sum of wealth inevitably attracted unwanted attention: dozens of attorneys descended upon Columbus–America, hoping to secure a piece of the golden booty for the numerous insurance companies, underwriters, and banks that claimed title to the ship and her payload. Thus began the first round of litigation over the treasures of the *S.S. Central America*.

The insurance companies initially succeeded in establishing ownership over the gold in the face of Columbus–America's claim under the law of finds. *CADG I*, 974 F.2d at 468. The case was remanded back to district court to determine a proper award for Thompson and his colleagues under the law of salvage. *Ibid.* The court indicated in no uncertain terms that Columbus–America should receive "by far the largest share of the treasure" as just compensation for their efforts. *Id.* at 468–69. Indeed, the group did receive the largest share—90% of a golden haul that remains today one of the largest treasure finds in history. *CADG II*, 56 F.3d at 562. As a salvor, Columbus–America never took title to the gold, but it remained in possession of the entire haul as the central marketing authority responsible for liquidating the treasure. *Id.* at 574–75. The Fourth [—8—] Circuit closed this chapter of the litigation by applauding Thompson's efforts: "What Thompson and Columbus–America have accomplished is, by any measure, extraordinary. We can say without hesitation that their story is a paradigm of

American initiative, ingenuity, and determination." *Id.* at 576.

C

One might have hoped that the Fourth Circuit's 1995 opinion would have marked the end of the litigation over the *Central America*. Alas, efforts to market the treasure generated further legal woes. Thompson initially tried to sell the gold through Christie's New York. These efforts failed and resulted in a lawsuit. Thompson looked next to the West Coast, signing an agreement in 1999 with California Gold Marketing Group, LLC on behalf of Recovery Limited and Columbus–America. By this time, Thompson's crew had grown nervous about not having been paid their share of the treasure. Thompson's lawyer responded to these concerns in a March 2000 letter:

> On the marketing front, retail sales have been very robust to date. Three of the largest numismatic dealers in the world are involved, and progress has been encouraging. (*Coin World* and *Numismatic News* have been carrying information about the gold tours, and should be a good source for announcements by the California Gold [Marketing] Group). . . .

> The California Gold [Marketing] Group's purchase of 92.4% of the treasure awarded to Columbus–America has resulted in settlements with Christie's and the Bank of California. The end result appears essentially to be the elimination of those claims, with a pay-off of approximately $43 million. (The newspaper reports on payments of $50 million and $100 million, respectively, are inaccurate).

> While the terms of the agreement are confidential, essentially it provides, in addition to the sums paid Christie's and the Bank of California, for a split of profits between Columbus–America and the California Gold [Marketing] Group, with the percentages varying depending on who procures the buyer's [sic] and the amount of sales made.

> To date, there has been no net profit to Columbus–America. The Group is very hopeful that profits may be obtained within the next 6–12 months, as sales progress.

> It has been, and remains, Tommy's intention to make payment to Don Craft and others of like standing their pro rata portion of the profits due to them under the Non–Disclosure Agreements simultaneously with [—9—] his receipt of any net profits. Tommy is grateful for the work done and is as anxious for net profits as anyone.

> We should have a much better idea of the nature and size of those net profits as sales progress over the next several months.

The plaintiffs allege that Thompson's lawyer further represented that Thompson retained a reversionary interest in the treasure, from which the plaintiffs would assuredly be paid. Subsequent litigation reveled, however, that Thompson sold this reversionary interest, allegedly in a June 2001 amendment to his agreement with California Gold Marketing Group.

D

The latest salvo of litigation began in 2005 and 2006, when various parties brought suit against the defendants in three separate actions filed in the Court of Common Pleas for Franklin County, Ohio. The matters were consolidated, and the defendants removed the action to the United States District Court for the Southern District of Ohio in April 2006. The plaintiffs involved in the instant appeal, referred to throughout the litigation as the "Williamson Plaintiffs," are a group of employees hired to assist in the location and recovery of the *Central America* (Michael E. Williamson, the estate of Don C. Craft,[4] Kirk

---

[4] Mr. Craft passed away early in the course of this litigation, and his estate was substituted as the successor party-in-interest.

O'Donnell, John Lettow, Timothy McGinnis, Fred Newton, William Watson, Chris Hancock, and Dale Schoeneman), as well as the company from which Thompson rented a side-scan sonar, International Deep Sea Survey, Inc. The plaintiffs brought suit against Thompson and the board of directors of Columbus Exploration, LLC[5] ("the individual defendants") and numerous business entities, including Recovery Limited, Columbus–America, and Columbus Exploration ("the entity defendants"). The plaintiffs demanded monetary relief for breach of their non-disclosure agreements, conversion of the recovered gold, and breach of fiduciary duty. The plaintiffs also requested the imposition of a constructive trust upon the [—10—] defendants and an accounting of the defendants' finances. The entity defendants answered by raising a host of affirmative defenses and lodging three counterclaims of their own: breach of contract, civil conspiracy, and unfair competition.

In early 2011, the parties filed cross-motions for summary judgment. In a detailed opinion, the district court: (1) granted summary judgment for all of the defendants as to plaintiffs' claims for conversion, formation of a constructive trust, breach of fiduciary duty, and request for an accounting; (2) granted summary judgment for three entity defendants and four individual defendants on the plaintiffs' breach-of-contract claims, thereby dismissing them from the case entirely; (3) granted summary judgment for the plaintiffs on all of the entity defendants' counterclaims; and (4) ruled that the remaining defendants will be judicially estopped from arguing that the plaintiffs did not perform their contractual obligations under the non-disclosure agreements. *Williamson v. Recovery Ltd. P'ship*, No. 2:06–CV–292, 2011 WL 2181813, at *32 (S.D. Ohio June 3, 2011). The remaining entity defendants gave timely notice of interlocutory appeal of the grant of summary judgment on their counterclaims. This appeal is before us as case number 11-3723.

After the entity defendants filed their initial appeal, the plaintiffs moved for prejudgment attachment to certain assets belonging to Columbus Exploration and Thompson ("the injunction defendants"), as well as a preliminary injunction to prevent both parties from divesting themselves of property that could be used to fulfill a judgment against them. The plaintiffs filed their motion after Columbus Exploration allegedly thwarted a state receivership action by filing a sham bankruptcy petition, which it withdrew several weeks later. In light of this, the plaintiffs sought a security interest in the $250,000 corpus of a severance trust established for the benefit of Thompson, in 500 commemorative gold restrike coins, and in other artifacts recovered from the *Central America*.

The location of the severance-trust corpus and the gold restrike coins was initially unknown to the plaintiffs. During the course of litigating the preliminary-injunction motion, it was discovered that both had gone missing. Over an objection to [—11—] the court's jurisdiction to entertain the motion, the district court: (1) gave the plaintiffs a prejudgment interest in seven crates of artifacts stored in a warehouse in Columbus, Ohio; (2) enjoined Thompson from transferring or selling any portion of the gold restrike coins or the severance-trust *res* in his possession or his residence in Vero Beach, Florida; and (3) enjoined Columbus Exploration from transferring or selling any assets that could be used to satisfy a judgment against it, other than those necessary in the ordinary course of its business. The district court further ordered Thompson to explain what happened to the severance-trust corpus and the gold restrike coins. When he failed to comply with a subsequent order to appear in person before the court, the judge issued a bench warrant for Thompson's arrest. He remains at large today. Through counsel, Thompson and Columbus Exploration took an interlocutory appeal of the injunction order, which is currently before the panel as case no. 12-3949.

---

[5] Columbus Exploration was formed in 1998 in order to market the recovered gold and fulfill the contractual obligations of Recovery Limited.

II

Neither of the orders appealed is final, and this matter accordingly falls outside our jurisdiction to hear appeals from final orders of the district court. *See* 28 U.S.C. § 1291. The plaintiffs do not contest our jurisdiction to hear the appeal of the salvage time bar and the preliminary injunction. They do, however, assert that we lack jurisdiction to hear the entity defendants' appeal of the summary adjudication of their counterclaims and the injunction defendants' prejudgment-attachment order. The entity defendants cite as a jurisdictional basis for the summary-judgment appeal 28 U.S.C. § 1292(a)(3), which gives us authority to hear appeals of "[i]nterlocutory decrees . . . determining the rights and liabilities of the parties to admiralty cases in which appeals from final decrees are allowed." For the order of prejudgment attachment, the injunction-defendants claim that the order had the "practical effect" of a preliminary injunction, and that we thus have jurisdiction under §1292(a)(1).

A

We have not had a prior opportunity to speak authoritatively on 28 U.S.C. §1292(a)(3). The plain language of the statute announces a rather broad exception to the final-judgment rule—the term "admiralty cases" appears to sweep up any claim [—12—] presented in a case in which admiralty jurisdiction has been invoked. The entity defendants argue the same, citing *Roco Carriers, Ltd. v. M/V Nurnberg Express*, 899 F.2d 1292 (2d Cir. 1990). In that case, the Second Circuit allowed Aid Export, a land-based transportation company brought into federal court on a claim pendent to a maritime-shipping suit, to bring an immediate appeal under of § 1292(a)(3) of a grant of summary judgment against it on a state-law conversion claim. *Id.* at 1297. Citing the use of the word "cases," as opposed to "claims," the Second Circuit held that § 1292(a) allowed the state-law defendant to bring an interlocutory appeal simply because its claim was part of a broader suit in admiralty. *Ibid.*

Such a reading gives us pause, however, as it would render the final-judgment rule a nullity in admiralty cases. The Supreme Court has cautioned lower courts to construe exceptions to § 1291 narrowly, so as not to "swallow the general rule that a party is entitled to a single appeal, to be deferred until final judgment has been entered." *Digital Equipment Corp. v. Desktop Direct, Inc.*, 511 U.S. 863, 868 (1994). Furthermore, it is widely accepted that Congress passed §1292(a)(3) with the peculiarities of maritime litigation in mind:

> In admiralty, trials were traditionally bifurcated. First, there would be a trial before the court on the issue of liability. If there was a finding of liability, there would then be a separate hearing before a special master to ascertain damages. These damages hearings were often both lengthy and costly. Congress intended 28 U.S.C. § 1292(a)(3) to permit parties to appeal the finding of liability on the merits, before undergoing the long, burdensome, and perhaps unnecessary damages proceeding. Section 1292(a)(3) was not intended to clutter the federal docket with interlocutory odds and ends.

City of Fort Madison v. Emerald Lady, 990 F.2d 1086, 1089 (8th Cir. 1993) (citations and internal quotation marks omitted). In light of this, the majority of our sister circuits have eschewed the reading adopted by *Roco Carriers* for a narrower interpretation that looks to the nature of each individual claim involved in the interlocutory appeal, as opposed to the nature of the broader suit. *Wingerter v. Chester Quarry Co.*, 185 F.3d 657, 664 (7th Cir. 1998); *Evergreen Int'l Corp. v. Standard Warehouse*, 33 F.3d 420, [—13—] 424–25 (4th Cir. 1994); *City of Fort Madison v. Emerald Lady*, 990 F.2d 1086, 1089 (8th Cir. 1993); *Bodden v. Osgood*, 879 F.2d 184, 186–87 (5th Cir. 1989).

Though the majority's interpretation is not without force, we cannot accept this reading of §1292(a)(3). Contextual exegesis notwithstanding, it is axiomatic that the clearest evidence of congressional intent is the plain language of statute itself. Where the text is plain and unambiguous, we must apply a statute according to its terms. *Carcieri v. Salazar*, 555 U.S. 379, 387 (2009). Section §1292(a)(3) allows for interlocutory appeal of decrees "determining the rights and liabilities of the parties to admiralty cases." There is no ambiguity in Congress's word choice, and we thus cannot adopt a reading that would effectively strike out the word "cases" and replace it with the word "claims." *See Roco Carriers*, 899 F.2d at 1297.

This plain-text reading is bolstered by Rule 9(h)(2) of the Federal Rules of Civil Procedure, which states: "A case that includes an admiralty or maritime claim within this subdivision (h) is an admiralty case within 28 U.S.C. §1292(a)(3)." Neither party cited this highly relevant provision or the compelling notes to Rule 9 from the 1997 Advisory Committee, which specifically and clearly address the issue before us:

A single case can include both admiralty or maritime claims and nonadmiralty claims or parties. This combination reveals an ambiguity in the statement in present Rule 9(h) that an admiralty "claim" is an admiralty "case." An order "determining the rights and liabilities of the parties" within the meaning of §1292(a)(3) may resolve only a nonadmiralty claim, or may simultaneously resolve interdependent admiralty and nonadmiralty claims. Can appeal be taken as to the nonadmiralty matter, because it is part of a case that includes an admiralty claim, or is appeal limited to the admiralty claim?

The courts of appeals have not achieved full uniformity in applying the §1292(a)(3) requirement that an order "determin[e] the rights and liabilities of the parties." It is common to assert that the statute should be construed narrowly, under the general policy that exceptions to the final judgment rule should be construed narrowly. This policy would suggest that the ambiguity should be resolved by limiting the interlocutory appeal right to orders that

determine the rights and liabilities of the parties to an admiralty claim.

A broader view is chosen by this amendment for two reasons. The statute applies to admiralty "cases," and may itself provide for [—14—] appeal from an order that disposes of a nonadmiralty claim that is joined in a single case with an admiralty claim. Although a rule of court may help to clarify and implement a statutory grant of jurisdiction, the line is not always clear between permissible implementation and impermissible withdrawal of jurisdiction. In addition, so long as an order truly disposes of the rights and liabilities of the parties within the meaning of §1292(a)(3), it may prove important to permit appeal as to the nonadmiralty claim. Disposition of the nonadmiralty claim, for example, may make it unnecessary to consider the admiralty claim and have the same effect on the case and parties as disposition of the admiralty claim. Or the admiralty and nonadmiralty claims may be interdependent. An illustration is provided by *Roco Carriers, Ltd. v. M/V Nurnberg Express*, 899 F.2d 1292 (2d Cir. 1990). Claims for losses of ocean shipments were made against two defendants, one subject to admiralty jurisdiction and the other not. Summary judgment was granted in favor of the admiralty defendant and against the nonadmiralty defendant. The nonadmiralty defendant's appeal was accepted, with the explanation that the determination of its liability was "integrally linked with the determination of non-liability" of the admiralty defendant, and that "section 1292(a)(3) is not limited to admiralty claims; instead, it refers to admiralty cases." 899 F.2d at 1297. The advantages of permitting appeal by the nonadmiralty defendant would be particularly clear if the plaintiff had appealed the summary judgment in favor of the admiralty defendant.

The parties do not dispute that Rule 9(h) has been properly invoked in this case—indeed, the plaintiffs argued this very point in the district court when they successfully challenged the defendants' attempt to force a jury trial. While the plaintiffs do argue that §1292(a)(3) applies only when the appellant has pled admiralty as the jurisdictional basis for the issues raised on appeal, such a requirement is without basis in either the text of the statute or the text of Rule 9.

The entity defendants claim that the only issue remaining for trial is the calculation of damages. The plaintiffs do not contest this, and our review of the record has revealed nothing to the contrary. Because the case before the court is an admiralty case under Rule 9(h) and because the district court's summary-judgment order determined the rights and liabilities of the parties, we hold that the order is amenable to interlocutory review under §1292(a)(3) and we will thus address the merits of the entity defendants' appeal in their entirety. [—15—]

B

We next turn to the injunction defendants' appeal of the order of prejudgment attachment and preliminary injunction. The principles to be applied here are relatively straightforward. To the extent that the district court issued a preliminary injunction, we have jurisdiction to review the order. 28 U.S.C. § 1292(a)(1). To the extent that it granted prejudgment security under the laws of Ohio, via Rule 64 of the Federal Rules of Civil Procedure, we lack jurisdiction to hear an immediate appeal. 15A Charles Alan Wright, Arthur R. Miller, et al., *Federal Practice and Procedure* § 3914.2 (West 2013) ("For many years it has been safe to say that generally appeal can be taken from orders that deny security but cannot be taken from orders that grant security."); *see also Hitachi Zosen Clearing, Inc. v. Tek–Matik, Inc.*, 846 F.2d 27, 28–29 (6th Cir. 1988).

According to its order of July 18, 2012, the district court granted the following pretrial relief:

1. The Court orders the attachment of seven (7) crates (or more) of artifacts warehoused on Joyce Avenue, Columbus, Ohio, and owned by Columbus Exploration LLC or any other Defendant Entity. These creates are not to be moved, encumbered or sold without further order of this Court.

2. The court issues a preliminary injunction against Thomas G. Thompson with regard to the five hundred (500) re-strike or commemorative gold coins transferred to him by Columbus Exploration, LLC. . . . [H]e shall not sell, encumber, transfer or diminish in value such coins. . . .

. . .

3. The Court issues a preliminary injunction against Thomas G. Thompson related to the Termination Trust. In the event that the funds received by Thompson from the Termination Trust are still in his possession, such funds are restrained from any transfer or dissipation of any kind subject to further order of this Court. . . .

4. The Court issues a preliminary injunction against Thomas G. Thompson regarding his house located at 135 9th Avenue, Vero Beach, Florida 32962. Thompson shall not sell, encumber, transfer or diminish the value of that real proper[t]y without further order of this Court.

5. The Court issues a preliminary injunction against the Defendant entities prohibiting them from making any transfer of assets beyond those within the normal or ordinary course of business for such [—16—] recurring expenses as are anticipated. Any other transfers require further approval of this Court after notice and hearing.

In large part, the district court ordered injunctive relief, reviewable under §1292(a)(1). The litigants disagree, however, on whether we may review the order insofar as it relates to the crates of artifacts warehoused in Columbus.

On first blush, it would appear that the plaintiffs are correct that we lack jurisdiction. The relief is styled as an "attachment" and granted under Ohio Revised Code § 2715, the section of the state code devoted exclusively to attachment to property. The injunction defendants counter that we must treat the putative attachment order as an injunction because it forbids encumbrance or disposal of the property, giving it the practical effect of an injunction. They correctly note that, for the purposes of determining our jurisdiction under § 1292(a)(1), we look past the labels used by the trial court and to the "nature of the order and the substance of the proceeding below to determine whether the rationale for denying appeal applies." *N.E. Ohio Coal. For Homeless & Serv. Employees Int'l Union, Local 1199 v. Blackwell*, 467 F.3d 999, 1005 (6th Cir. 2006). Orders that have the practical effect of an injunction are subject to interlocutory appeal under § 1292(a)(1) "only if the order has a 'serious, perhaps irreparable, consequence' and the order can be 'effectively challenged' only by means of an immediate appeal." *Booher v. N. Ky. Univ. Bd. of Regents*, 163 F.3d 395, 397 (6th Cir. 1998) (quoting *Carson v. American Brands, Inc.*, 450 U.S. 79, 84 (1981)).

Even if we were to assume that this portion of the order had the practical effect of an injunction, the injunction defendants do not explain how the order results in serious harm to them or why interlocutory appeal is the only avenue of relief available to them. Issues adverted to in a perfunctory manner, without some effort to develop an argument, are deemed forfeited. *United States v. Johnson*, 440 F.3d 832, 846 (6th Cir. 2006). Additionally, it is clear from the record that the district court sought to make the order as minimally invasive as possible, stating that though it was specifically ordering the artifacts to "stay put," the court would timely consider, and be inclined to grant, any reasonable request to make use of the artifacts. We see no serious or irreparable [—17—] consequence flowing from the attachment order, regardless of whether it had an injunctive element to it, and we therefore decline to entertain these issues under § 1292(a)(1).

III

Having determined our jurisdiction, we now turn to a complex procedural issue. The entity defendants argue that the entirety of the plaintiffs' case is time barred under 46 U.S.C. § 80107(c):

A civil action to recover remuneration for giving aid or salvage services must be brought within 2 years after the date the aid or salvage services were given, unless the court in which the action is brought is satisfied that during that 2-year period there had not been a reasonable opportunity to seize the aided or salvaged vessel within the jurisdiction of the court or within the territorial waters of the country of the plaintiff's residence or principal place of business.

According to the entity defendants, the plaintiffs provided services to assist in the salvage of the *Central America* and, by the plain text of the statute, their suit for compensation is subject to a two-year statute of limitation. The entity defendants urge a broad reading of the statute, citing in support the words immediately preceding "salvage services"—"[a] civil action to recover remuneration." The plaintiffs claim that this is not a salvage action and they do not seek a salvage award. Rather, they assert that this is a simple maritime-contract dispute: they complied with the non-disclosure agreements by holding Thompson's works in confidence, but he did not pay according to the terms of the contract.

To be sure, salvage actions have long presented numerous complexities for the federal courts. Add to this the factual peculiarities of a recovery operation for treasures long, and assumed forever, lost at the bottom of the ocean, and even the most seasoned jurist can find himself navigating uncharted waters. We may resolve this issue, however, by noticing two basic points. First, the plaintiffs are not suing on their employment contracts. Rather, they are suing on their non-disclosure agreements, in which they exchanged confidentiality for a percentage of the net recovery from the *Central America.* [—18—] Under no conceivable definition of the term may such a contract be deemed an agreement to provide "salvage services."

Second, to the extent that the entity defendants would have us consider the broader nature of the plaintiffs' job descriptions, it is a fundamental principle of admiralty that one who provides services pursuant to a contract of employment may not be considered a "pure" salvor. Contract salvors are not entitled to a number of special protections afforded to pure salvors, including the right to a salvage award and the right to seize a vessel pending payment. Reading the limitations provision in context with the remainder of the statute, which includes a tolling provision for those who have been unable to arrest the aided or salved vessel, §80107(c) applies only to pure salvors. Accordingly, the limitations provision cannot apply to the plaintiffs.

A

The term "salvage services" is not defined in Title 46. However, the term "salvage" has a long-accepted definition within the law of admiralty:

> Salvage is well defined as the compensation allowed to persons by whose assistance a ship or vessel, or the cargo of the same, or the lives of the persons belonging to the ship or vessel, are saved from danger or loss in cases of shipwreck, derelict capture, or other marine misadventures.

> Other jurists define it as the service which volunteer adventurers spontaneously render to the owners, in the recovery of property from loss or damage at sea under the responsibility of making restitution and with a lien for their reward.

> Persons who render such service are called salvors, and a salvor is defined to be a person who, without any particular relation to the ship in distress, proffers useful service and gives it as a volunteer adventurer without any pre-existing contract that connected him with the duty of employing himself for the preservation of the vessel.

> Enough appears in those definitions to show that the elements necessary to constitute a valid salvage claim are as follows: (1.) A marine peril to the property to be rescued. (2.) Voluntary service not owed to the property as matter of duty. (3.) Success in saving the property or some portion of it from the impending peril.

The Clarita and the Clara, 90 U.S. (23 Wall.) 1, 16 (1874) (footnotes omitted). [—19—]

We may glean from this definition a simple, yet fundamental, characteristic of a salvage action: the assistance provided must be on a volunteer basis, that is, provided without expectation of compensation under a pre-existing agreement. Volunteer, or "pure," salvors hold special place in maritime law that is "utterly at variance with terrene common law." 3A *Benedict on Admiralty* § 1 (Lexis 2013). Two unique entitlements of a pure salvor are the right to a liberal salvage award, typically in excess of the *quantum meruit* of the service provided, *The Blackwall*, 77 U.S. (10 Wall.) 1, 13–14 (1870), and the right to obtain a lien upon and arrest the aided or salved vessel, *The Sabine*, 101 U.S. 384, 386 (1880).

If, however, the services for which the plaintiff seeks payment are due within the scope of a valid contract, he is not entitled to an award as a pure salvor. *See The Camanche*, 75 U.S. (8 Wall.) 448, 477 (1869); *accord Solana v. GSF Dev. Driller I*, 587 F.3d 266, 271 (5th Cir. 2009); *Flagship Marine Servs., Inc. v. Belcher Towing Co.*, 966 F.2d 602, 605 (11th Cir. 1992). Though the mere existence of an agreement to provide a given type of service will not necessarily defeat a claim for a pure salvage award, *Fort Myers Shell &*

Dredging Co. v. Barge NBC 512, 404 F.2d 137, 139 (5th Cir. 1968), "a contract to pay a given sum for the services to be rendered, or a binding engagement to pay at all events, whether successful or unsuccessful in the enterprise, will operate as a bar to a meritorious claim for salvage." *The Camanche*, 75 U.S. (8 Wall.) at 477. Loss of status as a pure salvor strips a plaintiff not only of his right to a salvage award, but also of his ability to seize the aided or salved vessel through a salvage lien. 3A *Benedict on Admiralty* § 159.

B

At the outset, it is questionable whether the plaintiffs are salvors of any kind vis-à-vis the entity defendants. The plaintiffs are not seeking compensation for any act that may even colorably be called salvage. Indeed, the *quid* for which they now seek the promised *quo* is no affirmative act at all—it is silence. The entity defendants ignore that the plaintiffs' breach-of-contract claims are predicated on an alleged breach of the non-disclosure agreements, in which the parties exchanged promises of confidentiality for [—20—] a percentage of the net recovery from the *Central America*. The entity defendants make no attempt to argue that the confidence held pursuant to the non-disclosure agreements constitutes "salvage services." As the previous discussion of "salvage" illuminates, this is with good reason: it would strain all credulity to accept that one who maintains secrecy of his employer's works and writings is the same as one who "assist[s]a ship or vessel, or the cargo of the same, or the lives of the persons belonging to the ship or vessel," thereby saving them "from danger or loss in cases of shipwreck, derelict capture, or other marine misadventures." *See The Clarita and the Clara*, 90 U.S. (23 Wall.) at 16.

The entity defendants' briefing ignores the plain distinction between the compensation due under the employment contract and the compensation due under the non-disclosure agreements, asserting that the plaintiffs' claims "arise from their having provided services in the salvage of the *SS Central America*." Appellant's Br. 34. They seemingly invite us to judge the nature of the plaintiffs'

claims based upon the broader context of the recovery operation. Even if we did, their argument would still fail. It is beyond debate that, to the extent that the plaintiffs provided any salvage services, they did so pursuant to pre-arranged agreements. Accordingly, they cannot be pure salvors. The question thus becomes whether the term "salvage services," as used in § 80107(c), refers solely to acts of pure salvage or includes acts of contractual salvage.

Though § 80107(c) does not define the term, and a precise definition of the term is not readily apparent, "[i]t is a fundamental canon of statutory construction that the words of a statute must be read in their context and with a view to their place in the overall statutory scheme." *Greenbaum v. EPA*, 370 F.3d 527, 535 (6th Cir. 2004) (quoting *FDA v. Brown & Williamson Tobacco Corp.*, 529 U.S. 120, 132–33 (2000)). The subordinate clause at the end of subsection (c) gives courts discretion to toll the two-year statute of limitations if "during that 2-year period there had not been a reasonable opportunity to seize the aided or salvaged vessel . . . ." Of course, a prejudgment lien on an aided or salved vessel is a privilege enjoyed specifically by pure salvors. *See The Sabine*, 101 U.S. at 386 ("Salvors, under the maritime law, have a lien upon the property [—21—] saved . . . . Such a remedy is the one usually pursued, and in view of the fact that the lien is maritime and exists quite independently of possession, it ordinarily affords the best mode of securing the payment of their salvage claims."). It would be exceedingly odd for Congress to have intended to bring both pure and contract salvors within the ambit § 80107(c)'s statute of limitation, and then, without providing any textual delineation, create a tolling provision that is relevant to only one of the two categories of salvors. The more sensible reading of the statute is that it applies only to the group of salvors to whom the entirety of the statute speaks—pure salvors. Accordingly, § 80107(c) cannot apply to the plaintiffs.

IV

The district court granted summary judgment against all three of the entity defendants' counterclaims. The court found that the evidence submitted by the entity defendants was either vague or irrelevant, and thus could not establish the elements of any of the counterclaims, even when viewed in a favorable light. We affirm that decision.

We review the district court's grant of summary judgment *de novo*. *Trs. of the Mich. Laborers' Health Care Fund v. Gibbons*, 209 F.3d 587, 590 (6th Cir. 2000). The decision below may be affirmed only if the pleadings, affidavits, and other submissions show "that there is no genuine dispute as to any material fact and the movant is entitled to judgment as a matter of law." Fed. R. Civ. P. 56(a). In determining whether a genuine issue of material fact exists, we draw all reasonable inferences in favor of the nonmoving party. *See Matsushita Elec. Indus. Co., Ltd. v. Zenith Radio Corp.*, 475 U.S. 574, 587–88 (1986).

The counterclaims are interlinked. The entity defendants claim that the plaintiffs breached their non-disclosure agreements and then conspired to file frivolous suits across the country, all alleging that the defendants were in fact the breaching party, as a means of frustrating business with the California Gold Marketing Group. The breach-of-contract counterclaim is the foundation upon which the civil-conspiracy and unfair- [—22—] competition counterclaims are built. If the breach-of-contract counterclaim does not survive summary judgment, then the remaining counterclaims are doomed as well.

As they did in the court below, the entity defendants refer us to two sets of documents to substantiate their counterclaims: declarations from their attorneys, Robert Robol and David Douglas; and an affidavit from plaintiff Timothy McGinnis, with two attached newspaper articles in which he is quoted discussing his work on the recovery of the *S.S. Central America*. The declarations from the two attorneys contain no evidence relevant to any of the entity defendants' counterclaims. Rather, they are oriented towards refuting the testimony of one of the plaintiffs' witnesses, James Shirley, a retired attorney who represented some of the plaintiffs early on in the litigation and upon whom the plaintiffs rely to introduce documents tending to prove their entitlement to compensation under the non-disclosure agreements.

The statements from McGinnis's affidavit are quotations from two newspaper articles appearing in the *Seattle Times*. In the first of these articles, McGinnis broadly discusses how the deep-sea-sonar scan worked. The second article states that "McGinnis has collected everything he could about the *U.S. Central America* [sic]" and that he has "17-year-old records and folded handwritten notes about the sunken ship" that he intends to pass on to his children. The newspaper clippings confirm the same.

Nothing in McGinnis's affidavit establishes any element of any of the counterclaims against any of the other plaintiffs. To the extent that the entity defendants offer the affidavit and the attached articles as proof that McGinnis himself breached his non-disclosure agreement, this represents nothing more than a scintilla of evidence. *See Hirsch v. CSX Trans., Inc.*, 656 F.3d 359, 362 (6th Cir. 2011). McGinnis's statements are highly generalized in nature and give no indication as to the substance of the documents in his possession. While it is not outside the realm of possibility that some of the documents are covered by the non-disclosure agreement, it is equally possible that they are nothing more than his personal, handwritten reflections on the adventures.

Without any evidence of the subject matter of these documents in the record, no reasonable factfinder could conclude that McGinnis violated his agreement without [—23—] engaging in a large degree of impermissible speculation. *See* Fed. R. Evid. 602. Accordingly, the plaintiffs are entitled to summary judgment on the entity defendants' breach-of-contract claim. Because the civil-conspiracy and unfair-competition counterclaims are predicated on the breach-of-contract counterclaim—and because both are wholly unsubstantiated by the record before us—the plaintiffs are entitled to summary judgment on those issues as well.

V

Finally, the injunction defendants, Thompson and Columbus Exploration, raise a plethora of issues with the district court's injunction order. They challenge the district court's jurisdiction to entertain the preliminary-injunction motion, its authority in equity to grant a preliminary injunction, and the proper exercise of the court's discretion in granting the injunction. They further assert that the $500 bond set by the district court was unconstitutionally low. We reject all of these arguments and affirm the district court.

A

1

The injunction defendants' first two arguments go to the district court's jurisdiction to entertain the plaintiffs' motion for a preliminary injunction and its authority in equity to issue the injunction. They first argue that the Supreme Court's decision in *Grupo Mexicano de Desarrollo v. Alliance Bond Fund*, 527 U.S. 308 (1999), prohibits the issuance of a preliminary injunction on the sale or transfer of assets absent a claim in equity or a valid judgment on which the plaintiff seeks to execute. While the holding of *Grupo Mexicano* provides a colorable basis for the merits of their argument, *id.* at 333, the injunction defendants run into a more basic problem—forfeiture.

Curiously, the injunction defendants seemingly frame the issue before this court as a jurisdictional argument. Appellant's Br. 20 ("[T]he Trial Court did not have jurisdiction in equity to issue a preliminary injunction."). To the extent that they intended to do so, they are several centuries too late in making this argument. *See* [—24—] Judiciary Act of 1789, 1 Stat. 74, 78 (vesting district courts with jurisdiction over "all suits of a civil nature at common law or in equity"). Perhaps the explanation for this odd presentation lies in the manner in which the injunction defendants presented their arguments in the court below. They spent a great deal of time arguing that the district court was deprived of jurisdiction to entertain the preliminary-

injunction motion due to the entity defendants' interlocutory appeal. However, they do not once suggest that, jurisdiction notwithstanding, the district court lacked *authority* to grant the equitable remedy of a preliminary injunction in order to protect a future potential remedy at law. This latter point is the crux of *Grupo Mexicano, see* 527 U.S. at 333 ("Because such a remedy was historically unavailable from a court of equity, we hold that the District Court had no *authority* to issue a preliminary injunction preventing petitioners from disposing of their assets pending adjudication of respondents' contract claim for money damages." (emphasis added)); yet they do not even once cite the opinion, let alone present the argument, in their pleadings below. Accordingly, their argument is forfeited before this court. *Jolivette v. Husted*, 694 F.3d 760, 770 (6th Cir. 2012) ("As a rule, we will not review issues if they are raised for the first time on appeal.").

2

The injunction defendants also argue that the district court was stripped of jurisdiction to entertain the preliminary-injunction motion when the entity defendants took an interlocutory appeal to this court. "The filing of a notice of appeal is an event of jurisdictional significance—it confers jurisdiction on the court of appeals and divests the district court of its control over those aspects of the case involved in the appeal." *Griggs v. Provident Consumer Disc. Co.*, 459 U.S. 56, 58 (1982); *see also United States v. Garcia–Robles*, 562 F.3d 763, 767–68 (6th Cir. 2009). This transfer of power, however, does not effect a total divestiture of jurisdiction from the district court: it retains jurisdiction to enforce its judgment, *City of Cookeville v. Upper Cumberland Elec. Membership Corp.*, 484 F.3d 380, 394 (6th Cir. 2007), to proceed with matters that will aid the appellate process, *Cochran v. Birkel*, 651 F.2d 1219, 1221 (6th Cir. 1981), and to adjudicate matters unrelated to the issues on appeal, *Weaver v. Univ. of* [—25—] *Cincinnati*, 970 F.2d 1523, 1528–29 (6th Cir. 1992). In *Weaver*, in particular, we held that "an appeal from an interlocutory order does not divest the trial court of jurisdiction to continue deciding other issues involved in the case." 970 F.2d at 1528–29.

The preliminary injunction here is one of those "other issues" over which the trial court retains jurisdiction. The plaintiffs moved for the injunction upon information that Columbus Exploration was approaching insolvency. The plaintiffs' desire for security is particularly understandable in light of the fact that the plaintiffs had information suggesting that Columbus Exploration was abusing the federal bankruptcy courts to evade a state receivership action.

The injunction defendants assert that the injunction is inextricably intertwined with their interlocutory appeal. However, it is a basic legal principle that the right and the remedy are two analytically distinct aspects of a suit. *Cf. Davis v. Passman*, 441 U.S. 228, 239 (1979) ("[T]he question whether a litigant has a 'cause of action' is analytically distinct and prior to the question of what relief, if any, a litigant may be entitled to receive."). Even if we accept *arguendo* the injunction defendants' assertion that their appeal may negate the plaintiffs' entitlement to a remedy by disproving their cause of action, the plaintiffs' efforts to ensure that a remedy may still be had if they prevail on appeal does not affect the merits of the defendants' appellate argument against the cause of action. We therefore affirm the district court's jurisdiction to entertain the request for a preliminary injunction.

B

We next move to the substance of the preliminary injunction. When considering a motion for a preliminary injunction, the district court must consider and balance four factors: "(1) whether the movant has a strong likelihood of success on the merits; (2) whether the movant would suffer irreparable injury without the injunction; (3) whether issuance of the injunction would cause substantial harm to others; and (4) whether the public interest would be served by issuance of the injunction." *Chabad of S. Ohio & Congregation Lubavitch v. City of Cincinnati*, 363 F.3d 427, 432 (6th Cir. 2004).

We review the district court's overall decision to grant the injunction for an [—26—] abuse of discretion, deferring to its fact finding under a clear-error standard and reviewing its decisions of law *de novo*. *Ibid.*

The injunction defendants claim that the district court erred as a matter of law in its analysis of the first, second, and fourth factors. Scrutiny of their argument reveals, however, that all of their complaints against the district court's ruling relate to its fact finding and general balancing of the factors. We must therefore give deference to the district court in our analysis of each of the defendants' arguments.

They first claim that the district court erred in finding that the plaintiffs had a substantial likelihood of success on the merits of their breach-of-contract claims. The district court previously held that all of the defendants are judicially estopped from claiming that the plaintiffs did not fulfill the terms of their non-disclosure agreements, as the defendants previously claimed in the initial round of litigation in the Fourth Circuit that their salvage award should take into account the money they will have to pay the plaintiffs pursuant to their non-disclosure agreements. *Williamson*, 2011 WL 2181813, at *24–25. Accordingly, the district court focused its injunction analysis on whether the plaintiffs had a substantial likelihood of showing a net recovery from the salvage operation, thus triggering the plaintiffs' contractual entitlements to a share of the profits. The court found a substantial likelihood of successfully proving profits by referring to data produced during an external audit of Recovery Limited and Columbus Exploration. The data revealed that Thompson and a number of outsiders, many of whom with a lower payment priority than the defendants, had received substantial sums of money despite repeated representations to the plaintiffs that no one had yet been paid. The injunction defendants offer no evidence demonstrating that the district court clearly erred in this determination.

The injunction defendants next charge that the court abused its discretion in finding that

Columbus Exploration's precarious financial situation demonstrated that the plaintiffs would suffer irreparable harm without the injunction. They claim that, regardless of Columbus Exploration's financial situation, the equitable remedy of an injunction is inappropriate in a situation such as this, where the ultimate remedy sought [—27—] by the plaintiffs is a remedy in law compensable with money. To a substantial degree, this is a repackaging of the defendants' forfeited *Grupo Mexicano* argument. It is sufficient to note, however, that the majority in *Grupo Mexicano* specifically reserved the question of whether an injunction to protect a legal remedy would be appropriate in cases where the defendants have engaged in fraudulent behavior, 527 U.S. at 325 n.7, and a number of our sister circuits have interpreted *Grupo Mexicano* to "exempt[] from its proscription against preliminary injunctions freezing assets cases involving . . . fraudulent conveyances." *Iantosca v. Step Plan Servs., Inc.*, 604 F.3d 24, 33 (1st Cir. 2010) (internal quotation marks omitted); *see also Johnson v. Couturier*, 572 F.3d 1067, 1083–84 (9th Cir. 2009); *Animale Grp., Inc. v. Sunny's Perfume, Inc.*, 256 F. App'x 707, 709 (5th Cir. 2007); *Kennedy Bldg. Assocs. v. CBS Corp.*, 476 F.3d 530, 535 (8th Cir. 2007). We agree and join our sister circuits.

The district court was well within its sound discretion to grant an injunction in this case. Indeed, the genesis of the motion for a preliminary injunction was a bankruptcy filing by Columbus Exploration that reeked of fraud. We further note that a panel of this circuit has previously upheld a substantial sanction against Columbus Exploration, Thompson, and others for their bad-faith failure to comply with a court-ordered audit. *See generally Williamson v. Recovery Ltd. P'ship*, 467 F. App'x 382 (6th Cir. 2012). The aforementioned audit itself, as referenced by the district court, suggests that Columbus Exploration engaged in a number of accounting irregularities and questionable financial transactions. And, though it occurred after the issuance of the injunction, it is a rather damning indictment of the defendants' behavior that one of the parties to this very issue, Thomas Thompson, is presently a wanted fugitive for his behavior during the course of this litigation.[6]

The injunction defendants also contend that the district court erred in finding that the public interest would be served by issuing the injunction. By the district court's own statement, the public-interest factor did not weigh heavily in the plaintiffs' favor. But [—28—] neither did it weigh against them. The injunction defendants' analysis of this factor consists of yet another block quote from *Grupo Mexicano*. Appellant's Br. 39. Their cursory analysis fails to demonstrate that the district court abused its discretion in assessing this element or in its overall decision to grant the injunction. We therefore affirm the district court.

C

As a final matter, the injunction defendants assert that the district court abused its discretion by setting a $500 bond for the preliminary injunction. The district court, however, did not set the bond for the preliminary injunction. It set the bond for the prejudgment attachment on the crates of artifacts. As discussed earlier, the injunction defendants have not demonstrated how the order results in serious or irreparable consequence to them, and we therefore do not have jurisdiction to entertain arguments on this issue. Furthermore, the district court explained that it chose to set this lower bond amount because it was leaving the crates in the possession of the defendants and allowing them wide latitude to move the court for permission to use the artifacts. This decision strikes us as eminently reasonable.

VI

For the foregoing reasons, we **AFFIRM** the judgments of the district court, except as to its order of prejudgment attachment of certain

---

[6] Though we decline to exercise our discretion to dismiss Thompson's appeal *sua sponte* under the fugitive-disentitlement doctrine, his flagrant contempt may well serve as a basis for this court and the district court to deny him future access to judicial process, unless and until he turns himself in.

artifacts, as to which we lack jurisdiction to entertain the appeal.

United States Court of Appeals
for the Sixth Circuit

No. 12-4377

MARATHON ASHLAND PETROLEUM
vs.
WILLIAMS

Upon Petition for Review of a Decision and Order of the Benefits Review Board. Nos. OWCP No. 06-1560; BRB No. 12-0051.

Decided: October 24, 2013

Citation: 733 F.3d 182, 1 Adm. R. 365 (6th Cir. 2013).

Before **COOK, GRIFFIN** and **KETHLEDGE,** Circuit Judges.

[—1—] **GRIFFIN,** Circuit Judge:

Petitioners Marathon Ashland Petroleum and Marathon Ashland Petroleum Company, LLC ("Marathon") appeal—for the second time—a decision of the Benefits Review Board of the U.S. Department of Labor affirming an order of an administrative law judge awarding permanent and total disability benefits to respondent Bill Williams under the Longshore and Harbor Workers' Compensation Act, [—2—] 33 U.S.C. § 901, et seq. In adjudicating Marathon's first petition for review, a panel of this court declined to address the substance of Marathon's challenge and instead remanded for further proceedings because we held that the administrative record was inadequate regarding the date on which Williams became eligible for benefits. *See Marathon Ashland Petroleum v. Williams,* 384 F. App'x 476 (6th Cir. 2010). On remand, the ALJ and the board discussed in great detail the precise date on which Williams became eligible for permanent and total disability benefits. In its second petition for review, Marathon advances the same arguments that the previous panel did not consider in the first petition, which are that the board erred in affirming the ALJ's findings that Williams is permanently and totally disabled and that he is unable to perform the alternative employment identified by Marathon's vocational expert. For the reasons that follow, we deny the petition and

grant Williams leave to file a motion for attorney fees under 33 U.S.C. § 928(a).

I.

The following background facts are taken from this court's previous opinion in *Marathon Ashland Petroleum v. Williams,* 384 F. App'x 476 (6th Cir. 2010).

Bill Williams had worked at Marathon's Ashland, Kentucky, facility for twenty-five years, most recently as a senior barge welder. His job required considerable overhead heavy lifting, such as repeatedly carrying 150-pound weights. Williams alleged that he sustained a long thoracic nerve injury to his right shoulder while replacing parts of a barge at work on February 13, 2003. He had been experiencing pains in his right shoulder and right arm six to eight months prior to the accident, and his injury was likely the result of the cumulative effect of his heavy lifting. Since the injury, Williams has not returned to work and has been seen by multiple physicians. These physicians, as explained more fully below, do not agree on a common diagnosis for Williams.

Three days after the accident, Williams began treatment with Dr. Michael Goodwin, an orthopedist, who ultimately diagnosed him with a long thoracic nerve problem. Dr. Goodwin continued to see Williams roughly once a month until Dr. Goodwin diagnosed him as permanently unable to work in July 2003. Despite this diagnosis, on March 30, 2004, Dr. Goodwin provided Williams with specific restrictions, including a prohibition on lifting more than five pounds with his right arm and all [—3—] overhead work. Dr. Goodwin wrote a letter to Marathon on June 22, 2005, indicating that Williams could not return to work as a welder, since it required heavy lifting and overhead work. Following an October 3, 2005, visit, Dr. Goodwin opined that Williams' condition would never improve.

Dr. Goodwin also referred Williams to Dr. John Brems, an orthopedist and shoulder specialist. On April 17, 2003, Dr. Brems recommended that Williams cease work until September 2003 and undergo an Electromyogram test ("EMG") in August to determine if the nerve was healing. Dr. Goodwin, however, did not perform the repeat EMG because, as he explained in his deposition testimony, he was more interested in clinical recovery than nerve studies.

On May 25, 2004, Marathon sent Williams to Dr. Michael Best, an orthopedic surgeon and expert in long thoracic nerve injuries. The visit, and another on March 1, 2005, lasted approximately five minutes each. Dr. Best agreed with Dr. Brems' treatment recommendation and had Williams undergo two EMGs and two functional capacity exams. Dr. Joseph Zerga performed the EMGs and concluded after Williams' EMG in July 2004 that Williams could not perform the work of a barge welder or any other work that required heavy lifting above shoulder-level on his right-hand side but could do activity that did not require heavy lifting. Dr. Zerga performed another EMG in November 2004 and concluded that Williams' nerve injury had healed.

Williams' second exam with Dr. Best, which occurred on March 1, 2005, showed that Williams' long thoracic nerve injury had healed. Dr. Best had Williams undergo functional capacity evaluations and concluded that Williams possessed a full range of motion with no strength deficit and had no long-term or permanent impairment. He therefore considered Williams capable of returning to his former welding position, which had since been modified to include the use of hoists and an additional individual to assist with lifting and carrying duties. Despite this conclusion, Dr. Best noted that Williams' efforts throughout testing were inconsistent and that he was unaware of the specifics of Williams' prior job description. Even more, Dr. Best later revised his prior opinion and concluded that Williams was not capable of meeting the demands of his former position and that his safe-work capabilities were within the medium to heavy work category.

Based on Dr. Best's March exam, Marathon sent Williams a return-to-work notice on May 12, 2005. Williams reported to work on May 31, 2005, but told Marathon officials that he could not perform his duties. In the meantime, Williams continued to refrain from working. More than a year later, Marathon had a vocational expert prepare a [—4—] transferable skills analysis/Labor Market Survey report to determine Williams' capabilities for alternate employment. The report noted that Williams could not return to his pre-injury employer as a welder/longshoreman, but listed nine alternate positions that he could perform. The expert completed a second Labor Market Survey on October 30, 2006, which listed ten employers within thirty miles of Ashland, Kentucky, who indicated they were hiring for positions Williams was capable of performing. Williams testified that he did not contact any of the prospective alternate employers because he had a foot gout ailment.

Following Williams' claim for Longshore Act benefits, the ALJ entered an order on May 7, 2008, awarding Williams total disability compensation under the [Act]. The ALJ determined that Williams reached maximum medical improvement ("MMI") on May 31, 2005. MMI is reached at that point where a physician believes that further treatment will not improve a claimant's condition. As a result, the ALJ awarded Williams temporary total disability benefits from February 15, 2003, through May 31, 2005, and permanent total disability benefits thereafter. The ALJ found that Williams could not return to his former barge-welding position at Marathon and that Marathon had not satisfied its burden of establishing the availability of suitable alternate employment. The ALJ credited Dr. Goodwin's opinion of October 5, 2005, that Williams' shoulder would never improve and discredited Dr. Best's opinion because he indicated he was unaware of the physical requirements of Williams' job. Furthermore, the ALJ credited Williams' own testimony.

Marathon appealed the ALJ's decision to the [benefits review board], which affirmed the decision on January 27, 2009. Marathon then petitioned this [c]ourt for review.

Id. at 477–78 (internal quotation marks and citation omitted).

After reviewing the administrative record, this court concluded: "we find the ALJ's reasoning for its conclusion that Williams reached MMI on May 31, 2005, and is therefore entitled to receive permanent disability benefits from that date, to be 'inadequate . . . to accommodate a thorough review.'" *Id.* at 479 (quoting *Dir., Office of Workers' Comp. Programs v. Congleton*, 743 F.2d 428, 429 (6th Cir. 1984)). Our court explained:

According to Dr. Best, Williams reached MMI on March 1, 2005. The parties stipulated that, according to Dr. Goodwin, Williams has yet to [—5—] reach MMI. Yet, Dr. Goodwin's office notes from October 3, 2005, indicate that he did not anticipate that Williams' shoulder would ever improve. The ALJ found that Williams' attempt to return to work on May 31, 2005, established that this was his date of MMI. We question whether this was appropriate. While Williams' inability to perform his prior job duties may indicate that he was permanently disabled as of May 31, 2005, it does not necessarily indicate that this was the date he reached MMI. Especially given that Williams was examined by Dr. Goodwin on two

occasions subsequent to May 31, 2005, we think the ALJ's explanation for establishing May 31, 2005, as the date of MMI needs to be more thoroughly explained.

Id. We therefore remanded for further administrative proceedings.

On remand, the ALJ determined that, based on Dr. Goodwin's controlling medical opinion, Williams reached MMI on October 3, 2005, not May 31, 2005. Other than altering the MMI date, the benefits award remained unchanged. The benefits review board affirmed, and Marathon's timely petition for review followed.

II.

A.

Our review of decisions of an ALJ and the benefits review board is limited. *Pittsburgh & Conneaut Dock Co. v. Dir., Office of Workers' Comp. Programs*, 473 F.3d 253, 258 (6th Cir. 2007). An ALJ's decision is reviewed to determine whether it is consistent with applicable law and supported by substantial evidence. *Id.* "Substantial evidence is more than a scintilla of evidence but less than a preponderance and is such relevant evidence as a reasonable mind might accept as adequate to support a conclusion." *Id.* at 259 (internal quotation marks and citation omitted). Our scope of review is "exceedingly narrow" when the question is whether the ALJ reached the correct result after weighing conflicting medical evidence. *Id.* (internal quotation marks and citation omitted). As for the board's decision, we review its legal conclusions de novo and independently review the record to see if it properly determined whether the ALJ's findings are supported by substantial evidence. *Id.* at 258. "The record must be [—6—] reviewed as a whole, including whatever in the record fairly detracts from its weight." *Id.* at 259 (internal quotation marks and citation omitted).

B.

The parties dispute whether the board erred in affirming the ALJ's determination that Williams was permanently and totally disabled as of October 3, 2005. Disability claims under the Longshore Act are governed by a burden-shifting scheme. *Morehead Marine Servs., Inc. v. Washnock*, 135 F.3d 366, 372 (6th Cir. 1998). A claimant establishes a prima facie case of total disability by showing that he can no longer perform his "usual work" because of a work-related injury. *Id.*; *see also Bunge Corp. v. Carlisle*, 227 F.3d 934, 941 (7th Cir. 2000) ("To gain an award of benefits for total disability under the [Longshore Act], a claimant must first establish a prima facie case by demonstrating that he cannot perform his prior employment due to the effects of a work-related injury."). A claimant's "usual work" is defined by his regular duties at the time of his injury. *Manigault v. Stevens Shipping Co.*, 22 Ben. Rev. Bd. Serv. 332 (1989). In determining whether a claimant can return to his "usual work," the ALJ must compare the claimant's medical restrictions with the physical requirements of his job. *See Newport News Shipbuilding & Dry Dock Co. v. Riley*, 262 F.3d 227, 232 (4th Cir. 2001) ("Whether an injury is a disability is determined by comparing the employee's medical restrictions to her job responsibilities."). If a claimant establishes a prima facie case, "the burden shifts to the employer to demonstrate the availability of suitable alternative employment that the claimant is capable of performing in the geographical area and that he or she could secure if he or she diligently tried." *Washnock*, 135 F.3d at 372; *see also Universal Mar. Corp. v. Moore*, 126 F.3d 256, 264 (4th Cir. 1997) (employer rebuts a prima facie case of disability "by presenting evidence of other jobs that are available in the relevant geographic market for which the claimant is physically and educationally qualified").

The board did not err in concluding that the record contains substantial evidence to support the ALJ's finding that Williams established a prima facie case because he cannot return to his "usual work" as a senior barge welder. First, Dr. Goodwin, [—7—]

Williams' treating doctor who is board certified in orthopedic surgery, testified that Williams would not be able to return to his previous position because his permanent right-shoulder weaknesses and functional limitations, which include a twenty-pound lift restriction upon his right arm and no overhead work, prevent him from performing the very heavy-duty work of a barge welder. Second, Williams, a twenty-five year veteran employee of Marathon, testified that there was simply "no way" he could return to his former position. The ALJ placed "great weight" on Williams' testimony. Third, Dr. Kleykamp, Williams' general care physician, opined that because Williams cannot lift or work overhead, he is unable to perform the duties associated with a senior barge welder.

Additionally, and contrary to Marathon's assertion, the board and the ALJ did not irrationally discount the conflicting medical opinion of Dr. Best, Marathon's review doctor. Although Dr. Best opined that Williams was fully healed and ready to return to work in March 2005 with no functional limitations, Williams treated with Dr. Goowin three times *after* Dr. Best last saw him, and Dr. Goodwin observed that the winging of Williams' right scapula was still present and opined that his patient had not yet recovered and was unlikely to ever fully recover. And although Dr. Best opined that Williams could return to work because his former position had since been modified to reduce his work load, as the board correctly noted, this opinion does not support a finding that he could return to the "usual work" Williams performed at the time of injury. Also, Williams testified that when he attempted to return to work in May 2005, he could not perform even the "modified" position. Ultimately, the ALJ acted within her discretion when crediting Williams' testimony and the medical opinion of his treating doctor over that of Marathon's review doctor. *See Bunge*, 227 F.3d at 940 ("[T]he ALJ determines the weight to be accorded to evidence and makes credibility determinations. Moreover, where the testimony of medical experts is at issue, the ALJ is entitled to accept any part of an expert's testimony or reject it completely."). Accordingly, the board did not err in affirming the ALJ's determination that Williams established a prima facie case of total disability. [—8—]

C.

Because Williams established a prima facie case, the burden shifts to Marathon to "demonstrate the availability of suitable alternative employment that the claimant is capable of performing in the geographical area and that he or she could secure if he or she diligently tried." *Washnock*, 135 F.3d at 372. To meet this burden, Marathon must offer sufficient evidence from which the ALJ could determine that there were jobs available in Williams' community that he could likely secure and realistically perform, taking into consideration his functional capabilities, age, background, education, and training. *See Bunge*, 227 F.3d at 941; *Moore*, 126 F.3d at 264; *Louisiana Ins. Guar. Ass'n v. Abbott*, 40 F.3d 122, 127 (5th Cir. 1994).

The board did not err in affirming the ALJ's determination that Marathon had failed to carry its burden of identifying "suitable alternative employment" that Williams is capable of performing. We conclude that the decision by the board is supported by substantial evidence. Marathon's vocational expert Julie Hathaway identified twenty jobs in two separate reports that she believed Williams could perform. However, she failed to consider Dr. Goodwin's work restrictions when drafting her report, which the ALJ determined were controlling. For example, Hathaway included a number of sedentary and light duty jobs in her report, but provided no information as to whether those jobs complied with Dr. Goodwin's restrictions, specifically the prohibition on overhead lifting. Instead, the jobs she identified are based on Dr. Best's opinion of Williams' abilities, which the ALJ afforded little weight. If—as is the case here—an employer's vocational expert does not identify jobs compatible with the claimant's work restrictions, the expert's opinion cannot satisfy the employer's burden of establishing suitable alternative employment. *Uglesich v. Stevedoring Servs. of America*, 24 Ben. Rev. Bd. Serv. 180 (1991). Put a different way, the jobs in Hathaway's

reports are truly "mirages" as Williams suggests because they are based on functional limitations contained in a discredited medical opinion and are not jobs that Williams can "realistically perform." *New Orleans (Gulfwide) Stevedores v. Turner*, 661 F.2d 1031, 1043 (5th Cir. 1981). The board therefore properly affirmed the ALJ's finding that [—9—] Marathon failed to rebut Williams' prima facie case of disability. Accordingly, we deny Marathon's petition for review.

III.

Finally, Williams requests leave to file a motion for appellate attorney fees. Pursuant to 33 U.S.C. § 928(a), a Longshore Act claimant who utilizes the services of an attorney and successfully prosecutes a disputed liability claim for benefits is entitled to an award of attorney fees for work done on appeal from the board. *See* 33 U.S.C. § 928(a) ("If the employer . . . declines to pay any compensation on . . . a claim . . . on the ground that there is no liability . . . and the person seeking benefits shall thereafter have utilized the services of an attorney at law in the successful prosecution of his claim, there shall be awarded . . . a reasonable attorney's fee against the employer . . . in an amount approved by the . . . court . . . which shall be paid directly by the employer . . . to the attorney for the claimant in a lump sum after the compensation order becomes final."); 20 C.F.R. § 702.132 ("Any person seeking a fee for services performed on behalf of a claimant with respect to claims filed under the [Longshore] Act shall make application therefor to the . . . court . . . before whom the services were performed[.]"); *see also Ford Aerospace & Commc'ns Corp. v. Boling*, 684 F.2d 640, 643 (9th Cir. 1982) (court of appeals has authority to grant attorney fees for work done on appeal from the board, but no authority to grant fees for work at the administrative level).

We grant the request by Williams to file a motion for appellate attorney fees. Williams may file within 21 days of the date of this opinion a motion for attorney fees, supported by an affidavit of counsel. Marathon may respond within 14 days thereafter. We retain further jurisdiction regarding the award of attorney's fees.

IV.

For these reasons, we deny the petition and grant respondent Williams leave to file a motion for attorney fees under 33 U.S.C. §928(a).

United States Court of Appeals for the Seventh Circuit

United States Court of Appeals
for the Seventh Circuit

No. 12-3310

BABA-DAINJA EL
vs.
AMERICREDIT FINANCIAL SERVICES, INC.

Appeal from the United States District Court for the
Northern District of Illinois, Eastern Division

Decided: March 20, 2013

Citation: 710 F.3d 748, 1 Adm. R. 372 (7ᵗʰ Cir. 2013).

Before **POSNER, WOOD,** and **TINDER,** Circuit Judges.

[—1—] **POSNER,** Circuit Judge:

The plaintiff bought a used pickup truck in 2011 for $28,000 and financed the purchase by means of a six-year installment contract that specified an interest rate of 23.9 percent. The dealer who sold him the truck assigned the contract to AmeriCredit. But after making the first installment the plaintiff sent his new creditor a copy of the installment contract that he had stamped "accepted for value and [—2—] returned for value for settlement and closure," and told AmeriCredit to collect the balance of the money due it under the contract from the U.S. Treasury. AmeriCredit repossessed the truck, sold it, and billed the plaintiff $11,322.28 to cover the difference between the price at which the truck had been resold and the unpaid balance on the installment contract.

The plaintiff responded by suing AmeriCredit and two of its officers in a federal district court in Illinois for $34 million in compensatory damages and $2.2 billion in punitive damages. Needless to say, he was proceeding pro se. The district judge couldn't make sense of the complaint and dismissed it as being frivolous. Frivolous it is, though not completely unintelligible. It has the earmarks of the "Sovereign Citizens" movement. As explained by the FBI, "Sovereign citizens view the USG [U.S. government] as bankrupt and without tangible assets; therefore, the USG is believed to use citizens to back US currency. Sovereign citizens believe the USG operates solely on a credit system using American citizens as collateral. Sovereign citizens exploit this belief by filing fraudulent financial documents charging their debt to the Treasury Department." Federal Bureau of Investigation, "Sovereign Citizens: An Introduction for Law Enforcement" 3 (Nov. 2010), http://info.publicintelligence.net/FBI-SovereignCitizens.pdf (visited March 6, 2013).

The plaintiff based federal jurisdiction on the admiralty and diversity jurisdictions of the federal courts. Admiralty jurisdiction over his case may seem [—3—] unavailable to him on two grounds: the case has nothing to do with maritime activities; and, "in the absence of diversity of citizenship, it is essential to jurisdiction that a substantial federal question should be presented." *Hagans v. Lavine*, 415 U.S. 528, 537 (1974); *see also Frederick v. Marquette National Bank*, 911 F.2d 1, 2 (7ᵗʰ Cir. 1990); *Beauchamp v. Sullivan*, 21 F.3d 789, 790 (7th Cir. 1994); *Dixon v. Coburg Dairy, Inc.*, 369 F.3d 811, 817 n. 5 (4th Cir. 2004). The first ground is solid, but not the second. Article III, section 2 of the Constitution confers federal jurisdiction over admiralty cases. But cases don't have to arise under federal law in order to be within the admiralty jurisdiction, *Romero v. International Terminal Operating Co.*, 358 U.S. 354 (1959)—they just have to involve maritime activities. Often, however, they do arise from federal law, either statutory or judge-made. It is unclear what the plaintiff's admiralty claim arises from, but clear that the claim is not within the admiralty jurisdiction because it has no relation to maritime activities. (The Sovereign Citizens movement does not recognize the limitation of the admiralty jurisdiction to maritime activities. *See* "Why We Are in the Admiralty Jurisdiction," Apr. 18, 2004, http://freedomschool.com/law/Admiralty.htm (visited March 7, 2013), where we read, for example, that "any of the actors working for the United States are vessels . . . . We are all vessels; human bags carrying 'sea water.' ")

Dismissals because of absence of federal jurisdiction ordinarily are without prejudice— "dismissal [for want of federal jurisdiction] with prejudice is inappropriate because such a dismissal may improperly prevent a litigant from refiling his complaint in another court that [—4—] does have jurisdiction..., and perhaps more essentially, once a court determines it lacks jurisdiction over a claim, it perforce lacks jurisdiction to make any determination of the merits of the underlying claim." *Brereton v. Bountiful City Corp.*, 434 F.3d 1213, 1217 (10th Cir. 2006). We added the qualifier "ordinarily" for two reasons. The first is the sensible remark in *Caribbean Broadcasting System, Ltd. v. Cable & Wireless P.L.C.*, 148 F.3d 1080, 1091 (D.C. Cir. 1998), that "in rare circumstances, a district court may use its inherent power to dismiss with prejudice (as a sanction for misconduct) even a case over which it lacks jurisdiction, and its decision to do so is reviewed for abuse of discretion." We return to this qualification at the end of the opinion.

Second, if the reason there's no federal jurisdiction is the plaintiff's having predicated jurisdiction on a frivolous federal claim, dismissal with prejudice is appropriate, *Beauchamp v. Sullivan*, *supra*, 21 F.3d at 790-91, for such a suit will go nowhere in any court. This almost certainly is the case insofar as the plaintiff's admiralty claim is concerned, if that claim is founded on federal law (though if not it's still outside admiralty jurisdiction, as we've pointed out). But he invoked diversity jurisdiction as well, and if there was diversity jurisdiction but the claim asserted was frivolous the case should have been dismissed with prejudice. When a case of which the court has jurisdiction is dismissed because it fails to state a claim (which a frivolous suit obviously fails to do), the dismissal is a merits determination and is therefore with prejudice. The difference between a federal-question case that is frivolous and a diversity case that is frivolous is that the latter case but [—5—] not the former is within federal jurisdiction, because a substantial claim is not a condition of diversity jurisdiction.

The district court dismissed the entire complaint without prejudice. Indeed, remarking that the "inordinately high interest rate" in the installment contract (almost 24 percent) might violate Illinois's usury law, he invited the plaintiff to file an amended complaint. The plaintiff did so but did not take the judge's hint about usury. Had he done so, he would soon have hit a dead end. Illinois does not recognize a common law claim for usury, *Tennant v. Joerns*, 160 N.E. 160, 162-63 (Ill. 1928) (per curiam); *Sweeney v. Citicorp Person-to-Person Financial Center, Inc.*, 510 N.E.2d 93, 98 (Ill. App. 1987), and the Illinois Motor Vehicle Retail Installment Sales Act, 815 ILCS 375/21, provides that "notwithstanding the provisions of any other statute, for motor vehicle retail installment contracts executed after September 25, 1981, there shall be no limit on the finance charges which may be charged, collected, and received." *See General Motors Acceptance Corp. v. Kettelson*, 580 N.E.2d 187 (Ill. App. 1991); *cf. In re Oakes*, 267 F.2d 516, 518 (7th Cir. 1959) (Illinois law). Instead the plaintiff refiled his original complaint with immaterial changes. The judge again dismissed the complaint, but this time ruled (incorrectly as we'll see) that it had successfully invoked diversity jurisdiction; and so this time he made the dismissal a dismissal on the merits and therefore with prejudice, as we suggested is the proper procedure when a claim within the diversity jurisdiction is frivolous.

AmeriCredit filed a counterclaim to the amended complaint, seeking the $11,322.28 that it was out plus [—6—] prejudgment interest and attorneys' fees. It did not seek, and could not, for a mere breach of contract, have obtained, punitive damages. *Morrow v. L.A. Goldschmidt Associates, Inc.*, 492 N.E.2d 181, 183 (Ill. 1986). (The two officers whom the plaintiff had sued were not counterclaimants; the $11,322.28 was owed to AmeriCredit, not to them.) It might have charged the plaintiff with fraud, in which event it could have sought punitive damages; but it did not. The plaintiff did not answer the counterclaim and eventually the judge entered a default judgment for $13,582, plus costs, in favor of AmeriCredit.

The plaintiff has appealed. The appeal tracks his submission in the district court. In their brief in response the defendants argue that the district court never acquired jurisdiction over the plaintiff's suit, because the only possible basis for federal jurisdiction was diversity of citizenship and the complaint didn't state a colorable claim for monetary relief in excess of $75,000, as the diversity statute requires. 28 U.S.C. § 1332(a).

If there is no jurisdiction over the plaintiff's suit, there would be jurisdiction over the counterclaim only if, were it filed as a free-standing suit, it would be within federal jurisdiction. *See Barefoot Architect, Inc. v. Bunge*, 632 F.3d 822, 836 (3d Cir. 2011); *Safeco Ins. Co. v. City of White House*, 36 F.3d 540, 546 (6th Cir. 1994). The defendants' counterclaim is based exclusively on state law, so the only basis of federal jurisdiction is the diversity jurisdiction, which requires that the parties be of diverse citizenship and the amount in controversy exceed $75,000. The defendants' brief asks us to affirm the default judgment but does not contend that the counter- [—7—] claim satisfied the amount in controversy requirement. The plaintiff's opening and reply briefs don't mention the counterclaim.

We ordered the defendants' brief stricken because it lacked an adequate jurisdictional statement. The defendants filed an amended brief. The jurisdictional statement in it states that the plaintiff's suit is within diversity jurisdiction because it "alleges that the matter in controversy exceeds the sum or value of $75,000.00, exclusive of interest and costs" and that the plaintiff is a citizen of Illinois and the three defendants are citizens of Delaware (AmeriCredit) and Texas (AmeriCredit and the two officers). The brief adds that the district court had supplemental jurisdiction over the counterclaim, 28 U.S.C. §1367, and repeats the request in the stricken brief that we affirm the default judgment.

The revised jurisdictional statement is riddled with errors. The fact that the plaintiff *alleged* an amount in controversy in excess of $75,000—in fact in excess of $2 billion—does not establish that this *is* the amount in controversy. "[I]f from the face of the pleadings, it is apparent, to a legal certainty, that the plaintiff cannot recover the amount [that is, an amount required to maintain a diversity suit] claimed or if, from the proofs, the court is satisfied to a like certainty that

the plaintiff never was entitled to recover that amount, . . . the suit will be dismissed." *St. Paul Mercury Indemnity Co. v. Red Cab Co.*, 303 U.S. 283, 289 (1938). It is a legal certainty that the plaintiff is entitled to recover nothing. Since his suit is therefore not within federal jurisdiction (for remember that his invocation of admiralty jurisdiction [—8—] is also groundless), the counterclaim cannot be within the district court's supplemental jurisdiction. That jurisdiction is limited to claims intimately related to claims that are within federal jurisdiction on some other ground. "[I]n *any civil action of which the district courts have original jurisdiction*, the district courts shall have supplemental jurisdiction over all other claims that are so related to claims in the action within such original jurisdiction that they form part of the same case or controversy under Article III of the United States Constitution." 28 U.S.C. §1367(a) (emphasis added); *see Kelly v. Fleetwood Enterprises, Inc.*, 377 F.3d 1034, 1040 (9ᵗʰ Cir. 2004).

Nor has the counterclaim, considered as an independent suit, been shown to be within federal jurisdiction. AmeriCredit has as we said no federal claim; and while there is complete diversity of citizenship, the amount in controversy alleged by AmeriCredit is below the statutory minimum; it is only $11,000 plus prejudgment interest. This is another bobble by AmeriCredit, though one without consequences. The loan contract required the plaintiff to pay "reasonable attorney's fees, costs and expenses incurred [by AmeriCredit] in the collection or enforcement of the debt," and when such expenses are sought as part of an underlying claim, rather than pursuant to a separate post-judgment right to "costs" or "fees" incurred in the litigation, they are considered part of the amount in controversy. *Missouri State Life Ins. Co. v. Jones*, 290 U.S. 199, 202 (1933); *Gardynski- Leschuck v. Ford Motor Co.*, 142 F.3d 955, 958 (7th Cir. 1998); *Manguno v. Prudential Property & Casualty Ins. Co.*, 276 F.3d 720, 723-24 (5th Cir. 2002); *Miera v. Dairyland* [—9—] *Ins. Co.* 143 F.3d 1337, 1340 (10th Cir. 1998); compare *Smith v. American General Life & Accident Ins. Co.*, 337 F.3d 888, 896-97 (7th Cir. 2003); *Hart v. Schering-Plough Corp.*, 253 F.3d 272, 273-74

(7th Cir. 2001); *Gardynski- Leschuck v. Ford Motor Co., supra*, 142 F.3d at 958-59; *Hall v. EarthLink Network, Inc.*, 396 F.3d 500, 506 (2d Cir. 2005); *Burns v. Windsor Ins. Co.*, 31 F.3d 1092, 1097 (11th Cir. 1994). Nevertheless it's inconceivable that AmeriCredit's claim was worth more than $75,000 exclusive of interest and costs when we consider the default judgment that AmeriCredit does not challenge as inadequate—a measly $13,582.75, plus costs.

So the judge should have dismissed the counterclaim for want of federal jurisdiction, though without prejudice because AmeriCredit should be allowed to refile it as a new suit in an Illinois state court. Not that that would be an ideal solution. The amount AmeriCredit would be suing for might be too small to make a suit worthwhile unless it would have an *in terrorem* effect that would make future debtors less inclined to try to stiff AmeriCredit, which seems unrealistic. Rather than file a counterclaim over which the district court had no jurisdiction, as AmeriCredit's lawyers should have realized from the get-go, or bring suit in state court, AmeriCredit could have asked the judge to impose sanctions on the plaintiff under Fed. R. Civ. P. 11 for filing a frivolous suit; it did not.

It might seem that an appropriate sanction would have been to award AmeriCredit the amount of the default judgment, on the theory that the plaintiff's frivolous suit foisted that cost on AmeriCredit. But that isn't [—10—] correct. Had the plaintiff simply failed to pay the $11,322.28 it owed AmeriCredit, AmeriCredit would have had to file a suit in state court if it wanted to collect the money. The harm it incurred by being sued frivolously by the plaintiff was the expense of defending against the plaintiff's suit—that was the expense it could have sought reimbursement of under Rule 11 but didn't.

Another possible sanction, as we suggested earlier, would have been dismissal of the plaintiff's second complaint with prejudice, so that he cannot refile his suit against AmeriCredit in state court; for the only motive of such a refiling could be harassment. The district judge did dismiss the second complaint with prejudice, but not as a sanction—instead on the erroneous ground that there was federal diversity jurisdiction and he was deciding the merits.

The judgment must therefore be vacated and the case remanded with directions that the judge (1) either dismiss the plaintiff's suit without prejudice or dismiss with prejudice, as a sanction (not requested by the defendant, but within the court's inherent authority); (2) vacate the default judgment in favor of AmeriCredit on its counterclaim; and (3) dismiss the counterclaim but without prejudice.

VACATED, AND REMANDED
WITH DIRECTIONS.

This page intentionally left blank

United States Court of Appeals for the Eighth Circuit

United States Court of Appeals
for the Eighth Circuit

No. 12-1720

IN RE AMERICAN RIVER TRANSP. CO.

Appeal from the United States District Court for the
Eastern District of Missouri

Decided: August 30, 2013

Citation: 728 F.3d 839, 1 Adm. R. 378 (8th Cir. 2013).

Before **RILEY**, Chief Judge, **WOLLMAN** and **MELLOY**,
Circuit Judges.

[—1—] **WOLLMAN**, Circuit Judge: [—2—]

American River Transportation Company (Artco) appeals from the district court's order dismissing its limitation complaint. We reverse and remand.

I.

On March 6, 2011, the M/V Julie White, a towboat owned by Artco, was pushing four barges southbound on the Mississippi River in the vicinity of Lock and Dam 25. The barges became separated from the M/V Julie White, allided with structures appurtenant to Lock and Dam 25, and then sank. The United States advised Artco that the barges had caused damage to Lock and Dam 25 and/or the structures appurtenant to it.

Artco salvaged and removed the sunken barges from the Mississippi River. Artco then filed a complaint seeking exoneration from, or limitation of liability for, claims arising from the allision pursuant to the Limitation of Shipowners' Liability Act, 46 U.S.C. §§ 30501-12 (the Limitation Act). In accordance with the Limitation Act, Artco sought to limit its liability to the value of the M/V Julie White, the four barges, and their freight, which Artco alleged had a total value of $1,322,837.85. The district court entered an order approving Artco's posted security, enjoining the prosecution of any suits related to the allision, and requiring Artco to provide notice to potential claimants advising them of the limitation action.

Artco provided notice to the United States of the limitation action. This notice mirrored the requirements of Federal Rule of Civil Procedure Supplemental Rule F(5). It informed the United States that as a potential claimant, if it wished to contest Artco's right to exoneration or limitation, it was required to file a proof of claim and answer to the limitation complaint by June 15, 2011. The United States did not file a proof of claim or answer. Instead, it appeared in the limitation action and filed a motion to dismiss the complaint under Rule 12(b)(6), arguing that its claims under the [—3—] Rivers and Harbors Act, 33 U.S.C. §§ 401-76, were not subject to limitation under the Limitation Act.

The district court agreed, holding that the government could seek an implied *in personam* cause of action under § 408 of the Rivers and Harbors Act and that such an action was not subject to the Limitation Act. *See* D. Ct. Order of Mar. 12, 2012, at 11. Because the government was the only potential claimant to Artco's limitation action, the district court dismissed the limitation complaint.

II.

Artco contends that the district court erred by entertaining the motion to dismiss the limitation complaint because the government lacked standing and by concluding that § 408 of the Rivers and Harbors Act provided an implied *in personam* cause of action.

The Limitation Act, formerly 46 U.S.C. §183, permits a vessel owner to file a complaint to limit its liability in the case of an accident and states that "the liability of the owner of a vessel for any claim, debt, or liability described in subsection (b) shall not exceed the value of the vessel and pending freight" when the loss or damage occurs "without the privity or knowledge of the owner." 46 U.S.C. § 30505(a), (b). For an explanation of the history and purpose of the Limitation Act, see *Lewis v. Lewis & Clark Marine, Inc.*, 531 U.S. 438, 446-48 (2001).

When first passed, the Limitation Act "did not establish a procedure to implement the limitations on liability that it established." *Am. Milling Co. v. Brennan Marine, Inc.*, 623 F.3d 1221, 1224 (8th Cir. 2010). "[T]he Supreme Court enacted rules to establish a uniform judicial procedure by which a vessel owner could seek to limit its liability under the Limitation Act. Over time, these rules were amended and relabeled, and Rule F was eventually adopted as part of the Federal [—4—] Rules of Civil Procedure." *Id.* (internal citations omitted). "As other courts have explained, 'Rule F evolved as a procedural device to implement the [Limitation Act].'" *Id.* (quoting *Bouchard Transp. Co., Inc. v. Updegraff*, 147 F.3d 1344, 1347 (11th Cir. 1998) (alteration in original)). Under Rule F(5), any claimant who wishes to contest a vessel owner's "right to exoneration from or the right to limitation of liability" must file a proof of claim and an answer to the complaint, unless the claim has included an answer.

Artco contends that the district court erred by allowing the government to file its motion to dismiss the limitation complaint without first filing a proof of claim and answer in accordance with Federal Rule of Civil Procedure Supplemental Rule F(5). The government argues that its claim under the Rivers and Harbors Act is not subject to the Limitation Act and that it is therefore not required to follow the procedural steps established in Rule F(5). The district court held that the government's claim was not subject to the Limitation Act, and implicitly rejected Artco's argument that the government was nevertheless required to comply with the procedural steps outlined in Rule F(5) prior to filing its motion to dismiss. *See* D. Ct. Order of Mar. 12, 2012, at 11. Rule F(5) is part of the Federal Rules of Civil Procedure, and we review the district court's interpretation of the rule *de novo. Am. Milling*, 623 F.3d at 1224.

"Admiralty and maritime law includes a host of special rights, duties, rules, and procedures." *Lewis*, 531 U.S. at 446. As discussed above, Rule F was created to implement the Limitation Act. *See Am. Milling*, 623 F.3d at 1224. After notice of a limitation complaint is issued either by publication or directly by mail, Rule F(5)

provides the process by which potential claimants must proceed.

> Claims shall be filed and served on or before the date specified in the notice provided for in subdivision (4) of this rule. Each claim shall specify the facts upon which the claimant relies in support of the claim, [—5—] the items thereof, and the dates on which the same accrued. If a claimant desires to contest either the right to exoneration from or the right to limitation of liability the claimant shall file and serve an answer to the complaint unless the claim has included an answer.

Fed. R. Civ. P. Supp. R. F(5).

Artco contends that a party does not have standing to appear in a limitation proceeding and file a motion to dismiss the limitation complaint unless it first complies with the requirements of Rule F(5). The government contends that it has Article III standing, which is all that is required. Although Article III establishes the "irreducible constitutional minimum of standing," *Lujan v. Defenders of Wildlife*, 504 U.S. 555, 560 (1992), a party may also be subject to prudential and statutory standing requirements, *see Miller v. Redwood Toxicology Lab., Inc.*, 688 F.3d 928, 933-34 (8th Cir. 2012).

The Federal Rules of Civil Procedure Supplemental Rules C and G have been deemed to create statutory standing requirements for challenging forfeiture actions. *See, e.g., United States v. 8 Gilcrease Lane*, 638 F.3d 297, 298 n.1 (D.C. Cir. 2011) (stating that a verified claim under Supplemental Rule C(6) is essential to conferring statutory standing upon a claimant in a forfeiture action); *United States v. $22,050.00*, 595 F.3d 318, 323 n.5 (6th Cir. 2010) (stating that strict compliance with Supplemental Rule G is a prerequisite for statutory standing to challenge a forfeiture action); *United States v. $148,840.00*, 521 F.3d 1268, 1273 n.3 (10th Cir. 2008) (stating that Supplemental Rule C(6) serves as the requirement for statutory standing in a forfeiture action); *United States v.*

$487,825.00, 484 F.3d 662, 664 (3d Cir. 2007) ("In order to stand before a court and contest a forfeiture, a claimant must meet both Article III and statutory standing requirements. To establish statutory standing in a forfeiture case, the claimant must comply with the procedural requirements set forth in Rule C(6)(a) and § 983(a)(4)(A)." (internal citation omitted)); *United States v. $103,387.27*, 863 F.2d 555, 560-61 n.10 (7th Cir. 1988) (noting that forfeiture actions [—6—] require Article III and statutory standing and that statutory standing is satisfied by meeting the requirements of Supplemental Rule C(6)); *United States v. $38,000.00*, 816 F.2d 1538, 1545 (11th Cir. 1987) ("The Supplemental Rules govern judicial forfeiture proceedings and establish the statutory standing requirements for these actions."); *see also United States v. Lot 65 Pine Meadow*, 976 F.2d 1155, 1157 (8th Cir. 1992) (although not invoking the term "statutory standing," holding that a party "lacked standing to contest the forfeiture" because he had failed to file a timely claim in accordance with Rule C(6)).

Similarly, we conclude that Rule F(5) creates statutory standing requirements for challenging limitation actions. The purpose of Rule F(5), much like that of Rules C(6) and G(5), is to bring all potentially interested parties into one proceeding to address competing claims to certain property. *Compare United States v. Three Parcels of Real Property*, 43 F.3d 388, 392 (8th Cir. 1994) ("The purpose of Rule C(6) is to inform the court that there is a claimant to the property who wants it back and intends to defend it." (internal quotation marks omitted)), *with White v. Sabatino*, 415 F. Supp. 2d 1163, 1180 (D. Haw. 2006) ("The purpose of [Rule F(5)] is to consolidate all pending and potential claims against the owner of the vessel in one Limitation proceeding."). Likewise, an examination of Rule F demonstrates that it provides a structure and procedures that are similar to those provided by Rules C and G.[1]

Moreover, although not explicitly declaring the claim requirement of Rule F(5) [—7—] a statutory standing requirement, several decisions have implicitly addressed it in this manner. *See, e.g., In re Triton*, 719 F. Supp. 2d 753, 757-58 (S.D. Tex. 2010) (potential claimants who had not filed claims under Rule F(5) lacked standing to seek dismissal of the limitation action); *In re Lenzi*, Civ. A. No. 89-4571, 1989 WL 146659, at *1 (E.D. Pa. Dec. 1, 1989) (concluding that party who filed an answer and a motion for summary judgment in a limitation complaint, but not a proper claim under Rule F(5), lacked standing to contest the right to limitation or exoneration). Accordingly, we conclude that filing a claim in accordance with Rule F(5) is a statutory standing requirement.

Furthermore, we reject the government's contention that this requirement is inapplicable when the claim at issue is not subject to the Limitation Act. In support of this proposition, the government relies primarily upon *United States v. CF Industries, Inc.*, 542 F. Supp. 952, 956 (D. Minn. 1982), in which limitation complaints were filed by the respective owners of a barge and a tug involved in an accident on the Mississippi River. *Id.* at 953-54. The actions were consolidated and transferred to the United States District Court for the Southern District of Illinois. Under the limitation proceedings, injunctions were issued enjoining the

---

[1] Admittedly, the language in Rule F(5) differs from that of current Rules C(6) and G(5), but the former version of Rule C(6) contained language similar to Rule F(5). *Compare* Fed. R. Civ. P. Supp. R. F(5) (2013) ("Claims shall be filed and served on

or before the date specified in the notice provided for in subdivision (4) of this rule. Each claim shall specify the facts upon which the claimant relies in support of the claim, the items thereof, and the dates on which the same accrued. If a claimant desires to contest either the right to exoneration from or the right to limitation of liability the claimant shall file and serve an answer to the complaint unless the claim has included an answer."), *with* Former Fed. R. Civ. P. Supp. R. C(6) (1992) ("The claimant of property that is the subject of an action in rem shall file a claim within 10 [—7—] days after process has been executed, or within such additional time as may be allowed by the court, and shall serve an answer within 20 days after the filing of the claim."). Former Rule C(6)'s similar language was also deemed to create standing requirements. *See Lot 65 Pine Meadow*, 976 F.2d at 1157; *United States v. One Dairy Farm*, 918 F.2d 310, 311-13 (1st Cir. 1990).

commencement and prosecution of any and all suits, actions, or proceedings related to the accident at issue in the limitation complaints. *Id.* at 954. Notwithstanding the injunctions, the government filed an action under the Clean Water Act (CWA) in the United States District Court for the District of Minnesota. The limitation plaintiffs filed motions to dismiss, contending that the government's claim was subject to the Limitation Act. *Id.* [—8—]

The district court held that the government's claim under the CWA was not subject to the Limitation Act and thus could be filed outside the limitation proceeding. *Id.* at 956. The limitation plaintiffs argued further that although the claims were not subject to the Limitation Act, the government was still obligated to request relief from the injunctions granted in the limitation proceedings before directly filing its action in the District of Minnesota. The district court rejected this argument as well, concluding:

> Although the United States has at times followed such a procedure, . . . it is not required to do so. The injunctions entered in the limitation actions were based on the authority of Supplemental Admiralty Rule F(3), and therefore were limited to enjoining "any claim subject to limitation in the action." Because the claim for the statutory penalty was not subject to limitation in the action, it falls beyond the scope of the injunctions. In addition, requiring the United States to initially enter the limitation actions would require the United States to go through costly, time consuming and unnecessary proceedings. Such a requirement would serve no purpose while unduly complicating the proceedings.

Id. at 956-57 (internal citations omitted).

Even assuming that the government's potential Rivers and Harbors Act claim is not subject to the Limitation Act, *CF Industries* does not lend support to the government's position. Contrary to the government's argument, the above-cited discussion in *CF*

Industries does not permit the government to intervene in a limitation proceeding without following the requirements established in Rule F. *CF Industries* and similar cases demonstrate only that the government need not appear in the limitation proceeding at all to assert its claims when those claims are not subject to the Limitation Act; it has no bearing on whether Rule F(5)'s claim requirement applies when a party does appear in a limitation action and attempts to contest the limitation complaint. *See,e.g., In re Complaint of Metlife Capital Corp.,* 132 F.3d 818, 821-24 (1st Cir. 1997) (concluding that claims under the Oil Pollution [—9—] Act were not subject to the Limitation Act or Rule F, and thus the claims could be filed in a collateral proceeding without abiding by the procedures set forth in Rule F).

Because the government chose to appear in the limitation action to contest the complaint, it was required to demonstrate that it had the requisite standing to do so. In this case, the government did not have statutory standing because it failed to file a claim in accordance with Rule F(5). The district court thus erred by entertaining the government's motion to dismiss the limitation complaint. Because we conclude that the government was without standing, we need not address the merits of the government's motion to dismiss, *i.e.,* whether § 408 of the Rivers and Harbors Act provides an *in personam* cause of action.

III. Conclusion

We reverse the district court's order dismissing Artco's limitation proceeding and remand the case to the district court for further proceedings in accordance with the views set forth in this opinion.

(Reporter's Note: Dissenting opinion on p. 382).

[—9—] **RILEY,** Chief Judge, dissenting:

Because I agree with the district court's well-reasoned decision, I respectfully dissent.

A. Injunction

The majority correctly recognizes "that the government need not appear in [a] limitation proceeding at all to assert its claims when those claims are not subject to the Limitation Act," *ante* at 8, but incorrectly implies that the government's appearance in *this* limitation proceeding was, therefore, futile. The actual language used in the limitation injunction issued in this case states: [—10—]

> IT IS . . . ORDERED that notice be given to *all* persons asserting *any* claims with respect to the [March 6, 2011 allision] in which the *United States of America*[] claims to have sustained damage to structures appurtenant to Lock and Dam 25. The court further admonishes all such parties to file their respective claims with the Clerk of this Court . . . on or before the 15th day of June, 2011; and
>
> . . .
>
> IT IS FURTHER ORDERED . . . that the institution and/or prosecution of *any suits, actions or legal proceedings of any nature or description whatsoever in any court whatsoever*, against [Artco] and/or the M/V Julie White in respect of any claim arising out of or connected with the [March 6, 2011 allision], except in *this proceeding*, are hereby stayed and restrained.

(Emphasis added).

Far from leaving the government free to initiate a suit "not subject to the Limitation Act," *ante* at 8, in a different proceeding, the all-encompassing language of the injunction prohibited the government from doing so except in "this proceeding." The injunction prohibited collateral *in personam* proceedings against Artco and *in rem* proceedings against the Julie White, enjoining all claims "whatsoever." This language was so sweeping the government reasonably could conclude the

injunction applied to claims under 33 U.S.C. §408. Rather than "'serv[ing] no purpose while unduly complicating the proceedings,'" *ante* at 8 (quoting *United States v. CF Indus., Inc.*, 542 F. Supp. 952, 957 (D. Minn. 1982)), the government's participation in this case served the purpose of freeing the government [—11—] from a burdensome injunction[2] and of eliminating the prospect of unduly complicated collateral proceedings.[3]

B. Standing

Even though the injunction placed a substantial burden on the government, the majority concludes the government lacked statutory standing to challenge the injunction. I disagree.

1. Statutory Standing

There is an elemental flaw in the majority's "conclu[sion] that [Federal Rules of Civil Procedure Supplemental] Rule F(5) creates *statutory* standing requirements for challenging limitation actions." *Ante* at 6 (emphasis added). Rule F(5) is not a *statute*. It is a court-created procedural *rule*. *See* 28 U.S.C. § 2072(a) ("The Supreme Court shall have the power to prescribe general *rules* of practice and procedure." (emphasis added)); *Sibbach v. Wilson & Co.*, 312 U.S. 1, 9-10 (1941) ("Congress has undoubted power to regulate the practice and procedure of federal courts, and may exercise that power by delegating to this or other federal courts authority to make *rules* not inconsistent with the *statutes* or Constitution of the United States." (emphasis added) (footnotes omitted)); *cf., e.g., Black's Law Dictionary* 1448 (8th ed. 2004) (defining "statute" as "[a] law passed by

---

[2] That is an injunction which exceeded the district court's authority under the Limitation Act, 46 U.S.C. §§ 30501-30512. *Compare* District Court Order, March 29, 2011, at 2 (enjoining *in rem* suits against "the M/V Julie White"), *with* 46 U.S.C. §30505 (limiting only the *in personam* liability of "the *owner* of a vessel" (emphasis added)).

[3] This is not to say the government was *required* to intervene before filing a collateral suit under 33 U.S.C. § 408, but it was certainly reasonable and appropriate for the government to do so given the risk of contempt proceedings if it ignored and then violated the injunction.

a *legislative* body" (emphasis added)). A specific statute provides that Rule F(5), like any other procedural rule, "*shall not [—12—] abridge, enlarge or modify any substantive right.*" 28 U.S.C. § 2072(b) (emphasis added). "[I]t is axiomatic that the Federal Rules of Civil Procedure do *not* create or withdraw federal jurisdiction." *Owen Equip. & Erection Co. v. Kroger*, 437 U.S. 365, 370 (1978) (emphasis added).

Though sharing the term "standing" with its Article III counterpart, statutory standing "has nothing to do with whether there is a case or controversy under Article III." *Steel Co. v. Citizens for a Better Env't*, 523 U.S. 83, 97 (1998). Rather, "statutory standing goes to the merits of the claim." *Miller v. Redwood Toxicology Lab., Inc.*, 688 F.3d 928, 934 (8th Cir. 2012). Statutory standing asks only "whether *this* plaintiff has a cause of action under the statute." *Steel Co.*, 523 U.S. at 97 n.2; *see also In re Athens/Alpha Gas Corp.*, 715 F.3d 230, 235 (8th Cir. 2013) ("[B]ecause the merits inquiry and the statutory standing inquiry often overlap, . . . it would be artificial to draw a distinction between the two."). Thus, "'[s]tatutory standing is simply statutory interpretation.'" *Miller*, 688 F.3d at 934 (quoting *Graden v. Conexant Sys., Inc.*, 496 F.3d 291, 295 (3d Cir. 2007)). *Statutory* standing depends on the *statute*.

The majority analogizes the "purpose," "structure[,] and procedures" of Rule F(5) to those of Rule G(5) and former Rule C(6).[4] *Ante* at 6. The majority's analogy ignores the critical distinction between Rule F(5) and these rules. Existing Rule G(5) and former Rule C(6) reflect statutory standing flowing from actual statutes. *See* 18 U.S.C. §983(a)(4)(A); 21 U.S.C. § 881(d). Rule G(5) and former Rule C(6) do not create statutory standing requirements independent from these statutes. *See Via Mat Int'l S. Am. Ltd. v. United States*, 446 F.3d 1258, 1264 (11th Cir.

---

[4] "The *in rem* forfeiture Supplemental Rules were renumbered in 2006. The provisions that are now located in Rule G were previously located in Rule C(6). Thus, the older cases discuss adherence to Rule C(6)." *United States v. $22,050.00*, 595 F.3d 318, 322 n.4 (6th Cir. 2010).

2006) (explaining "[s]tatutory standing under Rule C(6) is not inherent to all forfeiture actions; it is only [—13—] required *if specifically invoked by statute*" (emphasis added)); *see also, e.g., United States v. $487,825.00*, 484 F.3d 662, 664 (3d Cir. 2007) ("To establish statutory standing in a forfeiture case, the claimant must comply with the procedural requirements set forth in Rule C(6)(a) and § 983(a)(4)(A)."); *United States v. $38,000.00*, 816 F.2d 1538, 1545 n.13 (11th Cir. 1987) (holding "judicial forfeitures are governed by the Supplemental Rules" because of § 881(d)). Rule G(5) and former Rule C(6) are procedural rules which alone cannot create statutory requirements. It is only because these rules apply the statutory requirements of 18 U.S.C. § 983 and 21 U.S.C. § 881 that a non-compliant claimant lacks statutory standing in forfeiture proceedings.

By contrast, nothing in the Limitation Act mandates compliance with Rule F(5). The Limitation Act does contain certain statutory standing requirements. *See, e.g.,* 46 U.S.C. §30511. But adherence to Rule F(5) is not one of them, which means Rule F(5) remains an ordinary procedural rule. It can neither confer nor withdraw statutory standing.

2. Standing To Challenge An Injunction

Even if the majority were correct that the government's decision not to file a claim under Rule F(5) meant the government was not a party to the limitation proceeding, it is well established that "[a] nonparty normally has standing to appeal when it is adversely affected by an injunction." *In re Piper Funds, Inc., Institutional Gov't Income Portfolio Litig.*, 71 F.3d 298, 301 (8th Cir. 1995); *see also Devlin v. Scardelletti*, 536 U.S. 1, 6-9, 14 (2002) (holding nonparty class members bound by a settlement order "have the power to bring an appeal without first intervening"). As there is no doubt the government had standing to *appeal* the limitation injunction without subjecting itself to Rule F(5)'s cumbersome requirements for becoming a "party," it makes no sense that the government would lack similar standing to challenge the injunction in the district court, especially given this court's distaste for [—14—] claims first litigated on appeal. *See, e.g., Orr v. Wal-Mart Stores, Inc.*, 297 F.3d 720, 725 (8th Cir. 2002).

The weight of circuit precedent agrees. *See, e.g., Samnorwood Indep. Sch. Dist. v. Tex. Educ. Agency*, 533 F.3d 258, 266 (5th Cir. 2008) (determining a nonparty had standing to bring a declaratory judgment challenging an injunction "because the equitable relief granted by the district courts placed a burden on the challenging party which gave them a personal stake in the litigation"); *United States v. Kirschenbaum*, 156 F.3d 784, 794 (7th Cir. 1998) ("[N]on-parties who are bound by a court's equitable decrees have a right to move to have the order dissolved, and other circuits have held that where a non-party is purportedly bound by an injunction, the non-party may bring an appeal rather than face the possibility of a contempt proceeding." (internal citation omitted)); *In re Estate of Ferdinand Marcos Human Rights Litig.*, 94 F.3d 539, 544 (9th Cir. 1996) (deciding a nonparty had standing where an injunction presented the nonparty "with the choice of either conforming its conduct to the dictates of the injunction or ignoring the injunction and risking contempt proceedings").

Because the limitation injunction gave the government the choice of appearing in "this proceeding" or risking uncertain collateral litigation, Artco essentially "'haled [the government] into district court despite [the government's] objections.'" *Piper*, 71 F.3d at 301 (quoting *SEC v. Wencke*, 783 F.2d 829, 834 (9th Cir. 1986)). Therefore, regardless of Rule F(5), "[e]quitable considerations clearly warrant giving standing" to the government to challenge the injunction in the district court. *Id.*

3. Rule F(5)

Even if a non-statutory procedural rule could deprive the government of statutory standing, Rule F(5) would not do so in this case. [—15—]

First, by its plain terms, Rule F(5) applies only to those filing claims in the *limitation action*. The first two sentences of the rule specify the requirements for asserting a claim in the limitation action, and the final sentence, like the preceding sentence, expressly applies only to *"claimant[s]*," establishing the procedure for those who have asserted "claims" in the limitation action but also wish to "contest either the right to exoneration from or the right to limitation of liability." Fed. R. Civ. P. Supp. R. F(5) (emphasis added). The purpose of Rule F(5) plainly is to ensure that an individual who chooses to file a claim under Rule F is not thereby barred from contesting the propriety of the limitation action. Nothing in Rule F bars a person who has *not* asserted a claim in the limitation action (i.e., a person who is not a "claimant") from "contest[ing] either the right to exoneration from or the right to limitation of liability" without filing a claim or answer.

Of course, a non-claimant may not challenge the propriety of a limitation action without having some minimum connection to the case. But the government's minimum connection here is not Rule F(5), it is Article III and 33 U.S.C. § 408. Rule F(5) can no more destroy the standing of one who has suffered an "injury in fact" which is "causal[ly] connect[ed]" to the "conduct complained of" and "likely" to "be redressed by a favorable decision," than it can confer standing on one who seeks a "speculative" remedy for a "conjectural" injury caused by "the independent action of some third party." *Lujan v. Defenders of Wildlife*, 504 U.S. 555, 560-61 (1992) (internal quotations and citations omitted).

Second, a Rule 12(b)(6) motion to dismiss "must be made *before* pleading if a responsive pleading is allowed." Fed. R. Civ. P. 12(b)(6) (emphasis added). If Rule F(5) required the government to file an answer (i.e., a responsive pleading) before filing a Rule 12(b)(6) motion, as the majority suggests, then the government could *never* file a Rule 12(b)(6) motion. Such an interpretation of Rule F(5) would give vessel owners free reign to commence limitation actions with ill-pled complaints. *Cf.* [—16—] Fed. R. Civ. P. Supp. R. G(5)(b) (requiring a claimant to file "an answer to the complaint *or a motion under Rule 12*" (emphasis added)).

Although the Supplemental Rules contain numerous specific pleading requirements, *see, e.g.*, Fed. R. Civ. P. Supp. R. B(1)(a), C(2), the Supplemental Rules contain no indication that admiralty and maritime claims are exempt from general federal pleading rules, *see* Fed. R. Civ. P. 8. To the contrary, "[t]he Federal Rules of Civil Procedure also apply to [admiralty and maritime claims] except to the extent they are inconsistent with the[] Supplemental Rules." Fed. R. Civ. P. Supp. R. A(2). Rule F(2)'s specific pleading requirements are in no way inconsistent with Rule 8(a)'s general requirements. A complaint filed under Rule F(2) must contain "enough heft to 'sho[w] that the pleader is entitled to relief,'" *Bell Atl. Corp. v. Twombly*, 550 U.S. 544, 557 (2007) (alteration in original) (quoting Fed. R. Civ. P. 8(a)(2)). And Rule 12(b)(6) authorizes motions to dismiss for "failure to state a claim upon which relief can be granted," permitting the government to test the legal sufficiency of the pleadings contained "within the four corners of [the] complaint." *Ashcroft v. Iqbal*, 556 U.S. 662, 674 (2009). Challenging the legal sufficiency of Artco's complaint is precisely what the government sought to do in this case.[5] Nothing in Rule F could deny the government standing to do so. [—17—]

C. Conclusion

Because (1) the government had standing to challenge the limitation injunction by moving to dismiss under Rule 12(b)(6) and (2) the government's 33 U.S.C. § 408 claim

---

[5] The best reading of Rule F(5), which harmonizes Rule F with Rule 8 and the "well-pleaded complaint" requirement, *Twombly*, 550 U.S. at 556-57, is that an answer is required to contest whether there is a genuine factual dispute related to "the right to exoneration from or the right to limitation of liability"—akin to a motion for summary judgment—whereas an answer is not required to contest whether the Rule F(2) complaint, based solely on the assertions contained therein, is sufficient "to state a claim to relief that is plausible on its face," *Twombly*, 550 U.S. at 570.

against Artco is not subject to the Limitation Act,[6] I would affirm.

---

[6] The district court's conclusion that 33 U.S.C. §408 gives the government an *in personam* remedy against Artco was a straightforward application of *Wyandotte Transp. Co. v. United States*, 389 U.S. 191 (1967), consistent with the relevant agency's regulations, *see* 33 C.F.R. § 209.170(e), and our court's longstanding practice, *see, e.g., United States v. Capital Sand Co.*, 466 F.3d 655, 658 (8th Cir. 2006) (affirming § 408 liability against a vessel owner); *United States v. Am. Commercial Barge Line Co.*, 988 F.2d 860, 861-62 (8th Cir. 1993) ("Under the Rivers and Harbors Act of 1899, the Company is strictly liable for the damage the [vessel] and its barges caused to the gate. This point was never contested."); *United States v. Logan & Craig Charter Serv., Inc.*, 676 F.2d 1216, 1219 (8th Cir. 1982) ("It is well recognized that private parties are strictly liable for damage to works protected under section 408.").

This page intentionally left blank

1 Adm. R.

United States Court of Appeals for the Ninth Circuit

United States Court of Appeals
for the Ninth Circuit

No. 12-35332

SHELL OFFSHORE, INC.
vs.
GREENPEACE, INC.

Appeal from the United States District Court for the
District of Alaska

Decided: March 12, 2013

Citation: 709 F.3d 1281, 1 Adm. R. 388 (9th Cir. 2013).

Before **KOZINSKI**, Chief Judge, **TASHIMA** and **SMITH**, Circuit Judges.

[—4—] **TASHIMA**, Circuit Judge:

Shell Offshore, Inc. and Shell Gulf of Mexico, Inc. (together, "Shell") hold multi-year oil and gas leases in the Outer Continental Shelf ("OCS"), located in the Arctic Ocean off the coast of Alaska. Greenpeace, Inc. ("Greenpeace USA") has publicly undertaken a campaign to "stop Shell" from drilling in the Arctic. The district court granted Shell's motion for a preliminary injunction, which prohibited Greenpeace USA from coming within a specified distance of vessels involved in Shell's Arctic OCS exploration and from committing various unlawful and tortious acts against those vessels. Greenpeace USA argues that the action is not justiciable, that the district court lacked subject matter jurisdiction to issue its order, and that the court erred in its application of *Winter v. Natural Resources Defense Council, Inc.*, 555 U.S. 7 (2008), to the merits of Shell's motion. We conclude that the action presents a justiciable case or controversy, that the district court had jurisdiction to issue its order, and that it did not abuse its discretion in doing so. Accordingly, we affirm. [—5—]

I. BACKGROUND

A. Greenpeace Efforts to Stop Arctic Drilling

Shell has presented evidence that Greenpeace USA and Greenpeace entities around the world are publicly committed to stopping Shell's exploration of its Arctic OCS leases. Indeed, the websites of virtually all Greenpeace organizations, including Greenpeace USA, prominently feature a campaign to "stop Shell."

But "stop Shell" is not merely a campaign of words and images. Greenpeace USA also uses so-called "direct actions" to achieve its goals, and its general counsel has conceded that direct action can include illegal activity. There is evidence that Greenpeace USA and its counterparts around the globe are united in the goal of stopping Shell. When Greenpeace activists forcibly boarded an oil rig off the coast of Greenland in 2010 and used their bodies to impede a drilling operation, Greenpeace USA's executive director described their conduct as "bold non-violent direct action" by "our activists." Greenpeace USA similarly endorsed the forcible boarding of a Shell vessel by Greenpeace New Zealand activists in February 2012, again referring to them as "our brave activists."

The record before the district court contained evidence that Greenpeace activists used illegal "direct action" to interfere with legal oil drilling activities on many such occasions. Several incidents involved Shell vessels that were subsequently named in the district court's preliminary injunction order and used in Shell's 2012 Arctic OCS drilling operation. *See Shell Offshore Inc. v. Greenpeace, Inc.*, [—6—] 864 F. Supp. 2d 839, 854–55 (D. Alaska 2012). These incidents were as follows:

1. Direct Action Against Shell's *Harvey Explorer* Vessel

Greenpeace USA activists unlawfully boarded the *Harvey Explorer*, a vessel that Shell contracted to use in its Arctic OCS operation, in May 2010. The vessel was in the Gulf of Mexico (and scheduled to depart for Alaska) when activists boarded it, unfurled banners, and painted slogans on its walls.[1]

---

[1] Greenpeace USA has admitted that its activists boarded the *Harvey Explorer*, but now argues—in passing—that the incident is "jurisdictionally irrelevant to the current case,"

2. Direct Action Against Cairn Energy's Arctic Drilling Operation

Shell adduced evidence that Greenpeace used direct action against another energy company, Cairn Energy, in order to prevent Cairn from conducting OCS oil and gas exploration activities in the Arctic Ocean. Greenpeace USA's executive director described the first such action in Greenpeace International's 2010 Annual Report:

> In August, our activists evaded Danish navy commanders and scaled Cairn's exploration rig off Greenland, halting the operation—we [—7—] knew that, due to very tight deadlines, even a minor delay could have a major effect; Cairn didn't find oil in 2010.

Dkt. 56-19 (Ex. 1015 at 0005).

In 2011, Greenpeace activists again boarded a Cairn vessel off the coast of Greenland. Approximately twenty such activists were arrested after climbing the rig, attaching themselves under the rig in a "survival pod," and hanging a few meters from the drill bit. A news report posted on the Greenpeace Africa website quoted one of the "climbers" as saying:

> There's no way Cairn can drill for oil while we're hanging next to their drill-bit, and it's going to be extremely difficult for them to remove our survival pod. To drill oil here would be dangerous insanity. We have to stop the Arctic oil rush.

Dkt. 56-25 (Ex. 1020 at 0001).

3. Direct Action Against Shell's *Noble Discoverer* Vessel

In February 2012, six Greenpeace New Zealand activists illegally boarded and occupied the Shell drillship *Noble Discoverer* while it stopped at New Zealand on its way to the Arctic Ocean. Activists equipped with survival gear scaled the 53-meter drilling tower, secured themselves to the rig, and unfurled "stop Shell" banners. They were arrested by New Zealand authorities four days later. Greenpeace USA, in its blog, endorsed the activists' conduct and described them as [—8—] "our brave activists." Dkt. 11-14 at 2. Its website described the incident as "only the first chapter in what will undoubtedly be an epic battle."

4. Direct Action Against Shell's *Nordica* and *Fennica* Vessels

In March 2012, Greenpeace activists boarded and occupied the *Nordica* and *Fennica*, two of Shell's "icebreaker" support vessels, while in port in Finland. Again in May 2012, Greenpeace activists twice boarded and occupied the *Nordica* while it transited through Swedish and Danish waters. Activists chained themselves to the vessel, dropped weights and other objects in the water to obstruct the vessel's propulsion, and created a human blockade using divers.

B. Preliminary Injunction

Shell was scheduled to begin federally-authorized exploration of its Arctic OCS leases in 2012. In the months leading up to the exploration, Shell first obtained a temporary restraining order and then a preliminary injunction that barred Greenpeace USA from coming within specified distances of named Shell vessels[2] involved in the OCS exploration. *See Shell Offshore Inc. v. Geenpeace, Inc.*, 2012 WL 1931537, at *16 (D. Alaska May 29, 2012) (amended order); *Shell Offshore*, 864 F. Supp. 2d at 855 (original order). The injunction also prevented Greenpeace USA from committing various tortious and illegal acts against those vessels and their [—9—] occupants.[3] By its own

---

[2] Including within 1000 meters of the *Noble Discoverer* and the *Kulluk*.

[3] The injunction barred Greenpeace from:

a. Breaking into or trespassing on [specified] vessels;

---

presumably because it took place in the Gulf of Mexico rather than the Arctic Ocean.

terms, the injunction expired on October 31, 2012—the last day of the 2012 Arctic Ocean open water season during which Shell would explore its OCS leases.

Greenpeace USA challenges the injunction on several grounds: (1) that the dispute does not present a justiciable case or controversy; (2) that the district court lacked subject matter jurisdiction; (3) that Shell has sued the wrong Greenpeace entity; and (4) that the district court based its ruling on legal standards and factual findings that were erroneous. We conclude that each of these contentions lacks merit.

II. STANDARD OF REVIEW

Our standard of review for preliminary injunction appeals is by now familiar: [—10—]

We review the district court's decision to grant or deny a preliminary injunction for abuse of discretion. Our review is limited and deferential. The district court's interpretation of the underlying legal principles, however, is subject to de novo review and a district court abuses its discretion when it makes an error of law.

Sw. Voter Registration Educ. Project v. Shelley, 344 F.3d 914, 918 (9th Cir. 2003) (en banc) (internal citations omitted); *see also United States v. Hinkson*, 585 F.3d 1247, 1251 (9th Cir. 2009) (en banc) (articulating our two-part test for abuse of discretion). We review findings of fact for clear error. *Thalheimer v. City of San Diego*, 645 F.3d 1109, 1115 (9th

---

    b.   Tortiously or illegally interfering with the operation, movement or progress of [specified] vessels;

    c.   Barricading, blocking, or preventing access to or egress from [specified] vessels;

    d.   Tortiously or illegally endangering or threatening any employee, contractor or visitor of Shell or any of its affiliates who is present on, or as they enter or exit, [specified] vessels.

Shell Offshore, 864 F. Supp. 2d at 855.

Cir. 2011). "Under this standard, [a]s long as the district court got the law right, it will not be reversed simply because the appellate court would have arrived at a different result if it had applied the law to the facts of the case." *Id.* (alteration in original) (internal quotation marks omitted).

We review standing, ripeness, and mootness de novo. *See Doe No. 1 v. Reed*, 697 F.3d 1235, 1238 (9th Cir. 2012); *Stormans, Inc. v. Selecky*, 586 F.3d 1109, 1119 (9th Cir. 2009). "[W]e have an independent obligation to consider mootness *sua sponte*." *NASD Dispute Resolution, Inc. v. Judicial Council*, 488 F.3d 1065, 1068 (9th Cir. 2007) (internal quotation marks omitted). [—11—]

III. JUSTICIABILITY

A. Standing and Ripeness

Greenpeace USA's justiciability arguments are hazy, but appear to challenge both Shell's standing to sue and the ripeness of the dispute. "Article III standing requires an injury that is actual or imminent, not conjectural or hypothetical. In the context of injunctive relief, the plaintiff must demonstrate a real or immediate threat of irreparable injury." *Cole v. Oroville Union High Sch. Dist.*, 228 F.3d 1092, 1100 (9th Cir. 2000) (internal quotation marks omitted). The same facts by which Shell has shown (1) a likelihood of success on the merits of its claim that Greenpeace USA would commit tortious or illegal acts against Shell's Arctic drilling operation in the absence of an injunction, and (2) that the resulting harm would be irreparable, necessarily establish that Shell has standing to seek injunctive relief. *See infra*, Parts V.B.1–2.

The dispute is also ripe because the facts are sufficiently developed and the nature of the dispute warrants prompt adjudication. *See Abbott Labs. v. Gardner*, 387 U.S. 136, 149 (1967) (explaining that the ripeness inquiry considers "the fitness of the issues for judicial decision and the hardship to the parties of withholding court consideration"). Shell presented undisputed evidence that it is only authorized to explore these leases during the narrow open water season of July through October, and the district court concluded that it faced irreparable harm absent injunctive relief; to withhold decision in such a context would work a serious hardship upon Shell. [—12—]

B. Mootness

It is undisputed that the preliminary injunction expired by its own terms on October 31, 2012—after oral argument, but before this Court could render a decision. So we must determine whether the action is moot.[4] We conclude that it falls within the mootness exception for disputes "capable of repetition, yet evading review." *NAACP, W. Region v. City of Richmond*, 743 F.2d 1346, 1353 (9th Cir. 1984) (internal quotation marks omitted).

In order for the exception to apply, "(1) the duration of the challenged action or injury must be too short to be fully litigated; and (2) there must be a reasonable likelihood that the same party will be subject to the action again." *Id.* As we recently explained, "[c]ases that qualify under prong one present controversies of inherently limited duration." *Doe No. 1*, 697 F.3d at 1240. An action is "fully litigated" if it is reviewed by this Court and the Supreme Court. *See Alcoa, Inc. v. Bonneville Power Admin.*, 698 F.3d 774, 786 87 (9th Cir. 2012).

A preliminary injunction limited to a single Arctic Ocean open water season, that bars Greenpeace USA from physically interfering with Shell's Arctic drilling operation, will never last long enough to allow full litigation because of the inherently limited duration of the open water season and, correspondingly, the drilling season. Under its multi-year [—13—] lease, Shell is legally authorized to drill only between July 10 and October 31 of each year. The now-expired preliminary

injunction against Greenpeace USA was by its own terms limited to a total duration of less than seven months, encompassing the drilling season, plus the time necessary for Shell vessels to transit to the Arctic Ocean.[5] Orders of such inherently limited duration will almost always evade full review. *See, e.g., United States v. Oregon*, 657 F.2d 1009, 1012 (9th Cir. 1985) (holding that American Indian tribe's appeal from an injunctive order banning salmon fishing in 1980 was not moot even though the spring salmon run of 1980 was over and the order was limited to that run).

Turning to the second prong, we have every reason to believe that the underlying wrong will recur. Shell has drilling rights under a multi-year lease, and there is no reason to believe that Greenpeace USA's "stop Shell" campaign was limited to the 2012 drilling season. We conclude that there is at minimum a "reasonable expectation that the same complaining party [will] be subject to the same action again." *Weinstein v. Bradford*, 423 U.S. 147, 149 (1975).

IV. JURISDICTION

The preliminary injunction at issue protects specific Shell vessels as they journey from shore-based facilities in the United States, through United States territorial waters, and into the waters of the U.S. Exclusive Economic Zone [—14—] ("EEZ") where rigs attach to the Arctic seabed and conduct exploration activities. Greenpeace USA does not challenge the district court's conclusion that, with regard to injunctive relief in the United States and its territorial waters, the court had subject matter jurisdiction based on diverse party citizenship. *See* 28 U.S.C. § 1332(a). Likewise, Greenpeace USA does not dispute that the Outer Continental Shelf Lands Act ("OCSLA") gave the court jurisdiction to grant injunctive relief while Shell's vessels are attached to the

---

[4] On November 1, 2012, Shell filed a motion to dismiss the appeal for mootness, on the grounds that the preliminary injunction had expired by its own terms. Greenpeace argued in response that the case fell within a mootness exception. Our ruling today that the case is not moot operates as a denial of Shell's motion to dismiss.

[5] The preliminary injunction ran from March 28, 2012, through October 31, 2012. *See Shell Offshore*, 864 F. Supp. 2d at 855. The district court did not explain why it so temporally limited the injunction. It appears, however, from its moving papers, that Shell sought a preliminary injunction only through the 2012 exploration drilling season.

seabed. *See* 43 U.S.C. § 1333(a)(1) (extending jurisdiction to the "seabed of the outer Continental Shelf and to . . . devices permanently or temporarily attached to the seabed, which may be erected thereon for the purpose of exploring for, developing, or producing resources therefrom").

Greenpeace USA is now solely appealing the district court's holding that under 28 U.S.C. § 1333, it had admiralty jurisdiction to enjoin conduct relating to vessels that were neither in U.S. territorial waters (where diversity jurisdiction extends) nor attached to the seabed (where OCSLA jurisdiction extends)—that is, vessels transiting through the U.S. EEZ.[6] We need not decide whether §1333 provides jurisdiction over this particular stretch of an oil rig's journey because a court can exercise supplemental jurisdiction over the entire constitutional case. *See* 28 U.S.C. §1367(a). The common nucleus of operative facts underlying Shell's claim for injunctive relief do not change when its vessels traverse an invisible line separating U.S. territorial waters from the waters of the U.S. EEZ, nor at the moment when its rigs detach from the seabed; this is therefore a single "case or [—15—] controversy" for the purposes of § 1367(a), and we conclude that the district court did not err in exercising jurisdiction over it.

V. DISCUSSION

A. Whether Greenpeace USA is the Proper Entity to Enjoin

A common thread in Greenpeace USA's various challenges is the argument that Greenpeace USA was not directly involved in any prior attacks on Shell vessels. But Shell does not need to show past injury by Greenpeace USA to establish standing or to succeed on the merits of its preliminary injunction motion. *See Diamontiney v. Borg*, 918 F.2d 793, 795 (9th Cir. 1990) ("[A]s commentators have noted, 'the injury need not have been inflicted when application [for an

injunction] is made or be certain to occur; a strong threat of irreparable injury before trial is an adequate basis.' Requiring a showing of actual injury would defeat the purpose of the preliminary injunction, which is to prevent an injury from occurring." (quoting 11 Charles Alan Wright et al., *Federal Practice and Procedure* § 2948 at 437–38 (1973)); *see also Restatement (Second) of Torts* § 933 cmt. (1)(b) ("[A] common method of proving a threat of a future tort is by proving a past tort under conditions that render its repetition or continuance probable. It is not necessary, however, to prove past wrong.").

Regardless, Greenpeace USA does not dispute evidence that its own activists carried out the attack on Shell's *Harvey Explorer*. And, although the record does not make clear which Greenpeace entity was directly responsible for multiple attacks on Cairn Energy vessels in the Arctic Ocean, [—16—] Greenpeace USA's executive director essentially took credit for it, describing the perpetrators as "our activists" and boasting that as a result of this direct action, "Cairn didn't find oil in 2010." Dkt. 56-19 (Exh. 1015 at 0005). Accordingly, the district court observed that although Shell had "not demonstrated that Greenpeace USA was directly involved in either the New Zealand or Finnish incidents" involving the *Noble Discoverer*, *Nordica*, and *Fennica*, other evidence showed that "stopping Shell and other oil companies from drilling in the Arctic is more likely than not one of the overall priority strategies of Greenpeace worldwide, as well as of Greenpeace USA." *Shell Offshore*, 864 F. Supp. 2d at 848. We see no clearly erroneous factual findings undergirding that conclusion.[7] [—17—]

---

[6] *See Shell Offshore*, 2012 WL 1931537, at *2. The district court did not reach the question of whether its diversity jurisdiction extended to the EEZ. *Id.* at *5 n.42.

[7] The dissent argues that Greenpeace USA's legal status is relevant to this appeal because "a person (or corporation) can be held legally responsible only for his own actions, absent extraordinary circumstances." Dissent at 25. But this truism, which the dissent derives from cases involving decisions on the merits, *see First Nat'l City Bank v. Banco Para El Comercio Exterior de Cuba (Bancec)*, 462 U.S. 611, 618 (1983) (appeal from dismissal of complaint on the merits); *NAACP v. Claiborne Hardware Co.*, 458 U.S. 886, 896 (1982) (appeal from judgment imposing damages liability), has no application to the present context

B. Grant of Preliminary Injunction

A plaintiff who seeks a preliminary injunction must show:

[1] that he is likely to succeed on the merits, [2] that he is likely to suffer irreparable harm in the absence of preliminary relief, [3] that the balance of equities tips in his favor, and [4] that an injunction is in the public interest.

Winter, 555 U.S. at 20.

The district court applied the correct legal standard and as our discussion below makes clear, it did so in a manner that was logical, plausible, and supported by the record. *See Hinkson*, 585 F.3d at 1251. As such, we conclude that the district court did not abuse its discretion in granting the preliminary injunction.

---

of an appeal from a preliminary injunctive order. To determine whether Shell has demonstrated a likelihood of success on the merits, we must engage in a probabilistic inquiry, an inquiry that simply was not addressed in *Claiborne Hardware* and *Bancec*.

The questionable nature of the dissent's reliance on merits-based decisions is further heightened by the limitations inherent in interlocutory review. Unlike review of a decision on the merits, our preliminary injunction decisions are both narrow in scope and rendered without benefit of a fully developed factual record. *See Ctr. for Biological Diversity v. Salazar*, — F.3d —, 2013 WL 440727, at *4 (9th Cir. Feb. 4, 2013). These limitations explain why, as we have observed time and again, preliminary injunctions decisions are just that— "preliminary." *Id.* at *3; [—17—] *Ranchers Cattlemen Action Legal Fund United Stockgrowers of Am. v. U.S. Dep't of Agric.*, 499 F.3d 1108, 1114 (9th Cir. 2007) (quoting *S. Or. Barter Fair v. Jackson Cnty.*, 372 F.3d 1128, 1136 (9th Cir. 2004)). In light of the important distinctions between review of a preliminary injunction versus a merits-based review, we fail to see how *Claiborne Hardware* and *Bancec* can be instructive.

1. Likelihood of Success on the Merits

Greenpeace USA challenges the district court's conclusion that Shell "demonstrated by a preponderance of the evidence that it is likely that Greenpeace USA would intend to commit tortious or illegal acts against Shell's Arctic drilling operations in the absence of preliminary injunctive relief." *Shell Offshore*, 864 F. Supp. 2d at 850. First, [—18—] Greenpeace USA argues that the district court erred by impermissibly shifting the burden of proof to it. The court explained that it "accorded a minor degree of weight to the fact that there is no sworn statement in this record from Greenpeace USA indicating that the organization will not attempt tortious or unlawful acts this summer against Shell" and that, to the contrary, its executive director stated publicly in March 2012 that "'[w]hatever happens in court, Greenpeace will continue to oppose Shell's plans peacefully and vigorously.'" *Id.* at 849. The district court's "weighing" of Greenpeace USA's silence amounts to an observation that contrary evidence offered by Shell stood unrefuted. There is consequently no error here.

Second, Greenpeace USA argues that Shell failed to meet its burden. The record before the district court contained evidence that: (1) Greenpeace USA forcibly boarded and defaced a Shell vessel, the *Harvey Explorer*, as part of its campaign to "stop Shell" from drilling in the Arctic; (2) on two occasions, activists that Greenpeace USA termed "our activists" employed unlawful and tortious means to stop another energy company (Cairn) from finding oil in the Arctic; (3) Greenpeace USA conceded that it uses "direct action"—including unlawful conduct—as means to an end; (4) Greenpeace USA and the global Greenpeace organization share the goal of stopping Shell from drilling in the Arctic; and (5) Greenpeace activists from other nations have on multiple occasions employed unlawful or tortious means to stop Shell from drilling in the Arctic. On these facts, we cannot say that the district court abused its discretion in concluding that Shell met its burden. *See Hinkson*, 585 F.3d at 1251. [—19—]

2. Likelihood of Irreparable Harm

The district court concluded that Shell demonstrated a likelihood of irreparable harm absent injunctive relief because "illegal or tortious efforts to board or interfere with [its] vessels would be likely to present unacceptable risks to human life, property and the environment." *Shell Offshore*, 864 F. Supp. 2d at 851 (internal quotation marks omitted). In support of these findings, the court considered evidence that actions of the sort undertaken by Greenpeace activists against Shell vessels in New Zealand, Finland, and Greenland pose risks to the safety of activists and vessel occupants alike. The court also found—and Greenpeace USA does not dispute—that "if Greenpeace USA successfully disrupted Shell's operation, calculating the amount of economic harm would be very difficult." *Id.*

Greenpeace USA offers nothing beyond conclusory statements and case summaries in support of its one-sentence argument that the "likelihood of future injury is speculative and cannot be based on matters that occurred in 1997,[8] or that involved entities that are not Greenpeace USA." The record provides ample support for the conclusion that Greenpeace USA has either undertaken directly, or embraced as its own, tactics that include forcible boarding of vessels at sea and the use of human beings as impediments to drilling operations. We find it too plain for debate that such tactics at minimum pose a serious risk of harm to human life, particularly if attempted in the extreme conditions of the Arctic Ocean, and that such harm could find no adequate remedy at law. [—20—] Accordingly, we find no abuse of discretion in the district court's conclusion. *See Hinkson*, 585 F.3d at 1251.

3. Balance of Equities

The district court concluded that "[b]y carefully tailoring preliminary injunctive relief to focus on illegal and tortious conduct, and minimizing any impact on Greenpeace USA's right to monitor the activities and

peacefully protest against Shell within the confines of the law, . . . the balance of the equities remains solidly tipped in Shell's favor." *Shell Offshore*, 864 F. Supp. 2d at 853. Greenpeace USA argues that the court erred by failing to apply a standard that would require the balance of hardships to tip "sharply" in Shell's favor.

Under *Winter*, a preliminary injunction movant must show, inter alia, that "the balance of equities tips in his favor." 555 U.S. at 20. But if a plaintiff can only show that there are "serious questions going to the merits"—a lesser showing than likelihood of success on the merits—then a preliminary injunction may still issue if the "balance of hardships tips *sharply* in the plaintiff's favor," and the other two *Winter* factors are satisfied. *Alliance for the Wild Rockies v. Cottrell*, 632 F.3d 1127, 1135 (9th Cir. 2011) (emphasis added). But the serious questions approach is inapplicable in this case because, as explained above, Shell demonstrated, and the district court found, a likelihood of success on the merits.

We conclude that the district court did not err in finding that the balance of equities favors Shell. Shell has an interest in conducting legally authorized exploration of its Arctic leases without dangerous interference from Greenpeace USA. [—21—] Greenpeace USA has a countervailing First Amendment right to protest Shell's drilling activities, and the injunction imposes safety zones around Shell vessels that prevent Greenpeace USA from exercising its rights in close proximity to those vessels. Greenpeace USA argues that this is an undue speech restriction, prohibited under *Schenck v. Pro-Choice Network of W.N.Y.*, 519 U.S. 357 (1997). We disagree.

The safety zones do not prevent Greenpeace USA from communicating with its target audience because, as the district court observed, Greenpeace USA has no audience at sea. And although the injunction imposes a safety "bubble" around Shell's vessels, Greenpeace USA's reliance on *Schenck* and its discussion of bubble zones around abortion clinics is sorely misplaced. Speech is, of

---

[8] We have searched the briefs in vain for clues as to which 1997 matters Greenpeace USA refers.

course, most protected in such quintessential public fora as the public sidewalks surrounding abortion clinics. *See id.* at 377. But the high seas are not a public forum, and the lessons of *Schenck* have little applicability there.

We conclude that, in light of the serious risk to human life and property posed by the conduct that the preliminary injunction enjoins, and given the narrow tailoring of the order, the district court did not abuse its discretion in finding that the scales of equity tip in Shell's favor.

4. Public Interest

Finally, we must decide whether the district court abused its discretion in concluding that an injunction is in the public interest. Congress has recognized a public interest in the "expeditious and orderly development" of the OCS, *see Amoco Prod. Co. v. Vill. of Gambell, AK*, 480 U.S. 531, 546 [—22—] n.11 (1987) (quoting 43 U.S.C. §1332(3)), and Shell's Arctic OCS project is authorized by law.

Greenpeace USA argues that the district court failed to consider the public interest in environmental protection before issuing the injunction. After reminding the court of the *Deepwater Horizon* disaster, Greenpeace USA argues that there is an amplified public interest in "allow[ing] the public, including Greenpeace USA, to monitor [oil drilling] activities." Finally, Greenpeace USA argues that OCSLA recognizes an interest in "public participation and environmental protection" that is furthered by groups like itself.

The district court considered the public interest in having Greenpeace USA monitor Shell's Arctic drilling activities. In fact, the court agreed with Greenpeace USA's OCSLA argument, stating that "OCSLA recognizes the important role that environmental organizations such as Greenpeace USA may play in legal proceedings regarding the development of the Outer Continental Shelf." *Shell Offshore*, 864 F. Supp. 2d at 852. The court also acknowledged that the injunction could impact "Greenpeace USA's otherwise

legal activities." *Id.* It responded by crafting a narrow injunctive order that prohibited only illegal and tortious conduct and by expressly inviting Greenpeace USA to

> seek to modify [the] order so as to permit Greenpeace to more closely monitor Shell's activities within the safety zones established by [the] order at such specific times, locations, and conditions that [the] court may order after each party has been accorded an opportunity to be heard on any such motion. [—23—]

Id. at 856. We cannot say that this treatment of public interest factors constituted an abuse of discretion.

CONCLUSION

The district court did not abuse its discretion in granting Shell's motion for a preliminary injunction, which is amply supported by the record. Consequently, the preliminary injunction order is **AFFIRMED**.

(Reporter's Note: Concurring opinion in part and dissenting opinion in part on p. 396).

[—23—] M. SMITH, Circuit Judge, concurring in part and dissenting in part:

I concur with Parts III and IV of the majority opinion that discuss justiciability and jurisdiction. I part ways with the majority, however, where it holds that Shell may impute the actions of other independent Greenpeace entities to Greenpeace USA in order to meet Shell's burden of proof.[1] Because I cannot support the imposition of legal sanctions on Greenpeace USA based, in significant part, on the conduct of others that Greenpeace USA does not control, I respectfully dissent.

I.

The majority claims that Greenpeace USA was properly enjoined because the "evidence showed that stopping Shell [—24—] and other oil companies from drilling in the Arctic is more likely than not one of the overall priority strategies of Greenpeace Worldwide, as well as of Greenpeace USA." (Maj. Op. at 16) (quoting *Shell Offshore Inc. v. Greenpeace, Inc.*, 864 F. Supp. 2d 839, 848 (D. Alaska 2012)). Of course, Greenpeace USA does not dispute that it seeks to stop Shell from drilling in the Arctic. Rather, Greenpeace USA disputes that Shell has presented sufficient evidence to show that Greenpeace USA will likely use *illegal methods* to achieve its goal. Because Greenpeace USA is unquestionably entitled to lawfully protest Shell's drilling activities, the real issue in this case is whether Shell has sufficiently proved that Greenpeace USA is likely to take "imminent" unlawful action unless it is enjoined. *See Lujan v. Defenders of Wildlife*, 504 U.S. 555, 560–61 (1992).

Relying heavily on evidence of previous unlawful encounters between "Greenpeace activists" and Shell, such as the boarding of the *Noble Discoverer* in New Zealand and the boarding of the *Nordica* and *Fennica* in Finland, the majority concludes that Shell has

met its burden. The majority's reliance on these acts is troubling, however, because even the majority admits that Greenpeace USA played no part in these events.[2] In order to sufficiently link these activities to Greenpeace USA, the majority advances two theories, both of which are ill-conceived. First, the majority claims that "Shell does not need to show past injury *by Greenpeace USA*" to be entitled to legal relief. (Maj. Op. at 15) (emphasis added). Alternatively, the majority claims that because Greenpeace USA reported on the unlawful actions of other Greenpeace [—25—] entities on its website, and made reference to the members of such Greenpeace groups as "our activists," Greenpeace USA "endorsed" those actions, thereby permitting us to hold Greenpeace USA responsible for the underlying conduct in this litigation. (Maj. Op. at 5). For the reasons discussed below, I disagree with both propositions.

A. The Separate Legal Status of Greenpeace USA Is Relevant to This Appeal

It is axiomatic that a plaintiff must sue the proper party in order to obtain relief. *See, e.g., Krupski v. Costa Crociere S.p.A.*, 130 S. Ct. 2485, 2494 (2010) ("[M]aking a deliberate choice to sue one party instead of another while fully understanding the factual and legal differences between the two parties is the antithesis of making a mistake concerning the proper party's identity.").[3] It is similarly well recognized that a person (or corporation) can be held legally responsible only for his own actions, absent extraordinary circumstances. *See, e.g., N.A.A.C.P. v. Claiborne Hardware Co.*, 458 U.S. 886, 920 (1982) ("Civil liability may not be imposed merely because an individual belonged to a

---

[1] As discussed more fully below, Greenpeace USA is one of sixteen independent voting members of Stichting Greenpeace Council (a.k.a., Greenpeace International), and is the only Greenpeace entity that is a party to this case.

[2] The record is clear that the *Noble Discoverer* was boarded by members of Greenpeace New Zealand, while the *Nordica* and *Fennica* were boarded by members of Greenpeace Nordic.

[3] *Leonard v. Parry*, 219 F.3d 25, 29 (1st Cir. 2000) ("[E]ven the most liberal interpretation of 'mistake' cannot include a deliberate decision not to sue a party whose identity plaintiff knew from the outset.") (quotation omitted); *Springman v. AIG Mktg., Inc.*, 523 F.3d 685, 690 (7th Cir. 2008) ("the maintenance for years of a suit against a party known by the plaintiff to be the wrong one to sue was an abuse of legal process").

group, some members of which committed acts of violence."); *First Nat. City Bank v. Banco Para El Comercio Exterior de Cuba (Bancec)*, 462 U.S. 611, 625 (1983) ("Separate legal personality has been described as an almost indispensable aspect of the public corporation."). Certainly Shell understands these **[—26—]** principles well—its own corporate disclosure statement takes up nearly a full page of its answering brief,[4] listing all of the subsidiaries and entities Shell admittedly relies on to limit its own liability.[5] Yet when it comes to Greenpeace USA, what is sauce for the goose is apparently not sauce for the gander.

The majority claims that Greenpeace USA can be held to account for the actions of legally separate Greenpeace entities. But well-established law, as well as basic fairness, dictates otherwise. As the Supreme Court noted in a similar case:

The taint of violence colored the conduct of some petitioners. They, of course, may be **[—27—]** held liable for the consequences of their violent deeds. The burden of demonstrating that it colored the entire collective effort, however, is not satisfied by evidence that violence occurred . . . Such a characterization must be supported by findings that adequately disclose the evidentiary basis for concluding that *specific parties* agreed to use unlawful means[.]

Claiborne Hardware Co., 458 U.S. at 933 (emphasis added).

Applying these principles to the case before us, Greenpeace USA should only be legally sanctioned for the actions of other independent entities on a sufficient showing that Greenpeace USA significantly coordinated with, encouraged, or controlled the actions of those groups. *See, e.g., id.* at 932–34 (the fact that certain activists engaged in unlawful conduct cannot be attributed to other protest organizers unless it could be shown that the latter had personally committed or authorized the unlawful acts); *Bancec*, 462 U.S. at 626–29 (explaining that "limited liability is the rule, not the exception," and thus one corporate entity may only be held liable for the actions of another "where a corporate entity is so extensively controlled by its owner that a relationship of principal and agent is created.").

The record here, however, does not demonstrate such pervasive control. Instead, the record indicates that Greenpeace USA functions as an operationally independent member of Stichting Greenpeace Council (a.k.a., Greenpeace International), the Amsterdam-based "parent" entity that licenses the Greenpeace name to groups like Greenpeace USA. Together with the other fifteen voting members of **[—28—]** Greenpeace International, Greenpeace USA helps set Greenpeace's worldwide campaign priorities, such as preventing oil drilling in the Arctic, or logging in the Amazon. But when it comes to the methods and tactics used to advance those priorities, the record makes clear that each Greenpeace licensee is autonomous, and free to choose the tactics most likely to resonate with its local constituency. Thus, while Greenpeace New Zealand and Greenpeace Nordic may seek to advance the global "stop Shell" campaign through the unlawful boarding of Shell vessels, Greenpeace USA may choose more benign tactics, like the

---

[4] Appellee Shell Offshore Inc. is a wholly owned subsidiary of SOI Finance Inc., which is a wholly owned subsidiary of Shell US E&P Investments LLC, which is a wholly owned subsidiary of Shell Oil Company, which, in turn, is a wholly owned subsidiary of Shell Petroleum Inc., which is a wholly owned subsidiary of Shell Petroleum N.V., which is a wholly owned subsidiary of Royal Dutch Shell plc. (Appellee's Corporate Disclosure Statement). Shell Offshore Inc. is itself the parent corporation of Enterprise Oil North America Inc., which in turn is the parent company of Shell Gulf of Mexico Inc., the other Shell appellee in this case. *Id.*

[5] Consider the following exchange with Shell's counsel at oral argument:

The Court: I am very well aware that Shell has thousands of corporate and other entities and I have never heard a Shell representative basically say these are all worthless; we should treat them all as just one entity.

Mr. Leppo: And I'm not saying that your honor . . . I will never make that argument.

letter-writing campaign Greenpeace USA admits it coordinated through its website.

Understood in its correct factual context, it is legally improper to impute the independent tactical choices of other Greenpeace licensees to Greenpeace USA in this litigation. Yet under the majority's newly announced rule, Greenpeace USA's separate legal status has no bearing on our decision. Of course, as previously noted, courts have consistently held just the opposite, and found that a party's *individual* culpability is a key factor in fashioning an appropriate legal remedy. *See, e.g., Claiborne Hardware Co.,* 458 U.S. at 932–34.[6] The majority does not adequately explain why this case should be decided any differently, and absent such justification, I cannot endorse its permissive and pernicious [—29—] new rule.[7] Without sufficient proof of what Greenpeace USA *itself* has done to threaten Shell's Arctic drilling operations, I would not grant a preliminary injunction.

B. Mere Endorsement of Criminal Conduct Cannot Support an Injunction

In addition to improperly relying on the direct evidence of illegal acts committed by non-party Greenpeace entities, the majority also relies on Greenpeace USA's "endorsement" of such acts to support its conclusion that Greenpeace USA was properly enjoined here. Put simply, the majority implies that Greenpeace USA can be enjoined, at least in part, because Greenpeace USA wrote favorably about the unlawful activities of groups like Greenpeace New Zealand, and described those groups' activists as "our activists." Again, I disagree.

My first ground for disagreement is factual. Although Shell tries its best to paint Greenpeace USA's statements as imminent threats, they are clearly no such thing. That Greenpeace USA officially referred to those members of Greenpeace New Zealand who unlawfully boarded the *Noble Discoverer* as "our brave activists," and described the incident as "only the first chapter in what will undoubtedly be an epic battle," is unremarkable. These statements say nothing about Greenpeace USA's *own* planned involvement [—30—] in any "epic battle," let alone shed light on Greenpeace USA's contemplated "battle" tactics. Rather, Greenpeace USA's statements are fully consistent with its claim that it plans to protest Shell's Arctic drilling using only legal methods.[8]

More importantly, however, the majority's "endorsement" test is legally ill-advised, because it is likely to have an unintended chilling effect on otherwise protected speech. No party to these proceedings claims that Greenpeace USA's blog posts fall outside the protections of the First Amendment. *See Brandenburg v. Ohio,* 395 U.S. 444, 447–48 (1969) ("advocacy of the use of force or of law violation except where such advocacy is directed to inciting or producing imminent lawless action" is protected under the Constitution); *Planned Parenthood of Columbia/Willamette, Inc. v. Am. Coal. of Life Activists,* 290 F.3d 1058, 1072 (9th Cir. 2002) (en banc) ("If ACLA had merely *endorsed* or encouraged the violent actions of others, its speech would be protected.") (emphasis added). Praising civil disobedience and promising further protest in no way rises to the level of incitement or a true threat. *See id.* at 1089 (Kozinski, J. dissenting) ("The difference between a true threat and protected

---

[6] *Scales v. United States,* 367 U.S. 203, 228–30 (1961); *Schware v. Bd. of Bar Exam. of State of N.M.,* 353 U.S. 232, 244 (1957); *Anderson v. Abbott,* 321 U.S. 349, 357–62 (1944); *Louisiana-Pacific Corp. v. ASARCO, Inc.,* 5 F.3d 431, 433–34 (9th Cir. 1993).

[7] Contrary to the majority's assertion in its own footnote seven, there is no justification for distinguishing between types of requested relief when considering whether a plaintiff has adequately sued the proper party. To obtain *any* legal relief, a plaintiff must sue the correct entity. Any other rule is simply nonsensical and contrary to long-established precedent. *See, e.g., Bancec,* 462 U.S. at 626–29.

[8] Contrary to what the district court found, Greenpeace USA denied that it intended to illegally interfere with Shell's activities. Greenpeace USA's sworn denial in its verified answer was all that was necessary, since Shell has the burden of proof in this case. *See Thalheimer v. City of San Diego,* 645 F.3d 1109, 1116 (9th Cir. 2011).

expression is this: A true threat warns of violence or other harm that the speaker *controls*.") (emphasis added). Yet by premising the grant of a preliminary injunction, at least in part, on Greenpeace USA's clearly protected political speech, the majority indirectly penalizes Greenpeace USA for [—31—] behavior that cannot be punished directly. Chief Judge Kozinski, now in the majority, stated the issue well in dissent: "Like *Claiborne Hardware*, this case involves a concerted effort by a variety of groups and individuals in pursuit of a common political cause. Some of the activities were lawful, others were not. In both cases, there was evidence that the various players communicated with each other and, at times, engaged in concerted action. The Supreme Court, however, held that mere association with groups or individuals who pursue unlawful conduct is an insufficient basis for the imposition of liability, unless it is shown that the defendants actually participated in or authorized the illegal conduct." *Id.* at 1095.

Because the record here does not show that Greenpeace USA actually participated in or authorized much of the illegal conduct relied on by the majority, I respectfully dissent.

No. 11-55823

CLEVO CO.
vs.
HECNY TRANSP., INC.

Appeal from the United States District Court for the Central District of California

Decided: April 26, 2013

Citation: 715 F.3d 1189, 1 Adm. R. 400 (9th Cir. 2013).

Before **GOODWIN** and **FLETCHER**, Circuit Judges, and **KORMAN**, Senior District Judge for the U.S. District Court for the Eastern District of New York, sitting by designation

[—3—] GOODWIN, Senior Circuit Judge:

Clevo Company appeals the district court's grant of summary judgment in favor of Hecny Transportation, Inc. We affirm.

I. BACKGROUND

A. CLEVO'S SALES AGREEMENT WITH AMAZON

Clevo is a Taiwan-based manufacturer of computer parts and accessories. In 2007, Clevo and a Brazilian entity, Amazon PC Industria e Comerciao de Microcomputadores, LTDA ("Amazon"), agreed that Clevo would manufacture and sell, and Amazon would buy, millions of dollars' worth of Clevo computer parts. Clevo and Amazon also agreed that the parts would be delivered to Amazon in multiple shipments; that Amazon would take delivery of each shipment in Brazil; and that Amazon would pay for each shipment in installments. The first installment, 10% of the shipment's price, would be paid pre-manufacture; another 20% installment would be paid before Clevo arranged shipment; and the remaining 70% balance would be paid after shipment but before Amazon took possession of the parts.

To protect its interest in receiving full payment, Clevo insisted that after it released a particular shipment for international carriage, Clevo would retain the original bills of lading for that shipment while awaiting Amazon's final 70% payment. Clevo and Amazon agreed that a shipment of parts would not be released to Amazon unless Amazon presented the original bills of lading. [—4—]

B. THE HECNY GROUP

Under Clevo and Amazon's negotiated terms, the Hecny Shipping Group ("Hecny Group") was designated to handle all of the contract shipments. The Hecny Group's members include multiple separate entities:

(1) Hecny Shipping, Limited ("Hecny Shipping"). Hecny Shipping is a non-vessel-operating common carrier ("NVOCC") based in Hong Kong, China. NVOCCs are "middlemen who typically arrange for relatively small shipments to be picked up from shippers, consolidate the . . . parcels, and ship them via a carrier or several carriers." Schoenbaum, *Admiralty & Maritime Law* (5th ed. 2012) § 7-7; *see also Kukje Hwajae Ins. Co. v. M/V Hyundai Liberty*, 294 F.3d 1171, 1176 (9th Cir. 2002), *vacated on other grounds by Green Fire & Marine Ins. Co. v. M/V Hyundai Liberty*, 543 U.S. 985 (2004).

(2) Hecny Transportation, Inc. ("Hecny Transportation"). Hecny Transportation is a freight forwarder with operations in Miami. A "freight forwarder acts as an intermediary between [a] shipper and [an] ocean carrier." Schoenbaum, *Admiralty & Maritime Law* § 7-7; *see also Constructores Tecnicos v. Sea-Land Serv., Inc.*, 945 F.2d 841 (5th Cir. 1991).

(3) Hecny Transportation (Shanghai) Limited ("Hecny Shanghai"). Hecny Shanghai is a China-based entity that takes delivery of Shanghai-originating shipments for the Hecny Group.

(4) HTI Transportes Internacionais Ltda. ("Hecny Brazil"). Hecny Brazil is a Manaus, Brazil-based freight [—5—] forwarder. Hecny Transportation maintained Hecny Brazil as its agent in Brazil, and Hecny Brazil maintained Hecny Transportation as its agent outside Brazil.

C. The Guarantee

In May 2007, Clevo began sending numerous shipments of computer parts to Amazon, and the parts were delivered without incident. But at the end of 2007, Clevo took additional measures to protect its right to payment and to formalize Hecny Transportation's role in the delivery process.

To that end, Clevo sent a document denominated "Guarantee Letter" to Hecny Transportation on December 21, 2007. The document stated:

We (Clevo Co.) will give sea shipments over to your agent in Shanghai (Hecny Shipping Limited) . . . .

. . . .

In order to protect Clevo's right of ownership, we request you to sign [sic] a guarantee letter which contains as following:

If you release any sea shipment to Amazon PC without our further notice, Hecny Transportation, Inc.-MIA must compensate Clevo all damage which we suffer.

For the purpose of protecting your right, on[] the other hand, provided that Clevo agree[s] to release sea shipment[s] to Clevo's customer, [—6—] Clevo will give you a notice by fax, and please work[] in accordance with International Transportation Rule.

Unless Clevo propose[s] a written notice to terminate this letter, the Parties have caused [it] to be executed . . . .

Notably, the text of the letter lacks any reference to a contractual statute of limitations or any other significant provisions limiting the parties' liability. But those omissions did not prevent Hecny Transportation from giving assent. Instead, a Hecny Transportation employee signed the letter and returned the signed copy (the "Guarantee") to Clevo.

After receiving the Guarantee, Clevo made multiple additional shipments of parts to Amazon between January 2008 and September 2008. Although the Hecny Group completed each of those shipments without any apparent difficulty, it would fare much worse when handling Clevo's next shipment, in October 2008.

D. Shipping the Goods

1. Clevo prepares the Goods and Hecny Shipping issues the Bills of Lading.

In October 2008, Clevo received an Amazon order for an additional $2,210,000 in parts (the "Goods"), as well as Amazon's pre-shipment payments. After manufacturing the Goods, Clevo delivered them to Hecny Shanghai for transport on or about October 23, 2008. Four days later, Hecny Shipping issued two bills of lading for the shipment (the "Bills of Lading"). [—7—]

Each of the Bills of Lading includes a front and back page. The front pages describe:

- the Goods;
- the name of the shipper ("CLEVO CO.");
- the consignee, Amazon;
- the port of loading and destination ("SHANGHAI" and "MANAUS", respectively); and
- the delivery agent ("HECNY TRANSPORTATION, INC. - MIA").

The back pages contain numerous Terms and Conditions of Contract ("Terms and Conditions").

Section 5 of the Terms and Conditions includes a *Himalaya* clause (the "*Himalaya* Clause"), which provides that:

[Hecny Shipping] shall be entitled to sub contract on any terms the whole or any part of the carriage . . . and any and all duties whatsoever . . . . [E]very such servant, agent and sub contractor shall have the benefit of all provisions herein for the benefit of [Hecny Shipping] as if such provisions were expressly for their benefit . . . .

Himalaya clauses are commonly used in bills of lading. *See Mori Seiki USA, Inc. v. M.V. Alligator Triumph*, 990 F.2d 444, 450 (9th Cir. 1993); *Norfolk S. Ry. v. James N. Kirby, Pty Ltd.*, 543 U.S. 14, 31–32, 20 n.2 (2004); *Adler v. Dickson (The Himalaya)* [1954] 2 Lloyd's Rep. 267; [1955] 1 Q.B. 158 (C.A.). [—8—]

Additionally, Section 21 of the Terms and Conditions states that Hecny Shipping "shall [be] discharged from all liability in respect of non-delivery[,] misdelivery[,] delay[,] loss[,] or damage unless suit is brought within 1 year after delivery of the Goods."

Clevo received the original Bills of Lading on or about October 27, 2008, and retained them, as Amazon had yet to pay the remaining 70% of the Goods' purchase price.

2. The Goods are transported and released.

At or around the time that Hecny Shipping issued the Bills of Lading, the Goods began their transit to Brazil. Hecny Shanghai arranged an initial sea transportation segment, during which the Goods traveled from Shanghai to Los Angeles. After the Goods arrived in Los Angeles, Hecny Transportation booked their motor transport to Miami, unloaded them, and staged them for air transportation between Miami and Manaus. Hecny Transportation then arranged for carrier Arrow Air, Inc. ("Arrow Air") to complete the Goods' final air transportation segment via two flights. For both flights, Hecny Transportation issued its own "house" air waybill, as well as a "master" air waybill on behalf of Arrow Air (the "Waybills").

Soon after the Goods arrived in Manaus, Hecny Transportation forwarded the Waybills to Hecny Brazil, and Hecny Brazil released those Waybills to Amazon. With the Waybills in hand, Amazon took delivery of the Goods in November 2008.

Hecny Brazil concedes that it never required Amazon to present the Bills of Lading prior to taking possession of the [—9—] Goods. For its part, Clevo never provided the Bills of Lading to Amazon and Clevo never notified any Hecny Group entity that it could release the Goods. Instead, Clevo retained the Bills of Lading while awaiting the final 70% balance of the Goods' purchase price.

3. Clevo discovers the improper delivery.

By January 2009, Clevo still had not received payment and emailed Hecny Transportation to ensure that the Goods were still being held. To Clevo's apparent surprise, a Hecny Transportation employee responded that the "sh[i]p[men]ts were moved to Manaus . . . . I have not received any request to hold the [shipments] in Miami."

Despite taking delivery of the Goods, Amazon never forwarded the outstanding purchase price to Clevo and instead filed for bankruptcy. On December 11, 2009, more than one year after the initial misdelivery to Amazon, Clevo sued numerous Hecny Group entities for the unpaid remainder of the Goods' purchase price.

II. DISCUSSION

A. JURISDICTION AND STANDARD OF REVIEW

The district court correctly concluded that it had original jurisdiction under 28 U.S.C. §1333, and we have jurisdiction under 28 U.S.C. § 1291. We review orders granting summary judgment *de novo, see Bamonte v. City of Mesa*, 598 F.3d 1217, 1220 (9th Cir. 2010), and therefore apply "the same principles as the district court: whether, with the evidence viewed in the light most favorable to the non-moving party, there are no genuine issues of material fact, so that the [—10—] moving party is entitled to a judgment as a matter of law." *Id.* (internal quotation marks omitted).

B. APPLICATION

Viewing the evidence in the light most favorable to Clevo, the record reflects that Hecny Transportation and its agent, Hecny Brazil, were required to obtain the original Bills of Lading from Amazon prior to releasing the Goods. And there is no dispute that the relevant Hecny entities never obtained those documents. Nevertheless, Hecny Transportation's liability to Clevo turns not on any failure in delivery but instead on the applicable statute of limitations. Put differently, because Clevo filed suit more than one year after the improper delivery, the central question is whether Clevo's claims are governed by the Guarantee, which establishes no express statute of limitations, or the Bills of Lading, which establish a one-year limit on suit.

We conclude that the Guarantee was initially effective to place Clevo and Hecny Transportation in direct contractual privity, without any contractually-created statute of limitations. But that initial relationship was modified when the Bills of Lading issued. Section 21 of the Terms and Conditions supplemented the terms of the Guarantee and created an express limitations period, providing that Hecny Shipping "shall [be] discharged from all liability in respect of . . . misdelivery . . . unless suit is brought within 1 year after delivery of the Goods."

By operation of the *Himalaya* Clause, the benefit of the one-year statute of limitations in the Bills of Lading extended beyond Hecny Shipping to Hecny Transportation as well. *See M.V. Alligator Triumph*, 990 F.2d at 450; *Kirby*, 543 U.S. at [—11—] 31–32. And because Hecny Transportation has asserted that provision in defense to suit, Clevo's claims are time-barred. We explain our reasoning in greater detail below.

1. The Guarantee was effective *ab initio* between Clevo and Hecny Transportation.

We first consider the nature and effect of the Guarantee. Hecny Transportation contends that the document cannot be considered a valid contract between it and Clevo, because the requisite elements of contract formation are absent here. Not so.

Basic principles in the common law of contracts readily apply in the maritime context. *See Kirby*, 543 U.S. at 23 ("federal common law . . . appl[ies]" where contract suit is "under . . . admiralty jurisdiction"); *Yang Ming Mar. Transp. Corp. v. Okamoto Freighters Ltd.*, 259 F.3d 1086, 1092 (9th Cir. 2001) ("familiar principles of contract interpretation govern" construction of maritime bill of lading). And the Guarantee presents the requisite elements of offer, acceptance, and consideration. *See* RESTATEMENT (SECOND) OF CONTRACTS §§ 17, 22, 24, 50.

Clevo made an offer by explaining proposed terms of conduct on its own letterhead; "request[ing]" Hecny Transportation "to sign" the document as a means of assent; and sending the document to Hecny Transportation. Hecny Transportation tendered an acceptance by signing the Guarantee and returning it to Clevo. And the parties' mutual assent accompanied a mutual exchange of promises as consideration. Viewing the Guarantee in the light most favorable to Clevo, *see Bamonte*, 598 F.3d at 1220, Clevo promised Hecny Transportation that, among other things, it [—12—] would provide future Amazon-destined shipments to Hecny Shanghai and Hecny Transportation. Clevo also vested in Hecny Transportation a direct breach-of-contract claim if Clevo failed to perform. In return, Hecny Transportation promised not to "release any sea shipment to Amazon . . . without [Clevo's] further notice" and to compensate Clevo for an improper release. Therefore, the signed Guarantee established a valid contract. As of December 2007, Clevo and Hecny Transportation were directly bound to an agreement that prescribed specific delivery instructions for Clevo's shipments but lacked any contractual statute of limitations.

However, ten months after the Guarantee was executed, Hecny Shipping issued the Bills of Lading.

2. The Bills of Lading supplemented the Guarantee.

The Bills of Lading, which directly bind Clevo,[1] describe a multifaceted, multimodal shipment of the Goods between Shanghai and Manaus, and provide additional details about the roles of Hecny Transportation and other Hecny Group entities during transport. The *Himalaya* Clause makes clear that Hecny Shipping is "entitled to sub contract on any terms the whole or any part of the carriage . . . and any and all duties whatsoever undertaken . . . in relation to the Goods," and the Clause also grants Hecny Shipping's agents and subcontractors "the benefit of all provisions [in the Bills] for the benefit of [Hecny Shipping] as if such provisions were expressly for their benefit." Moreover, the front page of each Bill of Lading describes a "Delivery Agent . . . Hecny [—13—] Transportation, Inc.-MIA," thereby further confirming that agents would be involved in handling Clevo's shipment. Thus, where the Guarantee provided a general outline of the relationship between Clevo and Hecny Transportation, the Bills of Lading supplement that outline, explain a division of labor, and identify Hecny Transportation's role in that division of labor.

In addition to providing these details, however, the Bills of Lading also add an express statute of limitations for shipping-related suits. Under the terms of Section 21, suits against Hecny Shipping for non-delivery, delay, loss, misdelivery, or damage to the Goods must be filed, if at all, within one year after delivery.[2]

---

[1] Clevo does not argue that it is not bound by the terms of the Bills of Lading.

[2] The terms of the Bills of Lading expressly permit Hecny Shipping to amend pre-existing contracts to which it was a stranger. In Section 5 of the Terms and Conditions, Hecny Shipping represented that it executed the Bills of Lading "not only on its own behalf but also as agent and trustee for [its] servants, agents, and sub contractors." Neither Clevo nor Hecny Transportation has attacked the validity of this agency representation.

3. The *Himalaya* Clause extends Hecny Shipping's one-year statute of limitations to Hecny Transportation.

Although the express language of Section 21 protects only Hecny Shipping from untimely suits, the *Himalaya* Clause extends the benefits of the one-year limitation to Hecny Transportation as well.

We previously explained that *Himalaya* clauses are "commonly used to extend a carrier's defenses and liability limitations to certain third parties performing services on its [—14—] behalf," *M.V. Alligator Triumph*, 990 F.2d at 450, and the Supreme Court has recently addressed *Himalaya* clauses in *Kirby*. *Kirby* teaches that where, as here, a *Himalaya* clause "indicates an intent to extend the [carrier's] liability limitation broadly" and describes the carrier's servants, agents, and subcontractors, there is "no reason to contravene the clause's obvious meaning," and the carrier's defenses should be extended to those servient parties. 543 U.S. at 31–32; *see also Kawasaki Kisen Kaisha Ltd. v. Regal-Beloit Corp.*, 130 S. Ct. 2433, 2439 (2010); *M.V. Alligator Triumph*, 990 F.2d at 450–51 (reviewing *Himalaya* clause and extending carrier's liability limitations to agent). Because: (1) the *Himalaya* Clause expressly permits "every . . . servant, agent and sub contractor [to] have the benefit of all provisions . . . for the benefit of" Hecny Shipping; (2) the one-year statute of limitations is such a provision; and (3) Hecny Transportation is such an agent, Hecny Transportation is thereby entitled to assert Section 21's time-bar.

4. Clevo's claims are time-barred.

Hecny Transportation's error in releasing the Goods to Amazon without first obtaining the original Bills of Lading is a misdelivery. *See C-ART, Ltd. v. Hong Kong Islands Lines Am., S.A.*, 940 F.2d 530, 533 (9th Cir. 1991) ("if the carrier delivers the goods to one other than the authorized holder of the bill of lading, the carrier is liable for misdelivery") (internal alterations and quotation marks omitted). And the Bills of Lading specifically bar all suits for "misdelivery . . . unless suit is brought within 1 year after delivery of the Goods." Because Clevo did not file suit against Hecny Transportation until December 11, 2009, more than one year after the misdelivery occurred, Clevo's claims are time-barred. [—15—]

III. CONCLUSION

The district court correctly granted summary judgment to Hecny Transportation.

AFFIRMED.

United States Court of Appeals
for the Ninth Circuit

No. 12-35266

INSTITUTE OF CETACEAN RESEARCH
vs.
SEA SHEPHERD CONSERVATION SOC'Y

Appeals from the United States District Court for the Western District of Washington

Decided: February 25, 2013
Amended: May 24, 2013

Citation: 725 F.3d 940, 1 Adm. R. 406 (9ᵗʰ Cir. 2013).

Before **KOZINSKI**, Chief Judge, and **TASHIMA** and **SMITH, JR.**, Circuit Judges.

[—5—] **KOZINSKI**, Chief Judge:

You don't need a peg leg or an eye patch. When you ram ships; hurl glass containers of acid; drag metal-reinforced ropes in the water to damage propellers and rudders; launch smoke bombs and flares with hooks; and point high-powered lasers at other ships, you are, without a doubt, a pirate, no matter how high-minded you believe your purpose to be.

Plaintiffs-Appellants (collectively, "Cetacean") are Japanese researchers who hunt whales in the Southern Ocean. The United States, Japan and many other nations are signatories to the International Convention for the Regulation of Whaling art. VIII, Dec. 2, 1946, 62 Stat. 1716, 161 U.N.T.S. 74, which authorizes whale hunting when conducted in compliance with a research permit issued by a signatory. Cetacean has such a permit from Japan. Nonetheless, it has been hounded on the high seas for years by a group calling itself Sea Shepherd Conservation Society and its eccentric founder, Paul Watson (collectively "Sea Shepherd"). Sea Shepherd's tactics include all of those listed in the previous paragraph. [—6—]

Cetacean sued under the Alien Tort Statute, 28 U.S.C. § 1350, for injunctive and declaratory relief. The statute provides a cause of action for "a tort . . . committed in violation of the law of nations or a treaty of the United States." 28 U.S.C. § 1350. Cetacean argues that Sea Shepherd's acts amount to piracy and violate international agreements regulating conduct on the high seas. The district court denied Cetacean's request for a preliminary injunction and dismissed its piracy claims. We have jurisdiction over the order denying the injunction pursuant to 28 U.S.C. § 1292(a). We also have jurisdiction to review the dismissal of the piracy claims because the district court's reasoning for dismissing them is "inextricably intertwined with" its reasons for denying the preliminary injunction. *Smith* v. *Arthur Andersen LLP*, 421 F.3d 989, 998 (9th Cir. 2005) (internal quotation marks omitted).

I. DISMISSAL OF THE PIRACY CLAIMS

We review the district court's dismissal of Cetacean's piracy claims de novo. *Manzarek* v. *St. Paul Fire & Marine Ins. Co.*, 519 F.3d 1025, 1030 (9th Cir. 2008). "[T]he definition of piracy under the law of nations . . . [is] spelled out in the UNCLOS, as well as the High Seas Convention," which provide almost identical definitions. *United States* v. *Dire*, 680 F.3d 446, 469 (4th Cir. 2012); *see* United Nations Convention on the Law of the Sea ("UNCLOS"), art. 101, Dec. 10, 1982, 1833 U.N.T.S. 397; Convention on the High Seas, art. 15, Apr. 29, 1958, 13 U.S.T. 2312, 450 U.N.T.S. 82. The UNCLOS defines "piracy" as "illegal acts of *violence* or detention, or any act of depredation, committed for *private ends* by the crew or the passengers of a private ship . . . and directed . . . on the high seas, against another ship . . . or against persons or property on board such ship." [—7—] UNCLOS art. 101 (emphasis added); *see also* Convention on the High Seas art. 15.

The district court's analysis turns on an erroneous interpretation of "private ends" and "violence." The district court construed "private ends" as limited to those pursued for "financial enrichment." But the common understanding of "private" is far broader. The term is normally used as an antonym to "public" (e.g., private attorney general) and often refers to matters of a personal nature that are not necessarily connected to finance (e.g., private property, private entrance, private understanding and invasion of privacy). *See Webster's New Int'l Dictionary* 1969 (2d. ed. 1939) (defining "private" to mean "[b]elonging to, or concerning, an individual person, company, or interest").

We give words their ordinary meaning unless the context requires otherwise. *See Leocal* v. *Ashcroft*, 543 U.S. 1, 8–9 (2004); Antonin Scalia & Bryan A. Garner, *Reading Law: The Interpretation of Legal Texts* 69 (2012). The context here is provided by the rich history of piracy law, which defines acts taken for private ends as those not taken on behalf of a state. *See* Douglas Guilfoyle, *Piracy Off Somalia: UN Security Council Resolution 1816 and IMO Regional Counter-Piracy Efforts*, 57 Int'l & Comp. L. Q. 690, 693 (2008) (discussing the High Seas Convention); Michael Bahar, *Attaining Optimal Deterrence at Sea: A Legal and Strategic Theory for Naval Anti-Piracy Operations*, 40 Vand. J. Transnat'l L. 1, 32 (2007); *see also Harmony* v. *United States*, 43 U.S. (2 How.) 210, 232 (1844) ("The law looks to [piracy] as an act of hostility . . . being committed by a vessel not commissioned and engaged in lawful warfare."). Belgian courts, perhaps the only ones to have previously considered the issue, have held that environmental activism qualifies as [—8—] a private end. *See* Cour de Cassation [Cass.] [Court of Cassation] *Castle John* v. *NV Mabeco*, Dec. 19, 1986, 77 I.L.R. 537 (Belg.). This interpretation is "entitled to considerable weight." *Abbott* v. *Abbott*, 130 S. Ct. 1983, 1993 (2010) (internal quotation marks omitted). We conclude that "private ends" include those pursued on personal, moral or philosophical grounds, such as Sea Shepherd's professed environmental goals. That the perpetrators believe themselves to be serving the public good does not render their ends public.

The district court's interpretation of "violence" was equally off-base. Citing no precedent, it held that Sea Shepherd's conduct is not violent because it targets ships and equipment rather than people. This runs afoul of the UNCLOS itself, which prohibits "violence . . . against another ship" and "violence . . . against persons or property." UNCLOS art. 101. Reading "violence" as extending to malicious acts against inanimate objects also comports with the commonsense understanding of the term, *see Webster's New Int'l Dictionary* 2846, as when a man violently pounds a table with his fist. Ramming ships, fouling propellers and hurling fiery and acid-filled projectiles easily qualify as violent activities, even if they could somehow be directed only at inanimate objects.

Regardless, Sea Shepherd's acts fit even the district court's constricted definition. The projectiles directly endanger Cetacean's crew, as the district court itself recognized. And damaging Cetacean's ships could cause them to sink or become stranded in glacier-filled, Antarctic waters, jeopardizing the safety of the crew. [—9—]

The activities that Cetacean alleges Sea Shepherd has engaged in are clear instances of violent acts for private ends, the very embodiment of piracy. The district court erred in dismissing Cetacean's piracy claims.

II. PRELIMINARY INJUNCTION

"A plaintiff seeking a preliminary injunction must establish [1] that he is likely to succeed on the merits, [2] that he is likely to suffer irreparable harm in the absence of preliminary relief, [3] that the balance of equities tips in his favor, and [4] that an injunction is in the public interest." *Winter* v. *Natural Res. Def. Council, Inc.*, 555 U.S. 7, 20 (2008). We review the district court's denial of the preliminary injunction for abuse of discretion. *Harris* v. *Bd. of Supervisors, L.A. Cnty.*, 366 F.3d 754, 760 (9th Cir. 2004). "A district court would necessarily abuse its discretion if it based its ruling on an erroneous view of the law or on a clearly erroneous assessment of the evidence." *Cooter & Gell* v. *Hartmarx Corp.*, 496 U.S. 384, 405 (1990).

A. Likelihood of Success

Cetacean sought its injunction pursuant to three international agreements: the Convention for the Suppression of Unlawful

Acts Against the Safety of Maritime Navigation ("SUA Convention"), art. 3, Mar. 10, 1988, S. Treaty Doc. No. 101-1, 1678 U.N.T.S. 222, the UNCLOS and the Convention on the International Regulations for Preventing Collisions at Sea ("COLREGS"), Oct. 20, 1972, 28 U.S.T. 3459, 1050 U.N.T.S. 18. [—10—]

1. The SUA Convention

The SUA Convention prohibits acts that endanger, or attempt to endanger, the safe navigation of a ship. SUA Convention art. 3. Cetacean presented uncontradicted evidence that Sea Shepherd's tactics could seriously impair its ability to navigate. The district court nonetheless concluded that, since Sea Shepherd has not yet disabled any of Cetacean's ships, it's unlikely it would succeed in the future. This was clear error. The district court overlooked the actual language of the Convention, which prohibits "endager[ing]" safe navigation. *Id.* This requires only that Sea Shepherd create dangerous conditions, regardless of whether the harmful consequences ever come about. *See Webster's New Int'l Dictionary* 843. As to whether Sea Shepherd's tactics actually are dangerous, the record discloses that it has rammed and sunk several other whaling vessels in the past. *See* Appendix.

The district court also erred by failing to recognize that Sea Shepherd, at the very least, *attempted* to endanger the navigation of Cetacean's ships. An attempt is sufficient to invoke the SUA Convention, even if unsuccessful. Sea Shepherd's repeated claims that its efforts are merely "symbolic" and "employed so as to ensure maximum safety" are disingenuous. How else can it explain that it has switched to metal-reinforced prop-fouling ropes? Reinforced ropes carry the same symbolic meaning as normal ropes, but they are far more destructive. Nor does symbolism require Sea Shepherd to bring its ships dangerously close to Cetacean's. The district court's conclusion that Cetacean wasn't likely to succeed on its SUA Convention claims rested on an implausible determination of the facts and an erroneous application of law; it was an abuse of discretion. *United* [—11—]

States v. *Hinkson*, 585 F.3d 1247, 1251 (9th Cir. 2009) (en banc).

2. The UNCLOS

For the reasons explained above, Part I, *supra*, the district court erred in its assessment of Cetacean's UNCLOS piracy claims, and consequently abused its discretion in assessing the likelihood of success on these claims. *See Cooter & Gell*, 496 U.S. at 405.

3. The COLREGS

The district court did find that Cetacean is likely to succeed on the merits of its claims under the COLREGS. The COLREGS state obligatory and universal norms for navigating ships so as to avoid collision. *Crowley Marine Services, Inc.* v. *Maritrans, Inc.*, 530 F.3d 1169, 1172–73 (9th Cir. 2008). Sea Shepherd deliberately navigates its ships dangerously close to Cetacean's ships. The district court's finding that this is likely a violation of the COLREGS is adequately supported by the record. *See Hinkson*, 585 F.3d at 1251.

B. LIKELIHOOD OF IRREPARABLE HARM

The district court determined that "injury is possible, but not likely," even though it found that the projectiles Sea Shepherd launches at Cetacean's ships "are an obvious hazard to anyone who [sic] they might hit" and that Sea Shepherd navigates its ships "in such a way that a collision is highly likely." Sea Shepherd itself adorns the hulls of its ships with the names and national flags of the numerous whaling vessels it has rammed and sunk. *See* Appendix. The district court's [—12—] observation that Cetacean hasn't yet suffered these injuries is beside the point. *See Helling* v. *McKinney*, 509 U.S. 25, 33 (1993). Cetacean's uncontradicted evidence is that Sea Shepherd's tactics could immobilize Cetacean's ships in treacherous Antarctic waters, and this is confirmed by common sense: A dangerous act, if committed often enough, will inevitably lead to harm, which could easily be irreparable. *Harris*, 366 F.3d at 766.

C. BALANCE OF EQUITIES

The district court correctly found that the balance of equities favors Cetacean. As it noted, "[a]bsent an injunction, the whalers will continue to be the victims of Sea Shepherd's harassment," but "Sea Shepherd ... points to no hardship that it will suffer if the court imposes an injunction."

D. PUBLIC INTEREST

"The public interest inquiry primarily addresses impact on non-parties rather than parties." *Bernhardt* v. *L.A. Cnty.*, 339 F.3d 920, 931 (9th Cir. 2003) (internal quotation marks omitted). This is particularly the case where "the impact of an injunction reaches beyond the parties, carrying with it a potential for public consequences." *Stormans, Inc.* v. *Selecky*, 586 F.3d 1109, 1139 (9th Cir. 2009). The primary public interests at issue here are the health of the marine ecosystem, *Winter*, 555 U.S. at 25–26; *see also Earth Island Inst.* v. *U.S. Forest Serv.*, 442 F.3d 1147, 1177 (9th Cir. 2006), and the safety of international waterways.

Where a valid law speaks to the proper level of deference to a particular public interest, it controls. *See Golden Gate Rest. Ass'n* v. *City & Cnty. of S.F.*, 512 F.3d 1112, 1126–27 [—13—] (9th Cir. 2008). Our laws defining the public interest in regards to whaling are the Whaling Convention Act and the Marine Mammal Protection Act, both of which permit whaling pursuant to scientific permits issued under the Whaling Convention. 16 U.S.C. § 1372; 16 U.S.C. §916c. Cetacean's activities are covered by such a permit and thus are consistent with congressional policy as to the marine ecosystem.

Our laws also reflect a strong public interest in safe navigation on the high seas. As already discussed, Sea Shepherd's activities clearly violate the UNCLOS, the SUA Convention and the COLREGS. *See* Part II.A, *supra*. As such, they are at loggerheads with the public interest of the United States and all other seafaring nations in safe navigation of the high seas.

The district court also considered the interest in keeping U.S. courts out of the international political controversy surrounding whaling. But enjoining piracy sends no message about whaling; it sends the message that we will not tolerate piracy. This is hardly a controversial view, as evidenced by a joint statement from the United States, Australia, the Netherlands and New Zealand condemning dangerous activities in the Southern Ocean. Joint Statement on Whaling and Safety at Sea from the Governments of Australia, the Netherlands, New Zealand, and the United States: Call for Responsible Behavior in the Southern Ocean Whale Sanctuary (Dec. 13, 2011), *available at* http://www.state.gov/r/pa/prs/ps/2011/12/1787 04.htm. Refusing the injunction sends the far more troublesome message that we condone violent vigilantism by U.S. nationals in international waters. [—14—]

The district court also rejected Cetacean's claims on international comity grounds. While there is a public interest in maintaining harmonious international relations, it's not a factor here. An Australian court has entered default judgment against Cetacean, purporting to enjoin it from whaling in Antarctic coastal waters over which Australia claims sovereignty. The district court's deference to Australia's judgment in that case was an abuse of discretion. *Asvesta* v. *Petroutsas*, 580 F.3d 1000, 1009 (9th Cir. 2009). To begin, the district court misunderstood the Australian judgment, which addressed the legality of Cetacean's activities, not Sea Shepherd's. Whatever the status of Cetacean's whaling under Australian law, it gives Sea Shepherd no license to engage in piracy. It is for Australia, not Sea Shepherd, to police Australia's court orders.

Additionally, comity applies only if the foreign court has competent jurisdiction. *Id.* at 1011. But the United States doesn't recognize Australia's claims of sovereignty over Antarctic waters. *See* Note from U.S. Deputy Representative to the United Nations, to Secretary-General of the United Nations (Dec. 3, 2004); Note from Embassy of the United States, to Australian Department of Foreign Affairs and Trade (Mar. 31, 1995). By according comity to Australia's judgment, we would implicitly recognize Australia's jurisdiction, in contravention of the stated position of our government. The conduct of foreign affairs is within the exclusive province of the Executive, *see United States v. Hooker*, 607 F.2d 286, 289 (9th Cir. 1979), and we must defer to its views, *see Willams v. Suffolk Ins. Co.*, 38 U.S. (13 Pet.) 415, 420 (1839); *cf. Mingtai Fire Ins. Co. v. United Parcel Serv.*, 177 F.3d 1142, 1147 (9th Cir. 1999). [—15—]

E. UNCLEAN HANDS

An injunction is an equitable remedy. *Winter*, 555 U.S. at 32. While the *Winter* factors "are pertinent in assessing the propriety of any injunctive relief," *id.*, traditional equitable considerations such as laches, duress and unclean hands may militate against issuing an injunction that otherwise meets *Winter*'s requirements. Here, however, the district court abused its discretion in denying the injunction based on unclean hands. *Seller Agency Council, Inc. v. Kennedy Ctr. for Real Estate Educ., Inc.*, 621 F.3d 981, 986 (9th Cir. 2010).

The district court held that Cetacean's hands are unclean because, "[i]n flouting the Australian injunction, the whalers demonstrate their disrespect for a judgment of a domestic court." Because neither the United States nor Japan recognizes Australia's jurisdiction over any portion of the Southern Ocean, Cetacean owes no respect to the Australian order. Moreover, the unclean hands doctrine requires that the plaintiff have "dirtied [his hands] in acquiring the right he now asserts, or that the manner of dirtying renders inequitable the assertion of such rights against the defendant." *Republic Molding Corp. v. B.W. Photo Utils.*, 319 F.2d 347, 349 (9th Cir. 1963). Cetacean has done nothing to acquire the rights to safe navigation and protection from pirate attacks; they flow automatically from customary international law and treaties. Nor is there anything remotely inequitable in seeking to navigate the sea lanes without interference from pirates.

* * *

The district court's orders denying Cetacean's preliminary injunction and dismissing its piracy claims are **REVERSED**. [—16—] The preliminary injunction we issued on December 17, 2012, *Inst. of Cetacean Research v. Sea Shepherd Conservation Soc'y*, 702 F.3d 573 (9th Cir. 2012), will remain in effect until further order of this court. Panels have broad discretion to reassign cases on remand when they feel justice or its appearance requires it. *See United States v. Quach*, 302 F.3d 1096, 1103–04 (9th Cir. 2002). The district judge has expressed strong and erroneous views on the merits of this high profile case. Without ourselves reaching any determination as to his ability to proceed impartially or impugning his integrity, to preserve the appearance of justice, we conclude reassignment is appropriate. *See Ellis v. U.S. Dist. Court (In re Ellis)*, 356 F.3d 1198, 1211 (9th Cir. 2004) (en banc). The appearance of justice would be served if the case were transferred to another district judge, drawn at random, and we so order in accordance with the standing orders of the Western District of Washington. The panel retains jurisdiction over any further appeals or writs involving this case.

(Reporter's Note: Concurring opinion in part and dissenting opinion in part on p. 411).

[—17—] Appendix

ER 279

[—18—]

ER 281

[—19—] M. SMITH, Circuit Judge, concurring in part and dissenting in part:

I concur in both the reasoning and the judgment of the panel opinion, reversing the district court's dismissal of Cetacean's piracy claims, and its failure to grant Cetacean a preliminary injunction. Even if one believes it is barbaric to harvest whales for any purpose at the beginning of the 21st century, as practiced by Cetacean, it is clearly permitted under international law. *See* International Convention for the Regulation of Whaling art. VIII, Dec. 2, 1946, 62 Stat. 1716, 161 U.N.T.S. 74. Sea Shepherd's piracy is not. *See* Maj. Op. at 5–14.

However, I respectfully dissent from the majority's decision to reassign this case to a different district judge. "We remand to a different judge only in unusual circumstances or when required to preserve the interests of justice." *United States v. Wolf Child*, 699 F.3d 1082, 1102 (9th Cir. 2012) (citing *United States v. Quach*, 302 F.3d 1096, 1103 (9th Cir. 2002)). Specifically, we employ a three-factor test to determine whether to remand a case to a different district judge:

(1) whether the original judge would reasonably be expected upon remand to have substantial difficulty in putting out of his or her mind previously expressed views or findings determined to be erroneous or based on evidence that must be rejected, (2) whether [—20—]

reassignment is advisable to preserve the appearance of justice, and (3) whether reassignment would entail waste and duplication out of proportion to any gain in preserving the appearance of fairness.

Id.; *see also Wyler Summit P'ship v. Turner Broad. Sys., Inc.*, 235 F.3d 1184, 1196 (9th Cir. 2000).

Applying these factors, I see no basis for reassigning this case. Our panel opinion is well-articulated, succinct, and absolutely clear as to what is required of the district judge on remand. Importantly, it leaves no room for any district judge to "have substantial difficulty . . . putting out of his or her mind previously expressed views." *Wolf Child*, 699 F.3d at 1102. The Sea Shepherds are pirates. Period. No district judge could fail to grasp the clarity and firmness of our opinion.

Moreover, the "appearance of justice" does not require reassignment. We have previously reserved reassignment for only the most egregious cases.[1] While the district judge [—21—] clearly erred in finding for the Sea Shepherds, there is absolutely no evidence in

---

[1] *See, e.g., United States v. Working*, 287 F.3d 801, 809–10 (9th Cir. 2002) (reassigning to different district judge where district court sentenced defendant to one day in jail following conviction for assault with the intent to commit first degree murder); *Quach*, 302 F.3d at 1103–04 (reassigning where district court previously suggested that the defendant was "fortunate" not to receive the death penalty, and where the court indicated that had the government moved for a downward departure, it would have denied the motion); *United Nat. Ins. Co. v. R&D Latex Corp.*, 141 F.3d 916, 919–20 (9th Cir. 1998) (reassigning where district judge had "twice granted summary judgment" to a party without articulating any reasons); *cf. Wyler Summit Partnership*, 235 F.3d at 1196 (refusing to remand to a different district judge even though district judge "adopted verbatim" one party's clearly biased proposed order); *United States v. Waknine*, 543 F.3d [—21—] 546, 560 (9th Cir. 2008) (refusing to reassign to a different district judge despite commission of significant procedural errors).

this record to suggest that he did so for an improper purpose, such as bias or prejudice.

Finally, because I do not believe "preserving the appearance of fairness" requires reassignment, the majority's decision will necessarily "entail waste and duplication out of proportion" to any benefits. *Wolf Child*, 699 F.3d at 1102. District judges, like circuit judges, occasionally make mistakes. Where, as here, there is no reason to suspect that the district judge will repeat those mistakes on remand, reassignment is inappropriate.

I respectfully dissent from the majority's decision to reassign this case to a different district judge.

United States Court of Appeals
for the Ninth Circuit

No. 12-35332

SHELL OFFSHORE, INC.
vs.
GREENPEACE, INC.

Appeal from the United States District Court for the
District of Alaska

Decided: July 10, 2013

Citation: 722 F.3d 1144, 1 Adm. R. 413 (9th Cir. 2013).

Before **KOZINSKI**, Chief Judge, **TASHIMA** and **SMITH**, Circuit Judges.

[—3—] ORDER

Chief Judge Kozinski votes to deny the petition for rehearing en banc and Judge Tashima so recommends. Judge Smith votes to grant the petition for rehearing en banc. The full court was advised of the petition for rehearing en banc, and a judge of the court called for a vote on whether to rehear the matter en banc. The majority of the nonrecused active judges[1] failed to vote in favor of en banc rehearing.

The petition for rehearing en banc is denied.

GOULD, Circuit Judge, joined by **PREGERSON**, **REINHARDT**, **WARDLAW**, **W. FLETCHER**, and **SMITH**, Circuit Judges, dissenting from denial of rehearing en banc:

In my view the dissent of Judge M. Smith has the better position as contrasted with the majority opinion. This case should have been reviewed en banc because the majority opinion offends important principles that transcend the case: (1) A party should not be enjoined because of its association with other entities; and (2) A party should not be enjoined because it, with what I would have previously thought was free speech, endorsed or claimed affinity with "activist" operations of other entities.

---

[1] Judges O'Scannlain, Graber, and Christen were recused and did not participate.

The majority opinion upholds a preliminary injunction against Greenpeace USA based in significant part on acts [—4—] committed by legally separate Greenpeace entities. In doing so, the decision disregards corporate norms of limited liability and relies on a guilt-by-association model that offends justice.

The panel majority dismissed Greenpeace USA's separate legal status as irrelevant to its review of the preliminary injunction, explaining that legal status is relevant only for decisions on the merits. *Shell Offshore, Inc. v. Greenpeace, Inc.*, 709 F.3d 1281, 1289 n.7 (9th Cir. 2013). I disagree. "Limited liability is the rule, not the exception." *First Nat. City Bank v. Banco Para El Comercio Exterior de Cuba*, 462 U.S. 611, 626 (1983) (quoting *Anderson v. Abbott*, 321 U.S. 349, 362 (1944)). There is no reason that rule is any more applicable at the merits stage than during review of the propriety of a preliminary injunction.

Moreover, under the preliminary-injunction analysis established by the Supreme Court in *Winter v. Natural Res. Def. Council*, 555 U.S. 7, 20 (2008), we must consider the likelihood of success on the merits of the underlying action to determine whether an injunction is appropriate. To determine the likelihood of success on the merits of Shell's claims, the majority should have considered whether Greenpeace USA can be held accountable for the acts of legally separate organizations by merely endorsing or supporting those acts. The panel majority did not do that, and, instead, assumed Greenpeace USA's guilt based on its association with and stated support for these other Greenpeace entities. We should be wary of such an assumption not only because it violates corporate norms on which modern commerce is based, but because it violates the bedrock principle that an individual should not be held accountable for the actions of his or her associates. [—5—]

The Supreme Court has cautioned against imposing legal sanctions based on statements that endorse or advocate for illegal activity because it is "alien to the traditions of a free society and the First Amendment itself."

NAACP v. Claiborne Hardware Co., 458 U.S. 886, 932 (1982); *see also Healy v. James*, 408 U.S. 169, 186 (1972) ("Guilt by association alone, without (establishing) that an individual's association poses the threat feared . . . is an impermissible basis upon which to deny First Amendment rights." (quotations omitted)). The First Amendment concern here is not whether the injunction is an undue restriction against Greenpeace USA's right to protest and monitor Shell's vessels at sea. *See Shell Offshore, Inc.*, 709 F.3d at 1291. It is that the majority's opinion imposes legal sanctions based on Greenpeace USA's statements that at most "mere[ly] advocate[d] the use of force or violence," *Claiborne Hardware Co.*, 458 U.S. at 927, or "endorsed" the violent acts of others, *Planned Parenthood of Columbia/Willamette, Inc. v. Am. Coal. of Life Activists*, 290 F.3d 1058, 1072 (9th Cir. 2002) (en banc). These statements of support are protected speech and should not have been a basis for enjoining Greenpeace USA. *See Claiborne Hardware Co.*, 458 U.S. at 928 (appeals to violence that do not in fact incite lawless action are protected speech). The panel majority's contrary conclusion will undermine the freedom of an organization to "stimulate [its] audience with spontaneous and emotional appeals for unity and action in a common cause." *Id.*

I would prefer to see our opinions give organizations like Greenpeace USA the breathing space to let their fortunes rise or fall based on their conduct, not on their association with [—6—] others and not on their free speech endorsement of others. I regret that we take another course that is contrary to what is or should be our law.

I respectfully dissent.

414

United States Court of Appeals
for the Ninth Circuit

No. 11-73172

SCHWIRSE

VS.

DIRECTOR, OFFICE OF WORKERS' COMPENSATION
PROGRAM

Petition for Review of an Order of the Benefits
Review Board

Decided: July 26, 2013

Citation: 736 F.3d 1165, 1 Adm. R. 415 (9th Cir. 2013).

Before **SILVERMAN, CLIFTON,** and **SMITH,** Circuit
Judges.

[—3—] **N.R. SMITH,** Circuit Judge:

3 U.S.C. § 903(c) precludes compensation to an injured employee if "the injury was occasioned solely by [his] intoxication." This language precludes recovery where the intoxication of the employee was the sole "legal cause" of the injury. "Legal cause" is the causal connection in fact, which extends not only to positive and active physical forces, but also to pre-existing passive conditions. *Cf. Exxon Co., U.S.A. v. Sofec, Inc.,* 517 U.S. 830, 837–39 (1996); *White v. Roper,* 901 F.2d 1501, 1505–06 (9th Cir. 1990). The Benefits Review Board (BRB) did not err when it affirmed the administrative law judge's (ALJ) denial of Schwirse's claim for compensation under the Longshore and Harbor Workers' Compensation Act (LHWCA) due to intoxication. We have jurisdiction to review the petition under 33 U.S.C. § 921(c); we deny the petition for review.

FACTS

Gary Schwirse was employed by Marine Terminals Corporation (MTC) as an A-registered longshoreman. On January 8, 2006, Schwirse drank two beers before going to [—4—] work at 8:00 a.m. Between 8:00 a.m. and 12:00 p.m., he drank an additional three beers. At lunch, Schwirse consumed four to five more beers. Between the end of lunch and the end of the day (approximately 4:00 p.m.),

Schwirse also drank more than half a pint of whiskey.

At approximately 4:30 p.m., Schwirse decided to relieve himself near the bull rail of MTC's dock. While doing so, Schwirse fell over the bull rail onto a concrete and steel ledge (approximately six feet below the rail). After Schwirse's fall, he was taken by ambulance to the hospital where he was diagnosed with acute alcohol intoxication (.29 serum level or .25 blood alcohol level), cannabis ingestion, and a severe scalp laceration to his right temple.

Thereafter, Schwirse sought compensation for his injury under the LHWCA. However, MTC refused to pay the compensation, arguing that he had no claim for compensation under the LHWCA. MTC asserted that Schwirse was precluded from receiving compensation under 33 U.S.C. §903(c), because his intoxication was the sole cause of his injury.

At the hearing before the ALJ on June 21, 2007, Schwirse stated that he could not remember the details of the incident. Instead, he asserted, based upon the statements of his coworkers (neither of whom testified), that the fall was due to tripping over a bright orange warning cone. However, in Schwirse's earlier deposition (taken on October 20, 2006), he recalled the facts differently. At that time, Schwirse stated that neither of his coworkers actually saw what happened; instead, he was the one, who specifically recalled seeing and tripping over a traffic cone at the bull rail's edge. The ALJ awarded Schwirse benefits. The ALJ determined that [—5—] Schwirse's injury was not caused solely by intoxication, because there was no direct proof that intoxication (and not something else) caused him to fall. MTC appealed the ALJ's decision to the BRB. The BRB reversed the ALJ, finding that the employer rebutted the presumption that the injury was caused by something other than intoxication. The BRB noted that "[i]t is not [the] employer's burden to prove on the record as a whole that intoxication was the sole cause of claimant's injury."

Schwirse filed a motion for reconsideration, arguing that the BRB's ruling incorrectly stated the employer's burden of proof. After review of the motion, the BRB agreed with Schwirse's argument, correcting its prior opinion. Instead, the BRB stated that the burden of proof is on the employer and remanded the matter back to the ALJ to make further findings and weigh the relevant evidence.

On remand, the ALJ weighed the conflicting evidence and determined that MTC had established that intoxication was the sole cause of Schwirse's fall. Relying on the testimony of the marine manager, the ALJ concluded that the bull rail was free of tripping or slipping hazards. The ALJ also credited the testimony of Drs. Burton and Jacobsen, physicians testifying on behalf of MTC, that the sole cause of Schwirse's fall was due to intoxication. The ALJ thus concluded that there was "no other explanation for [Schwirse's] industrial injury than his intoxication." The ALJ also rejected Schwirse's alterative argument that the concrete and metal [—6—] slab (on which he fell) caused the injury rather than his intoxication.[1]

The BRB affirmed the decision.

DISCUSSION

"The Longshore Act is a comprehensive scheme to provide compensation for the disability or death of employees resulting from injuries occurring upon the navigable waters of the United States." *Price v. Stevedoring Servs. of Am., Inc.*, 697 F.3d 820, 823 (9th Cir. 2012) (internal quotation marks omitted); *see also* 33 U.S.C. § 903(a). However, "[n]o compensation shall be payable if the injury was occasioned solely by the intoxication of the employee." 33 U.S.C. § 903(c). Despite this exclusion, the LHWCA provides that "a claim for compensation . . . shall be presumed, in the

---

[1] We further note that Schwirse presented no argument or evidence that the concrete and metal slab (on which he fell) was defective, and that such defect caused his injury to any extent. He only argued that the fall (onto a concrete and metal slab) caused his injury.

absence of substantial evidence to the contrary . . . [t]hat the injury was *not* occasioned solely by the intoxication of the injured employee." 33 U.S.C. § 920(c) (emphasis added). "[T]he employer may rebut the presumption . . . by presenting substantial evidence that is specific and comprehensive enough to sever the potential connection between the disability and the work environment." *Hawaii Stevedores, Inc. v. Ogawa*, 608 F.3d 642, 651 (9th Cir. 2010) (internal quotation marks omitted). The ALJ then "determines as a matter of law whether substantial rebuttal evidence has been presented." *Id.* If the ALJ determines that the employer rebutted the presumption, "the presumption in favor of the [—7—] claimant 'falls out of the case' and the ALJ moves to the third and final step of weighing the evidence as a whole 'to determine whether the claimant has established the necessary causal link between the injury and employment.'" *Id.* (quoting *Bath Iron Works Corp. v. Fields*, 599 F.3d 47, 54–55 (1st Cir. 2010)). "This final determination is a question of fact." *Id.*

1. The BRB did not err in interpreting 33 U.S.C. § 903(c).

This case turns, in part, on an interpretation of the LHWCA. We have held that "[t]he Board's interpretation of the LHWCA is a question of law reviewed de novo and is not entitled to any special deference." *Stevedoring Servs. of Am. v. Price*, 382 F.3d 878, 883 (9th Cir. 2004) (citing *Stevedoring Servs. of Am. v. Dir., OWCP*, 297 F.3d 797, 801–02 (9th Cir. 2002)). However, we "respect the Board's interpretation . . . if it 'is reasonable and reflects the underlying policy of the statute.'" *Id.* at 883 (quoting *Kelaita v. Dir., OWCP*, 799 F.2d 1308, 1310 (9th Cir. 1986)).

Under 33 U.S.C. § 903(c), "[n]o compensation shall be payable if the injury was occasioned solely by the intoxication of the employee." Breaking the phrase into its parts, the LHWCA defines "injury" as:

> accidental injury or death arising out of and in the course of employment, and such occupational disease or infection as

arises naturally out of such employment or as naturally or unavoidably results from such accidental injury, and includes an injury caused by the willful act of a third person [—8—] directed against an employee because of his employment.

33 U.S.C. § 902(2). This definition does not fully address the language we must interpret here, whether the "injury was occasioned solely by" a cause, in this case intoxication. The term "injury" is modified by "occasioned solely by," which requires us to determine whether intoxication was the "legal cause" of the injury (a "but for" analysis).

The "occasioned solely by" phrase is not defined by the statute. In determining whether an employee's injury was "occasioned solely by" intoxication, we take guidance from those admiralty cases determining proximate cause. *See Exxon*, 517 U.S. at 839. By analogy, we determine whether intoxication was the only or "sole" cause by (1) looking at the act that caused the accident and (2) determining whether there were any superseding or intervening causes that contributed to the injury. *Id.* at 837–39.

This interpretation is consistent with the BRB's application of a two-part test for determining whether the employer met its burden in establishing that intoxication was the sole cause of the accident. *See Sheridon v. Petro-Drive, Inc.*, 18 BRBS 57, *2 (1986). First, the employer must establish "that the employee was drunk at the time of the accident." *Id.* (quoting *Shearer v. Niagara Falls Power Co.*, 150 N.E. 604, 605 (N.Y. 1982)). Second, the employer must establish that the employee "fell *owing to his drunkenness* and was injured." *Id.* (emphasis added).

We therefore hold that an injury "occasioned solely by" intoxication means that the legal cause of the injury was intoxication, regardless of the surface material of the landing [—9—] on which the intoxicated person fell. In other words, as aptly stated by the BRB, "[i]f intoxication was the sole cause of the claimant's fall, then intoxication also was the sole cause of the claimant's injury."

Instead, Schwirse argues an all-encompassing definition of the term injury. Relying on *Johnson v. Dir., Office of Workers Compensation Programs*, 911 F.2d 247, 250 (9th Cir. 1990), Schwirse argues that Congress used the term "accident," to mean the "event causing the harm," where it intended to limit compensation to the sole cause of the fall. In other words, by using the term "injury," Congress intended to incorporate the "harmful physical consequences of that event." Thus, Schwirse's definition would suggest that, because he hit the concrete surface rather than the river or a featherbed, his injury was not solely occasioned by intoxication. In other words, his "accident" may have been caused by intoxication, but harmful physical consequences of the fall (the injury) was caused by hitting the concrete and metal slab.

We reject Schwirse's interpretation. Accepting Schwirse's broad definition of the term "injury" would violate a "cardinal principle of statutory construction." *See TRW Inc. v. Andrews*, 534 U.S. 19, 31 (2001). In particular, if "we [were] to adopt [Schwirse's] construction of the statute, the express [intoxication] exception would be rendered insignificant, if not wholly superfluous." *Id.* (internal quotation marks and alternations omitted). Schwirse's interpretation of the term "injury" would read out the phrase "occasioned solely by" and preclude the application of §903(c). Nearly every "harm" would not be "occasioned solely by the intoxication" but rather by some further cause, such as the ground. Further, as noted by the [—10—] Supreme Court, "Life is too short to pursue every event to its most remote, 'but-for,' consequences, and the doctrine of proximate cause provides a rough guide for courts in cutting off otherwise endless chains of cause-and-effect." *Pac. Operators Offshore, LLP v. Valladolid*, 132 S. Ct. 680, 692 (2012). We therefore conclude that the most logical way to interpret § 903(c) and § 920(c) of the LHWCA is to interpret the phrase "occasioned solely by" to limit the analysis to the sole causal factor of the injury.

2. The BRB did not err in affirming the ALJ's finding that MTC produced sufficient evidence to rebut the statutory presumption that Schwirse's injury was not solely caused by intoxication.

In considering a claim for disability benefits under the LHWCA, the ALJ is required to follow a three part process. First, the claimant must show that he sustained an injury in the course and scope of his employment. *See Albina Engine & Machine v. Dir., OWCP*, 627 F.3d 1293, 1298 (9th Cir. 2010). If an injury is established, a presumption arises that the injury was not occasioned solely by intoxication. *See* 33 U.S.C. § 920(c); *see also Albina Engine*, 627 F.3d at 1298. Second, the employer must present "substantial evidence" to rebut that presumption. *See* 33 U.S.C. § 920; *see also Albina Engine*, 627 F.3d at 1298. Lastly, if the employer successfully rebuts the presumption, the ALJ must then evaluate whether the claimant met his burden of persuasion by a preponderance of the evidence that the record as a whole justifies awarding benefits.[2] *Albina Engine*, 627 F.3d at 1298. [—11—]

The Board must accept the ALJ's findings of fact if they are supported by "substantial evidence in the record considered as a whole." 33 U.S.C. § 921(b)(3); *see also Container Stevedoring Co. v. Dir., OWCP*, 935 F.2d 1544, 1546 (9th Cir. 1991). The Supreme Court has defined "substantial evidence" as "more than a mere scintilla. It means such relevant evidence as a reasonable mind might accept as adequate to support a conclusion." *Universal Camera Corp. v. NLRB*, 340 U.S. 474, 477 (1951). We conduct an independent review to

determine if the Board adhered to this standard. *Bumble Bee Seafoods v. Dir., OWCP*, 629 F.2d 1327, 1329 (9th Cir. 1980).

Reviewing the BRB's decision, we conclude the BRB adhered to this standard and did not err in affirming the ALJ's denial of compensation under the LHWCA. First, there is no dispute that Schwirse sustained an injury while at work. Thus, a presumption arises that Schwirse's injury was not occasioned solely by intoxication. The BRB correctly concluded that substantial evidence in the record supported the ALJ's conclusion that Schwirse's employer rebutted the presumption that intoxication was not the sole cause of Schwirse's injury. The BRB stated the correct standard of review regarding the ALJ's findings of facts. The BRB noted that the ALJ "found sufficient evidence, in the form of the opinions of Drs. Burton and Jacobsen, the testimony of Mr. Yockey, and photographs of the accident site . . . ." Based on [—12—] this evidence, the ALJ ruled out any tripping hazards and then relied on the expertise of doctors to conclude intoxication was the sole cause. There was no evidence of any superseding or intervening cause of the injury. Further, there is no question that a foreseeable consequence of falling is that one may hit the pre-existing surface material. It is also foreseeable that the surface material surrounding the dock was hard and would cause significant injury. A preference that one may fall on more forgiving material (such as a featherbed or water) does not alter the "legal cause" of the injury. Thus, absent evidence of the surface material being unforeseeably defective, the "legal cause" is limited to the reason for his fall and the foreseeable consequences of that fall. Here, the ALJ found that the only known cause for Schwirse's injury was the fall off the bull rail attributable solely to his drunkenness. Thus the BRB did not err in concluding substantial evidence supported the ALJ's conclusions.

We further find no error in the BRB's conclusion that Schwirse's employer does not have to "rule out" all other possible causes of injury in order to rebut the presumption under 33 U.S.C. § 920(c). As noted by the BRB, the employer "need not negate every

---

[2] Having rebutted the presumption that the claimant's injury was not occasioned solely by intoxication under the substantial evidence standard, the employer does not further bear the burden of proving that the [—11—] employee's injury was caused solely by intoxication under the preponderance of the evidence standard. *Albina Engine* clearly establishes that after the employer rebuts the presumption by substantial evidence, the burden shifts to the claimant to prove entitlement to benefits by a preponderance of the evidence. To the extent that it placed the burden at the latter stage on the employer, the BRB erred.

hypothetical cause." *Sheridon*, 18 BRBS 57, *3. To hold otherwise would contradict the statutory language, which only requires "substantial evidence" to rebut the presumption. *See Ortco Contractors, Inc. v. Charpentier*, 332 F.3d 283, 288 (5th Cir. 2003) ("[T]he BRB *cannot* require employers to rebut a [33 U.S.C. § 920(a)] presumption by 'ruling out' every conceivable connection between the injury and the claimant's employment. The LHWCA requires a *lower* evidentiary standard than this—the employer must adduce only *substantial evidence* that the injury was not work-related."). **[—13—]**

Lastly, BRB correctly concluded that the ALJ's decision to deny disability benefits, based on the record as a whole, was proper. As the Supreme Court stated in *Del Vecchio v. Bowers*,

> If the employer alone adduces evidence which tends to support the theory [contrary to the presumption], the case must be decided upon that evidence. Where the claimant offers substantial evidence in opposition, . . . the issue must be resolved upon the whole body of proof pro and con; and if it permits an inference either way upon the question . . . , the Deputy Commissioner and he alone is empowered to draw the inference; his decision as to the weight of the evidence may not be disturbed by the court.

296 U.S. 280, 286–87 (1935) (footnotes omitted). The only alleged cause of Schwirse's injury that was supported by substantial evidence was Schwirse's intoxication. The ALJ properly "weigh[ed] the evidence as a whole 'to determine whether [Schwirse had] established the necessary causal link between the injury and employment.'" *Hawaii Stevedores*, 608 F.3d at 651 (citation omitted).

PETITION DENIED.

United States Court of Appeals for the Ninth Circuit

No. 12-56298

TOBAR
vs.
UNITED STATES

Appeal from the United States District Court for the Southern District of California

Decided: September 25, 2013

Citation: 731 F.3d 938, 1 Adm. R. 420 (9th Cir. 2013).

Before **PREGERSON, GRABER,** and **CHRISTEN,** Circuit Judges.

[—4—] **GRABER,** Circuit Judge:

Patrolling in international waters, the United States Coast Guard suspected the crew of an Ecuadorian fishing boat of illicit activities. With the authorization of Ecuadorian authorities, the Coast Guard boarded the boat, searched for drugs, and towed the boat to Ecuador. The Ecuadorian crew, who are Plaintiffs here, allege that agents of Defendant United States harmed Plaintiffs and their property in violation of the Federal Tort Claims Act ("FTCA"), the Suits in Admiralty Act ("SAA"), and the Public Vessels Act ("PVA"). The district court held that the government had not waived its sovereign immunity, and it dismissed the case. In an earlier appeal, we affirmed in part, vacated in part, and remanded for further proceedings. *Tobar v. United States*, 639 F.3d 1191 (9th Cir. 2011). In particular, we remanded for the district court to accept further evidence and briefing on the issue whether reciprocity with Ecuador exists—a statutory condition under 46 U.S.C. § 31111 to the government's waiver of sovereign immunity. *Id.* at 1200.

On remand, the parties submitted, among other documents, affidavits by experts in Ecuadorian law. Unpersuaded that reciprocity exists, the district court again held that the government had not waived its sovereign immunity. The district court also held, in the alternative, that Plaintiffs' claims fell within the "discretionary function exception" to the government's waiver of sovereign immunity. Plaintiffs timely appeal the judgment dismissing the action. [—5—]

We review de novo whether the government has waived its sovereign immunity. *Harger v. Dep't of Labor*, 569 F.3d 898, 903 (9th Cir. 2009). We disagree with the district court's analysis of the experts' affidavits. We hold that, on the evidence submitted by the parties, reciprocity with Ecuador exists. We agree with the district court that the "discretionary function exception" applies generally to Plaintiffs' claims, because most of the actions by the Coast Guard were discretionary. But we hold that, under the facts here, the government may have violated its non-discretionary policy of paying damages to the owner of the boat. To the extent that Plaintiffs can establish that the United States violated that mandatory obligation, sovereign immunity does not bar this action. Accordingly, we affirm in part, vacate in part, and remand for further proceedings.

DISCUSSION

We must determine whether reciprocity with Ecuador exists and, if so, whether the discretionary function exception bars Plaintiffs' claims. We address those issues in turn.[1] [—6—]

A. *Reciprocity with Ecuador*

The PVA's waiver of sovereign immunity is conditioned on the following reciprocity requirement:

> A national of a foreign country may not maintain a civil action under this chapter unless it appears to the

---

[1] Plaintiffs also argue that the district court abused its discretion by denying further discovery. Because Plaintiffs have not identified relevant information that discovery could have uncovered, we hold that the district court did not abuse its discretion. *See Quinn v. Anvil Corp.*, 620 F.3d 1005, 1015 (9th Cir. 2010) ("We review district court rulings on discovery matters for abuse of discretion.").

satisfaction of the court in which the action is brought that the government of that country, in similar circumstances, allows nationals of the United States to sue in its courts.

46 U.S.C. § 31111. As we held in the first appeal, where, as here, the suit falls within the scope of the PVA, claims brought under the FTCA and SAA also must meet that reciprocity requirement. *Tobar*, 639 F.3d at 1197 (citing *United States v. United Cont'l Tuna Corp.*, 425 U.S. 164 (1976), and *Taghadomi v. United States*, 401 F.3d 1080 (9th Cir. 2005)).

The relevant question is whether Ecuador, "in similar circumstances, allows nationals of the United States to sue in its courts." 46 U.S.C. § 31111. The determination of foreign law is a legal question. *Tobar*, 639 F.3d at 1200.

Plaintiffs originally submitted evidence only that Ecuador has an "open court" system and that foreigners have equal access to the courts. We held that those statements were insufficient because they failed to address whether Ecuador would assert sovereign immunity: "The documents demonstrate that a foreign citizen can bring suit to the same extent as an Ecuadorian citizen, but the documents do not address the key issue here: whether the Ecuadorian [—7—] government would waive sovereign immunity in similar circumstances." *Id.* at 1199.

On remand, Plaintiffs submitted affidavits by three experts in Ecuadorian law, and the government submitted an affidavit by one such expert. Neither party challenges the experts' credentials.

Plaintiffs' experts made two new points. First, according to Plaintiffs' experts, the concept of "sovereign immunity" as understood in common-law nations does not exist in Ecuadorian law, because Ecuador is a civil-law nation. Second, Plaintiffs' experts stated that, accordingly, there would be no legal impediment to a United States citizen's suing the Ecuadorian government in similar circumstances; reciprocity exists.

Those affidavits establish that, in similar circumstances, a United States citizen would be able to sue Ecuador in Ecuadorian courts. Accordingly, reciprocity exists. 46 U.S.C. § 31111.

The government's arguments to the contrary are unpersuasive. On the first point, concerning the existence of sovereign immunity in Ecuadorian law, the government asserts that sovereign immunity does indeed exist in Ecuadorian law, and it faults Plaintiffs' experts for providing "unsupported" conclusions to the contrary. But the affidavits themselves *are* support—they are sworn statements by legal experts on Ecuadorian law. *See* Fed. R. Civ. P. 44.1 ("In determining foreign law, the court may consider any relevant material or source, including testimony, whether or not submitted by a party or admissible under the Federal Rules of Evidence."). Moreover, the government's expert offered only [—8—] one statement concerning sovereign immunity in Ecuadorian law: "Regardless of what one argues about the role, if any[,] [s]overeign immunity plays in Ecuadorian law, I can say that there is nothing in the Constitution of Ecuador (1998 Constitution would be applicable given the date of the casualty in 2005) which would absolutely guarantee reciprocity as to the hypothetical action." (Emphases omitted.) In other words, the government's expert declined to contest the proposition that sovereign immunity does not exist in Ecuador. Read narrowly, the expert demurs; read broadly, he implicitly concedes that Plaintiffs' experts are correct that sovereign immunity does not exist in Ecuadorian law. If, as the government asserts, sovereign immunity exists in Ecuadorian law, we would expect its expert simply to say so.[2] [—9—]

---

[2] Plaintiffs' experts correctly identify sovereign immunity as a creature of common law, rather than civil law. *See, e.g.*, 33 Charles Alan Wright & Charles H. Koch, Jr., *Federal Practice and Procedure* § 8403, at 418 (3d ed. 2006) (tracing the roots of the doctrine to Blackstone: "Blackstone took to be a fundamental principle that 'the King can do no wrong.'"); *id.* at 419 ("This body of law crossed the Atlantic and a similar principle evolved in U.S. law."); *accord* Erwin Chemerinsky, *Federal Jurisdiction* § 9.2.1, at 629 (5th ed. 2007) ("The

Nor does the government identify any other Ecuadorian legal source in support of its position. The government cites cases in which Ecuador has waived *foreign* sovereign immunity as a defendant in a case in United States court. *Jota v. Texaco Inc.*, 157 F.3d 153, 162–63 (2d Cir. 1998); *Aquamar S.A. v. Del Monte Fresh Produce N.A.*, 179 F.3d 1279, 1300 (11th Cir. 1999). But *foreign* sovereign immunity concerns the right of a foreign nation (or agency) to sovereign immunity *in courts of the United States*. The doctrine of sovereign immunity at issue here is different. We must determine the extent to which a nation can use its sovereign immunity as a defense *in its own courts*. Nothing in the United States cases cited by the government concerns the question whether Ecuador applies the concept of sovereign immunity *in its own court system*. That Ecuador may choose to waive or retain sovereign immunity when it finds itself as a defendant in United States courts simply does not speak to whether that defense is available in courts of its own jurisdiction.

Turning to the second point—that reciprocity exists because there would be no legal impediment to filing suit if the nationalities were reversed—the government's response rests on a misunderstanding of the relevant inquiry. The government's expert repeatedly demurs, or implicitly concedes, the legal point; instead, he focuses only on whether, *as a practical matter*, litigation in Ecuadorian courts would succeed:

It is my opinion that a hypothetical action as described above in paragraph 2, could hardly (or never) be successful, and could hardly (or never) result in a money judgment against the Ecuadorian military or Ecuadorian [—10—] government entities. In other words, *as a practical matter*, there is no reciprocity.

. . . .

Whether reciprocity may exist to whatever degree as a legal matter based on Constitutional and legal rules, *as a practical matter*, I believe it will be very hard, not to say impossible, to get a judicial decision against the government of Ecuador or the Navy. One must assume that if intended suits against the government and its military are actually permitted, it would be *practically*, not to say unthinkably, unlikely to get a favorable decision to hypothetical plaintiffs, especially now when the executive branch is reorganizing the entire judiciary system. In other words, no reciprocity exists *as a practical matter*.

. . . .

Even if reciprocity could be said to exist in Ecuador as a matter of Constitutional and legal rules, *as a practical matter*, its existence would be unimaginably difficult to achieve.

(Paragraph numbering omitted; emphases altered.) The expert never explains what those practical considerations are.[3] [—11—] In any event, the unspecified practical limitations on the potential *success* of a suit do not speak to the relevant legal inquiry here: whether a citizen of the United States would be *allowed to sue. See* 46 U.S.C. § 31111 (querying whether the foreign government, "in similar

---

principle of sovereign immunity is derived from English law, which assumed that 'the King can do no wrong.'"). Although we have found no source describing the difference between common-law nations and civil-law nations with respect to sovereign immunity in a nation's own courts, we note that, traditionally, civil-law nations took a more lenient view of access to the courts in the realm of *foreign* sovereign immunity. *See* Letter from Jack B. Tate, Acting Legal Advisor, Department of State, to Acting Attorney General Philip B. Perlman, May 19, 1952, *reprinted in Alfred Dunhill of London, Inc. v. Republic of Cuba*, 425 U.S. 682, 711–15 (1976); *Williams v. Shipping Corp. of India*, 653 F.2d 875, 878 (4th Cir. 1981) (describing the doctrine).

---

[3] For example: Are the filing deadlines strict? Is discovery against Ecuador limited? Are suits against the government disfavored? Are the filing fees expensive? Would the government seek to resolve the dispute [—11—] through political channels? Is there a presumption in favor of the government?

circumstances, allows nationals of the United States to sue in its courts").[4]

The government's final arguments fare no better. The government argues that it is not clear from the affidavits by Plaintiffs' experts whether they considered the precise context—in particular, the fact that the challenged actions were taken by the United States *military*. Although the experts did not specifically mention the military, they were aware of the facts of this case and assessed reciprocity in that light. For example, one expert reached his conclusions only after stating: "I have reviewed the facts and information on file with the case of Tobar, et al v. The United States." Moreover, the experts' conclusions did not depend on the precise nature of the underlying facts, because their reasoning was that sovereign immunity simply does not exist in Ecuadorian law.

The government also argues, as stated by its expert, that there is no "absolute guarantee" of reciprocity in the Ecuadorian constitution. But that is not the proper inquiry. There need not be a constitutional guarantee to meet the [—12—] statute's reciprocity requirement. Section 31111 asks only whether the foreign government, "in similar circumstances, allows nationals of the United States to sue in its courts." On the evidence submitted by the parties, we hold that reciprocity exists under 46 U.S.C. §31111.

B. *Discretionary Function Exception*

1. *Applicability to the PVA*

The FTCA waives sovereign immunity for certain categories of claims, subject to specified exceptions, including the "discretionary function exception":

> Any claim based upon an act or omission of an employee of the Government, exercising due care, in the execution of a statute or regulation, whether or not such statute or regulation be valid, or based upon the exercise or performance or the failure to exercise or perform a discretionary function or duty on the part of a federal agency or an employee of the Government, whether or not the discretion involved be abused.

28 U.S.C. § 2680(a). The exception "marks the boundary between Congress' willingness to impose tort liability upon the United States and its desire to protect certain governmental activities from exposure to suit by private individuals." *United States v. S.A. Empresa de Viacao Aerea Rio Grandense (Varig Airlines)*, 467 U.S. 797, 808 (1984).

Neither the SAA nor the PVA expressly contains the "discretionary function exception." Nevertheless, in *Earles* [—13—] *v. United States*, 935 F.2d 1028, 1032 (9th Cir. 1991), we joined eight sister circuits in holding that the exception applies to claims brought under the SAA. "Were we to find the discretionary function exception not to be applicable to the SAA, we would subject all administrative and legislative decisions concerning the public interest in maritime matters to independent judicial review in the not unlikely event that the implementation of those policy judgments were to cause private injuries." *Id.* (internal quotation marks and alterations omitted). The same reasoning applies to claims under the PVA: If Congress' intent to exempt discretionary functions from independent judicial review is given effect, the discretionary function exception must apply to the PVA as well. *Cf. Koohi v. United States*, 976 F.2d 1328, 1336 (9th Cir. 1992) (incorporating the FTCA's "combatant activities" exception into the PVA because, "if Congress's manifest intent to maintain sovereign immunity from liability arising from the combatant activities of maritime vessels is to be given meaningful effect, the combatant activities exception must be incorporated into the PVA").

---

[4] We need not and do not decide whether a country with a demonstrably corrupt court system, where legal permission to sue is but an empty gesture, would qualify under the statute. There is neither evidence nor argument in this case that such would be the "practical" reason for the projected lack of success in the hypothetical Ecuadorian litigation.

Not surprisingly, then, all three sister circuits to have considered the issue have held that the discretionary function exception applies to claims under the PVA. *Thames Shipyard & Repair Co. v. United States*, 350 F.3d 247, 254 (1st Cir. 2003); *B & F Trawlers, Inc. v. United States*, 841 F.2d 626, 630 (5th Cir. 1988); *U.S. Fire Ins. Co. v. United States*, 806 F.2d 1529, 1534–35 (11th Cir. 1986), *abrogated in part by United States v. Gaubert*, 499 U.S. 315 (1991), *as recognized in Cranford v. United States*, 466 F.3d 955, 959 (11th Cir. 2006); *see also McMellon v. United States*, 387 F.3d 329, 334–49 (4th Cir. 2004) (en banc) (conducting an extensive analysis of the FTCA, SAA, and PVA to conclude, in reasoning that applies equally to the PVA, that [—14—] the SAA incorporates the discretionary function exception). We join our sister circuits in holding that the discretionary function exception also applies to the PVA's waiver of sovereign immunity.

2. *Application of the Discretionary Function Exception*

The Supreme Court decided a series of cases concerning the scope of the discretionary function exception, culminating in its 1991 decision in *Gaubert*, 499 U.S. 315. *See also Berkovitz ex rel. Berkovitz v. United States*, 486 U.S. 531 (1988); *Varig Airlines*, 467 U.S. 797; *Indian Towing Co. v. United States*, 350 U.S. 61 (1955); *Dalehite v. United States*, 346 U.S. 15 (1953). After *Gaubert*, the courts have followed a two-step analysis when considering whether the discretionary function exception applies. *See Terbush v. United States*, 516 F.3d 1125, 1129 (9th Cir. 2008) (citing *Berkovitz*, 486 U.S. at 536–37). The first step asks "whether the challenged actions involve an 'element of judgment or choice.'" *Id.* (quoting *Gaubert*, 499 U.S. at 322). The exception will not apply if "a federal statute, regulation, or policy specifically prescribes a course of action for an employee to follow." *Berkovitz*, 486 U.S. at 536. Otherwise, the analysis proceeds to the second step.

The second step asks "'whether that judgment is of the kind that the discretionary function exception was designed to shield,' namely, 'only governmental actions and decisions based on considerations of public policy.'" *Terbush*, 516 F.3d at 1129 (quoting *Berkovitz*, 486 U.S. at 536–37); *see also Varig Airlines*, 467 U.S. at 814 (describing the inquiry as whether the decision is "grounded in social, economic, and political policy"). This inquiry requires a determination of [—15—] where the activity falls on the spectrum from non-policy activities (such as driving a car) to policy-related ones (such as drafting regulations). *Whisnant v. United States*, 400 F.3d 1177, 1181 (9th Cir. 2005).

a. *First Step: "Element of Judgment or Choice"*

"[T]he discretionary element is not met where a federal statute, regulation, or policy specifically prescribes a course of action for an employee to follow." *Myers ex rel. L.M. v. United States*, 652 F.3d 1021, 1028 (9th Cir. 2011) (internal quotation marks omitted). "An agency does not retain discretion whether to act where a statute or policy directs *mandatory and specific action* and the agency has no lawful option but to adhere to the directive." *Bailey ex rel. Estate of Bailey v. United States*, 623 F.3d 855, 860 (9th Cir. 2010) (emphasis added). The statute authorizing the actions taken here speaks in pertinent part only in general terms and does not direct mandatory and specific action:

> The Coast Guard *may* make inquiries, examinations, inspections, searches, seizures, and arrests upon the high seas and waters over which the United States has jurisdiction, for the prevention, detection, and suppression of violations of laws of the United States. For such purposes, commissioned, warrant, and petty officers *may at any time* go on board of any vessel subject to the jurisdiction, or to the operation of any law, of the United States, address inquiries to those on board, examine [—16—] the ship's documents and papers, and examine, inspect, and search the vessel and use all necessary force to compel compliance.

14 U.S.C. § 89(a) (emphases added).

Indeed, Plaintiffs do not assert that § 89(a) prescribes a specific course of action. Instead, they assert that the government violated its own *regulations and policies*. In particular,[5] the U.S. Coast Guard Maritime Law Enforcement Manual provides: "When acting pursuant to flag State authorization, the boarding State may not exceed the terms of the authorization. Such authorization may be contained in a pre-existing written agreement or may be provided on an ad hoc basis." That policy does not afford any discretion: "the boarding State *may not exceed* the terms of the authorization." (Emphasis added.) Here, the specific authorization to board and inspect Plaintiffs' boat[6] contained the following condition: "If there are no drugs on board, and there are damages or losses sustained by the vessel, in accordance to the U.S. laws and in a manner complying with international laws, the owner of the vessel will be compensated, as long as neither the vessel nor the crew have been involved in illicit actions." That directive, too, is specific and mandatory: The owner "*will be* compensated," so long as the specified conditions are met. (Emphasis [—17—] added.) By carrying out its activities with respect to Plaintiffs' boat, the government accepted that mandatory obligation.

Accordingly, to the extent that Plaintiffs demonstrate that all of the specified conditions have been met, their claims are not barred by the discretionary function exception. In their complaint, Plaintiffs allege that there were no drugs on board, that there were damages and losses sustained by the vessel, that some Plaintiffs owned the boat, and that neither the vessel nor the crew had been involved in illicit actions. Because the district court dismissed this action on the pleadings, we take as true the allegations in the complaint. *Cell Therapeutics Inc. v. Lash*

Grp. Inc., 586 F.3d 1204, 1206 n.2 (9th Cir. 2010). In this procedural posture, then, those elements have been satisfied.[7]

It is less clear that Plaintiffs have exhausted their administrative remedies, as required by the policy: "in accordance to the U.S. laws and in a manner complying with international laws, the owner of the vessel will be compensated." The complaint alleges that Plaintiffs "filed a claim for injuries with the United States Navy and Coast Guard" and that the government took no action on that claim within six months, "tantamount to denial of the claim." At oral argument, the government's lawyer suggested that the administrative denial of Plaintiffs' claim resulted from Plaintiffs' failure to provide documentation of damages. In [—18—] order to prove that the government violated its non-discretionary duty to pay damages to the owner, Plaintiffs must demonstrate that it met the administrative requirements imposed by federal law. But these issues cannot be decided on the pleadings.

Two additional, related restrictions warrant mention. First, the non-discretionary duty requires the government to pay damages to "*the owner*" of the boat. (Emphasis added.) Because the government's non-discretionary duty applies only to the owner of the boat, the only Plaintiffs who can benefit from the policy are the owners. Second, the nondiscretionary duty pertains to "damages or losses sustained by the vessel." Plaintiffs have alleged a wide range of injuries, including physical damages to the boat itself and reputational damages to crew members resulting from "public ridicule." Because the parties have not briefed the issue, we express no view on the extent of "damages or losses" encompassed by the non-discretionary duty to pay.

---

[5] We have considered Plaintiffs' arguments carefully, but we have uncovered no other regulation or policy that directs a mandatory and specific course of action that is relevant here.

[6] The United States' request for Ecuador's authorization to search this specific Ecuadorian boat is contained in a letter that lists the condition quoted in the text above. The record contains no suggestion that Ecuador's grant of authorization differed from the request.

---

[7] Because we conclude that the manual, in conjunction with the letter, prescribed a non-discretionary course of action, we need not consider whether the government voluntarily assumed a non-discretionary contractual duty. *See Bell v. United States*, 127 F.3d 1226, 1229 (10th Cir. 1997).

b. Second Step: "Based on Considerations of Public Policy"

Plaintiffs also argue that, even if the government did not violate a non-discretionary duty, the discretionary function exception nevertheless is inapplicable, because any discretionary judgments were not "based on considerations of public policy." This step considers the discretionary judgment at issue and asks "whether that judgment is of the kind that the discretionary function exception was designed to shield, namely, only governmental actions and decisions based on considerations of public policy." *Terbush*, 516 F.3d at 1129 (internal quotation marks omitted). As discussed above, 14 U.S.C. § 89(a) confers discretion on the Coast [—19—] Guard crew in carrying out the boarding and inspection of vessels on the high seas. "[I]f a regulation allows the employee discretion, the very existence of the regulation creates a *strong presumption* that a discretionary act authorized by the regulation involves consideration of the same policies which led to the promulgation of the regulations." *Gaubert*, 499 U.S. at 324 (emphasis added); *see also id.* ("When established governmental policy, as expressed or implied by statute, regulation, or agency guidelines, allows a Government agent to exercise discretion, it must be presumed that the agent's acts are grounded in policy when exercising that discretion.").

Two sister circuits have held, in actions similar to this one, that the second step was met. In *B & F Trawlers*, 841 F.2d at 627, the Coast Guard discovered a ship carrying marijuana and began towing the ship. During the towing, a fire broke out on the ship, and the Coast Guard eventually sank the ship. *Id.* The Fifth Circuit held that the Coast Guard's actions concerned public policy. *Id.* at 631. The court reasoned that "the discretionary activity is the enforcement of narcotics laws on the high seas" and that "the discretionary function exception in principle shields from tort liability the Coast Guard's apprehension and transportation of drug-running vessels." *Id.* at 631–32.

Similarly, in *Mid-South Holding Co. v. United States*, 225 F.3d 1201, 1203 (11th Cir.

2000), the Customs Service searched a ship that later sank, allegedly because of the Custom Service's negligent actions while conducting the search. The Eleventh Circuit held that the second step was met because "the decision to board and search a vessel is the product of the balancing of various compelling policy considerations." *Id.* at 1205. After block-quoting the [—20—] reasoning of the Fifth Circuit in *B & F Trawlers*, the court held:

> The considerations cited by the Fifth Circuit apply with equal force here. The Customs Service, faced with escalating enforcement duties and limited resources, must decide how best to effectuate our nation's anti-narcotics laws. In so doing, the Customs Service necessarily exercises discretion in choosing whether to board and search a vessel, weighing the costs of implementing such activities against the likelihood of an enforcement success. The discretionary function exception was designed to prevent judicial "second guessing" of exactly this type of policy-based decision.

Id. at 1206 (citations omitted).

In our view, the reasoning of the Fifth and Eleventh Circuits applies equally here.[8] The

---

[8] Plaintiffs' attempts to distinguish those cases fall flat. Plaintiffs point out that the Fifth Circuit in *B & F Trawlers* remanded the case to determine whether the Coast Guard had violated any regulations. But a violation of a regulation concerns the first step, discussed above, not the second step. Turning to *Mid-South Holding*, Plaintiffs insist that the Eleventh Circuit's discussion concerned a different exception, the "Customs exception," and not the discretionary function exception. Plaintiffs are mistaken. The district court had analyzed the law enforcement exception without mention of a "customs exception," but the Eleventh Circuit expressly declined to reach that issue because it resolved the case on the ground of the discretionary function exception. *Mid-South Holding*, 225 F.3d at 1207–08. The entire discussion concerns the discretionary function exception. *Id.* at 1205–07. In sum, Plaintiffs offer [—21—] no factual or legal distinction between this case and *B & F Trawlers*

challenged actions—the **[—21—]** boarding, searching, and towing of the ship—all fall under policy considerations of enforcement of domestic drug laws, "minimization of intrusion on the privacy and property interests of searched parties," general considerations of foreign relations, as well as "weighing the costs of [boarding and searching the ship] against the likelihood of an enforcement success." *Id.* at 1206–07. "Although the attendant details could be characterized as mundane or as disengaged from any substantial policy consideration, they are nonetheless critical to the performance of the discretionary scheme and, accordingly, are entitled to the protection of the discretionary function exception." *Id.* at 1207.

We therefore hold that, to the extent that Plaintiffs' claims fall outside the non-discretionary duty to pay damages, their claims are barred by the discretionary function exception.

CONCLUSION

On the evidence submitted in this case, reciprocity with Ecuador exists because, in similar circumstances, nationals of the United States are able to sue Ecuador in Ecuadorian courts. Accordingly, the government's waiver of sovereign immunity is not barred by the reciprocity requirement. The government's waiver of sovereign immunity also is not barred by the discretionary function exception to the extent that Plaintiffs' claims result from the failure of the government to meet its non-discretionary duty to pay damages, contained in Ecuador's authorization to board Plaintiffs' vessel and incorporated by reference in the Coast **[—22—]** Guard Maritime Law Enforcement Manual. Otherwise, the discretionary function exception bars Plaintiffs' claims.

AFFIRMED in part, VACATED in part, and REMANDED for further proceedings. The parties shall bear their own costs on appeal.

---

and *Mid-South Holding*, and we cannot discern a meaningful distinction.

No. 12-35392

COURTNEY
vs.
GOLTZ

Appeal from the United States District Court for the Eastern District of Washington

Decided: December 2, 2013

Citation: 736 F.3d 1152, 1 Adm. R. 428 (9th Cir. 2013).

Before **HAWKINS**, **THOMAS**, and **NGUYEN**, Circuit Judges.

[—3—] NGUYEN, Circuit Judge:

James and Clifford Courtney challenge Washington statutes that require a certificate of "public convenience and necessity" ("PCN") in order to operate a ferry on Lake Chelan in central Washington state. The Courtneys claim that these state laws abridge their right to use the navigable waters of the United States, in violation of the Privileges or Immunities Clause of the Fourteenth Amendment. The **[—4—]** Washington Utilities and Transportation Commission and its various officers and directors (collectively, "WUTC") successfully moved to dismiss the case and this appeal followed.

The Courtneys' first claim for relief challenges the constitutionality of the PCN requirement as applied to the provision of public ferry service on Lake Chelan. We hold that the Privileges or Immunities Clause of the Fourteenth Amendment does not encompass a right to operate a public ferry on intrastate navigable waterways and affirm the district court's dismissal of this claim. The Courtneys' second claim challenges the PCN requirement as applied to the provision of boat transportation services on Lake Chelan solely for patrons of specific businesses. As to this claim, we find that the district court properly abstained from deciding the issue under the *Pullman* doctrine, but that it should have retained jurisdiction instead of dismissing the claim. Therefore, we vacate

and remand the second claim with instructions that the district court retain jurisdiction over the constitutional challenge.

BACKGROUND

I

James and Clifford Courtney are fourth-generation residents of Stehekin, a small unincorporated community on the northwest end of Lake Chelan in central Washington state. Lake Chelan is a narrow, fifty-five-mile long lake, which has been designated by the Army Corps of Engineers as a "navigable water of the United States." The northwest portion of Lake Chelan, including Stehekin, is part of the Lake Chelan National Recreation Area. Although it is only **[—5—]** accessible by boat, plane, or foot, Stehekin has long been a summer destination for tourists. *See* WUTC, *Appropriateness of Rate and Service Regulation of Commercial Ferries Operating on Lake Chelan* 3–4 (2010), *available at* http://www.wutc.wa.gov/webimage.nsf/0/d068a7290f85512a882576ac007e2d73/ ("Ferry Report"). The Courtneys and their siblings own and operate several businesses in Stehekin, which provide lodging and recreational activities such as white water rafting tours and horseback riding.

Most tourists and residents reach Stehekin by way of a public ferry operated by the Lake Chelan Boat Company. The state has regulated ferry service on Lake Chelan since 1911. By the 1920s, there were at least four different ferry companies offering services on Lake Chelan. Then, in 1927, the Washington legislature enacted a law that conditioned the right to operate a ferry service upon certification that such service was required by "public convenience and necessity."[1] **[—6—]**

---

[1] The Courtneys cite a 1927 *Seattle Daily Times* article in support of their argument that the legislature's goal in passing the PCN requirement was to protect existing ferry owners from competition, and have asked that we take judicial notice of this article. Because we do not rely upon the article, we deny the motion.

The Ferry Report describes the rationale for the regulation as follows: for certain industries that

II

A

In its current form, Washington Revenue Code § 81.84.010 dictates that a "commercial ferry may not operate any vessel or ferry for the public use for hire between fixed termini or over a regular route upon the waters within [Washington] . . . without first applying for and obtaining from the [WUTC] a certificate declaring that public convenience and necessity require such operation." Wash. Rev. Code § 81.84.010(1). In order to obtain a PCN certificate, a potential ferry operator must prove that its proposed operation is required by "public convenience and necessity," and that it "has the financial resources to operate the proposed service for at least twelve months." Id. § 81.84.020(1)–(2). If the territory in which the applicant desires to set up operation is already served by a commercial ferry company, no PCN certificate may be granted unless the applicant proves that the existing certificate holder: "[(a)] has failed or refused to furnish reasonable and adequate service[; (b)] has failed to provide the service described in its certificate or tariffs after the time allowed to initiate service has elapsed[;] or [(c)] has not objected to the issuance of the certificate as prayed for." Id. § 81.84.020(1).

B

Since the statute's enactment, only one PCN certificate has been issued for providing ferry services on Lake Chelan. It is now held by Lake Chelan Recreation, Inc. d/b/a Lake [—7—] Chelan Boat Company.[2] In 1997, James Courtney applied for a PCN certificate

---

"typically have very high capital costs, benefit from economies of scale, and provide an indispensable service to the public[,] . . . the legislature has made a judgment that the public's interest in reliable and affordable service is best served by a single, economically regulated provider whose owners can make the sizeable investments needed to initiate and maintain service without the threat of having customers drawn away by a competing provider." Ferry Report 11.

[2] At least four potential ferry operators have applied for a PCN certificate over the last sixty years, but all were denied by the WUTC after Lake Chelan Boat Company objected to the applications.

to operate a commercial ferry out of Stehekin. The Lake Chelan Boat Company objected, and the WUTC denied Courtney's application, finding that the Lake Chelan Boat Company provided "reasonable and adequate service," the proposed service might "tak[e] business from" the company, and Courtney failed to satisfy the financial responsibility requirement. Courtney did not seek judicial review of the WUTC's decision. See Wash. Rev. Code §§ 34.05.570, 34.05.574.

In 2006, James Courtney explored the possibility of starting an on-call boat service out of Stehekin, which he thought might fall within the "charter service" exemption to the PCN requirement. Because the proposed service would need to utilize federally owned docks, Courtney applied to the United States Forest Service for a special-use permit, which required confirmation that the proposed service was actually exempt from the PCN requirement. The WUTC initially opined that a PCN certificate would not be needed for the proposed on-call boat service, but changed its mind after the Lake Chelan Boat Company objected to the proposal. Several months later, the WUTC again reversed course, indicating that the proposed service would be exempt from the PCN requirement. However, no formal decision was ever rendered. WUTC's executive director, David Danner, did not respond to the Forest Service's request for an advisory opinion on this issue. [—8—]

In 2008, Clifford Courtney wrote to David Danner, inquiring whether various other kinds of boat transportation services (distinct from the proposed on-call service) would require a PCN certificate. The suggested services included (a) one in which Clifford would charter a boat and offer transportation as part of a package for guests who intended to stay at his ranch and go river rafting, and (b) a scenario in which he would purchase his own vessel in order to transport patrons of his various Stehekin-based businesses. Danner responded that such services would require a certificate because they would still be "for the public use for hire," and that it "[did] not matter whether the transportation [Clifford] would provide [was] 'incidental to'" other businesses. However, Danner noted that his response merely reflected the opinion of the WUTC staff and Courtney was free to pursue a formal declaratory ruling by the commissioners provided that "the existing certificate holder . . . agree[d] to participate" in the proceeding. Were Courtney simply to proceed with the proposed service, the WUTC could initiate a "classification proceeding," during which Clifford would be required to testify and prove that his activities did not require a PCN certificate. The WUTC also orally confirmed to Courtney that his proposed services would likely require a PCN certificate.

C

In 2009, after Clifford Courtney wrote to the governor and several state legislators regarding the PCN requirement, the legislature directed the WUTC to conduct a study on the regulation of commercial ferry services on Lake Chelan. The report by the WUTC, which issued in January 2010, concluded that Lake Chelan Boat Company was providing satisfactory service and recommended that there be no change [—9—] to the existing laws and regulations. The WUTC noted that there might be flexibility under the existing law to permit some competition by exempting certain services from the PCN certificate requirement, provided that any such service would not "significantly threaten" the existing certificate holder's business.

D

In October 2011, the Courtneys sued the WUTC and various commissioners and directors in their official capacities, seeking declaratory and injunctive relief pursuant to 42 U.S.C. § 1983 and 28 U.S.C. § 2201. The Courtneys claimed that the PCN requirement abridges their right to use the navigable waters of the United States under the Privileges or Immunities Clause of the Fourteenth Amendment, and is therefore unconstitutional.

The WUTC moved to dismiss the Courtneys' complaint pursuant to Federal Rule of Civil Procedure 12(b)(6), and the district court granted the motion. The district court dismissed the Courtneys' first claim—challenging the constitutionality of the PCN requirement as applied to the provision of public ferry service on Lake Chelan—with prejudice. The district court concluded that it was unclear that the "right to use the navigable waters of the United States" was "truly a *recognized* Fourteenth Amendment right," and that even if it was, it did not extend to protect the right "to operate a ferry service open to the public." The district court dismissed the Courtneys' second claim—challenging the constitutionality of the PCN requirement as applied to provision of boat transportation services on Lake Chelan solely for patrons of specific businesses—without prejudice. As to the second claim, the court held that the Courtneys lacked standing; their [—10—] claim was unripe; and, notwithstanding its ripeness finding, the court would abstain pursuant to *Railroad Commission of Texas v. Pullman Co.*, 312 U.S. 496 (1941).

DISCUSSION

I

To state a claim for relief under 42 U.S.C. §1983, the Courtneys must allege facts that, if true, constitute a violation of a right guaranteed by the United States Constitution. *Balistreri v. Pacifica Police Dep't*, 901 F.2d 696, 699 (9ᵗʰ Cir. 1990). Their claim for declaratory relief under 28 U.S.C. § 2201 similarly requires that the Courtneys allege facts that, if true, would violate federal law. *See Skelly Oil Co. v. Phillips Petroleum Co.*, 339 U.S. 667, 672 (1950).

"We review *de novo* a district court's dismissal for failure to state a claim under Federal [Rule of] Civil [Procedure] 12(b)(6)." *Aguayo v. U.S. Bank*, 653 F.3d 912, 917 (9th Cir. 2011). In doing so, we take all factual allegations in the complaint as true and construe them in the light most favorable to the Courtneys. *See id.*

II

A

The Courtneys argue that the district court erred in dismissing their first claim relating to the provision of public ferry service because the Privileges or Immunities Clause of the Fourteenth Amendment protects the right "to use the [—11—] navigable waters of the United States."[3] We agree with the district court that even if the Privileges or Immunities Clause recognizes a federal right "to use the navigable waters of the United States," the right does not extend to protect the Courtneys' use of Lake Chelan to operate a commercial public ferry.

In its seminal decision interpreting the Privileges or Immunities Clause of the Fourteenth Amendment—the *Slaughter-House Cases*, 83 U.S. 36 (1872)—the Supreme Court upheld a Louisiana statute that granted a private company the exclusive right to operate a slaughter-house on the Mississippi River. *Id.* at 58–61, 83. In doing so, the Court distinguished between rights that accompany state citizenship and those that exist by virtue of United States citizenship. *Id.* at 72–77. The Court explained that the Fourteenth Amendment protects "the privileges or immunities of citizens of *the United States*," which are distinct from those that exist by virtue of *state* citizenship. *Id.* at 73–74 (emphasis in original). [—12—]

The "privileges *and* immunities" referred to in Article IV are conferred by *state* citizenship and consist of those rights "which are

---

[3] Section I of the Fourteenth Amendment reads:

All persons born or naturalized in the United States, and subject to the jurisdiction thereof, are citizens of the United States and of the state wherein they reside. *No state shall make or enforce any law which shall abridge the privileges or immunities of citizens of the United States*; nor shall any state deprive any person of liberty, or property, without due process of law; nor deny to any person within its jurisdiction the equal protection of the laws.

U.S. Const. amend. XIV, § 1 (emphasis added).

fundamental; which belong of right to the citizens of all free governments, and which have at all times been enjoyed by citizens of the several States which compose this Union, from the time of their becoming free, independent, and sovereign." *Id.* at 76 (first emphasis added, second emphasis in original). They fall under "the following general heads: protection by the government, with the right to acquire and possess property of every kind, and to pursue and obtain happiness and safety, subject, nevertheless, to such restraints as the government may prescribe for the general good of the whole." *Id.* (internal quotation marks omitted).

By contrast, the "privileges *or* immunities" discussed in the Fourteenth Amendment consist of rights "which ow[e] their existence to the Federal government, its National character, its Constitution, or its laws." *Id.* at 79 (emphasis added). In analyzing the legislative history of the Thirteenth and Fourteenth Amendments, the Court noted that "the one pervading purpose" of the amendments was to ensure "the freedom of the slave race, the security and firm establishment of that freedom, and the protection of the newly-made freeman and citizen from the oppressions of those who had formerly exercised unlimited dominion over him." *Id.* at 71.

B

The Supreme Court in the *Slaughter-House Cases* ultimately concluded that the rights asserted by the butchers were rights "which belong to citizens of the States as such," and therefore the Court did not need to "defin[e] the privileges and immunities of citizens of the United States which no State can abridge, until some case involving those [—13—] privileges [made] it necessary to do so." *Id.* at 78–79. However, the Court suggested some examples of inherently federal privileges, such as the right "to demand the care and protection of the Federal government over his life, liberty, and property when on the high seas . . .[,] [t]he right to peaceably assemble and petition for redress of grievances, . . . [and t]he *right to use the navigable waters of the United States*, however they may penetrate the territory of the several States." *Id.* at 79 (emphasis added).

The Courtneys' case is predicated entirely on the Supreme Court's passing reference to a "right to use the navigable waters of the United States"—a phrase that has yet to be interpreted by a single federal appellate court in the privileges or immunities context. As such, the boundaries of the term "use" have not been established. Still, we are not faced with an entirely blank slate. The historical backdrop upon which the Supreme Court enunciated the navigable waterway right strongly suggests that the Court did not intend a panoptic definition of the term. Moreover, our Privileges or Immunities Clause jurisprudence does not support an interpretation that would foreclose states from regulating public transportation upon their intrastate navigable waterways. Thus, even if we assume that the examples of rights deriving from national citizenship set forth by the Supreme Court in the *Slaughter-House Cases* are not mere dicta, we nevertheless find that the right "to use the navigable waters of the United States" does not include a right to operate a public ferry on Lake Chelan.

Turning to the historical context, Article 4 of the Northwest Ordinance of 1787 established navigable waters within newly federal territory as "common highways" that would be "forever free," even in the event portions of the [—14—] Northwest Territory were incorporated into newly formed States. Ordinance of 1787 art. IV; *Econ. Light & Power Co. v. United States*, 256 U.S. 113, 118–19 (1921) ("The public interest in navigable streams . . . does not arise from custom or implication, but has a very definite origin[;] [b]y article 4 of the compact in the Ordinance of July 13, 1787 . . . it was declared: 'The navigable waters . . . shall be common highways, and forever free . . . as to the citizens of the United States . . . .'").

Cases interpreting the language in the Northwest Ordinance emphasize the states' responsibility to avoid destroying navigable waters or rendering them *unnavigable*.[4] The Supreme Court has explicitly held that the Ordinance did [—15—] not prevent states from granting exclusive ferry franchises, so long as such franchises did not encroach on the federal commerce power. *See Fanning v. Gregoire*, 16 How. (U.S.) 524, 534 (1853) (holding that "the free navigation of the Mississippi river . . . does not . . . interfere with the police power of the States, in granting ferry licenses"); *Conway v. Taylor*, 66 U.S. 603, 635 (1861) (noting that "[since] before the Constitution had its birth, the States have exercised the power to establish and regulate ferries," not Congress, and that "the authority [to do so] lies within the scope of 'that immense mass' of undelegated powers which 'are reserved to the States respectively[]'").

In light of the foregoing, a reasonable interpretation of the right to "use the navigable waters of the United States," and the one we adopt, is that it is a right to

---

[4] *See, e.g., Ill. River Packet Co. v. Peoria Bridge Ass'n*, 38 Ill. 467, 479 (1865) ("The ordinance does not mean that the river and its navigation shall be . . . free from all and every condition, but only that it shall be free from obstruction . . . ."); *Nedtweg v. Wallace*, 237 Mich. 14, 20 (1926) ("[T]he [1787] ordinance accomplished no more than to preserve the rivers and lakes as common highways and in no sense prevents the state from granting the soil under navigable waters to private owners. The state is sovereign of the navigable waters within its boundaries, bound, however, in trust, to do nothing in hindrance of the public right of navigation, hunting, and fishing." (citation omitted)); *Sewers v. Hacklander*, 219 Mich. 143, 150 (1922) (holding that Article 4 of the Northwest Ordinance has "no bearing upon riparian rights and ownership, except [if] there is an interference with navigation"); *Hogg v. Zanesville Canal & Mfg. Co.*, 5 Ohio 410, 416 (1832) ("Every citizen of the United States has a perfect right to its free navigation. A right derived, not from the legislature of Ohio, but from a superior source. With this right the legislature can not interfere. In other words, they can not, by any law which they may pass, impede or obstruct the navigation of this river."); *Spooner v. McConnell*, 22 F. Cas. 939, 945 (Ohio C.C. 1838) ("[T]he legislature may improve . . . the navigable rivers of the state, and authorize the construction of any works on them which shall not materially obstruct their navigableness.").

navigate the navigable waters of the United States. Here, it is clear that the Courtneys wish to do more than simply navigate the waters of Lake Chelan. Indeed, they are not restrained from doing so in a general sense. Rather, they claim the right to utilize those waters for a very specific professional venture. While navigation of Lake Chelan is a necessary component of the Courtneys' proposed activity, it is neither sufficient to achieve their purpose nor the cause of their dissatisfaction. The Supreme Court in the *Slaughter-House Cases* declined to define the plaintiffs' asserted rights broadly, finding that the statute did not prohibit the butchering of animals in general because it was specifically "the slaughter-house privilege, which [was] mainly relied on to justify the charges of gross injustice to the public, and invasion of private right." *Slaughter-House Cases*, 83 U.S. at 61. Similarly here, the district court correctly identified the actual privilege at stake as a ferry operation privilege, not a broad navigation privilege. Were navigation all the Courtneys wished to do, **[—16—]** they would not need the WUTC's permission and this dispute would never have arisen. We find it exceedingly unlikely that the Supreme Court in the *Slaughter-House Cases* contemplated operation of a public ferry as part of the right "to use the navigable waters of the United States," so as to divest the states of their historic authority to regulate public transportation on intrastate navigable waterways.

Indeed, the *Slaughter-House* decision, itself, contains suggestions that contradict such an understanding. In discussing the nature of the states' police power, the majority noted that, with respect to "laws for regulating the internal commerce of a State, and those which respect . . . ferries . . . [, n]o direct general power . . . is granted to Congress; and consequently they remain subject to State legislation." *Id.* at 63 (quoting *Gibbons v. Ogden*, 22 U.S. (Wheaton) 1, 203 (1824)) (internal quotation marks omitted). Moreover, while the dissenting minority disagreed with the majority's acceptance of a slaughter-house monopoly, it seemed to approve of ferry franchises, stating that

[i]t is the duty of the government to provide suitable roads, bridges, and ferries for the convenience of the public, and if it chooses to devolve this duty to any extent . . . upon particular individuals or corporations, it may of course stipulate for such exclusive privileges . . . as it may deem proper, without encroaching upon the freedom or the just rights of others.

Id. at 88 (Field, J., dissenting). **[—17—]**

Further, the driving force behind this litigation is the Courtneys' desire to operate a particular business using Lake Chelan's navigable waters—an activity driven by economic concerns. We have narrowly construed the rights incident to United States citizenship enunciated in the *Slaughter-House Cases*, particularly with respect to regulation of intrastate economic activities. *See, e.g., Merrifield v. Lockyer*, 547 F.3d 978, 983–84 (9th Cir. 2008).[5]

C

Finally, although the *Slaughter-House* Court acknowledged that "the right to engage in one's profession of choice" was a "fundamental" privilege belonging to "citizens of all free governments," it "made it very clear" that such a right "[was] *not* protected by the Privileges or Immunities Clause if [it was] not of a 'federal' character." *Id.* at 983 (emphasis added) (citations omitted).

---

[5] In *Merrifield*, we upheld a pest-control licensing requirement under the Privileges or Immunities Clause, despite the appellant's contention that the license requirement "infringe[d] on his right to practice his chosen profession." 547 F.3d at 983. We noted that the Supreme Court's decision in *Saenz v. Roe*, 526 U.S. 489 (1999), "represents the Court's only decision qualifying the bar on Privileges or Immunities claims against 'the power of the State governments over the rights of [their] own citizens,'" *id.* at 983 (quoting *Slaughter-House Cases*, 83 U.S. at 77); that "[*Saenz*] was limited to the right to travel[,]" *id.* at 984; and that "[t]he Court has not found other economic rights protected by [the Privileges or Immunities C]lause," *id.* We have made clear that this "limitation on the Privileges or Immunities Clause" remains in effect. *See id.*

Operation of a ferry service is not inherently "federal" in character. To the contrary, the regulation of ferry operation has traditionally been the prerogative of state and local authorities. *See, e.g., Gloucester Ferry Co. v. Pennsylvania*, 114 U.S. 196, 215–17 [—18—] (1885) (recognizing that "[t]he power of the states to regulate matters of internal police includes the establishment of ferries" so long as regulations do not burden interstate commerce); *Can. Pac. Ry. Co. v. United States*, 73 F.2d 831, 833 (9th Cir. 1934) (explaining that "[a]t common law a franchise was necessary to the creation of a ferry and . . . an integral part of the definition"); *Kitsap Cnty. Transp. Co. v. Manitou Beach-Agate Pass Ferry Ass'n*, 30 P.2d 233, 234–35, 237 (Wash. 1934) (finding a state PCN requirement to be within the state's police power in order to serve "the best interests of the traveling public at large").

In this case, the state of Washington has a vital interest in regulating traffic on its navigable waterways. As the WUTC noted in its Ferry Report, "[t]he combination of statutory protection from competition, on the one hand, and stringent regulation of rates and terms of service, on the other, has historically been adopted for industries believed to have characteristics of a 'natural monopoly.'" Ferry Report 11 (citing Charles F. Phillips, Jr., *The Regulation of Public Utilities* 49–73 (3d ed. 1993)). The PCN requirement creates precisely the kind of ferry franchise that has existed with approval since before the *Slaughter-House Cases* were decided. *See, e.g., Conway*, 66 U.S. at 633–35.

The Courtneys contend that ferry operation on Lake Chelan is "nationalized" because of the "national character of the forum in which such a ferry operates," and that Lake Chelan is "uniquely federal" due to its incorporation into "the federal Lake Chelan National Recreation Area." However, the Courtneys provide no actual authority for the proposition that the Lake Chelan National Recreation Area renders unconstitutional state regulation of ferry service on wholly intrastate waterways. The Lake Chelan National Recreation [—19—] Area does not appear to contemplate preemption of state ferry

regulations, and the federal government has in the past refrained from exercising exclusive jurisdiction over its National Recreation Areas. *See* 16 U.S.C. § 90a-1; *see also Silas Mason Co. v. Tax Comm'n of Wash.*, 302 U.S. 186, 244 (1937) (finding that "the evidence is clear that the Federal Government contemplated the continued existence of state jurisdiction consistent with federal functions" with respect to the federal Grand Coulee Dam site in Lake Roosevelt); 36 C.F.R. § 7.55 (setting forth regulations for Lake Roosevelt as a National Recreation Area).

D

At the end of the day, the state legislation the Courtneys challenge is narrow in scope, merely restricting the operation of commercial public ferries to those who obtain a PCN certificate. The PCN requirement does not constrain the Courtneys from traversing Lake Chelan in a private boat for private purposes. *See* Wash. Rev. Code § 81.84.010(1) (restricting ferry operation "for the public use for hire"). Nor does it affect their ability to operate a commercial freight transportation service. *See id.* For that matter, the Courtneys are free to operate a commercial ferry service so long as they apply for and obtain a PCN certificate. *See id.* Although the Courtneys have apparently found the PCN requirement to be a difficult hurdle to surmount, "the hardship, impolicy, or injustice of state laws is not necessarily an objection to their constitutional validity." *Mo. Pac. Ry. Co. v. Humes*, 115 U.S. 512, 520–21 (1885). Because we hold that the Privileges or Immunities Clause of the Fourteenth Amendment does not protect a right to operate a public ferry on Lake Chelan, we affirm the district court's dismissal of the Courtneys' first claim for relief. [—20—]

III

The district court declined to express an opinion as to whether the right to use the navigable waters of the United States covers the use of such waters for private boat services for patrons of specific businesses or groups of businesses. Instead, it found that the Courtneys lacked standing, the claim was unripe, and the issue was appropriate for abstention under the doctrine enunciated in *Railroad Commission of Texas v. Pullman Co.*, 312 U.S. 496 (1941). We disagree as to standing[6] and need not reach the ripeness issue because we find that the district court did not abuse its discretion in abstaining from considering the claim under the *Pullman* doctrine. However, we conclude that the district court should have retained jurisdiction over the Courtneys' case and vacate and remand with instructions that it do so.

The *Pullman* doctrine is "based on the avoidance of needless friction between federal pronouncements and state policies." *Reetz v. Bozanich*, 397 U.S. 82, 87 (1970) (internal quotation marks omitted). It vests federal courts with discretion[7] to abstain from adjudicating disputes that hinge on [—21—] significant and unsettled questions of state law. *See Pullman*, 312 U.S. at 499–500.

Abstention under *Pullman* is an appropriate course where

> (1) the case touches on a sensitive area of social policy upon which the federal courts ought not enter unless no alternative to its adjudication is open, (2) constitutional adjudication plainly can be avoided if a definite ruling on the state issue would terminate the controversy, and (3) the possible determinative issue of state law is uncertain.

---

[6] Although a close question, the threat of a classification proceeding, Washington Supreme Court precedent, and the economic loss the Courtneys have already suffered from having to refrain from purchasing a vessel for which they had negotiated favorable terms make their fear of enforcement and injury sufficiently actual to confer standing here.

[7] The district court incorrectly stated that a federal court "must abstain" from considering a federal constitutional question if the *Pullman* requirements are satisfied. To the contrary, its ultimate decision to abstain is discretionary under such circumstances. *See Potrero Hills Landfill, Inc. v. Cnty. of Solano*, 657 F.3d 876, 889 (9th Cir. 2011) ("*Pullman* is a discretionary doctrine that flows from the court's equity powers.").

Confederated Salish v. Simonich, 29 F.3d 1398, 1407 (9th Cir. 1994). The court "has no discretion to abstain in cases that do not meet the requirements." *Fireman's Fund Ins. Co. v. City of Lodi*, 302 F.3d 928, 939 (9th Cir. 2002).

A

The array of cases dealing with waterways and water-based transportation in Washington state suggests that regulation of water traffic is indeed a sensitive issue of social policy in Washington. *See Rancho Palos Verdes Corp. v. City of Laguna Beach*, 547 F.2d 1092, 1094 (9th Cir. 1976) (pointing to the "array of state constitutional provisions and statutes" involving land use planning as evidence that it is "a sensitive area of social policy" in California). Given the ubiquity of waterways in Washington, and the unique importance of water navigation in the Lake Chelan area specifically, it follows that regulation of water routes and resources in the area would be of great concern to the state. *See Reetz*, 397 U.S. at 87 (noting that "fish resources" was [—22—] "an asset unique in its abundance in Alaska," and that "the management [of fish resources was] a matter of great state concern").

B

In addition, "[a] state court decision . . . could conceivably avoid any decision under the Fourteenth Amendment and would avoid any possible irritant in the federal-state relationship." *Id.* at 86–87. If, for example, the WUTC issues a declaratory order that the "charter" boat service proposed by the Courtneys is not "for the public use for hire," within the meaning of Washington Revised Code § 81.84.010(1), the PCN requirement would not apply to them and the claim would be rendered moot. The Courtneys have challenged the state statutory scheme *as applied* to their proposed transportation services. A decision by the WUTC that the Courtneys do *not* need a PCN certificate to operate their proposed services would obviate the need for this constitutional challenge.

Moreover, even if the WUTC concludes that the PCN requirement applies to the

Courtneys' proposed services, a contrary ruling by the Washington Supreme Court could also potentially render their constitutional challenge unnecessary. *See England v. La. State Bd. of Med. Examiners*, 375 U.S. 411, 424 (1964) (Douglas, J., concurring) ("Where state administrative action is challenged, a federal court will normally not intervene where there is an adequate state court review which is protective of any federal constitutional claim."). **[—23—]**

C

Finally, as discussed above, it is not clear whether the PCN requirement applies to the private boat transportation services the Courtneys wish to provide. An issue of state law is "uncertain" if "a federal court cannot predict with any confidence how the state's highest court would decide an issue of state law." *Pearl Inv. Co. v. City and Cnty. of S.F.*, 774 F.2d 1460, 1465 (9th Cir. 1985).

The PCN requirement in Washington Revised Code § 81.84.010 only applies to vessels or ferries "for the public use for hire." That phrase has yet to be applied in a formal agency opinion or by any state court to the services the Courtneys propose. The WUTC's 2010 Ferry Report indicated that it "might reasonably conclude that a boat service offered on Lake Chelan (and elsewhere) in conjunction with lodging at a particular hotel or resort, and which is not otherwise open to the public, does not require a certificate under [Washington Revised Code § 81.84.010]," but also that "the commission could . . . decide not to adopt that interpretation." Ferry Report 15. Notwithstanding allegations in the Courtneys' complaint that suggest the WUTC would hold them subject to the PCN requirement, it remains unclear how the Washington Supreme Court would interpret the statutory provision at issue with respect to the Courtneys' proposed services.[8] **[—24—]**

---

[8] The Washington Supreme Court's decision in *Kitsap* dealt with a private club that initiated a boat transportation service reserved for its members and their guests only. 30 P.2d at 235. The court concluded that the service was still considered a "common carrier" and was subject to

D

In light of the foregoing, the district court did not abuse its discretion in abstaining from adjudication of the Courtneys' second claim for relief. Nevertheless, the district court should have retained jurisdiction over the case pending resolution of the state law issues, rather than dismissing the case without prejudice. We have generally considered dismissal inappropriate following *Pullman* abstention. *See Fireman's Fund Ins. Co.*, 302 F.3d at 940 ("If a court invokes *Pullman* abstention, it should stay the federal constitutional question until the matter has been sent to state court for a determination of the uncertain state law issue." (internal quotation marks and citation omitted)); *Columbia Basin Apt. Ass'n v. City of Pasco*, 268 F.3d 791, 802 (9th Cir. 2001) (same); *Int'l Bhd. of Elec. Workers, Loc. Union No. 1245 v. Pub. Serv. Comm'n of Nev.*, 614 F.2d 206, 213 (9th Cir. 1980) (finding dismissal following *Pullman* abstention improper pending Nevada courts' resolution of state issues); *Santa Fe Land Improvement Co. v. City of Chula Vista*, 596 F.2d 838, 841 (9th Cir. 1979) ("If the court abstains under *Pullman*, retention of jurisdiction, and not dismissal of the action, is the proper course."). **[—25—]**

---

the PCN requirement. *Id.* In doing so, the court emphasized that the "club boat" was, in practice, essentially a competing public ferry service. *Id.* at 236. *Kitsap* is the only Washington case to have disapproved of a "private **[—24—]** charter" service, and the WUTC recognized that "a boat service offered . . . in conjunction with lodging at a particular hotel or resort, and which is not otherwise open to the public, [might] not require a certificate." Ferry Report 15. The "shuttle" and "charter" services proposed by the Courtneys would be appurtenant to their Stehekin-based businesses and presumably be operated solely for patrons of these businesses. However, the Courtneys' complaint does not provide specific details regarding their proposed boat services, and it is therefore difficult to compare those services to the "club boat" scenario. Thus, the *Kitsap* case does not help us predict with any confidence how the Washington Supreme Court would rule on this issue.

The Supreme Court has found dismissal without prejudice following *Pullman* abstention to be appropriate where Texas law precluded a grant of state declaratory relief if a federal court retained jurisdiction. *See Harris Cnty. Comm'rs Ct. v. Moore*, 420 U.S. 77, 88 n.14 (1975). The same does not appear to be true, however, in Washington. *See Rancho Palos Verdes Corp.*, 547 F.2d at 1096 (distinguishing California law from Texas law and the *Harris* decision in holding that the district court should have retained jurisdiction following *Pullman* abstention); *Brown v. Vail*, 623 F. Supp. 2d 1241, 1247 (W.D. Wash. 2009) (retaining jurisdiction following exercise of *Pullman* abstention, citing, *inter alia*, *Columbia Basin*, 268 F.3d at 802).

Despite its proper invocation of the *Pullman* doctrine, the district court erred in dismissing the Courtneys' second claim. Therefore, we vacate and remand the Courtneys' second claim with directions that the district court enter an order retaining jurisdiction over the constitutional claim. *See Isthmus Landowners Ass'n, Inc. v. California*, 601 F.2d 1087, 1090–91 (9th Cir. 1979) (finding failure to retain jurisdiction after *Pullman* abstention to be reversible error).

CONCLUSION

The district court's dismissal of the Courtneys' first claim for relief is **AFFIRMED**. The dismissal of their second claim for relief is **AFFIRMED** in part, **VACATED** in part, and **REMANDED** with instructions that the district court retain jurisdiction over the constitutional question.

The parties shall bear their own costs of appeal.

This page intentionally left blank

United States Court of Appeals for the Eleventh Circuit

United States Court of Appeals
For the Eleventh Circuit

No. 10-13623

LOBO
vs.
CELEBRITY CRUISES, INC.

Appeals from the United States District Court for the Southern District of Florida

Decided: January 7, 2013

Citation: 704 F.3d 882, 1 Adm. R. 440 (11ᵗʰ Cir. 2013).

[—3—] Before TJOFLAT, PRYOR, and RIPPLE,* Circuit Judges.

*Honorable Kenneth F. Ripple, United States Circuit Judge for the Seventh Circuit, sitting by designation.

TJOFLAT, Circuit Judge:

I.

A.

In *Lobo v. Celebrity Cruises, Inc.* ("*Lobo I*"), 448 F.3d 891 (11ᵗʰ Cir. 2007), we held that the Convention on the Recognition and Enforcement of Foreign Arbitral Awards ("Convention") and its implementing legislation, 9 U.S.C. §§ 202-208, super[s]eded the Seaman's Wage Act, 46 U.S.C. § 10313, and required the District Court to grant a motion to compel arbitration of a foreign seaman's claim for wages allegedly due under a collective bargaining agreement. We accordingly affirmed the District Court's order compelling the arbitration of a cabin steward's [—4—] claim for wages—in the form of tips passengers paid for his services—that his employer, a cruise line, allegedly withheld.[1]

The cabin steward was Inacio Lobo. After his case was submitted to arbitration, Lobo became dissatisfied with the representation his union, Federazione Italianan Transporti ("FIT"), was providing him; so he returned to the District Court—this time with a class

action[2] against the union and the cruise line under § 301 of the Labor Management Relations Act ("LMRA"), 29 U.S.C. § 185,[3] asserting both hybrid and non-hybrid claims for the tips he and other cabin stewards had not received.[4] *Lobo v Celebrity Cruises, Inc.* ("*Lobo II*"), No. 08-23386 (S.D. Fl. 2008). His hybrid claim against his employer, Celebrity Cruises, Inc. ("Celebrity"), was that it breached the wage provisions of the collective bargaining agreement ("CBA") it had with FIT. His hybrid claim against FIT was [—5—] that it breached the duty of fair representation it owed him under § 9(a) of the National Labor Relations Act ("NLRA"), 29 U.S.C. §159.[5] Lobo's non-hybrid claim was lodged against FIT; it replicated the § 9(a) allegations of the hybrid claim.

Lobo and the members of the putative class were citizens and residents of India. FIT is an Italian union. Celebrity is a Liberian corporation; its cruise ships are registered in the Bahamas. The defendants, citing *Benz v. Compania Naviera Hidalgo, S.A.*, 353 U.S.

---

[1] *Lobo I* was brought as a class action, but the plaintiff did not seek class certification.

[2] As in *Lobo I*, the plaintiff did not seek class certification.

[3] Lobo's complaint invoked the District Court's subject matter jurisdiction under 28 U.S.C. § 1331 (federal question) and 28 U.S.C. § 1333 (admiralty).

[4] A hybrid claim is a suit in which a plaintiff may simultaneously assert a claim against his employer and a claim against his union. This type of claim supersedes the Convention and permits a suit in federal court. *See DelCostello v. Int'l Brotherhood of Teamsters*, 462 U.S. 151, 163-65, 103 S.Ct. 2281, 2290-92, 76 L.Ed.2d 476 (1983) ("Ordinarily ... an employee is required to attempt to exhaust any grievance or arbitration remedies provided in the collective-bargaining agreement.... [But] when the union representing the employee in the grievance/arbitration procedure ... breach[es] its duty of fair representation ... an employee may bring suit against both the employer and the union, notwithstanding the outcome or finality of the grievance or arbitration proceeding.").

[5] This claim arises under federal common law. *See Marquez v. Screen Actors Guild, Inc.*, 525 U.S. 33, 44, 119 S.Ct. 292, 299, 142 L.Ed.2d 242 (1998) ("When a labor organization has been selected as the exclusive representative of the employees in a bargaining unit, it has a duty, implied from its status under § 9(a) of the NLRA as the exclusive representative of the employees in the unit, to represent all members fairly.").

138, 77 S.Ct. 699, 1 L.Ed.2d 709 (1957) and *McCulloch v. Sociedad Nacional de Marineros de Honduras*, 372 U.S. 10, 83 S.Ct. 671, 9 L.Ed.2d 547 (1963), separately moved the District Court to dismiss Lobo's complaint under Federal Rule of Civil Procedure 12(b)(6) for failure to state a claim for relief. FIT also moved the court to dismiss it from the case under Federal Rule of Civil Procedure 12(b)(5) for insufficient service of process. In an order entered on September 10, 2009, the court granted FIT's Rule 12(b)(5) motion and dismissed the complaint against it without prejudice. It agreed with both defendants that *Benz* foreclosed Lobo's hybrid claims; as *Benz* explicitly held, the [—6—] LMRA does not apply to labor disputes between foreign crew members and a foreign ship owner. 353 U.S. at 143, 77 S.Ct. at 702. The court therefore dismissed the complaint as to Celebrity with prejudice.

B.

After perfecting service of process on FIT, Lobo filed an amended complaint against FIT alone. He reasserted a non-hybrid breach of fair representation claim under § 9(a) as well under federal common law. He also added a state law claim for breach of a duty of "good faith and fair dealing."[6] FIT moved the District Court to dismiss the amended complaint under Federal Rule of Civil Procedure 12(b)(1) for lack of subject matter jurisdiction. On July 7, 2010, the court granted the motion. In its view, since the non-hybrid claim could not be brought under the LMRA and NLRA, the court lacked the subject matter jurisdiction needed to entertain the amended complaint. On July 8, 2010, the District Court, in conformance with its orders of September 10, 2009, and July 7, 2010, entered final judgment in favor of Celebrity and FIT.

---

[6] Lobo brought the state law claim under the District Court's supplemental jurisdiction, 28 U.S.C. § 1367. The CBA contained a provision stating that the agreement was to be construed under Florida law. The amended complaint alleged that parties to a contract are obligated to deal with one another in good faith and fairly.

C.

[—7—] While *Lobo II* was pending in the District Court, John Gomez and none of the cabin stewards named in that case brought a class action against Celebrity under the Seaman's Wage Act, seeking damages in the amount of the tips Celebrity had allegedly withheld. *Gomez v. Celebrity Cruises, Inc.*, No. 09-22991 (S.D. Fl. 2009).[7] Rather than invoking the arbitration provision of the CBA, Celebrity moved the court to dismiss the case under the doctrine of *res judicata*. Celebrity argued that the plaintiffs should have, but did not, assert their Seaman's Wage Act claim in *Lobo II*. The District Court agreed and on December 23, 2009, dismissed the case with prejudice.[8]

Gomez and the nine other cabin stewards who had joined him in *Lobo II* and *Gomez* (the "Stewards") appealed the District Court's judgment in both cases, Appeal Nos. 10-13623 and 10-10406, respectively. We address the appeals separately, beginning with *Lobo II*.

II.

[—8—] A.

The hybrid claims in *Lobo II* were dismissed under Rule 12(b)(6) for failure to state a claim. We review Rule 12(b)(6) dismissals *de novo*, accepting the allegations in the complaint as true and construing them in the light most favorable to the plaintiff. *Hill v. White*, 321 F.3d 1334, 1335 (11th Cir. 2003).

The District Court dismissed the Stewards' hybrid claims against Celebrity and FIT after determining that the Supreme Court's decisions in *Benz* and *McCullough* foreclosed the application of the LMRA and the NLRA to

---

[7] Inacio Lobo was not included as a named plaintiff because he and Celebrity had settled the claim he had brought in *Lobo I* and, again, in *Lobo II*.

[8] The court did so without having first certified the plaintiffs' class.

wage disputes between foreign ships and foreign seamen.[9] We agree.

It is well-settled that these statutes do not apply to wholly-foreign disputes. In *Benz*, the Supreme Court concluded that "Congress did not fashion [the LMRA] to resolve labor disputes between nationals of other countries operating ships under foreign laws. The whole background of the Act is concerned with industrial strife between American employers and employees." 353 U.S. at 143-44, 77 S.Ct. at 702. The *Benz* court found this legislative history compelling as "inescapably describ[ing] the boundaries of the Act as including only the workingmen of our own country and its possessions." *Id.* at 144, 77 S.Ct. at 703. Similarly, the [—9—] Supreme Court has held that the NLRA does not extend to foreign crews working aboard foreign ships because such an application would interfere with the "internal management and affairs" of the ship. *McCulloch*, 372 U.S. at 20-21, 83 S.Ct. at 677. Thus, as the Supreme Court indicated in *Spector v. Norwegian Cruise Line Ltd.*, 545 U.S. 119, 130, 125 S.Ct. 2169, 2177, 162 L.Ed.2d 97 (2005), *Benz* and *McCulloch* stand for the proposition that "[a]bsent a clear statement of congressional intent, general statutes [like the LMRA or the NLRA] may not apply to foreign-flag vessels insofar as they regulate matters that involve only the internal order and discipline of the vessel."

We need not labor long to determine whether a wage dispute between a foreign-flag vessel and its foreign crew falls within the internal affairs of a ship. *Benz* and *McCulloch* have plainly answered that question. *See Benz*, 353 U.S. at 142-44, 77 S.Ct. at 701-02 (holding the LMRA inapplicable to the picketing of a foreign ship operated entirely by foreign seamen); *McCulloch*, 372 U.S. at 12-13, 83 S.Ct. at 672-73 (holding that the National Labor Relations Board could not

order a union election because the NLRA did not apply to foreign seamen aboard foreign vessels). As the Supreme Court has made clear, the LMRA and NLRA do not apply to "wage disputes arising on foreign vessels between nationals of other [—10—] countries," even when "the vessel comes within our territorial waters."[10] *Benz*, 353 U.S. at 142, 77 S.Ct. at 702.

Here, the Stewards are engaged in a wage dispute with their employer, Celebrity, and their labor union, FIT. All parties in this dispute are foreign. The holdings of *Benz* and *McCulloch* control.

The Stewards contend that *Benz* is inapplicable. They attempt to distinguish the case by noting that *Benz* concerned the picketing of ships, whereas the Stewards' claim concerns a contractual breach over wages. The seamen in *Benz*, however, were picketing because they "demanded that their term of service be reduced, their wages be increased, and more favorable conditions of employment be granted." 353 U.S. at 139, 77 S.Ct. at 700. Just like the Stewards, the *Benz* plaintiffs were engaged in (among other things) a wage dispute arising from their employment contract with their foreign-flag vessel. The LMRA does not apply to these disputes.

The Stewards next argue that, even if *Benz* is on point, it was implicitly overruled by *Hellenic Lines, Ltd. v. Rhoditis*, 398 U.S. 306, 90 S.Ct. 1731, 26 L.Ed.2d 252 (1970). According to the Stewards, *Hellenic Lines* replaced the *Benz* [—11—] and *McCulloch* "internal affairs" framework with a choice of law analysis determined by the points of contact an employer has with the United States. This mode of analysis was rejected by the Supreme Court in *McCulloch*. 372 U.S. at 19 n. 9, 83 S.Ct. at 676 n. 9 (noting that points of contact analysis is inappropriate when application of the NLRA would interfere with

---

[9] The LMRA was actually a series of amendments to the NLRA. Because the implied duty of fair representation has been found under §9(a) of the original NLRA, and the vehicle to bring a hybrid claim has been found under the later addition of § 301 of the LMRA, we join the parties and the District Court in distinguishing between the acts.

[10] The Stewards raise the argument that the presumption against extraterritorial application should not apply here. This contention is inapposite. The question of applicability turns on the identity of parties, not whether their conduct occurred within United States territory.

the internal order of the ship, though could be applied to contexts arising under the Jones Act). *Hellenic Lines* did not disturb *McCulloch's* holding. In *Hellenic Lines*, the Supreme Court found that tort claims brought under the Jones Act could be maintained by a foreign seaman against a foreign ship. 372 U.S. at 308-310, 83 S.Ct. at 1733-34. The Supreme Court, however, has not extended the *Hellenic Lines* analysis to maritime contract cases—such as this case—and this court has expressly declined to do so. *See Dresdner Bank AG v. M/V Olympia Voyager*, 446 F.3d 1377, 1381 (11th Cir. 2006) (declining to extend the *Lauritzen* [*v. Larsen*, 345 U.S. 571, 73 S.Ct. 921, 97 L.Ed. 1254 (1953)] and *Hellenic Lines* points of contact analysis to maritime contracts). Indeed, the Supreme Court reaffirmed the reasoning of *Benz* and *McCulloch* in *Spector*—a case post-dating *Hellenic Lines*—where it determined the applicability of the Americans with Disabilities Act to foreign ships. 545 U.S. at 129-30, 125 S.Ct. at 2177. The analysis in *Benz* and *McCulloch* continues to be the relevant inquiry.

The Stewards claim that, even if *Benz* and *McCulloch* control, the internal [—12—] affairs of Celebrity's ships would not be disrupted were we to apply the LMRA and the NLRA to this dispute. They argue that applying these statutes would merely compel the paying of wages, not affect the "movement and functioning" of the ships. This argument misapprehends the internal affairs inquiry. Federal courts are not charged with predicting the operational consequences of applying these statutes on a case-by-case basis. Nor have the Stewards presented support suggesting otherwise. To adopt this reasoning would lead to the kind of inquiry into the "internal order and discipline" that *McCulloch* concluded would be "entirely infeasible in actual practice." 372 U.S. at 19, 83 S.Ct. at 676. Because the Supreme Court has already determined that wage disputes between a foreign vessel and its foreign crew fall within the internal affairs of a ship, we are foreclosed from revisiting the question. *Benz*, 353 U.S. at 142-43, 77 S.Ct. at 702.

The Stewards also contend that applying these statutes will not negatively impact international comity. This argument addresses the canon of statutory construction applied in *Benz* and *McCulloch* that, absent an express statement from Congress, we do not construe statutes to extend to disputes between foreign parties where the United States maintains no interest. *See Spector*, 545 U.S. at 131-32, 125 S.Ct. at 2178 ("It is reasonable to presume Congress intends no interference with matters that are primarily of concern only to the ship and the foreign state in [—13—] which it is registered."). The Supreme Court has refused to disrupt this rule unless clearly instructed by Congress, *Benz*, 353 U.S. at 147, 77 S.Ct. at 704, particularly where, as here, the legislative record bears no mention of foreign application. *See Windward Shipping (London) Ltd. v. Am. Radio Ass'n, AFL-CIO*, 415 U.S. 104, 113, 94 S.Ct. 959, 964, 39 L.Ed.2d 195 (1974) ("We are even more reluctant to attribute to Congress an intention to disrupt this comprehensive body of law by construction of an Act unrelated to maritime commerce and directed solely at American labor relations.").

This canon is rooted in a general concern for international comity. Nevertheless, the Stewards argue that this canon should be applied on a case-by-case basis and not under these facts. They argue that, unlike in *McCulloch* where Honduras had a strong interest in applying its laws to Honduran citizens, the Bahamas has no interest in applying its labor laws here because the Stewards are citizens of India, not the Bahamas.

A case-specific inquiry into the effect on international relations is not permitted. Though the *McCulloch* court had occasion to illustrate how the application of these statutes could readily arouse international discord, *see* 372 U.S. at 21, 83 S.Ct. at 677, the case-specific facts of a particular dispute do not govern the analysis. *Benz* clearly illustrates that the concern for international [—14—] comity in these cases is general in nature and not allayed by a case-by-case, effects-oriented inquiry. Though that case was about the LMRA, the *Benz* court recounted the international rancor that was aroused when Congress proposed certain amendments to the Seamen's Wage Act[11]—a statute unrelated to the LMRA. The Court explained that the extension of the LMRA to disputes between foreign parties had the potential to create an analogous reaction. The Court mentioned no brewing international backlash over the potential extension of the LMRA itself; it merely used the Seaman's Wage Act tensions to illustrate the potential for international discord were the Court to apply generally-worded statutes to wholly-foreign disputes without express instruction from Congress. *See Benz*, 353 U.S. at 146, 77 S.Ct. at 703-04. An actual or imminent international quarrel therefore is not necessary to deny the application of these statutes; Congress must speak clearly regardless of the specific facts of a particular case. We would upend this principle were we to entertain the Stewards' argument here.

Lastly, the Stewards contend that § 301 of the LMRA is coextensive with the remedies under the Seaman's Wage Act, which expressly permits foreign seamen to bring suit against foreign ships. The Stewards base this argument on [—15—] *U.S. Bulk Carriers, Inc. v. Arguelles*, 400 U.S. 351, 357, 91 S.Ct. 409, 413, 27 L.Ed.2d 456 (1971), which held that §301 functions as "optional remedy" to seamen in addition to those available under the Seaman's Wage Act. The holding in *Bulk Carriers* was a narrow one: the Court held that the express remedy in the Seaman's Wage Act was not implicitly overruled by the addition of arbitration procedures in § 301 of the LMRA; rather, the LMRA merely afforded seamen an additional path to recovery. *Id.* at 357-58, 91 S.Ct. at 413. Furthermore, the plaintiff in *Bulk Carriers* was an alien resident of Baltimore that was represented by an American union and worked aboard an American ship. *Arguelles v. U.S. Bulk Carriers, Inc.*, 408 F.2d 1065, 1066, 1068 (4th Cir. 1969). Because the dispute in *Bulk Carriers* involved an American ship and an American union, there is no justification for

reading that case as extending § 301 to disputes between foreign parties. *See Int'l Longshoremen's Local 416, AFL-CIO v. Ariadne Shipping Co.*, 397 U.S. 195, 199-200, 90 S.Ct. 872, 874, 25 L.Ed.2d 218 (1970) (holding that American residents hired by a foreign ship to work on an American dock did not involve the internal affairs of a foreign ship).[12] [—16—]

B.

Next, we address the District Court's decision to dismiss the Stewards' non-hybrid claims under Rule 12(b)(1). We review dismissal for lack of subject matter jurisdiction *de novo*. *Sinaltrainal v. Coca-Cola Co.*, 578 F.3d 1252, 1260 (11th Cir. 2009). In its July 7, 2010, order, the District Court considered the applicability of the judicially-created duty of fair representation. Finding no other source for the duty of fair representation other than in the NLRA and finding the NLRA inapplicable to the Stewards' case, the District Court dismissed the Stewards' claim under Rule 12(b)(1) for lack of subject matter jurisdiction.

To determine whether a complaint states a federal cause of action is a merits question. *Morrison v. Nat'l Australia Bank, Ltd.*, __ U.S. __, 130 S.Ct. 2869, 2877, 177 L.Ed.2d 535 (2010). "Subject-matter jurisdiction, by contrast, refers to a tribunal's power to hear a case." *Id.* (internal quotation marks omitted). Where a plaintiff's well-pleaded complaint alleges a cause of action arising under federal law, subject matter jurisdiction exists for a federal court to determine whether the allegations entitle him to relief. *City of Chicago v. Int'l Coll. of Surgeons*, 522 U.S. 156, 163, 118 S.Ct. 523, 529, 139 L.Ed.2d 525

---

[11] These amendments would have extended the Seaman's Wage Act to advance payments given to foreign seaman by foreign vessels. *See Benz*, 353 U.S. at 146, 77 S.Ct. at 703-04.

[12] The Stewards have also presented plain meaning and legislative purpose arguments. They are foreclosed by *Benz* and *McCulloch*. *Benz*, 353 U.S. at 144, 77 S.Ct. at 702-03 (noting the complete absence of legislative history indicating the LMRA's application to disputes between foreign parties); *McCulloch*, 372 U.S. at 19-20, 83 S.Ct. at 676-77 (rejecting a literal reading of the NLRA's language given the extensive legislative history suggesting the Act applies only to American workingmen and their employers).

(1997); *see Bell v. Hood*, 327 U.S. 678, 682, 66 S.Ct. 773, 776, 90 L.Ed. 939 (1946) ("Jurisdiction ... is not defeated ... by the possibility that the averments might fail to state a cause of [—17—] action on which petitioners could actually recover."). Because the Stewards sufficiently alleged a breach of the federal common law duty of fair representation under the NLRA, the District Court had subject matter jurisdiction to hear the case under 28 U.S.C. § 1331. *See Marquez*, 525 U.S. at 49, 119 S.Ct. at 302 ("[W]hen a plaintiff alleges a breach of the duty of fair representation, this claim is cognizable in ... federal court.").

Nevertheless, we affirm the dismissal of the fair representation claim under Rule 12(b)(6) for failure to state a claim.[13] *See Lucas v. W.W. Grainger, Inc.*, 257 F.3d 1249, 1256 (11th Cir. 2001) ("[W]e may affirm [the District Court's] judgment on any ground that finds support in the record.") (internal quotation marks omitted).

The Stewards contend that even if the hybrid mechanism of § 301 of the LMRA is inapplicable, they can still maintain a non-hybrid claim against FIT under § 9(a) of the NLRA. They argue that our precedent dictates that the NLRA applies when a foreign union engages in wrongful conduct through its agents [—18—] within the United States. To support this contention, the Stewards look to our decision in *Dowd v. Int'l Longshoremen's Assoc., AFL-CIO*, 975 F.2d 779 (11th Cir. 1992). *Dowd* does not support this argument. *Dowd* concerned the application of the NLRA to an American labor union that induced a foreign union to pressure foreign importers to establish a secondary boycott in the United

States. *Id.* at 781. The application of the NLRA to the American union in that case— and the noticeable absence of NLRA claims against the foreign union—actually supports the argument that the NLRA does not apply to the Stewards' claims. Indeed, in *Dowd* we restated the Supreme Court's holding in *McCulloch*. 975 F.2d at 788 ("[T]he NLRA does not regulate the practices of owners of foreign vessels which are temporarily present in an American port with regard to foreign employees working on these vessels."). The Stewards have failed to identify a source for the duty of fair representation other than the NLRA. Because the NLRA does not apply when its application would only concern the internal affairs of a foreign vessel, the Stewards cannot bring a fair representation claim under it here.

III.

We now move to *Gomez*. The doctrine of *res judicata*, or claim preclusion, bars the parties to an action from litigating claims that were or could have been [—19—] litigated in a prior action between the same parties. *Jaffree v. Wallace*, 837 F.2d 1461, 1466 (11th Cir. 1988). The party asserting claim preclusion as a defense must establish four elements: (1) the prior decision must have been rendered by a court of competent jurisdiction; (2) there must have been a final judgment on the merits; (3) both cases must involve the same parties or their privies; and (4) both cases must involve the same causes of action. *In re Piper Aircraft Corp.*, 244 F.3d 1289, 1296 (11th Cir. 2001). We review a claim preclusion decision *de novo*. *Id.* at 1295.

The question before us is whether the dismissal of the LMRA claim in *Lobo II* precluded the Stewards from bringing a claim under the Seaman's Wage Act in *Gomez*. The parties agree that the District Court exercised competent jurisdiction and that the actions involve the same parties. The parties dispute whether the District Court's order dismissing the LMRA claim was a final judgment on the merits and whether the cases share the same cause of action.

---

[13] Though the District Court had jurisdiction to hear the fair representation claim, this does not revive the Stewards' state law claim for breach of good faith and fair dealing. The District Court indicated that even if it had original jurisdiction it would decline to exercise supplemental jurisdiction over the Stewards' state law claim. We need not disturb this disposition. *See Raney v. Allstate Ins. Co.*, 370 F.3d 1086, 1089 (11th Cir. 2004) ("We have encouraged district courts to dismiss any remaining state claims when ... the federal claims have been dismissed prior to trial.").

A.

We agree with the Stewards that the District Court's September 10, 2009, order dismissing the LMRA claims in *Lobo II* was not a final judgment. Although the Stewards appealed that order, we dismissed the appeal for lack of jurisdiction [—20—] because the order was not final or immediately appealable. This order was not claim preclusive. *See First Ala. Bank, N.A. v. Parsons Steel, Inc.*, 825 F.2d 1475, 1480 n. 5 (11th Cir. 1987) ("Nonappealable interlocutory orders are not entitled to collateral estoppels or res judicata effect.").[14] Nevertheless, we take judicial notice of the District Court's entry of judgment on July 8, 2010, in *Lobo II*. This judgment rendered the September 10, 2009, dismissal final.

We also conclude that the September 10, 2009, order was an adjudication on the merits because the order was a Rule 12(b)(6) dismissal with prejudice. *Hall v. Tower Land & Inv. Co.*, 512 F.2d 481, 483 (5th Cir. 1975) ("[G]ranting defendant's motion to dismiss for plaintiff's failure to state a claim upon which relief can be granted operates as an adjudication on the merits."); *see Citibank, N.A. v. Data Lease Fin. Corp.*, 904 F.2d 1498, 1501 (11th Cir. 1990) ("[D]ismissal of a complaint with prejudice satisfies the requirement that there be a judgment on the merits."). The Stewards' contention that a judgment on the merits occurs only [—21—] when the rendering court has addressed the substance of every claim to be later precluded is baseless. The District Court's judgment of July 8, 2010, constitutes a final adjudication on the merits as to Celebrity.[15]

B.

Next, the parties dispute whether the cause of action in *Gomez* is the same as the one in *Lobo II*. A cause of action is the same for *res judicata* purposes if it "arises out of the same nucleus of operative fact, or is based upon the same factual predicate, as a former action." *Piper*, 244 F.3d at 1297. The Stewards argue that there is no common nucleus of operative fact here because the LMRA claim in *Lobo II* arose out of Celebrity's conduct during the arbitration and not out of the company's failure to pay wages. But claim preclusion "applies not only to the precise legal theory presented in the prior case, but to all legal theories and claims arising out of the same nucleus of operative fact." *NAACP v. Hunt*, 891 F.2d 1555, 1561 (11th Cir. 1990).

The test for a common nucleus of operative fact is "whether the same facts are involved in both cases, so that the present claim could have been effectively [—22—] litigated with the prior one." *Piper*, 244 F.3d at 1301. A comparison of the complaints reveals that the facts in the LMRA claim in *Lobo II* and the Seaman's Wage Act claim in *Gomez* were alleged verbatim. This satisfies the same cause of action requirement.

IV.

We affirm the District Court in Appeal No. 10-13623. Because the Stewards are foreign employees involved in an internal wage dispute with a foreign ship, neither the LMRA nor the NLRA apply to the Stewards'

---

[14] Celebrity correctly observes that the categories of appealable orders and orders entitled to preclusive effect do not always overlap. Yet the differences between the two arise not because some preclusive orders are non-final, but because some non-preclusive orders are nonetheless appealable. *See, e.g.*, 18 *Moore's Federal Practice – Civil* §131.30[2][c][i] (3d ed. 2010) ("The Supreme Court has construed the term 'final decision' to embrace some collateral orders the effect of which cannot be rectified on appeal from final judgment. Furthermore, 28 U.S.C. § 1292 provides for appeals of certain interlocutory orders. Even though such matters are 'appealable,' they could not be the basis for claim preclusion." (footnotes omitted)). 9 U.S.C. § 16(a)(1) is particularly on point: interlocutory orders denying a motion to compel arbitration are generally appealable.

[15] The Stewards also argue that the District Court's dismissal of the claim against Celebrity in *Lobo II* was "purely a dismissal for lack of subject matter jurisdiction"—and thus lacks claim-preclusive effect. In its September 10, 2009 order, the District Court dismissed the Stewards' hybrid claim against Celebrity for failure to state a claim, not for lack of subject matter jurisdiction. The Stewards' characterization of the District Court's September 10, 2009, order is meritless.

challenges. Since their claims are dependent upon the protections of those acts, the District Court properly dismissed their claims against Celebrity and FIT in *Lobo II*.

We affirm the District Court in Appeal No. 10-10406. Because the Stewards could have raised their Seaman's Wage Act claim in *Lobo II* but did not, we affirm the District Court's order in *Gomez* to dismiss the claim as barred by the doctrine of *res judicata*.

AFFIRMED

United States Court of Appeals
for the Eleventh Circuit

No. 11-15060

AQUA LOG, INC.
VS.
LOST AND ABANDONED PRE-CUT LOGS

Appeal from the United States District Court for the
Middle District of Georgia

Decided: February 15, 2013

Citation: 709 F.3d 1055, 1 Adm. R. 448 (11ᵗʰ Cir. 2013).

Before **TJOFLAT, COX**, Circuit Judges, and **MOTZ**,* District Judge.

*Honorable J. Frederick Motz, United States District Judge for the District of Maryland, sitting by designation.

[—3—] **COX**, Circuit Judge:

These cases present a question that is almost as old as the doctrine of admiralty jurisdiction itself. As Justice Daniel posed it in 1857, "[T]he inquiry is naturally suggested, what are navigable waters?" *Jackson v. The Steamboat Magnolia*, 61 U.S. (20 How.) 296, 320 (1857) (Daniel, J., dissenting). Today, we answer that question as follows: a waterway is navigable for admiralty-jurisdiction purposes if, in its present state, it is capable of supporting commercial activity. [—4—]

I. FACTS & PROCEDURAL HISTORY

These consolidated appeals concern segments of two Georgia waterways—a two river-mile stretch of the Flint River and a one river-mile stretch of Spring Creek. The Flint River segment is bounded by a bridge at State Highway 37 at Newton, Georgia at its northern end and Bainbridge, Georgia at its southern end. The Flint River empties into Lake Seminole, which lies on the border between Georgia and Florida. The Flint River south of Bainbridge is currently used in interstate commerce, but the two river-mile stretch at issue here is not currently used in interstate commerce. Spring Creek is a tributary of the Flint River. (References in this opinion to the Flint River and Spring Creek should be understood as only addressing the two river-mile stretch of the Flint River and the one river-mile stretch of Spring Creek at issue in these cases.)

Historically, commercial vessels used both the Flint River and Spring Creek for transportation. The parties agree that the Flint River was used to transport commercial vessels and that Spring Creek was capable of transporting commercial vessels. Although currently there is no commercial activity on these waterways, the parties agree that the Flint River and Spring Creek can, in their present states, transport commercial vessels loaded with freight in the regular course of trade for at least part of the year. [—5—]

During the late nineteenth century and early twentieth century, loggers transported their commercially harvested logs by floating them down rivers. Inevitably, some of the logs sank to the bottom. Today, there is an increased demand for these sunken logs because they produce superior furniture, flooring, and musical instruments. Such submerged logs are at the heart of this appeal.

Aqua Log, a company that finds, removes, and sells submerged logs, has located a number of submerged logs that have been abandoned by their original owners at the bottom of the Flint River and Spring Creek. Aqua Log estimates that there are hundreds of submerged logs at the bottoms of the waterways.

Aqua Log, through its president, has located and removed two logs from the Flint River, using the Flint River to transport the logs. It has also removed one log from Spring Creek, using Spring Creek to transport that log. Aqua Log wishes to remove all of the submerged logs and sell them.

So, in August 2007, Aqua Log, invoking the court's admiralty[1] jurisdiction, brought three

---

[1] The terms "admiralty" and "maritime" are "virtually synonymous." Bryan Garner, *A Dictionary of Modern Legal Usage* 29 (2d ed. 1995). We therefore use the terms interchangeably.

in rem actions[2] seeking a salvage award for the logs or, in the alternative, an award of title to the logs based on the American Law of Finds. The [—6—] State of Georgia intervened and claimed ownership of the logs. Georgia moved for summary judgment, arguing that the court lacks subject-matter jurisdiction because the Flint River and Spring Creek are not navigable waters. The district court agreed and granted summary judgment in favor of Georgia. Specifically, the court held that a waterway is only navigable for admiralty jurisdiction purposes when there is evidence of present or potential commercial activity on that waterway. Finding that no commercial activity currently occurs on the Flint River and Spring Creek and that Aqua Log failed to present evidence of any planned commercial activity, the court determined that it lacked subject-matter jurisdiction and granted summary judgment in favor of Georgia. Aqua Log appeals.

II. ISSUES ON APPEAL

This appeal presents two issues: first, whether the district court erred in requiring evidence of present or planned commercial activity on a waterway for it to be considered navigable for admiralty-jurisdiction purposes; and second, whether the Flint River and Spring Creek are navigable waterways.

III. STANDARD OF REVIEW

Georgia raised the issue of subject-matter jurisdiction in its motion for summary judgment. Subject-matter jurisdiction, however, is more appropriately addressed in a motion to dismiss pursuant to Federal Rule of Civil Procedure [—7—] 12(b)(1). As a result, we will treat the district court's grant of summary judgment for lack of subject-matter jurisdiction as a dismissal under Rule 12(b)(1). *See United States v. Blue Cross & Blue Shield of Ala., Inc.*, 156 F.3d 1098, 1101 n.7 (11th Cir. 1998) (treating a district court's grant of summary judgment for lack of subject-matter jurisdiction as a dismissal under Rule 12(b)(1)). We review de novo the district

court's dismissal for lack of subject-matter jurisdiction. *Broward Gardens Tenants Ass'n v. U.S. Envtl. Prot. Agency*, 311 F.3d 1066, 1072 (11th Cir. 2002).

IV. CONTENTIONS OF THE PARTIES

Aqua Log contends that the district court applied the wrong test to determine navigability and asks us to adopt a test that defines navigable waters as those waters that are merely capable of being used for commercial purposes. If we adopt that test, Aqua Log contends, then the Flint River and Spring Creek are navigable waterways, and the district court has subject-matter jurisdiction.

Georgia, on the other hand, urges us to adopt the district court's test for navigability—that a waterway is navigable only if it currently supports commercial activity or if there is evidence of planned commercial activity on that waterway. And because the Flint River and Spring Creek do not currently support commercial [—8—] activity and no such activity is planned, the district court properly concluded that the waterways are not navigable and that it lacked subject-matter jurisdiction.

V. DISCUSSION

The Constitution delegates jurisdiction over admiralty cases to the federal courts. U.S. Const. art. III, § 2. This power is codified in 28 U.S.C. § 1333(1), which gives Article III courts "original jurisdiction . . . of . . . [a]ny civil case of admiralty or maritime jurisdiction." Federal admiralty jurisdiction extends to all navigable waters. *Ex parte Garnett*, 141 U.S. 1, 15, 11 S. Ct. 840, 843 (1891); Grant Gilmore, Jr. & Charles L. Black, *The Law of Admiralty* 31–32 (2d ed. 1975) ("[T]he admiralty jurisdiction of the United States extends to all waters, salt or fresh, with or without tides, natural or artificial, which are in fact navigable in interstate or foreign water commerce."). Thus, for a court to have admiralty jurisdiction, the body of water in question must be navigable. Both Aqua Log and Georgia agree that for the court to have admiralty jurisdiction in these in rem actions,

---

[2] Case No. 11-15060 and Case No. 11-15076 involve the Flint River, while Case No. 11-15078 involves Spring Creek.

the waterways where the res (the submerged logs) are located must be navigable.

Aqua Log seeks a salvage award for the submerged logs or, in the alternative, title to the logs. Aqua Log contends that if the court does not have admiralty jurisdiction, then it will not be able to pursue its claims, which are [—9—] unique to maritime law. For the court to have admiralty jurisdiction, the Flint River and Spring Creek must be navigable. Thus, we must decide (A) what test applies to determine the navigability of a waterway for admiralty-jurisdiction purposes and (B) whether the Flint River and Spring Creek meet that test. We address each issue in turn.

A.

We first consider what test applies to determine if a body of water is navigable for admiralty-jurisdiction purposes.[3] The parties have not called to our attention any Eleventh Circuit precedent addressing this issue.

The district court defined navigable waters as those waters with evidence of present or potential commercial activity. Relying on *Seymour v. United States*, 744 F. Supp. 1161 (S.D. Ga. 1990), the court reasoned that the purpose of admiralty jurisdiction is to promote and protect commercial activity and that, in the absence of such commercial activity, the federal interest in protecting and promoting commercial activity no longer exists. And so, according to the district [—10—] court, admiralty jurisdiction should extend only to those waterways with present or planned commercial activity.

The district court's opinion is well-reasoned, but we respectfully disagree with the court's holding. And, we are not writing on a clean slate. We are bound by the Fifth Circuit's decision in *Richardson v. Foremost Ins. Co.*, 641 F.2d 314 (5th Cir. Apr. 1981),

aff'd sub nom. Foremost Ins. v. Richardson, 457 U.S. 668, 102 S. Ct. 2654 (1982). The Fifth Circuit decided *Richardson* on April 2, 1981, and under our precedent, Fifth Circuit cases decided before October 1, 1981, bind us. *Bonner v. City of Prichard*, 661 F.2d 1206, 1209 (11th Cir. 1981) (en banc).

In *Richardson*, the Fifth Circuit addressed whether a tort claim based on a collision between two pleasure boats on a waterway that was "seldom, if ever, used for commercial activity" fell within the federal courts' admiralty jurisdiction. 641 F.2d at 315–16. The court noted that for admiralty jurisdiction to exist in a tort case, two requirements must be met: (1) there must be a significant relationship between the alleged wrong and traditional maritime activity (the nexus requirement) and (2) the tort must have occurred on navigable waters (the location requirement). *Id.* at 315. Concluding that both requirements had been met, the Fifth Circuit held that the district court had admiralty jurisdiction over the tort claim. *Id.* at 316. The court determined that the nexus requirement had been met [—11—] because boats "are engaged in traditional maritime activity when a collision between them occurs on navigable waters." *Id.* As to the location requirement, the court concluded that the tort occurred on navigable waters even though the waterway was seldom, if ever, used for commercial activity. *Id.* Specifically, the court said:

> We note additionally from the record that the place where the accident occurred is seldom, if ever, used for commercial activity. That does not cause us to vary from our holding. . . . It would be introducing another note of uncertainty to hold that admiralty jurisdiction extends only to a stretch of navigable water that presently functions as a commercial artery. . . . If the waterway is capable of being used in commerce, that is a sufficient threshold to invoke admiralty jurisdiction.

---

[3] We note that the term "navigable" has different meanings in different contexts. *Kaiser Aetna v. United States*, 444 U.S. 164, 170–72, 100 S. Ct. 383, 388–89 (1979). In this case, we are concerned only with term as it used to establish the limits of the jurisdiction of the federal courts over admiralty and maritime cases.

Id. We are bound by this holding.[4] And the fact that *Richardson* considered whether admiralty jurisdiction extends to a tort case does not change this conclusion. Whether in a tort case or in a salvage case, the waterway at issue must be navigable. [—12—]

Neither Georgia nor the district court undertakes to distinguish this holding in *Richardson*.[5] Instead, Georgia and the district court rely on cases from three of our sister circuits that they argue support a test for navigability that requires evidence of present or potential commercial activity. Specifically, they point to the Seventh Circuit's decision in *Chapman v. United States*, 575 F.2d 147 (7th Cir. 1978) (en banc), the Eighth Circuit's decision in *Livingston v. United States*, 627 F.2d 165 (8th Cir. 1980), and the Ninth Circuit's decision in *Adams v. Montana Power Co.*, 528 F.2d 437 (9th Cir. 1975). Georgia and the district court read these cases as adopting a test for navigability that requires current commercial activity. But each case also contains language that suggests they adopt a test for navigability that looks to whether the waterway at issue is simply capable of supporting commercial activity. *See Livingston*, 627 F.2d at 169–70 ("[T]he concept of 'navigability' in admiralty is properly limited to describing a *present capability* of waters to sustain commercial shipping." (emphasis added)); *Chapman*, 575 F.2d at 151 ("We hold that a recreational boating accident does not give rise to a claim within the admiralty jurisdiction when it occurs on waters that . . . are not in fact used for

commercial navigation and are *not susceptible* of such use in their present [—13—] state." (emphasis added)); *Adams*, 528 F.2d at 439 ("A waterway is navigable provided that it is used or *susceptible of being used* as an artery of commerce." (emphasis added)).

Nevertheless, even if these cases are understood to mean what the district court and Georgia suggest, there is substantial precedent to the contrary in our sister circuits. *See Cunningham v. Dir., Office of Workers' Comp. Programs*, 377 F.3d 98, 108 (1st Cir. 2004) (noting that for admiralty-jurisdiction purposes, navigability is understood to describe a present capability of a waterway to sustain commerce); *LeBlanc v. Cleveland*, 198 F.3d 353, 359 (2d Cir. 1999) (looking to whether the waterway is "presently used, or is presently capable of being used, as an interstate highway for commercial trade" in determining whether it is navigable); *Price v. Price*, 929 F.2d 131, 134 (4th Cir. 1991) (adopting a test that considers whether the body of water at issue is capable of supporting commercial activity); *Finneseth v. Carter*, 712 F.2d 1041, 1044 (6th Cir. 1983) (considering whether the waterway "is used or capable or susceptible of being used as an interstate highway for commerce" when deciding whether it is navigable).

On appeal, Georgia argues that a test for navigability that looks to whether there is evidence of current or planned commercial activity on the waterway strikes the appropriate balance between protecting commercial maritime activity and [—14—] respecting the ability of the states to regulate their own affairs by not applying substantive maritime law (which applies when admiralty jurisdiction is invoked) in the absence of actual commercial activity.

While sound policy reasons support the test proposed by Georgia, the navigability test announced in *Richardson* is supported by equally sound policy. A test for navigability that looks to whether a waterway is capable of supporting commercial activity promotes and encourages maritime commerce.

---

[4] The Fifth Circuit's definition of navigability is a holding. A holding is both the result of the case "and those portions of the opinion necessary to that result." *United States v. Kaley*, 579 F.3d 1246, 1253 n.10 (11th Cir. 2009) (quoting *Seminole Tribe of Fla. v. Florida.*, 517 U.S. 44, 67, 116 S. Ct. 1114, 1129 (1996)). The Fifth Circuit concluded that the district court erroneously dismissed the tort case for lack of subject-matter jurisdiction. To reach this result, it had to determine that both requirements for admiralty jurisdiction over tort cases—the nexus and location requirements—were met.

[5] While we agree with the district court that *Richardson* primarily focused on the nature of the action and actors, *Richardson* nevertheless addressed the character of the water where the tort occurred and we are bound by that holding.

The primary focus of maritime law is to protect and encourage commercial maritime activity. *See Sisson v. Ruby*, 497 U.S. 358, 367, 110 S. Ct. 2892, 2898 (1990) ("The fundamental interest giving rise to maritime jurisdiction is 'the protection of maritime commerce.'" (quoting *Foremost Ins. Co. v. Richardson*, 457 U.S. 668, 674, 102 S. Ct. 2654, 2658 (1982))). When admiralty jurisdiction is invoked, a uniform body of federal maritime law applies. *Yamaha Motor Corp., U.S.A. v. Calhoun*, 516 U.S. 199, 206, 116 S. Ct. 619, 623 (1996) ("With admiralty jurisdiction . . . comes the application of substantive maritime law." (quoting *E. River S.S. Corp. v. Transamercia Delavel Inc.*, 476 U.S. 858, 864, 106 S. Ct. 2295, 2298–99 (1986))). This body of law serves to protect commercial activity by ensuring that uniform rules of conduct are in place. *Exec. Jet Aviation, Inc. v. City* [—15—] *of Cleveland*, 409 U.S. 249, 269–70, 93 S. Ct. 493, 505 (1972). The Supreme Court has said:

> The law of admiralty has evolved over many centuries, designed and molded to handle problems of vessels relegated to ply the waterways of the world, beyond whose shores they cannot go. That law deals with navigational rules—rules that govern the manner and direction those vessels may rightly move upon the waters. When a collision occurs or a ship founders at sea, the law of admiralty looks to those rules to determine fault, liability, and all other questions that may arise from such a catastrophe. Through long experience, the law of the sea knows how to determine whether a particular ship is seaworthy, and it knows the nature of maintenance and cure. It is concerned with maritime liens, the general average, captures and prizes, limitation of liability, cargo damage, and claims for salvage.

Id. Finding admiralty jurisdiction when a waterway is capable of supporting commercial activity creates a "climate conducive to commercial maritime activity." *Finneseth*, 712 F.2d at 1046. That is, commercial activity could begin on such a waterway and immediately have uniform rules in place without having to determine whether commercial activity currently takes place on that waterway.

Moreover, a test for navigability that requires actual commercial activity is unpredictable and is therefore not conducive to maritime commerce. If actual commercial activity is the test, the application of substantive maritime law becomes contingent on the presence or absence of commercial activity. *Price*, 929 F.2d at 133–34 ("Rules governing conduct on navigable waters cannot remain uniform or have any certainty if their applicability is dependent on whether, on any [—16—] given day, commercial maritime activity is being conducted on the waters."). A test that requires evidence of actual or likely commercial activity fails to provide the predictability that encourages maritime commerce. And predictability in the courts is valuable.

We are mindful that the *Richardson* test may expand admiralty jurisdiction into waterways that may never be used for commercial maritime activities. However, the broad federal interests in protecting and promoting maritime commerce justify this potential encroachment. "If the waterway is capable of being used in commerce, that is a sufficient threshold" to conclude that it is navigable for admiralty-jurisdiction purposes. *Richardson*, 641 F.2d at 316.

B.

We next address whether the Flint River and Spring Creek are capable of supporting commercial activity and are therefore navigable waters. We easily answer this question because both Aqua Log and Georgia agree that the Flint River and Spring Creek are capable of supporting commercial activity. (*See* No. 11-15078, Dkt. 43-1 at 3; No. 11-15076, Dkt. 60-11 at 2; No. 11-15060, Dkt. 65-19 at 2.) Therefore, we conclude that these are navigable waters for admiralty-jurisdiction purposes. [—17—]

VI. CONCLUSION

Because the segments of the Flint River and Spring Creek at issue in these cases are capable of supporting commercial activity, they are navigable waters for admiralty-jurisdiction purposes. We therefore hold that the district court erred in concluding that the waterways are not navigable and dismissing these cases for lack of subject-matter jurisdiction on that ground.[6] Accordingly, we reverse and remand for proceedings consistent with this opinion.

REVERSED AND REMANDED.

---

[6] The district court decided it lacked subject-matter jurisdiction solely on the basis that the Flint River and Spring Creek are not navigable waters. We express no opinion on whether there are any other requirements necessary for its claims to fall within federal admiralty jurisdiction.

United States Court of Appeals
for the Eleventh Circuit

No. 12-15204

WALLACE

vs.

NCL (BAHAMAS) LTD.

Appeal from the United States District Court for the
Southern District of Florida

Decided: October 1, 2013

Citation: 733 F.3d 1093, 1 Adm. R. 454 (11ᵗʰ Cir. 2013).

[—2—] Before **TJOFLAT** and **WESLEY**, Circuit Judges, and **PROCTOR**, United States District Judge for the Northern District of Alabama, sitting by designation.

PROCTOR, District Judge:

A passenger's time spent on a cruise ship is typically very relaxing, at least until it is time to disembark. In this case, the defendant-appellee NCL (Bahamas) Ltd., ("NCL") decided to make that last day of the voyage less stressful for its customers. To accomplish this goal, NCL implemented a new policy, called "Freestyle" cruising, which permits passengers to stay aboard for a longer time after the ship has docked on the last day of their voyage. Passengers, who would normally disembark very early, are allowed to stay on board until as late as 10:30 a.m. That is the good news.

The bad news, at least for the NCL employees who worked as senior stateroom stewards aboard the cruise ships, is that on that same day, while one group of passengers is leisurely disembarking, another group of passengers is eager to board and begin their cruise ship experience. Due to the arrival of these new passengers, NCL required the senior stateroom stewards to have all of the cabins cleaned by 2:00 p.m. This made it much more difficult for the senior stewards to timely complete their work. That is, although they began their work shifts at 7:00 a.m., for the most part, they were unable to begin cleaning the cabins until as late as 10:30 a.m. because the departing group of passengers was still enjoying their [—3—] Freestyle cruise. This in turn allowed scant time to complete the

assigned cleaning work by 2:00 p.m. In light of the substantial workload and the shortened time frame within which to complete it, most of the senior stewards adopted the practice of hiring helpers (out of their own pocket) to assist them in completing their work on embarkation day.

This appeal involves the claims of six senior stateroom stewards ("Seafarers") who worked aboard cruise ships operated by NCL. They assert that NCL has not paid them their full wages because their compensation does not take into account the amounts they were required to pay their helpers to complete their work on embarkation days. Consequently, they contend NCL is liable for compensatory and penalty wages under the Seaman's Wage Act, 46 U.S.C. § 10313, et seq. ("the Act"). The district court awarded them compensatory but not penalty wages. The only substantive issue in this appeal concerns the Seafarers' argument that the district court erred in not awarding them penalty wages.[1] After careful review, and with the benefit of oral argument, we affirm. [—4—]

---

[1] In their briefing, the Seafarers argue that they are entitled to post-trial class certification under Federal Rule of Civil Procedure 23. Although NCL responded to this argument in its brief, we see no reason to substantively address the class certification question. Consistent with the magistrate judge's recommendation, the district court found that the predominance requirement of Federal Rule of Civil Procedure 23(b)(3) was not satisfied. The district court noted that in order to pursue their theory of the case, the Seafarers would be required to introduce an overwhelming amount of individualized proof as to two issues: (1) whether and why a particular senior steward hired helpers; and (2) what, if any, damages a particular senior steward suffered. The district court concluded that the issue of damages in this case is entirely fact specific, and demands a member-by-member analysis. The Seafarers have not addressed, much [—4—] less contested, these findings in their briefing on appeal. Moreover, the Seafarers did not press this issue at oral argument. Finally, we have carefully reviewed the record and find no error in the district court's Rule 23 findings. For these reasons, and because their class certification argument is wholly without merit, we conclude the district court did not err in denying the motion for class certification. Therefore, the focus of this opinion is devoted to the penalty wage issue.

I. BACKGROUND

A. Procedural History

This case originally was filed by thirty-two current and former employees of NCL. They asserted claims under the Seaman's Wage Act for unpaid wages and penalty wages, and also have advanced a state law claim for breach of the implied contractual covenant of good faith and fair dealing. Their state law claim involves allegations surrounding their employment and collective bargaining agreements. After amendments to the pleadings and substantial motion practice, the number of plaintiffs and claims was narrowed, and the district court ordered the claims of the Seafarers (*i.e.*, six of the plaintiffs[2]) to be tried first.

The Seafarers' claims were tried in the district court without a jury. On September 7, 2012, the district court entered its Findings of Fact and Conclusions [—5—] of Law. The district court found in favor of the Seafarers on their claims for unpaid wages under 46 U.S.C. §10313 (f) and for breach of the implied covenant of good faith and fair dealing. The district court, however, found in favor of NCL, and against the Seafarers, on the claim for penalty wages under 46 U.S.C. §10313 (g). After liquidating the amount of prejudgment interest, the district court entered its partial final judgment with respect to the Seafarers' claims on October 1, 2012.[3] This appeal followed.

---

[2] Those six plaintiffs are the appellants here and include Abraham Wallace, Adrian Nash, Pauline Haughton, John George James, Glenford Palmer, and Everol Barrant. The claims of the remaining plaintiffs remain to be tried.

[3] Abraham Wallace was awarded $14,400.00 in damages plus $5,186.71 in prejudgment interest. Adrian Nash was awarded $14,400.00 in damages plus $4,869.56 in prejudgment interest. Glenford Palmer was awarded $13,650.00 in damages and $4,689.65 in prejudgment interest. Everol Barrant was awarded $9,450.00 in damages plus $2,552.58 in prejudgment interest. Pauline Haughton was awarded $14,700.00 in damages plus $4,949.12 in prejudgment interest. John James was awarded $6,150.00 in damages plus $1,704.34 in prejudgment interest.

B. The District Court's Findings of Fact

NCL owns and operates a fleet of nine cruise ships. The Seafarers worked on these vessels as senior stateroom stewards during the relevant time period—between May 14, 2006 and June 14, 2009. The Seafarers each signed an employment contract with NCL, under which NCL hired them for ten months. During these ten months, the Seafarers lived on board the cruise ships. They would then take two months of vacation before signing new employment contracts with the same terms and conditions. The Seafarers' employment contracts all incorporated the collective bargaining agreement executed by NCL and the Norwegian Seafarers' Union for Catering Personnel, a labor organization which [—6—] represents all of the senior stewards. The collective bargaining agreement established senior stewards' pay rates and guaranteed that NCL employees would be entitled to one hundred percent of their wages minus approved deductions each month.

On embarkation day (the day a cruise ends, passengers disembark, and new passengers board), senior stewards had to clean between 30 and 35 cabins[4] before new passengers arrived. On these days, their responsibilities included: (1) stripping the beds of linens and sheets; (2) separating the linens and sheets; (3) making the beds; (4) dusting the cabins; (5) sanitizing the cabin's handrails, door handles, closet doors, frequently touched areas, and telephones; (6) cleaning any used coffee pots and ice buckets; (7) separating the garbage into bottles, cans, paper, and plastic; (8) taking garbage to the incinerator; and (9) vacuuming the cabin and hallways. NCL had rigorous standards that required "immaculate" cabins and a quality control system to randomly check for cleanliness.

In 2000, NCL implemented its Freestyle cruising policy, which permitted passengers to stay on board later on embarkation day. This policy was designed to maximize relaxation for passengers. Prior to this time, NCL required

---

[4] Although there was some dispute over how many beds 30 to 35 cabins contained, senior stewards had to strip and make at least 70 beds.

passengers to disembark by 8:00 or 8:30 a.m. With Freestyle cruising, passengers could stay as long (or almost as long) as they wished. The senior stewards technically started [—7—] their work at 7:00 a.m. on embarkation day, but under the Freestyle cruise system, passengers would leave their cabins much later. Indeed, few passengers would leave before 8:30 a.m., and most passengers did not disembark until 9:30 or 10:30 a.m. Because new passengers would venture to their rooms soon after boarding, NCL required that all cabins be cleaned by 2:00 p.m. This caused problems for NCL senior stewards on embarkation day. One NCL supervisor noted that with the Freestyle "concept we also advertise relax[ing] debark[ation] which puts another stress" on embarkation day.

Although junior stewards[5] worked alongside the senior stewards, they offered little or no help, and in fact had their own separate work responsibilities. The senior stewards therefore had to complete a substantial workload in a shortened timeframe. And, if they failed to finish their assignments or rushed their work, they faced a quality control process that could lead to verbal and written reprimands. Thus, the senior stewards had to hire helpers to complete their duties on embarkation day.

In making the finding that the senior stewards needed to hire helpers to finish their work on embarkation day in a timely manner, the district court [—8—] reviewed the testimony of various witnesses and the paper record. The district court discredited the testimony of four NCL witnesses who testified that senior stewards could finish their work

without hiring a helper.[6] The district court found two NCL witnesses on this issue, Cesar Lanic and Ronald Alcaraz, were credible and believable.[7]

The district court also commented that at least one voyage note indicates that the senior stewards complained about the need for helpers on embarkation day. Further, NCL employees mentioned in various e-mails that the senior stewards needed to hire helpers. In one e-mail, a former NCL hotel-operations director wrote that, because they had not hired helpers the day before, the senior stewards [—9—] "were a bit negligent with their staterooms." Another e-mail noted that all senior stewards hired helpers except those lucky enough to have helpers assigned to them (and paid for) by NCL.

---

[5] Although, technically, the titles NCL uses for the relevant categories of employees aboard its cruise ships are "senior stateroom steward" and "stateroom steward," the trial judge referred to this latter position group, stateroom stewards (who worked alongside the senior stewards) as "junior stewards" and called senior stateroom stewards "senior stewards." He did so apparently to avoid the confusing use of very similar sounding titles. For ease of reference and clarity, we use these same designations.

[6] Cesar Hapa, an executive housekeeper at NCL testified that senior stewards could finish their work on time without help. However, the district court discredited this testimony because Hapa articulated a bias when he blamed nationality for the Seafarers' inability to complete their work. Michelle Dognon-Bertino, a former NCL hotel-operations director, also testified that the senior stewards could finish their work without helpers. But, the district court found she lacked credibility because she initially signed a sworn statement in which she said the senior stewards needed helpers to finish their work and made an about-face on nearly everything written in her sworn statement. Clyde Harbin, a NCL executive housekeeper, testified that he knew the senior stewards opted to hire helpers but despite knowing of the issue regarding helpers did nothing about it. Patrycja Kosla, a senior NCL housekeeping trainer, testified that she trained junior and senior stewards to work together. However, the district court did not find her testimony persuasive because of the antagonistic stance she took in response to the questions posed by plaintiffs' trial counsel on cross examination, resulting in illogical responses. For example, the trial court questioned her testimony that she would voluntarily give up twenty-five percent of her salary.

[7] Lanic and Alcaraz testified that they could clean all cabins without helpers. However, Lanic and Alcaraz had junior stewards who helped them, and they also admitted they sometimes too hired helpers. Although the district court found the men to be "outliers" (i.e., their success in completing their assignments was unique as compared to the vast majority of other senior stewards), it did find their testimony believable.

Based upon these documents and the trial testimony, the district court concluded that it was necessary for senior stewards to hire helpers to complete the work assigned to them on embarkation day. After making these findings of fact, the district court then explained its conclusions of law.

C. The District Court's Conclusions of Law

The district court concluded that the NCL had wrongfully withheld the Seafarers' wages in violation of the Seaman's Wage Act, but did not award penalty wages. As to compensatory wages, the district court determined that during the relevant claim period, NCL created a situation where it was nearly impossible for the Seafarers to clean all of their assigned cabins without "hiring" helpers. Therefore, the trial court concluded that NCL violated the Seaman's Wage Act by assigning the Seafarers an amount of work that could not be completed without the Seafarers using some of their wages to pay for helpers, and in turn not compensating them in a manner that accounted for the payments they were required to make to their helpers. Thus, the district court concluded that NCL owed the Seafarers an amount in compensatory damages equal to the money they [—10—] used to pay helpers to complete the work on time. According to the district court, NCL's actions, in practice, constituted a withholding of wages under 46 U.S.C. § 10313(f). This finding is not challenged on appeal.

On the other hand, the district court concluded that a dispute existed about whether the back wages were owed and determined the Seafarers were not entitled to penalty wages under 46 U.S.C. § 10313(g). The district court provided two reasons for so holding. First, NCL had a reasonable belief the Seafarers' claimed wages were not due them. That is, from a technical viewpoint, NCL paid the Seafarers their full wages earned for the hours they themselves actually worked, even though it created a situation that forced the Seafarers to use some of that money to compensate helpers. Second, at least two senior stewards, Lanic and Alcaraz, told NCL they could complete their work without the aid of helpers because junior stewards

helped them do so. Thus, the district court concluded that NCL had not acted arbitrarily, willfully, or unreasonably, and did not award penalty wages.

II. DISCUSSION

As explained above, the primary issue on appeal is whether the district court erred in failing to award the Seafarers penalty wages. The Seafarers contest the district court's ruling and argue that the district court should have awarded penalty wages because: (1) NCL did not meet its burden to show that the failure to pay was [—11—] with sufficient cause; (2) the district court's finding that NCL violated the common law duty of good faith and fair dealing necessitates a finding of bad faith withholding of wages; and (3) the district court's other findings of fact demonstrate NCL's conduct was indeed arbitrary, willful, or unreasonable. For the reasons explained in detail below, we reject each of these arguments.

A. Standard of Review[8]

The standard of review that we apply when a party claims a trial court erred in its fact finding is a familiar one. "We review a district court's factual findings when sitting without a jury in admiralty under the clearly erroneous standard." *Venus Lines Agency, Inc. v. CVG Int'l Am., Inc.*, 234 F.3d 1225, 1228 (11th Cir. 2000). Federal Rule of Civil Procedure 52(a) dictates that we may review a district court's factual findings only for clear error:

---

[8] The Seafarers maintain the standard of review is *de novo*. However, a review of their arguments makes clear that in this appeal they actually are contesting the findings of fact made by the district court (and upon which it based its penalty wages ruling). Thus, we find the operative standard of review is whether the trial court's fact finding is clearly erroneous. But, even if we reviewed *de novo* the district court's conclusion of law that the Seafarers are not entitled to penalty wages, ("We review [admiralty bench trial] conclusions of law *de novo*."). *See Venus Lines Agency, Inc.*, 234 F.3d 1225, 1228 (11th Cir. 2000). Based upon an examination of the record, we would affirm.

(1) *In General*. In an action tried on the facts without a jury or with an advisory jury, the court must find the facts specially and state its conclusions of law separately. The findings and conclusions may be stated on the record after the close of the evidence or may appear in an opinion or a memorandum of decision filed by the court. . . . [—12—]

(6) *Setting Aside the Findings*. Findings of fact, whether based on oral or other evidence, must not be set aside unless clearly erroneous, and the reviewing court must give due regard to the trial court's opportunity to judge the witnesses' credibility.

Fed.R.Civ.P. 52(a)(1),(6). This is a "highly deferential standard of review." *Renteria-Marin v. Ag-Mart Produce, Inc.*, 537 F.3d 1321, 1324 (11th Cir. 2008) (citing *Holton v. City of Thomasville Sch. Dist.*, 425 F.3d 1325, 1350 (11th Cir. 2005) and Fed. R. Civ. P. 52(a)). "A finding of fact is clearly erroneous when the entirety of the evidence leads the reviewing court to a definite and firm conviction that a mistake has been committed." *Dresdner Bank AG v. M/V Olympia Voyager*, 446 F.3d 1377, 1380 (11th Cir. 2006)(citation omitted); *see also Anderson v. City of Bessemer City, N.C.*, 470 U.S. 564, 573-74 (1985) ("If the district court's account of the evidence is plausible in light of the record viewed in its entirety, the court of appeals may not reverse it even though convinced that had it been sitting as the trier of fact, it would have weighed the evidence differently. Where there are two permissible views of the evidence, the factfinder's choice between them *cannot* be clearly erroneous.") (emphasis added) (citation omitted).

B. Analysis

1. Seaman's Wage Act

Before discussing the merits of this appeal, we begin by reviewing the law applicable to the Seafarers' claims. The Seaman's Wage Act provides the following regarding payment of wages: "At the end of a voyage, the master shall [—13—] pay each seaman the balance of wages due the seaman within 24 hours after the cargo has been discharged or within 4 days after the seaman is discharged, whichever is earlier." 46 U.S.C. § 10313(f). The statute further states that where a shipowner withholds a seafarer's wages and lacks "sufficient cause" for doing so, "the master or owner shall pay to the seaman 2 days' wages for each day payment is delayed." 46 U.S.C. § 10313(g). Under section 10313(f), the seaman is entitled to reimbursement of all wages unlawfully withheld by the shipowner. If the shipowner's withholding is found to be "without sufficient cause," section 10313(g) requires payment of additional penalty wages.

Once the Seafarers established their wages were wrongfully withheld, the burden of proof shifted to NCL to show that the delay in payment was justified (that is, it was not without sufficient cause). *See Arguelles v. U.S. Bulk Carriers, Inc.*, 408 F.2d 1065, 1070 (4th Cir. 1969)("If delay in payment of wages is established the burden of proof is on the ship owner to show that his delay was justified."), *aff'd*, 400 U.S. 351 (1971). "The phrase, 'without sufficient cause,' as used in [§ 10131(g) and its predecessor] means more than the absence of a valid defense to the claim for wages. Otherwise, it adds nothing to the meaning of the statute. In other words, a wrongful withholding alone does not establish the absence of sufficient cause." *See Larkins v. Hudson Waterways Corp.*, 640 F.2d 997, 999 (9th Cir. 1981)(internal citation omitted); *see also Chretien v. Exxon Co.*, [—14—] *U.S.A.*, 863 F.2d 182, 184 (1st Cir. 1988) (quoting *Larkins*, 640 F.2d at 999)(same); *Henry v. S/S Bermuda Star*, 863 F.2d 1225, 1241 n.70 (5th Cir. 1989) ("We do caution at this juncture that the double wage penalty is not triggered merely by a wrongful withholding."); *Swain v. Isthmian Lines, Inc.*, 360 F.2d 81, 83 n.5 (3d Cir. 1966) ("It is well settled that the mere existence of an unlawful withholding does not, in and of itself, establish the absence of sufficient cause for that withholding.").

Courts have historically characterized a withholding as "without sufficient cause" when premised on willful, unreasonable, or arbitrary conduct. *See Griffin v. Oceanic*

Contractors, Inc., 458 U.S. 564, 572, 102 S.Ct. 3245, 3250 (1982) (noting that the purpose of the penalty wages provision is to deter "negligent or arbitrary delays in payment"); *McCrea v. United States*, 294 U.S. 23, 30, 55 S.Ct. 291, 294 (1935) ("The statute thus confers no right to recovery double wages where the delay in payment of wages was not in some sense arbitrary, willful, or unreasonable."); *Mateo v. The M/S Kiso*, 41 F.3d 1283, 1289 (9th Cir. 1994) ("'Without sufficient cause' has been characterized by admiralty courts as arbitrary, unwarranted, unjust, and unreasonable conduct."); *Vinieris v. Byzantine Maritime Corp.*, 731 F.2d 1061, 1063-64 (2d Cir. 1984) (recovery of penalty wages requires there "to be a showing of 'conscious misconduct' on the part of the [—15—] ship's Captain, . . . which was arbitrary, unwarranted, unreasonable, unjust, and willful")(citation omitted).

The phrase "without sufficient cause" must be taken to mean something more than merely valid defenses to a wage claim. Its meaning, in effect, is a wil[l]ful, unreasonable and arbitrary attitude upon the part of the master or shipowner in refusing to pay earned wages to the seamen. It may be a high-handed or capricious action, although not necessarily so. "Without sufficient cause" has been characterized by admiralty courts as arbitrary, unwarranted, unjust, and unreasonable conduct.

The presence of good faith or moral justification for refusal to pay undoubtedly has considerable effect in the determination of whether the master['s] or shipowner's action was or was not "without sufficient cause." Generally, where the refusal or failure to pay wages results from an honest difference of opinion arising from a matter in dispute—a dispute about which honest men are apt to differ—the courts will be loathe to declare a penalty when later one of the disputants has been proved wrong.

. . . [A] showing of good faith upon the part of the master or owner, together with reasonable cause for failure to pay wages due, undoubtedly carries considerable influence in determining whether such refusal is not without sufficient cause. Where the master or owner has acted in a reasonable manner throughout and without any showing of arbitrariness or unjustness, where he had an honest doubt as to the justification of the demand, and where the facts and circumstances surrounding the wage demand are susceptible to an honest doubt as to the justness of the seaman's demand, it cannot be said that the refusal is without sufficient cause.

Mateo, 41 F.3d at 1289-90 (quoting 1 Martin J. Norris, *The Law of Seamen* § 17:5, at 517-19, 17:6, at 519 (4th ed. 1985)(citations omitted)); *see also Henry v. S/S Bermuda Star*, 863 F.2d 1225, 1241 n.70 (5th Cir. 1989) ("We do caution at this juncture that the double penalty is not triggered merely by a wrongful [—16—] withholding."). Additionally, courts have explained that penalty wages are not recoverable if the shipowner had a reasonable belief that the wages were not due, if the shipowner committed an error in judgment, or if there was a dispute as to the wages owed. *See Byzantine Maritime Corp.*, 731 F.2d at 1063-64.

Mindful that we must liberally construe the provisions of the Seaman's Wage Act in favor of the Seafarers, *see, e.g., Isbrandtsen Co. v. Johnson*, 343 U.S. 779, 782 (1952) ("Whenever congressional legislation in aid of seamen has been considered here since 1872, this Court has emphasized that such legislation is largely remedial and calls for liberal interpretation in favor of the seamen."), after careful review we conclude that the district court's factual findings which formed the basis of its decision not to award penalty wages were not clearly erroneous.

2. The District Court's Findings of Fact Are Not Clearly Erroneous

Initially, we pause to note the precise reasons why the district court concluded that NCL satisfied its burden to show its actions did not demand penalty wages. In part, this is necessary because the Seafarers have incorrectly asserted that the district court's sole ground for denying penalty wages was because two senior stewards, Lanic and Alcaraz, informed NCL that junior stewards helped clean the cabins. In fact, the district court provided two reasons for concluding that the Seafarers were not entitled to penalty wages. First, the district court found that NCL had a reasonable belief the wages were not due. That is, the trial court [—17—] concluded that in a practical sense NCL had in fact paid the Seafarers the wages they were due for the work they actually performed, even though the company created a situation where they had to use some of that money to compensate helpers.[9] Notably, the district

---

[9] NCL maintains that the Seafarers have waived any argument on appeal related to this first finding on the penalty wage issue because they did not address it in their initial brief. Although they may not have explicitly addressed the trial court's first finding, we find implicit references to it in the Seafarers' initial brief. For example, the Seafarers cite to evidence that they believe demonstrated that NCL did not have a reasonable belief that the wages were not due. But even if they had not addressed the issue in their initial brief, we do not agree with NCL that the first finding was a separate legal ground upon which the district court based its conclusion not to award penalty wages. Rather, the district court's conclusion on this issue was based upon a number of factors that formed part of a single analysis. *See Little v. T-Mobile USA, Inc.*, 691 F.3d 1302, 1307 (11th Cir. 2012) ("In [*Gray ex. rel Alexander v. Bostic*, 613 F.3d 1041 (11th Cir. 2010)]. . . . [t]he district court...did not state independently adequate alternative grounds for its ruling; it blended a number of factors into its decision. . . . Here, the district court's decision was not in a single pot with blended ingredients but instead was in a number of pots containing different ingredients."). In this case, the factors that formed the basis of the court's two specific findings on the penalty wage issue were part of a single judicial determination—whether NCL's withholding of wages was "without sufficient cause." Therefore, we find the Seafarers have not

court observed that (1) the Seafarers' theory of back wage liability, although a winning one, was novel and (2) its own research had not uncovered any opinion (published or unpublished) in which a shipowner was held liable under the Act for failing to compensate seaworkers for amounts paid to others. Second, the district court found that Lanic and Alcaraz told NCL they could complete their work using junior stewards, who helped clean the cabins. Based upon both of these grounds, the district court found the Seafarers were not entitled to penalty wages. [—18—]

a. The Rule 52 Record Evidence Supports the Trial Court's Finding

The Seafarers' contention that NCL presented no credible evidence demonstrating its withholding of wages was with sufficient cause cuts no ice at all. The district court found that NCL presented two credible witnesses at trial on the issue of whether the senior stewards could finish their work without hiring helpers. It bears repeating that one of the grounds upon which the district court concluded the Seafarers were not entitled to penalty wages was the testimony of Lanic and Alcaraz.

Contrary to the Seafarers' arguments, the adverse credibility findings the district court made as to other NCL witnesses are irrelevant to the Rule 52(a) question before us, as that particular testimony did not inform the district court's decision not to award penalty wages. The district court credited the testimony of the two senior stewards who testified that they told NCL they were able to finish their work on embarkation day. Although they may have been "outliers" (and, in fact, were even classified as such by the district court), that designation is simply not determinative. The district court found their testimony believable, and based (at least in part) upon that evidence, the district court found the Seafarers were not entitled to penalty wages. Our role is not to decide that factual issue *de novo*. *See Zenith Radio Corp.*

---

waived any challenges as to the trial court's initial finding.

v. Hazeltine Research Inc., 395 U.S. 100, 123 (1969). Here, to be sure, there were at least two permissible views of the trial evidence. One [—19—] such view (which was not adopted by the district court) would have allowed the trier of fact to discredit Lanic and Alcaraz's testimony for one of at least two reasons: (1) because they were outliers; or (2) because other witnesses testified that completing the work without the aid of helpers was impossible. But the point that the Seafarers fail to acknowledge is that the district court took a different, yet equally permissible view of the evidence—that despite their status as outliers, Lanic and Alcaraz were credible witnesses on an important issue of fact. Where, as here, we are presented with two permissible views of this testimony, we cannot say the district court, sitting as a trier of fact, was clearly erroneous in adopting one view over the other. *See Anderson*, 470 U.S. at 574.

b. That the Seafarers Prevailed on Their Common Law Duty of Good Faith and Fair Dealing Claim is Inapposite

The Seafarers also argue that because they prevailed on their common law claim for breach of the common law duty of good faith and fair dealing, it follows that NCL acted in bad faith under the Seaman's Wage Act, thus warranting the imposition of penalty wages. The Seafarers' argument is off the mark.

In reaching its conclusion that NCL violated the duty of good faith and fair dealing, the district court explained that under Florida law,[10] a breach of this duty occurs "where one party to a contract uses its discretion to make it difficult for the [—20—] other party to fulfill his contractual obligations." The district court noted that the Seafarers' payment to helpers did not constitute an approved deduction under their collective bargaining agreement. The district court also stated that NCL had wide discretion in deciding how much work and

how much time was required of the senior stewards on embarkation day, as well as how much help the senior stewards were entitled to receive. Moreover, the district court found that the Seafarers could not have expected that their jobs would require them to pay, out of pocket, helpers to assist in the completion of their work. Thus, the district court concluded that NCL violated its duty of good faith and fair dealing.

The Seafarers contend that this finding necessarily compels the conclusion that NCL acted in bad faith for purposes of the penalty wages provision of the Seaman's Wage Act. However, this is simply not the case. Notably, the district court did not find that NCL acted in "bad faith" in connection with its conclusion that NCL breached its duty of good faith and fair dealing.[11] Moreover, even if it [—21—] had concluded NCL acted in bad faith for purposes of this common law claim, bad faith in the penalty wages context is measured against a different legal standard.

To determine whether a delay in payment under the Seaman's Wage Act was reasonable, courts have applied a *subjective* test based upon good faith. *See Bender v. Waterman S.S. Corp.*, 166 F.2d 428, 428 (3rd Cir. 1948) (concluding that the "sufficient cause" referred

---

[10] The record reflects that the parties waived any choice of law issues by agreeing that Florida law applied to all disputes arising under the collective bargaining agreement.

[11] The Seafarers point to Florida law explaining that the absence of good faith constitutes bad faith. *See Continental Cas. Co. v. City of Jacksonville*, 550 F. Supp. 2d 1312, 1337 ([M.D.]Fla. 2007) ("Conceptually, 'good faith' is generally not applied by itself without resort to the very concept being defined or to its reverse concept of 'bad faith' . . . . Essentially, good faith and bad faith are two sides of the same coin. Put differently, the absence of 'good faith' constitutes 'bad faith,' and qualitative descriptions of 'good faith' conduct are often compared to qualitative descriptions of 'bad faith' conduct composed of terms that are simply the antonyms of terms used to describe 'good faith.'")(citations omitted). This proposition is, at the same time, unremarkable and of no help to the Seafarers here. The authority that the Seafarers' rely upon for the conclusion that the absence of good faith necessarily leads to a finding of bad faith is helpful only in the context of analyzing their common law claims. It is inapposite to the discussion of whether NCL engaged in bad faith in connection with the Seafarers' federal claim for penalty wages.

to in the penalty wages provision need not amount to a valid legal defense to the claim for wages); *Byzantine Maritime Corp.*, 731 F.2d at 1063-64 (noting that the penalty wages provision should not be imposed "where payment is withheld in good faith under a reasonable belief that it is not due, where there is a bona fide dispute as to the amount owed, or where there has been an honest error of judgment in this regard") (citations omitted)). In contrast, under Florida law, in the context of the common law duty of good faith and fair dealing, a finding of "bad faith" is an objective one that does not require a showing of subjective bad faith. *See Vila & Son Landscaping Corp. v. Posen Constr., Inc.*, 99 So. 3d 563, 567 (Fla. Dist. Ct. App. 2012).

Because the legal standards are different, we cannot say the district court erred in failing to award penalty wages on the basis of its finding that NCL violated the common law duty of good faith and fair dealing. Moreover, the district indicated that it appeared a dispute existed over whether the wages were [—22—] owed. Indeed, in support of its conclusion regarding penalty wages, the district court noted that NCL had in fact fully paid the wages that the Seafarers claimed for their *own* work—it just created a situation where the Seafarers had to use some of those wages to pay helpers for assistance in timely completing that work. The district court concluded that a dispute existed over whether the wages were actually due and that NCL had a reasonable belief the wages were properly withheld. We conclude the district court did not commit clear error in these critical findings, and that these findings support its conclusion that penalty wages were not due, even if NCL breached the state-law duty of good faith and fair dealing.

c. The Trial Court's Findings of Fact on the Underlying Wage Claims Do Not Undermine Its Fact Finding on the Penalty Wages Question

Finally, the Seafarers argue that based upon the district court's other findings of fact and the record as a whole, they are entitled to penalty wages. The extremely deferential

standard of review that we must employ and our own examination of the record lead us to the exact opposite conclusion.

The district court made two key findings of fact related to the Seafarers' back wage claims: that (1) NCL created a situation where it was nearly impossible for the Seafarers to clean their assigned cabins without helpers on embarkation [—23—] day; and (2) NCL knew of the need for helpers to be utilized to complete most of the work. Based upon these findings, the district court found that although it technically paid full wages to the Seafarers for their own actual work performed, NCL was liable to the Seafarers for compensatory damages equal to the amount each paid to hire helpers to finish their work. However, these findings are of no avail to the Seafarers in connection with their penalty wages claim. They are simply not evidence of any willful, arbitrary, or willful misconduct on the part of NCL. Accordingly, we cannot say the district court erred by failing to award penalty wages based upon these findings.

As explained in detail above, the district court made findings of fact which are supported by the record, and upon which it based its decision not to award penalty wages. That conclusion will not be disturbed based upon other findings that have no bearing on the penalty wages analysis at issue below and on this appeal.

The Seafarers have pointed to the following evidence which they assert entitles them to penalty wages: (1) testimony from an NCL corporate representative that he could not provide a name of a senior steward who could clean his or her cabins on embarkation day without hiring a helper; (2) internal e-mails between NCL management stating that they knew helpers were used to clean cabins; (3) helper audits performed in 2006 to track the hours they helped senior [—24—] stewards on embarkation day to determine if those helpers' extra work hours were in violation of International Labour Organization regulations; and (4) a financial analysis performed by NCL to estimate how much it cost the company to pay for the senior stewards' helpers. However, again, the Seafarers ignore the testimony of Lanic and Alcaraz, which the district court found to be believable,[12] as well as the fact that this evidence was considered by the district court. We cannot conclude that the evidence necessitated a finding of an arbitrary, willful, or unreasonable withholding of wages, particularly in light of the district court's finding that a good faith dispute existed over whether the wages were actually owed as NCL actually paid the wages but created a situation where the Seafarers [—25—] had to use some of those wages to hire others to help them complete their embarkation day duties.

The district court weighed the evidence, and found that although it was rare for a senior steward not to use helpers, NCL knew that some senior stewards were able to finish their work on their own or with the assistance of junior stewards. Thus, after reviewing the record and hearing oral argument, we conclude that the district court's findings upon which it based its conclusion not to award penalty wages were not clearly erroneous.

IV. CONCLUSION

For the reasons set for above, the partial judgment of the district court is **AFFIRMED**.

---

[12] Nor can [we] say that the district court clearly erred based upon one executive's testimony that he could not provide the name of a senior steward who completed his or her work without a helper. Likewise, the audits and financial analysis merely demonstrate what the district court found—that NCL knew a situation existed requiring senior stewards to hire helpers to finish cleaning cabins on embarkation days. Just as these record facts do not show that the district court clearly erred in its penalty wages findings, neither does the district court's determination that the testimony of Hapa, Dongon-Bertino, Harbin, and Kosla was not credible establish any Rule 52(a) error. The trial court's findings on issues related to the underlying wage claim simply do not undermine its credibility findings regarding the testimony of Lanic and Alcaraz. It merely shows that the district court concluded that those four witnesses were not credible in testifying that all of the senior stewards were able to complete their work without hiring a helper. (Again, the district court necessarily found that the vast majority of the senior stewards were not assisted by junior stewards.). Moreover, regardless of the district court's findings as to the lack of credibility of Hapa, Dongon-Bertino, Harbin, and Kosla, that did not in any way affect its view of the credibility and believability of Lanic and Alcaraz. Even in light of the rejected testimony of the other four witnesses, Lanic and Alcaraz's testimony makes "the district court's account of the events . . . plausible" in determining whether NCL acted with sufficient cause. *See Anderson*, 470 U.S. at 573-74. Therefore, we readily conclude that the district court did not make clearly erroneous findings of fact.

This page intentionally left blank

United States Court of Appeals for the District of Columbia Circuit

United States Court of Appeals
for the District of Columbia Circuit

No. 12-1080

CITY OF OAKLAND
vs.
FEDERAL MARITIME COMM'N

On Petition for Review of an Order of the Federal
Maritime Commission

Decided: July 26, 2013

Citation: 724 F.3d 224, 1 Adm. R. 466 (D.C. Cir. 2013).

Before **HENDERSON,** and **BROWN,** Circuit Judges,
and **GINSBURG,** Senior Circuit Judge.

[—2—] BROWN, Circuit Judge:

The City of Oakland manages a port on lands granted by the State of California to benefit its citizens. This arrangement implicates the public trust doctrine, an ancient delineation of the states' rights in (among other things) their tidelands. But what happens when the public trust doctrine bumps into the Eleventh Amendment? Oakland believes it is entitled to a share of the State's sovereign immunity for its management of the port and has asked us to review the Federal Maritime Commission's contrary conclusion. We agree with the Commission, however, and deny Oakland's petition.

I

A

When California joined the Union in 1850, it acquired ownership of all underwater land within its borders subject to the ebb and flow of the tide—otherwise known as "tidelands." *See Phillips Petroleum Co. v. Mississippi,* 484 U.S. 469, 476 (1988). This was simply a consequence of joining the Union, though California, with its miles of coast, may have benefitted more than others. **[—3—]**

Yet California did not acquire proprietary rights in these lands; instead, under the so-called public trust doctrine, it took the tidelands in trust for its citizens. *See Dist. of*

Columbia v. Air Fla., Inc., 750 F.2d 1077, 1082 (D.C. Cir. 1984). Although the trust objectives have evolved over time, California currently holds the tidelands in trust for "statewide public purposes" like commerce, navigation, fishing, natural preservation, and "other recognized uses." CAL. PUB. RES. CODE § 6009(a). *See generally Nat'l Audubon Soc'y v. Superior Court,* 658 P.2d 709, 718–24 (Cal. 1983) (describing the public trust doctrine and its application in California).[1] California's authority over the tidelands is subordinate to this trust but is otherwise absolute. CAL. PUB. RES. CODE § 6009(b).

California has repeatedly exercised its authority over the tidelands by granting discrete portions to various municipalities. We are concerned with only one of these grants. In 1911, it conveyed certain stretches to the city of Oakland to be maintained as a "public harbor for all purposes of commerce and navigation." 1911 Cal. Stat. 1258.[2] Oakland did not thereby gain plenary authority over the tidelands, however; it took the land subject to the public trust, *see Nat'l Audubon Soc'y,* 658 P.2d at 721, as well as the conditions **[—4—]** expressly enumerated in the grant, which were generally consistent with the public trust doctrine. For example, the grant included a proviso retaining for the people of California an "absolute right to fish in the waters of said harbor, with the right of convenient access to said waters over said land." 1911 Cal. Stat. at 1259.

Oakland responded to the grant in 1927 by establishing the Port Department, a municipal agency charged with "the comprehensive and adequate development of the Port of Oakland through continuity of

---

[1] The doctrine is not unique to California, *see, e.g., Ill. Cent. R.R. Co. v. Illinois,* 146 U.S. 387, 452 (1892), but its contours are defined by state law. *Air Fla., Inc.,* 750 F.2d at 1082.

[2] In fact, California had already granted Oakland a stretch of land "between high tide and ship channel" in 1852, a portion of "salt, marsh and tide lands" in 1874, and a stretch of "salt marsh and tide lands" in 1909. *See* 1909 Cal. Stat. 665; 1874 Cal. Stat. 132; 1852 Cal. Stat. 180. None of this land, we are told, has anything to do with the case.

control, management and operation." Charter of the City of Oakland § 700 (2008). The Port Department is run by the Board of Port Commissioners, a seven-member body of "bona fide" Oakland residents nominated by the city mayor and appointed and removable by the city council. *Id.* §§ 701–03. It acts "for and on behalf of" Oakland. *Id.* § 706.

It also acts subject to the oversight of California's State Lands Commission, the agency vested with "[a]ll jurisdiction and authority remaining in the State" over granted tidelands. CAL. PUB. RES. CODE §6301.[3] The State Lands Commission monitors and audits public land grantees like the Port Department to ensure compliance with the public trust doctrine and land grant. *See id.* §§ 6009(c), 6301.

B

SSA Terminals, LLC ("SSA"), occupies three berths in the Oakland port. At some point SSA concluded the Port [—5—] Department failed to consider it when looking for a tenant to occupy five open berths of choice port real estate. To make matters worse, the Port Department ultimately leased those berths to one of SSA's competitors under terms more favorable than those governing SSA's lease. SSA therefore filed a complaint with the Federal Maritime Commission alleging the Port Department violated the Shipping Act. *See* 46 U.S.C. §§ 41102(c), 41106(2)–(3) (requiring marine terminal operators to follow "just and reasonable" regulations and practices, and prohibiting them from discriminating against or "unreasonably" refusing to deal with a party).

Oakland tried to, but could not, convince the Administrative Law Judge to dismiss the complaint on grounds of sovereign immunity. Much to Oakland's dismay, the Commission was equally unsympathetic and rejected its sovereign immunity argument on appeal, so Oakland filed this petition for review.

---

[3] The three-member State Lands Commission consists of two statewide elected officers and one member of the governor's cabinet. *See* CAL. PUB. RES. CODE § 6101; *see also* CAL. CONST. art. 5, §§ 2, 9, 11; CAL. GOV. CODE § 13000 *et seq.*

II

The Eleventh Amendment protects states from suit without their consent. *Alden v. Maine*, 527 U.S. 706, 730 (1999). The sovereign immunity provided by the Amendment draws on principles of federalism and comity, *see Alden*, 527 U.S. at 728–29; *Idaho v. Coeur d'Alene Tribe of Idaho*, 521 U.S. 261, 268 (1997), and protects both state dignity and state solvency, *see Hess v. Port Auth. Trans-Hudson Corp.*, 513 U.S. 30, 52 (1994). It restrains not only the courts, but also certain federal agencies like the Commission. *Fed. Mar. Comm'n v. S.C. State Ports Auth.*, 535 U.S. 743, 760 (2002).

Determining what entities are entitled to claim immunity tracks a simple constitutional line: Eleventh Amendment sovereign immunity belongs to the states. *Lake Country* [—6—] *Estates, Inc. v. Tahoe Reg'l Planning Agency*, 440 U.S. 391, 400 (1979); *see LaShawn A. v. Barry*, 87 F.3d 1389, 1393 n.4 (D.C. Cir. 1996) (en banc). This means that when the state is not named as a defendant, sovereign immunity attaches only to entities that are functionally equivalent to states (often called "arms of the state") or when, despite procedural technicalities, the suit effectively operates against the state as the real party in interest. *See N. Ins. Co. of N.Y. v. Chatham Cnty.*, 547 U.S. 189, 193 (2006); *Regents of Univ. of Cal. v. Doe*, 519 U.S. 425, 429 (1997); *Lake Country Estates, Inc.*, 440 U.S. at 400. These kinds of suits may offend the state's dignity or assault its solvency no less than if the state were itself the named defendant. *See, e.g., Coeur d'Alene Tribe of Idaho*, 521 U.S. at 269–70, 281–82.

And so a puzzle. Oakland recognizes, as it must, that municipalities are not protected by the Eleventh Amendment even though they exercise a "slice of state power," *Lake Country Estates, Inc.*, 440 U.S. at 400 (internal quotation marks omitted); *see also P.R. Ports Auth. v. Fed. Mar. Comm'n*, 531 F.3d 868, 881–84 (D.C. Cir. 2008) (Williams, J., concurring), and it neither denies it is a municipality nor claims the Port Department is anything other than a municipal agency. Oakland likewise concedes it is not an arm of the State, thereby surrendering its ability to argue that the Port Department is structurally entitled to sovereign immunity. *See P.R. Ports Auth.*, 531 F.3d at 873 ("[A]n entity either is or is not an arm of the State: The status of an entity does not change from one case to the next based on the nature of the suit, the State's financial responsibility in one case as compared to another, or variable factors."). And the Port Department's funds—which are managed by the city treasurer—are used only to finance bonds, maintain and operate Port Department facilities, and compensate employees, with any surplus potentially going into Oakland's [—7—] general treasury. *See* Charter of the City of Oakland §§ 717, 720. Why, then, would Oakland be entitled to Eleventh Amendment protection?

Oakland seeks safe passage through these shoals by relying on a novel reading of the public trust doctrine. Its argument has two parts, each of which it believes sufficient to trigger the Eleventh Amendment. First, Oakland explains, the Port Department functions as a "subordinate governmental agenc[y] of the state" because the State of California exercises "virtually complete control" over Port Department's administration of the tidelands—which because of the public trust doctrine is essentially a non-delegable state duty. Pet'r's Br. 36, 38, 40 (internal quotation marks omitted). Second, Oakland reasons, any judgment against the Port Department would be paid with State funds because revenues generated from public trust lands are part of the public trust and must be used for "State purposes." Pet'r's Br. 42. Unfortunately for Oakland, its reliance on cases granting immunity to state agents adds nothing to the conversation. Those cases establish the unremarkable proposition that but for Eleventh Amendment protection, a state, which can act only through its agents, may be liable for (or otherwise impacted by) the actions of one. *See P.R. Ports Auth.*, 531 F.3d at 878–79 ("[S]overeign immunity can apply in a particular case if the entity was acting as an agent of the State or if the State would be obligated to pay a judgment against an entity in that case."); *see also Alden*, 527 U.S. at

756–57; *Shands Teaching Hosp. & Clinics, Inc. v. Beech St. Corp.*, 208 F.3d 1308, 1311 (11th Cir. 2000) (holding that a Medicare fiscal intermediary may be immune "only to the extent that a judgment would expose the government to financial liability or interfere with the administration of government programs"). And worse, we do not think the public trust doctrine changes Oakland's Eleventh Amendment calculus: it appears California's dignity [—8—] and fisc would survive any suit against the Port Department untroubled. *See Hess*, 513 U.S. at 47 (invoking state dignity and solvency as analytical lodestars).

California retains ultimate responsibility for protecting its public trust property, *see Ill. Cent. R.R. Co. v. Illinois*, 146 U.S. 387, 453–54 (1892); *Nat'l Audubon Soc'y*, 658 P.2d at 723–24, and it may vindicate its responsibility by passing legislation modifying or terminating the tidelands grant to Oakland, *see Mallon v. City of Long Beach*, 282 P.2d 481, 487 (Cal. 1955). The legislature has in fact tweaked Oakland's grant twenty-four times during the past century, and if it revokes the grant entirely, the tidelands will revert to the State. *Id.* The same holds true for port revenues, which are part of the public trust. *City of Long Beach v. Morse*, 188 P.2d 17, 20 (Cal. 1947).

But until California exercises this authority, the Port Department will continue to manage the tidelands however it sees fit within the limits fixed by the public trust and tidelands grant. *See Nat'l Audubon Soc'y*, 658 P.2d at 723; *People ex. rel. Webb v. Cal. Fish Co.*, 138 P. 79, 83, 88 (Cal. 1913). All liability for port-related debts likewise belongs to the Port Department, and nothing in the record suggests California must or would intervene if the Port Department cannot handle its debts. *See* 1911 Cal. Stat. at 1259 (requiring Oakland to improve the port "without expense to the state"); Charter of the City of Oakland §717(3)(Ninth) (permitting transfer of surplus revenue and income generated by the port to the "General Fund of the City" to the extent the surplus is not needed for port-related purposes).[4] [—9—]

Thus, while the State may alter certain parameters constraining the Port Department's actions, the record contains no reason to think it can do more. Certainly none of the twenty-four amendments to the tidelands grant have affected the day-to-day management of the port.[5] *See also* [—10—] CAL. PUB. RES. CODE § 6308 (requiring joinder of the state as a "necessary party defendant"

___

[4] Oakland believes a judgment against the Port Department would operate against the state treasury under California probate law, which grants trustees the right to repayment from the trust for [—9—] expenditures that either were "properly incurred in the administration of the trust" or that "benefited the trust." CAL. PROB. CODE § 15684. We are unpersuaded that the public trust doctrine implies a trust relationship within the meaning of the probate code.

[5] Through these amendments, the legislature granted additional land, reserved for itself mineral rights and the right to use the land for highways, permitted Oakland to convey land to various military and educational institutions, extended the allowed length of granted franchises and leases, approved land use relating to other public trust purposes and certain land exchanges, and authorized use of revenue generated by public trust land for certain additional purposes that would nonetheless promote the public trust. *See* 2005 Cal. Stat. 5244; 2004 Cal. Stat. 4233; 1986 Cal. Stat. 5065; 1981 Cal. Stat. 3919; 1965 Cal. Stat. 3892; 1961 Cal. Stat. 2553; 1960 Cal. Stat. 319; 1957 Cal. Stat. 1902; 1955 Cal. Stat. 1936; 1953 Cal. Stat. 1908; 1945 Cal. Stat. 686; 1943 Cal. Stat. 2189; 1941 Cal. Stat. 2236; 1939 Cal. Stat. 1261; 1939 Cal. Stat. 1260; 1939 Cal. Stat. 1258; 1937 Cal. Stat. 2500; 1937 Cal. Stat. 752; 1937 Cal. Stat. 335; 1937 Cal. Stat. 115; 1931 Cal. Stat. 1346; 1923 Cal. Stat. 416; 1919 Cal. Stat. 1088; 1917 Cal. Stat. 63. Suggestively, one of these modifications purported to permit, but not require, Oakland to convey particular parcels of the public trust lands to the State for various transportation projects. *See* 1937 Cal. Stat. 335 (characterizing the legislation as an "urgency measure necessary for the immediate preservation of the public peace, health and safety"). If the legislature has the sort of control Oakland believes, one might wonder why it did not just reach out and take the land. Of course, if the State can modify Oakland's land grant, one might also wonder whether it could simply run the port directly—but we have no reason to explore these what-ifs.

in any proceeding "*involving the title to or the boundaries of* tidelands" (emphasis added)). To the extent the State *can* do more, its power appears to derive from the State's general relationship with municipalities rather than the public trust doctrine. *See, e.g., Mallon*, 282 P.2d at 487. And that is not enough to claim the attention of the Eleventh Amendment. *See Hess*, 513 U.S. at 47.

It is perhaps for these reasons that the State Lands Commission, though vested with all of California's jurisdiction and authority over the tidelands, has limited and only indirect control of the Port Department—and apparently only to the extent necessary to ensure compliance with the public trust and land grant. *See* CAL. STATE LANDS COMM'N, PUBLIC TRUST POLICY 3 (2001); *see also* CAL. PUB. RES. CODE § 6305. If it concludes the Port Department violated the terms of the public trust or land grant, it may advise the Port Department of that fact, report the violation to the state legislature, or sue to enjoin the violation. CAL. STATE LANDS COMM'N, PUBLIC TRUST POLICY 3; *see* CAL. PUB. RES. CODE §6306. The State Lands Commission, as the California attorney general put it in an amicus brief to the Commission, is simply the legislature's "day-to-day eyes and ears." Far from establishing an agency relationship, California's relationship with the Port Department—its ability to control Oakland's management of the port only to the extent Oakland violates the public trust or tidelands grant—suggests the opposite. *See, e.g.,* RESTATEMENT (THIRD) OF AGENCY §§ 1.01 cmts. f, g, 1.04(10) (2006).

Without any record evidence suggesting suits against the Port Department effectively target the State of California, we will not distort the Eleventh Amendment by mantling [—11—] Oakland with sovereign immunity. *Cf. Fresenius Med. Care Cardiovascular Res., Inc. v. P.R. & Caribbean Cardiovascular Ctr. Corp.*, 322 F.3d 56, 63 (1st Cir. 2003) ("It would be every bit as much an affront to the state's dignity and fiscal interests were a federal court to find erroneously that an entity was an arm of the state, when the state did not structure the entity to share its sovereignty."). The State of California had the opportunity to claim a dignity or financial interest when the Commission invited it to submit an amicus brief explaining the Port Department's status under state law, but nowhere did the State assert any interest in Oakland's immunity—a strong signal that California does not view suits against the Port Department as a threat to its sovereign interests. *Cf. Lake Country Estates, Inc.*, 440 U.S. at 401, 407 (looking to state briefs disclaiming intent to confer immunity on bi-state compact); *Morris v. Wash. Metro Area Transit Auth.*, 781 F.2d 218, 224–25 (D.C. Cir. 1986) (similar). Indeed, the State spoke up only after the Commission affirmatively asked it to do so, and it fell silent after Oakland filed its petition for review. This is telling and, we think, representative of Oakland's rights in and responsibilities for the tidelands.

III

For the reasons stated, Oakland's petition for review is

Denied.

Tables of Authority

This page intentionally left blank

Table of Cases

This page intentionally left blank

Table of Cases [1]

---

[1] Cases named solely after ships, *see, e.g., The Pennsylvania*, 86 U.S. (19 Wall.) 125 (1873), are alphabetized under the letter "T." Cases where the United States is the plaintiff are alphabetized by defendant under the letter "U."

C

D

G

H

I

L

M

N

O

P

S

T

U

V

W

Y

Z

This page intentionally left blank

Table of Statutes and Rules

This page intentionally left blank

Table of Statutes and Rules [1]

Treaties/International

Federal

Constitution

Miscellaneous

---

[1] As cited in the opinions reported.

RULES

REGULATIONS

STATE

Index

This page intentionally left blank

INDEX

A

B

C

N

O

P

Q

R

S

T

U

V

W

Z

This page intentionally left blank